Fodor's 2009

Beadles

SOUTHERN
CALIFORNIA

Where to Stay and Eat
for All Budgets

Must-See Sights
and Local Secrets

Ratings You Can Trust

Excerpted from *Fodor's California 2009*

Fodor's Travel Publications   New York, Toronto, London, Sydney, Auckland

www.fodors.com

FODOR'S SOUTHERN CALIFORNIA 2009

Editors: Michael Nalepa, Amy Wang, Paul Eisenberg, Maria Teresa Hart, Molly Moker

Editorial Contributors: Cheryl Crabtree, Roger J. Grody, Maria C. Hunt, Marlise Elizabeth Kast, Tanja Kern, Amanda Knoles, Lina Lecaro, Kathy A. McDonald, Stef McDonald, Jane Onstott, Reed Parsell, Charyn Pfeuffer, Laura Randall, AnnaMaria Stephens, Kastle Waserman, Bobbi Zane

Production Editor: Jennifer DePrima
Maps & Illustrations: David Lindroth, Mark Stroud, *cartographers*; Bob Blake, Rebecca Baer, *map editors;* William Wu, *information graphics*
Design: Fabrizio La Rocca, *creative director;* Guido Caroti, Siobhan O'Hare, *art directors*; Tina Malaney, Chie Ushio, Ann McBride, Jessica Walsh, *designers*; Melanie Marin, *senior picture editor*
Cover Photo (Joshua Tree National Park): Eliot Cohen
Production Manager: Angela L. McLean

COPYRIGHT

ISBN 978-1-4000-0806-3

ISSN 1543-1037

SPECIAL SALES

This book is available at special discounts for bulk purchases for sales promotions or premiums. Special editions, including personalized covers, excerpts of existing books, and corporate imprints, can be created in large quantities for special needs. For more information, write to Special Markets/Premium Sales, 1745 Broadway, MD 6-2, New York, New York 10019, or e-mail specialmarkets@randomhouse.com.

AN IMPORTANT TIP & AN INVITATION

Although all prices, opening times, and other details in this book are based on information supplied to us at press time, changes occur all the time in the travel world, and Fodor's cannot accept responsibility for facts that become outdated or for inadvertent errors or omissions. So **always confirm information when it matters,** especially if you're making a detour to visit a specific place. Your experiences—positive and negative—matter to us. If we have missed or misstated something, **please write to us.** We follow up on all suggestions. Contact the Southern California editor at editors@fodors.com or c/o Fodor's at 1745 Broadway, New York, NY 10019.

PRINTED IN THE UNITED STATES OF AMERICA

10 9 8 7 6 5 4 3 2 1

Be a Fodor's Correspondent

Your opinion matters. It matters to us. It matters to your fellow Fodor's travelers, too. And we'd like to hear it. In fact, we need to hear it.

When you share your experiences and opinions, you become an active member of the Fodor's community. That means we'll not only use your feedback to make our books better, but we'll publish your names and comments whenever possible. Throughout our guides, look for "Word of Mouth," excerpts of your unvarnished feedback.

Here's how you can help improve Fodor's for all of us.

Tell us when we're right. We rely on local writers to give you an insider's perspective. But our writers and staff editors—who are the best in the business—depend on you. Your positive feedback is a vote to renew our recommendations for the next edition.

Tell us when we're wrong. We're proud that we update most of our guides every year. But we're not perfect. Things change. Hotels cut services. Museums change hours. Charming cafés lose charm. If our writer didn't quite capture the essence of a place, tell us how you'd do it differently. If any of our descriptions are inaccurate or inadequate, we'll incorporate your changes in the next edition and will correct factual errors at fodors.com immediately.

Tell us what to include. You probably have had fantastic travel experiences that aren't yet in Fodor's. Why not share them with a community of like-minded travelers? Maybe you chanced upon a beach or bistro or B&B that you don't want to keep to yourself. Tell us why we should include it. And share your discoveries and experiences with everyone directly at fodors.com. Your input may lead us to add a new listing or highlight a place we cover with a "Highly Recommended" star or with our highest rating, "Fodor's Choice."

Give us your opinion instantly at our feedback center at www.fodors.com/feedback. You may also e-mail editors@fodors.com with the subject line "Southern California Editor." Or send your nominations, comments, and complaints by mail to Southern California Editor, Fodor's, 1745 Broadway, New York, NY 10019.

You and travelers like you are the heart of the Fodor's community. Make our community richer by sharing your experiences. Be a Fodor's correspondent.

Tim Jarrell, Publisher

CONTENTS

ABOUT THIS BOOK

Our Ratings

Sometimes you find terrific travel experiences, and sometimes they just find you. But usually the burden is on you to select the right combination of experiences. That's where our ratings come in.

As travelers we've all discovered a place so wonderful that its worthiness is obvious, a place is so unique that superlatives don't do it justice. These sights, properties, and experiences get our highest rating, **Fodor's Choice**, indicated by orange stars.

Black stars highlight sights and properties we deem **Highly Recommended**, places that our writers, editors, and readers praise for consistency and excellence.

By default, there's another category: any place we include in this book is by definition worth your time, unless we say otherwise. And we will.

Disagree with any of our choices? Care to nominate a place or suggest that we rate one more highly? Visit our feedback center at www.fodors.com/feedback.

Budget Well

Hotel and restaurant price categories from ¢ to $$$$ are defined in the opening pages of each chapter. For attractions, we always give standard adult admission fees; reductions are usually available for children, students, and senior citizens. Want to pay with plastic? **AE, D, DC, MC, V** following restaurant and hotel listings indicate whether American Express, Discover, Diners Club, MasterCard, and Visa are accepted.

Restaurants

Unless we state otherwise, restaurants are open for lunch and dinner daily. We mention dress only when there's a specific requirement and reservations only when they're essential or not accepted—it's always best to book ahead.

Hotels

Hotels have private bath, phone, TV, and air-conditioning and operate on the European Plan (aka EP, meaning without meals), unless we specify that they use the Continental Plan (CP, with a Continental breakfast), Breakfast Plan (BP, with a full breakfast), or Modified American Plan (MAP, with breakfast and dinner) or are all-inclusive (including all meals and most activities).

We always list facilities but not whether you'll be charged an extra fee to use them.

Many Listings
- ★ Fodor's Choice
- ★ Highly recommended
- ⊠ Physical address
- ✢ Directions
- ⌖ Mailing address
- ☎ Telephone
- 🖷 Fax
- ⊕ On the Web
- ✆ E-mail
- 💷 Admission fee
- ☺ Open/closed times
- Ⓜ Metro stations
- ▤ Credit cards

Hotels & Restaurants
- 🏨 Hotel
- ➡ Number of rooms
- ◿ Facilities
- ❍ Meal plans
- ✕ Restaurant
- ⌫ Reservations
- ⌦ Smoking
- ⌷ BYOB
- ✕🏨 Hotel with restaurant that warrants a visit

Outdoors
- ⚐ Golf
- ⚠ Camping

Other
- ℂ Family-friendly
- ⇨ See also
- ⊠ Branch address
- ☞ Take note

1

Experience Southern California

Venice Beach, Los Angeles

WORD OF MOUTH

I know many people want to see the glitzy stuff that CA has to offer, but there is some real natural beauty, too. Just take the time to drive down Pacific Coast Highway and look at the water.

—canterbury

WHAT'S NEW IN SOUTHERN CALIFORNIA

Kidding Around

California's theme parks work overtime to keep current. That's why Legoland launched Land of Adventure—with four rides, including Lost Kingdom Adventure—and the interactive Sea Life Aquarium in 2008. A new Sheraton hotel, with direct access to a back entrance to Legoland, also opened in 2008. Disneyland, exploiting its high-grossing movies, has a new play zone based on *Pirates of the Caribbean,* and a new submarine attraction based on *Finding Nemo.* Disney has also opened the Dream Suite, originally designed for the Disney family; lucky guests selected at random may get a chance to spend the night there.

Leave the Driving to Amtrak

Riding the rails can be a very satisfying experience, particularly in California where the distances between destinations can run into the hundreds of miles. You can save money on gas and parking, avoid freeway traffic, and see some of the best the state has to offer. The best trip is on the new, luxuriously appointed Coast Starlight, a long-distance train with sleeping cars that runs between Seattle and Los Angeles, passing some of California's most beautiful coastline as it hugs the beach.

Head for the Hills

Things are looking up for visitors to California's alpine recreation areas, thanks to a host of enhancements. As part of a fittingly gigantic redevelopment project, Mammoth Mountain opened its Top of the Sierra Interpretive Center in spring of 2007 (at an altitude of 11,053 feet, they do mean *top*); and the Westin Monache condominium-hotel, anchor of the Village at Mammoth, is expected to open in time for the upcoming ski season.

Wedding Bells Are Ringing

The State Supreme Court legalized same-sex marriages in June 2008, making California the second state in the nation to go this route, and the decision has the state tourism industry salivating at the prospect of a huge new market. Couples are booking weddings and honeymoons at a record rate. Expect to see the welcome mat out for same-sex couples at all of California's most romantic resorts—from Yosemite to Newport and Laguna beaches to Palm Springs (and, of course, West Hollywood).

Homegrown Hospitality

Agritourism in California isn't new (remember, Knott's Berry Farm once *was* a berry farm), but it is on the rise, with farm tours and agricultural festivals sprouting up everywhere. In the Central Valley, America's number-one producer of stone fruit, you can travel themed tourist routes (like Fresno County's Blossom Trail) and tour herb gardens, fruit orchards, organic dairies, and pumpkin patches. In Southern California public gardens bloom abundantly year-round.

State of the Arts

California's beauty-obsessed citizens aren't the only ones opting for a fresh look these days: its esteemed art museums are also having a bit of work done. Following a trend set by the Getty Villa in L.A. (which debuted its "extreme makeover" in 2006), Long Beach's Museum of Latin American Art doubled its exhibition space in 2007. Meanwhile, the Museum of Contemporary Art in San Diego (MCASD Downtown) has expanded into new digs, and the city's arts-oriented New Children's Museum opened in 2008.

WHEN TO GO

Because they offer activities indoors and out, the top Californian cities rate as all-season destinations. Ditto for Southern California's coastal playgrounds. Blessed with near-constant swimsuit weather, they lure beach bums year-round. (Die-hard sun worshippers, however, should note that a marine overcast called "June gloom" often descends in early summer).

Dying to see Death Valley? It's best appreciated in spring when desert blooms offset its austerity and temperatures are still manageable. Yosemite is ideal in the late spring because roads closed in winter are reopened, the summer crowds have yet to arrive, and the park's waterfalls—swollen with melting snow—run fast.

Snowfall makes winter peak season for skiers in Mammoth Mountain, where runs typically open around Thanksgiving. (They sometimes remain in operation into June, so you may avoid the crowds—and have the opportunity to ski in your T-shirt.)

Climate

Geography is the key to California's climate. Remember this is a *big* state: one that covers roughly as much ground as Italy and Greece combined. Moreover, its topography is unusually diverse. Traveling the length of it north to south, you'll encounter everything from mist-shrouded redwood forests and fertile valleys to parched (but profoundly beautiful) deserts. It's difficult to generalize much about the state's weather beyond saying that precipitation comes in winter and summers are dry in most places. As a rule, inland regions are hotter in summer and colder in winter, compared with coastal areas, which are relatively cool year-round. As you climb into the mountains, seasonal variations are more apparent: winter brings snow (at elevations above 3,000 feet), autumn is crisp, spring can go either way, and summer is sunny and warm, with only an occasional thundershower.

Forecasts

National Weather Service (⊕ *www.wrh.noaa. gov*). **Weather Channel** (⊕ *www.weather.com*).

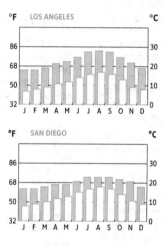

Microclimates

Mountains separate the California coastline from the state's interior, and the weather can sometimes vary dramatically within a 15-minute drive. Day and nighttime temperatures can also vary greatly. In August, Palm Springs' thermometers can soar to 110°F at noon, and drop to 75°F at night. Bottom line: bring along a jacket, you never know when you're going to need it.

WHAT'S WHERE

The following numbers refer to chapters.

2 San Diego. Planeloads of visitors head here to see the world-famous zoo and Sea-World, as well as the historic Gaslamp Quarter and Mexican-inflected Old Town.

3 Orange County. The real O.C. is a diverse destination with premium resorts, first-rate restaurants, strollable waterfront communities, and kid-friendly attractions.

4 Los Angeles. Love it or hate it (and there are many, many reasons to love it), L.A. is a world-class metropolis.

5 Channel Islands National Park. Only 60 mi northwest of Los Angeles, this park seems worlds away.

6 The Inland Empire. Head here for alpine respite in Wrightwood and Idyllwild, seasonal escapes in the San Bernardino Mountains and Lake Arrowhead, and winery tours in the Temecula Valley.

7 Palm Springs & the Southern Desert. Golf the finest courses, lounge at fabulous resorts, and experience ethereal deserts.

8 Joshua Tree National Park. Proximity to urban areas—and great rock climbing—makes this one of the most visited national parks.

9 Death Valley National Park. The desert is vast, lonely—and stunning.

10 The Mojave Desert. In this hardscrabble country, stark beauty compensates for material pleasures.

11 The Southern Sierra. Sawtooth mountains and deep powder combine to create outstanding skiing conditions.

12 Yosemite National Park. The views immortalized by Ansel Adams—of towering granite monoliths, verdant glacial valleys, and lofty waterfalls—are still camera-ready.

13 Sequoia & Kings Canyon National Parks. Ancient redwoods towering above jagged mountains will take your breath away.

14 The Central Valley. Travelers along Highway 99 will enjoy scattered attractions like Forestiere Underground Gardens and the wineries of Lodi.

15 The Central Coast. Swanky Santa Barbara, Hearst Castle, and Big Sur sit along this scenic 200-mi route.

16 Monterey Bay Area. Postcard-perfect Monterey, Victorian-flavored Pacific Grove, surfer paradise Santa Cruz, and exclusive Carmel share this gorgeous stretch of coast.

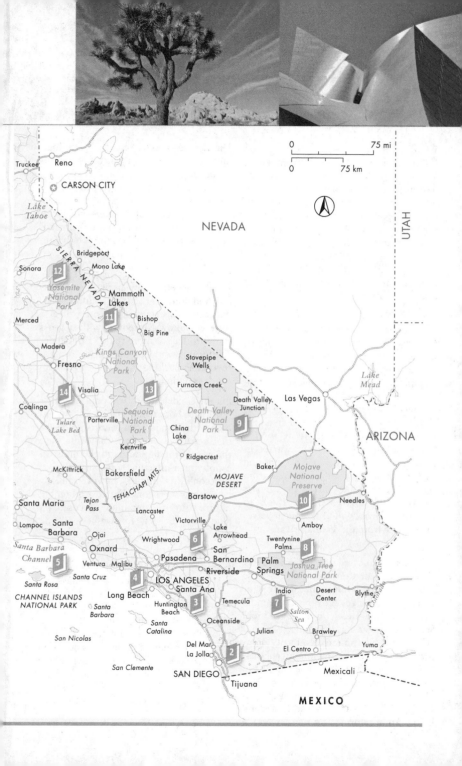

CALIFORNIA TODAY

The People

California is as much a state of mind as a state in the union—a kind of perpetual Promised Land that has represented many things to many people. In the 18th century, Spanish missionaries came seeking converts. In the 19th, miners rushed here to search for gold. And, in the years since, a long line of Dust Bowl farmers, land speculators, Haight-Ashbury hippies, migrant workers, dot-commers, real estate speculators, and would-be actors came chasing their own dreams.

The result is a population that leans toward idealism—without necessarily being as liberal as you might think. (Remember, this is Ronald Reagan's old stomping ground.) And despite the stereotype of the blue-eyed, blond surfer, California's population is not homogeneous either. Ten million people who live here (over 28% of Californians) are foreign born—including Governor Schwarzenegger. Almost half hail from neighboring Mexico; another third emigrated from Asia, following the waves of Chinese workers who arrived in the 1860s to build the railroads and subsequent waves of refugees from the Vietnam War.

The Politics

What's blue and red and green all over? California: a predominantly Democratic state with a red-hot Republican governor and an aggressive "go green" agenda. Since winning office in 2003, Arnold Schwarzenegger has introduced several environmental initiatives—most notably placing strict controls on greenhouse gas emissions—that have been lauded in some quarters and decried in others. Also on the legislative table are such controversial issues as universal health care and immigration reform.

The debates these issues generate, logically enough, lead to a fair bit of infighting in Sacramento. But that isn't stopping Californians from taking them to the national level. Residents of this large, rich, heavily populated state—which certainly contributes its fair share to the federal budget—will tell you that's only fair.

The Economy

Leading all other states in terms of the income generated by agriculture, tourism, and industrial activity, California has the country's strongest and most diverse state economy. Moreover, with a gross state product of more than $1.6 trillion, California would be one of the top ten economies *in the world* if it were an independent nation.

But the Golden State's economic history is filled with boom-and-bust cycles—beginning with the mid-19th-century gold rush that started it all—and California (and the rest of the nation) is in the midst of a downturn affecting some segments of the economy. Optimists, however, already have their eyes on the next potential boom: "green companies" focused on alternative energy, renewables, electric cars, and the like.

The Culture

Cultural organizations thrive in California, and you'll find world-class art museums; ballet-, opera-, and theater companies; and symphonies throughout the state. But California's *real* forte is pop culture, and L.A. and its environs are the chief arbiters. Movie, TV, and video production have long been centered here (Hollywood celebrated 100 years of filmmaking in 2007). Capitol Records set up shop in L.A. in the 1940s, and this area

has been instrumental in the music industry ever since.

And while these industries continue to influence national trends, today they are only part of the pop culture equation. Online "communities" have their says as well—YouTube, MySpace, and Facebook are California creations.

The Parks and Preserves

Cloud-spearing redwood groves, snow-tipped mountains, canyon-slashed deserts, primordial lava beds, and a seemingly endless coast: California's natural diversity is staggering—and efforts to protect it started early. The first national park here was established in 1890, and the National Park Service now oversees 30 sites in California (more than in any other state). When you factor in 278 state parks—which encompass underwater preserves, wildlife reserves, dune systems, and other sensitive habitats—the number of acres involved is almost as impressive as the topography itself.

Due to encroaching development and pollution, keeping these natural treasures in pristine condition is an ongoing challenge. For instance, Sequoia and Kings Canyon (which is plagued by pesticides and other agricultural pollutants blown in from the San Joaquin Valley) has been named America's "smoggiest park" by the National Parks Conservation Association, and the Environmental Protection Agency has designated it as an "ozone non-attainment area with levels of ozone pollution that threaten human health."

The Cuisine

California gave us McDonald's, Denny's, Carl's Jr., Taco Bell, and, of course, In-N-Out Burger. Fortunately for those of us with fast-clogging arteries, the state also kick-started the organic food movement. Back in the 1970s, California-based chefs put American cuisine on the culinary map by focusing on freshly prepared seasonal ingredients.

Today, this focus has spawned the "locavore" movement—followers try to only consume food produced within a 100-mi radius of where they live, since processing and refining food and transporting goods over long distances is bad for both the body and the environment.

This isn't much of a restriction in California, where a huge variety of crops grow year-round. Some 350 cities and towns have certified farmers' markets—and their stalls are filled to overflowing. California has been America's top agricultural producer for the last 50 years, growing more fruits and vegetables than any other state. Dairies and ranches also thrive here, and fishing fleets harvest fish and shellfish from the rich waters offshore.

QUINTESSENTIAL SOUTHERN CALIFORNIA

The Beach

California's beach culture is, in a word, legendary. Of course, it only makes sense that folks living in a state with a 1,264-mi coastline (a hefty portion of which sees the sun upward of 300 days a year) would perfect the art of beach-going. True aficionados begin with a reasonably fit physique, plus a stylish wardrobe consisting of flip-flops, bikinis, wet suits, and such. Mastery of at least one beach skill—surfing, boogie boarding, kayaking, Frisbee tossing, power walking, or soaking up some rays—is also essential. As a visitor, though, you need only a swimsuit and some rented equipment for most sports. You can then hit the beach almost anywhere, thanks to the California belief in coastal access as a birthright. The farther south you go, the wider, sandier, and sunnier the beaches become; moving north they are rockier and foggier, with colder and rougher surf.

The Unusual

Maybe the constantly perfect weather or the looming threat of earthquakes makes Southern Californians a little crazy. Whatever the reason, many have a pronounced appetite for the unusual, the off-center, even the bizarre. Witness the Integratron, a domed time machine with UFO landing strip, near Joshua Tree National Park (itself filled with natural oddities). Or San Luis Obispo's Madonna Inn, where you can sleep in a faux-cave and stir pink sugar into your coffee. Marta Becket performs solo in her Amargosa Opera House outside Death Valley National Park, where Scotty's Castle stands in pointless Moorish-style splendor way out in the desert. Idiosyncratic creations large and small litter the Southern California landscape—many of them designed to attract visitors, others simply personal expressions.

Californians live in such a large and splashy state that they sometimes seem to forget about the rest of the country. They've developed a distinctive culture all their own, which you can delve into by doing as the locals do.

The Automobile

Americans may have a love affair with the automobile, but Californians have an out-and-out obsession. Even when gas prices rev up and freeway traffic slows down, their passion burns as hot as ever. You can witness this ardor any summer weekend at huge classic- and custom-car shows held statewide. Even better, you can feel it yourself by taking the wheel. Drive to the sea following Laguna Canyon Road to Laguna Beach; trace an old stagecoach route through the mountains above Santa Barbara on Highway 154; track migrating whales up the coast to Big Sur; or take 17-Mile Drive along the precipitous edge of the Monterey Peninsula. Glorious for the most part, but authentically congested in some areas in the south, Highway 1 runs almost the entire length of the state.

The Outdoors

One of California's greatest assets—the mild year-round weather enjoyed by most of the state—inspires residents to spend as much time outside as they possibly can. To be sure, they have a tremendous enthusiasm for every imaginable outdoor sport, and, up north especially, fresh-air adventures are extremely popular (which may explain why everyone there seems to own at least one pair of hiking boots). But, overall, the California-alfresco creed is more broadly interpreted. Indeed, the general rule when planning any activity is "if it can happen outside, it will!" *Plein air* vacation opportunities include dining on patios, decks, and wharves; shopping in street markets or elaborate open-air malls; hearing almost any kind of music at moonlight concerts; touring the sculpture gardens that grace major art museums; and celebrating everything from gay pride to garlic at outdoor fairs.

TOP SOUTHERN CALIFORNIA ATTRACTIONS

San Diego

(A) San Diego is a thoroughly modern metropolis set on the sunny Pacific, filled with tourist attractions (think the zoo and SeaWorld) and blissful beaches. But this is also a city steeped in history—in 1769 Spaniards established a settlement here at Old Town, site of the first Spanish outpost and now a state park dedicated to illustrating San Diego's raucous early days. The city's rousing downtown dining and entertainment district, the Gaslamp Quarter, is a contemporary recreation of bawdy Stingaree of the late 1800s.

Los Angeles

(B) Tinsel Town, Lala Land, City of Angels: L.A. goes by many names and has many personas. Recognized as America's capital of pop culture, it also has high-brow appeal with arts institutions like the Getty Center, the Geffen Contemporary, Walt Disney Concert Hall, the Norton Simon Museum, and Huntington Library. But you can go wild here, too—and not just on the Sunset Strip. Griffith Park, Will Rogers State Historic Park, and Malibu Lagoon State Beach all offer a natural break from the concrete jungle.

Channel Islands National Park

(C) This five-island park northwest of Los Angeles is a remote but accessible eco escape. There are no phones, no cars, and no services—but there are over 2,000 species of plants and animals (among them blue whales and brown pelicans), plus ample opportunities for active pursuits. On land, hiking tops the itinerary. Underwater preserves surround the park, so snorkeling, scuba diving, fishing, and kayaking around lava tubes and natural arches are other memorable options.

Palm Springs

(D) Celebrities used to flee to the desert for rest, relaxation, a few rays of sun, and

indulgence in some high jinks beyond the watchful eyes of the media. You don't have to spend much time in Palm Springs to realize those days are *long* gone. In this improbably situated bastion of Bentleys and bling, worldly pleasures rule. Glorious golf courses, tony shops and restaurants, decadent spa resorts—they're all here. Solitude seekers can still slip away to Joshua Tree National Park or Anza-Borrego Desert State Park.

Death Valley

(E) On the surface, a vacation in Death Valley sounds about as attractive as a trip to hell. Yet for well-prepared travelers, the experience is more awe inspiring than ominous. Within the largest national park in the contiguous United States you'll find the brilliantly colored rock formations of Artists Palette, the peaks of the Panamint Mountains, and the desolate salt flats of Badwater, 282 feet below sea level. You can't get any lower than this in the Western Hemisphere—and, in summer, you can't get much hotter.

Yosemite National Park

(F,G) Nature looms large here, both literally and figuratively. In addition to hulking Half Dome, the park is home to El Capitan (the world's largest exposed granite monolith, rising 3,593 feet above the glacier-carved valley floor) and Yosemite Falls (North America's tallest cascade). In Yosemite's signature stand of giant sequoias—the Mariposa Grove—even the trees are Bunyanesque. Needless to say, crowds can be super-size, too, as this is one of America's most popular national parks. And if you haven't had your fill of natural wonders, two more parks—Sequoia and Kings Canyon—are just to the south.

SOUTHERN CALIFORNIA'S TOP EXPERIENCES

Hit the Road

Kings Canyon Highway, Redwood Highway, Tioga Pass, 17-Mile Drive, the Lake Tahoe loop: California has some splendid and challenging roads. You'll drive through a tunnel formed by towering redwood trees on the Redwood Highway. If you venture over the Sierras by way of Tioga Pass (through Yosemite in summer only), you'll see emerald green meadows, gray granite monoliths, and pristine blue lakes . . . and very few people.

Ride a Wave

Surfing—which has influenced everything from fashion to moviemaking to music—is a quintessential California activity. You can find great surf breaks anywhere along the coast between Santa Cruz and San Diego. But one of the best places to try it is Huntington Beach. Lessons are widely available. If you're not ready to hang ten, you can hang out at "Surf City's" International Surfing Museum or stroll the Surfing Walk of Fame.

Think Globally, Eat Locally

Over the years California cuisine has evolved from a mere trend into a respected gastronomic tradition: one that pairs local, often organic or sustainable, ingredients with techniques inspired by European, Asian, and, increasingly, Middle Eastern cuisine.

Embrace Your Inner Eccentric

Maybe the looming threat of earthquakes makes Californians a little crazy. Maybe they're just quirky. In any case, if you can't beat 'em, join 'em. Begin by touring Hearst Castle—the beautifully bizarre estate William Randolph Hearst built above San Simeon. Scotty's Castle, a Moorish confection in Death Valley, offers a variation on the theme; as does Marta Becket's one-woman Armargosa Opera House.

Get Reel

In L.A. it's almost obligatory to do some Hollywood-style stargazing. Cue the action with a behind-the-scenes tour of one of the dream factories. (Warner Bros. Studios' five-hour deluxe version, which includes lunch in the commissary, is just the ticket for cinephiles.) Other must-sees include the Kodak Theatre, home of the Academy Awards; Grauman's Chinese Theatre, where celebs press hands into cement for posterity's sake; Hollywood Boulevard's star-paved Walk of Fame; and the still iconic Hollywood sign.

Go Wild

California communities host hundreds of annual events, but some of the best are organized by Mother Nature. The most famous is the "miracle migration" that sees swallows flock back to Mission San Juan Capistrano each March. Masses of monarch butterflies reliably arrive in Pacific Grove for their winter vacation every October; and, in an event worthy of *Ripley's Believe It or Not,* grunion fish come onshore to spawn along select SoCal beaches March through May.

People-Watch

Opportunities for world-class people-watching abound in California. Just saunter along the century-old boardwalk in time-warped, resiliently boho Santa Cruz. Better yet, hang around L.A.'s Venice Boardwalk, where chainsaw jugglers, surfers, fortune-tellers, and well-oiled bodybuilders take beachfront exhibitionism to a new high (or low, depending on your point of view). The result is pure eye candy.

FAQ

I'm not particularly active. Will I still enjoy visiting a national park? Absolutely, the most popular parks really do have something for everyone. Take Yosemite. When the ultrafit embark on 12-hour trail treks, mere mortals can hike Cook's Meadow—an easy 1-mi loop that's also wheelchair accessible. If even that seems too daunting, you can hit the highlights (Yosemite Falls, Half Dome, El Capitan, and more) on a $22 bus tour; hop on a free shuttle; or drive yourself to sites like Glacier Point or the Mariposa Grove of Giant Sequoias.

What's the single best place to take the kids? Well, that depends on your children's ages and interests, but for its sheer smorgasbord of activities, San Diego is hard to beat. Between the endless summer weather and sites such as SeaWorld, the San Diego Zoo, and Legoland (about 30 minutes away), California's southernmost city draws families in droves.

Once you've covered the mega-attractions, enjoy an easy-to-swallow history lesson in Old Town or the Maritime Museum. Want to explore different ecosystems? La Jolla Cove has kid-friendly tidal pools and cliff caves; while Anza-Borrego Desert State Park is a doable two-hour drive east. That being said, there are kid-friendly attractions all over the state—your kids are going to have to try really hard to be bored.

California sounds expensive. How can I save on sightseeing? If you're focusing on the big three cities, consider taking a pass—a Go Card Pass (☎800/887–9103 ⊕www. gocardusa.com), that is. Sold in one-day to one-week versions, they're priced from $45 and cover dozens of tours and attractions in San Diego or L.A. CityPass (☎888/330–5008 ⊕www.citypass.com) includes admission and some upgrades for main attractions in Hollywood and Southern California. Many museums set aside free-admission days. Prefer the great outdoors? An $80 America the Beautiful annual pass (☎888/275–8747 ⊕www. nps.gov) admits you to every site under the National Park Service umbrella. Better yet, depending on the property, passengers in your vehicle get in free, too.

Any tips for a first-time trip into the desert? The desert's stark, sun-blasted beauty will strip your mind of everyday clutter. But it is a brutal, punishing place for anyone ill-prepared. So whether it's your first or 15th visit, the same dos and don'ts apply. Stick to a state or national park. Pick up pamphlets at its visitor center and *follow the instructions* they set out. Keep your gas tank full. Bring lots of water and drink at least two gallons a day—even if you're not thirsty. Wear a hat and sunscreen, and don't expect to move too fast at midday when the sun is kiln-hot.

I'm not crazy about spending 14 nights in hotels. Any alternatives? If you want to pretend you're lucky enough to live in California, try a vacation rental. Aside from providing privacy, a rental lets you set your own schedule and cook at your leisure (you'll save money, plus it's a great excuse to stock up on that fine California produce!). HomeAway (⊕www. homeaway.com) is a good place for house hunting. It lists more than 4,000 condos, cottages, beach houses, ski chalets, and villas.

For more information on California trip planning, see the Essentials sections in each chapter and at the back of the book.

GREAT ITINERARIES

SOUTHERN CALIFORNIA DREAMING

Los Angeles, Palm Springs & San Diego

Day 1: Arrival/Los Angeles

As soon as you land at LAX, make like a local and hit the freeway. Even if downtown L.A.'s top-notch art, history, and science museums don't tempt you, the hodgepodge of art-deco, beaux-arts, and futuristic architecture begs at least a drive-by. Heading west, Wilshire Boulevard cuts through a historical and cultural cross-section of the city. Two stellar sights on its Miracle Mile are the encyclopedic Los Angeles County Museum of Art and the fossil-filled La Brea Tar Pits. Come evening, the open-air Farmers' Market and its many eateries hum. Hotels in Beverly Hills or West Hollywood beckon, just a few minutes away.

Day 2: Hollywood & the Movie Studios

Every L.A. tourist should devote at least one day to the movies and take at least one studio tour. For fun, choose the special-effects theme park at Universal Studios Hollywood; for the nitty-gritty, choose Warner Bros. Studios. Nostalgic musts in half-seedy, half-preening Hollywood include the Walk of Fame along Hollywood Boulevard, the celebrity footprints cast in concrete outside Grauman's Chinese Theatre, and the 1922 Egyptian Theatre (Hollywood Boulevard's original movie palace). When evening arrives, West Hollywood's restaurants are stoked up and the Sunset Strip club scene couldn't get any hotter—the parking nightmare proves it.

Day 3: Beverly Hills & Santa Monica

Even without that extensive art collection, the Getty Center's pavilion architecture, hilltop gardens, and frame-worthy L.A. views would make it a dazzling destination. Descend to the sea via Sunset Boulevard for lunch along Santa Monica's Third Street Promenade, followed by a ride on this historic carousel on the pier. The buff and the bizarre meet on the boardwalk at Venice Beach (strap on some Rollerblades if you want to join them!). Rodeo Drive in Beverly Hills specializes in exhibitionism with a heftier price tag, but voyeurs are still welcome.

Day 4: Los Angeles to Palm Springs

Freeway traffic permitting, you can drive from the middle of L.A. to the middle of the desert in a couple of hours. Somehow in harmony with the harsh environment, mid-century "modern" homes and businesses with clean, low-slung lines define the Palm Springs style. The city seems far away, though, when you hike in hushed Tahquitz or Indian canyons; cliffs and palm trees there shelter rock art, irrigation works, and other remnants of Agua Caliente culture. If your boots aren't made for walking, you can always practice your golf game or indulge in some spa treatments at an area resort instead.

Day 5: The Desert

If riding a tram up an 8,516-foot mountain for a stroll or even a snowball fight above the desert sounds like fun to you, then show up at the Palm Springs Aerial Tramway before the first morning tram leaves (later, the line can get discouragingly long). Afterward stroll through the Palm Springs Art Museum where you can see a shimmering display of contemporary studio glass, an array of enormous Native American baskets, and signifi-

cant works of 20th-century sculpture by Henry Moore and others.

Day 6: Palm Springs to San Diego

South through desert and mountains via the Palms to Pines Highway on your way to San Diego, you might pause in the Temecula Valley for lunch at a local winery. Otherwise go straight for the city's nautical heart by exploring the restored ships of the Maritime Museum at the waterfront downtown. Victorian buildings—and plenty of other tourists—surround you on a stroll through the Gaslamp Quarter, but the 21st century is in full swing at the leviathan Horton Plaza retail and entertainment complex. Plant yourself at a downtown hotel and graze your way through the neighborhood's many restaurants and nightspots.

Day 7: San Diego Zoo & Coronado

Malayan tapirs in a faux-Asian rain forest, polar bears in an imitation Arctic—the San Diego Zoo maintains a vast and varied collection of creatures in a world-renowned facility comprised of meticulously designed habitats. Come early, wear comfy shoes, and stay as long as you can stand the droves of children. Boutique-y Coronado—anchored by the

grand Hotel Del Coronado—offers a more adult antidote. Tea, cocktails, or perhaps dinner at the Del makes a civilized end to an untamed day.

Day 8: SeaWorld & Old Town

Resistance is futile: you're going to SeaWorld. So what if it screams commercial? This humongous theme park, with its walk-through shark tanks and peppy killer-whale shows, also screams fun. Surrender to the experience and try not to sit in anything sticky. Also touristy (but with genuine historical significance), Old Town drips with Spanish and Mexican heritage. Soak it up in the plaza at Old Town San Diego State Historic Park; then browse the stalls and shops outside the park of Bazaar del Mundo and San Diego Avenue.

Day 9: La Jolla to Laguna Beach

Positioned above an idyllic cove, La Jolla invites lingering. So slow down long enough to enjoy its shop-lined streets, sheltered beaches, and cultural institutions like the low-key Birch Aquarium at Scripps and the well-curated Museum of Contemporary Art. At Mission San Luis Rey, in Oceanside, and Mission San Juan Capistrano, you can glimpse life as

it was during the Spanish colonial days. Once a haven for artists, Laguna Beach still abounds with galleries. Its walkable downtown streets would abut busy Main Beach Park if the Pacific Coast Highway didn't run through the middle of town.

Day 10: Catalina Island

Having spent so much time looking at the ocean, it's high time you got out *on* it—a quick excursion to Catalina, 75 minutes from the coast, will do the trick. Get an early start, catching the ferry from Newport Beach, then use the day to explore this nostalgia-inducing spot. The harbor town of Avalon has a charming, retro feel, while the island's mountains, canyons, and coves are ideal spots for outdoor adventures. Take the 4:30 boat back to the mainland and overnight in Anaheim.

Day 11: Disneyland

Disney's original park is a blast even without kids in tow. So go ahead: skirt the lines at the box office—advance-purchased ticket in hand—and storm the gates of the Magic Kingdom. You can cram the highlights into a single day if you arrive at opening time with a strategy already mapped out. Alternately, you can spend your final full day next door at Disneyland's sister park, California Adventure, which is a fitting homage to the Golden State. In either case, cap your holiday with a nighttime toast at Downtown Disney.

Day 12: Departure/Los Angeles

Pack up your mouse gear and give yourself ample time to reach the airport. Without traffic the 35-mi drive from Anaheim to LAX *should* take about 45 minutes.

TIPS

❶ If you don't have 12 days to spare, or if really hot weather bothers you, cut this itinerary down to 10 days by skipping the Palm Springs segment and going directly to San Diego from Los Angeles. It's a 120-mi drive on Interstate 5.

❷ Don't get shut out of anything you really want to see, and don't waste precious vacation time standing in line. Make reservations and purchase tickets in advance whenever possible. Discounted multi-venue packages are widely available.

❸ No matter how carefully you plan your movements to avoid busy routes at peak hours, you will inevitably encounter heavy traffic in L.A., Orange County, and San Diego.

❹ Allow yourself twice as much time as you think you'll need to negotiate LAX.

San Diego

Balboa Park

WORD OF MOUTH

"San Diego is one of the most interesting places in the USA to visit. We loved to look at the incoming ships and drive the coast. . . . So much to see besides the Balboa Park museums and all the rest."

—JJ5

"The Zoo (in my opinion) is a must! It was our favorite part of the trip. . . . We LOVED San Diego and decided that it was the city of friendly people as everyone was so nice."

—travelmonkey

ME TO
EGO

TOP REASONS TO GO

★ **Beautiful beaches:** San Diego's shore shimmers with crystalline Pacific waters rolling up to some of the prettiest stretches of sand on the West Coast.

★ **Good eats:** Taking full advantage of the region's bountiful vegetables, fruits, herbs, and seafood, San Diego's chefs surprise, dazzle, and delight diners with inventive California-colorful cuisine.

★ **History lessons:** The well-preserved and reconstructed historic sites in California's first European settlement help you imagine what the area was like when Spanish and Portuguese explorers first arrived.

★ **Stellar shopping:** Horton Plaza, the Gaslamp Quarter, Seaport Village, Coronado, Old Town . . . it seems like no matter where you go in San Diego, you'll find great places to do a little browsing.

★ **Urban oasis:** Balboa Park contains 1,200 acres waiting to be explored, including most of San Diego's museums and its world-famous zoo.

1 Downtown. San Diego's downtown area is delightfully urban and accessible, filled with walkable A-list attractions like the Gaslamp Quarter, Horton Plaza, and the harbor.

2 Old Town. The former pueblo of San Diego—California's first permanent European settlement— is now preserved as a state historic park.

3 La Jolla. This luxe, bluff-top enclave fittingly means "the jewel" in Spanish. Come here for fantastic upscale shopping and unspoiled stretches of the coast.

4 Mission Bay. Home to 27 mi of shoreline (and SeaWorld), this 4,600 acre aquatic park is San Diego's monument to sports and fitness.

5 Coronado. Home to the Hotel Del, this islandlike peninsula is a favorite celebrity haunt. Boutique-filled Orange Street and Silver Strand State Beach are two great stops.

2

GETTING ORIENTED

Exploring San Diego may be an endless adventure, but there are limitations, especially if you don't have a car. San Diego is more a chain of separate communities than a cohesive city, and many of the major attractions are separated by some distance. Walking is good for getting an up-close look at how San Diegans live, but true Southern Californians use the freeways that crisscross the county. Interstate 5 runs a direct north–south route through the coastal communities from Orange County in the north to the Mexican border. Interstates 805 and 15 do much the same inland. Interstate 8 is the main east–west route. Routes 163, 52, and 94 serve as connectors.

SAN DIEGO PLANNER

Getting Around

If you're going to drive around San Diego, study a map before you hit the road. The freeways are convenient and fast most of the time, but if you miss your turnoff or get caught in commuter traffic, you'll experience a none-too-pleasurable hallmark of Southern California living—freeway madness.

Public transportation has improved a great deal in the past decade: the San Diego Trolley, which runs as far south as San Ysidro, has expanded in the north from Old Town to beyond Mission San Diego and San Diego State University; commuter *Coaster* trains run frequently between downtown San Diego and Oceanside, with convenient stops in Del Mar, Encinitas, Carlsbad, and other charming coastal towns; and the bus system covers almost all of the county. Making connections to see the various sights is time-consuming, however. Since the coast is itself a major attraction, consider staying there if you're carless. The great distances between sights render taxis prohibitively expensive for general transportation, although cabs are useful for getting around once you're in a given area. Old Town Trolley Tours has a hop-on, hop-off route of popular spots around the city.

About the Restaurants

Because of its multiethnic population, you can find cuisine from nearly every part of the world in San Diego. Local specialties include fish tacos and spiny lobster. While "Appropriate Dress Required" signs are sometimes displayed in the entrances to restaurants, this generally means nothing more than clean and reasonably neat clothing. Meals cost less in San Diego than in other major metropolitan areas, but you may find more expensive entrées in districts like La Jolla, the Gaslamp Quarter, and Little Italy. Reservations are always a good idea; we mention them only when they're essential or not accepted.

About the Hotels

When you make reservations, ask about specials. Many hotels promote discounted weekend packages to fill rooms after convention and business customers leave town. High season is summer, and rates are lowest in the fall. Since the weather is great year-round, don't expect substantial discounts in winter. That being said, you can find affordable rooms in even the most expensive areas. If an ocean view is important, request it when booking, but be aware that it will cost significantly more than a non-ocean-view room. You can save on hotels and attractions by visiting the San Diego Convention & Visitors Bureau Web site (www.sandiego.org) for a free Vacation Planning Kit with a Travel Value Coupon booklet.

WHAT IT COSTS				
¢	$	$$	$$$	$$$$
Restaurants				
under $10	$10–$18	$19–$27	$28–$35	over $35
Hotels				
under $100	$100–$199	$200–$299	$300–$400	over $400
Dining prices are for a main course at dinner, excluding 7.75% tax. Lodging prices are for a standard double room in high (summer) season, excluding 10.5% tax.				

Updated
by Maria
Hunt, Marlise
Elizabeth
Kast, Amanda
Knoles, Jane
Onstott,
AnnaMaria
Stephens,
Bobbi Zane

SAN DIEGO IS A BIG city—second only to Los Angeles in population—with a small-town feel. It also covers a lot of territory, roughly 400 square mi of land and sea. To the north and south of the city are 70 mi of beaches. Inland, a succession of chaparral-covered mesas are punctuated with deep-cut canyons that step up to savannalike hills, separating the verdant coast from the arid Anza-Borrego Desert.

The San Diego area, the birthplace of California, was claimed for Spain by explorer Juan Rodríguez Cabrillo in 1542 and eventually came under Mexican rule. You'll find reminders of San Diego's Spanish and Mexican heritage throughout the region——in architecture and place-names, in distinctive Mexican cuisine, and in the historic buildings of Old Town.

In 1867 developer Alonzo Horton, who called the town's bayfront "the prettiest place for a city I ever saw," began building a hotel, a plaza, and prefab homes on 960 downtown acres. The city's fate was sealed in 1908, when President Theodore Roosevelt's Great White Fleet sailed into the bay. The U.S. Navy, impressed by the city's excellent harbor and temperate climate, decided to build a destroyer base on San Diego Bay in the 1920s. The newly developed aircraft industry soon followed (Charles Lindbergh's plane Spirit of St. Louis was built here). The military, which operates many bases and installations throughout the county, continues to contribute to the local economy.

EXPLORING SAN DIEGO

BALBOA PARK

Overlooking downtown and the Pacific Ocean, 1,200-acre Balboa Park is the cultural heart of San Diego, where you'll find most of the city's museums and its world-famous zoo. Most first-time visitors see only these attractions, but Balboa Park is really a series of botanical gardens. Kate Sessions, the "Mother of Balboa Park," made sure that both developed and undeveloped acreage here bloomed with the purple blossoms of the jacaranda tree, palms, and hundreds of varieties of other trees.

Historic buildings dating from San Diego's 1915 Panama–California International Exposition are strung along the park's main east–west thoroughfare, El Prado, which leads from 6th Avenue eastward over the Laurel Street Bridge (also known as the Cabrillo Bridge), the park's official gateway.

Parking near Balboa Park's museums is no small accomplishment. If you end up parking a bit far from your destination, consider the stroll back through the greenery part of the day's recreation. Alternatively, you can just park at Inspiration Point on the east side of the park, off Presidents Way. Free trams run from there to the museums every 8–10 minutes, 9:30–5:30 daily.

SIGHTS TO SEE

❶ Alcazar Garden. The gardens surrounding the Alcazar Castle in Seville, Spain, inspired the landscaping here; you'll feel like royalty resting on the benches by the exquisitely tiled fountains. The flower beds are ever-changing horticultural exhibits featuring more than 6,000 annuals for a nearly perpetual bloom. Bright orange-and-yellow poppies appear in spring and deep rust and crimson chrysanthemums arrive in fall. ✉ *1439 El Prado.*

OFF THE BEATEN PATH

Hillcrest. Northwest of Balboa Park, Hillcrest is San Diego's center for the gay community and artists of all types. It truly is one of the city's most interesting neighborhoods. University, 4th, and 5th avenues are filled with cafés, a superb collection of restaurants (including many outstanding ethnic eateries), and boutiques (among which are several indie bookstores selling new and used books along 5th below University).

❹ Reuben H. Fleet Science Center. The Fleet Center's clever interactive exhibits are artfully educational. You can reconfigure your face to have two left sides, or, by replaying an instant video clip, watch yourself coming and going at different speeds. The IMAX Dome Theater, the world's first, screens exhilarating nature and science films. A 23-passenger motion simulator ride takes you on a journey into exciting realms. The Nierman Challenger Learning Center—a realistic mock mission-control and futuristic space station—is a big hit. ✉ *1875 El Prado* ☎ *619/238–1233* ⊕ *www.rhfleet.org* ✉ *Gallery exhibits $8, gallery exhibits and IMAX film $12.50* ☉ *Daily 9:30; closing hrs vary from 5 to 9, call ahead.*

Fodor'sChoice
★

❷ San Diego Museum of Art. Known primarily for its Spanish Baroque and Renaissance paintings, including works by El Greco, Goya, Rubens, and van Ruisdael, San Diego's most comprehensive art museum also has strong holdings of South Asian art, Indian miniatures, and contemporary California paintings. An outdoor Sculpture Court and Garden exhibits both traditional and modern pieces. The IMAGE (Interactive Multimedia Art Gallery Explorer) system allows you to call up the highlights of the museum's collection on a computer screen and custom-design a tour, call up historical information on the works and artists, and print color reproductions. The museum's goal is to "connect people to art and art to people," so its exhibits tend to have broad appeal, and if traveling shows from other cities come to town, you can expect to see them here. Lectures, concerts, and film events are also on the roster. Free docent tours are offered throughout the day. ✉ *1450 El Prado* ☎ *619/232–7931* ⊕ *www.sdmart.org* ✉ *$10* ☉ *Tues.–Sun. 10–6; Memorial Day–Labor Day until 9 Thurs.*

❸ San Diego Zoo. Balboa Park's—and perhaps the city's—most famous attraction is its 100-acre zoo, and it deserves all the press it gets. Nearly 4,000 animals of some 800 diverse species roam in hospitable, expertly crafted habitats that replicate natural environments as closely as possible. The flora in the zoo, including many rare species, is even more costly than the fauna. Walkways wind over bridges and past waterfalls

Fodor'sChoice
★

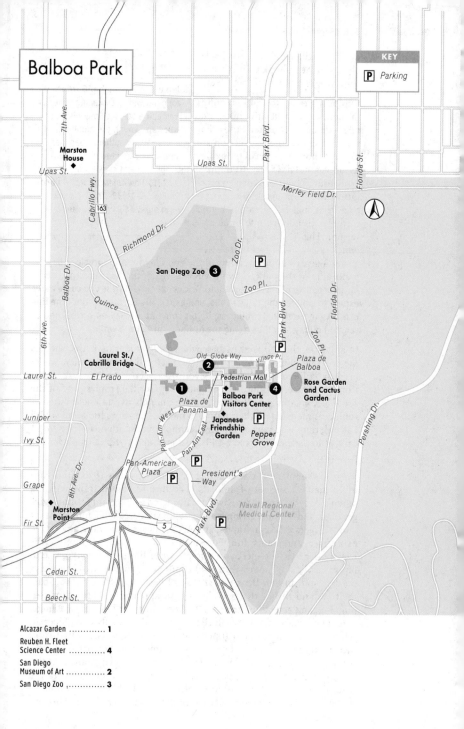

Balboa Park

ringed with tropical ferns; elephants in a sandy plateau roam so close you're tempted to pet them.

Exploring the zoo fully requires the stamina of a healthy hiker, but open-air double-decker buses that run throughout the day let you zip through three-quarters of the exhibits on a guided 35- to 40-minute, 3-mi tour. There are also express buses, used for quick transportation, that make five stops around the grounds and include some narration. The Skyfari Aerial Tram, which soars 170 feet above the

> **TRANQUIL BREAK**
>
> **Japanese Friendship Garden.** A koi pond with a cascading water wall and a 60-foot-long wisteria arbor are among the highlights of Balboa Park's authentic Japanese garden, designed to inspire contemplation and evoke tranquility. ✉ *2215 Pan American Rd., Balboa Park* ☎ *619/232-2721* ⊕ *www. niwa.org* ✍ *$4* ☾ *Tues.–Sun. 10–4.*

ground, gives a good overview of the zoo's layout and, on clear days, a panorama of the park, downtown San Diego, the bay, and the ocean, far past the San Diego–Coronado Bridge. ■ TIP➡ Unless you come early, expect to wait for the regular bus, and especially for the top tier—the line can take more than 45 minutes; if you come at midday on a weekend or school holiday, you'll be doing the in-line shuffle for a while.

In any case, the zoo is at its best when you wander its paths, such as the one that climbs through the huge, enclosed **Scripps Aviary,** where brightly colored tropical birds swoop between branches just inches from your face, and into the neighboring **Gorilla Tropics,** one of the zoo's bioclimatic zone exhibits, where animals live in enclosed environments modeled on their native habitats. The zones look and sound natural, thanks in part to modern technology: the sounds of the tropical rain forest emerge from a 144-speaker sound system that plays CDs recorded in Africa.

The zoo's simulated Asian rain forest, **Tiger River,** has 10 exhibits with more than 35 species of animals. The mist-shrouded trails winding down a canyon into Tiger River are bordered by fragrant jasmine, ginger lilies, and orchids, giving you the feeling of descending into an Asian jungle. Tigers, Malayan tapirs, and Argus pheasants wander among the exotic trees and plants. **Ituri Forest**—a 4-acre African rain forest at the base of Tiger River—lets you glimpse huge but surprisingly graceful hippos frolicking under water, and buffalo cavorting with monkeys on dry land. In **Sun Bear Forest** playful beasts constantly claw apart the trees and shrubs that serve as a natural playground for climbing, jumping, and general merrymaking. At the popular **Polar Bear Plunge,** where you can watch the featured animals take a chilly dive, Siberian reindeer, white foxes, and other Arctic creatures are separated from their predatory neighbors by a series of camouflaged moats. The lush, tropical environment at **Absolutely Apes,** where orangutans and siamangs climb, swing, and generally live almost as they would in the wild, is lined with 110-foot-long and 12-foot-high viewing windows that offer a unique opportunity to see these endangered apes close up.

"PANDA-MONIUM"

The San Diego Zoo currently has more giant pandas than any other zoo in the United States, and is the only zoo in North America to have had four successful panda births. The zoo's first success was Hua Mei, born in 1999 and the first giant panda cub born in the United States to survive to adulthood. Hua Mei's mother, Bai Yun, then had a second cub, a male, Mei Sheng, in August 2003. Two years later, in August 2005, Bai Yun and Gao Gao, her mate, became the parents of the cute-ster Su Lin, a female. In August 2007 Bai Yun gave birth to her fourth cub, Zhen Zhen, which appropriately means "precious." The female cub was just four ounces at birth, about the size of a stick of butter! When fully grown, Zhen Zhen will weigh between 220 and 330 pounds.

Hua Mei and Mei Sheng (who left in November 2007) now live in China, but Su Lin, Zhen Zhen, and their parents are generally available for viewing from 9 to 4:15 each day at the Giant Panda Research Station. All pandas in the U.S. are on loan from China, and even babies born here pass to China's control after their third birthday. By the time of your visit, China may have decided that Su Lin should come home or be sent elsewhere. After Hua Mei was returned to China in 2004, she became a mother herself, to a set of twins born in September 2004, then to a second set of twins in August 2005—truly blessed events considering there are presumed to be only 1,500 pandas still remaining in the wild. Expect lines at the panda exhibit to be long, so arrive early.

The San Diego Zoo houses the largest number of koalas outside Australia, and they remain major crowd pleasers even though they are overshadowed by the pandas and especially the baby pandas that result from the work of the zoo's department of Conservation and Research for Endangered Species.

For a hands-on experience there's the **Children's Zoo,** where goats and sheep beg to be petted. There is one viewer-friendly nursery where you may see various baby animals bottle-feed and sleep peacefully in large baby cribs. Children can see entertaining creatures of all sorts nearby at the Wegeforth National Park Sea Lion Show in Wegeforth Bowl and at the Wild Ones Show in Hunte Amphitheater, both put on daily.

Joan B. Kroc's **Monkey Trails and Forest Tales** spans three acres representing African and Asian forests. This is the largest and most elaborate animal habitat in the zoo's history. You can follow an elevated trail at treetop level and trek paths on the forest floor, observing some of nature's most unusual and threatened animals and birds, including African mandrills, Asia's clouded leopard, the rare pygmy hippopotamus, Visayan warty pigs from the Philippines, weaver birds that build the most elaborate nests of any species, not to mention flora such as endangered mahogany trees, rare, exotic orchids, and insect-eating plants.

Set to debut in spring 2009, the zoo's newest exhibit, Elephant Odyssey, highlights animals of the past, present, and future. The 7-acre habitat features relatives of animal species that dotted the Southern California landscape more than 10,000 years ago, such as elephants, lions, and wild horses.

The zoo rents strollers, wheelchairs, and cameras; it also has a first-aid office, a lost and found, and an ATM. It's best to avert your eyes from the two main gift shops until the end of your visit; you can spend a half day just poking through the wonderful animal-related posters, crafts, dishes, clothing, and toys. There is one guilt-alleviating fact if you buy too much: some of the profits of your purchases go to zoo programs. Audio tours, behind-the-scenes tours, walking tours, tours in Spanish, and tours for people with hearing or vision impairments are available; inquire at the entrance. Lastly, when you've finished here, you haven't seen it all until you've seen the San Diego Wild Animal Park, the zoo's 1,800-acre extension to the north at Escondido. ⊠*2920 Zoo Dr.* ☎*619/234–3153, 888/697–2632 Giant panda hotline* ⊕*www. sandiegozoo.org* ⬛*$24.50 includes zoo, Children's Zoo, and animal shows; $34 includes above, plus guided bus tour, unlimited express bus rides, and round-trip Skyfari Aerial Tram rides; zoo free for children under 12 in Oct.; $60 pass good for admission to zoo and San Diego Wild Animal Park within 5 days* ▤*AE, D, MC, V* ⊙*July–Sept., daily 9–9; Sept.–May, daily 9–4; Children's Zoo and Skyfari ride generally close 1 hr earlier.*

DOWNTOWN

Downtown is San Diego's Lazarus. Written off as moribund by the 1970s, downtown is now one of the city's prime draws. The turnaround began in the late 1970s with the revitalization of the Gaslamp Quarter Historic District and massive redevelopment that gave rise to the Horton Plaza shopping center and the San Diego Convention Center, as well as to elegant hotels, upscale condominium complexes, and trendy restaurants and cafés. Although many consider downtown to be the 16½-block Gaslamp Quarter, it actually comprises eight neighborhoods, also including East Village, Little Italy, and Embarcadero.

Considered the liveliest of the bunch, Gaslamp's Fourth and Fifth avenues are riddled with trendy nightclubs, swanky lounge bars, chic restaurants, and boisterous sports pubs. Nearby, the most ambitious of the downtown projects is East Village, encompassing 130 blocks between the railroad tracks up to J Street, and from 6th Avenue east to around 10th Street. Sparking the rebirth of this former warehouse district was the 2004 construction of the San Diego Padres' baseball stadium, PETCO Park. As the city's largest downtown neighborhood, East Village is continually broadening its boundaries with its urban design of redbrick cafés, spacious galleries, rooftop bars, sleek hotels, and warehouse restaurants.

There are reasonably priced ($4–$7 per day) parking lots along Harbor Drive, Pacific Highway, and lower Broadway and Market Street. Most restaurants offer valet parking at night, but beware of fees of $15 and up.

SIGHTS TO SEE

❶ Embarcadero. The bustle of Embarcadero comes less these days from the activities of fishing folk than from the throngs of tourists, but this waterfront walkway—comprised of Seaport Village and the San Diego Convention Center—remains the nautical soul of the city. There are several seafood restaurants here, as well as sea vessels of every variety—cruise ships, ferries, tour boats, and Navy destroyers.

On the north end of the Embarcadero at Ash Street you'll find the **Maritime Museum.** South of it, the **B Street Pier** is used by ships from major cruise lines—San Diego has become a major cruise-ship port, both a port of call and a departure point. The cavernous Cruise Ship Terminal has a cruise-information center. The occasional sight of several massive vessels lined up side-by-side is unforgettable, but note that security is tight on embarkation days, and only passengers with tickets are allowed in the cruise terminal on such occasions.

Tickets for harbor tours and whale-watching trips are sold at the foot of Broadway Pier. The terminal for the Coronado Ferry lies just beyond, between Broadway Pier and B Street Pier. One block south of Broadway Pier at Tidelands Park is Military Heritage Art, a collection of works that commemorate the service of the U.S military.

Lining the pedestrian promenade between the Cruise Ship Terminal and Hawthorn Street are 30 "urban trees" sculpted by local artists. Docked at the Navy pier is the decommissioned USS *Midway,* now the home of the San Diego Aircraft Carrier Museum. **Tuna Harbor,** at the foot of G Street, was once the hub of one of San Diego's earliest and most successful industries, commercial tuna fishing. The industry has moved far away to the western Pacific, so these days there are more pleasure boats than tuna boats tied up at the G Street Pier, but the United States Tuna Foundation still has offices here. The pleasant Tuna Harbor Park offers a great view of boating on the bay and across to any aircraft carriers docked at the North Island naval base.

The next bit of seafront greenery is a few blocks south at **Embarcadero Marina Park North,** an 8-acre extension into the harbor from the center of Seaport Village. It's usually full of kite fliers, in-line skaters, and picnickers. Seasonal celebrations, including San Diego's Parade of Lights, the Port of San Diego Big Balloon Parade, the Sea and Air Parade, and the Big Bay July 4 Celebration, are held here and at the similar **Embarcadero Marina Park South.**

Providing a unique shopping experience, **Seaport Village** covers 14 acres of waterfront retail stores, restaurants, and cafés. Even window-shoppers are treated to a pleasant experience with 4 mi of cobblestone paths, trickling fountains, and beautiful gardens.

The **San Diego Convention Center,** on Harbor Drive between 1st and 6th avenues, is a waterfront landmark designed by Canadian architect Arthur Erickson. The backdrop of blue sky and sea complements the building's nautical lines. The center often holds trade shows that are open to the public, and tours of the building are available.

⑤ Gaslamp Quarter Historic District. When the move for downtown redevelopment gained momentum in the 1970s, there was talk of bulldozing the Gaslamp's Victorian-style buildings and starting from scratch. (The district has the largest collection of Commercial Victorian–style buildings in the country.) History buffs, developers, architects, and artists formed the Gaslamp Quarter Council, however, and gathered funds from the government and private benefactors to clean up and preserve the quarter, restoring the finest old buildings and attracting businesses and the public back to its heart. Their efforts have paid off. Former flophouses have become choice office buildings, and the area is filled with hundreds of trendy shops, restaurants, and nightclubs.

William Heath Davis House (⊠ *410 Island Ave., at 4th Ave., Gaslamp Quarter* ☎ *619/233–4692*), one of the first residences in town, houses the Gaslamp Quarter Historical Foundation, the district's curator. Before Alonzo Horton came to town, Davis, a prominent San Franciscan—born in Honolulu to a Boston shipping family—had made an unsuccessful attempt to develop the waterfront area. In 1850 he had this prefab saltbox-style house shipped around Cape Horn and assembled in San Diego (it originally stood at State and Market streets). Audio-guided ($10) and brochure-guided ($5) museum tours are available during museum hours, which are Tuesday–Saturday 10–6, Sunday 10–3. Regularly scheduled two-hour walking tours of the historic district leave from the house on Saturday at 11 and cost $10. The museum also provides detailed self-guided tour maps of the district for free.

The Victorian **Horton Grand Hotel** (⊠ *311 Island Ave.* ☎ *619/544–1886*) was created in the mid-1980s by joining together two historic hotels, the Brooklyn Kahle Saddlery Hotel and the Grand Horton Hotel, built in the boom days of the 1880s; Wyatt Earp stayed at the Brooklyn Kahle Saddlery Hotel while he was in town speculating on real estate ventures and opening gambling halls. The two hotels were not originally located at this address; they were once about four blocks away but were dismantled and reconstructed to make way for Horton Plaza. A small Chinese Museum behind the lobby serves as a tribute to the surrounding Chinatown district, a collection of modest structures that once housed Chinese laborers and their families.

The majority of the quarter's landmark buildings are on 4th and 5th avenues, between Island Avenue and Broadway. If you don't have much time, stroll down 5th Avenue, where highlights include the **Louis Bank of Commerce Building** (No. 835), the **Old City Hall Building** (No. 664), the **Nesmith-Greeley Building** (No. 825), and the **Yuma Building** (No. 631). The Romanesque-revival **Keating Hotel** (⊠ *432 F St., at 5th Ave., Gaslamp Quarter*) was designed by the same firm that created the famous Hotel Del Coronado. At the corner of 4th Avenue and F Street, peer into the Hard Rock Cafe, which occupies a restored turn-of-the-20th-century tavern with a 12-foot mahogany bar and a spectacular stained-glass domed ceiling.

The section of G Street between 6th and 9th avenues has become a haven for galleries; stop in one of them to pick up a map of the downtown arts district. Just to the north, on E and F streets from 6th to 12th avenues, the evolving Urban Art Trail has added pizzazz to drab city thoroughfares by transforming such things as trash cans and traffic controller boxes into canvases. For additional information about the historic area, call the **Gaslamp Quarter Association** (☎619/233–5227) or log on to their Web site www.gaslamp.org. ✉ *Between 4th and 6th Aves., from Broadway to Harbor Dr.*

6 **Horton Plaza.** This downtown shopping, dining, and entertainment
★ mecca fronts Broadway and G Street from 1st to 4th avenues and covers more than six city blocks. Designed by Jon Jerde and completed in 1985, Horton Plaza is far from what one would imagine a shopping center—or city center—to be. A collage of pastels with elaborate, colorful tile work on benches and stairways, banners waving in the air, and modern sculptures marking the entrances, Horton Plaza rises in uneven, staggered levels to six floors; great views of downtown from the harbor to Balboa Park and beyond can be had here.

Macy's and Nordstrom department stores anchor the plaza, and an eclectic assortment of more than 130 clothing, sporting-goods, jewelry, book, and gift shops flank them. Other attractions include the country's largest Sam Goody music store, a movie complex, restaurants, and a long row of take-out ethnic food shops and dining patios on the uppermost tier—and the respected San Diego Repertory Theatre below ground level. In 2008 the Balboa Theater, contiguous with the shopping center, reopened its doors after a $26.5 million renovation. The historic 1920s theater seats 1,500 and offers live arts and cultural performances throughout the week.

The mall has a multilevel parking garage; even so, lines to find a space can be long. Entering the parking structure on G Street rather than 4th Avenue generally means less traffic and more parking space. Parking validation is complimentary whether you spend a bundle or just window-shop. Validation machines throughout the center allow for three hours' free parking; after that it's $6 per hour. If you use this notoriously confusing fruit-and-vegetable–themed garage, be sure to remember at which produce level you've left your car. If you're staying downtown, the Old Town Trolley Tour will drop you directly in front of Horton Plaza. ✉ *324 Horton Plaza* ☎ *619/238–1596* ⊕ *www.westfield. com/hortonplaza* ⊗ *Mon.–Fri. 10–9, Sat. 10–8, Sun. 11–7.*

3 **International Visitor Information Center.** One of the two visitor information centers operated by the San Diego Convention and Visitors Bureau (the other is in La Jolla), this is the best resource for information on the city. The staff members and volunteers who run the center speak many languages and dispense information on hotels, restaurants, and tourist attractions, including those in Tijuana, and provide discount coupons for many. Stop by when visiting the Embarcadero, since it's just across from Broadway Pier. ✉ *10401/3 W. Broadway, at Harbor Dr.* ☎ *619/236–1212* ⊕ *www.sandiego.org* ⊗ *June–Sept., daily 9–5; Oct.–May, daily 9–4.*

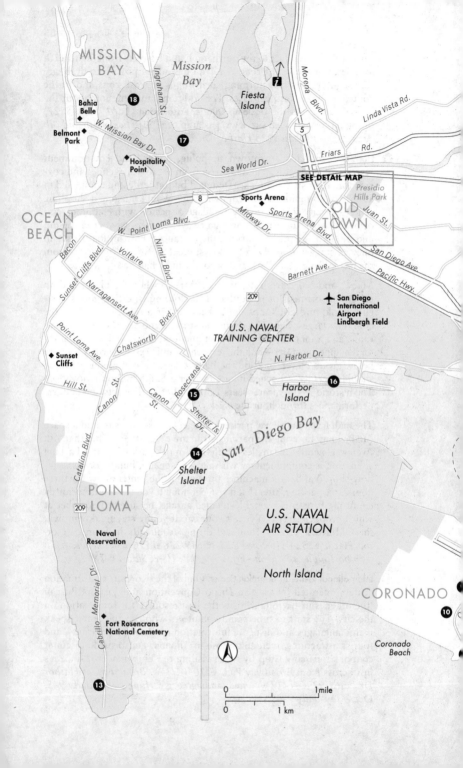

Central San Diego & Mission Bay

2

San Diego River

8

163

805

BUS 8

University Ave.

Park Blvd.

Florida St.

Idaho St.

Upas St.

Morley Field Dr.

SEE DETAIL MAP

Balboa Park

Pershing Dr.

San Diego Museum of Man ◆

San Diego Natural History Museum ◆

Spreckles Organ Pavilion ◆

Balboa Park Municipal Golf Course

Date St.

Cabrillo Fwy.

8th Ave.

1

2

3

4

5

6

7

Ash St.

Russ Blvd.

Spreckles Theater

6th Ave.

10th Ave.

12th Ave.

16th Ave.

4th Ave.

24th Ave.

25th Ave.

Broadway

Market St.

DOWNTOWN

8

Embarcadero Marina Park North

Nazill South

◆ San Diego Convention Center

Imperial Ave.

28th St.

32nd St.

National Ave.

Harbor Dr.

5

75

Main St.

3rd St.

San Diego-Coronado Bay Bridge

NATIONAL CITY

75

9

Orange Ave.

Pomona Ave.

Glorietta Bay Inn

11

12

Silver Strand Blvd.

KEY

🚤 Ferry

ℹ️ Tourist information

② Maritime Museum. A must for anyone with an interest in nautical history, this collection of six restored and replica ships affords a fascinating glimpse of San Diego during its heyday as a commercial seaport. The museum's headquarters are the *Berkeley,* an 1898 ferryboat moored at the foot of Ash Street. The steam-driven ship, which served the Southern Pacific Railroad in San Francisco until 1958, played its most important role during the great earthquake of 1906, when it saved thousands of people from the fires that had engulfed San Francisco by carrying them across San Francisco Bay to Oakland. Its ornate carved-wood paneling, stained-glass windows, and plate-glass mirrors have been restored, and its main deck serves as a floating museum, with permanent exhibits on West Coast maritime history and complementary rotating exhibits.

FodorsChoice ★

If you crave more than a dockside experience, you can take to the water in the museum's other sailing ship, the *Californian*, a replica of a 19th-century revenue cutter that patrolled the shores of California. Designated the state's official tall ship, it can be boarded for a variety of half- and full-day sails (weather permitting) on weekends. (Typically, weekday cruises are reserved for schoolchildren.) Tickets may be purchased online or at the museum on the day of sail. Full-day sails leave at 10 AM and half-day sails leave between 1 and 4 PM. They're most popular on sunny days, when it's recommended to show up at least one hour ahead of desired departure. ⊠ *1492 N. Harbor Dr.* ☎ *619/234–9153* ⊕ *www.sdmaritime.org* ⊠ *$14 includes entry to all ships except the Californian* ⊙ *9–8, until 9 PM in summer.*

④ Museum of Contemporary Art, San Diego. The downtown branch of the city's modern art museum has assumed a personality of its own. Its postmodern, cutting-edge exhibitions are perfectly complemented by the steel-and-glass transportation complex of which it is a part. Four small galleries in the two-story building host rotating shows, some from the permanent collection in the older La Jolla branch, others loaned from far-flung international museums. A new downtown expansion opened nearby in January 2007, featuring an education room for hands-on interactive art activites. ■TIP➔**If you get the chance, stop by TNT (Thursday Night Thing), an eclectic series of free events held at 7 pm the first Thursday of each month. Happenings include live bands, DJ lessons, films, or interpretive artists.** ⊠ *1001 Kettner Blvd.* ☎ *619/234–1001* ⊕ *www.mcasd.org* ⊠ *$10; ages 25 and under are free* ⊙ *Mon.–Fri. 11–5, Thurs. until 7. Closed Tues.*

⑦ Seaport Village. On a prime stretch of waterfront that spreads out across 14 acres connecting the harbor with hotel towers and the convention center, the three bustling shopping plazas of Seaport Village are designed to reflect the New England clapboard and Spanish mission architectural styles of early California. A ¼-mi boardwalk that runs along the bay and 4 mi of paths lead to specialty shops—everything from a kite store and swing emporium to a shop devoted to hot sauces—as well as snack bars and restaurants, many with harbor views; there are about 75 in all. Seaport Village's shops are open daily 10 to 9 (10 to 10 in summer); a few eateries open early for breakfast, and many have extended nighttime hours, especially in summer. (It must be noted that most of the eateries here serve only passable or even mediocre fare, charging prices that rival or exceed those of the city's better restaurants.) Live music can be heard daily from 12 to 4 at the main food court. Additional free concerts take place every Sunday from 1 to 4 at the East Plaza Gazebo of Seaport Village. If you happen to visit San Diego during the first weekend in December, be sure to check out Deck the Palms. The family event features a tropically transformed Seaport Village, complete with sand sculptures, decorated palm trees, and a surfing Santa.

The **Seaport Village Carousel** has 54 animals—lots of horses plus a giraffe, dragon, elephant, dog, and others—hand-carved and hand-painted by Charles Looff in 1895. (This is a replacement for Seaport Village's previous historic carousel, also a Looff, which was sold to a private collector in 2004.) Tickets are $2. Strolling clowns, balloon sculptors, mimes, musicians, and magicians are also on hand throughout the village to entertain kids. ⊠ *849 W. Harbor Dr.* ☏*619/235–4014, 619/235–4013 events hotline, 619/239–1228 carousel information* ⊕*www.seaportvillage.com.*

CORONADO

Although it's actually an isthmus, easily reached from the mainland if you head north from Imperial Beach, Coronado has always seemed like an island and is often referred to as such. Located just 15 mi east of downtown San Diego, Coronado was a small sandbar until the late 1900s and was named after Mexico's Coronado Islands.

As if freeze-framed in the 1950s, Coronado's quaint appeal is captured in its old-fashioned storefronts, well-manicured gardens, and charming Ferry Landing Marketplace. Today's residents, many of whom live in grand Victorian homes handed down for generations, can usually be seen walking their dogs or chatting with neighbors in this safe, non-gated community. Naval Air Station North Island was established in 1911 on Coronado's north end, across from Point Loma, and was the site of Charles Lindbergh's departure on the transcontinental flight that preceded his famous solo flight across the Atlantic. Coronado's long relationship with the U.S. Navy and its desirable real estate have made it an enclave for military personnel; it's said to have more retired admirals per capita than anywhere else in the United States.

The streets of Coronado are wide, quiet, and friendly, with lots of neighborhood parks where young families mingle with the area's many senior citizens. Grand old homes face the waterfront and the Coronado Municipal Golf Course, under the bridge at the north end of Glorietta Bay; it's the site of the annual July 4 fireworks display. Community celebrations and concerts take place in Spreckels Park on Orange Avenue.

Coronado is accessible via the arching blue 2.2-mi-long San Diego–Coronado Bay Bridge, which handles some 68,000 cars each day. The view of the harbor, downtown, and the island is breathtaking, day and night. Until the bridge was completed in 1969, visitors and residents relied on the Coronado Ferry, which today has become quite popular with bicyclists, who shuttle their bikes across the harbor and ride Coronado's wide, flat boulevards for hours.

San Diego's Metropolitan Transit System runs a shuttle bus, No. 904, around Coronado; you can pick it up where you disembark the ferry and ride it out as far as Silver Strand State Beach. Buses start leaving from the ferry landing at 10:30 AM and run once an hour on the half hour until 6:30 PM. Bus No. 901 runs daily between the Gaslamp Quarter and Coronado.

You can board the ferry, operated by **San Diego Harbor Excursion** (☎619/234–4111, 800/442–7847 in CA ⊕www.sdhe.com), at the Broadway Pier on the Embarcadero in downtown San Diego; you'll arrive at the Ferry Landing Marketplace in Coronado. Boats depart every hour on the hour from the Embarcadero and every hour on the half hour from Coronado, daily 9–9 from San Diego (9 AM –10 PM Friday and Saturday), 9:30–9:30 from Coronado (9:30 AM –10:30 PM Friday and Saturday); the fare is $3 each way, 50¢ extra for bicycles. Buy tickets at the Broadway Pier or the Ferry Landing Marketplace. In addition to nightly dinner cruises and seasonal whale-watching tours, San Diego Harbor Excursion also offers water-taxi service weekdays 2–10, and weekends 11–11. Later hours can be arranged. The taxi can run between any two points in San Diego Bay. The fare is $7 per person. Call ☎619/235–8294 to book.

SIGHTS TO SEE

⑩ **Coronado Museum of History and Art.** The neoclassical First Bank of Commerce building, constructed in 1910, holds the headquarters and archives of the Coronado Historical Association, a museum, the Coronado Visitor Center, the Coronado Museum Store, and Tent City Restaurant. The collection celebrates Coronado's history with photographs and displays of its formative events and major sights. Two galleries have permanent displays, while a third hosts traveling exhibits; all offer interactive activities for children and adults. For information on the town's historic houses, pick up a copy of the inexpensive *Promenade Through the Past: A Brief History of Coronado and Its Architectural Wonders* at the museum gift shop. The book traces a 60-minute walking tour of the architecturally and historically significant buildings that surround the area. The tour departs from the museum lobby on Wednesday at 2 PM and Friday at 10:30 AM and costs $10. ✉*1100 Orange Ave.* ☎*619/435–7242* ⊕*www.coronadohistory.org* 🎫*Donations accepted* ⊙ *Weekdays 9–5, Sat.–Sun. 10–5.*

⑧ **Ferry Landing Marketplace.** This collection of shops at the ferry landing is on a smaller—and generally less interesting—scale than Seaport Village, but you do get a great view of the downtown San Diego skyline. Located along the San Diego Bay, the little shops and restaurants resemble the gingerbread domes of the Hotel Del Coronado. If you want to rent a bike or in-line skates, stop in at **Bikes and Beyond**

(✉ *1201 1st St. #122* ☎*619/435–7180*). ✉*1201 1st St., at B Ave.,* ☎*619/435–8895.*

❶ **Hotel Del Coronado.** One of San Diego's best-known sites, the hotel has been a National Historic Landmark since 1977. It has a colorful history, integrally connected with that of Coronado itself. The Del, as natives call it, was the brainchild of financiers Elisha Spurr Babcock Jr. and H.L. Story, who saw the potential of Coronado's virgin beaches and its view of San Diego's emerging harbor. They purchased a 4,100-acre parcel of land in 1885 for $110,000 and threw a lavish July 4 bash for prospective investors in their hunting and fishing resort. By the end of the year they had roused public interest—and had an ample return on their investment. The hotel opened in 1888, just 11 months after construction began.

Fodor's Choice ★

SOUL OF THE CITY

❾ **Orange Avenue.** Coronado's business district and its village-like heart, Orange Avenue is surely one of the most charming spots in Southern California. Slow-paced and very "local" (the city fights against chain stores), it's a blast from the past, although entirely up-to-date in other respects. The **Coronado Visitor Center** (✉*1100 Orange Ave.* ☎*619/437–8788* ⊕ *www.coronadovisitorscenter.com*) is open weekdays 9–5, Saturday 10–5, and Sunday 10–5 year-round.

The Del's distinctive red-tile roofs and Victorian gingerbread architecture have served as a set for many movies, political meetings, and extravagant social happenings. It's speculated that the Duke of Windsor may have first met Wallis Simpson here. Eleven presidents have been guests of the Del, and the film *Some Like It Hot*—starring Marilyn Monroe, Jack Lemmon, and Tony Curtis—used the hotel as a backdrop. Tours of the Del are available Tuesday at 10:30 AM and Friday–Sunday at 2 PM. Reservations are required through the Coronado Visitor Center. (☎*619/437–8788* ⊕*www.coronadovisitorscenter.com*) ✉*1500 Orange Ave.* ☎*619/435–6611* ⊕*www.hoteldel.com.*

❷ **Silver Strand State Beach.** The stretch of sand that runs along Silver Strand Boulevard from the Hotel Del Coronado to Imperial Beach is a perfect family gathering spot, with restrooms and lifeguards. The shallow shoreline and minimal crowds also make it a popular spot for kitesurfing. Don't be surprised if you see groups exercising in military style along the beach; this is a training area for the U.S. Navy's SEAL teams. Across from the beach are the Coronado Cays, an exclusive community popular with yacht owners and celebrities, and the Loews Coronado Bay Resort.

HARBOR AND SHELTER ISLANDS & POINT LOMA

The populated outcroppings that jut into the bay just west of downtown and the airport demonstrate the potential of human collaboration with nature. Point Loma, Mother Nature's contribution to San Diego's attractions, has always protected the center city from the Pacific's tides and waves. It's shared by military installations, funky motels and fast-food shacks, stately family homes, huge estates, and private marinas packed with sailboats and yachts. Newer to the scene, Harbor and Shelter islands are landfill. Created out of sand dredged from the San Diego Bay in the second half of the past century, they've become tourist hubs—their high-rise hotels, seafood restaurants, and boat-rental centers looking as solid as those anywhere else in the city.

SIGHTS TO SEE

⑬ ⟳ ★ Cabrillo National Monument. This 160-acre preserve marks the site of the first European visit to San Diego, made by 16th-century explorer Juan Rodríguez Cabrillo (circa 1498–1543)—historians have never conclusively determined whether he was Spanish or Portuguese. Cabrillo, who had earlier gone on voyages with Hernán Cortés, landed at this spot, which he called San Miguel, in 1542. Today the site, with its rugged cliffs and shores and outstanding overlooks, is one of the most frequently visited of all the national monuments.

The **visitor center** presents films and lectures about Cabrillo's voyage, the sea-level tide pools, and migrating gray whales. **Interpretive stations** with recorded information in six languages—including, appropriately enough, Portuguese—have been installed along the walkways that edge the cliffs. The moderately steep **Bayside Trail**, 2½-mi round-trip, winds through coastal sage scrub, curving under the cliff-top lookouts and taking you ever closer to the bay-front scenery. You cannot reach the beach from this trail and must stick to the path to protect the cliffs from erosion and yourself from thorny plants and snakes—including rattlers. You'll see prickly pear cactus and yucca, black-eyed Susans, fragrant sage, and maybe a lizard or a hummingbird. The climb back is long but gradual, leading up to the **Old Point Loma Lighthouse.**

The western and southern cliffs of Cabrillo National Monument are prime whale-watching territory. A sheltered **viewing station** has wayside exhibits describing the great gray whales' yearly migration from Baja California to the Bering and Chukchi seas near Alaska. High-powered telescopes help you focus on the whales' water spouts. More accessible sea creatures can be seen in the **tide pools** at the foot of the monument's western cliffs. Drive north from the visitor center to Cabrillo Road on the left, which winds down to the Coast Guard station and the shore. ⊠ *1800 Cabrillo Memorial Dr., Point Loma* ☎ *619/557–5450* ⊕ *www.nps.gov/cabr* ☜ *$5 per car, $3 per person entering on foot or by bicycle, entrance pass allows unlimited admissions for 1 wk from date of purchase; free for Golden Age and Golden Access passport and holders of Cabrillo National Monument Pass and National Parks Pass holders* ⊗ *Park daily 9–5.*

⑯ Harbor Island. Following the success of nearby Shelter Island—created in 1950 out of material left behind from dredging a channel in San Diego Bay during the 1930s—the U.S. Navy decided to use the residue that resulted from digging berths deep enough to accommodate aircraft carriers to build another recreational island; the result is the 1½-mi-long peninsula known as Harbor Island. Restaurants and high-rise hotels now line its inner shore. The bay shore has pathways, gardens, and picnic spots for sightseeing or working off the calories from the various indoor or outdoor food fests held here. On the west point, Tom Ham's Lighthouse restaurant has a U.S. Coast Guard–approved beacon shining from its tower.

⑮ Scott Street. Running along Point Loma's waterfront from Shelter Island to the old Naval Training Center on Harbor Drive, this thoroughfare is lined with deep-sea fishing charters and whale-watching boats. It's a good spot to watch fishermen (and women) haul marlin, tuna, and puny mackerel off their boats.

⑭ Shelter Island. In 1950 San Diego's port director thought there should be some use for the sand and mud the Works Project Administration dredged up during the course of deepening a ship channel in the 1930s and '40s. He decided it might be a good idea to raise the shoal that lay off the eastern shore of Point Loma above sea level, landscape it, and add a 2,000-foot causeway to make it accessible. His hunch paid off. Shelter Island—actually a peninsula—now supports towering mature palms, a cluster of resorts, restaurants, and side-by-side marinas. It's the center of San Diego's yacht-building industry, and boats in every stage of construction are visible in the yacht yards. A long sidewalk runs from the landscaped lawns of the **San Diego Yacht Club** (tucked down Anchorage Street off Shelter Island Drive) past boat brokerages to the hotels and marinas that line the inner shore, facing Point Loma. On the bay side, fishermen launch their boats or simply stand on shore and cast. Families relax at picnic tables along the grass, where there are fire rings and permanent barbecue grills. Within walking distance is the huge Friendship Bell, given to San Diegans by the people of Yokohama, Japan, in 1960.

MISSION BAY & SEAWORLD

Mission Bay Park is San Diego's monument to sports and fitness. This 4,600-acre aquatic park has 27 mi of shoreline including 19 of sandy beach. Playgrounds and picnic areas abound on the beach and low grassy hills of the park. On weekday evenings joggers, bikers, and skaters take over. In the daytime, swimmers, water-skiers, anglers, and boaters—some in single-person kayaks, others in crowded powerboats—vie for space in the water. The San Diego Crew Classic, which takes place in late March or April, fills this area of the bay with teams from all over the country. One Mission Bay caveat: swimmers should note signs warning about water pollution; on occasions when heavy rains or other events cause pollution, swimming is strongly discouraged.

SIGHTS TO SEE

⑰ ⓒ SeaWorld San Diego. One of the world's largest marine-life amusement parks, SeaWorld is spread over 189 tropically landscaped bayfront acres—and it seems to be expanding into every available square inch of space with new exhibits, shows, and activities. The biggest attraction in its 40 years of existence opened on Memorial Day 2004: **Journey To Atlantis** involves a cruise on an eight-passenger "Greek fishing boat" down a heart-stopping 60-foot plunge to explore a lost,

FodorsChoice ★

sunken city. After this journey serenaded by dolphins calls, you view a 130,000-gallon pool, home to exotic Commerson's dolphins, a small black-and-white South American species known for speed and agility.

The majority of SeaWorld's exhibits are walk-through marine environments. Kids get a particular kick out of the **Shark Encounter,** where they come face-to-face with sandtiger, nurse, bonnethead, black-tipped, and white-tipped reef sharks by walking through a 57-foot clear acrylic tube that passes through the 280,000-gallon shark habitat. The hands-on **California Tide Pool** exhibit gives you a chance to get to know San Diego's indigenous marine life. At **Forbidden Reef** you can feed bat rays and

go nose-to-nose with creepy moray eels. At **Rocky Point Preserve** you can view bottlenose dolphins, as well as Californian sea otters. At **Wild Arctic,** which starts out with a simulated helicopter ride to a research post at the North Pole, beluga whales, walruses, and polar bears can be viewed in areas decked out like the wrecked hulls of two 19th-century sailing ships. **Manatee Rescue** lets you watch the gentle-giant marine mammals cavorting in a 215,000-gallon tank. Various **freshwater and saltwater aquariums** hold underwater creatures from around the world. And for younger kids who need to release lots of energy, **Sesame Street Bay of Play at SeaWorld,** opened in 2008, is a hands-on fun zone that features three family-friendly Sesame Street–themed rides.

SeaWorld's highlights are its large-arena entertainments. You can get front-row seats if you arrive 30 minutes in advance, and the stadiums are large enough for everyone to get a seat in the off-season. Introduced in 2006 and starring the ever-beloved Shamu the Killer Whale, **Believe** features synchronized whales and brings down the house. Another favorite is *Sesame Street Presents Lights, Camera, Imagination! in 4-D,* a new film that has Cookie Monster, Elmo, and other Sesame Street favorites swimming through an imaginary ocean and flying through a cinematic sky. **Clyde and Seamore's Risky Rescue,** the sea lion and otter production, also is widely popular.

Not all the shows are water-oriented. **Pets Rule!** showcases the antics of more common animals like dogs, cats, birds, and even a pig. One segment of the show actually has regular house cats climbing ladders and hanging upside down as they cross a high wire. The majority of the animals used in the show were adopted from shelters.

Trainer for a Day gives you a first-hand look at how SeaWorld's trainers work, and allows you to help them with everything from food preparation to training techniques. The $545 fee may seem hefty, but it buys a once-in-a-lifetime opportunity. A less expensive treat ($36 adults, $19 children) is the **Dine With Shamu** package, which includes a buffet lunch or dinner and allows you the thrill of eating while the whales swim up to you or happily play nearby.

Shipwreck Rapids, SeaWorld of San Diego's first adventure ride, offers plenty of excitement—but you may end up getting soaked. For five minutes, nine "shipwrecked" passengers careen down a river in a raft-like inner tube, encountering a series of obstacles, including several waterfalls. There's no extra charge, making this one of SeaWorld's great bargains—expect long lines. Those who want to head to higher ground might consider the **Skytower,** a glass elevator that ascends 265 feet; the views of San Diego County are especially spectacular in early morning and late evening. The **Bayside Skyride,** a five-minute aerial tram ride that leaves from the same spot, travels across Mission Bay. Combined admission for the Skytower and the tram is $5. The fact that Anheuser-Busch is the park's parent company is evident in the presence of the beer company's signature Clydesdales, huge horses that you can visit in their "hamlet" when they're not putting on demonstrations or parading through the park.

SeaWorld is chockablock with souvenir shops and refreshment stands (the only picnic grounds are outside the park entrance), so it's hard to come away from here without spending a lot of money on top of the hefty entrance fee. The San Diego 3-for-1 Ticket ($109 for adults, $86 for children ages 3 to 9) offers five consecutive days of unlimited admission to SeaWorld, the San Diego Zoo, and the San Diego Wild Animal Park. This is a good idea, because if you try to get your money's worth by fitting everything in on a single day, you're likely to end up tired and cranky. Many hotels, especially those in the Mission Bay area, also offer SeaWorld specials that may include rate reductions or two days' entry for the price of one. ⊠ *500 Sea World Dr., near west end of I–8, Mission Bay* ☎ *800/257–4268* ⊕ *www.seaworld.com* ⊠ *$59 adults, $49 kids; parking $10 cars, $6 motorcycles, $15 RVs and campers; 1-hr behind-the-scenes walking tours $12 extra* ⊟ *AE, D, MC, V* ⊙ *Daily 10–dusk; extended hrs in summer.*

⑱ Vacation Isle. Ingraham Street bisects this island, providing two distinct experiences for visitors. The west side is taken up by the Paradise Point Resort & Spa, but you don't have to be a guest to enjoy the hotel's lushly landscaped grounds and bay-front restaurants. The water-ski clubs congregate at **Ski Beach** on the east side of the island, where there's a parking lot as well as picnic areas and restrooms. Ski Beach is the site of the annual Thunderboat Regatta, held in September. At a pond on the south side of the island, children and young-at-heart adults take part year-round in motorized miniature boat races. ⊠ *Mission Bay.*

OLD TOWN

San Diego's Spanish and Mexican roots are most evident in Old Town, the area north of downtown at Juan Street, near the intersection of Interstates 5 and 8, that was the first European settlement in Southern California. Although Old Town was largely a 19th-century phenomenon, the pueblo's true beginnings took place much earlier and on a hill overlooking it, where soldiers from New Spain established a military outpost in May 1769. Two months later Father Junípero Serra established the first of the California missions, San Diego de Alcalá.

On San Diego Avenue, the district's main drag, art galleries and expensive gift shops are interspersed with tacky curio shops, restaurants, and open-air stands selling inexpensive Mexican pottery, jewelry, and blankets. The Old Town Esplanade on San Diego Avenue between Harney and Conde streets is the best of several mall-like affairs constructed in mock Mexican-plaza style. Shops and restaurants also line Juan and Congress streets.

Access to Old Town is easy, thanks to the nearby Transit Center. Ten bus lines stop here, as do the San Diego Trolley and the Coaster commuter rail line. Two large parking lots linked to the park by an underground pedestrian walkway ease some of the parking congestion, and signage leading from I–8 to the Transit Center is easy to follow.

SIGHTS TO SEE

5 El Campo Santo. The old adobe-wall cemetery established in 1849 was until 1880 the burial place for many members of Old Town's founding families—as well as for some gamblers and bandits who passed through town. ⊠*North side of San Diego Ave. S., between Arista and Ampudia Sts., Old Town.*

1 Junípero Serra Museum. The hill on which San Diego's original Spanish presidio (fortress) and California's first mission were perched is now the domain of a Spanish mission–style museum established, along with Presidio Park, by department store magnate and philanthropist George Marston in 1929 to commemorate the history of the site from the time it was occupied by the Kumeyaay Indians through its Spanish, Mexican, and American periods. Artifacts include Kumeyaay baskets, Spanish riding gear, and a painting that Father Serra would have viewed in Mission San Diego de Alcalá. The education room has hands-on stations where kids can grind acorns in *metates* (stones used for grinding grain), dig for buried artifacts with archaeology tools, or dress up in period costumes—one represents San Diego founding father Alonzo Horton. Ascend the tower to compare the view you'd have gotten before 1929 with the one you have today. The museum, now operated by the San Diego Historical Society, is at the north end of Presidio Park, near Taylor Street. ⊠*2727 Presidio Dr.* ☎*619/297–3258* ⊕*www.sandiegohistory. org* ☞*$5* ⊙ *Weekdays 11–3; weekends 10–4:30.*

3 Old Town San Diego State Historic Park. The six square blocks on the site of San Diego's original pueblo are the heart of Old Town. Most of the 20 historic buildings preserved or re-created by the park cluster around

Old Town Plaza, bounded by Wallace Street on the west, Calhoun Street on the north, Mason Street on the east, and San Diego Avenue on the south. The plaza is a pleasant place to rest, plan your tour of the park, and watch passersby. San Diego Avenue is closed to vehicle traffic here.

The **Robinson-Rose House** (☎619/220–5422), on Wallace Street facing Old Town Plaza, was the original commercial center of Old San Diego, housing railroad offices, law offices, and the first newspaper press. Built in 1853 but in ruins at the end of the 19th century, it has been reconstructed and now serves as the park's visitor center and administrative headquarters. It contains a model of Old Town as it looked in 1872, as well as various historic exhibits. Just behind the Robinson-Rose House is a replica of the Victorian-era Silvas-McCoy house, originally built in 1869.

The **Casa de Estudillo** (✉4001 Mason St., Old Town), the largest and most elaborate of the original adobe homes, was built on Mason Street in 1827 by the commander of the San Diego Presidio, José Maria Estudillo. The **San Diego Union Museum** (✉Twigg St. and San Diego Ave., Old Town) is in a New England–style, wood-frame house prefabricated in the eastern United States and shipped around Cape Horn in 1851.

The building has been restored to replicate the newspaper's offices of 1868, when the first edition of the *San Diego Union* was printed.

Also worth exploring in the plaza area are the free **Dental Museum, Mason Street School, Wells Fargo History Museum, First San Diego Courthouse, Casa de Machado y Silvas Commercial Restaurant Museum,** and the **Casa de Machado Y Stewart.** Ask at the visitor center for locations.

❷ Presidio Park. The hillsides of the 40-acre green space overlooking Old Town from the north end of Taylor Street are popular with picnickers, and many couples have taken their wedding vows on the park's long stretches of lawn, some of the greenest in San Diego. You may encounter enthusiasts of the sport of grass-skiing gliding over the grass and down the hills on their wheeled-model skis. It's a nice walk from Old Town to the summit if you're in good shape and wearing the right shoes—it should take about half an hour. You can also drive to the top of the park via Presidio Drive, off Taylor Street.

If you do decide to walk, look in at the Presidio Hills Golf Course on Mason Street. It has an unusual clubhouse that incorporates the ruins of Casa de Carrillo, the town's oldest adobe, constructed in 1820. At the end of Mason Street, veer left on Jackson Street to reach the **Presidio Ruins,** where adobe walls and a bastion have been built above the foundations of the original fortress and chapel. Also on-site are the 28-foot-high Serra Cross, built in 1913 out of brick tiles found in the ruins, and a bronze statue of Father Serra. Before you do much poking around here, however, it's a good idea to get some historical perspective at the Junípero Serra Museum, just to the east. Take Presidio Drive southeast of the museum and you'll come to the site of Fort Stockton, built to protect Old Town and abandoned by the United States in 1848. Plaques and statues also commemorate the Mormon Battalion, which enlisted here to fight in the battle against Mexico. ✉*1 block north of Old Town.*

❹ Thomas Whaley Museum. Thomas Whaley was a New York entrepreneur who came to California during the gold rush. He wanted to provide his East Coast wife with all the comforts of home, so in 1857 he had Southern California's first two-story brick structure built, making it the oldest double-story brick building on the West Coast. The house, which served as the county courthouse and government seat during the 1870s, stands in strong contrast to the Spanish-style adobe residences that surround the nearby historic plaza and marks an early stage of San Diego's "Americanization." A garden out back includes many varieties of Old Garden roses from before 1867, when roses were first hybridized. The place is perhaps most famed, however, for the ghosts that are said to inhabit it. ✉*2476 San Diego Ave.* ☎*619/297-7511* ⊕*www.whaley house.org* ✉*$6 before 5, $10 after 5.* ☉*Sept.–May, Mon.–Tues. 10–5, Thurs.–Sun. 10–10; June–Aug., daily 10–10.*

LA JOLLA

La Jollans have long considered their village to be the Monte Carlo of California, and with good cause. Its coastline curves into natural coves backed by verdant hillsides covered with homes worth millions. Although La Jolla is a neighborhood of the city of San Diego, it has its own postal zone and a coveted sense of class; the ultra-rich from around the globe own second homes here—the seaside zone between the neighborhood's bustling downtown and the cliffs above the Pacific has a distinctly European flavor—and old-monied residents maintain friendships with the visiting film stars and royalty who frequent the area's exclusive luxury hotels and private clubs. Development and construction have radically altered the once serene and private character of the village, but it has gained a cosmopolitan air that makes it a popular vacation resort.

To reach La Jolla from I–5, if you're traveling north, take the La Jolla Parkway (formerly known as Ardath Road) exit, which veers into Torrey Pines Road, and turn right onto Prospect Street. If you're heading south, get off at the La Jolla Village Drive exit, which also leads into Torrey Pines Road. For those who enjoy meandering, the best way to approach La Jolla from the south is to drive on Mission Boulevard through Mission and Pacific beaches, past the crowds of in-line skaters, bicyclists, and sunbathers. The clutter and congestion ease up as the street becomes La Jolla Boulevard. Road signs along La Jolla Boulevard and Camino de la Costa direct drivers and bicyclists past homes designed by such respected architects as Frank Lloyd Wright and Irving Gill. As you approach the village, La Jolla Boulevard turns into Prospect Street.

Prospect Street and Girard Avenue, the village's main drags, are lined with expensive shops and office buildings. Through the years the shopping and dining district has spread to Pearl and other side streets.

SIGHTS TO SEE

3 Birch Aquarium at Scripps. The largest oceanographic exhibit in the United States, maintained by the Scripps Institution of Oceanography, sits at the end of a signposted drive leading off North Torrey Pines Road just north of La Jolla Village Drive. More than 60 tanks are filled with colorful saltwater fish, and a 70,000-gallon tank simulates a La Jolla kelp forest. Besides the fish themselves, attractions include a gallery based on the institution's ocean-related research, and interactive educational exhibits on climate change and global warming. A concession sells food, and there are outdoor picnic tables. ⊠ *2300 Expedition Way* ☎ *858/534–3474* ⊕ *www.aquarium.ucsd.edu* ⊠ *$11, parking free for 3 hrs* ☉ *Daily 9–5, last ticket sold at 4:30.*

4 La Jolla Caves. It's a walk of 145 sometimes slippery steps down a tunnel to Sunny Jim, the largest of the caves in La Jolla Cove and the only one reachable by land. This is a one-of-a-kind local attraction and worth the time if you have a day or two to really enjoy La Jolla. The man-made tunnel took two years to dig, beginning in 1902; later a shop was built at its entrance. Today La Jolla Cave Store, a throwback to that

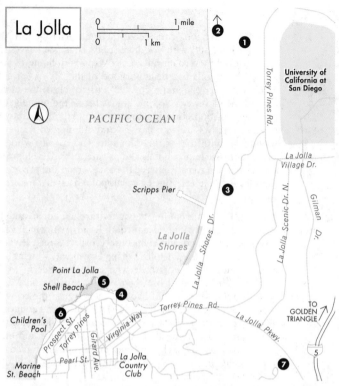

early shop, is still the entrance to the cave, which was named Sunny Jim after a 1920s cartoon character. The shop sells souvenirs and jewelry and watercolors by local artists. ⊠ *1325 Cave St.* ☎ *858/459–0746* ⊕ *www.cavestore.com* ⊠ *$4* ⊙ *Daily 9–5; extended summer hours.*

❺ **La Jolla Cove.** This shimmering blue inlet is what first attracted everyone ♻ to La Jolla, from Native Americans to the glitterati; it's the secret to the ★ village's enduring cachet. You'll find the cove—as locals always refer to it, as though it were the only one in San Diego—beyond where Girard Avenue dead-ends into Coast Boulevard, marked by towering palms that line a promenade where people strolling in designer clothes are as common as Frisbee throwers.

Smaller beaches appear and disappear with the tides, which carve small coves in cliffs covered with ice plants. Pathways lead down to the beaches. Keep an eye on the tide to avoid getting trapped once the waves come in. A long layer of sandstone stretching out above the waves provides a perfect sunset-watching spot. Be careful, these rocks can get slippery.

An underwater preserve at the north end of La Jolla Cove makes the adjoining beach the most popular one in the area. On summer days, when water visibility reaches up to 20 feet, the small beach is covered with blankets, towels, and umbrellas, and the lawns at the top of the stairs leading down to the cove are staked out by groups of scuba divers, complete with wet suits and tanks. The **Children's Pool,** at the south end of the park, has a curving beach protected by a seawall from strong currents and waves. Since the pool and its beach have become home to an ever-growing colony of harbor seals, it's seldom utilized by swimmers, especially due to the questionable levels of bacteria. It is however the best place on the coast to view these engaging creatures. If you want to take a dip, it is best to head just north of Children's Pool to the pristine waters of La Jolla Cove. ■ **TIP→ Make sure to walk through Ellen Browning Scripps Park, past the groves of twisted junipers to the cliff's edge. Perhaps one of the open-air shelters overlooking the sea will be unoccupied, and you can spread your picnic out on a table and enjoy the scenery.** ✛ *From Torrey Pines Road, turn right on Prospect, then right on Coast Blvd. The park is located at the bottom of the hill* ☎ *619/235–1169* ⊕ *www.sandiego.gov/park* ⊙ 4 AM–8 PM.

❼ Mount Soledad. La Jolla's highest spot can be reached by taking Nautilus Street to La Jolla Scenic Drive South and then turning left. Proceed a few blocks to the park, where parking is plentiful and the views are astounding, unless the day is hazy, as it can be along the coast. The top of the mountain is an excellent vantage point from which to get a sense of San Diego's geography: looking down from here you can see the coast from the county's northern border to the south far beyond downtown. ✉ *6905 La Jolla Scenic Dr. S.*

❻ Museum of Contemporary Art, San Diego. The oldest section of La Jolla's ★ branch of San Diego's modern art museum was originally a residence, designed by Irving Gill for philanthropist Ellen Browning Scripps in 1916. In the mid-1990s, the compound was updated and expanded by architect Robert Venturi and his colleagues at Venturi, Scott Brown and Associates, who respected Gill's original geometric structure and clean, mission-style lines while adding their own distinctive touches. The result is a striking contemporary building that looks as though it's always been here. California artists figure prominently in the museum's permanent collection of post-1950s art, but the museum also includes examples of every major art movement since that time—works by Andy Warhol, Robert Rauschenberg, Frank Stella, Joseph Cornell, and Jenny Holzer, to name a few. ✉ *700 Prospect St.* ☎ *858/454–3541* ⊕ *www. mcasd.org* 💲 *$10, free every Thur. 5–7* ⊙ *Thurs. 11–7, Fri.–Tues. 11– 5. Closed Wed.*

❶ Salk Institute. The world-famous biological-research facility founded by polio vaccine developer Jonas Salk sits on 26 cliff-top acres. The twin structures that modernist architect Louis I. Kahn designed in the 1960s in consultation with Dr. Salk used poured concrete and other low-maintenance materials to clever effect. The thrust of the laboratory–office complex is outward toward the Pacific Ocean, an orientation that is accentuated by a foot-wide "Stream of Life" that flows through the center of a travertine marble courtyard between the buildings. Architects-to-be and building buffs enjoy the free tours of the property; call ahead to book, because the tours take place only when enough people express interest. You can, however, stroll at will through the dramatic courtyard—simultaneously monumental and eerie. ⊠*10010 N. Torrey Pines Rd.* ☎*858/453–4100 Ext. 1200* ⊕*www.salk.edu* ✉*Free* ⊙*Grounds weekdays 9–5; architectural tours Mon., Wed., and Fri. at noon. Reservations required.*

❷ Torrey Pines State Beach and Reserve. *Pinus torreyana,* the rarest native pine tree in the United States, enjoys a 1,700-acre sanctuary at the northern edge of La Jolla. About 6,000 of these unusual trees, some as tall as 60 feet, grow on the cliffs here. The park is one of only two places in the world (the other is Santa Rosa Island, off Santa Barbara) where the Torrey pine grows naturally. The reserve has several hiking trails leading to the cliffs, 300 feet above the ocean; trail maps are available at the park station. Wildflowers grow profusely in spring, and the ocean panoramas are always spectacular. When in this upper part of the park, respect the various restrictions. Not permitted: picnicking, smoking, leaving the trails, dogs, alcohol, or collecting plant specimens.

You can unwrap your sandwiches, however, at Torrey Pines State Beach, just below the reserve. When the tide is out, it's possible to walk south all the way past the lifeguard towers to Black's Beach over rocky promontories carved by the waves (avoid the bluffs, however; they're unstable). **Los Peñasquitos Lagoon** at the north end of the reserve is one of the many natural estuaries that flow inland between Del Mar and Oceanside. It's a good place to watch shorebirds. Volunteers lead guided nature walks at 10 and 2 on most weekends. ⊠*N. Torrey Pines Rd.* ⊹*exit off I–5 onto Carmel Valley Rd. going west, then turn left (south) on Old Hwy. 101* ☎*858/755–8219* ✉*Parking $8* ⊙*Daily 8–dusk.*

WHERE TO EAT

CORONADO & SOUTH BAY

AMERICAN

$$$–$$$$ ✕ **1500 Ocean.** The fine dining restaurant at Hotel Del Coronado offers
Fodor'sChoice   a memorable evening that showcases the best organic and naturally
★   raised ingredients the Southland has to offer. Chef Brian Sinnott, who honed his technique in San Francisco, presents sublimely subtle dishes such as crisply fried squash blossoms stuffed with ricotta and basil, local rockfish in tomato shellfish broth, and duck confit with black kale and cranberry beans. The interior, at once inviting and elegant, evokes a posh cabana, while the terrace offers ocean views. An excellent international wine list and equally clever desserts and artisan cheeses complete the experience. ⊠*Hotel Del Coronado, 1500 Orange Ave.* ☎*619/522-8490* ✉*AE, D, DC, MC, V* ⊙*No lunch.*

FRENCH

$$–$$$ ✕**Chez Loma.** This is widely considered one of the most romantic restaurants in Southern California, and it's a favorite with guests at nearby Hotel Del Coronado. Tucked away on a side street, the restaurant is

in a former house with lots of windows, soft lighting, and an upstairs Victorian parlor where coffee and dessert are served. The more elaborate dishes among the carefully prepared French bistro menu are boeuf bourguignon, rack of lamb with balsamic marinade, and filet mignon. A specially priced early dinner menu and two choices of fixed-price menus for $38 or $45 offer more value. There's sidewalk dining and Sunday brunch, too. ⊠*1132 Loma Ave.* ☎*619/435–0661* ▤*AE, D, MC, V* ✆*No lunch.*

DOWNTOWN

AMERICAN

$$$–$$$$
Fodor'sChoice
★
✕**Molly's Restaurant.** Tucked away on the ground floor of the Marriott Marina, Molly's attracts in-the-know locals and guests with its fine California cuisine paired with an award-winning wine list. The dinner-only restaurant done in dark wood and marble makes an intimate setting for Chef Timothy Au's eggplant napoleon with prosciutto and tomato confit, Maine lobster cannelloni, and Niman Ranch pork chop with apple confit and broccoli rabe. Wine lovers will revel in sommelier Lisa Redwine's (seriously) list of boutique wines from California, Oregon, and Washington. Large-format bottles and vertical tastings are a specialty; so are wine dinners created to showcase collectors' cellars. Reservations are advised. ⊠*333 W. Harbor Dr., Downtown* ☎*619/230–8909* ▤*AE, D, DC, MC, V* ✆*No lunch.*

CAFÉS

¢
★
✕**Bread on Market.** The baguettes at this artisanal bakery near the PETCO Park baseball stadium are every bit as good as the ones you'd buy in Paris. Focaccia and other superior loaves are the building blocks for solid but pricey sandwiches, which range from Genoa salami and sweet butter to a vegan sandwich with locally grown avocado. The menu extends to a daily soup, a fruit-garnished cheese plate, and an appetizing Mediterranean salad. Snackers gravitate here for fudge-textured brownies, almond biscotti, and other irresistible sweets. During baseball season, the "take-me-out-to-the-ballgame" box lunch offers a choice of sandwich, chips, a freshly baked cookie, and a bottle of water for $10.75. ⊠*730 Market St., East Village* ☎*619/795–2730* ▤*MC, V* ✆*Closed Sun. No dinner.*

FRENCH

$$$–$$$$
★
✕**Bertrand at Mister A's.** Restaurateur Bertrand Hug's sumptuous 12th-floor dining room offers serene decor, contemporary paintings, and a view that stretches to Mexico and San Diego Bay, making it perfect for a sunset cocktail. Chef Stephane Voitzwinkler creates luxurious and similarly priced seasonal dishes such as sautéed foie gras, Dover sole, and Kobe flatiron steak with béarnaise. The dessert list encompasses a galaxy of sweets. Service, led by the charming Hug, is expert and attentive. ⊠*2550 5th Ave., Middletown* ☎*619/239–1377* ⌂*Reservations essential* ▤*AE, DC, MC, V* ✆*No lunch weekends.*

$$$–$$$$
★
✕**Le Fontainebleau.** On the second floor of the elegant Westgate Hotel, this restaurant is worthy of the famous chateau for which it is named.

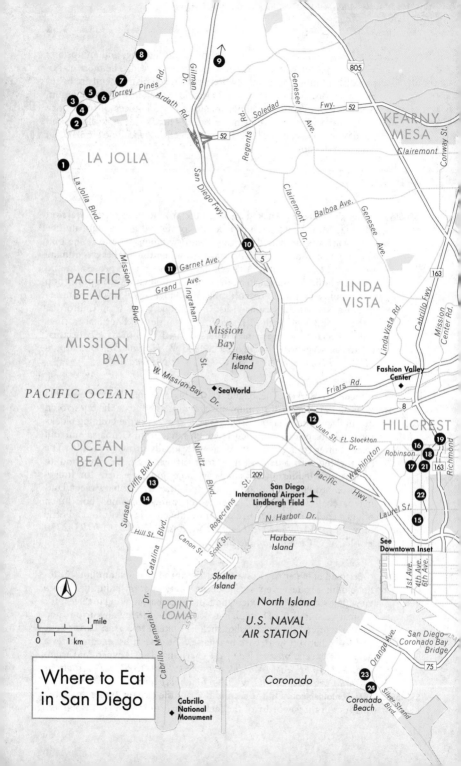

Where to Eat in San Diego

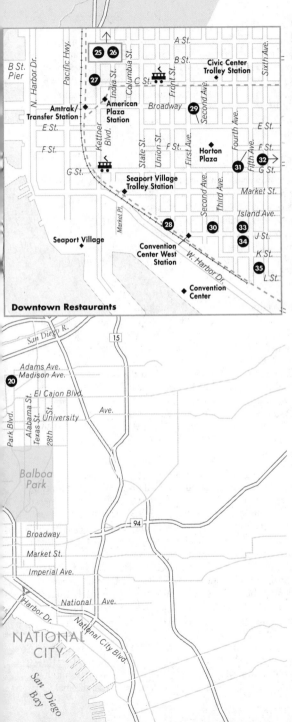

Downtown Restaurants

2

Normandy-born chef Fabrice Hardel writes seasonal menus, but usually offers classics like chateaubriand for two, Dover sole meunière, and French steak au poivre, dramatically flambéed at your table. Pairing the multi-course tasting menu with specially selected wines costs in excess of $100 per person, a price that seems not unreasonable when accompanied by the live harp or piano music that is a Fontainebleau staple. ⊠ *1055 2nd Ave., Downtown* ☎ *619/557–3655* ⊟ *AE, D, DC, MC, V* ⊘ *No lunch.*

INDIAN

$ ✕ **Monsoon.** An exceptionally attractive restaurant, Monsoon delights with features such as a room-centering waterfall that splashes like a cloudburst from a bower of hanging plants. Folding doors allow some tables to share the outdoor atmosphere of the terrace, but at a distance from the sidewalk. The menu offers many dishes not easily found at local Indian eateries, including a sweetly spiced mango soup, and "balti"-style lamb with tomato, garlic, ginger, and coconut. The dozens of curries and similar dishes are spiced to taste, and baked-to-order breads should not be missed. ⊠ *729–733 4th Ave., Gaslamp Quarter* ☎ *619/234–5555* ⊟ *AE, D, DC, MC, V.*

MEXICAN

$$–$$$ ✕ **Candelas.** The scents and flavors of imaginative Mexican cuisine with a European flair permeate this handsome, romantic restaurant and nightspot in the shadow of San Diego's tallest residential towers. Candles glow everywhere around the small, comfortable dining room. There isn't a burrito or taco in sight. Fine openers such as cream of black bean and beer soup, and salad of watercress with bacon and pistachios warm diners up for local lobster stuffed with mushrooms, jalapeño peppers, and aged tequila; or tequila-flamed jumbo prawns over creamy, seasoned goat cheese. The adjacent bar pours many elegant tequilas and has become a popular, often jam-packed nightspot. ⊠ *416 3rd Ave., Downtown* ☎ *619/702–4455* ⊟ *AE, D, DC, MC, V* ⊘ *No lunch weekends.*

SEAFOOD

$$$–$$$$ ✕ **Oceanaire Seafood Room.** Engineered to recall an oceanliner from the ★ 1940s—there are tubes of Brylcreem in the men's room, for goodness sake—Oceanaire is a bit put-on, but admirable for the long bar serving up classic cocktails, oysters, and sashimi, and a carefully prepared menu that offers up to 25 daily "fresh catches," and many specialties ranging from convincing Maryland crab cakes and oysters Rockefeller to richly stuffed California sole, a luxurious one-pound pork chop, and irresistible hash brown potatoes. Chef Brian Malarkey creates a daily menu that may include the deliciously hot, spice-fired "angry" lobster. Service is a casual thing in San Diego, which makes the professional staff here all the more notable. ⊠ *400 J St., Gaslamp Quarter* ☎ *619/858–2277* ⊟ *AE, D, DC, MC, V* ⊘ *No lunch.*

¢–$ ✕ **The Tin Fish.** On the rare rainy day, the staff takes it easy at this eatery ★ less than 100 yards from the PETCO Park baseball stadium (its 100-odd seats are all outdoors). Musicians entertain some evenings, making this a lively spot for dinners of grilled and fried fish and shellfish, as

2

well as seafood burritos and tacos. The quality here routinely surpasses that at grander establishments—for instance, the bread used for sandwiches stuffed with fried oysters and the like is baked on the premises. Service hours vary with the day of the week, the weather, and whether it's baseball season or not, but generally Tin Fish is open from 11 to 8 Sunday through Thursday and until 11 PM on weekends. ⊠*170 6th Ave., Gaslamp Quarter* ☎*619/238–8100* ⟁*Reservations not accepted* ⊟*AE, D, MC, V.*

STEAK HOUSES

$$$–$$$$ ✕**Rainwater's on Kettner.** San Diego's premier homegrown steak house ★ also ranks as the longest-running of the pack, not least because it has the luxurious look and mood of an old-fashioned Eastern men's club. The cuisine is excellent: open with the signature black-bean soup with Madeira. Continue with the tender, expertly roasted prime rib, superb veal liver with onions and bacon, broiled free-range chicken, fresh seafood, or the amazingly succulent pork chops, all served in vast portions with plenty of hot-from-the-oven cornsticks on the side. The prime steaks sizzle, as does the bill. The well-chosen wine list has pricey but superior selections. ⊠*1202 Kettner Blvd., Downtown* ☎*619/233–5757* ⊟*AE, MC, V* ⊗*No lunch weekends.*

THAI

$–$$ ✕**Rama.** Gauzy draperies, murals of Thai dancers, and a rock wall **Fodor'sChoice** flowing with water create a dreamy rain-forest effect in the back room ★ of this excellent newcomer to the Gaslamp Quarter's booming restaurant row. One of the best Thai restaurants in San Diego, Rama combines professional service with a kitchen that understands the subtle demands of spicing the myriad dishes. The tart, pungent, spiced-to-order (as everything can be) *talay* (seafood soup—it literally means "ocean") pairs well with a crispy duck salad as a light meal for two. Dozens of curries and stir-fries take the tastebuds on exciting adventures in flavor. The front dining room is now a private club, so reservations are advised. ⊠*327 4th Ave., Gaslamp Quarter* ☎*619/501–8424* ⊟*AE, D, DC, MC, V.*

LITTLE ITALY

ITALIAN

$$–$$$ ✕**Po Pazzo.** An eye-catching new creation from leading Little Italy res- **Fodor'sChoice** taurateurs Joe and Lisa Busalacchi, Po Pazzo earns its name, which ★ means "a little crazy," mixing a bar with a restaurant serving modern Italian fare. A steak house with an accent, this stylish eatery offers attractive salads and thick cuts of prime beef, as well as a top-notch presentation of veal saltimbocca, and risotto in an osso buco "sauce" that defines richness. It's fun but pricey, although at lunch the Kobe beef burger with fresh-from-the-fat fries is an affordable way to enjoy the experience. ⊠*1917 India St., Little Italy* ☎*619/238–1917* ⊟*AE, D, DC, MC, V* ⊗*No lunch weekends.*

$–$$ ✕**Buon Appetito.** This charmer serves Old World–style cooking in a ★ casual but decidedly sophisticated environment. Choose a table on the breezy sidewalk or in an indoor room jammed with art and fellow diners. Baked eggplant *all'amalfitana,* in a mozzarella-topped tomato sauce, is a dream of a dish, and in San Diego, tomato sauce doesn't get better than this. Consider also veal with tuna sauce, branzino (sea bass) in a mushroom sauce, hearty seafood cioppino, and expert osso buco paired with affordable and varied wines. The young Italian waiters' good humor makes the experience fun. ⊠*1609 India St., Little Italy* ☎*619/238–9880* ▤*AE, MC, V.*

UPTOWN

AMERICAN

$ ✕**Hash House A Go Go.** Expect to wait an hour or more for weekend
Fodor'sChoice breakfast at this trendy Hillcrest eatery, whose walls display photos of
★ farm machinery and other icons of Middle America, but whose menu takes an up-to-the-minute look at national favorites. The oversized portions are the main draw here; at breakfast, huge platters carpeted with fluffy pancakes sail out of the kitchen, while at noon customers favor the overflowing chicken potpies crowned with flaky pastry. The parade of old-fashioned good eats continues at dinner with hearty meat and seafood dishes, including the grand sage-flavored fried chicken, bacon-flavored waffles, and hot-maple-syrup combinations. ⊠*3628 5th Ave., Hillcrest* ☎*619/298–4646* ▤*AE, MC, V.*

¢–$ ✕**Hob Nob Hill.** That Hob Nob never seems to change suits San Diego
★ just fine; this is the type of place where regulars delight in ordering the same meal they've been ordering for 20 years. With its dark-wood booths and patterned carpets, the restaurant seems suspended in the 1950s, but you don't need to be a nostalgia buff to appreciate the bargain-price American home cooking—dishes such as pecan rolls, fried chicken, and corned beef like your mother never really made. The crowds line up morning, noon, and night. Reservations are suggested for Sunday breakfast. ⊠*2271 1st Ave., Middletown* ☎*619/239–8176* ▤*AE, D, MC, V.*

CAFÉS

¢ ✕**Bread & Cie.** There's a brisk East Coast air to this artsy, urban bakery
★ and café that put itself on the map by being one of San Diego's first and best artisan bread bakers. Owner Charles Kaufman is a former New Yorker and filmmaker, who gave Bread & Cie a sense of theater by putting bread ovens imported from France on center stage. The mix includes warm focaccia covered in cheese and vegetables, crusty loaves of black olive bread, gourmet granola with Mediterranean yogurt, bear claws, and first-rate cinnamon rolls. Lunch on house-made quiche, paninis filled with pastrami, turkey, and pesto, or Brie and honey, washed down with tea, coffee, and upscale soft drinks. ⊠*350 University Ave., Hillcrest* ☎*619/683–9322* ▤*D, MC, V.*

INDIAN

$ ✕**Bombay Exotic Cuisine of India.** Notable for its elegant dining room
★ with a waterfall, Bombay employs a chef whose generous hand with raw and cooked vegetables gives each course a colorful freshness remi-

niscent of California cuisine, though the flavors definitely hail from India. Try the tandoori lettuce-wrap appetizer and any of the stuffed *kulchas* (a stuffed flatbread). The unusually large selection of curries may be ordered with meat, chicken, fish, or tofu. The curious should try the *dizzy noo shakk,* a sweet and spicy banana curry. Try a *thali,* a plate that includes an entrée, traditional sides, naan, dessert, and tea. ⊠*Hillcrest Center, 3960 5th Ave., Suite 100, Hillcrest* ☎*619/298–3155* ▤*AE, D, DC, MC, V.*

ITALIAN

$–$$ ✕**Sambuca Italian Bistro.** This cozy, candlelit restaurant, with reason-
★ able prices and a well-prepared menu, differs more than a bit from the competition. Dishes marked "signature" are particularly noteworthy, like the Sambuca shrimp appetizer with a lime-garlic sauce. Creamy flavors make the four-cheese fusilli pasta with lobster an extravagant treat, while there's delicious subtlety to the roasted chicken with brandied Gorgonzola sauce. There are daily specials on weekdays. ⊠*3888 4th Ave., Hillcrest* ☎*619/298–8700* ▤*AE, D, MC, V.*

MEXICAN

$–$$ ✕**Ortega's, A Mexican Bistro.** Californians have long flocked to Puerto
★ Nuevo, the "lobster village" south of San Diego in Baja California. When a member of the family that operates several Puerto Nuevo restaurants opened Ortega's, it became an instant sensation, since it brought no-nonsense, authentic Mexican fare straight to the heart of Hillcrest. The specialty of choice is a whole lobster prepared Baja-style and served with superb beans, rice, and made-to-order tortillas, but there are other fine options, including melt-in-the-mouth carnitas (slowly cooked pork), made-at-the-table guacamole, and grilled tacos filled with *huitlacoche* corn mushrooms and Mexican herbs. The pomegranate margaritas are a must, as is the special red salsa if you like authentic spice. ⊠*141 University Ave., Hillcrest* ☎*619/692–4200* ▤*AE, MC, V.*

¢ ✕**El Zarape.** There's a humble air to this cozy Mexican taqueria, but one
★ bite of the signature scallop tacos and you'll realize something special is happening in the kitchen. Seared bay scallops mingle with tangy white sauce and shredded cheese in a satiny corn tortilla. Or perhaps you'll prefer sweet pieces of lobster meat in oversize quesadillas; burritos filled with chiles rellenos, or the original beef, ham, and pineapple Aloha burrito. No matter, nearly everything is fantastic at this busy under-the-radar eatery that's part of a developing independent restaurant row in University Heights. Mexican beverages, including the sweet-tart hibiscus-flower drink *jamaica* and the cinnamon rice drink *horchata,* and house-made flan and rice pudding round out the menu. ⊠*4642 Park Blvd., University Heights* ☎*619/692–1652* ▤*AE, MC, V.*

BEACHES

AMERICAN

¢–$ ✕ **Hodad's.** No, it's not a flashback. The 1960s live on at this fabulously
☺ funky burger joint founded in that era: an unrepentant hippie crowd
★ sees to it. Walls are covered with license plates, and the amiable servers with tattoos. Still, this is very much a family place, and Hodad's
clientele often includes toddlers and octogenarians. Huge burgers are
the thing, loaded with onions, pickles, tomatoes, lettuce, and condi-
ments, and so gloriously messy that you might wear a swimsuit so
you can stroll to the beach for a bath afterward. The mini-hamburger
is good, the double bacon cheeseburger absolutely awesome, as are
the onion rings and seasoned potato wedges. ✉ *5010 Newport Ave.,
Ocean Beach* ☎ *619/224–4623* ⊟ *AE, MC, V.*

GERMAN

$–$$ ✕ **Kaiserhof.** Without question this is the best German restaurant in San
★ Diego County, and the lively bar and beer garden work to inspire a
sense of *Gemütlichkeit* (happy well-being). Tourist board–style posters
of Germany's romantic destinations hang on the wall, Spaten and Pau-
laner flow from the tap. Gigantic portions are accompanied by such side
dishes as potato pancakes, bread dumplings, red cabbage, and spaetzle.
Entrées include sauerbraten, Wiener schnitzel, goulash, a great Reuben
sandwich, and smoked pork chops, plus excellent daily specials such
as crisp pork schnitzel with tart red cabbage. Weekday happy hour
includes German beers on tap and a generous buffet. Reservations are a
good idea. ✉ *2253 Sunset Cliffs Blvd., Ocean Beach* ☎ *619/224–0606*
⊟ *AE, MC, V* ☺ *Closed Mon. No lunch Tues.–Thurs.*

ITALIAN

$–$$ ✕ **Caffe Bella Italia.** Contemporary Italian cooking as prepared in Italy—
an important point in fusion-mad San Diego—is the rule at this simple
restaurant near one of the principal intersections in Pacific Beach. The
menu presents Neapolitan-style macaroni with sausage and artichoke
hearts in spicy tomato sauce, pizzas baked in a wood-fired oven, pap-
pardelle with a creamy Gorgonzola and walnut sauce, plus formal
entrées like chicken breast sautéed with balsamic vinegar, and slices of
rare filet mignon tossed with herbs and topped with arugula and Parmesan shavings. Impressive daily specials include beet-stuffed ravioli in
creamy saffron sauce. ✉ *1525 Garnet Ave., Pacific Beach* ☎ *858/273–
1224* ⊟ *AE, D, DC, MC, V* ☺ *No lunch Sun. and Mon.*

JAPANESE

$–$$ ✕ **Sushi Ota.** Wedged into a minimall between a convenience store and
★ a looming medical building, Sushi Ota initially seems less than auspi-
cious. Still, San Diego–bound Japanese businesspeople frequently call
for reservations before boarding their trans-Pacific flights. Look closely
at the expressions on customers' faces as they stream in and out of the
doors, and you can see the eager anticipation and satisfied glows that
are products of San Diego's best sushi. Besides the usual California roll
and tuna and shrimp sushi, sample the sea urchin or surf clam sushi,
and the soft-shell crab roll or the omakase menu. Sushi Ota offers

the cooked as well as the raw. There's additional parking behind the mall. It's hard not to notice that Japanese speakers get the best spots, and servers can be abrupt. ⊠*4529 Mission Bay Dr., Pacific Beach* ☎*858/270–5670* ♨*Reservations essential* ▤*AE, D, MC, V* ⊘*No lunch Sat.–Mon.*

LA JOLLA

AMERICAN

$$$–$$$$
Fodor'sChoice
★

✕**George's California Modern.** Formerly George's at the Cove, a $2.6 million makeover brought a new name and sleek updated look to this eternally popular restaurant overlooking La Jolla Cove. Hollywood types and other visiting celebrities can be spotted in the sleek main dining room with its wall of windows. Simpler, more casual preparations of fresh seafood, beef, and lamb reign on the new menu chef Trey Foshee enlivened with seasonal produce from local specialty growers. Give special consideration to imaginatively garnished, citrus-cured yellowtail, succulent garlic-roasted chicken, chickpea-crusted petrale sole, and spice-braised Duroc pork shoulder. For more informal dining and a sweeping view of the coast, try the rooftop Ocean Terrace. ⊠*1250 Prospect St.* ☎*858/454–4244* ♨*Reservations essential* ▤*AE, D, DC, MC, V* ⊘*No lunch.*

$$–$$$
★

✕**Nine-Ten.** Many long years ago, the elegant Grande Colonial Hotel in the heart of La Jolla "village" housed a drugstore owned by actor Gregory Peck's father. In the sleekly contemporary dining room that now occupies the space, acclaimed Chef Jason Knibb serves satisfying seasonal fare at breakfast, lunch, and dinner. At night the perfectly executed menu can take extravagant turns, as with the appetizers of Maine scallops with cauliflower custard, brown butter, and capers, or lobster risotto, and creative ones, as with the entrées of duck breast with forbidden black rice and *sous vide* salmon in an orange–olive oil emulsion. Pastry Chef Amy O'Hara is newly arrived from San Francisco, and skilled at creating ephemeral and delicious desserts; her caramelized bananas with coconut ice cream is sublime. ⊠*910 Prospect St.* ☎*858/964–5400* ▤*AE, D, DC, MC, V.*

ASIAN

$$–$$$
★

✕**Roppongi Restaurant and Sushi Bar.** A hit from the moment it opened, Roppongi serves global cuisine with strong Asian notes. The contemporary dining room, done in wood tones and accented with a tropical fish tank, Buddhas, and other Asian statuary, has a row of comfortable booths along one wall. It can get noisy when crowded; tables near the bar are generally quieter. Order the imaginative Euro-Asian tapas as appetizers, or combine them for a full meal. Equally delicious are the Roppongi crab stack and the Asian pear arugula salad. Good entrées are wasabi-crusted filet mignon and hibachi-grilled sea bass. The creative sushi bar rocks. ⊠*875 Prospect St.* ☎*858/551–5252* ▤*AE, D, DC, MC, V.*

$$–$$$
Fodor'sChoice
★

✕**Zenbu.** There's a cool California vibe to this cozy, moodily lighted sushi and seafood restaurant that serves some of the freshest fish in town and attracts a who's who of La Jolla. Restaurateur Matt Rimel runs a commercial fishing company, and uses his connections to bring varied seafood from all over the world that excels whether raw or cooked. Seasonal specialties include buttery Croatian and Spanish *otoro* tuna belly and local sea urchin fresh from its spiny shell. Sushi, which can be pricey, ranges from simple nigiri to beautiful sashimi plates and original rolls like Salmon Spider, which combines soft-shell crab with fresh salmon. Cooked dishes run from noodle bowls and Montana prime sirloin seared at the table on a hot stone to whole fried rockfish or local spiny lobster dynamite. ⊠*7660 Fay Ave., Suite 1* ☎*858/454–4540* ▤*AE, D, DC, MC, V* ⊗*No lunch.*

CAFÉ

¢–$ ✕**Michele Coulon Dessertier.** A "dessertier" confects desserts, a job that
★   Michele Coulon does exceedingly well with organic produce and imported chocolate in the back of a small, charming shop in the heart of La Jolla. Moist chocolate-chip scones, the colorful raspberry pin-wheel *bombe* (a molded dessert of cake, jam, almond macaroons, and ice-cream filling), the berry-frangipane tart, and a decadent chocolate mousse cake are a few treats. This is not just a place for dessert, however. Lunch is served weekdays (the store is open 9–4), and the simple menu includes quiche Lorraine (baked fresh daily) and salads. ⊠*7556 Fay Ave.* ☎*858/456–5098* ▤*AE, D, MC, V* ⊗*Closed Sun. No dinner.*

FRENCH

$$$–$$$$ ✕**Marine Room.** Gaze at the ocean from this venerable La Jolla Shores
★   mainstay and, if it's during an especially high tide, feel the waves race across the sand and beat against the glass. Long-running chef Bernard Guillas takes a bold approach to combining ingredients. Creative seasonal menus score with "trilogy" plates that combine three meats, sometimes including game, in distinct preparations. Exotic ingredients show up in a variety of dishes, including zatar-spiced prawns, hibiscus infusion with ahi tuna, and rosehips with a rack of lamb. ⊠*2000 Spindrift Dr.* ☎*858/459–7222* ▤*AE, D, DC, MC, V.*

$$$ ✕**Tapenade.** Named after the Provençal black olive-and-anchovy paste,
Fodor's Choice   Tapenade specializes in the fresh cuisine of the south of France. The
★   sunny cuisine matches the unpretentious, light, and airy room, lined with 1960s French movie posters, in which it is served. Fresh ingredients, a delicate touch with sauces, and an emphasis on seafood characterize the menu, which changes frequently. If you're lucky, it may include boar stewed in red wine (possibly the single best entrée in San Diego), lobster in a lobster-corn sauce flavored with Tahitian vanilla, pan-gilded sea scallops, and desserts like chocolate fondant. The two-course "Riviera Menu" served at lunch for $19.95 is a fabulous steal. ⊠*7612 Fay Ave.* ☎*858/551–7500* ▤*AE, DC, MC, V* ⊗*No lunch weekends.*

ITALIAN

$ ✕**Osteria Romantica.** The name means "Romantic Inn," and with a
Fodor's Choice   sunny location a few blocks from the beach in La Jolla Shores, the look
★   does suggest a trattoria in Positano. The kitchen's wonderfully light hand shows up in the tomato sauce that finishes the scampi La Jolla

2

Shores and other dishes, and in the pleasing Romantica salad garnished with figs and walnuts. Savory pasta choices include lobster-filled *mezzelune* (half moons) in saffron sauce, and wonderfully rich spaghetti *alla carbonara,* while main events might be chicken with fennel or a nice plate of breaded veal scallops crowned with chopped arugula and tomatoes. The warm, informal service suits the neighborhood. ⊠*2151 Avenida de la Playa* ☎*858/551–1221* ⊟*AE, D, DC, MC, V.*

SEAFOOD

$$$–$$$$ ✕**Blue Coral Seafood & Spirits.** This upscale, fairly new seafood restau-
Fodor'sChoice rant at the Hyatt Aventine complex is off to a swimming start with its
★ menu of fresh fish, inventive cocktails, and modern decor highlighted by a blue coral–inspired glass sculpture. At the bar, natural juices and fruit-infused spirits enliven cocktails such as the Blueberry Drop and the Coral Cocktail. Settle into one of the raised half-moon banquettes to experience a creative menu of classically inspired dishes, such as clam chowder spiked with herbs and bacon or a three-way crab tasting; à la carte entrées include subtle petrale sole in chive butter, pepper-crusted mahimahi, and tender filet mignon with balsamic sauce. Sides include addictive blue-cheese-and-apple slaw and lobster macaroni and cheese. A fantastic list of 60 wines by the glass makes for interesting reading and sipping; be sure to make reservations, because it's already a "spot" Thursday through Saturday. ⊠*8990 University Center La.* ☎*858/453–2583* ⊟*AE, D, DC, MC, V* ☺*No lunch.*

OLD TOWN

MEXICAN

$–$$ ✕**Zocalo Grill.** Try for a table by a fireplace on the covered terrace, but
★ the contemporary cuisine tastes just as good anywhere in the spacious and handsome eatery. Instead of cooking the carnitas (in this case, chunks of pork) the traditional way, simmering them in well-seasoned lard, Zocalo braises them in a mixture of honey and Guinness beer and serves the dish with mango salsa and avocado salad. Recommended starters include artichoke fritters and crisp shrimp skewers with pineapple-mango relish. The Seattle surf and turf roasts wild salmon and forest mushrooms on a cedar plank. This is one of the best bets in Old Town. ⊠*2444 San Diego Ave.* ☎*619/298–9840* ⊟*AE, DC, MC, V.*

WHERE TO STAY

CORONADO

$$$$ ▦**Coronado Island Marriott Resort.** Near San Diego Bay, this snazzy hotel has rooms with great downtown skyline views. A $15 million renovation in 2007 brings a revamped lobby with sofas for lounging, grounds with tropical plants, a redesigned pool area with firepits, and large rooms and suites in low-slung buildings redone in a cheerful island-inspired fashion. The resort runs $6 water taxis that drop you off downtown. **Pros:** Spectacular views; hotel spa; close to water taxis.

Cons: Not in downtown Coronado; difficult to find. ⊠*2000 2nd St. 92118* ☎*619/435–3000 or 800/543–4300* ⊕*www.marriotthotels.com/ sanci* ⇆*273 rooms, 27 suites* ♿*In-room: Wi-Fi. In-hotel: restaurant, room service, bar, tennis courts, pools, gym, spa, beachfront, water sports, bicycles, laundry service, concierge, parking (fee), no-smoking rooms* ▭*AE, D, DC, MC, V.*

$$$$ 🏨**Glorietta Bay Inn.** The main building on this property is an Edwardian-style mansion built in 1908 for sugar baron John D. Spreckels, who once owned much of downtown San Diego. Rooms in the mansion and in the newer motel-style buildings are quaintly furnished, some have patios or balconies. The inn is adjacent to the Coronado harbor and near many restaurants and shops, but is much smaller and quieter than the Hotel Del across the street. Tours ($12) of the island's historical buildings depart from the inn three mornings a week. Continental breakfast in the morning and ginger snaps and lemonade in the afternoon are served daily. **Pros:** Great views; friendly staff; close to beach. **Cons:** Mansion rooms are small; lots of traffic nearby. ⊠*1630 Glorietta Blvd. 92118* ☎*619/435–3101 or 800/283–9383* ⊕*www.glorietta bayinn.com* ⇆*100 rooms* ♿*In-room: kitchen (some), refrigerator, DVD, dial-up. In-hotel: pool, bicycles, no elevator, laundry service, concierge, parking (fee), no-smoking rooms* ▭*AE, MC, V.*

$$$–$$$$ 🏨**Hotel Del Coronado.** The Victorian-styled "Hotel Del," situated along
Fodor'sChoice   28 oceanfront acres, is as much of a draw today as it was when it
★   opened in 1888. The resort is always alive with activity, as guests— including U.S. presidents, European royalty, and celebrities—and tourists marvel at the fanciful architecture, surrounding sparkling sand, and gorgeous ocean views. About half of the resort's accommodations are in the more charming, original Victorian building, where each room is unique in size and footprint. Rooms in the California Cabana buildings and Ocean Towers, built in the mid-1970s, have a Pottery Barn–style look with marble bathrooms and more contemporary furnishings. These rooms are closer to the pool and the beach, making them a good option for families with children. In 2007 the hotel added several luxury enhancements, including a new spa with an infinity pool and Beach Village: 78 lavish beachfront villas and cottages that feature fully equipped kitchens, fireplaces, spa-style baths with soaking tubs, Bose sound systems, and private ocean-view terraces. The signature restaurant, 1500 Ocean, serves southern coastal cuisine in an elegant beachfront cabana setting. **Pros:** Romantic; on the beach; hotel spa. **Cons:** Some rooms are small; expensive dining; public areas are very busy. ⊠*1500 Orange Ave. 92118* ☎*800/468–3533 or 619/435–6611* ⊕*www.hoteldel.com* ⇆*757 rooms, 65 suites, 43 villas, 35 cottages* ♿*In-room: safe, refrigerator (some), Ethernet. In-hotel: 5 restaurants, room service, bars, pools, gym, spa, beachfront, water sports, bicycles, children's programs (ages 4–12), laundry service, concierge, airport shuttle, parking (fee), no-smoking rooms* ▭*AE, D, DC, MC, V.*

DOWNTOWN

$$$$
★
Omni San Diego Hotel. The product of burgeoning downtown growth, this modern masterpiece occupies the first 21 floors of a 32-story high-rise overlooking PETCO Park baseball stadium. Though built for the business traveler, the hotel attracts a fair share of sports fans (it's connected to the stadium by a sky bridge). The modern lobby is simply stunning; all rooms have windows that open to the breeze, and most have views of the ocean, bay, the downtown skyline, or the PETCO outfield. Pleasantly decorated, rooms include DVD players and soothing sound machines. The pool terrace has a stone fireplace, outdoor dining, and a tanning area. **Pros:** Baseball game views; good location; modern setting. **Cons:** Busy; crowded during baseball season. ⊠ *675 L St., Gaslamp Quarter* ☎ *619/231–6664 or 800/843–6664* ⊕ *www. omnisandiegohotel.com* ⤴ *478 rooms, 33 suites* ♿ *In-room: safe, DVD, dial-up, Wi-Fi. In-hotel: restaurant, room service, bar, pool, gym, laundry service, concierge, public Wi-Fi, parking (fee), some pets allowed (fee), no-smoking rooms* ⊟ *AE, D, DC, MC, V.*

$$$$
San Diego Marriott Hotel and Marina. This 25-story twin-tower hotel next to the convention center has everything a businessperson—or leisure traveler—could want. As a major site for conventions, the complex can be hectic and impersonal, and the hallways can be noisy. Lending some tranquillity are the lagoon-style pools nestled between cascading waterfalls. The standard rooms are smallish, but pay a bit extra for a room with a balcony overlooking the bay and you can have a serene, sparkling world spread out before you. The fine dining restaurant Molly's and its gourmet shop are worth a visit. Seaport Village and a trolley station are nearby. **Pros:** Great location; many amenities; good restaurant. **Cons:** Small rooms; very busy. ⊠ *333 W. Harbor Dr., Embarcadero* ☎ *619/234–1500 or 800/228–9290* ⊕ *www.marriott hotels.com/sandt* ⤴ *1,300 rooms, 54 suites* ♿ *In-room: refrigerators (some), dial-up. In-hotel: 2 restaurants, room service, bars, tennis courts, pools, gym, laundry facilities, concierge, executive floor, parking (fee), no-smoking rooms* ⊟ *AE, D, DC, MC, V.*

$$$$
Fodor's Choice
★
U.S. Grant. Stepping into the regal U.S. Grant not only puts you in the lap of luxury but also back into San Diego history; the 99-year-old building is on the National Register of Historic Sites. A 2006 remodeling reintroduced the hotel's original grandeur and opulence. The lobby is a confection of luxurious French fabrics, crystal chandeliers, and Italian Carrera–marble floors. Guests sip tea and martinis here Thursday through Sunday afternoons. Rooms feature custom Italian linens, operatic lighting, and original French and Native American artwork, and the sunny baths are elegantly designed with marble-tile shower enclosures and stone sinks. The Grant Grill restaurant reopened in January 2007, boasting a fusion of grilled specialties and fresh regional cuisine. The venue's 1940s-style New York decor has a glamorous appeal, with African mahogany walls and plush seating. **Pros:** Modern rooms; great location; near shopping and restaurants. **Cons:** The hotel's many special events get hectic. ⊠ *326 Broadway, Downtown* ☎ *619/232–3121 or 800/237–5029* ⊕ *www.usgrant.net* ⤴ *270 rooms, 47 suites* ♿ *In-room: safe, Ethernet, Wi-Fi. In-hotel: restaurant, room service, bar,*

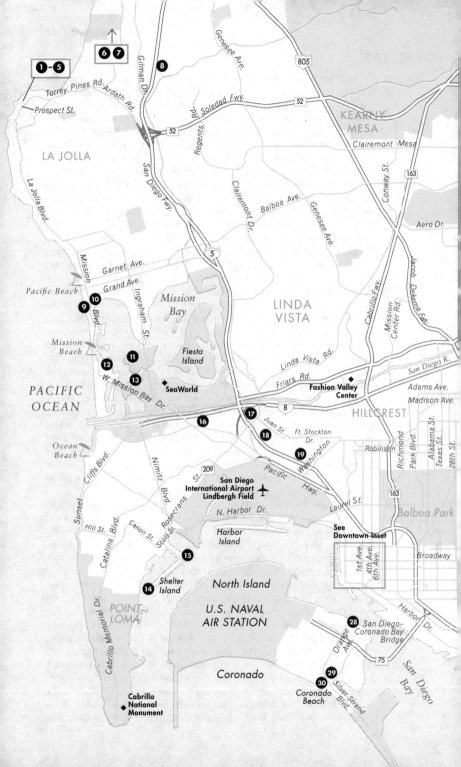

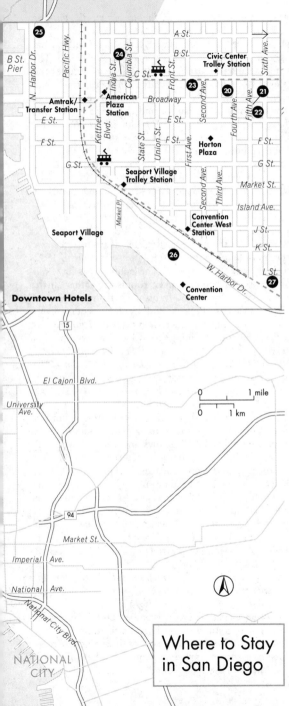

2

Downtown Hotels

Where to Stay in San Diego

gym, laundry service, concierge, public Wi-Fi, airport shuttle, parking (fee), no-smoking rooms ▤AE, D, DC, MC, V.

$$$$

FodorsChoice

★

🏨**Westgate Hotel.** A modern high-rise near Horton Plaza hides what must be the most opulent Old World–style hotel in San Diego. The lobby, modeled after the anteroom at Versailles, is done in antiques and Baccarat chandeliers. Rooms are individually furnished with Italian marble counters and bath fixtures with 24-karat-gold overlays. From the ninth floor up the views of the harbor and city are breathtaking, but some views have been obscured by newer buildings. Afternoon tea, with or without champagne, is served in the lobby to the accompaniment of piano and harp music. The San Diego Trolley stops right outside the door. **Pros:** Elegant rooms; grand lobby; near shopping. **Cons:** Formal atmosphere; somewhat gritty neighborhood. ⊠*1055 2nd Ave., Gaslamp Quarter* ☎*619/238–1818, 800/221–3802* ⊕*www.westgate hotel.com* ⟿*223 rooms* ⌂*In-room: DVD, Ethernet. In-hotel: 2 restaurants, room service, bar, gym, spa, concierge, airport shuttle, parking (fee), no-smoking rooms* ▤AE, D, DC, MC, V.

$$$–$$$$

🏨**Gaslamp Plaza Suites.** On the National Register of Historic Places, this 11-story structure a block from Horton Plaza was built in 1913 as one of San Diego's first "skyscrapers." The public areas have old marble, brass, and mosaics. Although most rooms are rather small, they are well decorated with dark-wood furnishings that give the hotel an elegant flair. You can enjoy the view and a complimentary Continental breakfast on the rooftop terrace. Book ahead if you're visiting in summer. **Pros:** Historic building; good location; well priced. **Cons:** Books up early; smallish rooms. ⊠*520 E St., Gaslamp Quarter* ☎*619/232–9500 or 800/874–8770* ⊕*www.gaslampplaza.com* ⟿*12 rooms, 52 suites* ⌂*In-room: refrigerator, DVD. In-hotel: restaurant, bar, laundry service, parking (fee), no smoking rooms* ▤AE, D, DC, MC, V* ❑CP.

$$$–$$$$

★

🏨**W Hotel.** Come here for the trendy decor and neon drinks, not the service. The W chain's urban finesse adapts to San Diego with nautical blue-and-white rooms with beach-ball pillows and goose-down comforters atop the beds. The Beach bar has a heated sand floor and fire pit, but the pool is tiny by San Diego standards. The lobby doubles as the futuristic Living Room lounge, a local hipster nightspot where nonguests have to wait behind a velvet rope. Be sure to get a room on an upper floor—the leather- and black-clad crowd parties into the night. The hotel restaurant, Rice, serves stylish Asian and Latin cuisine, and the Away Spa caters to both body and spirit. **Pros:** Large lobby; modern rooms; spa. **Cons:** Spotty service; not centrally located. ⊠*421 West B St., Downtown* ☎*619/398–3100 or 877/822–0000* ⊕*www.whotels. com/sandiego* ⟿*258 rooms, 16 suites* ⌂*In-room: safe, DVD, dial-up, Wi-Fi. In-hotel: restaurant, room service, bars, gym, spa, concierge, parking (fee), no-smoking rooms* ▤AE, D, MC, V.

$$–$$$

🏨**Holiday Inn San Diego on the Bay.** A December 2007 renovation brought new beds and bath fixtures to this hotel on the Embarcadero, overlooking San Diego Bay. The hotel, made up of three high-rise towers reached by dated elevators, has spacious rooms with balconies and hard-to-beat views. Although the hotel grounds are nice, if fairly sterile, the bay is just across the street and offers boat rides, restaurants, and picturesque walking areas. The hotel is very close to the airport and Amtrak station. The English-style Elephant and Castle Pub is a great place for food, drink, and meeting people. **Pros:** Large rooms; great views. **Cons:** Not centrally located. ✉ *1355 N. Harbor Dr., Embarcadero* ☎ *619/232–3861 or 800/877–8920* ⊕ *www.holiday-inn.com* ⇥ *600 rooms, 10 suites* ⬧ *In-room: Wi-Fi. In-hotel: 3 restaurants, room service, bar, pool, gym, laundry facilities, public Wi-Fi, airport shuttle, parking (fee), no-smoking rooms* ▭ *AE, D, DC, MC, V.*

¢   **500 West.** An $8 million renovation in 2004 transformed San Diego's historic 1924 Armed Services YMCA Building into this hip, urban boutique hotel. Catering to the style-conscious, the hotel has tiny rooms big on quality, with flat-screen TVs, platform beds, Michael Graves–designed lighting, and a postmodern decor. It has mostly single rooms and very few doubles, and all rooms share detached private bathrooms. The Grand Central Café serves breakfast and lunch daily, and the hotel lobby has wireless Internet. Weekly tenants can use a gourmet kitchen equipped with a Viking range and Sub-Zero fridge; there's also a common area with tables and vending machines. The YMCA gym is still downstairs and may account for the sometimes funny smell in the lobby; guests can use it for $5 a day or $15 a week. **Pros:** Near shops and restaurants; modern room decor; kitchen. **Cons:** Small rooms; few double rooms; above YMCA. ✉ *500 W. Broadway, Downtown* ☎ *619/234–5252 or 866/500–7533* ⊕ *www.500westhotel.com* ⇥ *259 rooms* ⬧ *In-room: Wi-Fi. In-hotel: restaurant, bar, gym, laundry facilities, public Wi-Fi* ▭ *MC, V.*

HARBOR ISLAND, SHELTER ISLAND & POINT LOMA

$$$–$$$$ **Kona Kai Resort.** This 11-acre property blends Spanish and Mediterranean styles. The spacious and light-filled lobby, with its neoclassical end tables, velvet sofas, and Oriental carpets over faded terra-cotta tiles, opens onto a lush esplanade that overlooks the hotel's adjacent marina. The rooms are well appointed, if a bit small, though most have balconies and look out onto either the marina or San Diego Bay. The attractive hotel is popular for business meetings. In summer, a two- to four-night minimum stay might be in effect. **Pros:** Quiet area; near marina; water views. **Cons:** Not centrally located; small rooms. ✉ *1551 Shelter Island Dr., Shelter Island* ☎ *619/221–8000 or 800/566–2524* ⊕ *www.resortkonakai.com* ⇥ *129 rooms, 5 suites* ⬧ *In-room: refrigerator, Wi-Fi. In-hotel: restaurant, room service, bar, tennis courts, pools, gym, spa, beachfront, bicycles, public Wi-Fi, airport shuttle, parking (fee), no-smoking rooms* ▭ *AE, D, DC, MC, V.*

$$–$$$ **Humphrey's Half Moon Inn & Suites.** This sprawling South Seas–style resort has grassy open areas with palms and tiki torches. A $20 million upgrade in early 2008 put new bedding, carpeting, flat-screen TVs, microwaves, and granite vanities in guest rooms. The rooms, some with kitchens and some with yacht-harbor or bay views, are decorated in a subtle natural color scheme. The Grand Marina Suite can accommodate up to eight in 1,000 square feet with a full kitchen. Locals

throng to Humphrey's for the brunch, jazz lounge, and the outdoor jazz and pop concerts from May through October. **Pros:** Water views; near marina; nightlife on property. **Cons:** Vast property; not centrally located. ⊠*2303 Shelter Island Dr., Shelter Island* ☎*619/224–3411 or 800/542–7400* ⊕*www.halfmooninn.com* ⟲*128 rooms, 54 suites* ⚒*In-room: safe, kitchen (some), refrigerator, Ethernet, dial-up. In-hotel: restaurant, room service, bar, pool, gym, bicycles, no elevator, laundry facilities, airport shuttle, parking (fee), no-smoking rooms* ▭*AE, D, DC, MC, V.*

$$ ▦ **Holiday Inn Express–SeaWorld Area.** In Point Loma near the West
★   Mission Bay exit off I–8, this is a surprisingly cute and quiet lodging option despite proximity to bustling traffic. The three-story building is only about a half mile from both SeaWorld and Mission Bay. Geared toward leisure travelers, rooms offer firm and soft pillows, and include standard sleeper sofas. Hot buffet breakfast is included. **Pros:** Near SeaWorld; free breakfast; good service. **Cons:** Not a scenic area; somewhat hard to find. ⊠*3950 Jupiter St., Sports Arena* ☎*619/226–8000 or 800/320–0208* ⊕*www.hiexpress.com* ⟲*71 rooms, 2 suites* ⚒*In-room: refrigerator, Ethernet. In-hotel: pool, laundry facilities, laundry service, public Wi-Fi, parking (no fee), no-smoking rooms* ▭*AE, D, DC, MC, V* ⦿*CP.*

OLD TOWN & VICINITY

$$–$$$ ▦ **Heritage Park Inn.** The beautifully restored mansions in Heritage Park
Fodor'sChoice   include this inn's romantic main 1889 Queen Anne–style house, as
★   well as the Italianate but plainer house of 1887 that serves as its extension. Rooms range from smallish to ample, and most are bright and cheery. A two-bedroom suite is furnished with period antiques, and there are also two junior suites. A full breakfast and afternoon tea are included. There's a two-night minimum stay on weekends, and weekly and monthly rates are available. Classic vintage films are shown nightly in the parlor on a small film screen. **Pros:** Historic area; tea service. **Cons:** Weekend minimum stay; no parking. ⊠*2470 Heritage Park Row 92110* ☎*619/299–6832 or 800/995–2470* ⊕*www.heritage parkinn.com* ⟲*9 rooms, 3 suites* ⚒*In-room: refrigerators (some). In-hotel: no elevator, public Wi-Fi, no-smoking rooms* ▭*AE, D, MC, V* ⦿*BP.*

$$–$$$ ▦ **Holiday Inn Express–Old Town.** Already an excellent value for Old
★   Town, this cheerful property throws in such perks as Continental breakfast and afternoon snacks. Rooms have a European look; a $1 million renovation in 2007 added new carpet, linens, and bathroom granite and fixtures. When you've had enough of the heated pool off the shaded courtyard, you can tackle the historic park's attractions and restaurants nearby. Priority Club members receive amenity bags with bottled water, granola bars, and fresh fruit. **Pros:** Good location; complimentary afternoon snack; Continental breakfast. **Cons:** Smallish rooms. ⊠*3900 Old Town Ave. 92110* ☎*619/299–7400 or 800/465–4329* ⊕*www.hioldtownhotel.com* ⟲*125 rooms, 4 suites* ⚒*In-room: refrigerator, Ethernet. In-hotel: pool, laundry facilities, laundry service,*

public Wi-fi, airport shuttle, parking (fee), no-smoking rooms ▤AE, D, DC, MC, V ⁙CP.

¢–$ 🏨**Western Inn–Old Town.** The three-story Western Inn, decorated in a
★   vaguely Spanish motif, is close to shops and restaurants, but far enough away from the main tourist drag that you don't have to worry about noise and congestion. The rooms won't win any design awards with their nonmatching multifloral decor, but they have new carpeting and furniture as of early 2008 and some have microwaves. There's a free Continental breakfast, and a barbecue area where you can cook for yourself. Bus, trolley, and Coaster stations are a few blocks away. **Pros:** Good location; quiet; free Continental breakfast. **Cons:** Dated rooms; no restaurant; not centrally located. ✉*3889 Arista St. 92110* ☎*619/298–6888 or 888/475–2353* ⊕*www.westerninn.com* ⇆*29 rooms, 6 suites* △*In-room: refrigerator (some), Wi-Fi. In-hotel: public Wi-Fi, parking (fee), no-smoking rooms* ▤*AE, D, DC, MC, V* ⁙*CP.*

LA JOLLA

$$$$ 🏨**Hotel Parisi.** A Zen-like peace welcomes you in the lobby, which has a
★   skylighted fountain and is filled with Asian art. The studio-style suites are decorated according to the principles of feng shui; you can order a massage, a yoga session, or the on-staff psychologist from room service. Favored by celebrities, the hushed, earth-tone suites have flat-screen TVs, granite bathrooms, Frette linens, and ergonomic tubs. The rooms are set back enough from the street noise, but in the ocean-view suites you have to look over buildings across the street to view the Pacific. A European buffet breakfast is served daily. **Pros:** Upscale amenities; modern decor; centrally located. **Cons:** One-room "suites"; snooty staff. ✉*1111 Prospect St. 92037* ☎*858/454–1511* ⊕*www.hotelparisi. com* ⇆*24 suites* △*In-room: safe, DVD, Wi-Fi. In-hotel: room service, parking (fee), no-smoking rooms* ▤*AE, D, MC, V* ⁙*CP.*

$$$$ 🏨**La Valencia.** This pink Spanish-Mediterranean confection drew Hol-
Fodor'sChoice   lywood film stars in the 1930s and '40s with its setting and views of
★   La Jolla Cove. Many rooms, although small, have a recently updated black, white, and neutral color scheme with colorful accents, mod brocade-pattern chairs, and flat-screen TVs. The personal attention provided by the staff, as well as the plush robes and grand bathrooms, make the stay even more pleasurable. The hotel is right in the middle of the shops and restaurants of La Jolla village. Rates are lower if you're willing to look out on the village rather than the ocean. Be sure to have a cocktail while gazing at the ocean in Le Sala and stroll the tiered gardens in back. **Pros:** Upscale rooms; views; near beach. **Cons:** Expensive; lots of traffic. ✉*1132 Prospect St. 92037* ☎*858/454–0771 or 800/451–0772* ⊕*www.lavalencia.com* ⇆*93 rooms, 10 suites, 15 villas* △*In-room: safe, DVD, Wi-Fi. In-hotel: 3 restaurants, room service, bar, pool, gym, laundry service, concierge, parking (fee), no-smoking rooms* ▤*AE, D, MC, V.*

$$$$ 🏨**Lodge at Torrey Pines.** This beautiful Craftsman-style lodge sits on
Fodor'sChoice   a bluff between La Jolla and Del Mar and commands a coastal view.
★   You know you're in for a different sort of experience when you see

the Scottish kilted doorman. The warm and understated rooms are spacious and furnished with antiques and reproduction turn-of-the-20th-century pieces. The service is excellent, and the restaurant, A.R. Valentien (named after a San Diego *plein-air* artist of the early 1900s), serves fine California cuisine. Beyond the grounds are the Torrey Pines Golf Course and scenic trails that lead to the Torrey Pines State Beach and Reserve. The village of La Jolla is a 10-minute drive away. **Pros:** Upscale rooms; good service; near golf. **Cons:** Not centrally located; expensive. ⊠*11480 N. Torrey Pines Rd. 92037* ☎*858/453–4420 or 800/995–4507* ⊕*www.lodgetorreypines.com* ⤴*164 rooms, 6 suites* ⚲*In-room: safe, kitchen (some), Ethernet. In-hotel: 2 restaurants, bars, golf course, pool, gym, spa, public Wi-Fi, parking (fee), no-smoking rooms* ☰*AE, D, DC, MC, V.*

$$$–$$$$
Fodor'sChoice
★

🏨**Grande Colonial.** This white wedding cake–style hotel has ocean views and is in the heart of La Jolla village. Built in 1913 and expanded and redesigned in 1925–26, the Colonial is graced with charming European details: chandeliers, a marble hearth, mahogany railings, oak furnishings, and French doors. In 2007, 18 club-level suites that include complimentary valet parking, luxury bath products, snack baskets, and full breakfast were added in areas called the Little Hotel by the Sea and Garden Terrace Suites done in cheerful tones of tangerine and lime. The hotel's restaurant, Nine-Ten, run by chef Jason Knibb, is well liked by locals for its fresh, seasonal California cuisine. **Pros:** Near shopping; near beach; superb restaurant. **Cons:** Somewhat busy street. ⊠*910 Prospect St. 92037* ☎*858/454–2181 or 800/826–1278* ⊕*www.the grandecolonial.com* ⤴ *52 rooms, 41 suites* ⚲*In-room: safe, kitchen (some), Wi-Fi. In-hotel: restaurant, room service, bar, pool, concierge, parking (fee), no-smoking rooms* ☰*AE, D, DC, MC, V.*

$$$–$$$$
Fodor'sChoice
★

🏨**Hilton La Jolla Torrey Pines.** The hotel blends discreetly into the Torrey Pines cliff top, overlooking the Pacific Ocean and the 18th hole of Torrey Pines Golf Course, site of the 2008 U.S. Open. Oversize accommodations are simple but elegant; most have balconies or terraces. The menu at the hotel's restaurant, the Torreyana Grille, changes with the seasons; Caesar salad and filet mignon are regulars, but you're likely to find lobster pot stickers and coffee-lacquered duck breast as well. **Pros:** Ocean view; near golf; large rooms. **Cons:** Not centrally located. ⊠*10950 N. Torrey Pines Rd. 92037* ☎*858/558–1500 or 800/774–1500* ⊕*www.hilton.com* ⤴*382 rooms, 12 suites* ⚲*In-room: safe, Wi-Fi. In-hotel: restaurant, room service, bars, tennis courts, pool, gym, laundry service, concierge, public Wi-Fi, parking (fee), no-smoking rooms* ☰*AE, D, DC, MC, V.*

$$$–$$$$
★

🏨**Hyatt Regency La Jolla.** The Hyatt is in the Golden Triangle area, about 10 minutes from the beach and the village of La Jolla. The postmodern design of architect Michael Graves's striking lobby continues in the spacious rooms, where warm cherrywood furnishings contrast with austere gray closets. Fluffy down comforters and cushy chairs and couches make you feel right at home, though, and business travelers appreciate the endless array of office and in-room services. The hotel's four trendy restaurants include Cafe Japengo. Rates are lowest on weekends. **Pros:** Many restaurants; modern rooms; upscale ameni-

2

ties. **Cons:** Busy hotel; not centrally located. ⊠*Aventine Center, 3777 La Jolla Village Dr.* ☎*858/552–1234 or 800/233–1234* ⊕*www.hyatt. com* ⇝*419 rooms, 20 suites* ⌂*In-room: safe, Ethernet, Wi-Fi. In-hotel: 4 restaurants, room service, bars, tennis courts, pool, gym, concierge, laundry service, parking (fee), no-smoking rooms* ☰*AE, D, DC, MC, V.*

$$$–$$$$ ⛱ **Scripps Inn.** You'd be wise to make reservations well in advance for this small, quiet inn tucked away on Coast Boulevard; its popularity with repeat visitors ensures that it's booked year-round. Lower weekly and monthly rates (not available in summer) make it attractive to long-term guests. Rooms are done in a beige beachy style, with plantation shutters, and all have ocean views; some have fireplaces and flat-screen TVs. Continental breakfast is served in the lobby each morning. **Pros:** Beach access; intimate; free parking. **Cons:** Spotty service; busy area. ⊠*555 S. Coast Blvd. 92037* ☎*858/454–3391* ⊕*www.jcresorts.com* ⇝*7 rooms, 7 suites* ⌂*In-room: safe, kitchen (some), DVD (some), Wi-Fi. In-hotel: no elevator, parking (no fee), no-smoking rooms* ☰*AE, D, DC, MC, V* ⎮◎⎮*CP.*

$$–$$$ ⛱ **La Jolla Inn.** One block from the beach and near some of the best shops and restaurants, this European-style inn with a delightful staff sits in a prime spot in the village of La Jolla. Many rooms have sweeping ocean views from their balconies; one spectacular penthouse suite faces the ocean, the other the village. Enjoy the delicious complimentary Continental breakfast in your room or on the upstairs sundeck. **Pros:** Near beach; good service; free parking. **Cons:** Keyed entry on village rooms; busy area; dated rooms. ⊠*1110 Prospect St. 92037* ☎*858/454–0133 or 888/855–7829* ⊕*www.lajollainn.com* ⇝*21 rooms, 2 suites* ⌂*In-room: kitchen (some), refrigerator, Ethernet, Wi-Fi. In-hotel: no elevator, laundry facilities, laundry service, parking (no fee), no-smoking rooms* ☰*AE, D, DC, MC, V* ⎮◎⎮*CP.*

MISSION BAY & THE BEACHES

$$$$ ⛱ **Paradise Point Resort & Spa.** The beautiful landscape at this 44-acre resort on Vacation Isle has been the setting for a number of movies. The botanical gardens have ponds, waterfalls, footbridges, waterfowl, and more than 600 varieties of tropical plants, a convincing backdrop for the Balinese spa. Many recreation activities are offered, including five pools, and there's access to a marina. The rooms' bright fabrics and plush carpets are cheery and many rooms overlook the water. **Pros:** Water views; pools; good service. **Cons:** Not near commercial areas; summer minimum stays; motel-thin walls. ⊠*1404 W. Vacation Rd., Mission Bay* ☎*858/274–4630 or 800/344–2626* ⊕*www.paradise point.com* ⇝*462 cottages* ⌂*In-room: safe, refrigerator, Ethernet. In-hotel: 3 restaurants, room service, bars, tennis courts, pools, gym, spa, beachfront, bicycles, concierge, parking (fee), no-smoking rooms* ☰*AE, D, DC, MC, V.*

$$$–$$$$ ⛱ **Bahia Resort Hotel.** This huge complex on a 14-acre peninsula in Mission Bay Park has studios and some suites with kitchens; many have wood-beam ceilings and a tropical theme. The hotel's Victorian-style

stern-wheeler, the *Bahia Belle,* offers guests complimentary cruises on the bay at sunset. Room rates are reasonable for a place so well located—within walking distance of the ocean—and with so many amenities, including use of the facilities at its sister hotel, the nearby Catamaran. **Pros:** Bay cruises; good value; free parking. **Cons:** Not centrally located. ⊠*998 W. Mission Bay Dr., Mission Bay* ☎*858/488–0551 or 800/576–4229* ⊕*www.bahiahotel.com* ⤴*243 rooms, 77 suites* ♿*In-room: kitchen (some), refrigerator, Ethernet. In-hotel: restaurant, room service, bars, tennis courts, pool, gym, concierge, public Wi-Fi, parking (no fee)* ▤*AE, D, DC, MC, V.*

$$$–$$$$
Fodor'sChoice
★
▣**Catamaran Resort Hotel.** Exotic macaw parrots perch in the lush lobby of this appealing hotel on Mission Bay. Tiki torches light the way through grounds thick with tropical foliage to the six two-story buildings and the 14-story high-rise. The South Seas theme continues in the room design, while the Catamaran Spa, where the almost 10,000-square-foot facilities are devoted to treatments such as Lomi Lomi massage and seaweed body wraps, has an Asian decor accented by beautiful mosaics, Buddhas, and gilt ceilings. The fitness center offers sweeping views of Mission Bay's beach; yoga and Pilates take place outside on the secluded lawn. A classical or jazz pianist plays nightly at the Moray Bar; the Atoll Restaurant serves fine cuisine, but the highlight is the Sunday brunch featuring Hawaiian dancers. Among the resort's many water-oriented activities are free cruises on Mission Bay aboard the *Bahia Belle* stern-wheeler. **Pros:** Recently upgraded rooms; spa; free cruises. **Cons:** Not centrally located. ⊠*3999 Mission Blvd., Mission Beach* ☎*858/488–1081 or 800/422–8386* ⊕*www.catamaran resort.com* ⤴*313 rooms* ♿*In-room: safe, kitchen (some), refrigerator (some), Ethernet, Wi-Fi. In-hotel: restaurant, room service, bar, pool, gym, spa, beachfront, bicycles, parking (fee), no-smoking rooms* ▤*AE, D, DC, MC, V.*

$$$–$$$$
▣**The Dana on Mission Bay.** There's a modern chic to the earth-toned lobby of this beach hotel, making it feel you've arrived somewhere much more expensive. The resort's rooms all have sofa sleepers—great for families—and bay views. The Bay View suites also have wet bars with granite counters and two flat-screen TVs. Some rooms are fairly standard hotel fare; be sure to ask for one of the newer Courtyard rooms, which are in two-story buildings without elevators. SeaWorld and the beach are within walking distance. The Marina Village Conference Center across the street offers meeting and banquet rooms with bay views. **Pros:** Free parking; water views; two pools. **Cons:** Slightly confusing layout; not centrally located. ⊠*1710 W. Mission Bay Dr., Mission Bay* ☎*619/222–6440 or 800/445–3339* ⊕*www.thedana.net* ⤴*259 rooms, 12 suites* ♿*In-room: refrigerator, Wi-Fi. In-hotel: 2 restaurants, room service, bar, pools, bicycles, laundry service, public Wi-Fi, airport shuttle, parking (fee), no-smoking rooms* ▤*AE, D, DC, MC, V.*

$$$
▣**Surfer Beach Hotel.** Choose this place for its great location—right on bustling Pacific Beach. Guest rooms were updated in 2006 but are still rather simple, though they include pillow-top beds, upholstered headboards, and retro accents and flat-screen TVs. Most have balconies, but

can look out on an ugly rooftop; get a higher room to take advantage of the ocean view. The slightly larger junior suites have leather sofas for lounging and wet bars with microwaves, refrigerators, and coffeemakers. While the two-bedroom Sunset Suite has bare bones decor, it includes a full kitchen and large sundeck that's perfect for warm-weather get-togethers. Take a break from the crowds on the beach and relax by the hotel's outdoor swimming pool. World Famous, the on-site restaurant, specializes in seafood and steaks and also serves up breakfast and lunch with an ocean view. **Pros:** Beach location; view rooms; pool. **Cons:** Busy area; dated rooms. ⊠ *711 Pacific Beach Dr., Pacific Beach* ☎ *858/483–7070 or 866/251–2764* ⊕ *www.surferbeachhotel. com* ↩ *52 rooms, 16 suites* ⌂ *In-room: refrigerator, Wi-Fi. In-hotel: restaurant, bar, pool, beachfront, laundry facilities, concierge, parking (fee), some pets allowed, no-smoking rooms* ⊟ *AE, D, DC, MC, V.*

NIGHTLIFE & THE ARTS

Years ago, San Diego scraped by on its daytime offerings. Fun after sundown consisted of neighborhood dives and a scattering of dance clubs and live music venues. That sleepy beach town vibe is as long gone as the red light district that once thrived where the tourist-friendly, nightlife-packed Gaslamp Quarter now stands.

Downtown is the obvious neighborhood for party animals of all ages. Its streets are lined with sleek lounges, massive nightclubs, and quirky dive bars. The Gaslamp Quarter is party central, with the most bars and clubs located on its 16-block stretch. The late-night commotion is spreading to East Village, the area surrounding PETCO Park, where new bars seem to crop up every other weekend. A few neighborhoods on the outskirts of downtown—Golden Hill and North and South Park, in particular—offer plenty of hip underground treasures for intrepid visitors.

The beach areas tend to cater to the casual and collegiate, though certain haunts have their share of former flower children and grizzled bikers. Hillcrest is the heart of San Diego's gay community, and home to loads of gay-popular bars. Coffeehouses are another important element of San Diego nightlife culture, especially for the under-21 set. Singer Jewel got her start in local coffee shops, and plenty of other acts have launched to fame from an active area music scene, including pop-punkers blink-182 and Grammy-winning gospel group Nickel Creek.

Locals rely on alt-weeklies like the *Reader* and *San Diego CityBeat*, as well as glossy monthlies like *San Diego* and *Riviera* magazines for nightlife info. You can't buy booze after 2 AM, which means last call is around 1:40. Smoking is only allowed outside, and even then it can be tricky. And be sure to hail a taxi if you've tied one on—drunk driving laws in California are stringent.

NIGHTLIFE

CASUAL BARS & PUBS

Fodor'sChoice ★ **The Waterfront** (✉*2044 Kettner Blvd., Little Italy* ☎*619/232–9656*) is San Diego's oldest neighborhood bar. It's not actually on the waterfront but has been the workingman's refuge in Little Italy since the days when the area was an Italian fishing community. Because the bar is considered a local landmark, developers actually constructed an apartment building around it rather than tear it down. It's also famous for its bar burgers, and it's still the hangout of working-class heroes, even if most of the collars are now white. There's live jazz and blues many evenings.

COFFEEHOUSES

★ **Brockton Villa Restaurant** (✉*1235 Coast Blvd., La Jolla* ☎*858/454–7393*), a palatial café overlooking La Jolla Cove, has indoor and outdoor seating, as well as scrumptious desserts and coffee drinks; the beans are roasted in San Diego. It closes at 9 most nights.

Fodor'sChoice ★ **Extraordinary Desserts** (✉*2929 5th Ave., Hillcrest* ☎*619/294–2132* ✉ *1430 Union St., Little Italy* ☎*619/294–7001*) lives up to its name, which explains why there's a line at this café, even though it has ample seating. Paris-trained Karen Krasne turns out award-winning cakes, tortes, and pastries of exceptional beauty (many are decorated with fresh flowers). The Japanese-theme patio invites you to linger over yet another coffee drink. A branch in Little Italy has a patio with teak chairs, a bar serving wine and bubblies, and a wider selection of savory nibbles.

Javanican (✉*4338 Cass St., Pacific Beach* ☎*858/483–8035*) serves the young beach-community set. Aside from a good cup of joe, live acoustic entertainment is a draw. Adventurous musicians can sign up to play at the open mike Monday nights. Other local musicians headline throughout the week.

DANCE CLUBS

★ **Cafe Sevilla** (✉*555 4th Ave., Gaslamp Quarter* ☎*619/233–5979*) brings a Latin flavor to the Gaslamp Quarter with its mix of contemporary and traditional Spanish and Latin American music. Get fueled up at the tapas bar before venturing downstairs for dancing. This is the best place in San Diego to take salsa lessons.

On Broadway (✉*615 Broadway, Gaslamp Quarter* ☎*619/231–0011*), a huge club in a former bank building, builds suspense with its velvet rope and suited security crew. On Friday and Saturday nights—the only nights it's open—sexily clad young professionals wait in a line that sometimes reaches around the block. Even the steep cover charges do little to discourage clubbers from waiting an hour or more. Drinks are pricey, and when the club is packed it can be near-impossible to order one from the sometimes unfriendly staff. But the cool decor—marble floors, Greek columns, and original vault doors mixed with modern design elements—make it worth a visit, as do the computerized light shows, Leviathan sound system, and skilled DJs.

Stingaree (⊠*6th Ave. and Island St., Gaslamp Quarter* ☏*619/544–0867*), a posh Gaslamp Quarter destination, occupies a historic warehouse in the former Red Light District. The owners spent a gazillion dollars creating this smashing three-story space with translucent "floating" staircases and floor-to-ceiling water walls. There's a high-end restaurant and a dance club inside (the music tends to be of the Top 40 variety). Dress nicely—the air of exclusivity at this hangout is palpable, and to further prove the point, drinks cost a fortune.

GAY

★ **Bourbon Street** (⊠*4612 Park Blvd., University Heights* ☏*619/291–0173*) is a popular place to meet old friends or make new ones. Several scenes exist in this one bar. The front area is a karaoke spot. The outdoor courtyard draws crowds that gather to watch and comment on whatever is showing on the large-screen TV. Weekends, a back area known as the Stable Bar has DJs who turn the small room into a makeshift dance floor.

Fodor'sChoice **Urban Mo's Bar and Grill** (⊠*308 University Ave., Hillcrest* ☏*619/491–
★ 0400*) rounds up country-music cowboys for line dancing and two-stepping on its wooden dance floor—but be forewarned, yee-hawers, Mo's can get pretty wild on Western nights. There are also techno and pop nights, but Mo's real allure is in the creative drinks (Parker Posey Cosmo, for example) and the breezy patio where love (or something like it) is usually in the air.

HIP LOUNGES & TRENDY SINGLES BARS

★ **Altitude Skybar** (⊠*660 K St., Gaslamp Quarter* ☏*619/696–0234*), at the San Diego Marriott Gaslamp Quarter, occupies the hotel's 22nd-story rooftop. It's a great spot not only to people-watch but also to admire the city skyline.

Pacific Beach Bar & Grill (⊠*860 Garnet Ave., Pacific Beach* ☏*858/272–4745*) is a block away from the beach. The popular nightspot has a huge outdoor patio, so you can enjoy star-filled skies as you party. The lines here on weekends are generally the longest of any club in Pacific Beach. There's plenty to see and do, from billiards and satellite TV sports to an interactive trivia game. The grill takes orders until 1 AM, so it's a great place for a late-night snack.

Fodor'sChoice The **W Hotel** (⊠*421 West B St., Downtown* ☏*619/398–3100*) has
★ three bars, and even after several years on the scene, they continue to lure the young bar-hopping set. The ground level Living Room, recently renovated by *Queer Eye*'s Thom Filicia, encourages lounging with plush chairs and couches. The scene is always charged at Magnet, adjacent to Rice restaurant. Have a late-night nosh and head for the beach—or, more accurately, Beach, the W's open-air rooftop with private beach cabanas, fire pits, and tons of heated sand covering the floor. Get here before 9 PM on weekends to avoid a queue.

JAZZ

★ **Clay's La Jolla** (⊠*7955 La Jolla Shores Dr., La Jolla* ☎*858/459–0541*) is the reincarnation of one of San Diego's most famous jazz venues, which closed in the mid-1990s, then returned half a decade later in a slightly different format. Perched on the top floor of the Hotel La Jolla, Clay's delivers an ocean view and a lineup of mostly jazz musicians (and the occasional DJ) Wednesday through Sunday.

★ **Croce's** (⊠*802 5th Ave., Gaslamp Quarter* ☎*619/233–4355*), the intimate jazz cave of restaurateur Ingrid Croce (widow of singer-songwriter Jim Croce), books superb acoustic-jazz musicians.

Humphrey's by the Bay (⊠*2241 Shelter Island Dr., Shelter Island* ☎*619/224–3577*), surrounded by water, is the summer stomping ground of musicians such as the Cowboy Junkies and Chris Isaak. From June through September this dining and drinking oasis hosts the city's best outdoor jazz, folk, and light-rock concert series. The rest of the year the music moves indoors for some first-rate jazz most Sunday, Monday, and Tuesday nights, with piano-bar music on most other nights.

LIVE MUSIC CLUBS

★ **Belly Up Tavern** (⊠*143 S. Cedros Ave., Solana Beach* ☎*858/481–8140*), a fixture on local papers' "best of" lists, has been drawing crowds of all ages since it opened in the mid-'70s. The "BUT's" longevity attests to the quality of the eclectic entertainment on its stage. Within converted Quonset huts, critically acclaimed artists play everything from reggae and folk to—well, you name it.

★ **'Canes Bar and Grill** (⊠*3105 Oceanfront Walk, Mission Beach* ☎*858/488–1780*) is closer to the ocean than any other music venue in town. Step outside for a walk on the beach, where the sounds of the national rock, reggae, and hip-hop acts onstage create a cacophony with the crashing waves. Step back inside to enjoy some of the cooler bands to pass through town.

FodorsChoice **Casbah** (⊠*2501 Kettner Blvd., Middletown* ☎*619/232–4355*), near
★ the airport, is a small club with a national reputation for showcasing up-and-coming acts. Nirvana, Smashing Pumpkins, and the White Stripes all played the Casbah on their way to stardom. Within San Diego, it's widely recognized as the headquarters of the indie rock scene. You can hear every type of band here—except those that sound like Top 40.

THE ARTS

You can buy half-price tickets to most theater, music, and dance events on the day of performance at **Times Arts Tix** (⊠*Horton Plaza, Gaslamp Quarter* ☎*619/497–5000*). Advance full-price tickets are also sold here. **Ticketmaster** (☎*619/220–8497*) sells tickets to many performances. Service charges vary according to the event, and most tickets are nonrefundable.

DANCE

★ **California Ballet Company** (☎ *858/560–6741*) performs high-quality contemporary and classical works September–May.

MUSIC

Fodor'sChoice **Copley Symphony Hall** (✉ *750 B St., Downtown* ☎ *619/235–0804*) has
★ great acoustics surpassed only by an incredible Spanish baroque interior. Not just the home of the San Diego Symphony Orchestra, the renovated 2,200-seat, 1920s-era theater has also presented such popular musicians as Elvis Costello and Sting.

La Jolla Music Society (☎ *858/459–3728*) presents internationally acclaimed chamber ensembles, orchestras, and soloists at Sherwood Auditorium, the Civic Theatre, Copley Symphony Hall, and the Stephen and Mary Birch North Park Theatre.

★ **San Diego Opera** (✉ *Civic Theatre, 3rd Ave. and B St., Downtown* ☎ *619/533–7000*) draws international artists. Its season runs January–May. Past performances have included *Die Fledermaus, Faust, Idomeneo,* and *La Bohème,* plus concerts by such talents as the late Luciano Pavarotti.

San Diego Symphony Orchestra (✉ *750 B St., Downtown* ☎ *619/235–0804*) puts on special events year-round, including classical concerts and summer and winter pops. Concerts are held at Copley Symphony Hall, except the Summer Pops series, which is held on the Embarcadero, beyond the San Diego Convention Center on North Harbor Drive.

★ **Spreckels Organ Pavilion** (✉ *Balboa Park* ☎ *619/702–8138*) holds a giant outdoor pipe organ donated to the city in 1914 by sugar magnates John and Adolph Spreckels. The beautiful Spanish Baroque pavilion hosts concerts by civic organist Carol Williams on most Sunday afternoons and on most Monday evenings in summer. Local military bands, gospel groups, and barbershop quartets also perform here. All shows are free.

Spreckels Theatre (✉ *121 Broadway, Downtown* ☎ *619/235–9500*), a designated-landmark theater erected in 1912, hosts comedy, dance, theater, and concerts. Good acoustics and old-time elegance make this a favorite local venue.

THEATER

Fodor'sChoice **La Jolla Playhouse** (✉ *University of California at San Diego, 2910 La*
★ *Jolla Village Dr., La Jolla* ☎ *858/550–1010*) crafts exciting and innovative productions under the new artistic direction of Christopher Ashley, May through March. Many Broadway shows, such as *Tommy* and *Jersey Boys,* have previewed here before heading for the East Coast. The playhouse has three stages: the Mandell Weiss Theatre has the main stage, the Mandell Weiss Forum is a thrust stage, and the Sheila and Hughes Potiker Theatre, opened in 2005, is a black-box theater.

★ **Lamb's Players Theatre** (✉ *1142 Orange Ave., Coronado* ☎ *619/437–0600*) has a regular season of five productions from February through

November and stages a musical, *Festival of Christmas*, in December. *An American Christmas* is the company's dinner-theater event at the Hotel Del Coronado.

Fodor'sChoice **Old Globe Theatre** (✉ *1363 Old Globe Way, Balboa Park* ☎ *619/234–*
★ *5623*) is the oldest professional theater in California, presenting classics, contemporary dramas, and experimental works at the historic Old Globe and its sister theaters, the intimate Cassius Carter Centre Stage and the outdoor Lowell Davies Festival Theater. The Old Globe also mounts a popular Shakespeare festival every summer at Lowell Davies.

SPORTS & THE OUTDOORS

BASEBALL

Long a favorite spectator sport in San Diego, where games are rarely rained out, baseball gained even more popularity in 2004 with the opening of PETCO Park, a stunning 42,000-seat facility right in the heart of downtown. The **San Diego Padres** (✉ *100 Park Blvd., Down-*
★ *town* ☎ *619/795–5000 or 877/374–2784* ⊕ *www.sandiegopadres. com*) slug it out for bragging rights in the National League West from April into October—they won the division in 2005 and 2006. Tickets are usually available on game day, but games with such rivals as the Los Angeles Dodgers and the San Francisco Giants often sell out quickly. For an inexpensive day at the ballpark, go for the $7 ($5 on the day of game) park pass and have a picnic on the grass, while watching the play on one of several giant-screen TVs.

BEACHES

Water temperatures are generally chilly, ranging from 55°F to 65°F from October through June, and 65°F to 75°F from July through September. For a surf and weather report, call 619/221–8824. Pollution, which has long been a problem near the Mexican border, is inching north and is generally worse near river mouths and storm drain outlets. The weather page of the *San Diego Union-Tribune* includes pollution reports along with listings of surfing and diving conditions.

Lifeguards are stationed at city beaches from Sunset Cliffs up to Black's Beach in the summertime, but coverage in winter is provided by roving patrols only. Pay attention to signs listing illegal activities; undercover police often patrol the beaches, carrying their ticket books in coolers. Glass containers are prohibited on all San Diego beaches if their purpose is to carry drinks, and fires are allowed only in fire rings or elevated barbecue grills. Alcoholic beverages—including beer—are completely banned on some city beaches. Imbibing in beach parking lots, on boardwalks, and in landscaped areas is also illegal. Although it may be tempting to take a starfish or some other sea creature as a souvenir from a tide pool, it upsets the delicate ecological balance and is illegal, too.

Finding a parking spot near the ocean can be hard in summer, but for the time being, unmetered parking is at all San Diego city beaches. Del Mar has a pay lot and metered street parking around the 15th Street beach.

Beaches are listed geographically, south to north.

CORONADO

Silver Strand State Beach. This quiet Coronado beach is ideal for families. The water is relatively calm, lifeguards and rangers are on duty year-round, and there are places to Rollerblade or ride bikes. Four parking lots provide room for more than 1,000 cars. Sites at a state campground ($25) for RVs are available by reservation (☎ *800/444–7275,* ⊕ *www.reserveamerica.com*). Foot tunnels under Route 75 lead to a bay-side beach, which affords great views of the San Diego skyline. ✦ *From San Diego–Coronado Bridge, turn left onto Orange Ave., which becomes Rte. 75, and follow signs, Coronado* ☎619/435–5184.

Coronado Beach. With the famous Hotel Del Coronado as a backdrop, ★ this stretch of sandy beach is one of San Diego County's largest and most picturesque. It's perfect for sunbathing, people-watching, or Frisbee. Exercisers include Navy SEAL teams, as well as the occasional Marine Recon unit, who have training runs on the beaches in and around Coronado. Parking can be difficult on the busiest days. There are plenty of restrooms and service facilities, as well as fire rings on the north end. ✦ *From the bridge, turn left on Orange Ave. and follow signs, Coronado.*

POINT LOMA

Sunset Cliffs. Beneath the jagged cliffs on the west side of the Point Loma peninsula is one of the more secluded beaches in the area. A few miles long, it's popular with surfers and locals. At the south end of the peninsula, near Cabrillo Point, tide pools teeming with small sea creatures are revealed at low tide. Farther north the waves lure surfers, and the lonely coves attract sunbathers. Stairs at the foot of Bermuda and Santa Cruz avenues provide beach access, as do some (treacherous at points) cliff trails. There are no facilities. A visit here is more enjoyable at low tide; check the local newspaper for tide schedules. ✦ *Take I–8 west to Sunset Cliffs Blvd. and head west.*

MISSION BAY & BEACHES

Ocean Beach. Much of this mile-long beach is a haven for volleyball players, sunbathers, and swimmers. The area around the municipal pier at the south end is a hangout for surfers and transients; the pier itself is open to the public 24 hours a day for fishing and walking, and there's a restaurant at the middle. The beach is south of the channel entrance to Mission Bay. You'll find fire rings as well as plenty of casual places to grab a snack on adjoining streets; limited parking is available. Swimmers should beware of strong rip currents around the main lifeguard tower. There's a dog beach at the north end where Fido can run leash-free. ✛ *Take I–8 west to Sunset Cliffs Blvd. and head west. A right turn off Sunset Cliffs Blvd. takes you to the water, Ocean Beach.*

★ **Mission Beach.** San Diego's most popular beach draws huge crowds on hot summer days but is lively year-round. The 2-mi-long stretch extends from the north entrance of Mission Bay to Pacific Beach. A wide boardwalk paralleling the beach is popular with walkers, joggers, roller skaters, bladers, and bicyclists. Surfers, swimmers, and volleyball players congregate at the south end. Scantily clad volleyball players practice on Cohasset Court year-round. Toward its north end, near the Belmont Park roller coaster, the beach narrows and the water becomes rougher. The crowds grow thicker and somewhat rougher as well. For parking, you can try for a spot on the street, but your best bets are the two big lots at Belmont Park. ✛ *Exit I–5 at Grand Ave. and head west to Mission Blvd. Turn south and look for parking near roller coaster at West Mission Bay Dr., Mission Beach.*

Pacific Beach/North Pacific Beach. The boardwalk of Mission Beach turns into a sidewalk here, but there are still bike paths and picnic tables along the beachfront. Pacific Beach runs from the north end of Mission Beach to Crystal Pier. North Pacific Beach extends from the pier north. The scene here is particularly lively on weekends. There are designated surfing areas, and fire rings are available. Parking can be a challenge, but there are plenty of restrooms, showers, and restaurants in the area. ✛ *Exit I–5 at Grand Ave. and head west to Mission Blvd. Turn north and look for parking, Pacific Beach.*

LA JOLLA

Tourmaline Surfing Park. This is one of the area's most popular beaches for surfing and sailboarding year-round. No swimming is allowed, and surfing etiquette is strongly enforced by the locals in and out of the water. There's a 175-space parking lot at the foot of Tourmaline Street that normally fills to capacity by midday. ✛ *Take Mission Blvd. north (it turns into La Jolla Blvd.) and turn west on Tourmaline St.*

Windansea Beach. The beach's sometimes towering waves (caused by an underwater reef) are truly world-class. With its incredible views and secluded sunbathing spots set among sandstone rocks, Windansea is also one of the most romantic of West Coast beaches, especially at sunset. ✛ *Take Mission Blvd. north (it turns into La Jolla Blvd.) and turn west on Nautilus St.*

Marine Street Beach. Wide and sandy, this strand often teems with sunbathers, swimmers, walkers, and joggers. The water is known as a great spot for bodysurfing, although the waves break in extremely shallow water and you'll need to watch out for riptides. ✛ *Accessible from Marine St., off La Jolla Blvd.*

Children's Pool. Because of the pool's location at the tip of the La Jolla peninsula, you can actually look east for unmatched panoramic views of the coastline and ocean. This shallow cove, protected by a seawall, has small waves and no riptide. The area just outside the pool is popular with scuba divers who explore the offshore reef when the surf is calm. Groups of harbor seals hang out along the beach, claiming it as their own during the winter pupping season. Court battles are currently raging between animal protection groups and citizens who want the pinnipeds to share the sand and stop fouling the water with their waste. Most recent court ruling (March 2008): seals: 1, kids, 0. Get back to your corners, guys. ✛ *Follow La Jolla Blvd. north. When it forks, stay to left, then turn right onto Coast Blvd.*

Shell Beach. North of Children's Pool is a small cove, accessible by stairs, with a relatively secluded beach. The exposed rocks off the coast have been designated a protected habitat for sea lions; you can watch them sun themselves and frolic in the water. ✛ *Continue along Coast Blvd. north from Children's Pool.*

Fodor'sChoice **La Jolla Cove.** This is one of the prettiest spots on the West Coast. A
★ palm-lined park sits on top of cliffs formed by the incessant pounding of the waves. At low tide the tide pools and cliff caves provide a destination for explorers. Divers, snorkelers, and kayakers can explore the underwater delights of the San Diego–La Jolla Underwater Park Ecological Reserve. The cove is also a favorite of rough-water swimmers. ✛ *Follow Coast Blvd. north to signs, or take La Jolla Village Dr. Exit from I–5, head west to Torrey Pines Rd., turn left, and drive downhill to Girard Ave. Turn right and follow signs.*

☺ **La Jolla Shores.** On summer holidays all access routes are usually closed,
★ so get here early—this is one of San Diego's most popular beaches. The lures are an incredible view of La Jolla peninsula, a wide sandy beach, an adjoining grassy park, and the gentlest waves in San Diego. In fact, several surf schools teach here, and kayak rentals are nearby. A concrete boardwalk parallels the beach. Arrive early to get a parking spot in the lot at the foot of Calle Frescota. ✉ *8200 Camino del Oro* ✛ *From I–5 take La Jolla Village Dr. west and turn left onto La Jolla Shores Dr. Head west to Camino del Oro or Vallecitos St. Turn right.*

★ **Black's Beach.** The powerful waves at this beach, officially known as Torrey Pines City Park Beach, attract world-class surfers, and its relative isolation appeals to nudist nature lovers (although by law nudity is prohibited) as well as gays and lesbians. Access to parts of the shore coincides with low tide. There are no lifeguards on permanent duty, although they do patrol the area between spring break and mid-October. Strong rip currents are common—only experienced swimmers should take the plunge. Storms have weakened the cliffs in the past few years; they're dangerous to climb and should be avoided. Part of the fun here is watching hang gliders and paragliders ascend from the glider port atop the cliffs. ✛ *Take Genesee Ave. west from I–5 and follow signs to glider port; easier access, via a paved path, available on La Jolla Farms Rd., but parking is limited to 2 hrs.*

DEL MAR

★ **Torrey Pines State Beach and Reserve.** One of San Diego's best beaches encompasses 12,000 acres of bluffs and bird-filled marshes. A network of meandering trails leads to the sandy shoreline below. Along the way enjoy the rare Torrey pine trees, found only here and on Santa

Rosa Island, offshore. The large parking lot is rarely full; there are bathrooms, showers, and lifeguards on patrol. Guided tours of the nature preserve here are offered on weekends. Torrey Pines tends to get crowded in summer, but heading south under the cliffs you'll run into isolated Black's Beach, above. ⊕ *Take Carmel Valley Rd. Exit west from I–5, turn left on Rte. S21* ☎ *858/755–2063* ⊕ *www.torreypine. org* ▱ *Parking $10.*

Del Mar Beach. The numbered streets of Del Mar, from 15th north to 29th, end at a wide beach popular with volleyball players, surfers, and sunbathers. Parking can be a problem in town; there's metered parking along the beach, making it challenging to stay for more than a few hours. The portion of Del Mar south of 15th Street is lined with cliffs and rarely crowded. Leashed dogs are permitted on most sections of the beach year-round; from October through May, dogs may run free at Rivermouth, Del Mar's northernmost beach. During the annual summer meeting of the Del Mar Thoroughbred Club, horse players sit on the beach in the morning, working on the *Daily Racing Form* before heading across the street to the track. Food, accommodations, and shopping are all within an easy walk of the beach. Because parking is at a premium, it's a great idea to bring a bike to cruise around the city before or after the beach. ⊕ *Take Via de la Valle Exit from I–5 west to Rte. S21 (also known as Camino del Mar in Del Mar) and turn left.*

ENCINITAS

★ **Swami's.** Palms and the golden lotus-flower domes of the nearby Self-Realization Center temple and ashram gave this picturesque beach its name. Extreme low tides expose tide pools that harbor anemones, starfish, and other sea life. Remember to look but don't touch; all sea life here is protected. The beach is also a top surfing spot; the only access is by a long stairway leading down from cliff-top Seaside Roadside Park, where there's free parking. On big winter swells, the bluffs are lined with gawkers watching the area's best surfers take on, and be taken down by, one of the best big waves in the county. Offshore, divers do their thing at North County's only underwater park, Encinitas Marine Life Refuge. ⊕ *Follow Rte. S21 north from Cardiff, or exit I–5 at Encinitas Blvd., go west to Rte. S21, and turn left.*

BICYCLING

On any given summer day **Route S21** from La Jolla to Oceanside looks like a freeway for cyclists. It's easily the most popular and scenic bike route around, never straying more than a quarter-mile from the beach. For more leisurely rides, **Mission Bay, San Diego Harbor,** and the **Mission Beach boardwalk** are all flat and scenic. For those who want to take their biking experience to the extreme, the **Kearny BMX** (✉ *3170 Armstrong St., Kearny Mesa* ☎ *6619/561–3824* ⊕ *www.kearnybmx.com*) has a dirt track where BMXers rip it up, racing three times a week, with time for practice beforehand.

Bike Tours San Diego (✉ *509 5th Ave., Downtown* ☎ *619/238–2444* ⊕ *www.bike-tours.com*) rents all types of bikes and conducts biking

tours in the downtown waterfront and Gaslamp area, to and around Coronado Island, up to Cabrillo National Monument, and elsewhere
★ in the city. **Hike Bike Kayak San Diego** (⊠ *2246 Ave. de la Playa, La Jolla* ☎ *858/551–9510 or 866/425–2925* ⊕ *www.hikebikekayak.com*) offers a wide range of guided bike tours, from easy excursions around Mission Bay and Coronado Island to slightly more rigorous trips through coastal La Jolla. Mountain-biking tours are available, and the company also rents bikes of all types (and can van-deliver them to your hotel).

Cheap Rentals Mission Beach (⊠ *3689 Mission Blvd., Mission Beach* ☎ *858/ 488–9070 or 800/941–7761* ⊕ *www.cheap-rentals.com*) is right on the boardwalk and has great daily and weekly prices for bike rentals, including beach cruisers, tandems, hybrids, and 2-wheeled baby carriers.

DIVING

Enthusiasts the world over come to San Diego to snorkel and scuba-dive off La Jolla and Point Loma. At La Jolla Cove you'll find the 6,000-acre
★ **San Diego–La Jolla Underwater Park Ecological Preserve.** Because all sea life is protected here, it's the best place to see large lobster, sea bass, and sculpin, as well as numerous golden garibaldi, the state marine fish. It's common to see hundreds of beautiful (and harmless) leopard sharks schooling at the north end of the cove, near La Jolla Shores, especially in summer. Farther north, off the south end of Black's Beach, the rim of **Scripps Canyon** lies in about 60 feet of water. The canyon plummets to more than 900 feet in some sections.

The HMCS *Yukon,* a decommissioned Canadian warship, was intentionally sunk off **Mission Beach** to create a diving destination. A mishap caused it to settle on its side, creating a surreal, M. C. Escher–esque diving environment. This is a technical dive and should be attempted by experienced divers only; even diving instructors have become disoriented inside the wreck. Another popular diving spot is **Sunset Cliffs** in Point Loma, where the sea life and flora are relatively close to shore. Strong rip currents make it an area best enjoyed by experienced divers. The *San Diego Union-Tribune* includes diving conditions on its weather page. For recorded diving information, contact the **San Diego City Lifeguard Service** (☎ *619/221–8824*).

Diving Locker (⊠ *6167 Balboa Ave., Clairemont Mesa* ☎ *858/292–0547* ⊕ *www.divinglocker.com*) has been a fixture in San Diego since 1958, making it the city's longest-running dive shop. **Scuba San Diego** (⊠ *1775 E. Mission Bay Dr., Mission Bay* ☎ *619/260–1880* ⊕ *www.scubasan diego.com*) is well regarded for its top-notch instruction and certification programs, as well as for guided dive tours of La Jolla Cove and La Jolla Canyon, as well as unguided charter boat trips to La Jolla's Wreck Alley or to the Coronado Islands (in Mexico, just south of San Diego).

FOOTBALL

The **San Diego Chargers** (⊠*9449 Friars Rd., Mission Valley* ☎*619/280–2121 or 877/242–7437* ⊕*www.chargers.com*), of the National Football League, fill Qualcomm Stadium from August through December. Games with AFC West rivals the Oakland Raiders are particularly intense.

GOLF

On any given day, it would be difficult to find a better place to play golf than San Diego. The climate—generally sunny, without a lot of wind—is perfect for the sport, and there are some 90 courses in the area, appealing to every level of expertise. Experienced golfers can play the same greens as PGA-tournament participants, and beginners or rusty players can book a week at a golf resort and benefit from expert instruction.

Most public courses in the area provide a list of fees for all San Diego courses. The **Southern California Golf Association** (☎*818/980–3630* ⊕*www.scga.org*) publishes an annual directory ($15) with detailed and valuable information on all clubs. Another good resource for golfers is the **Public Links Golf Association of Southern California** (☎*714/994–4747* ⊕*www.plga.org*), which details the region's public courses on its Web site.

COURSES

The following is not intended to be a comprehensive list but provides suggestions for some of the best places to play in the area. The adult public's greens fees are included for each course; carts (in some cases mandatory), instruction, and other costs are additional. Rates go down during twilight hours.

The **Balboa Park Municipal Golf Course** (⊠*2600 Golf Course Dr., Balboa Park* ☎*619/239–1660* ⊕*www.balboaparkgolf.com*) is in the heart of Balboa Park, making it convenient for downtown visitors. Greens fee: $21–$35.

★ **Coronado Municipal Golf Course** (⊠*2000 Visalia Row, Coronado* ☎*619/435–3121 Ext. 4* ⊕*www.golfcoronado.com*) has 18 holes, a driving range and putting green, equipment rentals, and a snack bar and sit-down restaurant. Views of San Diego Bay and the Coronado Bridge from the back nine makes this course popular—but rather difficult to get on unless you reserve a tee time, 3 to 14 days in advance, for an additional $38. Greens fee alone is $25, seven days a week, plus cart rental if desired.

FodorśChoice ★ **Four Seasons Aviara Golf Club** (⊠*7100 Four Seasons Point, Carlsbad* ☎*760/603–6800* ⊕*www.fourseasons.com*) is a top-quality course with 18 holes (designed by Arnold Palmer), a driving range, equipment rentals, and views of the protected adjacent Batiquitos Lagoon and the Pacific Ocean. Carts fitted with GPS systems that tell you the distance to the pin, among other features, are included in the cost. Greens fees: $215–$235.

2

★ **La Costa Resort and Spa** (✉2100 Costa del Mar Rd., Carlsbad ☎760/438–9111 or 800/854–5000 ⊕www.lacosta.com), one of the premier golf resorts in Southern California, has two 18-hole PGA-rated courses, a driving range, a clubhouse, equipment rentals, an excellent golf school, and a pro shop. After a full day on the links you can wind down with a massage, steam bath, and dinner at the exclusive spa resort that shares this verdant property. Greens fees: $195–$205, with a discount for resort guests.

Mission Bay Golf Resort (✉2702 N. Mission Bay Dr., Mission Bay ☎858/581–7880) has 18 holes, a driving range, equipment rentals, and a snack bar. A not-very-challenging executive (pars 3 and 4) course, Mission Bay is lighted for night play with final tee time at 7:45 PM. Greens fees: $22–$28.

★ **Rancho Bernardo Inn and Country Club** (✉17550 Bernardo Oaks Dr., Rancho Bernardo ☎858/675–8470 Ext. 1 ⊕www.ranchobernardoinn.com) has an 18-hole course, driving range, equipment rentals, and a restaurant; the course is managed by JC Golf, which has a golf school as well as several other respected courses throughout Southern California open to guests of Rancho Bernardo Inn. The restaurant here, El Bizcocho, lays out one of the best Sunday brunches in the county. Greens fees: $85–$110.

Fodor'sChoice **Torrey Pines Golf Course** (✉11480 N. Torrey Pines Rd., La Jolla ☎858/452–3226 or 800/985–4653 ⊕www.torreypinesgolfcourse.com) has a driving range and equipment rentals, and is one of the best public golf courses in the United States. Home to the 2008 U.S. Open and the site of the Buick Invitational since 1968, Torrey Pines has views of the Pacific from many of its 36 holes. The par-72 South Course receives rave reviews from the touring pros. Designed by Rees Jones, it has more length and more challenges than the North Course and, fittingly, commands higher greens fees. It's not easy to get a good tee time here, as professional brokers buy up the best ones. A full-day or half-day Instructional Golf Playing Package includes cart, greens fee, and a golf-pro escort for the first 9 holes. Greens fees on the South Course run $145–$181, the North Course $51–$64.

SAILING & BOATING

★ **Carlsbad Paddle Sports** (✉2002 S. Coast Hwy., Oceanside ☎760/434–8686 ⊕www.carlsbadpaddle.com) handles kayak sales, rentals, and instruction for coastal North County. **Harbor Sailboats** (✉2040 Harbor Island Dr., Harbor Island ☎619/291–9568 or 800/854–6625 ⊕www.harborsailboats.com) rents sailboats from 22 to 47 feet long for open-ocean adventures. **Seaforth Boat Rentals** (✉1715 Strand Way, Coronado ☎619/437–1514 or 888/834–2628 ✉1641 Quivira Rd., Mission Bay ☎619/223–1681 ✉333 West Harbor Dr. Gate 1, Downtown ☎619/239–2628) has kayaks, Jet Skis, fishing skiffs, and power boats from 10 feet to 20 feet in length as well as sailboats from 16 to 36 feet. They also can hook you up with a skipper.

SURFING

If you're a beginner, consider paddling in the waves off Mission Beach, Pacific Beach, Tourmaline Surfing Park, La Jolla Shores, Del Mar, or Oceanside. More experienced surfers usually head for Sunset Cliffs, the La Jolla reef breaks, Black's Beach, or Swami's in Encinitas. All necessary equipment is included in the cost of all surfing schools. Beach area Y's offer surf lessons and surf camp in the summer months and during

★ spring break. **Surf Diva Surf School** (✉ *2160 Avenida de la Playa, La Jolla* ☎ *858/454–8273* ⊕ *www.surfdiva.com*) offers clinics, surf camps, surf trips, and private lessons especially formulated for girls and women. Clinics and trips are for women only, but guys can book private lessons from the nationally recognized staff.

★ Many local surf shops rent both surf and bodyboards. **Cheap Rentals Mission Beach** (✉ *3689 Mission Blvd., Mission Beach* ☎ *858/488–9070 or 800/941–7761* ⊕ *www.cheap-rentals.com*) is right on the boardwalk, just steps from the waves. **Star Surfing Company** (✉ *4652 Mission Blvd., Pacific Beach* ☎ *858/273–7827* ⊕ *www.starsurfingco.com*) can get you out surfing around the Crystal Pier. **Hansen's** (✉ *1105 S. Coast Hwy. 101, Encinitas* ☎ *760/753–6595 or 800/480–4754* ⊕ *www.hansen surf.com*) is just a short walk from Swami's beach.

SHOPPING

CORONADO

FodorśChoice **Ferry Landing Marketplace.** A staggering view of San Diego's downtown
★ skyline across the bay, 30 boutiques, and a Tuesday afternoon farmers' market provide a delightful place to shop while waiting for a ferry. ✉ *1201 1st St., at B Ave.* ☎ *619/435–8895* ⊕ *www.coronadoferry landing.com.*

DOWNTOWN

Seaport Village. Quintessentially San Diego, this waterfront complex of more than 70 shops and restaurants has sweeping bay views, fresh breezes, and great strolling paths. Horse and carriage rides, an 1895 Looff carousel, and frequent public entertainment are side attractions. The Seaport is within walking distance of hotels, the San Diego Convention Center, and San Diego Trolley, and there's also an easily accessible free parking lot. ✉ *W. Harbor Dr. at Kettner Blvd.* ☎ *619/235–4014* ⊕ *www.spvillage.com.*

★ **Westfield Horton Plaza.** Within walking distance of most downtown hotels, Horton Plaza is bordered by Broadway, 1st Avenue, G Street, and 4th Avenue. The multilevel shopping, dining, and entertainment complex is an open-air visual delight, with a terra-cotta color scheme and flag-draped facades. There are department stores, including Macy's and Nordstrom; fast-food counters; upscale restaurants; the Lyceum Theater; cinemas; a game arcade; and 140 other stores. Park in the plaza garage and any store where you make a purchase will validate your parking ticket, good for three free hours. ⊠ *324 Horton Plaza* ☎ *619/238–1596* ⊕ *www.westfield.com/hortonplaza.*

GASLAMP QUARTER

Long a place where fine restaurants and clubs have catered to conventioneers and partying locals, the historic heart of San Diego has recently seen an explosion of specialty shops, art galleries, and boutiques take up residence in the Victorian buildings and renovated warehouses along 4th and 5th avenues. Some stores in this area tend to close early, starting as early as 5 PM. But a trip to the Gaslamp to shop is worth it. Here, you'll find the usual mall denizens as well as hip fashion boutiques and gift shops, even for your pup.

UPTOWN

Located north and northeast of downtown, the Uptown area includes Hillcrest, North Park, South Park, Mission Hills, and University Heights. The boundaries between the neighborhoods tend to blur, but you'll find that each area has unique shops. Hillcrest has a large gay community and boasts many avant-garde apparel shops alongside gift, book, and music stores. North Park, east of Hillcrest, is a retro buff's paradise with many resale shops, trendy boutiques, and stores that sell a mix of old and new. University Avenue offers a mélange of affordably priced furniture, gift, and specialty stores appealing to college students, singles, and young families. South Park's 30th, Juniper, and Fern streets have everything from the hottest new denim lines to baby gear and craft supplies. The shops and art galleries in upscale Mission Hills, west of Hillcrest, have a modern and sophisticated ambience that suits the well-heeled residents just fine.

LA JOLLA

Known as San Diego's Rodeo Drive, La Jolla's chic boutiques, art galleries, and gift shops line narrow twisty streets that are often celebrity-soaked. Prospect Street and Girard Avenue are the primary shopping stretches, and North Prospect is chockablock with art galleries. The Upper Girard Design District stocks home decor accessories and luxury furnishings. Parking is tight in the village and store hours vary widely, so it's wise to call in advance. Most shops on Prospect Street stay open until 10 PM on weeknights to accommodate evening strollers. On the east side of I–5, office buildings surround Westfield UTC, where you'll find department and chain stores.

OLD TOWN

Located north of downtown off I–5, Old Town is tourist-focused, but the festival-like ambience and authentic Mexican restaurants also make it a popular destination for locals. At Old Town Historic Park, you'll feel like a time traveler as you visit shops housed in restored adobe buildings. Farther down the street you'll find stores selling Mexican blankets, piñatas, and glassware. Old Town Festival Marketplace offers live entertainment, local artists selling their wares from carts, and a market crammed with unique apparel, home decor, toys, jewelry, and food. Dozens of stores sell San Diego logo merchandise and T-shirts at discounted prices, and you'll find great deals on handcrafted jewelry, art, and leather accessories.

SIDE TRIPS TO NORTH COUNTY

CARLSBAD

6 mi from Encinitas on Rte. S21, 36 mi north of downtown San Diego on I–5.

Once-sleepy Carlsbad, lying astride I–5 at the north end of a string of beach towns extending from San Diego to Oceanside, has long been popular with beach goers and sun seekers. On a clear day in this village you can take in sweeping ocean views that stretch from La Jolla to Oceanside by walking the 2-mi-long seawalk running between the Encina power plant and Pine Street. En route, you'll find several stairways leading to the beach and quite a few benches. More recently, however, much of the attention of visitors to the area has shifted inland, east of I–5, to LEGOLAND California and other attractions in its vicinity—two of the San Diego area's most luxurious resort hotels, one of the last remaining wetlands along the Southern California coast, a discount shopping mall, golf courses, the cattle ranch built by movie star Leo Carrillo, and colorful spring-blooming Flower Fields at Carlsbad Ranch.

Ⓒ **LEGOLAND California,** the centerpiece of a development that includes
Fodor'sChoice resort hotels and a designer discount shopping mall, offers a full day
★ of entertainment with more than 50 rides and attractions for pint-size fun-seekers and their parents. The mostly outdoor experience is best appreciated by kids ages 2 to 10, who often beg to ride the mechanical horses around the Royal Joust again and again or to take just one more turn through the popular Volvo Jr. Driving School. Miniland USA, an animated collection of U.S. cities and other areas constructed entirely of Lego blocks, captures the imaginations of all ages. Kids get a chance to dig for buried fossils on Dino Island, which holds the Dig Those Dinos paleontological play area as well as the Coastersaurus, a junior roller coaster. At the Fun Town Fire Academy, families compete at fire fighting by racing in a model fire truck and hosing down a simulated burning building. Also in Fun Town, besides the driving school, with miniature cars, is the Skipper School, with miniature boats. In Splash Battle, kids cruise through pirate-infested waters past exploding volcanoes; Treasure Falls, a mini-flume log ride with a 12-foot soaking plunge; and Pirate Shores, water-fight headquarters. Lost Kingdom Adventure, LEGOLAND'S first dark ride (meaning indoors) and part of a new four-ride block opened in 2008, features the adventures of

popular LEGO mini-figure Johnny Thunder battling the bad guys in an Egyptian temple with the help of riders using laser blasters to accumulate points and ultimately capture Sam Sinister and find the treasure. Also part of the mix are stage shows and restaurants with kid-friendly buffets. ✉*1 LEGOLAND Dr. ⊹ exit I–5 at Cannon Rd. and follow signs east ¼ mi* ☎*760/918–5346* ⊕*www.legolandca.com* ☎*$60, additional fees for some rides* ⊗*Hrs vary; call for information.*

WHERE TO STAY

$$$$
☾
Fodor'sChoice
★

▣ **Four Seasons Resort Aviara.** This hilltop resort on 30 acres offers one of the most sublime views in Southern California. Stroll out to the pool overlooking Batiquitos Lagoon, where the panorama stretches endlessly from lagoon to the Pacific. If you watch for a while you may catch sight of one of the 130 species of birds that inhabit the wetland. The quietly elegant Aviara is one of the most luxurious hotels in the San Diego area, with gleaming marble corridors, original artwork, crystal chandeliers, and enormous flower arrangements. Rooms have every possible amenity: oversize closets, private balconies or garden patios, and marble bathrooms with double vanities and deep soaking tubs. The resort is exceptionally family-friendly, providing a wide selection of in-room amenities designed for the younger set. Kids also have their own pool, plus nature walks with wildlife demonstrations. The on-site golf course is considered one of the best in California, and jazz concerts are presented on the lawn on summer Friday evenings. **Pros:** Unbeatable location, fabulous service. **Cons:** A little stiff. ✉*7100 Four Seasons Point* ☎*760/603–6800 or 800/332–3442* ⊕*www.fourseasons.com/ aviara* ⇆*329 rooms, 44 suites* ⚘*In-room: safe, refrigerator, DVD (some), Ethernet, Wi-Fi. In-hotel: 4 restaurants, room service, bars, golf course, tennis courts, pools, gym, spa, children's programs (ages 4–12), laundry service, concierge, public Internet, Wi-Fi, parking (fee), some pets allowed (fee), no-smoking rooms* ▤*AE, D, DC, MC, V.*

ESCONDIDO

8 mi north of Rancho Bernardo on I–15, 31 mi northeast of downtown San Diego on I–15.

☾
Fodor'sChoice
★

San Diego Wild Animal Park is an extension of the San Diego Zoo, 35 mi to the south. The 1,800-acre preserve in the San Pasqual Valley is designed to protect endangered species from around the world. Exhibit areas have been carved out of the dry, dusty canyons and mesas to represent the animals' natural habitats in various parts of Africa, the Australian rain forest, the Asian swamps, and the Asian plains.

The best way to see these preserves is to take the 60-minute, 5-mi monorail ride on the Wgasa Bushline Railway (included in the price of admission). The 1¼-mi-long **Kilimanjaro Safari Walk** winds through some of the park's hilliest terrain in the East Africa section, with observation decks overlooking the elephants and lions. A 70-foot suspension bridge spans a steep ravine, leading to the final observation point and a panorama of the entire park and the San Pasqual Valley. Along the trails of 32-acre **Heart of Africa** you can travel in the footsteps of an early explorer through forests and lowlands, across a floating bridge to a research station where an expert is on hand to answer questions; finally you arrive at Panorama Point for an up-close-and-personal view of cheetahs, a chance to feed the giraffes, and a distant glimpse of the expansive savanna where rhinos, impalas, wildebeest, oryx, and beautiful migrating birds reside. At **Condor Ridge,** the Wild Animal Park, which conducts captive breeding programs to save rare and endangered species, shows off one of its most successful efforts, the California condor. ⊠ *15500 San Pasqual Valley Rd.* ✛ *Take I–15 north to Via Rancho Pkwy. and follow signs, 6 mi* ☎*760/747–8702* ⊕*www.sandiego zoo.org/wap* ▱*$28.50 includes all shows and monorail tour; $60 combination pass grants entry within 5 days of purchase to San Diego Zoo and San Diego Wild Animal Park; parking $8* ⊙ *Mid-June–Labor Day, daily 9–8; mid-Sept.–mid-June, daily 9–4* ⊟*D, MC, V.*

SAN DIEGO ESSENTIALS

AIRPORTS & TRANSFERS

The major airport is San Diego International Airport, called Lindbergh Field locally. The airport's three-letter code is SAN. Major airlines depart and arrive at Terminal 1 (east) and Terminal 2 (west); commuter flights identified on your ticket with a 3000 sequence flight number depart from a third terminal, the commuter terminal. A red shuttle bus provides free transportation between terminals. ⇨ *California Essentials for airline contact information.*

Airport Information **San Diego International Airport** (☎*619/400–2400* ⊕*www.san.org*).

Shuttles & Buses **Cloud 9 Shuttle** (☎*800/974–8885* ⊕*www.cloud9shuttle. com*). **Coronado Livery** (☎*619/435–6310*). **Five Star** (☎*619/294–3300 or 866/281–4288* ⊕*www.fivestarshuttle.com*). **San Diego Transit** (☎*619/233–3004, 619/234–5005 TTY and TDD* ⊕*www.sdcommute.com*).

BUS & TROLLEY TRAVEL

The Greyhound terminal is downtown at Broadway and 1st Avenue, a block from the Civic Center trolley station.

San Diego County is served by a coordinated, efficient network of bus and rail routes that includes service to Oceanside in the north, the Mexican border at San Ysidro, and points east to the Anza-Borrego Desert. Under the umbrella of the Metropolitan Transit System, there are two major transit agencies: San Diego Transit and North County Transit District (NCTD). The bright-orange trolleys of the San Diego Trolley light-rail system serve downtown San Diego, Mission Valley, Old Town, South Bay, the U.S. border, and East County. The trolley system connects with San Diego Transit bus routes.

Bus Information **Greyhound** (☎*619/515–1100* ⊕*www.greyhound.com*). **North County Transit District** (☎*800/266–6883* ⊕*www.sdcommute.com*). **San Diego Transit** (☎*619/233–3004, 619/234–5005 TTY and TDD* ⊕*www.sdcommute.com*). **Transit Store** (☎*619/234–1060*).

2

CAR TRAVEL

When traveling in the San Diego area, it pays to consider the big picture to avoid getting lost. Water lies to the west of the city. To the east and north, mountains separate the urban areas from the desert. Interstate 5, which stretches from Canada to the Mexican border, bisects San Diego. Interstate 8 provides access from Yuma, Arizona, and points east. Drivers coming from Nevada and the mountain regions beyond can reach San Diego on I–15. During rush hour there are jams on I–5 and on I–15 between I–805 and Escondido.

TAXIS

Taxi stands are at shopping centers and hotels; otherwise you must call and reserve a cab. The companies listed below do not serve all areas of San Diego County. If you're going someplace other than downtown, ask if the company serves that area.

Taxi Companies **Orange Cab** (☎ 619/291-3333 ⊕ www.orangecabsandiego. com). **Silver Cabs** (☎ 619/280-5555). **Yellow Cab** (☎ 619/234-6161 ⊕ www. driveu.com).

TRAIN TRAVEL

Amtrak serves downtown San Diego's Santa Fe Depot with daily trains to and from Los Angeles, Santa Barbara, and San Luis Obispo. Connecting service to Oakland, Seattle, Chicago, Texas, Florida, and points beyond is available in Los Angeles. Amtrak trains stop in San Diego North County at Solana Beach and Oceanside.

Coaster commuter trains, which run between Oceanside and San Diego Monday–Saturday, stop at the same stations as Amtrak plus others.

Information **Amtrak** (☎ 800/872-7245 ⊕ www.amtrak.com). **Coaster** (☎ 800/266-6883 ⊕ www.sdcommute.com). **Metrolink** (☎ 800/371-5465 ⊕ www.metrolinktrains.com). **Oceanside Train Station** (☎ 760/722-4622 ⊕ www. sdcommute.com). **Santa Fe Depot** (☎ 619/239-9021). **Solana Beach Amtrak Station** (☎ 858/259-2697).

TOURS

RECOMMENDED TOURS/ GUIDES

Information **Bike Tours San Diego** (☎ 619/238-2444 ⊕ www.bike-tours.com). **Daytripper** (☎ 619/299-5777 or 800/679-8747 ⊕ www.daytripper.com). **Five Star Tours** (☎ 619/232-5040 or 800/553-8687 ⊕ www.efivestartours.com). **San Diego Scenic Tours** (☎ 858/273-8687 ⊕ www.sandiegoscenictours.com). **Secret San Diego** (☎ 619/917-6037 ⊕ www.wheretours.com).

BOAT TOURS

Information **Classic Sailing Adventures** (☎ 800/659-0141 ⊕ www.classic sailingadventures.com). **H&M Landing** (☎ 619/222-1144 ⊕ www.hmlanding. com). **Hornblower Cruises & Events** (☎ 619/234-8687 or 800/668-4322 ⊕ www.hornblower.com). **San Diego Harbor Excursion** (☎ 619/234-4111 or 800/442-7847 ⊕ www.sdhe.com). **Seaforth Sportfishing** (☎ 619/223-1681 ⊕ www.seaforthboatrental.com).

BUS & TROLLEY TOURS

Information **Centre City Development Corporation Downtown Information Center** (☎ 619/235-2222 ⊕ www.ccdc.com). **Gray Line San Diego** (☎ 800/331-5077 ⊕ www.sandiegograyline.com). **Old Town Trolley Tours** (☎ 619/298-8687 ⊕ www.trolleytours.com).

WALKING Information **Coronado Walking Tours** (☎ *619/435–5993*). **Gaslamp Quarter**
TOURS **Historical Foundation** (☎ *619/233–4692* ⊕ *www.gaslampquarter.org*). **Offshoot**
Tours (☎ *619/239–0512* ⊕ *www.balboapark.org*). **Urban Safaris** (☎ *619/944–*
9255 ⊕ *www.walkingtoursofsandiego.com*).

VISITOR INFORMATION

Citywide **San Diego Convention & Visitors Bureau** (☎ *619/232–3101* ⊕ *www.*
sandiego.org). **San Diego Convention & Visitors Bureau International Visitor**
Information Center (☎ *619/236–1212* ⊕ *www.sandiego.org*). **San Diego Visi-**
tor Information Center (☎ *619/276–8200 for recorded information* ⊕ *www.*
infosandiego.com).

San Diego County **California Welcome Center Oceanside** (☎ *760/721–1011*
or 800/350–7873 ⊕ *www.oceansidechamber.com*). **Carlsbad Convention &**
Visitors Bureau (☎ *800/227–5722* ⊕ *www.visitcarlsbad.com*). **Coronado Visitor**
Center (☎ *619/437–8788* ⊕ *www.coronadovisitorcenter.com*). **Del Mar Regional**
Chamber of Commerce (☎ *858/793–5292* ⊕ *www.delmarchamber.org*). **Encini-**
tas Chamber of Commerce (☎ *760/753–6041* ⊕ *www.encinitaschamber.com*).
Promote La Jolla, Inc. (☎ *858/454–5718* ⊕ *www.lajollabythesea.com*).

Orange County & Catalina Island

WITH DISNEYLAND AND KNOTT'S BERRY FARM

Laguna Beach

WORD OF MOUTH

"Say what you will about 'service' at Disney, but in all the years we
have stayed on-property we have yet to hear the word 'no' when
we have asked if something is possible."

—Voyager2006

WELCOME TO ORANGE COUNTY & CATALINA ISLAND

TOP REASONS TO GO

★ **Disney magic:** Walking down Main Street, U.S.A. with Cinderella's Castle straight ahead, you really will feel like you're in one of the happiest places on earth.

★ **Beautiful beaches:** Surf, swim, sail, or just relax on one of the state's most breathtaking stretches of coastline.

★ **Catalina Island:** Just a short hydrofoil away, Catalina feels 1,000 mi away from California. Wander around charming Avalon, or explore the unspoiled beauty of the island's wild interior.

★ **The fine life:** Some of the state's wealthiest communities are in coastal Orange County, so spend at least part of your stay here experiencing how the other half lives.

★ **Family fun:** Spend some quality time with the kids riding roller coasters, eating ice cream, fishing off ocean piers, and bodysurfing.

1 Anaheim. If you think you've "been there, done that" by visiting the mouse's Orlando outpost, think again. Disneyland has a unique place in the company's legend: it's the only kingdom to be overseen by Walt himself.

2 Newport Beach. This is one of the priciest pieces of real estate in the world. The island-dotted harbor is packed with huge yachts, and you won't find more Mercedes-Benzes per capita anywhere else on the planet.

3 Huntington Beach. Head here for surfing—even if you're just watching. The town is home to the International Surfing Museum, the Surfing Walk of Fame, and the U.S. open professional surf competition.

4 Laguna Beach. There's room for everyone in one of California's most welcoming towns. A longtime artist community, this gallery-packed destination has a beautiful cove and canyon and spectacular resort hotels.

GETTING ORIENTED

3

Like Los Angeles, Orange County stretches over a large area, lacks a singular focal point, and has limited public transportation. You'll need a car and a sensible game plan to make the most of your visit. Try staying at a mid-point location such as Irvine or Costa Mesa, both equidistant from inland tourist attractions and the coast. These towns are less crowded than Anaheim and less expensive than the beach cities. Of course, if you can afford it, staying at the beach is always recommended.

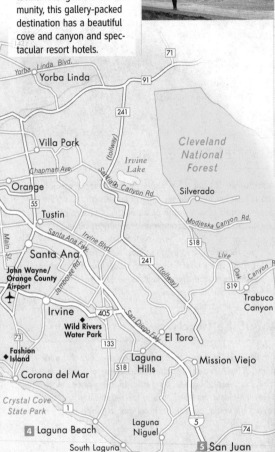

Disneyland

5 Mission San Juan Capistrano. Step back in time and visit this chapter in Southern California's colonial history, the largest California structure built by the Spanish.

ORANGE COUNTY & CATALINA ISLAND PLANNER

Car Travel

The San Diego Freeway (I–405), the coastal route, and the Santa Ana Freeway (I–5), the inland route, run north–south through Orange County. South of Laguna, I–405 merges into I–5 (called the San Diego Freeway south from this point). A toll road, the 73 Highway, runs 15 mi from Newport Beach to San Juan Capistrano; it costs $3 and is usually less jammed than the regular freeways. Do your best to avoid freeways during rush hours (6–9 AM and 3:30–6:30 PM).

Highways 55 and 91 head west to the ocean and east into the mountains and desert. Highway 91, which goes to inland points, has some express lanes for which drivers pay a toll, ostensibly to avoid the worst of rush-hour traffic. If you have three or more people in your car, though, you can use the Highway 91 express lanes most of the day for free (the exception being 4 PM–6 PM on weekdays, when you pay half fare). Highway 55 leads to Newport Beach. The Pacific Coast Highway (Highway 1) allows easy access to beach communities and is the most scenic route.

About the Restaurants

Restaurants in Orange County are typically more casual than in L.A. You'll rarely see men in jackets and ties. Of course, there's also a swath of supercasual places along the beachfronts—fish-taco takeout, taquerias, burger joints—that won't mind if you wear flip-flops. Reservations are recommended for the nicest restaurants. Many places don't serve past 11 PM, and locals tend to eat early. Remember that according to California law, smoking is prohibited in all enclosed areas.

About the Hotels

In most cases, you can take advantage of some of the facilities of luxury resorts, such as restaurants or spas, without being an overnight guest. As a rule, lodging prices tend to rise the closer the hotels are to the beach. If you are looking for value, consider a hotel that is inland along the I–405 corridor.

WHAT IT COSTS				
¢	$	$$	$$$	$$$$
Restaurants				
under $7	$7–$12	$12–$22	$22–$32	over $32
Hotels				
under $75	$75–$125	$125–$200	$200–$325	over $325

Restaurant prices are per person for a main course, excluding 8.25% sales tax. Hotel prices are for two people in a standard double room in nonholiday high season on the European Plan (no meals) unless otherwise noted. Taxes (9%–14%) are extra. In listings we always name the facilities available, but we don't specify whether they cost extra. When pricing accommodations, always ask about what's included.

Updated
by Charyn
Pfeuffer and
Laura Randall

FEW OF THE CITRUS GROVES that gave Orange County its name remain. This region south and east of Los Angeles is now ruled by tourism and high-tech business instead of farmers. With its tropical flowers and palm trees, the stretch of coast between Seal Beach and San Clemente is often called the California Riviera. Exclusive Newport Beach, artsy Laguna, and the surf town of Huntington Beach are the stars, but lesser-known gems on the glistening coast—such as Corona del Mar—are also worth visiting. Offshore, meanwhile, lies gorgeous Catalina Island, a terrific spot for diving, snorkeling, and hiking. And despite a building boom that began in the 1990s, the area is still a place to find wilderness trails, canyons, greenbelts, and national parks.

DISNEYLAND RESORT

🕒 *26 mi southeast of Los Angeles, via I–5.*

Fodor'sChoice
★

The snowcapped Matterhorn, the centerpiece of the Magic Kingdom, punctuates the skyline of **Anaheim.** Since 1955, when Walt Disney chose this once-quiet farming community for the site of his first amusement park, Disneyland has attracted more than 450 million visitors and thousands of workers, and Anaheim has been their host. To understand the symbiotic relationship between Disneyland and Anaheim, you need only look at the $4.2 billion spent in a combined effort by the Walt Disney Company and Anaheim, the latter to revitalize the city's tourist center and run-down areas, the former to expand and renovate the Disney properties into what is known now as **Disneyland Resort.** The resort is a sprawling complex that includes Disney's two amusement parks; three hotels; and Downtown Disney, a shopping, dining, and entertainment promenade. Anaheim's tourist center includes Angel Stadium of Anaheim, home of baseball's World Series Champion Los Angeles Angels of Anaheim; Arrowhead Pond, which hosts concerts and the hockey team the Anaheim Ducks; and the enormous Anaheim Convention Center.

GETTING THERE

Disneyland is about a 30-mi drive from either LAX or downtown. From LAX, follow Sepulveda Boulevard south to the I–105 freeway and drive east 16 mi to the I–605 north exit. Exit at the Santa Ana Freeway (I–5) and continue south for 12 mi to the Disneyland Drive exit. Follow signs to the resort. From downtown, follow I–5 south 28 mi and exit at Disneyland Drive. ✉ *1313 Harbor Blvd., Anaheim* ☎ *714/781–4565* ⊕ *www.disneyland.com.*

The **Anaheim Orange County Visitor & Convention Bureau** is a good source for maps and news on the area. ✉ *800 W. Katella Ave., Anaheim* ☎ *714/765–8888* ⊕ *www.anaheimoc.org.*

Disneyland Resort Express offers daily nonstop bus service between LAX, John Wayne Airport, and Anaheim. Reservations are not required. The cost is $19 one way for adults, $16 for children. ☎ *714/978–8855* ⊕ *www.airportbus.com.*

TIMING

Disneyland and Disney's California Adventure are open daily, 365 days a year; hours vary, depending on the season, but typically Disneyland opens at 8 AM and Disney's California Adventure at 10 AM. Guests at Disney hotels and those with a multiple-day Park Hopper pass are often allowed in an hour ahead of the official opening time. Disneyland stays open as late as midnight on weekends and in the summer, but it's always a good idea to check the Web site or call ahead.

If you plan to visit for more than a day, you can save money by buying three-, four-, and five-day Park Hopper tickets that grant same-day "hopping" privileges between Disneyland and Disney's California Adventure. You get a discount on the multiple-day passes if you buy online through the Disneyland Web site. A one-day Park Hopper pass costs $91 for anyone 10 or older, $81 for kids ages 3–9. Admission to either park (but not both) is $66 or $53 for kids 3–9; kids under 3 are free. Don't forget to factor in parking costs; $11 for cars, $13 for RVs.

DISNEYLAND

PARK NEIGHBORHOODS

☾ MAIN STREET, U.S.A.

FodorsChoice Walt's hometown of Marceline, Missouri, was the inspiration behind
★ this romanticized image of small-town America, circa 1900. It opens half an hour before the rest of the park, so it's a good place to explore if you're getting an early start to beat the crowds. The sidewalks are lined with a penny arcade and shops that sell everything from tradable pins to Disney-theme clothing and photo supplies. **Main Street Cinema** offers a cool respite from the crowds and six classic Disney animated shorts, including Steamboat Willie. There's rarely a wait to enter. Board the **Disneyland Railroad** here to save on walking; it tours all the lands, plus offers unique views of Splash Mountain and the Grand Canyon and Primeval World dioramas.

NEW ORLEANS SQUARE

A mini–French Quarter with narrow streets, hidden courtyards, and live street performances, this is home to two iconic attractions and the Cajun-inspired Blue Bayou restaurant. **Pirates of the Caribbean** now features Jack Sparrow and the cursed Captain Barbossa, in a nod to the blockbuster movies of the same name, plus enhanced special effects and battle scenes (complete with cannonball explosions). Nearby **Haunted Mansion** continues to spook guests with its stretching room and "doombuggy" rides (plus there's now an expanded storyline for the beating-heart bride). Its *Nightmare Before Christmas* holiday overlay is an annual tradition. Don't forget to check out the beautiful animation art at **Disney Gallery**, where free tours (no reservation required) are available in the afternoon. This is a good area to get a casual bite to eat; the clam chowder in sourdough bread bowls, sold at the French Market Restaurant and Royal Street Veranda, is a popular choice.

FRONTIERLAND

Located between Adventureland and Fantasyland, Frontierland transports you to the wild, wild West with its rustic buildings, shooting gallery, mountain range, and foot stompin' dance hall. The marquee attraction, **Big Thunder Mountain Railroad,** is a relatively tame roller coaster ride (no steep descents) that takes the form of a runaway mine car as it rumbles past desert canyons and an old mining town. Tour the Rivers of America on the **Mark Twain Riverboat** in the company of a grizzled old river pilot or circumnavigate the globe on the **Sailing Ship Columbia,** though its operating hours are usually limited to weekends. You can also raft over from here to Pirate's Lair on **Tom Sawyer Island,** which now features pirate-theme caves, treasure hunts, and music along with plenty of caves and hills to climb and explore. If you don't mind tight seating, have a snack at the Golden Horseshoe Restaurant while enjoying the always-entertaining comedy and bluegrass show of Billy Hill and the Hillybillies. Children won't want to miss **Big Thunder Ranch,** a small petting zoo of real pigs, goats, and cows beyond Big Thunder Mountain.

CRITTER COUNTRY

Down-home country is the theme in this shady corner of the park, where Winnie the Pooh and Davy Crockett make their homes. So does **Splash Mountain,** a classic flume ride accompanied by music and appearances by Br'er Rabbit and other characters from *Song of the South*. Don't forget to check out your photo (the camera snaps close-ups of each car just before it plunges into the water) on the way out. The patio of the popular Hungry Bear Restaurant has great views of Tom Sawyer's Island and Davy Crockett's Explorer Canoes.

ADVENTURELAND

Modeled after the lands of Africa, Polynesia, and Arabia, this tiny tropical paradise is worth braving the crowds that flock here for the ambience and better-than-average food. Sing along with the animatronic birds and tiki gods in the **Enchanted Tiki Room,** sail the rivers of the world with joke-cracking skippers on **Jungle Cruise,** and climb the Disneyodendron semperflorens (aka always-blooming Disney tree) to **Tarzan's Treehouse,** where you'll walk through scenes, some interactive, from the 1999 animated film. Cap off the visit with a wild jeep ride at **Indiana Jones Adventure,** where the special effects and decipherable hieroglyphics distract you while you're waiting in line. The kebabs at Bengal Barbecue and pineapple whip at Tiki Juice Bar are some of the best fast-food options in the park.

FANTASYLAND

Sleeping Beauty's Castle marks the entrance to Fantasyland, a visual wonderland of princesses, spinning teacups, flying elephants, and other classic storybook characters. Rides and shops (such as the princess-theme Once Upon a Time and Gepetto's Toys and Gifts) take precedence over restaurants in this area of the park, but outdoor carts sell everything from churros to turkey legs. Tots love the **King Arthur Carousel, Casey Jr. Circus Train,** and **Storybook Land Canal Boats.** This is also home to **Mr. Toad's Wild Ride, Peter Pan's Flight,** and **Pinocchio's Daring Journey,** classic, movie-theater-dark rides that immerse riders in Disney fairytales and appeal to adults and kids alike. The Abominable Snowman pops up on the **Matterhorn Bobsleds,** a roller coaster that twists and turns you up and around a made-to-scale model of the real Swiss mountain. Anchoring the east end of Fantasyland is **It's a Small World,** a smorgasbord of dancing animatronic dolls, cuckoo clock–covered walls, and variations of the song everyone knows by heart. Across the way, little princesses and knights can partake in a coronation ceremony, dancing, and storytelling by a Disney Princess at the **Disney Princess Fantasy Faire.** Check the daily guide for times.

MICKEY'S TOONTOWN
Geared toward small fry, this lopsided cartoonlike downtown, complete with cars and trolleys that invite exploring, is where Mickey, Donald, Goofy, and other classic Disney characters hang their hats. One of the most popular attractions is **Roger Rabbit's Car Toon Spin,** a twisting, turning cab ride through the Toontown of Who Framed Roger Rabbit? You can also walk through **Mickey's House** to meet and be photographed with the famous mouse, take a low-key ride on **Gadget's Go Coaster,** or bounce around the fenced-in playground in front of **Goofy's House.**

TOMORROWLAND
This popular section of the park underwent a complete refurbishment in 1998 and continues to tinker with its future with the regular addition of new or enhanced rides. The newest attraction, **Finding Nemo's Submarine Voyage** updates the old Submarine Voyage ride with the exploits of Nemo, Dory, Marlin, and other characters from the Pixar film. Try to visit this popular ride early in the day if you can and be prepared for a wait. The interactive **Buzz Lightyear Astro Blasters** lets you zap your neighbors with laser beams and compete for the highest score. Hurtle through the cosmos on **Space Mountain,** refurbished in 2005, and take a shuttle ride on Endor in **Star Wars.** There are also mainstays like the futuristic **Astro Orbiter** rockets, **Innoventions,** a self-guided tour of the latest toys of tomorrow, and **Honey, I Shrunk the Audience,** a 3-D film featuring Rick Moranis. Disneyland Monorail and Disneyland Railroad both have stations here. There's also a video arcade, and the dancing water fountain makes a perfect playground for kids on hot summer days.

OTHER ATTRACTIONS
Besides the eight lands, the daily live-action shows and parades are always crowd pleasers. **Fantasmic!** is a musical, fireworks, and laser show in which Mickey and friends wage a spellbinding battle against Disneyland's darker characters; and the daytime and nighttime Parade of Dreams features just about every animated Disney character ever drawn. ■TIP→ **Arrive early to secure a good view; if there are two shows scheduled for the day, the second one tends to be less crowded. A fireworks display sparks up Friday and Saturday evenings.** Brochures with maps, available at the entrance, list show- and parade times.

DISNEY'S CALIFORNIA ADVENTURE

☾
★
The sprawling 55-acre Disney's California Adventure, right next to Disneyland (their entrances face each other), pays tribute to the Golden State with four theme areas. In an effort to attract more crowds, the park began a major five-year overhaul in late 2007 that will infuse more of Walt Disney's spirit throughout the park and add a host of new attractions, including a nighttime water-effects show and a 12-acre section called Cars Land based on the Pixar film. The first new attraction, an interactive adventure ride called Toy Story Mania! and hosted by Woody, Buzz Lightyear, and friends opened at Paradise Pier in 2008.

PARK NEIGHBORHOODS

PARADISE PIER

This section re-creates the glory days of California's seaside piers. If you're looking for thrills, the **California Screamin'** roller coaster takes its riders from 0 to 55 MPH in about four seconds and proceeds through scream tunnels, steeply angled drops, and a 360-degree loop. **Sun Wheel**, a giant Ferris wheel, provides a good view of the grounds at a more leisurely pace. **Mulholland Madness** is a fun tribute to L.A.'s crazy traffic cycles. There's also carnival games, a fish-themed carousel, and Ariel's Grotto, where future princesses can dine with the mermaid and her friends (reservations a must).

HOLLYWOOD PICTURES BACKLOT

With a main street modeled after Hollywood Boulevard, a fake blue-sky backdrop, and real soundstages, this area celebrates California's most famous industry. **Disney Animation** gives you an insider's look at the work of animators and how they create characters. **Turtle Talk with Crush** lets kids have an unrehearsed talk with computer-animated Crush, a sea turtle from *Finding Nemo*. The Hyperion theater hosts **Aladdin—A Musical Spectacular**, a 45-minute live performance with terrific visual effects. ■TIP➔**Plan on getting in line about half an hour in advance: the show is well worth the wait**. On the latest film-inspired ride, **Monsters, Inc. Mike & Sulley to the Rescue**, you climb into taxis and travel the streets of Monstropolis on a mission of safely returning Boo to her bedroom. A major draw for older kids is the looming *Twilight Zone Tower of Terror*, which drops riders 13 floors.

A BUG'S LAND

Inspired by the 1998 film *A Bug's Life*, this section skews its attractions to an insect's point of view. Kids can cool off (or get soaked) in the water jets and giant garden hose of **Princess Dot Puddle Park**, spin around in giant takeout Chinese food boxes on **Flik's Flyers**, and hit the bug-shaped bumper cars on **Tuck and Roll's Drive 'Em Buggies**. The short show *It's Tough to Be a Bug!* gives you a 3-D look at insect life.

GOLDEN STATE

Celebrate California's history and natural beauty with nature trails, a winery, and a tortilla factory (with free samples). The area of Condor Flats has **Soarin' Over California**, a spectacular simulated hang-glider ride over California terrain, and the **Redwood Creek Challenge**

Trail, a challenging trek across net ladders and suspension bridges. The film *Golden Dreams* is a sentimental dash through California history narrated by Whoopi Goldberg. **Grizzly River Run** simulates the river rapids of the Sierra Nevadas; be prepared to get soaked. The Wine Country Trattoria is a great place for a relaxing outdoor lunch.

OTHER ATTRACTIONS

Downtown Disney is a 20-acre promenade of dining, shopping, and entertainment that connects the Disneyland Resort hotels and theme parks. Restaurant-nightclubs here include the **House of Blues,** which spices up its Delta-inspired ribs and seafood with various live music acts on an intimate two-story stage. At **Ralph Brennan's Jazz Kitchen** you can dig into New Orleans–style food and music. Sports fans gravitate to **ESPN Zone,** a sports bar–restaurant–entertainment center with American grill food, interactive video games, and 175 video screens telecasting worldwide sports events. There's also an **AMC** multiplex movie theater with stadium-style seating that plays the latest blockbusters and, naturally, a couple of kids' flicks. Promenade shops sell everything from Disney goods to antique jewelry; don't miss **Vault 28,** a hip boutique that sells one-of-kind vintage and couture clothes and accessories from Disney, Betsey Johnson, and other designers. ⊠*Disneyland Dr. between Ball Rd. and Katella Ave., Anaheim* ☎*714/300–7800* ⊕*www.disneyland. com* 🎟*Free* ⊙*Daily 7 AM–2 AM; hrs at shops and restaurants vary.*

WHERE TO STAY & EAT

An Anaheim Resort Transit (ART) bus can take you around town for $3. The buses run every 10 minutes during peak times, 20 minutes otherwise. They go between major hotels, Disney attractions, the Anaheim Convention Center, and restaurants and shops. See the ART Web site (⊕*www.rideart.org*) for more information. In addition, many hotels are within walking distance of the Disneyland Resort.

$$$–$$$$ ✕**Anaheim White House.** Several small dining rooms are set with crisp linens and candles in this flower-filled 1909 mansion. The northern Italian menu includes steak, rack of lamb, and fresh seafood. Try the Gwen Stefani Ravioli, lobster-filled pasta on a bed of ginger and citrus. A three-course prix-fixe "express" lunch, served weekdays, costs $24. ⊠*887 S. Anaheim Blvd., Anaheim* ☎*714/772–1381* ▤*AE, MC, V* ⊙*No lunch weekends.*

$$$–$$$$ ✕**Napa Rose.** In sync with its host hotel, Grand Californian, this restau-
★   rant is done in a lovely Arts and Crafts style. The contemporary cuisine here is matched with an extensive wine list (600 bottles on display). For a look into the open kitchen, sit at the counter and watch the chefs as they whip up signature dishes such as Gulf of California rock scallops in a sauce of lemon, lobster, and vanilla and spit-roasted prime rib of pork with ranch-style black beans. A four-course, $80 prix-fixe menu changes weekly. ⊠*Grand Californian Hotel, 1600 S. Disneyland Dr.* ☎*714/300–7170* ▤*AE, D, DC, MC, V.*

$$–$$$ ✕**Catal Restaurant & Uva Bar.** Famed chef Joachim Splichal takes a more casual approach at this bi-level Mediterranean spot—with tapas breaking into the finger-food territory. At the Uva (Spanish for "grape") bar on the ground level, you can graze on olives and Spanish ham, choosing

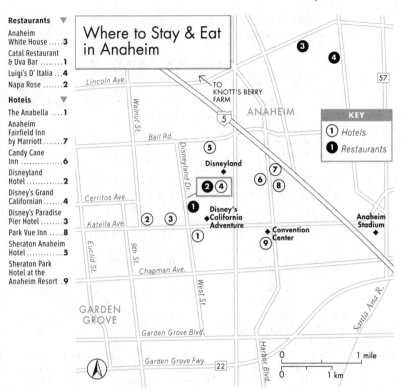

Where to Stay & Eat in Anaheim

KEY

① *Hotels*

❶ *Restaurants*

from 40 wines by the glass. Upstairs, Catal's menu spans paella, rotisserie chicken, and salads. ⊠*1580 Disneyland Dr., Suite 103, Downtown Disney* ☎*714/774–4442* ▤*AE, D, DC, MC, V.*

$–$$ ✕**Luigi's D'Italia.** Despite the simple surroundings—red vinyl booths and plastic checkered tablecloths—Luigi's serves outstanding Italian cuisine: spaghetti marinara, veal Parmesan, homemade pizza, and all the classics. Kids will feel right at home here; there's even a children's menu. It's an easy five-minute drive from Disneyland, but less crowded and expensive than many restaurants adjacent to the park. ⊠*801 S. State College Blvd., Anaheim* ☎*714/490–0990* ▤*AE, D, DC, MC, V.*

$$$$ ⊞**Disney's Grand Californian.** The newest of Disney's Anaheim hotels,
Fodor'sChoice this Craftsman-style luxury property has guest rooms with views of the
★ California Adventure park and Downtown Disney. They don't push the Disney brand too heavily; rooms are done in dark woods with amber-shaded lamps and just a small Bambi image on the shower curtain. Restaurants include the Napa Rose dining room and Storytellers Cafe, where Disney characters entertain children at breakfast. Of the three pools, the one shaped like Mickey Mouse is just for kids, plus there's an evening child activity center, and portable cribs are in every room. Room-and-ticket packages are available. The new Mandara spa has a couple's suite with Balinese-inspired art and textiles. In late 2007 the resort began an expansion project that will add 200 new rooms

and 50 Disney Vacation Club villas to the property. **Pros:** Large, gorgeous lobby; fresh-baked cookies upon arrival; direct access to California Adventure. **Cons:** The self-parking lot is across the street from the hotel; standard rooms are on the small side. ⌂*1600 S. Disneyland Dr., Disneyland Resort* ☎*714/956–6425* 📠*714/300–7701* ⊕*www. disneyland.com* ⚏*701 rooms, 44 suites* ⚐*In-room: safe, refrigerator, Ethernet. In-hotel: 2 restaurants, room service, bars, pools, gym, concierge, children's programs (ages 5–12), laundry service, parking (fee), no-smoking rooms* ⊟*AE, D, DC, MC, V.*

$$$–$$$$ 🏨**Disneyland Hotel.** Not surprisingly, the first of Disney's three hotels is the one most full of Magic Kingdom magic, with Disney-theme memorabilia and Disney music. Check out the Peter Pan–theme pool, with its wooden bridge, 110-foot waterslide, and relaxing whirlpool. The cove pools' sandy shores are great for sunning and playing volleyball. East-facing rooms in the Sierra Tower have the best views of the park, while west-facing rooms look over gardens. At Goofy's Kitchen, kids can dine with Disney characters. Room-and-ticket packages are available. **Pros:** Disney theme is everywhere; great kids' activities. **Cons:** Uninviting lobby; lots of kids means the noise level is high at all hours. ⌂*1150 Magic Way, Disneyland Resort* ☎*714/778–6600* 📠*714/956–6582* ⊕*www.disneyland.com* ⚏*990 rooms, 60 suites* ⚐*In-room: safe, refrigerator, Ethernet. In-hotel: 5 restaurants, room service, bars, pools, gym, spa, concierge, children's programs (ages 5–12), laundry service, airport shuttle, public Wi-Fi, parking (fee), no-smoking rooms* ⊟*AE, D, DC, MC, V.*

$$$–$$$$ 🏨**Disney's Paradise Pier Hotel.** The Paradise Pier has many of the same Disney touches as the Disneyland Hotel, but it's a bit quieter and tamer. From here you can walk to Disneyland or pick up a shuttle or monorail. SoCal style manifests itself in seafoam-green guest rooms with lamps shaped like lifeguard stands, and surfboard motifs. A wooden roller coaster–inspired waterslide takes adventurers to a high-speed splashdown. Room-and-ticket packages are available. **Pros:** First-rate concierge; friendly service. **Cons:** Small pool area; it's a 15-minute walk to Disneyland despite its location within the Disney resort area. ⌂*1717 S. Disneyland Dr., Disneyland Resort* ☎*714/999–0990* 📠*714/776–5763* ⊕*www.disneyland.com* ⚏*489 rooms, 45 suites* ⚐*In-room: safe, refrigerator, Ethernet. In-hotel: 2 restaurants, room service, bars, pool, gym, concierge, children's programs (ages 5–12), laundry service, public Wi-Fi, parking (fee), no-smoking rooms* ⊟*AE, D, DC, MC, V.*

$$–$$$ 🏨**Sheraton Anaheim Hotel.** If you're hoping to escape from the commer-
★   cial atmosphere of the hotels near Disneyland, consider this sprawling replica of a Tudor castle. In the flower- and plant-filled lobby you're welcome to sit by the grand fireplace, watching fish swim around in a pond. Rooms are sizable; some first-floor rooms open onto interior gardens and a pool area. A shuttle to Disneyland is available. **Pros:** Large, attractive lobby and spacious rooms with comfortable beds. **Cons:** Confusing layout; hotel sits close to a busy freeway and is not within walking distance of Disneyland. ⌂*900 S. Disneyland Dr., Anaheim* ☎*714/778–1700 or 800/325–3535* 📠*714/535–3889* ⊕*www.*

starwoodhotels.com ₪*460 rooms and 29 suites* ☆*In-room: refrigerators, safes, Wi-Fi. In-hotel: restaurant, room service, bar, pool, gym, laundry facilities, laundry service, parking (fee), no-smoking rooms* ▤*AE, D, DC, MC, V.*

$-$$ ⬚**Candy Cane Inn.** One of the Disneyland area's first hotels (deeds
★ were executed Christmas Eve, hence the name), the Candy Cane is one of Anaheim's most relaxing properties. Rooms are spacious and understated, while the palm-fringed pool is especially inviting. Premium rooms have two queen beds, microwaves, and coffeemakers. The hotel is just around the corner from Disneyland's main gate. A free Disneyland shuttle runs every half hour. **Pros:** Proximity to Disneyland; friendly service; well-lighted, landscaped property. **Cons:** Rooms and lobby are on the small side; all rooms face parking lot. ✉*1747 S. Harbor Blvd., Anaheim* ☎*714/774–5284 or 800/345–7057* 📠*714/772–5462* ⊕*www.candycaneinn.net* ₪*171 rooms* ☆*In-room: refrigerator, Wi-Fi. In-hotel: pool, spa, no elevator, laundry facilities, laundry service, parking (no fee), no-smoking rooms* ▤*AE, D, DC, MC, V* ⎥⎢*CP.*

$-$$ ⬚**Sheraton Park Hotel at the Anaheim Resort.** Sheraton took over this hotel in 2006 and freshened up the decor in guest rooms and public spaces. The handsome rooms are decorated in rich navy and brown and have private balconies with views of Disneyland or the surrounding area. You can also relax in the nicely landscaped outdoor area or take a dip in the oversize pool. It's about a 15-minute walk to Disneyland. **Pros:** Luxury lodging; large fitness center overlooks pool; most rooms have excellent views. **Cons:** Impersonal lobby; elevators can be slow when it's busy. ✉*1855 S. Harbor Blvd., Anaheim* ☎*714/750–1811 or 800/716–6199* 📠*714/971–3626* ⊕*www.starwoodhotels.com/sheraton* ₪*483 rooms, 7 suites* ☆*In-room: refrigerator, Wi-Fi. In-hotel: restaurant, room service, bar, pool, spa, laundry facilities, laundry service, parking (fee), no-smoking rooms* ▤*AE, D, DC, MC, V.*

¢-$$ ⬚**The Anabella.** This Spanish Mission–style hotel on the convention center campus is a good value, with junior suites going for as little as $69. Though their decor is more traditional than Mission-style, the suites are spacious with granite bathrooms and sleeper sofas. The interior rooms (away from Katella Avenue) are quieter. The hotel's Oasis, with a hot tub and pool, plus an adults-only pool, is a perfect place for relaxing. **Pros:** Attentive service; landscaped grounds; pet-friendly rooms. **Cons:** Some say the room walls are thin; it's a long walk to Disneyland's main gate. ✉*1030 W. Katella Ave., Anaheim* ☎*714/905–1050 or 800/863–4888* 📠*714/905–1054* ⊕*www.anabellahotel.com* ₪*308 rooms and 50 suites* ☆*In-room: safe, refrigerator, Wi-Fi. In-hotel: restaurant, room service, bar, pools, gym, spa, laundry facilities, laundry service, executive floor, parking (fee)* ▤*AE, D, DC, MC, V.*

$ ⬚**Anaheim Fairfield Inn by Marriott.** Attentive service and proximity to Disneyland (a 10-minute walk away) make this high-rise hotel a big draw for families. Most of the spacious rooms come with sleeper sofas as well as beds. In summer keep an eye out for the magician who roams the premises, entertaining adults and kids alike. **Pros:** Proximity to Disneyland; close to many restaurants; the lobby offers fruit-infused drinking water and a TV showing Disney movies. **Cons:** Small pool abuts the parking lot; lack of green space. ✉*1460 S. Harbor Blvd., Anaheim* ☎*714/772–6777 or 800/228–2800* 📠*714/999–1727* ⊕*www.marriott. com* ↝*467 rooms* ♿*In-room: refrigerator. In-hotel: restaurant, room service, pool, laundry facilities, laundry service, parking (no fee), no-smoking rooms* ▤*AE, D, DC, MC, V.*

¢–$ 🏨 **Park Vue Inn.** This bougainvillea-trimmed two-story Spanish-style inn is one of the closest hotels you'll find to Disneyland's main gate. Rooms were renovated in 2007, and most feature two queen beds, desks, and large TVs. **Pros:** Easy walk to Disneyland and many restaurants; good value. **Cons:** All rooms face the parking lot; some complain about early-morning street noise. ✉*1570 S. Harbor Blvd., Anaheim* ☎*714/772–3691 or 800/334–7021* 📠*714/956–4736* ⊕*www.parkvueinn.com* ↝*82 rooms, 6 suites* ♿*In-room: refrigerator. In-hotel: Wi-Fi, pool, gym, laundry facilities, parking (no fee), no-smoking rooms* ▤*AE, D, DC, MC, V.*

KNOTT'S BERRY FARM

🕐 *25 mi south of Los Angeles, via I–5, in Buena Park.*

★

The land where the boysenberry was invented (by crossing red raspberry, blackberry, and loganberry bushes) is now occupied by Knott's Berry Farm. In 1934, Cordelia Knott began serving chicken dinners on her wedding china to supplement her family's income. Or so the story goes. The dinners and her boysenberry pies proved more profitable than husband Walter's berry farm, so the two moved first into the restaurant business and then into the entertainment business. The park is now a 160-acre complex with 100-plus rides, dozens of restaurants and shops, and even a brick-by-brick replica of Philadelphia's Independence Hall. While it has some good attractions for small children, the park is best known for its roster of awesome thrill rides. And, yes, you can still get that boysenberry pie (and jam, juice—you name it).

GETTING THERE

Knott's is an easy 10-minute drive from Disneyland or a 30-minute drive from downtown Los Angeles. Take I–5 to Beach Boulevard and head south 3 mi; follow the park entrance signs on the right. ✉*8039 Beach Blvd., Buena Park* ✛*Between La Palma Ave. and Crescent St., 2 blocks south of Hwy. 91* ☎*714/220–5200* ⊕*www.knotts.com.*

TIMING

The park is open June–mid-Sept., daily 9 AM*–midnight; mid-September–May the park usually opens at 10* AM *and closes between 5 and 8* PM *on weekdays, and between 10* PM *and midnight on weekends. Call ahead or check Web site to confirm hours.* You can see the park in a day, but plan to start early and finish fairly late. Traffic can be heavy, so factor in time for delays.

■**TIP→ If you think you'll only need a few hours at the main park, you can save money by coming after 4** PM**, when admission fees drop to $25.** This deal is offered any day the park is open after 6. A full-day pass for adults is $50; Southern California residents pay $34 and children 3–11 are $20. Tickets can be purchased online and printed out ahead of time, to avoid waiting in line.

PARK NEIGHBORHOODS

GHOST TOWN

Clusters of authentic old buildings relocated from their original mining-town sites mark this section of the park. You can stroll down the street, stop and chat with a blacksmith, pan for gold (for a fee), crack open a geode, check out the chalkboard of a circa-1875 schoolhouse, and ride an original Butterfield stagecoach. Looming over it all is **GhostRider**, Orange County's first wooden roller coaster. Traveling up to 56 MPH and reaching 118 feet at its highest point, the park's biggest attraction is riddled with sudden dips and curves, subjecting riders to forces up to three times that of gravity. The **Calico Mine** ride descends into a replica of a working gold mine. The **Timber Mountain Log Ride** is a worthwhile flume ride, especially if you're with kids who don't make the height requirements for the flumes at Disneyland. Also found here is the park's newest thrill ride, the Pony Express, a roller coaster that lets riders saddle up on packs of "horses" tethered to a platforms that take off on a series of hairpin turns and travel up to 38 MPH. Don't miss the **Western Trails Museum**, a dusty old gem full of Old West memorabilia, plus menus from the original chicken restaurant, and Mrs. Knott's antique button collection. **Calico Railroad** departs regularly from Ghost Town station for a round-trip tour of the park (bandit hold-ups notwithstanding).

CAMP SNOOPY

It can get gridlocked on weekends, but small fry love this miniature High Sierra wonderland where the *Peanuts* gang hangs out. They can push and pump their own mini-mining cars on **Huff and Puff**, zip around a pint-size racetrack on **Charlie Brown Speedway**, and hop aboard **Woodstock's Airmail**, a kids' version of the park's Supreme Scream ride. Most of the rides here are geared toward kids only, leaving parents to cheer them on from the sidelines. **Sierra Sidewinder**, a roller coaster that opened near the entrance of Camp Snoopy in spring 2007, is aimed at older children with spinning saucer-type vehicles that go a maximum speed of 37 MPH.

BOARDWALK

Not-for-the-squeamish thrill rides and skill-based games dominate the scene at **Boardwalk**. Go head over heels on the **Boomerang** roller coaster, then do it again—backward. The **Perilous Plunge**, billed as the world's tallest, steepest, and—thanks to its big splash—wettest thrill ride, sends riders down an almost-vertical chute. The 1950s hot rod–theme **Xcelerator** launches you hydraulically into a super-steep U-turn, topping out at 205 feet. On the Western-theme **Silver Bullet**, riders are sent to a height of 146 feet and then back down 109 feet. Riders spiral, corkscrew, fly into a cobra roll, and experience overbanked curves. **Supreme Scream** propels you 254 feet in the air, then plunges you straight back down again in three terrifying seconds. Boardwalk is also home to a string of test-your-skill games that are fun to watch whether you're playing or not, and Johnny Rockets, the park's newest restaurant.

FIESTA VILLAGE

Over in **Fiesta Village** are two more musts for adrenaline junkies: **Montezooma's Revenge,** a roller coaster that goes from 0 to 55 MPH in less than five seconds, and **Jaguar!,** which simulates the motions of a cat stalking its prey, twisting, spiraling, and speeding up and slowing down as it takes you on its stomach-dropping course. There's also **Hat Dance,** a version of the spinning teacups but with sombreros, and a 100-year-old **Dentzel Carousel,** complete with an antique organ and menagerie of hand-carved animals.

WILD WATER WILDERNESS

Just like its name implies, this section is home to **Big Foot Rapids,** a splash-fest of white-water river rafting over towering cliffs, cascading waterfalls, and wild rapids. Don't miss the visually stunning show at **Mystery Lodge,** which tells the story of Native Americans in the Pacific Northwest with lights, music, and beautiful images.

Knott's Soak City Water Park is directly across from the main park on 13 acres next to Independence Hall. It has a dozen major water rides; the latest is **Pacific Spin,** an oversize waterslide that drops riders 75 feet into a catch pool. There's also a children's pool, 750,000-gallon wave pool, and funhouse. Soak City is only open late May through late September.

WHERE TO STAY & EAT

$$$$ ✕**Pirate's Dinner Adventure.** During this interactive pirate-theme dinner show, 150 actors/singers/acrobats (some quite talented) perform on a galleon while you eat a three-course meal. Food—shrimp, roast chicken, salad, mixed veggies, and unlimited soda, beer, and wine—is mediocre and seating is tight, but kids love making a lot of noise to cheer on their favorite pirate, and the action scenes are breathtaking. ⊠*7600 Beach Blvd., Buena Park* ☎*866/439–2469* ⊟*AE, D, MC, V.*

$$ ✕**Mrs. Knott's Chicken Dinner Restaurant.** Cordelia Knott's fried chicken and boysenberry pies drew crowds so big that Knott's Berry Farm was built to keep the hungry customers occupied while they waited. The restaurant's current incarnation (outside the park's entrance) still serves crispy fried chicken, along with tangy coleslaw, mashed potatoes, and Mrs. Knott's signature chilled cherry-rhubarb compote. The wait, unfortunately, can be two-plus hours on weekends; another option is to order a bucket of the same tasty chicken from the adjacent takeout counter and have a picnic at the duck pond next to Independence Hall across the street. ⊠*Knott's Berry Farm, 8039 Beach Blvd., Buena Park* ☎*714/220–5080* ⊟*AE, D, DC, MC, V.*

$–$$ ▥**Knott's Berry Farm Resort Hotel.** Knott's Berry Farm took over this high-rise hotel on park grounds from the Radisson chain in 2006 and renovated the rooms and lobby. The second-floor "camp rooms" are decorated in a Camp Snoopy motif and come with telephone bedtime stories. Shuttle service to Disneyland is available. Ask about packages that include entry to Knott's Berry Farm. **Pros:** Easy access to Knott's Berry Farm; great kids' activities. **Cons:** Lobby and hallways can be noisy and chaotic. ⊠*7675 Crescent Ave., Buena Park* ☏*714/995–1111 or 866/752-2444* 🖷*714/828-8590* ⊕*www.knottshotel.com* ⤳*320 rooms, 16 suites* ⚘*In-room: safes, high-speed Internet. In-hotel: restaurant, room service, bar, tennis court, pool, gym, concierge, laundry facilities, parking (fee), public Wi-Fi* ▭*AE, D, DC, MC, V.*

THE COAST

3

HUNTINGTON BEACH

40 mi southeast of Los Angeles, I–5 south to I–605 south to I–405 south to Beach Blvd.

Once a sleepy residential town with little more than a string of rugged surf shops, Huntington Beach has transformed itself into a resort destination. The town's appeal is its broad white-sand beaches with often-towering waves, complemented by a lively pier, shops, and restaurants on Main Street and the luxurious Hilton Waterfront Beach Resort and the Hyatt Regency.

Huntington Pier stretches 1,800 feet out to sea, well past the powerful waves that made Huntington Beach reach for the title of America's "Surf City." A farmers' market is held on Friday; an informal arts fair sets up most weekends. At the end of the pier sits **Ruby's** (☏*714/969–7829* ⊕*www.rubys.com*), part of a California chain of 1940s-style burger joints.

The **Pierside Pavilion** (⊠*PCH across from Huntington Pier*) has shops, restaurants, bars with live music, and a theater complex. The best surf-gear source is **Huntington Surf and Sport Pierside** (☏*714/841–4000*), next to the pier, staffed by true surf enthusiasts.

Just up Main Street from the pier, the **International Surfing Museum** pays tribute to the sport's greats with the Surfing Hall of Fame, which has an impressive collection of surfboards and related memorabilia. They've even got the Bolex camera used to shoot the 1966 surfing documentary *The Endless Summer.* ⊠*411 Olive Ave., Huntington Beach* ☏*714/960-3483* ⊕*www.surfingmuseum.org* 🎫*Free, $1 suggested donation for students, $2 for adults* ☉*Year-round weekdays noon–5, weekends 11–6.*

★ **Bolsa Chica Ecological Reserve** beckons wildlife lovers and bird-watchers with an 1,180-acre salt marsh that is home to 200 species of birds, including great blue herons, snowy and great egrets, and brown pelicans. Throughout the reserve are trails for bird-watching, including a comfortable 1½-mi loop. Free guided tours depart from the walking bridge the first Saturday of each month at 9 AM. ⊠*Entrance on PCH 1 mi south of Warner Ave., opposite Bolsa Chica State Beach at traffic light* ☏*714/846-1114* ⊕*www.bolsachica.org* 🎫*Free* ☉*Daily dawn–dusk.*

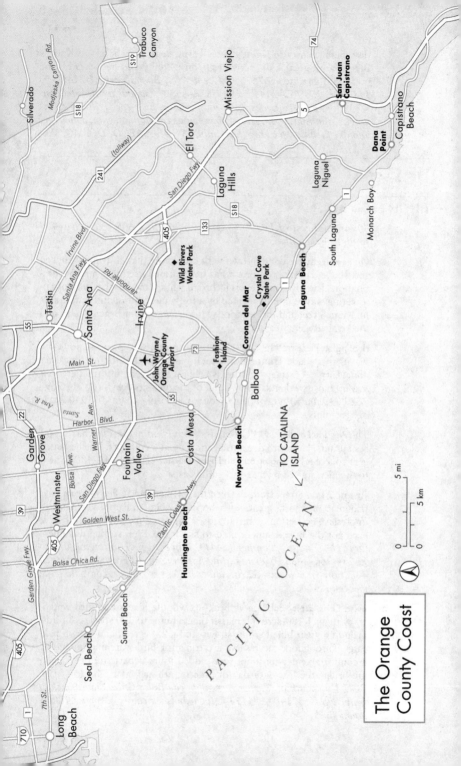

The Orange County Coast

WHERE TO STAY & EAT

$-$$ ✕**Lou's Red Oak BBQ.** You won't find any frills at Lou's—just barbecue
★ pork, grilled linguica, rotisserie chicken, and a lot of beef. Try the tri-
tip, either as an entrée or on a sandwich served "original style" on a
toasted bun smothered with garlic butter. ✉*21501 Brookhurst St.,
Huntington Beach* ☎*714/965–5200* ⊕*www.lousbbq.com* ▤*MC, V.*

$$$$ ▦**Hyatt Regency Huntington Beach Resort and Spa.** Sprawling along the
★ Pacific Coast Highway, almost every room in this Andalusia-style hotel
has an ocean view as well as a private balcony or terrace. With a nod
to California's Mission period, the hotel surrounds courtyards with
outdoor firepots and fountains. Artwork with a beach theme is by local
artists in guest rooms and public spaces. This Hyatt aims to create a village atmosphere, and to a large extent it has succeeded with the village
shopping area. Beach access is via a bridge over the PCH. **Pros:** Located
close to beach; responsive staff; family-friendly. **Cons:** Partial ocean-
view rooms are partial view at best; pesky resort and daily valet fees.
✉*21500 PCH92648* ☎*714/698–1234 or 800/554–9288* ⊕*www.*
huntingtonbeach.hyatt.com ⊷*517 rooms, 57 suites* ♿*In-room: safe,*
Ethernet, Wi-Fi. In-hotel: 3 restaurants, gym, spa, water sports, bicy-
cles, children's programs (ages 3–12), laundry service, executive floor,
public Wi-Fi, airport shuttle, parking (fee), no-smoking rooms ▤*AE,*
D, DC, MC, V.

$$$-$$$$ ▦**Hilton Waterfront Beach Resort.** Conveniently situated smack dab
across the street from the beach and within walking distance of Main
Street, this Mediterranean-style Hilton attracts a varied clientele—sin-
gles, families, couples, and business travelers. All guest rooms have
private balconies; oceanfront rooms boast views of Catalina Island. A
heated free-form pool, exotic landscaping, and sand volleyball court
add to the resort vibe. **Pros:** Within walking distance of several res-
taurants; excellent brunch buffet; oceanfront views. **Cons:** No self-
parking; decor is slightly dated; noise can be an issue. ✉*21100 PCH,*
Huntington Beach ☎*714/845–8000 or 800/822–7873* ⊕*www.water*
frontresort.com ⊷*266 rooms, 24 suites* ♿*In-room: safe, refrigerator,*
Wi-Fi, room service. In-hotel: restaurant, bar, tennis court, pool, gym,
children's programs (ages 5–12), executive floor, airport shuttle, park-
ing (fee), no-smoking rooms ▤*AE, D, DC, MC, V.*

SPORTS & THE OUTDOORS

BEACHES **Huntington City Beach** (☎*714/536–5281*) stretches for 3 mi north and
south of the pier from Bolsa Chica State Beach to Huntington State
Beach on the south. The beach is most crowded around the pier; ama-
teur and professional surfers brave the waves daily on its north side.
As you continue south, **Huntington State Beach** (☎*714/536–1454*) paral-
lels the PCH. On the state and city beaches there are changing rooms,
concessions, lifeguards, Wi-Fi services for park visitors with wireless-
enabled laptops and ample parking; the state beach also has barbe-
cue pits. At the northern section of the city, **Bolsa Chica State Beach**
(☎*714/846–3460*) has barbecue pits and RV campsites and is usually
less crowded than its southern neighbors.

SURFING **Corky Carroll's Surf School** (☎714/969–3959 ⊕www.surfschool.net) organizes lessons, weeklong workshops, and surfing trips. You can rent surf- or boogie boards at **Dwight's** (☎714/536–8083), one block south of the pier. **HB Wahine** (✉301 Main St. ☎714/330–3350) specializes in girls-only surf lessons, sells boards designed specially for them (narrower), and has hip surfing clothes, too.

O SOLE MIO IN THE O.C.

Try a one-hour gondola cruise with the Gondola Company of Newport (☎949/675–1212, ⊕ www.gondolas.com). It costs $85 for two and is frequently voted as the best place to take a date in Orange County.

NEWPORT BEACH

6 mi south of Huntington Beach, PCH.

★ **Newport Harbor,** which shelters nearly 10,000 small boats, may seduce even those who don't own a yacht. Spend an afternoon exploring the charming avenues and surrounding alleys.

Within Newport Harbor are eight small islands, including Balboa and Lido. The houses lining the shore may seem modest, but this is some of the most expensive real estate in the world. Marine Avenue, Balboa Island's main street, has shops, restaurants, and places to try the Balboa Bar: a slab of vanilla ice cream that has been dipped first in chocolate and then in a topping of your choice such as hard candy, Oreo crumbs, or peanut butter bark. Sugar & Spice, one of several ice-cream parlors that serve the concoction, claims to have invented it in 1945. As you stroll the perimeters of the island, you can see houses that range in style from Moderne, designed by John Lautner, to the more traditional Cape Cod. Several grassy areas on primarily residential Lido Isle have views of Newport Harbor. In evidence of the upper-crust Orange County mind-set, each is marked PRIVATE COMMUNITY PARK.

Newport Pier, which juts out into the ocean near 20th Street, is the heart of Newport's beach community and a popular fishing spot. Street parking is difficult at the pier, so grab the first space you find and be prepared to walk. A stroll along West Ocean Front reveals much of the town's character. On weekday mornings, head for the beach near the pier, where you're likely to encounter dory fishermen hawking their predawn catches, as they've done for generations. On weekends the walk is alive with kids of all ages on in-line skates, skateboards, and bikes dodging pedestrians and whizzing past fast-food joints, shops, and bars.

Newport's best beaches are on **Balboa Peninsula,** where many jetties pave the way to ideal swimming areas. The most intense bodysurfing place in Orange County and arguably on the West Coast, known as the **Wedge,** is at the south end of the peninsula. Created by accident in the 1930s when the Federal Works Progress Administration built a jetty to protect Newport Harbor, the break is pure euphoria for highly skilled bodysurfers. ■TIP→Since the waves generally break very close to shore and rip currents are strong, lifeguards strongly discourage visitors from attempting it—but it sure is fun to watch an experienced local ride it.

The **Balboa Pavilion,** on the bay side of the peninsula, was built in 1905 as a bath- and boathouse. Today it houses a restaurant and shops and serves as a departure point for harbor and whale-watching cruises. Look for it on Main Street, off Balboa Boulevard. Adjacent to the pavilion is the three-car ferry that connects the peninsula to Balboa Island. In the blocks around the pavilion you'll find restaurants, beach-side shops, and the small **Fun Zone**—a local kiddie hangout with a Ferris wheel and a nautical museum. On the other side of the narrow peninsula is **Balboa Pier.** On its end is the original branch of Ruby's, a 1940s-esque burger-and-shake joint.

The **Newport Harbor Nautical Museum** has exhibits on the history of the harbor as well as of the Pacific as a whole. For lovers of ship models, there are more than $3 million worth, some dating to 1798; one is made entirely of gold and silver. Another fun display is a virtual deep-sea fishing machine. New exhibits include a touch tank holding local sea creatures and a virtual sailing simulator. ⊠ *600 E. Bay Ave., Newport Beach* ☎ *949/675–8915* ⊕ *www.nhnm.org* 🎟 *Free* ⊘ *Daily 10–6, closed Tues.*

Shake the sand out of your shoes to head inland to the ritzy **Fashion Island** outdoor mall, a cluster of arcades and courtyards, complete with koi pond, inside in a sea of parking spaces. Although it doesn't have quite the international-designer clout of South Coast Plaza, it has the luxe department store Neiman Marcus and expensive spots like L'Occitane, Kate Spade, Ligne Roset, and Design Within Reach. Chains, restaurants, and the requisite movie theater fill out the rest. ⊠ *410 Newport Center Dr., between Jamboree and MacArthur Blvds., off PCH, Newport Beach* ☎ *949/721–2000* ⊕ *www.shopfashionisland.com.*

★ The **Orange County Museum of Art** gathers a collection of modernist paintings and sculpture by California artists and cutting-edge, international contemporary works. Works by such key California artists as Richard Diebenkorn, Ed Ruscha, Robert Irwin, and Chris Burden are included in the collection. The museum also displays some of its digital art, Internet-based art, and sound works in the Orange Lounge, a satellite gallery at South Coast Plaza; free of charge, it's open the same hours as the mall. ⊠ *850 San Clemente Dr., Newport Beach* ☎ *949/759–1122* ⊕ *www.ocma.net* 🎟 *$10* ⊘ *Wed.–Sun. 11–5, Thurs. 11–8.*

WHERE TO STAY & EAT

$$$–$$$$ ✕**The Cannery.** This 1920s cannery building still teems with fish, but ★ now they go into dishes on the eclectic Pacific Rim menu rather than being packed into crates. Settle in at the sushi bar, dining room, or patio before choosing between sashimi or oven-roasted Chilean sea bass. The menu also lists a selection of steaks and ribs. On Tuesday night a selection of 50 wines is sold at 50% off. ⊠ *3010 Lafayette Rd., Newport Beach* ☎ *949/566–0060* ⊕ *www.cannerynewport.com* ▤ *AE, D, DC, MC, V.*

$$–$$$ ✕ **3-Thirty-3.** If there's a nightlife "scene" to be had in Newport Beach, this is it. Swank and stylish, the "small bites, big tastes" menu attracts a convivial crowd—both young and old—for midday, sunset, and late-night dining. Try the lollipop lamb chops as a starter. Hungrier guests may enjoy the Kobe beef Gorgonzola burger or the 10-ounce ultimate halibut fillet. ✉*333 Bayside Dr.* ☎*949/673–8464* ⊕*www.3 thirty3nb. com* ▭*AE, MC, V.*

$$$$ ▥ **The Island Hotel.** A suitably stylish hotel in a very chic neighborhood
★ (it's across the street from the Fashion Island shopping center), the 20-story tower caters to luxury seekers by offering weekend golf packages in conjunction with the nearby Pelican Hill golf course. Guest rooms have outstanding views, private bars, and original art. The spa does its bit for luxury with a "pearl powder facial." For gustatory richness, try the Pavilion restaurant's contemporary menu, with choices such as potato-crusted Chilean sea bass. **Pros:** Proximity to Fashion Island; 24-hour exercise facilities; first-class spa. **Cons:** Steep valet parking prices; some rooms have views of the mall; pricey. ✉*690 Newport Center Dr., Newport Beach* ☎*949/759–0808 or 866/554–4620* ⊕*www.the islandhotel.com* ⌕*295 rooms, 82 suites* ↻*In-room: Wi-Fi. In-hotel: 2 restaurants, room service, bar, tennis courts, pool, gym, spa, concierge, some pets allowed (fee)* ▭*AE, D, DC, MC, V.*

$$$ ▥ **Hyatt Regency Newport Beach.** The best aspect of this grande dame of Newport hotels is its lushly landscaped acres: 26 of them, overlooking the Back Bay. When booking your room, suite, or bungalow, let them know your preference of bay, golf course, garden, or pool views. Most rooms have patios or balconies. **Pros:** Recent renovation in many of the rooms; good quality linens and bedding; centrally located for shopping. **Cons:** Self-park is far from main property; 10-minute drive to beach. ✉*1107 Jamboree Rd.* ☎*949/729–1234* ᵬ*949/644–1552* ⊕*newport-beach.hyatt.com* ⌕*388 rooms, 11 suites, 4 bungalows* ↻*In-room: safe, refrigerator, Ethernet. In-hotel: restaurant, room service, bar, golf course, tennis courts, pool, gym, spa, bicycles, airport shuttle, public Wi-Fi, laundry service* ▭*AE, D, DC, MC, V.*

SPORTS & THE OUTDOORS

BOAT RENTALS You can tour Lido and Balboa isles by renting kayaks ($15 an hour), sailboats ($45 an hour), small motorboats ($65 an hour), and electric boats ($75–$90 an hour at **Balboa Boat Rentals** (✉*510 E. Edgewater Ave., Newport Beach* ☎*949/673–7200* ⊕*www.boats4rent.com*). You must have a driver's license, and some knowledge of boating is helpful; rented boats must stay in the bay.

BOAT TOURS **Catalina Passenger Service** (✉*400 Main St., Newport Beach* ☎*949/673–5245* ⊕*www.catalinainfo.com*), at the Balboa Pavilion, operates daily 90-minute round-trip passage to Catalina Island for $61. Call first; winter service is often available only on weekends. **Hornblower Cruises & Events** (✉*2431 West Coast Hwy., Newport Beach* ☎*949/646–0155 or 888/467–6256* ⊕*www.hornblower.com*) books three-hour weekend dinner cruises with dancing for $68 Friday, $72 Saturday; the two-hour Sunday brunch cruise is $49.50.

GOLF **Newport Beach Golf Course** (✉*3100 Irvine Ave., Newport Beach* ☎*949/ 852–8681* ⊕*www.npbgolf.com*), a par-59 executive course, is lighted for night play. Rates start at $17. Reservations are accepted up to one week in advance, but walk-ins are accommodated when possible.

SPORTFISHING In addition to a complete tackle shop, **Davey's Locker** (✉*Balboa Pavilion, 400 Main St., Newport Beach* ☎*949/673–1434* ⊕*www.daveys locker.com*) operates sportfishing trips starting at $36, as well as private charters and, in winter, whale-watching trips for $25.

3

CORONA DEL MAR

2 mi south of Newport Beach, via Hwy. 1.

A small jewel on the Pacific Coast, Corona del Mar (known by locals as "CDM") has exceptional beaches that some say resemble their majestic northern California counterparts.

Corona del Mar State Beach (☎*949/644–3151* ⊕*www.parks.ca.gov*) is actually made up of two beaches, Little Corona and Big Corona, separated by a cliff. Facilities include fire pits, volleyball courts, food stands, restrooms, and parking. ■**TIP➔ Two colorful reefs (and the fact that it's off-limits to boats) make Corona del Mar great for snorkelers and for beachcombers who prefer privacy.**

Fodor'sChoice ★ Midway between Corona del Mar and Laguna, stretching along both sides of Pacific Coast Highway, **Crystal Cove State Park** is a favorite of local beachgoers and wilderness trekkers. It encompasses a 3½-mi stretch of unspoiled beach and has some of the best tide-pooling in southern California. Here you can see starfish, crabs, and other sea life on the rocks. The park's 2,400 acres of backcountry are ideal for hiking, horseback riding, and mountain biking, but stay on the trails to preserve the beauty. Environmental camping is allowed in one of the three campgrounds. Bring water, food, and other supplies; there's a pit toilet but no shower. Open fires and pets are forbidden. Parking costs $8. **Crystal Cove Historic District** holds a collection of 13 handmade historic rental cottages decorated and furnished to reflect the 1935–55 beach culture that flourished here. On the sand above the high tide line and on a bluff above the beach, the cottages offer a funky look at beach life 50 years ago. Cottages, at $165 per night for four people, can be reserved up to six months in advance from **Reserve America** (☎*800/444–7275* ⊕*www.reserveamerica.com*). Beach culture also flourishes in the district's two restaurants, the **Beachcomber at Crystal Cove Café** (☎*949/376–6900* ⊕*www.thebeachcombercafe.com*) and the Shake Shack. **The Store** (☎*949/376–8762*), holding works by local *plein air* artists and fine art photography, completes the picture. ☎*949/494–3539* ⊕*www.crystalcovestatepark.com* ☾*Daily 6–dusk.*

LAGUNA BEACH

Fodor'sChoice ★ *10 mi south of Newport Beach on Hwy. 1; 60 mi south of Los Angeles, I–5 south to Hwy. 133, which turns into Laguna Canyon Rd.*

Even the approach tells you that Laguna Beach is exceptional. Driving in along Laguna Canyon Road from the I–405 freeway gives you the chance to cruise through a gorgeous coastal canyon, large stretches of which remain undeveloped (⇨ *see the Laguna Coast Wilderness Park in Sports & the Outdoors, below*). After winding through the canyon, you'll arrive at a glistening wedge of ocean, at the intersection with the PCH.

There's a definite creative slant to this tight-knit community. The California *plein air* art movement coalesced here in the early 1900s; by 1932 an annual arts festival was established. Art galleries now dot the village streets, and there's usually someone daubing up in Heisler Park, overlooking the beach. The town's main street, Pacific Coast Highway, is referred to as either South Coast or North Coast Highway, depending on the address. From this waterfront, the streets slope up steeply to the residential areas. All along the highway and side streets, you'll find dozens of fine art and crafts galleries, clothing boutiques, and jewelry shops.

Laguna's central beach gives you a perfect slice of local life. A stocky 1920s lifeguard tower marks **Main Beach Park,** at the end of Broadway at South Coast Highway. A wooden boardwalk separates the sand from a strip of lawn. Walk along this, or hang out on one of its benches, to watch people bodysurfing, playing sand volleyball, or scrambling around one of two half-basketball courts. The beach also has children's play equipment, picnic areas, restrooms, and showers. Across the street is a lovely old movie theater.

The **Laguna Art Museum** displays American art, with an emphasis on California artists and works. Special exhibits change quarterly. ■ TIP→**Galleries throughout the area stay open late in coordination with the museum on the first Thursday of each month (visit ⊕ www.firstthursdaysartwalk. com for more information).** A free shuttle service runs from the museum to galleries and studios. ⊠ *307 Cliff Dr., Laguna Beach* ☎ *949/494–8971* ⊕ *www.lagunaartmuseum.org* ⊠*$10* ⊘ *Daily 11–5.*

WHERE TO STAY & EAT

$$$$ ✕**Studio.** In a nod to Laguna's art history, Studio has food that entices
★   the eye as well as the palate. You can't beat the location, on a 50-foot bluff overlooking the Pacific Ocean—every table has an ocean view. Executive chef James Boyce changes the menu daily to reflect the seafood and the fresh ingredients on hand (he even has a "personal forager"). Among the standouts you might find grilled rib-eye steak and a salad of seared Catalina yellowtail with Hawaiian green papaya and lemongrass. A prix-fixe tasting menu is $125; with wine it's $175. Nonalcoholic beverages can be paired with the food, too. ⊠ *Montage Hotel, 30801 S. Coast Hwy.* ☎ *949/715–6420* ⩍ *Reservations essential* ▤ *AE, D, DC, MC, V* ⊘ *Closed Mon. No lunch.*

$$–$$$ ✕**Five Feet.** Others have attempted to mimic this restaurant's innovative
★   blend of Chinese and French cooking styles, but Five Feet remains the leader of the pack. Among the standout dishes is the house catfish. The setting is pure Laguna: exposed ceiling, open kitchen, high noise level,

and brick walls hung with works by local artists. ⊠*328 Glenneyre St., Laguna Beach* 🕾*949/497–4955* 🖃*AE, D, DC, MC, V* ⊘*No lunch.*

¢–$ ✕**The Stand.** If an eatery can be called typically Laguna, this is it. Only organic vegan ingredients are used in preparations. There are around 20 spaces to eat outside, read the supplied tracts and newspapers, and maybe argue a point or two. Smoothies, salads, and pita sandwiches are favorites. The Stand is open 7–7 daily. ⊠*238 Thalia St., near PCH* 🕾*949/494–8101* 🖃*AE, D, MC, V.*

$$$$ 🏨**Montage Resort & Spa.** Laguna's connection to the Californian *plein air* artists is mined for inspiration at this head-turning, fancy hotel. The Montage uses the local Craftsman style as a touchstone. Shingled buildings ease down a bluff to the cove beaches; inside, works by contemporary and early-20th-century California artists snare your attention. Guest rooms balance ease and refinement; all have ocean views and amenities such as CD/DVD players and extra-deep tubs. Of the restaurants, Studio is the fanciest, with more sweeping Pacific views and a refined contemporary menu. At the oceanfront spa and fitness center, you can indulge in a sea-salt scrub, take a yoga class, or hit the lap pool. **Pros:** Top-notch service; central beach location; free fitness classes. **Cons:** Pricey; cuisine can be inconsistent. ⊠*30801 S. Coast Hwy., Laguna Beach* 🕾*949/715–6000 or 888/715–6700* ⊕*www. montagelagunabeach.com* ➘*262 rooms, 51 suites* ♿*In-room: safe, DVD, Ethernet. In-hotel: 3 restaurants, room service, bars, pools, gym, spa, beachfront, concierge, children's programs (ages 5–12), laundry service, parking (fee)* 🖃*AE, MC, V.*

FodorsChoice ★

$$$$ 🏨**Surf & Sand Resort.** One mile south of downtown, this Laguna Beach ★ property has been updated, made over, and is now even more fantastic than longtime locals remember. On an exquisite stretch of beach with thundering waves and gorgeous rocks, this is a getaway for those who want a boutique hotel experience without all the by-the-books formalities. Instead, expect clean white decor in the rooms, private balconies, slumber-worthy beds within earshot of the ocean, and a small, yet full-service spa—all within walking distance of downtown Laguna. The cuisine at Splashes is top notch, focusing on seasonal California cuisine. **Pros:** Easy access to beach; intimate property; new gym facilities. **Cons:** Expensive valet parking; the surf is quite loud. ⊠*1555 S. Coast Hwy., Laguna Beach* 🕾*949/497–4477 or 888/869–7569* ⊕*www.surfand sandresort.com* ➘*155 rooms, 13 suites* ♿*In-room: no a/c (some), safes, refrigerators (some), DVD, Ethernet. In-hotel: restaurant, room service, bar, pool, gym, spa, beachfront, concierge, children's programs (ages 5–12), laundry service, parking (fee)* 🖃*AE, D, DC, MC, V.*

SPORTS & THE OUTDOORS

BEACHES There are a handful of lovely beaches around town besides the Main Beach. **Aliso Creek County Beach** (🕾*714/834–2400* ⊕*www.ocparks. com/alisobeach*), in south Laguna, has a playground, fire pits, parking, food stands, and restrooms. **1,000 Steps Beach,** off South Coast Highway at 9th Street, is a hard-to-find locals' spot with great waves. There aren't really 1,000 steps down (it just seems that way). **Woods Cove,** off South Coast Highway at Diamond Street, is especially quiet during the week. Big rock formations hide lurking crabs. Climbing the steps to leave, you can see a Tudor-style mansion that was once the home of Bette Davis.

BICYCLES Mountain bikes and helmets can be rented at **Rainbow Bicycles** (⊠*485 N. Coast Hwy., Laguna Beach* ☎*949/494–5806* ⊕*www.teamrain.com*).

HIKING The **Laguna Coast Wilderness Park** (☎*949/923–2235* ⊕*www.lagunacan yon.org*) is spread over 19 acres of fragile coastal territory, including the canyon. The trails are great for hiking and mountain biking and are open daily, weather permitting. Docent-led hikes are given regularly; call for information.

WATER
SPORTS
Because its entire beach area is a marine preserve, Laguna Beach is ideal for snorkelers. Scuba divers should head to the Marine Life Refuge area, which runs from Seal Rock to Diver's Cove. Rent bodyboards at **Hobie Sports** (⊠*294 Forest Ave., Laguna Beach* ☎*949/497–3304* ⊕*www.hobie.com*).

SHOPPING

Forest and Ocean avenues and Glenneyre Street are full of art galleries and fine jewelry and clothing boutiques.

DANA POINT

10 mi south of Laguna Beach, via PCH.

Dana Point's claim to fame is its small-boat marina tucked into a dramatic natural harbor and surrounded by high bluffs.

Dana Point Harbor (☎*949/923–2255* ⊕*www.danapointharbor.com*) was first described more than 100 years ago by its namesake, Richard Henry Dana, in his book *Two Years Before the Mast*. At the marina are docks for small boats, marine-oriented shops, restaurants, and boat and bike rentals. In early March a **whale festival** (☎*949/472–7888 or 888/440–4309* ⊕*www.festivalofwhales.org*) celebrates the passing gray whale migration with concerts, 40-foot-long balloon whales on parade, films, sports competitions, and a weekend street fair.

At the south end of Dana Point, **Doheny State Beach** (☎*949/496–6171, 714/433–6400 water quality information* ⊕*www.dohenystatebeach. org*) is one of Southern California's top surfing destinations, but there's a lot more to do within this 61-acre area. Divers and anglers hang out at the beach's western end, and during low tide, the tide pools beckon both young and old. You'll also find five indoor tanks and an interpretive center devoted to the wildlife of the Doheny Marine Refuge. There are food stands and shops, picnic facilities, volleyball courts, and a pier for fishing. The beachfront campground here is one of the most popular in the state with 120 no-hookup sites that rent for $26–$35 per night; essential reservations from Reserve America (☎*800/444–7275*). ■**TIP→Be aware that the waters here periodically do not meet health standards established by California (warning signs are posted if that's the case).**

WHERE TO STAY & EAT

$$–$$$ ✕**Wind & Sea.** An unblocked marina view makes this a great place for lunch—and looking out on the Pacific might put you in the mood for a retro cocktail like a mai tai. Of the entrées, try the macadamia-crusted mahimahi. On warm days, patio tables beckon you outside. ✉*34699 Golden Lantern St., Dana Point* ☎*949/496–6500* ▭*AE, MC, V.*

$$$$
Fodor'sChoice
★
Ritz-Carlton, Laguna Niguel. Take Ritz-Carlton's top-tier level of service coupled with an unparalleled view of the Pacific and you're in the lap of complete luxury at this opulent resort. Rooms are well-appointed and spacious; tricked out with oversize plasma TVs, private balconies and posh marble bathrooms. Splurge for the Club Level where the list of included extra amenities is exhaustingly long. Service is impeccable for all guests, as every need is anticipated. Dine at Restaurant 162, where the focus is on California cuisine, highlighting fresh fish and seafood, or bone up on your wine knowledge at ENO, the property's wine, cheese, and chocolate tasting room. Beyond the panoramic views of the Pacific and opulent gardens, guests stroll down perfectly manicured trails to pristine white sand. **Pros:** Beautiful grounds/views; luxurious bedding; seamless service. **Cons:** Some rooms are small; resort and parking fees. ✉*1 Ritz-Carlton Dr., Dana Point* ☎*949/240–2000 or 800/240–2000* ⊕*www.ritzcarlton.com* ↻*363 rooms, 30 suites* ⟳*In-room: safe, refrigerator (some), DVD, Ethernet. In-hotel: 3 restaurants, room service, bar, tennis courts, pools, gym, spa, beachfront, children's programs (ages 5–12), laundry service, executive floor, public Wi-Fi, concierge, airport shuttle, parking (fee)* ▭*AE, D, DC, MC, V.*

SPORTS & THE OUTDOORS

Inside Dana Point Harbor, **Swim Beach** has a fishing pier, barbecues, food stands, parking, restrooms, and showers. Rental stands for surfboards, windsurfers, small powerboats, and sailboats can be found near most of the piers.

Dana Wharf Sportfishing & Whale Watching (✉*34675 Golden Lantern St., Dana Point* ☎*949/496–5794* ⊕*www.danawharfsportfishing.com*) runs charters and whale-watching excursions from early December to late April. Tickets cost $29; reservations are required. **Hobie Sports** (✉*24825 Del Prado, Dana Point* ☎*949/496–2366*) rents surfboards and boogie boards.

On **Capt. Dave's Dolphin Safari** (✉ *24440 Dana Point Harbor Dr., Dana Point* ☎*949/488–2828* ⊕*www.dolphinsafari.com*), you have a good chance of getting a water's-eye view of resident dolphins and migrating whales if you take one of these tours on a 35-foot catamaran. Dave, a marine naturalist–filmmaker, and his wife run the safaris year-round. The endangered blue whale is sometimes seen in summer. Reservations are required for the safaris, which last 2½ hours and cost $49.

SAN JUAN CAPISTRANO

5 mi north of Dana Point, via Hwy. 7; 60 mi north of San Diego, via I–5.

San Juan Capistrano is best known for its historic mission, where the swallows traditionally return each year, migrating from their winter haven in Argentina, but these days they are more likely to choose other local sites for nesting. St. Joseph's Day, March 19, launches a week of fowl festivities. After summering in the arches of the old stone church, the swallows head south on St. John's Day, October 23. Along Camino Capistrano are also antiques stores ranging from pricey to cheap.

If you arrive by train, you'll be dropped off across from the mission at the San Juan Capistrano depot. With its appealing brick café and preserved Santa Fe cars, the depot retains much of the magic of early American railroads. If driving, park near Ortega and Camino Capistrano, the city's main streets.

Fodor'sChoice
★
Mission San Juan Capistrano, founded in 1776 by Father Junípero Serra, was one of two Roman Catholic outposts between Los Angeles and San Diego. The Great Stone Church, begun in 1797, is the largest structure created by the Spanish in California. Many of the mission's adobe buildings have been preserved to illustrate mission life, with exhibits of an olive millstone, tallow ovens, tanning vats, metalworking furnaces, and the padres' living quarters. The gardens with their fountains are a lovely spot in which to wander. The bougainvillea-covered Serra Chapel is believed to be the oldest church still standing in California and is the only building remaining in which Father Serra actually led Mass. Mass takes place daily at 7 AM in the chapel. ⊠ *Camino Capistrano and Ortega Hwy., San Juan Capistrano* ☎ *949/234–1300* ⊕ *www.missionsjc. com* ☜ *$9* ☉ *Daily 8:30–5.*

WHERE TO STAY & EAT

$–$$ ✕ **The Ramos House Cafe.** It may be worth hopping the Amtrak for San Juan Capistrano just for the chance to have breakfast or lunch at what many call the restaurant with the best food in Orange County. Here's your chance to visit one of Los Rios Historic District's simple, board and batten homes dating back to 1881. This café sits practically on the railroad tracks across from the depot—nab a table on the patio and dig into a hearty breakfast, such as the mountainous wild-mushroom scramble or the mac 'n' cheese with smoked chicken. Every item on the menu illustrates chef-owner John Q. Humphreys's creative hand. ⊠ *31752 Los Rios St., San Juan Capistrano* ☎ *949/443–1342* ▤ *AE, D, DC, MC, V* ☉ *Closed Mon. No dinner.*

$$ ▥ **Mission Inn San Juan Capistrano.** "Quaint" is the best word to describe this intimate 20-room B&B on a 2-acre century-old family orchard where you can pick oranges right off the trees. Conveniently located within walking distance of the Mission, playhouse, and old-town shopping, each room of this cozy establishment is named for one of the California missions. Rooms are romantic in decor, albeit a touch dated—think lavish bedding, ornate mirrors, lighting fixtures and headboards; some rooms have electric fireplaces. **Pros:** Great location; clean rooms; beautiful grounds. **Cons:** Walls are thin; rooms can be noisy due to proximity to freeway; service isn't always responsive. ✉*26891 Ortega Hwy.* ☎*949/234–0249* ⊕*www.missioninnsjc.com* ⇌*20 rooms* ⚫*In-room: refrigerator, Wi-Fi (some). In-hotel: pool, no elevator, public Wi-Fi, parking (no fee), some pets allowed, no kids under 12* ▭*AE, D, MC, V* ⦿*CP.*

ORANGE COUNTY ESSENTIALS

3

AIRPORTS

The county's main facility is John Wayne Airport Orange County (SNA), which is served by 11 major domestic airlines and 3 commuter lines. Long Beach Airport (LGB) serves four airlines, including its major player, JetBlue. It's roughly 20–30 minutes by car from Anaheim. *For details on other L.A. County airports, including Los Angeles International Airport (LAX), see* ⇨ *the Essentials chapter.*

Airport Information **John Wayne Airport Orange County** (✉ *MacArthur Blvd. at I-405, Santa Ana* ☎ *949/252-5200* ⊕ *www.ocair.com*). **Long Beach Airport** (✉ *4100 Donald Douglas Dr., Long Beach* ☎ *562/570-6555* ⊕ *www.longbeach. gov/airport/*).

AIRPORT TRANSFERS

The only transfer service from John Wayne or LAX to Orange County coastal cities is provided by SuperShuttle, which can be expensive. Fares, determined by distance, are for the first person in a party; add $9 for additional persons. You'll pay $18 from John Wayne to Newport Beach and $33 to Laguna Niguel. Fares to the same destinations from LAX are $46 and $58 per person, respectively. Airport Bus and Prime Time Airport Shuttle provide transportation from John Wayne and LAX to the Disneyland area of Anaheim. Fares average about $13 per person from John Wayne and $15 to $20 from LAX.

Shuttles **Airport Bus** (☎ *800/938-8933* ⊕ *www.airportbus.com*). **Prime Time Airport Shuttle** (☎ *800/262-7433* ⊕ *www.primetimeshuttle.com*). **SuperShuttle** (☎ *714/517-6600* ⊕ *www.supershuttle.com*).

BUS TRAVEL

The Orange County Transportation Authority will take you virtually anywhere in the county, but it will take time; OCTA buses go from Knott's Berry Farm and Disneyland to Huntington Beach and Newport Beach. Bus 1 travels along the coast; buses 701 and 721 provide express service to Los Angeles.

Fares for the OCTA local routes are $1.25 per boarding; you can also get a $3 local day pass (valid only on the date of purchase). Day passes can be purchased from bus drivers upon boarding. Express bus fare between Orange County and L.A. is $3.75 a pop, $2.50 if you have a day pass. The bus-fare boxes take coins and dollar bills, but you must use exact change.

Bus Information **Greyhound** (☎ *714/999-1256 or 800/231-2222* ⊕ *www. greyhound.com*). **Los Angeles MTA** (☎ *213/626-4455* ⊕ *www.mta.net*). **Orange County Transportation Authority (OCTA)** (☎ *714/636-7433* ⊕ *www.octa.net*).

TRAIN TRAVEL

Amtrak makes daily stops in Orange County at Fullerton, Anaheim, Santa Ana, Irvine, San Juan Capistrano, and San Clemente. Metrolink is a weekday commuter train that runs to and from Los Angeles and Orange County, starting as far south as Oceanside and stopping in Laguna Niguel, Tustin, San Juan Capistrano, San Clemente, Irvine, Santa Ana, Orange, Anaheim, and Fullerton. The Metrolink system is divided into a dozen zones; the fare you pay depends on how many zones you cover. Buy tickets from the vending machines at each station. Ticketing is on an honor system.

Train Information **Amtrak** (☎ *800/872–7245* ⊕ *www.amtrak.com*). **Metrolink** (☎ *800/371–5465* ⊕ *www.metrolinktrains.com*).

VISITOR INFORMATION

Contacts **Anaheim-Orange County Visitor and Convention Bureau** (⊠ *Anaheim Convention Center, 800 W. Katella Ave., Anaheim* ☎ *714/765–8888* ⊕ *www.anaheimoc.org*). **Costa Mesa Conference and Visitors Bureau** (✉ *Box 5071, Costa Mesa, 92628* ☎ *714/435–8530 or 866/918–4749* ⊕ *www.travelcostamesa.com*). **Huntington Beach Conference and Visitors Bureau** (⊠ *301 Main St., Suite 208, Huntington Beach 92648* ☎ *714/969–3492* ⊕ *www.surfcityusa.com*). **Laguna Beach Visitors Bureau** (⊠ *252 Broadway, Laguna Beach 92651* ☎ *949/497–9229 or 800/877–1115* ⊕ *www.lagunabeachinfo.org*). **Newport Beach Conference and Visitors Bureau** (⊠ *110 Newport Center Dr., Suite 120, Newport Beach 92663* ☎ *949/719–6101 or 800/942–6278* ⊕ *www.visitnewportbeach.com*). **San Juan Capistrano Chamber of Commerce and Visitors Center** (⊠ *31421 La Matanza St., San Juan Capistrano 92693* ☎ *949/493–4700* ⊕ *www.sanjuanchamber.com*).

CATALINA ISLAND

Just 22 mi out from the L.A. coastline, across from Newport Beach and Long Beach, Catalina has virtually unspoiled mountains, canyons, coves, and beaches; best of all, it gives you a glimpse of what undeveloped Southern California once looked like.

Summer, weekends, and holidays, Catalina crawls with thousands of L.A.–area boaters, who tie their vessels at protected moorings in Avalon and other coves. Although Catalina is not known for its beaches, sunbathing and water sports are big draws; divers and snorkelers come for the exceptionally clear water surrounding the island. The main town, Avalon, is a charming, old-fashioned beach community, where yachts bob in the crescent-shaped bay. Wander beyond the main drag and you'll find brightly painted little bungalows fronting the sidewalks, with the occasional golf cart purring down the street.

Cruise ships sail into Avalon twice a week and smaller boats shuttle between Avalon and Two Harbors, a small isthmus cove on the island's western end. You can also take bus excursions beyond Avalon. Roads are limited and nonresident vehicles prohibited, so hiking (by permit only) and cycling are the only other means of exploring.

Although Catalina can be seen in a day, several inviting hotels make it worth extending your stay for one or more nights. A short itinerary might include breakfast along the boardwalk, a tour of the interior, a snorkeling excursion at Casino Point, and dinner in Avalon.

AVALON

A 1- to 2-hr ferry ride from Long Beach, Newport Beach, or San Pedro; a 15-min helicopter ride from Long Beach or San Pedro.

Avalon, Catalina's only real town, extends from the shore of its natural harbor to the surrounding hillsides. Most of the city's activity, however, is centered along the pedestrian mall on Crescent Avenue, and most sights are easily reached on foot. Private cars are restricted and rental cars aren't allowed, but taxis, trams, and shuttles can take you anywhere you need to go. Bicycles and golf carts can be rented from shops along Crescent Avenue.

A walk along **Crescent Avenue** is a nice way to begin a tour of the town. Vivid art deco tiles adorn the avenue's fountains and planters—fired on the island by the now-defunct Catalina Tile Company, the tiles are a coveted commodity.

Head to the **Green Pleasure Pier,** at the center of Crescent Avenue, for a good vantage point of Avalon. At the top of the hill you'll spot a big white building, the Inn at Mt. Ada, now a top-of-the-line B&B but originally built by William Wrigley Jr. for his wife. On the pier you'll find the Catalina Island Chamber of Commerce, snack stands, the Harbor Patrol, and scads of squawking seagulls.

★ On the northwest point of Avalon Bay (looking to your right from Green Pleasure Pier) is the majestic landmark **Casino.** This circular white structure is one of the finest examples of art deco architecture anywhere. Its Spanish-inspired floors and murals gleam with brilliant blue and green Catalina tiles. In this case, *casino,* the Italian word for "gathering place," has nothing to do with gambling. Rather, Casino life revolves around the magnificent ballroom. The same big-band dances that made the Casino famous in the 1930s and '40s still take place several times a year.

Santa Catalina Island Company leads tours of the Casino, lasting about 55 minutes, for $16. You can also visit the **Catalina Island Museum,** in the lower level of the Casino, which investigates 7,000 years of island history; or stop at the **Casino Art Gallery** to see works by local artists. First-run movies are screened nightly at the **Avalon Theatre,** noteworthy for its classic 1929 theater pipe organ. ⊠*1 Casino Way, Avalon* ☎*310/510–2414 museum* ⊕*www.catalina.com/museum.html* ☎*310/510–0808 art gallery, 310/510–0179 Avalon Theatre* ✑*Museum $4, art gallery free* ☉*Museum: daily 10–5. Art gallery: mid-Mar.–Dec., daily 10:30–4; Jan.–mid-Mar., Tues. and Thurs.–Sun. 10:30–4.*

In front of the Casino are the crystal-clear waters of the **Casino Point Underwater Park,** a marine preserve protected from watercraft where

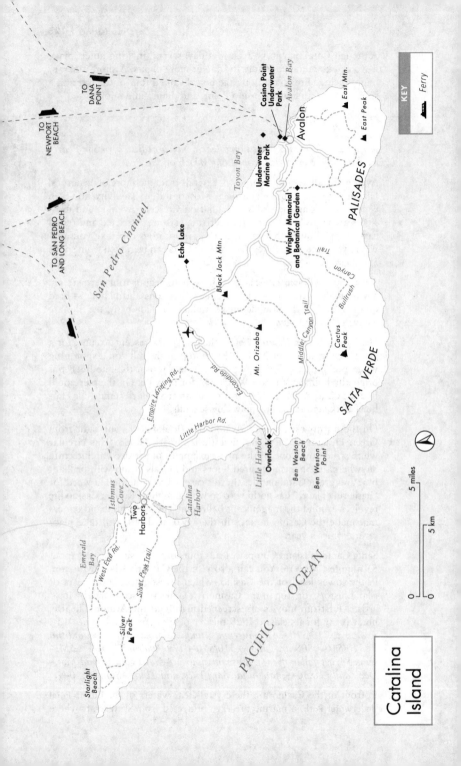

moray eels, bat rays, spiny lobsters, halibut, and other sea animals cruise around kelp forests and along the sandy bottom. It's a terrific site for scuba diving, with some shallow areas suitable for snorkeling. Scuba and snorkeling equipment can be rented on and near the pier. The shallow waters of **Lover's Cove**, east of the boat landing, are also good for snorkeling.

Two miles south of the bay via Avalon Canyon Road is **Wrigley Memorial and Botanical Garden.** Here you'll find plants native to Southern California, including several that grow only on Catalina Island: Catalina ironwood, wild tomato, and rare Catalina mahogany. The Wrigley family commissioned the garden as well as the monument, which has a grand staircase and a Spanish mausoleum inlaid with colorful Catalina tile. (The mausoleum was never used by the Wrigleys, who are buried in Los Angeles.) Taxi service from Avalon is available, or you can take a tour bus from the downtown Tour Plaza or ferry landing. ⊠ *Avalon Canyon Rd., Avalon* ☎ *310/510–2595* ⊕ *www.catalina.com/memorial. html* ☎ *$5* ⊙ *Daily 8–5.*

WHERE TO STAY & EAT

$$$–$$$$ ✕**Catalina Country Club.** The spring-training clubhouse built for the Chicago Cubs now does duty as a restaurant for surf-and-turf standbys. Much of the fare here is organic, including the roasted wild boar, alas not from the island's fabled herd (it was removed for environmental reasons). The adjacent bar is great for an after-dinner drink; it connects to the old Cubs locker room. ⊠ *1 Country Club Dr., Avalon* ☎ *310/510–7404* ⌕ *Reservations essential* ▤ *AE, D, DC, MC, V.*

$$–$$$ **Channel House.** Locals and tourists alike flock to this Avalon institu-
★   tion. The ambience is decidedly romantic with most tables offering bay views. An intimate patio, an elegant Victorian-style dining room, and live piano music on weekend evenings do their part to add to the ambience. Locally caught sand dabs, swordfish, and Caesar salads are all popular picks. Be sure to call ahead and confirm hours during the off-season. ⊠ *205 Crescent Ave., Avalon* ☎ *310/510–1617* ▤ *AE, D, MC, V* ⊙ *Closed Mon. mid-Oct.–Easter* ⊙ *Daily 11–3, 4:30–close.*

$ ✕**Eric's on the Pier.** This little snack bar has been an Avalon family–run institution since the 1920s. It's a good place to people-watch while munching a breakfast burrito, buffalo burger, or a hot dog. While most of the action is outside, you can sit down at a table inside and dine on a bowl of homemade clam chowder in a bread bowl or an order of fish-and-chips. ⊠ *Green Pier No. 2, Avalon* ☎ *310/510–0894* ▤ *AE, MC, V.*

$$$$ ⊞**Inn on Mt. Ada.** Staying in the mansion where William Wrigley Jr.
Fodor'sChoice   once lived gives you all the comforts of a millionaire's home—at a mil-
★   lionaire's prices, beginning at $400 a night in summer. Breakfast, lunch, beverages, snacks, and use of a golf cart are included. The guest rooms are traditional and elegant; some have fireplaces, and all have water views. The hilltop view of the curve of the bay is spectacular, and service is discreet. **Pros:** The Windsor room—with views of both the ocean and the bay; cookies and hor d'oeuvres in the evening; first-class ser-

vice. **Cons:** Rooms and bathrooms are on the small side; pricey. ✉*398 Wrigley Rd., Avalon* ☎*310/510–2030 or 800/608–7669* ⊕*www. innonmtada.com* ↩*6 rooms* ⅋*In-room: no a/c, no phone, DVD, VCR (some), Wi-Fi. In-hotel: public Wi-Fi, no kids under 14, no-smoking rooms, heliport and dock shuttle service* ▤*MC, V* ⊺*MAP.*

$$–$$$ ⊞ **Hotel Villa Portofino.** Steps from the beach and the Pleasure Pier, this hotel strikes a discreet note. Rooms are named after Italian cities, and most are decorated in deep jewel tones. Some ocean-facing rooms have open balconies, fireplaces, and marble baths. Courtyard rooms, opening on a central courtyard, have no exterior windows. You can sunbathe on the private deck, or ask for beach towels and chairs to take to the cove. **Pros:** Romantic; very close to the beach; incredible sun deck. **Cons:** Ground floor rooms can be noisy, although location is quiet in general; some rooms are on the small side. ✉*111 Crescent Ave., Avalon* ☎*310/510–0555 or 800/346–2326* ⊕*www.hotelvillaportofino. com* ↩*34 rooms* ⅋*In room: refrigerator, Wi-Fi. In hotel: no elevator* ▤*AE, D, DC, MC, V* ⊺*CP.*

NIGHTLIFE

El Galleon (✉*411 Crescent Ave., Avalon* ☎*310/510–1188*) has microbrews, bar nibbles, and karaoke. **Luau Larry's** (✉*509 Crescent Ave., Avalon* ☎*310/510–1919*), famous for the potent blue Whicky Whacker cocktail, comes alive with boisterous tourists and locals on summer weekends.

SPORTS & THE OUTDOORS

BICYCLING   Bike rentals are widely available in Avalon starting at $5 per hour and $12 per day. Look for rentals on Crescent Avenue and Pebbly Beach Road such as **Brown's Bikes** (✉*107 Pebbly Beach Rd., next to Island Rentals, Avalon* ☎*310/510–0986* 🖷*310/510–0747* ⊕*www.catalina biking.com*). To bike beyond the paved roads of Avalon, you must buy an annual permit from the Catalina Conservancy. Individual passes cost $50; family passes cost $75. You may not ride on hiking paths.

DIVING &   The Casino Point Underwater Park, with its handful of wrecks, is best
SNORKELING   suited for diving. Lover's Cove is better for snorkeling (no scuba diving allowed), but you'll share the area with glass-bottom boats. Both are protected marine preserves. **Catalina Divers Supply** (✉*Green Pleasure Pier* ☎*310/510–0330* ⊕*www.catalinadiverssupply.com*) rents equipment, runs guided scuba and snorkel tours, gives certification classes, and more. It has an outpost at Casino Point.

HIKING   ■**TIP**➜**If you plan to backpack overnight, you'll need a camping reservation. The interior is dry and desertlike; bring plenty of water and sunblock.**

Permits from the **Santa Catalina Island Conservancy** (✉*3rd and Claressa Sts., Avalon* ☎*310/510–2595* ⊕*www.catalinaconservancy.org*) are required for hiking into Catalina Island's interior. The permits are free and can be picked up at the main house of the conservancy or at the airport. You don't need a permit for shorter hikes, such as the one from Avalon to the Botanical Garden. The conservancy has maps of the island's east-end hikes, such as Hermit's Gulch Trail. It's possible to hike between Avalon and Two Harbors, starting at the Hogsback Gate, above Avalon, though the 28-mi journey has an elevation gain of 3,000 feet and is not for the weak. ■TIP→**For a pleasant 4-mi hike out of Avalon, take Avalon Canyon Road to Wrigley Gardens and follow the trail to Lone Pine. At the top, you'll have an amazing view of the Palisades cliffs and, beyond them, the sea.**

Another hike option is to take the **Airport Shuttle Bus** (☎310/510–0143) from Avalon to the airport for $17 round-trip. The 10-mi hike back to Avalon is mostly downhill, and the bus is an inexpensive way to see the interior of the island.

HORSEBACK RIDING Horseback riders can wrangle four-legged transportation for scenic trail rides. Reservations must be made at the **Catalina Stables** (✉600 Avalon Canyon Rd., Avalon ☎310/510–0478), which has guided rides starting at $42 for a half hour.

CATALINA ISLAND ESSENTIALS

AIR TRAVEL
Island Express helicopters depart hourly from San Pedro and Long Beach (8 AM–dusk). The trip takes about 15 minutes and costs $82 one-way, $156 round-trip (plus tax). Reservations a week in advance are recommended.

Airlines & Contacts **Island Express** (☎800/228–2566 ⊕www.islandexpress.com).

BOAT & FERRY TRAVEL
Two companies offer ferry service to Catalina Island. The boats have both indoor and outdoor seating and snack bars. Excessive baggage is not allowed, and there are extra fees for bicycles and surfboards. The waters around Santa Catalina can get rough, so if you're prone to seasickness, come prepared.

Catalina Express makes an hour-long run from Long Beach or San Pedro to Avalon and a 90-minute run from Dana Point to Avalon with some stops at Two Harbors. Round-trip fare for the various routes costs $60. Service from Newport Beach to Avalon is available through Catalina Passenger Service. Boats leave from Balboa Pavilion at 9 AM (in season), take 75 minutes to reach the island, and cost $57 round-trip. Return boats leave Catalina at 4:30 PM. Reservations are advised in summer and on weekends for all trips. ■TIP→**Keep an eye out for dolphins, which sometimes swim alongside the ferries.**

FARES & SCHEDULES
Boat & Ferry Information **Catalina Express** (☎800/481–3470 ⊕www.catalina express.com). **Catalina Passenger Service** (☎949/673–5245 or 800/830–7744 🖷949/673–8340 ⊕www.catalinainfo.com).

GOLF CARTS
Golf carts constitute the island's main form of transportation for sightseeing in the area, but they can't be used on the streets in town. You can rent them along Avalon's Crescent Avenue and Pebbly Beach Road for

about $40 per hour with a $30 deposit, payable via cash or traveler's checks only.

Local Agencies **Island Rentals** (⊠ *125 Pebbly Beach Rd., Avalon* ☎ *310/510–1456*).

LODGING

Between Memorial Day and Labor Day be sure to make reservations before heading here. After late October, rooms are much easier to find on shorter notice, rates drop dramatically, and many hotels offer packages that include transportation from the mainland and/or sightseeing tours.

TOURS

Santa Catalina Island Company runs the following Discovery Tours: a summer-only coastal cruise to Seal Rocks; the *Flying Fish* boat trip (summer evenings only); a comprehensive inland motor tour (which includes an Arabian horse performance); a tour of Skyline Drive; a Casino tour; a scenic tour of Avalon; a glass-bottom-boat tour, an undersea tour on a semisubmersible vessel; and a tour of the Botanical Garden. Reservations are highly recommended for the inland tours. Tours cost $15.25 to $99. There are ticket booths on the Green Pleasure Pier, at the Casino, in the plaza, and at the boat landing. Catalina Adventure Tours, which has booths at the boat landing and on the pier, arranges similar excursions at comparable prices.

The Santa Catalina Island Conservancy organizes custom ecotours and hikes of the interior. Naturalist guides drive open Jeeps through some gorgeously untrammeled parts of the island. Tours start at $98 per person for a three-hour trip (three-person minimum); you can also book half- and full-day tours. The tours run year-round.

Contacts **Catalina Adventure Tours** (☎ *310/510–2888* 🖷 *310/510–2797* ⊕ *www.catalinaadventuretours.com*). **Santa Catalina Island Company** (☎ *310/510–8687 or 800/626–1496* ⊕ *www.scico.com*). **Santa Catalina Island Conservancy** (⊠ *3rd and Claressa Sts., Avalon* ☎ *310/510–2595* ⊕ *www.catalinaconservancy.org*).

VISITOR INFORMATION

Tourist Information **Catalina Island Visitors' Bureau** (⊠ *Green Pleasure Pier, Box 217, Avalon* ☎ *310/510–1520* 🖷 *310/510–7606* ⊕ *www.catalina.com*).

Los Angeles

Los Angeles International Airport

WORD OF MOUTH

"The Getty Center is THE museum for children. When we were there in April, the place was crawling with families picnicking on the grounds—it was a delight to see. The galleries are varied, the views are spectacular, and the gardens are wonderful."

—happytrailstoyou

WELCOME TO LOS ANGELES

TOP REASONS TO GO

★ **Hollywood magic:**
A massive chunk of the world's entertainment is developed, written, filmed, edited, distributed, and sold here; you'll hear people discussing the "Industry" wherever you go.

★ **The beach:** Getting some sand on the floor of your car is practically a requirement here, and the beach is an integral part of the SoCal lifestyle.

★ **Chic shopping:** From Beverly Hills' Rodeo Drive and Downtown's Fashion District to the funky boutiques of Los Feliz, Silver Lake, and Echo Park, L.A. is a shopper's paradise.

★ **Trendy restaurants:** Celebrity is big business here, so it's no accident that the concept of the celebrity chef is a key part of the city's dining scene.

★ **People-watching:** Celeb-spotting in Beverly Hills, trying to get past the velvet rope at hip clubs, hanging out on the Venice Boardwalk . . . there's always something (or someone) interesting to see.

1 Hollywood. Go ahead, let yourself get a little star struck. Catch a flick at Grauman's Chinese Theater, pay your respects to your favorite star's Walk of Fame plaque, and check out Hollywood & Highland's Kodak Theater, home of the Academy Awards.

2 Downtown. A neighborhood in transition, LA's downtown is home to spectacular modern architecture, ethnic neighborhoods, and some of the city's key cultural institutions.

3 Beverly Hills. Go for the glamour, the restaurants, and the scene. You'll see plastic surgery, scads of sushi spots, a parade of custom cars, and, of course, lots of conspicuous consumption.

4 Santa Monica, Venice & Malibu. Hugging the Santa Monica bay in an arch, these desirable beach communities move from ultrarich, ultracasual Malibu to bohemian/seedy Venice, with liberal, Mediterranean-style Santa Monica in the middle.

5 The Valley. Home of several of the big studios, this is where the movie (and TV) magic happens. Though some locals shudder at the thought, if you're a film buff, you really should visit the Valley.

GETTING ORIENTED

Looking at a map of sprawling Los Angeles, first-time visitors are sometimes overwhelmed. Where to begin? What to see first? And what about all those freeways? Here's some advice: relax. Begin by setting your priorities—movie and television buffs should first head to Hollywood, Universal Studios, and a taping of a television show. Beach lovers and nature types might start out in Santa Monica or Venice or Malibu, or spend an afternoon in Griffith Park, one of the largest city parks in the country. Culture vultures should make a beeline for the twin Gettys (the center in Brentwood and the villa near Malibu), the Los Angeles County Museum of Art (LACMA), or the Norton Simon Museum. And urban explorers might begin with Downtown Los Angeles.

4

LOS ANGELES PLANNER

When to Go

Almost any time of the year is the right time to go to Los Angeles; the climate is mild and pleasant year-round. Winter brings crisp, sunny, unusually smogless days from about November to May (expect brief rains from December to April). Los Angeles summers, which are virtually rainless, can lead to air-quality alerts. Prices skyrocket and reservations are a must when tourism peaks from July through early October.

Driving

Most freeways are known by a name and a number; for example, the San Diego Freeway is I-405, the Hollywood Freeway is U.S. 101, the Ventura Freeway is a different stretch of U.S. 101, the Santa Monica Freeway is I-10, and the Harbor Freeway is I-110. It helps, too, to know which direction you're traveling; say, west toward Santa Monica or east toward Downtown Los Angeles. Distance in miles doesn't mean much, depending on the time of day you're traveling: the short 10-mi distance between the San Fernando Valley and Downtown Los Angeles might take an hour to travel during rush hour but only 20 minutes at other times.

About the Restaurants

Dining out in Los Angeles tends to be a casual affair, and even at some of the most expensive restaurants you're likely to see customers in jeans (although this is not necessarily considered in good taste). Despite its veneer of decadence, L.A. is not a particularly late-night city for eating. (The reenergized Hollywood dining scene is emerging as a notable exception.) The peak dinner times are from 7 to 9, and most restaurants won't take reservations after 10. Generally speaking, restaurants are closed either Sunday or Monday; a few are shuttered both days. Most places—even the upscale spots—are open for lunch on weekdays, when Hollywood megadeals are conceived.

About the Hotels

When looking for a hotel, don't write off the pricier establishments immediately. Price categories are determined by "rack rates"—the list price of a hotel room, which is usually discounted. Specials abound, particularly downtown on the weekends. Many hotels have packages that include breakfast, theater tickets, spa services, or exotic rental cars. Pricing is very competitive, so always check out the hotel Web site in advance for current special offers. When making reservations, particularly last-minute ones, check the hotel's Web site for exclusive Internet specials or call the property directly.

WHAT IT COSTS

¢	$	$$	$$$	$$$$
Restaurants				
under $7	$7–$12	$12–$22	$22–$32	over $32
Hotels				
under $75	$75–$125	$125–$200	$200–$325	over $325

Dining prices are per person for a main course or equivalent combination of smaller plates, excluding 8.25% sales tax. Lodging listings are the top selections of their type in each price category. Prices are based on the range between the least and most expensive standard double rooms in nonholiday high season, on the European Plan (no meals) unless otherwise noted. Taxes (9%–15.5%) are extra. When pricing accommodations, always ask what's included.

Updated
by Roger J.
Grody, Lina
Lecaro, Kathy
A. McDonald,
Stef
McDonald,
Laura Randall,
Kastle
Waserman

LOS ANGELES IS AS MUCH a fantasy as it is a physical city. A mecca for face-lifts, film noir, shopping starlets, beach bodies, and mind-numbing traffic, it sprawls across 467 square mi; add in the surrounding five-county metropolitan area, and you've got an area of more than 34,000 square mi. Contrary to popular myth, however, that doesn't mean you have to spend all your time in a car. In fact, getting out of your car is the only way to really get to know Los Angeles. We've divided the major sightseeing areas into 10 driving and walking tours that take you through the various entertainment-industry-centered, financial, beach-front, wealthy, and fringe neighborhoods and minicities that make up the vast L.A. area. But remember, no single locale—whether it be Malibu, Downtown, Beverly Hills, or Burbank—fully embodies Los Angeles. It's in the mix that you'll discover the city's character.

4

EXPLORING LOS ANGELES

DOWNTOWN LOS ANGELES

Once the lively heart of Los Angeles, Downtown has been a glitz-free businessman's domain of high-rises for the past few decades. But if there's one thing Angelinos love, it's a makeover, and now city planners have put the wheels in motion for a dramatic revitalization. Glance in every direction and you'll find construction crews building luxury lofts and retail space in hopes of attracting new high-class residents.

WHAT TO SEE

❽ Bradbury Building. Stunning wrought-iron railings, ornate moldings, a
★ Victorian-style skylighted atrium that rises almost 50 feet, and bird-cage elevators that seem to cry out for white-gloved, brass-buttoned operators: it's easy to see why the Bradbury leaves visitors awestruck. Designed in 1893 by a novice architect who drew his inspiration from a science-fiction story and a conversation with his dead brother via a Ouija board, the office building was originally the site of turn-of-the-20th-century sweatshops, but now houses a variety of businesses that try to keep normal working conditions despite the barrage of daily tourist visits and filmmakers. For that reason, visits are limited to the lobby and the first-floor landing. The building is open daily 9–5 for a peek, as long as you don't wander beyond visitor-approved areas. ✉*304 S. Broadway, southeast corner Broadway and 3rd St., Downtown* ☎*213/626–1893.*

⓫ California African-American Museum. Works by 20th-century African-American artists and contemporary works of the African diaspora are the backbone of this museum's permanent collection. Its exhibits document the African-American experience from Emancipation and Reconstruction through the 20th century, especially as expressed by artists in California and elsewhere in the West. Special musical as well as educational and cultural events are offered the first Sunday of every month. ✉*600 State Dr., Exposition Park* ☎*213/744–7432* ⊕*www.caamuseum.org* 🎟*Free, parking $6* ⊗*Tues.–Sat. 10–5, Sun. 11–5.*

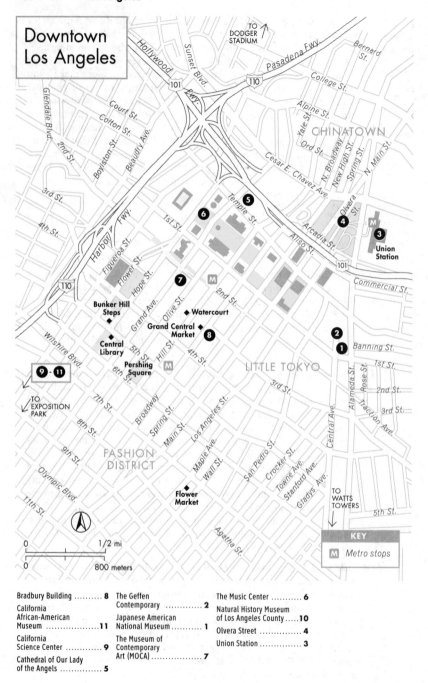

Downtown Los Angeles

TO DODGER STADIUM

CHINATOWN

Union Station

Bunker Hill Steps

Watercourt

Grand Central Market

Central Library

Pershing Square

TO EXPOSITION PARK

LITTLE TOKYO

FASHION DISTRICT

Flower Market

TO WATTS TOWERS

0   1/2 mi

0   800 meters

KEY

Ⓜ Metro stops

9 **California Science Center.** You're bound to see excited kids running up to the dozens of interactive exhibits here that illustrate the relevance of science to everyday life, from bacteria to airplanes. Clustered in different "Worlds," this center provides opportunities to examine such topics as structures and communications, where you can be an architect and design your own building and learn how to make it earthquake-proof; to "Life" itself, where Tess, the 50-foot animatronic star of the exhibit "Body Works," dramatically demonstrates how the body's organs work together. Air and Space Exhibits show what it takes to go to outer space with Gemini 11, real capsule flown into space by Pete Conrad and Dick Gordon in September 1966. An IMAX theater shows large-format releases. ⊠ *700 State Dr., Exposition Park 90037* ☎ *213/744–7400 or 323/724–3623* ⊕ *www.casciencectr.org* ✉ *Free, except for IMAX, prices vary; parking $6* ☉ *Daily 10–5.*

5 **Cathedral of Our Lady of the Angels.** Controversy surrounded Spanish

Fodor'sChoice architect José Rafael Moneo's unconventional, costly, austere design
★ for the seat of the Archdiocese of Los Angeles. But judging from the swarms of visitors and the standing-room-only holiday Masses, the church has carved out a niche for itself in Downtown's daily life. Opened in 2002, the ocher-concrete cathedral looms up by the Hollywood Freeway. The plaza in front is relatively austere, glaringly bright on sunny days; a children's play garden with bronze animals helps relieve the stark space. Imposing bronze entry doors, designed by local artist Robert Graham, are decorated with multicultural icons and New World images of the Virgin Mary. The canyonlike interior of the church is spare, polished, and airy. By day, sunlight illuminates the sanctuary through translucent curtain walls of thin Spanish alabaster, a departure from the usual stained glass. Artist John Nava used residents from his hometown of Ojai, California, as models for some of the 135 figures in the tapestries that line the nave walls. Make sure to go underground to wander the bright, somewhat incongruous, mazelike white-marble corridors of the mausoleum. Free guided tours start at the entrance fountain at 1 on weekdays. There's plenty of underground visitor parking; the vehicle entrance is on Hill Street. ■TIP→ **The café in the plaza has become one of Downtown's favorite lunch spots, as you can pick up a fresh, reasonably priced meal to eat at one of the outdoor tables.** ⊠ *555 W. Temple St., Downtown* ☎ *213/680–5200* ⊕ *www.olacathedral.org* ✉ *Free, parking $3 every 20 min, $14 maximum* ☉ *Mon.–Fri. 6:30–6, Sat. 9–6, Sun. 7–6.*

2 **The Geffen Contemporary.** Originally opened in 1982 as a temporary
★ exhibit hall while the **Museum of Contemporary Art (MOCA)** was under construction at California Plaza, this large flexible space, designed by architect Frank Gehry, charmed visitors with its antiestablishment character and lively exhibits. Thanks to its hit reception, it remains one of two satellite museums of the MOCA (the other is outside the Pacific Design Center in W. Hollywood). Named the Geffen Contemporary, after receiving a $5 million gift from the David Geffen Foundation, this museum houses a sampling of MOCA's permanent collection and usually one or two offbeat exhibits that provoke grins from even the stuffi-

est museum goer. Call before you visit as the museum sometimes closes for installations. ✉*152 N. Central Ave., Downtown* ☎*213/626–6222* ⊕*www.moca-la.org* ☜*$8, free with MOCA admission on same day and on Thurs.* ⊙*Mon. and Fri. 11–5, Thurs. 11–8, weekends 11–6.*

❶ **Japanese American National Museum.** What was it like to grow up on a sugar plantation in Hawaii? How difficult was life for Japanese-Americans interned in concentration camps during World War II? These questions are addressed by changing exhibits at this museum in Little Tokyo. Insightful volunteer docents are on hand to share their own stories and experiences. The museum occupies an 85,000-square-foot adjacent pavilion as well as its original site in a renovated 1925 Buddhist temple. Exhibits for 2009 include "Glorious Excess," featuring the work of Linkin Park musician/artist Mike Shinoda January–March, and a Kokeshi doll exhibition June–September. ✉*369 E. 1st St., at Central Ave., next to Geffen Contemporary, Downtown* ☎*213/625–0414* ⊕*www.janm.org* ☜*$8, free Thurs. 5–8 and 3rd Thurs. of month* ⊙*Tues., Wed., and Fri.–Sun. 11–5, Thurs. 11–8.*

❼ **The Museum of Contemporary Art (MOCA).** The MOCA's permanent collection of American and European art from 1940 to the present divides itself between three spaces: this linear red-sandstone building at California Plaza, the **Geffen Contemporary**, in nearby Little Tokyo, and the satellite gallery at W. Hollywood's **Pacific Design Center**. Likewise, its exhibitions are split between the established and the cutting-edge. Works by heavy hitters such as Mark Rothko, Franz Kline, Susan Rothenberg, Diane Arbus, and Robert Frank are part of the permanent collection which are rotated into exhibits at different times, while at least 20 themed shows are featured annually. The museum occasionally closes for exhibit installation. ✉*250 S. Grand Ave., Downtown* ☎*213/626–6222* ⊕*www.moca.org* ☜*$8, free on same day with Geffen Contemporary admission and on Thurs.* ⊙*Mon. and Fri. 11–5, Thurs. 11–8, weekends 11–6.*

FodorsChoice ★

❻ **The Music Center.** L.A.'s major performing arts venue since its opening in 1964, the Music Center is also now Downtown's centerpiece. Home to the Los Angeles Philharmonic, the Los Angeles Opera, the Center Theater Group, and the Los Angeles Master Chorale, the Music Center is also a former site of the Academy Awards. The center's crown jewel is the **Walt Disney Concert Hall**. Designed by Frank Gehry, the Hall opened in 2003 and instantly became a stunning icon of the city. The gorgeous stainless-steel-clad structure soars lyrically upward, seeming to defy the laws of engineering. Free tours of the Music Center are available by volunteer docents, "the Symphonians," who provide a wealth of architectural and behind-the-scenes information while escorting you through elaborate, art-punctuated VIP areas. ✉*135 N. Grand Ave., at 1st St., Downtown* ☎*213/972–7211, 213/972–4399 for tour information* ⊕*www.musiccenter.org* ☜*Free* ⊙*Free tours Tues.–Fri. 10–1:30, Sat. 10–noon.*

FodorsChoice ★

❿ **Natural History Museum of Los Angeles County.** With more than 35 million specimens, this is the third-largest museum of its type in the United

States. Since 1913, the museum has boasted a rich collection of toric fossils and extensive bird, insect, and marine-life exhibits. I stones shimmer in the Gem & Mineral Hall. An elaborate diorama exhibit shows North American and African mammals in detailed replicas of their natural habitats. Exhibits typifying various cultural groups include pre-Columbian artifacts and a display of crafts from the South Pacific. The Ralph M. Parsons Discovery Center & Insect Zoo encourages kids to do hands-on exploration of the museum's collections. In spring 2008, the museum opened its first public paleontological preparation laboratory. This innovative lab features "Thomas," a nearly 70% complete, 65 million-year-old T. rex excavated during field expeditions in southeastern Montana. ✉ *900 Exposition Blvd., Exposition Park* ☎ *213/763–3466* 🌐 *www.nhm.org* 🎟 *$9, free 1st Tues. of month* ⏲ *Weekdays 9:30–5, weekends 10–5.*

4

❹ ★ **Olvera Street.** This busy pedestrian block tantalizes with piñatas, mariachis, and fragrant Mexican food. As the major draw of the oldest section of the city, known as **El Pueblo de Los Angeles,** Olvera Street has come to represent the rich Mexican heritage of L.A. It had a close shave with disintegration in the early 20th century, until the socialite Christine Sterling walked through in 1926. Jolted by the historic area's decay, Sterling fought to preserve key buildings and led the transformation of the street into a Mexican-American marketplace. Today this character remains; vendors sell puppets, leather goods, sandals, serapes (woolen shawls), and handicrafts from stalls that line the center of the narrow street. On weekends, the restaurants are packed as musicians play in the central plaza. The weekends that fall around two Mexican holidays, Cinco de Mayo (May 5) and Independence Day (September 16), also draw huge crowds. TIP→ **To see Olvera Street at its quietest, visit late on a weekday afternoon, when long shadows heighten the romantic feeling of the passageway.** For information, stop by the **Olvera Street Visitors Center** (✉ *622 N. Main St., Downtown* ☎ *213/628–1274* 🌐 *www.olvera-street.com*), in the Sepulveda House, a Victorian built in 1887 as a hotel and boardinghouse. The center is open Monday–Saturday 10–3. Free 50-minute walking tours leave here at 10, 11, and noon Tuesday–Saturday.

❸ ★ **Union Station.** Evoking an era when travel and style went hand in hand, Union Station will transport you to another destination, and another time. Built in 1939 and designed by City Hall architects John and Donald Parkinson, it combines Spanish colonial revival and art deco styles that have retained their classic warmth and quality. The waiting hall's commanding scale and enormous chandeliers have provided the setting for countless films, TV shows, and music videos. Once the key entry point into Los Angeles prior to LAX, Union Station is worth a visit even if you don't plan to go anywhere but merely want to wallow in the ambience of one of the country's last great rail stations. The indoor restaurant, **Traxx,** offers a glamorous vintage setting for lunch and dinner. ✉ *800 N. Alameda St., Downtown.*

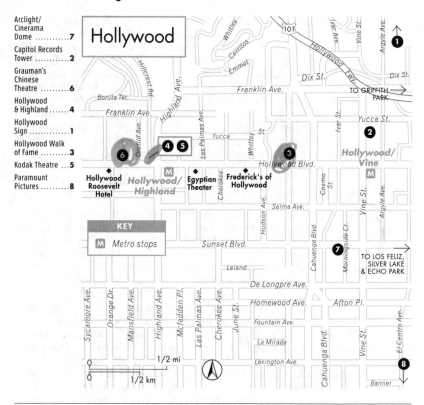

HOLLYWOOD

Hollywood is where the Tinseltown mythology of Los Angeles was born. And like Downtown, Hollywood is in the first stage of an extreme makeover designed to lure hipsters and big money back into the fold.

WHAT TO SEE

❼ Arclight/Cinerama Dome. Film buffs and preservationists breathed a sigh of relief when the Arclight complex opened its doors and rewrote the book on cushy movie going. With plush stadium seating, reserved seats for some showings, state-of-the-art sound, an usher who welcomes you and introduces the film, and snack bars that cook up their own fresh caramel corn, the Arclight justifies its high ticket prices ($11–$14, depending on the hour you go). Built next to the restored geodesic Cinerama Dome, a curved-screen architectural icon, the complex also caters to film lovers with special director's Q&A nights as well as exhibits of movie costumes and photography throughout the lobby. Even though there are 14 other theaters in the complex, many films sell out quickly. Your best chance at prime seating is to order tickets online and to choose a seat in advance. Parking is $2 in the adjacent garage with a movie ticket purchase and validation. ⊠ *6360 Sunset Blvd., at Vine St., Hollywood* ☎ *323/464–4226* ⊕ *www.arclightcinemas.com.*

Griffith Park

With so much of Los Angeles paved in cement and asphalt, 4,100-acre Griffith Park stands out as a special place. It's the largest municipal park and urban wilderness area in the United States. On warm weekends, there are parties, barbecues, mariachi bands, and strolling vendors selling fresh fruit. Joggers, cyclists, and walkers course its roadways, and golfers play its four municipal courses. Within the park there are three tennis courts, horse stables, a collection of vintage locomotive and railroad cars called Travel Town, and pony rides.

The park, which was named after Col. Griffith J. Griffith, a mining tycoon who donated 3,000 acres of land to the city for the park in 1896, has been used as a film and television location since the early days of motion pictures. One early Hollywood producer advised, "A tree is a tree, a rock is a rock, shoot it in Griffith Park."

After a major fire in May 2007, many hiking and equestrian trails were closed (for safety reasons, for replanting, and for the natural wildlife). Things are getting back to normal, but it's a good idea to check the park's blog (⊕ www.lagriffithpark.blogspot.com) for updates before visiting.

Griffith Park is accessible in several places: off Los Feliz Boulevard at Western Canyon Avenue, Vermont Avenue, Crystal Springs Drive, and Riverside Drive; from the Ventura/134 Freeway at Victory Boulevard, Zoo Drive, or Forest Lawn Drive; from the Golden State Freeway (I–5) at Los Feliz Boulevard and Zoo Drive. The park is open from 5 AM to 10 PM. Information (☎ 323/644–6661) and for emergencies, call the **ranger station** (☎ 323/913–7390) on Crystal Springs Drive, near the merry-go-round.

4

❷ **Capitol Records Tower.** According to legend, singer Nat King Cole and songwriter Johnny Mercer suggested that the record company's headquarters should be shaped to look like a stack of 45s, and their comment produced this lasting symbol of '50s chic. Or so the story goes. Architect Welton Becket claimed he just wanted to design a structure that economized space, and in so doing, he created the world's first cylindrical office building. On its south wall, L.A. artist Richard Wyatt's mural *Hollywood Jazz, 1945–1972* immortalizes musical greats Duke Ellington, Billie Holiday, Ella Fitzgerald, and Miles Davis. The recording studios are underneath the parking lot; all kinds of major artists, including Frank Sinatra, the Beatles, and Radiohead, have filled the echo chambers with sound. At the top of the tower, a blinking light spells out "Hollywood" in Morse code. Due to tightened security, the building is not open to the public. ✉ *1750 N. Vine St., Hollywood.*

❻ ★ **Grauman's Chinese Theatre.** A place that inspires the phrase "only in Hollywood," this fantasy of Chinese pagodas and temples has become a shrine to stardom. Although you have to buy a movie ticket to appreciate the interior trappings, the courtyard is open to the public. Here you'll find those oh-so-famous cement hand- and footprints. This tradition is said to have begun at the theater's opening in 1927, with the premiere of Cecil B. DeMille's *King of Kings,* when actress Norma

Talmadge just happened to step into wet cement. Now more than 160 celebrities have contributed imprints for posterity, including some odd-ball specimens, such as ones of Whoopi Goldberg's dredlocks and Betty Grable's legs. Recent inductees include the cast and director of *Ocean's 13*, the Harry Potter kids, and Will Smith. The main theater itself is worth visiting, if only to see a film in the same seats as hundreds of celebrities who have attended big premieres here. You could also take a $12 tour that takes you around the theaters and the VIP lounge. If it's movies you want, six more theaters are next to the Hollywood & Highland complex with every modern movie-going comfort. ⊠*6925 Hollywood Blvd., Hollywood* ☎*323/461–3331, 323/463–9576 for tours* ⊕*www.manntheatres.com.*

❹ **Hollywood & Highland.** Now an extremely busy tourist attraction (read: ★ not a lot of locals), this hotel-retail-entertainment complex was a dramatic play to bring glitz, foot traffic, and commerce back to Hollywood. The design pays tribute to the city's film legacy with a grand staircase leading up to a pair of white stucco 33-foot-high elephants, a nod to the 1916 movie *Intolerance*. (Something tells us that the reference is lost on most visitors.) ■TIP➡**Pause at the entrance arch, Babylon Court, which frames the Hollywood sign in the hills above for a picture-perfect view.** There are plenty of clothing stores and eateries—and you may find yourself ducking into these for a respite from the crowds and street artists. On the sidewalk below you could encounter everything from a sidewalk evangelist to a guy dressed as Spider-Man posing for pictures. In the summer and during Christmas vacation, special music programs and free entertainment keep strollers entertained. A Metro Red Line station provides easy access to and from other parts of the city, and there's plenty of underground parking accessible from Highland Avenue. ⊠*Hollywood Blvd. and Highland Ave., Hollywood* ⊕*www.hollywoodandhighland.com* ⊞*Parking $2 with validation* ⊗*Mon.–Sat. 10–10, Sun. 10–7.*

❶ **Hollywood Sign.** With letters 50 feet tall, Hollywood's trademark sign ★ can be spotted from miles away. The sign, which originally read HOLLYWOODLAND, was erected on Mt. Lee in the Hollywood Hills in 1923 to promote a real-estate development. In 1949 the "land" portion of the sign was taken down. By 1973, the sign had earned landmark status, but since the letters were made of wood, its longevity came into question. A makeover project was launched and the letters were auctioned off (rocker Alice Cooper bought the O, singing cowboy Gene Autry sponsored an L) to make way for a new sign made of sheet metal. Inevitably, the sign has drawn pranksters who have altered it over the years, albeit temporarily, to spell out HOLLYWEED (in the 1970s, to commemorate lenient marijuana laws), GO NAVY (before a Rose Bowl game), and PEROTWOOD (during the 1992 presidential election). A fence and surveillance equipment have since been installed to deter intruders. Use caution if driving up to the sign on residential streets since many cars speed around the blind corners. ⊕*www.hollywoodsign.org.*

❸ **Hollywood Walk of Fame.** Along Hollywood Boulevard runs a trail of ★ affirmations for entertainment-industry overachievers. On this mile-

long stretch of sidewalk, inspired by the concrete handprints in i.
of Grauman's Chinese Theatre, the names are embossed in brass, ea.
at the center of a pink star embedded in dark-gray terrazzo. They're
not all screen deities; many stars commemorate people who worked in
a technical field. More than 1,600 stars have been immortalized since
the first batch was placed in 1960, though that honor doesn't come
cheap—upon selection by a special committee, the personality in question (or more likely his or her movie studio or record company) pays
about $15,000 for the privilege. To aid you in spotting celebrities you're
looking for, stars are identified by one of five icons: a motion-picture
camera, a radio microphone, a television set, a record, or a theatrical
mask. Contact the **Hollywood Chamber of Commerce** (✉ *7018 Hollywood
Blvd.* ☏ *323/467–6412* ⊕ *www.hollywoodchamber.net*) for celebrity-
star locations and information on future star installations.

❺ Kodak Theatre. Follow the path of red-carpet Hollywood royalty to the
★ home of the Academy Awards. While taking a half-hour tour of this
famous setting isn't cheap, it's a worthwhile expense for movie buffs
who just can't get enough insider information. The tour guides share
plenty of behind-the-scenes tidbits about Oscar ceremonies as they take
you through the theater. You'll get to step into the VIP George East-
man Lounge, where celebrities mingle on the big night and get a bird's-
eye view from the balcony seating. (Be sure to ask how Oscar got his
name.) The interior design was inspired by European opera houses, but
underneath all the trimmings, the space has some of the finest technical systems in the world. Although you may not make it in for the
Oscar show itself, you can always come here for a musical or concert
performance by the likes of Alicia Keys or the Dixie Chicks. ✉ *6801
Hollywood Blvd., Hollywood* ☏ *323/308–6300* ⊕ *www.kodaktheatre.
com* ▦ *Tours $15 Tours daily 10:30–2:30.*

❽ Paramount Pictures. With a history dating to the early 1920s, this stu-
FodorsChoice dio was home to some of Hollywood's most luminous stars, including
★ Rudolph Valentino, Mae West, Mary Pickford, and Lucille Ball, who
filmed episodes of *I Love Lucy* here. The lot still churns out memorable movies and TV shows, including *Forrest Gump, Titanic,* and
Star Trek. You can take a studio tour (reservations required) led by
friendly guides who walk and trolley you around the back lots. As well
as gleaning some gossipy history (see the lawn where Lucy and Desi
broke up), you'll spot the sets of TV and film shoots in progress, including such hits as *Entertainment Tonight, Dr. Phil,* and *Everybody Hates
Chris.* You can also be part of the audience for live TV tapings. Tickets
are free; call for listings and times. ✉ *5555 Melrose Ave., Hollywood*
☏ *323/956–1777* ⊕ *www.paramount.com/studio* ▦ *Tours weekdays
by reservation only, $35.*

WILSHIRE BOULEVARD, MUSEUM ROW & FARMERS MARKET

The three-block stretch of Wilshire Boulevard known as Museum Row,
east of Fairfax Avenue, racks up five intriguing museums and a prehistoric tar pit to boot. Only a few blocks away are the historic Farmers

On the map:
Wilshire Boulevard, Museum Row & Farmers Market

❶ Pan Pacific Park — 1st St. — The Wilshire Country Club

Southwest Museum at LACMA West ❸

❹ ❷ Miracle Mile — Wilshire Blvd.

Craft and Folk Art Museum (CAFAM)

0 ——— 1/2 mile
0 ——— 500 meters

Market and The Grove shopping mall, a great place to people-watch over breakfast. Wilshire Boulevard itself is something of a cultural monument—it begins its grand 16-mi sweep to the sea in Downtown Los Angeles. ■TIP➔**Finding parking along Wilshire Boulevard can present a challenge any time of the day; you'll find advice on the information phone lines of most attractions.**

WHAT TO SEE

❶ **Farmers Market & The Grove.** The saying "Meet me at 3rd and Fairfax" became a standard line for generations of Angelenos who ate, shopped, and spotted the stars who drifted over from the studios for a breath of unpretentious air. Starting back in 1934 when two entrepreneurs convinced oil magnate E.B. Gilmore to open a vacant field for a bare-bones market, this spot became a humble shop for farmers selling produce out of their trucks. From this seat-of-the-pants situation grew a European-style open-air market and local institution at the corner of 3rd Street and Fairfax Avenue. Now the market includes 110 stalls and more than 20 counter-order restaurants, plus the landmark 1941 Clock Tower. In 2002 a massive expansion called The Grove opened; this highly conceptualized outdoor mall has a pseudo-European facade, with cobblestones, marble mosaics, and pavilions. Los Angeles history gets a nod with the electric steel-wheeled Red Car trolley, which shuttles two blocks through the Farmers Market and The Grove. If you hate crowds, try visiting the Grove before noon for the most comfortable shopping experience. **The Grove really dazzles around Christmas, with an enormous Christmas tree and a nightly faux snowfall until New Year's Day.** ⊠*Farmers Market, 6333 W. 3rd St.; The Grove, 189 The Grove Dr., Fairfax District* ☎*323/933–9211; Farmers Market, The Grove* ☎*323/900–8080* ⊕*www.farmersmarketla.com* ⊙*Farmers Market weekdays 9–9, Sat. 9–8, Sun. 10–7; The Grove Mon.–Thurs. 10–9, Fri. and Sat. 10–10, Sun. 11–8.*

❸ ★ **La Brea Tar Pits.** Do your children have dinos on the brain? Show them where dinosaurs come from by taking them to the stickiest park in town. About 40,000 years ago, deposits of oil rose to the earth's surface, collected in shallow pools, and coagulated into asphalt. In the early 20th century, geologists discovered that all that goo contained the largest collection of Pleistocene, or Ice Age, fossils ever found at one location: more than 600 species of birds, mammals, plants, reptiles, and insects. Roughly 100 tons of fossil bones have been removed in excavations over the last seven decades, making this one of the world's most famous fossil sites. You can see most of the pits through chain-link fences. Pit 91 is the site of ongoing excavation; tours are available, and you can volunteer to help with the excavations in summer. There are several pits scattered around Hancock Park and the surrounding neighborhood; construction in the area has often had to accommodate them. And in nearby streets and along sidewalks, little bits of tar occasionally ooze up, unstoppable. The nearby ⇨**Page Museum at the La Brea Tar Pits** displays fossils from the tar pits. ⊠*Hancock Park, Miracle Mile* ⊕*www.tarpits.org* ✉*Free.*

❷ Los Angeles County Museum of Art (LACMA). Serving as the focal point of the museum district along Wilshire Boulevard, LACMA's vast, encyclopedic collection of more than 100,000 objects dating from ancient times to the present is widely considered one of the most comprehensive in the western United States. Since opening in 1965 the museum has grown from three buildings to seven, stretching across a 20-acre campus. As part of an ambitious 10-year facelift plan that is becoming a work of art on its own, entitled "Transformation," the museum is on a mission to integrate the seven buildings and outdoor spaces into a coherent whole. Phase one began with the opening of the impressive Broad Contemporary Art Museum (BCAM) in early 2008. With three vast floors, BCAM's purpose is to more fully integrate contemporary art into LACMA's program and explore the interplay of contemporary art and traditional art.

Fodor's Choice ★

With rotating displays from its permanent collection, at any time it's possible to see items from LACMA's abundant holdings of works by leading Latin American artists, including Diego Rivera and Frida Kahlo; prominent Southern California artists; collections of Islamic and European art; paintings by Henri Matisse and Rene Magritte; and works by Paul Klee and Wassily Kandinsky, who taught at Germany's Bauhaus school in the 1920s; art representing the ancient civilizations of Egypt, the Near East, Greece, and Rome; plus a vast costume and textiles collection dating back to the 16th century.

The Pavilion for Japanese Art showcases scrolls, screens, drawings, paintings, textiles, and decorative arts from Japan; it's a particularly peaceful space, with natural light and a fountain on the ground floor that fills the building with the sound of flowing water. The Bing Center holds a research library, resource center, and film theater. The Boone's Children's Gallery on the soon-to-be "transformed" LACMA West end maintains an art-making mission through classes, interactive displays, and brightly colored decor. ⚠**Temporary exhibits sometimes require tickets purchased in advance, so check the calendar ahead of time.** ⊠*5905 Wilshire Blvd., Miracle Mile* ☏*323/857–6000* ⊕*www.lacma.org* ✉*$12, free 2nd Tues. of month, after-5 policy: "pay what you wish."* ⊙*Mon., Tues., and Thurs. noon–8, Fri. noon–9, weekends 11–8.*

❹ **Petersen Automotive Museum.** You don't have to be a gearhead to appreciate this building full of antique and unusual cars. The Petersen is likely
to be one of the coolest museums in town with its take on some of the
most unusual creations on wheels and rotating exhibits of the icons
who drove them. ⊠ *6060 Wilshire Blvd., Miracle Mile* ☎ *323/930–
2277* ⊕ *www.petersen.org* ⊒ *$10* ☉ *Tues.–Sun. 10–6.*

Fodor'sChoice
★

WEST HOLLYWOOD

West Hollywood is not a place to see things (like museums or movie
studios) as much as it is a place to do things—like go to a nightclub,
eat at a world-famous restaurant, or attend an art gallery opening. Also
thriving is an important interior-design and art-gallery trade. West Hollywood has always attracted the mavericks and the disenfranchised,
and in the 1980s, a coalition of seniors, gays, and lesbians spearheaded
a grassroots effort to bring cityhood to West Hollywood, which was
still an unincorporated part of Los Angeles County. The coalition succeeded in 1984, and today West Hollywood is one of the most progressive cities in Southern California. It's also one of the most gay-friendly
cities anywhere, with one-third of its population estimated to be either
gay or lesbian.

WHAT TO SEE

❹ **Avenues of Art and Design.** Established in 1996, the area where Melrose
Avenue and Robertson and Beverly boulevards become their own little
district creates the Avenues of Art & Design with the distinction of
being where fine, decorative, and culinary arts cater to the aestheti-
cally minded. Clustered here are more than 300 businesses, including
more than 30 art galleries; 100 antique, contemporary furniture, and
interior design stores; and 40 restaurants. While most galleries in this
pedestrian-friendly area are very high-end, it doesn't cost anything to
window-shop. For one Saturday in June, the Avenues of Art & Design
hosts the annual Art & Design Walk to give shoppers a chance to
let loose in some of the hottest boutiques like John Varvatos, Phyllis
Morris, James Perse, and Williams-Sonoma Home. ■TIP➔ **Periodically,
usually on the first Saturday evening of the month, several of the galleries
host group-opening receptions, known as Gallery Walks, to premiere new
exhibits and artists. Contact the West Hollywood Convention and Visitors
Bureau for information.** ☎ *310/289–2525 or 800/368–6020* ⊕ *www.
avenuesartdesign.com.*

❸ **Pacific Design Center.** Cesar Pelli designed these two architecturally
intriguing buildings, one sheathed in blue glass (known as the Blue
Whale), the other in green (the Green Whale). Together, they house 150
design showrooms, making this the largest interior design complex in
the western United States. Though focused on the professional trade
(meaning only pro decorators can shop the showrooms), the PDC has
become more open over the past few years, with public events and
some showroom access. Construction started on the new red building
in the fall of 2007 with plans to open sometime at the end of 2010. The
Downtown Museum of Contemporary Art has a small satellite **MOCA**

Gallery (☎310/289–5233 ⊕*www.moca.org*) here that showcases current artists and designers and hosts exhibit-related talks. Three cafés on the premises are also open to the public. ✉*8687 Melrose Ave., West Hollywood* ☎*310/657–0800* ⊕*www.pacificdesigncenter.com* ⊙*Weekdays 9–5.*

5 **Sunset Boulevard.** One of the most fabled avenues in the world, Sunset Boulevard began humbly enough in the 18th century as a route from El Pueblo de Los Angeles (today's Downtown L.A.) to the ranches in the west and then to the Pacific Ocean. Now as it winds its way across the L.A. basin to the ocean, it cuts through gritty urban neighborhoods and what used to be the working center of Hollywood's movie industry. In West Hollywood, it becomes the sexy and seductive Sunset Strip, then slips quietly into the tony environs of Beverly Hills and Bel-Air, twisting and winding past gated estates. Continuing on past UCLA in Westwood, through Brentwood and Pacific Palisades, Sunset finally descends to the beach, the edge of the continent, and the setting sun.

6 **Sunset Strip.** For 60 years the Hollywood's night owls have headed for
★ the 1¾-mi stretch of Sunset Boulevard between Crescent Heights Boulevard on the east and Doheny Drive on the west, known as the Sunset Strip. In the 1930s and '40s, stars such as Tyrone Power, Errol Flynn, Norma Shearer, and Rita Hayworth came for wild evenings of dancing and drinking at nightclubs like Trocadero, Ciro's, and Mocambo. By the '60s and '70s, the Strip had become the center of rock and roll for acts like Johnny Rivers, the Byrds, and the Doors. The '80s punk riot gave way to hair metal lead by Mötley Crüe and Guns N' Roses on the stages of the **Whisky A Go-Go** (✉*8901 Sunset Blvd., West Hollywood* ☎*310/652–4202* ⊕*www.whiskyagogo.com*) and **The Roxy** (✉*9009 Sunset Blvd., West Hollywood* ☎*310/276–2222* ⊕*www. theroxyonsunset.com*). Nowadays it's the **Viper Room** (✉*8852 Sunset Blvd., West Hollywood* ☎*310/358–1880* ⊕*www.viperroom.com*), the **House of Blues** (✉*8430 Sunset Blvd., West Hollywood* ☎*323/848–5100* ⊕*www.hob.com*), and the **Key Club** (✉*9039 Sunset Blvd., West Hollywood* ☎*310/274–5800* ⊕*www.keyclub.com*), where you'll find on-the-cusp actors, rock stars, club-hopping regulars, and out-of-towners all mingling over drinks and live music. Parking and traffic around the Strip can be tough on weekends, expect to pay around $10–$25 to park, which can take a bite out of your partying budget, but the time and money may be worth it if you plan to make the rounds—most clubs are within walking distance of each other.

BEVERLY HILLS & CENTURY CITY

If you only have a day to see L.A., see Beverly Hills. Love it or hate it, it delivers on a dramatic, cinematic scale of wealth and excess. Beverly Hills is the town's biggest movie star, and she always lets those willing to part with a few bills into her year-round party. Just remember to bring your sunscreen, sunglasses . . . and money for parking. Boutiques and restaurants line the palm tree–fringed sidewalks. People tend to stroll, not rush. Shopping ranges from the accessible and familiar

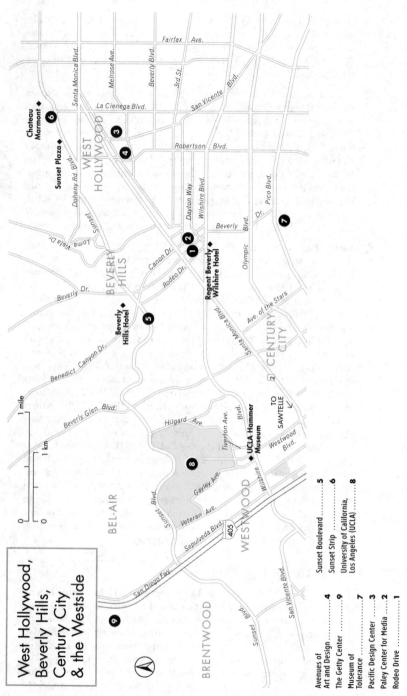

**West Hollywood,
Beverly Hills,
Century City
& the Westside**

(Pottery Barn) to the unique, expensive, and architectural. (Prada on Rodeo Drive).

A few blocks west on Santa Monica Boulevard is Beverly Hills' down brother, Century City. If Beverly Hills is about spending money, Century City is about making it. This collection of glass office towers and a favorite outdoor mall is home to entertainment companies, law firms, and investment corporations. It's a peculiarly precise place, with angular fountains, master-planned boulevards, and pedestrian bridges connecting lawyers to their turkey tahini wraps.

WHAT TO SEE

❷ Paley Center for Media. Formerly the Museum of Television and Radio, ★ this institution changed its name in 2007 with a look toward a future that encompasses all media in the ever-evolving world of entertainment and information. Reruns are taken to a curated level in this sleek stone-and-glass building, designed by Getty architect Richard Meier. A sister to the New York location, the Paley Center carries a duplicate of its collection: more than 100,000 programs spanning eight decades. Search for your favorite commercials and television shows on easy-to-use computers. A radio program listening room provides cozy seats supplied with headphones playing snippets of a variety of programming from a toast to Dean Martin to an interview with John Lennon. Frequent seminars with movers 'n' shakers from the film, television and radio world are big draws, as well as screenings of documentaries and short films. Free parking is available in the lot off Santa Monica Blvd. ⊠ *465 N. Beverly Dr., Beverly Hills* ☎ *310/786–1000* ⊕ *www. paleycenter.org* ⊗ *Wed.–Sun. noon–5.*

❶ Rodeo Drive. The ultimate shopping indulgence—Rodeo Drive is one of FodorsChoice Southern California's bona fide tourist attractions; here you can shop ★ for five-digit jewelry or a $35 handbag. The arts of window-shopping and window displays play out among the retail elite: Tiffany & Co., Gucci, Jimmy Choo, Valentino, Harry Winston, Prada . . . you get the picture. Several nearby restaurants have patios where you can sip a drink while watching career shoppers in their size 2 threads saunter by with shopping bags stuffed with superfluous delights. At the southern end of Rodeo Drive (at Wilshire Boulevard) is **Via Rodeo,** a curvy cobblestone street designed to resemble a European shopping area or a Universal Studio backlot—take your pick. The holidays bring a special magic to Rodeo and the surrounding streets with twinkling lights, swinging music, and colorful banners. ⊠ *Beverly Hills.*

THE WESTSIDE

For some privileged Los Angelenos, the city begins west of La Cienega Boulevard, where keeping up with the Joneses becomes an epic pursuit. Chic, attractive neighborhoods with coveted postal codes—Bel-Air, Brentwood, Westwood, West Los Angeles, and Pacific Palisades—are home to power couples pushing power kids in power strollers. Still, the Westside is rich in culture—and not just entertainment-industry culture. It's home to UCLA, the monumental Getty Center, and the engrossing Museum of Tolerance.

WHAT TO SEE

9 ☉ **The Getty Center.** With its curving walls and isolated hilltop perch, the Getty Center resembles a pristine fortified city of its own. You may have been lured up by the beautiful views of L.A. (on a clear day stretching all the way to the Pacific Ocean), but the architecture, uncommon gardens, and fascinating art collections will be more than enough to capture and hold your attention. When the sun is out, the complex's rough-cut travertine marble skin seems to soak up the light. You'll need to do some advance planning, since parking reservations are sometimes required during vacation periods, but the experience is well worth the effort.

Fodor'sChoice ★

Getting to the center involves a bit of anticipatory lead-up. At the base of the hill, a pavilion disguises the underground parking structure. From there you either walk or take a smooth, computer-driven tram up the steep slope, checking out the Bel-Air estates across the humming 405 freeway. The five pavilions that house the museum surround a central courtyard and are bridged by walkways. From the courtyard, plazas, and walkways, you can survey the city from the San Gabriel Mountains to the ocean.

Inside the pavilions are the galleries for the permanent collections of European paintings, drawings, sculpture, illuminated manuscripts, and decorative arts, as well as American and European photographs. The Getty's collection of French furniture and decorative arts, especially from the early years of Louis XIV (1643–1715) to the end of the reign of Louis XVI (1774–92), is renowned for its quality and condition; you can see a pair of completely reconstructed salons. In the paintings galleries, a computerized system of louvered skylights allows natural light to filter in, creating a closer approximation of the conditions in which the artists painted. Notable among the paintings are Rembrandt's *The Abduction of Europa,* Van Gogh's *Irises,* Monet's *Wheatstack, Snow Effects,* and *Morning,* and James Ensor's *Christ's Entry into Brussels.*

If you want to start with a quick overview, pick up the brochure in the entrance hall that guides you to 15 highlights of the collection. There's also an instructive audio tour ($3) with commentaries by art historians. Art information rooms with multimedia computer stations contain more details about the collections. The complex includes an upscale restaurant (reservations required) with panoramic window views, and two outdoor coffee bars. ■ TIP→On-site parking is subject to availability and usually fills up by late afternoon on holidays and summer weekends, so try to come early in the day. You may also take public transportation (MTA Bus 561 or Santa Monica Big Blue Bus 14). ✉ *1200 Getty Center Dr., Brentwood* ☎ *310/440–7300* ⊕ *www.getty.edu* ✉ *Free, parking $8* ☉ *Tues.–Thurs. and Sun. 10–6, Fri. and Sat. 10–9.*

7 **Museum of Tolerance.** Using interactive technology, this important museum (part of the Simon Wiesenthal Center) challenges visitors to confront bigotry and racism. One of the most affecting sections covers the Holocaust, with film footage of deportation scenes and simulated sets of concentration camps. Each visitor is issued a "passport" bearing the name of a child whose life was dramatically changed by the German Nazi rule and by World War II; as you go through the exhibit, you learn the fate of that child. Anne Frank artifacts are part of the museum's permanent collection. Interactive exhibits include the "Millennium Machine," which engages visitors in finding solutions to human rights abuses around the world, and the "Point of View Diner," a re-creation of a 1950s diner, red booths and all, that "serves" a menu of controversial topics on video jukeboxes. Recent renovations brought a new youth action floor and revamped 300-seat theater space. To ensure a visit to this popular museum, make reservations in advance (especially for Friday, Sunday, and holidays) and plan to spend at least three hours there. Testimony from Holocaust survivors is offered at specified times. Museum entry stops at least two hours before the actual closing time. A photo ID is required for admission, and all visitors must go through a security search. ⊠ *9786 W. Pico Blvd., just south of Beverly Hills* ☎ *310/553–8403* ⊕ *www.museumoftolerance.com* ⌦ *$13* ☉ *Sun.– Thurs. 11–4, Fri. 11–3.*

❽ University of California, Los Angeles (UCLA). With spectacular buildings such as a Romanesque library, the parklike UCLA campus makes for a fine stroll through one of California's most prestigious universities. In the heart of the north campus, the **Franklin Murphy Sculpture Garden** contains more than 70 works of artists such as Henry Moore and Gaston Lachaise. The **Mildred Mathias Botanic Garden,** which contains some 5,000 species of plants from all over the world in a 7-acre outdoor garden, is in the southeast section of the campus and is accessible from Tiverton Avenue. West of the main-campus bookstore, the **Morgan Center Hall of Fame** displays the sports memorabilia and trophies of the university's athletic departments. Many visitors head straight to the **Fowler Museum at UCLA** (☎ *310/825–4361* ⊕ *www.fowler.ucla.edu*), which presents exhibits on the world's diverse cultures and visual arts, especially those of Africa, Asia, Oceania, and Native and Latin America. Museum admission is free; use parking lot 4 off Sunset Boulevard ($8). It's open Wednesday–Sunday noon–5, Thursday until 8 PM.

Campus maps and information are available at drive-by kiosks at major entrances daily, and free 90-minute walking tours of the campus are given on weekdays at 10:15 and 2:15 and Saturday at 10:15. Call 310/825–8764 for reservations, which are required several days to two weeks in advance. The campus has cafés, plus bookstores selling UCLA Bruins paraphernalia. The main-entrance gate is on Westwood Boulevard. Campus parking costs $8. ⊠ *Bordered by Le Conte, Hilgard, and Gayley Aves. and Sunset Blvd., Westwood* ⊕ *www.ucla.edu.*

SANTA MONICA, VENICE & MALIBU

Hugging the Santa Monica Bay in an arch, the desirable communities of Malibu, Santa Monica, and Venice move from the ultrarich, ultracasual Malibu to the bohemian/seedy Venice. What they have in com-

mon, however, is cleaner air, mild temperatures, horrific traffic, and an emphasis on the beach-focused lifestyle that many people consider the hallmark of Southern California.

WHAT TO SEE

⑤ Getty Villa Malibu. Feeding off the cultures of ancient Rome, Greece, and Etruria, the remodeled Getty Villa opened in 2006 with much fanfare—and some controversy concerning the acquisition and rightful ownership of some of the Italian artifacts on display. The antiquities are astounding, but on a first visit even they take a backseat to their environment. This megamansion sits on some of the most valuable coastal property in the world. Modeled after an Italian country home, the Villa dei Papiri in Herculaneum, the Getty Villa includes beautifully manicured gardens, reflecting pools, and statuary. The largest and most lovely garden, the Outer Peristyle, gives you glorious views over a rectangular reflecting pool and geometric hedges to the Pacific. The new structures blend thoughtfully into the rolling terrain and significantly improve the public spaces, such as the new outdoor amphitheater, gift store, café, and entry arcade. ■**TIP→An advance timed entry ticket is required for admission. Tickets are free and may be ordered from the Web site or by phone.** ⊠*17985 Pacific Coast Hwy., Pacific Palisades*

*Fodor's*Choice
★

☎ *310/440–7300* ⊕ *www.getty.edu* 🎟 *Free, reservations required. Parking $8, cash only* ☉ *Thurs.–Mon. 10–5.*

❹ Malibu Lagoon State Beach. Bird-watchers, take note: in this 5-acre marshy area you could spot egrets, blue herons, avocets, and gulls. (You'll need to stay on the boardwalks so as not to disturb their habitats.) The path leads out to a rocky stretch of beach and makes for a pleasant stroll. You're also likely to spot a variety of marine life. The lagoon is open 24 hours and is particularly enjoyable in the early morning and at sunset. The parking lot has limited hours but street-side parking is usually available at off-peak times. ✉ *23200 Pacific Coast Hwy., Malibu.*

❶ Santa Monica Pier. Souvenir shops, a psychic adviser, carnival games, arcades, eateries, and **Pacific Park** are all part of this truncated pier at the foot of Colorado Boulevard below Palisades Park. The pier's trademark 46-horse Looff Carousel, built in 1922, has appeared in several films, including *The Sting.* Free concerts are held on the pier in summer. ✉ *Colorado Ave. and the ocean, Santa Monica* ☎ *310/458–8900* ⊕ *www.santamonicapier.org* 🎟 *Rides $1* ☉ *Carousel hrs vary depending on season and weather conditions, call ahead.*

❷ Third Street Promenade. Stretch your legs along this pedestrians-only
★ three-block stretch of 3rd Street, just a whiff away from the Pacific, lined with jacaranda trees, ivy-topiary dinosaur fountains, strings of lights, and branches of nearly every major U.S. retail chain. Outdoor cafés, street vendors, movie theaters, and a rich nightlife make this a main gathering spot for locals and visitors, as well as street musicians and performance artists. Plan a night just to take it all in or take an afternoon for a long people-watching stroll. There's plenty of parking in city structures on the streets flanking the promenade. ✉ *3rd St. between Wilshire Blvd. and Broadway, Santa Monica* ⊕ *www.third streetpromenade.com.*

❸ Venice Boardwalk. "Boardwalk" may be something of a misnomer—it's
Fodor'sChoice really a five-block section of paved walkway—but this L.A. mainstay
★ delivers year-round action. Bicyclists zip along and bikini-clad rollerbladers attract crowds as they put on impromptu demonstrations, vying for attention with magicians, fortune-tellers, a chain-saw juggler, and sand mermaids. At the adjacent Muscle Beach, bulging bodybuilders with an exhibitionist streak pump iron at an outdoor gym. You can rent in-line skates, roller skates, and bicycles (some with baby seats) at the south end of the boardwalk (officially known as Ocean Front Walk), along Washington Street near the Venice Pier.

THE SAN FERNANDO VALLEY

Some Angelenos swear, with a sneer, that they have never set foot in "the Valley." But without the dreaded Valley, the world would be without Disney, Warner Bros., Universal Studios, NBC, *Seinfeld, Desperate Housewives,* and a large chunk of pornography. In fact, nearly 70% of all entertainment productions in L.A. happen here. That means that some very rich entertainment executives regularly undergo sweltering

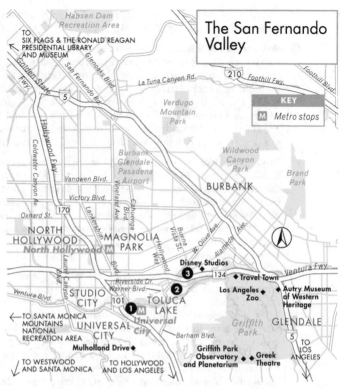

The San Fernando Valley

KEY

Ⓜ Metro stops

summer temperatures, smog, and bumper-to-bumper traffic on their trek from their Westside and Malibu compounds to their less glamorous workplaces.

WHAT TO SEE

❸ **NBC Television Studios.** In the entertainment sector of Burbank, the NBC studios is home to some of TVs most popular talk shows, soap operas, and news broadcasts. An hour-long tour gives you behind-the-scenes access to shows including the *Tonight Show with Jay Leno, Days of Our Lives,* the *Ellen DeGeneres Show, Access Hollywood,* and L.A. studios for the *Today Show* and other news programs. If you'd like to be part of a live studio audience, free tickets are available for tapings of the various NBC shows. ✉*3000 W. Alameda Ave., Burbank* ☎*818/840–3537* ☞*Tours $8.50.*

★ **The Ronald Reagan Presidential Library and Museum.** On 100 acres high up in the hills of Simi Valley is the final resting place of President Ronald Reagan, along with an extensive museum that chronicles his early days as a Hollywood movie star, the two terms he served as governor of California, and his journey to the presidency. A massive new pavilion shelters the Air Force One plane that flew Reagan and six other presidents from 1973–2001. Give yourself a good three hours to get through it all; a guided tour is your best bet. Don't forget to step outside to take time to enjoy the spectacular views and pay your respects at Reagan's gravesite. The library holds more than 50 million pages of presidential papers, photographs, film, video, audio, and books. It takes at least half an hour to drive here from Downtown L.A. ✉*40 Presidential Dr., Simi Valley* ☏*800/410–8354* ⊕*www.reaganfoundation. org* ⊡*$12* ⊗*Daily 10–5.*

Santa Monica Mountains National Recreation Area. The line that forms the boundary of the San Fernando Valley is one of the most famous thoroughfares in this vast metropolis. **Mulholland Drive** cuts through the Santa Monica Mountains National Recreation Area, a vast parkland that stretches along the top and west slopes of the Santa Monica Mountains from Hollywood to the Ventura County line. Driving the length of the hilltop road is slow and can be treacherous, but the rewards are sensational views of valley and city on each side and expensive homes along the way. The park incorporates several local and state parks, including Will Rogers and Malibu Lagoon. Large scenic portions of these oak-studded hills were owned at one time by such Hollywood stars as Ronald Reagan and Bob Hope. They provided location sites for many movies; the grassy rolling hillside continues to serve as a stand-in for the Wild West. Sets at the **Paramount Ranch** backlot (✉*2813 Cornell Rd., Agoura Hills, 91301*) have been preserved and continue to be used as location sites. Rangers regularly conduct tours of the Paramount Ranch, where you can see sets used by *MASH* and *Dr. Quinn, Medicine Woman.* This expansive area provides plenty of hiking and picnicking trails. Pick up a map in the ranger's station. To reach Mulholland Drive from Hollywood, go via Outpost Drive off Franklin Avenue or Cahuenga Boulevard west via Highland Avenue north. Note that it changes from Mulholland Drive to Mulholland Highway when you cross Calabasas. It ends at the coast north of Zuma Beach near Ventura. Keep an eye out for riders on horses as well as deer, raccoons, or a rare mountain lion along the way. Note: The visitor center is located outside of the park area. ✉*401 W. Hillcrest Dr., Thousand Oaks 91360* ☏*805/370–2301* ⊡*Free* ⊗*Daily 9–5.*

❶ **Universal Studios Hollywood.** While most first-time Los Angeles visitors ⟳ consider this to be a must-see stop, bear in mind there many other ★ attractions that define Hollywood without the steep prices and tourist traps found here. Despite the amusement park clichés, hard-core sightseeing and entertainment junkies will make this required visiting. ■ **TIP➔** If you get here when the park opens, you'll likely save yourself from long waits in line—arriving early pays off.

The first-timer favorite is the tram tour, during which you can experience the parting of the Red Sea, take a trip to old Mexico and Little Israel, duck from spitting creatures in Jurassic Park, visit *Desperate Housewives* neighborhood and Dr. Seuss's "Whoville," escape a thunderstorm and flood; see the airplane wreckage of *War of the Worlds*, see the still-creepy *Psycho* house, meet a 30-foot-tall version of King Kong; be attacked by the ravenous killer shark of *Jaws* fame; and survive an all-too-real simulation of an earthquake that measures 8.3 on the Richter scale, complete with collapsing earth. The trams have audio-visual monitors that play video clips of the TV shows and movies shot on the sets you pass by as this guided trip circles the 415-acre complex all day long. ■TIP→This tram ride is usually the best place to start, since it's on the lower level of the park, which gets really crowded in the afternoon.

Many attractions are based on Universal films and television shows, designed to give you a thrill in one form or another. Take your pick from the bone-rattling roller coaster *Revenge of the Mummy—The Ride*, the virtual world of *Terminator 2: 3D*, visit a jungle full of dinosaurs in *Jurassic Park—The Ride*, which includes an 84-foot water drop, or experience a simulated warehouse fire in *Backdraft* that is so real you can feel the heat.

Shrek 4-D reunites the film's celebrity voices to pick up where the movie left off in a 15-minute trailer of 3-D animation shown in an action simulation theater. *Fear Factor* Live and the House of Horrors are guaranteed to provide screams, while the Animal Actors show provides milder entertainment courtesy of some talented furry friends. The newest attraction based on the *Simpsons* animated series, opened in summer 2008, takes you on a journey like no other through their Springfield neighborhood in a ride that only the beloved, albeit cantankerous, Krusty the Klown could dream up.

Throughout the park you'll wander through prop-style settings of a French Village or travel back in time to the good ol' '50s, as costumed characters mingle with guests and pose for photos. Aside from the park, CityWalk is a separate venue, where you'll find a slew of shops, restaurants, nightclubs, and movie theaters, including IMAX 3-D. ⊠*100 Universal City Plaza, Universal City* ☎*818/622–3801* ⊕*www. universalstudioshollywood.com* ✉*$64, parking $10* ⊙*Contact park for seasonal hrs.*

❷ **Warner Bros. Studios.** If you're looking for a more authentic behind-the-scenes look at how films and TV shows are made, head to this major studio center. There aren't many bells and whistles here, but you'll get a much better idea of production work than you will at Universal Studios. You start with a short film on Warner Bros. movies and TV shows, then hop into a tram for a ride through the sets and soundstages of such favorites as *Friends, Gilmore Girls, ER, Casablanca,* and *Rebel Without a Cause.* You'll see the bungalows where icons such as Marlon Brando and Bette Davis spent time between shots, and the current production offices for Clint Eastwood and George Clooney. You might even spot a celeb or see a shoot in action—tours change from day to day depending on the productions taking place on the lot. Reservations are required. Call at least one week in advance and ask about provisions for people with disabilities; children under 8 are not admitted. Tours are given at least every hour, more frequently from May to September. A five-hour deluxe tour is available for $150, which includes a VIP lunch and allows visitors to spend more time on the sets, thus more ops for behind-the-scenes peeks and star spotting. ⊠*3400 W.*

SIX FLAGS MAGIC MOUNTAIN

True thrill seekers looking for "monster" rides and breathtaking roller coasters come to this anti-Disney amusement park for several of the biggest, fastest, and scariest in the world. The aptly named Scream, for instance, drops you 150 feet and tears through a 128-foot vertical loop. Superman: The Escape is a 41-story coaster that hurtles you from 0 to 100 mph in less than seven seconds. On Riddler's Revenge, the world's tallest and fastest stand-up roller coaster, you stand for a mile-long 65-mph total panic attack. Batman the Ride puts you on ski lift-style trains suspended from a track above to provide a zero-gravity, nothing-under-your-feet, flying experience as you sail through hairpin turns and vertical loops. In 2008, the Park's popular coaster, X, was transformed and reopened as X2, complete with sleeker trains and a one-of-a-kind tunnel and light show. Beloved children's icon Thomas The Tank Engine and his friends entertain kids at Thomas Town or take them to meet their favorite Looney Tunes characters in Bugs Bunny World. Shows, dining, parades, younger kids' rides, and those scream-inducing roller coasters make it a full day on this massive park (be sure to wear your walking shoes and brace yourself for some of the hilly areas).

Weekends are peak times here, so be prepared to stand in line for the more popular rides. (In warm weather, be sure you have sunscreen and water.) Save $20 and pass the long lines upon arrival by purchasing and printing your tickets ahead of time from the Web site. This place is also popular with teenagers so be prepared to pass plenty of loud packs, or just send your own here to have a day away from the parents. If your trip falls during one of L.A.'s heat waves and you need a place to cool down (and don't mind communal pools), you can hop over to its sister theme park, Six Flags Hurricane Harbor, right next door, and for $16.99 take a slippery cool trip down its massive waterslides. Rumor has it Six Flags is possibly selling and closing the park in the near future to make way for condos and homes in this desirable location—so call ahead. ✉ *26101 Magic Mountain Pkwy., off I–5, 25 mi northwest of Universal Studios and 36 mi outside L.A., Valencia* ☎ *661/255–4100* ⊕ *www.sixflags.com* ✎ *$60, parking $15* ☉ *Mid-Mar.–mid-Sept., daily; mid-Sept.–early Mar., weekends; call for hrs.*

Riverside Dr., Burbank ☎*818/972–8687* ⊕*www.wbsf.com* ✎*$45* ☉ *Weekdays 8:30–4.*

PASADENA AREA

Although seemingly absorbed into the general Los Angeles sprawl, Pasadena is a separate and distinct city. Noted for its Tournament of Roses, seen around the world each New Year's Day, the city brims with noteworthy spots, from its gorgeous Craftsman homes to its exceptional museums, particularly the Norton Simon and the Huntington Library, Art Collections, and Botanical Gardens. Where else can you see a Chaucer manuscript and rare cacti in one place?

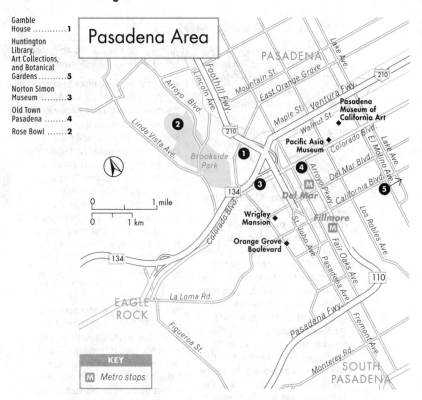

WHAT TO SEE

❶ **Gamble House.** Built by Charles and Henry Greene in 1908, this is a
★ spectacular example of American Arts and Crafts bungalow architecture. The term *bungalow* can be misleading, since the Gamble House is a huge three-story home. To wealthy Easterners such as the Gambles (as in Procter & Gamble), this type of vacation home seemed informal compared with their mansions back home. What makes admirers swoon is the incredible amount of handcraftsmanship, including a teak staircase and cabinetry, Greene & Greene–designed furniture, and an Emil Lange glass door. The dark exterior has broad eaves, with sleeping porches on the second floor. An hour-long, docent-led tour of the Gamble's interior will draw your eye to the exquisite details. If you want to see more Greene & Greene homes, buy a self-guided tour map of the neighborhood in the bookstore. ⊠ *4 Westmoreland Pl., Pasadena* ☎ *626/793-3334* ⊕ *www.gamblehouse.org* ✉ *$10* ☉ *Thurs.–Sun. noon–3; tickets go on sale Thurs.–Sat. at 10, Sun. at 11:30. 1-hr tour every 20 min.*

❺ **Huntington Library, Art Collections, and Botanical Gardens.** If you have time
Fodor's Choice for only one stop in the Pasadena area, it should be the Huntington,
★ built in the early 1900s as the home of railroad tycoon Henry E. Huntington. Henry and his wife, Arabella (who was his aunt by marriage),

voraciously collected rare books and manuscripts, botanical specimens, and 18th-century British art. The institution they established became one of the most extraordinary cultural complexes in the world. ■TIP➜ Ongoing gallery renovations occasionally require some works from the permanent collection to be shifted to other buildings for display.

Among the highlights are John Constable's intimate *View on the Stour near Dedham* and the monumental *Sarah Siddons as the Tragic Muse,* by Joshua Reynolds. In the Virginia Steele Scott Gallery of American Art you can see paintings by Mary Cassatt, Frederic Remington, and more.

The library contains more than 700,000 books and 4 million manuscripts, including such treasures as a Gutenberg Bible, the Ellesmere manuscript of Chaucer's *Canterbury Tales,* George Washington's genealogy in his own handwriting, scores of works by William Blake, and a world-class collection of early editions of Shakespeare. You'll find some of these items in the Library Hall with more than 200 important works on display. In 2006 the library acquired more than 60,000 rare books and reference volumes from the Cambridge, Massachusetts–based Bundy Library, making the Huntington the source of one of the biggest history of science collections in the world.

Although the art collections are increasingly impressive here, don't resist being lured outside into the stunning Botanical Gardens. From the main buildings, lawns and towering trees stretch out toward specialty areas. The 10-acre Desert Garden, for instance, has one of the world's largest groups of mature cacti and other succulents, arranged by continent. Visit this garden on a cool morning or in the late afternoon—a hot midday walk may be a little too authentic. In the Japanese Garden, an arched bridge curves over a pond; the area also has stone ornaments, a Japanese house, a bonsai court, and a Zen rock garden. There are collections of azaleas and 1,500 varieties of camellias. The 3-acre rose garden is displayed chronologically, so the development leading to modern varieties of roses can be observed; on the grounds is the charming **Rose Garden Tea Room,** where traditional afternoon tea is served. There are also herb, palm, and jungle gardens, plus the Shakespeare Garden, which blooms with plants mentioned in Shakespeare's works.

The Rose Hills Foundation Conservatory for Botanical Science, a massive greenhouse-style center with dozens of kid-friendly, hands-on exhibits, illustrates plant diversity in various environments. (These rooms are quite warm and humid, especially the central rotunda, which displays rain-forest plants.) The new Bing Children's Garden is a tiny tots' wonderland filled with opportunities for children to explore the ancient elements of water, fire, air, and earth. A classical Chinese Garden "Liu Fang Yuan" (or Garden of Flowing Fragrance) opened in spring 2008, the largest of its kind outside China. Work on this will continue for the next several years. A 1¼-hour guided tour of the botanical gardens is led by docents at posted times, and a free brochure with map and highlights is available in the entrance pavilion. ✉*1151 Oxford Rd., San Marino* ☎*626/405–2100* ⊕*www.huntington.*

org ⊠*$15 weekdays, $20 weekends, free 1st Thurs. of month* ⏱*Tues.–*
Fri. noon–4:30, weekends 10:30–4:30.

❸ **Norton Simon Museum.** Long familiar to television viewers of the New
Fodor'sChoice Year's Day Rose Parade, this low-profile brown building is more than
★ just a background for the passing floats. It's one of the finest small
museums anywhere, with an excellent collection that spans more than
2,000 years of Western and Asian art. It all began in the 1950s when
Norton Simon (Hunt-Wesson Foods, McCalls Corporation, and Canada Dry) started collecting the works of Degas, Renoir, Gauguin, and
Cézanne. His collection grew to include old masters, impressionists,
and modern works from Europe and Indian and Southeast Asian art.
After he retired, Simon reorganized the failing Pasadena Art Institute
and continued to assemble one of the world's finest collections.

Today the Norton Simon Museum is richest in works by Rembrandt,
Goya, Picasso, and, most of all, Degas: this is one of the only two
U.S. institutions to hold the complete set of the artist's model bronzes
(the other is New York's Metropolitan Museum of Art). Renaissance,
baroque, and rococo masterpieces include Raphael's profoundly spiritual *Madonna with Child with Book* (1503), Rembrandt's *Portrait of
a Bearded Man in a Wide-Brimmed Hat* (1633), and a magical Tiepolo
ceiling, *The Triumph of Virtue and Nobility Over Ignorance* (1740–
50). The museum's collections of impressionist (Van Gogh, Matisse,
Cézanne, Monet, Renoir) and cubist (Braque, Gris) works are extensive. Several Rodin sculptures are placed throughout the museum.
Head down to the bottom floor to see rotating exhibits and phenomenal Southeast Asian and Indian sculptures and artifacts, where graceful pieces like a Ban Chiang blackware vessel date to well before 1000
BC. Don't miss a living artwork outdoors: the garden, conceived by
noted southern California landscape designer Nancy Goslee Power.
The tranquil pond was inspired by Monet's gardens at Giverny. ⊠*411
W. Colorado Blvd., Pasadena* ☎*626/449–6840* ⊕*www.nortonsimon.
org* ⊠*$8* ⏱*Wed., Thurs., and Sat.–Mon. noon–6, Fri. noon–9.*

❹ **Old Town Pasadena.** Once the victim of decay, the area was revitalized
★ in the 1990s as a blend of restored 19th-century brick buildings with
a contemporary overlay. A phalanx of chain stores has muscled in, but
there are still some homegrown shops and plenty of tempting cafés and
restaurants. In the evening and on weekends, streets are packed with
people, and Old Town crackles with energy. The 12-block historic district is anchored along Colorado Boulevard between Pasadena Avenue
and Arroyo Parkway.

❷ **Rose Bowl.** With an enormous rose, the city of Pasadena's logo, adorned
on its exterior, it's hard to miss this 100,000-seat stadium, host of many
Super Bowls and home to the UCLA Bruins. Set in Brookside Park at
the wide bottom of an arroyo, the facility is closed except during games
and special events such as the monthly Rose Bowl Swap Meet, which is
considered the granddaddy of West Coast flea markets. ⊠*1001 Rose
Bowl Dr. at Rosemont Ave., Pasadena* ☎*626/577–3100* ⊕*www.rose*

bowlstadium.com ⊠*$7 from 9* AM *on, $10 for 8–9* AM *entrance, $15 for 7–8* AM *entrance.* ⊙*Flea market 2nd Sun. of month 9–4:30.*

LONG BEACH

Long Beach, long stuck in limbo between Los Angeles and Orange County in the minds of visitors, is steadily rebuilding its place in the Southern California scheme. Founded as a seaside resort in the 19th century, the city boomed in the early 20th century as oil discoveries drew in Midwesterners and Dust Bowlers. Bust followed boom and the city took on a somewhat raw, industrial, neglected feel. But a long-term redevelopment plan begun in the 1970s has finally come to fruition, turning the city back to its resort roots.

4

WHAT TO SEE

☾ **Aquarium of the Pacific.** Sea lions, nurse sharks, and octopuses, oh my!—this aquarium focuses primarily on ocean life from the Pacific Ocean, with a detour into Australian birds. The main exhibits include lively sea lions, a crowded tank of various sharks, and ethereal sea dragons, which the aquarium has successfully bred in captivity. Most impressive is the multimedia attraction, *Whales: A Journey with Giants.* This panoramic film shows in the aquarium's Great Hall, and when the entire core of the aquarium goes dark, you suddenly feel as if you're swimming with the giants. Ask for showtimes at the information desk. For a nonaquatic experience, head over to Lorikeet Forest, a walk-in aviary full of the friendliest parrots from down under. Buy a cup of nectar and smile as you become a human bird perch. Since these birds spend most of their day feeding, you're guaranteed a noisy—and possibly messy—encounter. (A sink, soap, and towels are strategically placed at the exhibit exit.) If you're a true animal lover, book an up-close-and-personal Animal Encounters Tour ($90) to learn about and assist in care and feeding of the animals; or find out how aquarium functions with the extensive Behind the Scenes Tour ($31.95); or just opt for an Overview Tour ($10) for a visit with all the details. ⊠*100 Aquarium Way, Long Beach* ☎*562/590-3100* ⊕*www.aquariumofpacific.org* ⊠*$20.95* ⊙*Daily 9–6.*

Queen Mary. This beautifully preserved ocean liner was launched in 1934 and made 1,001 transatlantic crossings before finally berthing in Long Beach in 1967. It has gone through many periods of renovations since, but in 1993, the RMS Foundation took over ownership and restored its original art deco style. Private investors "Save the Queen" took over in early 2008 with plans to oversee ongoing renovations.

On board, you can take one of five tours, such as the informative Behind the Scenes walk or the downright spooky Ghost and Legends tour. You could stay for dinner at one of the ship's restaurants, partake in the utterly English tradition of afternoon tea ($35–$40, monthly themes, call for reservations ☎ *562/499-1772*), or even spend the night in one of the wood-panel rooms. ⊠*1126 Queens Hwy., Long Beach* ☎*562/435-3511* ⊕*www.queenmary.com* ⊠*Tours $24.95–*

$31.95, includes a self-guided audio tour ⊙ *Call for times and frequency of guided tours.*

WHERE TO EAT

BEVERLY HILLS, CENTURY CITY & HOLLYWOOD

BEVERLY HILLS

$-$$
DELI

✕**Barney Greengrass.** Unlike your corner lox-and-bagel joint, this *haute* deli on the fifth floor of Barneys department store has an appropriately runway-ready aesthetic: limestone floors, mahogany furniture, and a wall of windows. On the outdoor terrace, at tables shaded by large umbrellas, you can savor flawless smoked salmon, sturgeon, and whitefish flown in fresh from New York. The deli closes at 6 PM. ⊠ *Barneys, 9570 Wilshire Blvd., Beverly Hills* ☎ *310/777–5877* ⊟ *AE, DC, MC, V.*

$$-$$$
ITALIAN

✕**Enoteca Drago.** High-flying Sicilian chef Celestino Drago scores with this sleek but unpretentious version of an *enoteca* (a wine bar serving small snacks). It's an ideal spot for skipping through an Italian wine list—more than 50 wines are available by the glass—and enjoying a menu made up of small plates such as deep-fried olives, an assortment of cheeses and *salumi*, ricotta-stuffed zucchini flowers, or *crudo* (Italy's answer to ceviche) from the raw bar. Although the miniature mushroom-filled ravioli bathed in foie gras–truffle sauce is a bit luxurious for an enoteca, it's one of the city's best pasta dishes. Larger portions and pizzas are also available here, but the essence of an enoteca is preserved. ⊠ *410 N. Cañon Dr., Beverly Hills* ☎ *310/786–8236* ⚑ *Reservations essential* ⊟ *AE, DC, MC, V.*

$$$$
JAPANESE
Fodor'sChoice
★

✕**Urasawa.** Shortly after celebrated sushi chef Masa Takayama packed his knives for the Big Apple, his soft-spoken protégé Hiroyuki Urasawa settled into the master's former digs. The understated sushi bar has precious few seats, resulting in incredibly personalized service. At a minimum of $275 per person for a strictly *omakase* (chef's choice) meal, Urasawa remains the priciest restaurant in town, but the endless parade of masterfully crafted, exquisitely presented dishes renders few regrets. The maple sushi bar, sanded daily to a satinlike finish, is the scene of a mostly traditional cuisine with magnificent ingredients. You might be served velvety bluefin toro paired with beluga caviar, slivers of foie gras to self-cook *shabu-shabu*–style, or egg custard layered with *uni* (sea urchin), glittering with gold leaf. This is also the place to come during *fugu* season, when the legendary, potentially deadly blowfish is artfully served to adventurous diners. ⊠ *2 Rodeo, 218 N. Rodeo Dr., Beverly Hills* ☎ *310/247–8939* ⚑ *Reservations essential* ⊟ *AE, DC, MC, V* ⊙ *Closed Sun. No lunch.*

$$$$
MODERN
Fodor'sChoice
★

✕**Spago Beverly Hills.** The famed flagship restaurant of Wolfgang Puck, Mr. Celebrity Chef himself, is justifiably a modern L.A. classic. The illustrious restaurant centers on a buzzing outdoor courtyard shaded by 100-year-old olive trees. From an elegantly appointed table inside, you can glimpse the exhibition kitchen and, on rare occasions, the affable owner greeting his famous friends (these days, compliments to the chef

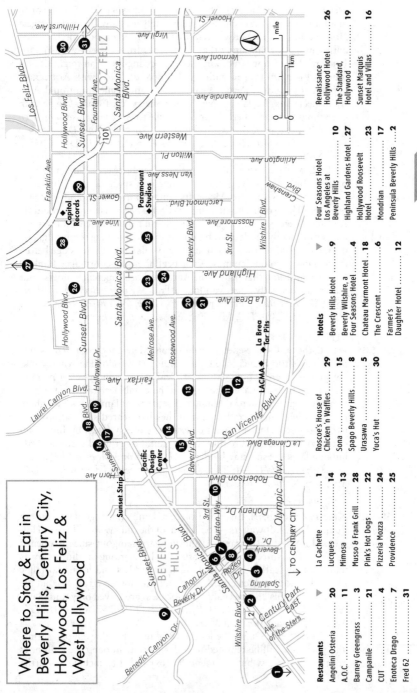

Where to Stay & Eat in Beverly Hills, Century City, Hollywood, Los Feliz & West Hollywood

Restaurants

Angelini Osteria	20
A.O.C.	11
Barney Greengrass	3
Campanile	21
CUT	4
Enoteca Drago	7
Fred 62	31
La Cachette	1
Lucques	14
Mimosa	13
Musso & Frank Grill	28
Pink's Hot Dogs	22
Pizzeria Mozza	24
Providence	25
Roscoe's House of Chicken 'n Waffles	29
Sona	15
Spago Beverly Hills	8
Urasawa	5
Yuca's Hut	30

Hotels

Beverly Hills Hotel	9
Beverly Wilshire, a Four Seasons Hotel	4
Chateau Marmont Hotel	18
The Crescent	6
Farmer's Daughter Hotel	12
Four Seasons Hotel Los Angeles at Beverly Hills	10
Highland Gardens Hotel	27
Hollywood Roosevelt Hotel	23
Mondrian	17
Peninsula Beverly Hills	2
Renaissance Hollywood Hotel	26
The Standard, Hollywood	19
Sunset Marquis Hotel and Villas	16

are directed to Lee Hefter). The people-watching here is worth the price of admission, but the clientele is surprisingly inclusive, from the biggest Hollywood stars to Midwestern tourists to foodies more preoccupied with vintages of Burgundy than with faces from the cover of *People*. Foie gras has disappeared, but the daily-changing menu might offer a four-cheese pizza topped with truffles, *côte de boeuf* with Armagnac-peppercorn sauce, Cantonese-style duck, and some traditional Austrian specialties. Acclaimed pastry chef Sherry Yard works magic with everything from an ethereal apricot soufflé to Austrian *kaiserschmarrn* (crème fraîche pancakes with fruit). ✉*176 N. Cañon Dr., Beverly Hills* ☎*310/385–0880* ⌂*Reservations essential* ▤*AE, D, DC, MC, V* ☽*No lunch Sun.*

$$$$
STEAK
Fodor'sChoice
★

✕**CUT.** In a true collision of artistic titans, celebrity chef Wolfgang Puck presents his take on steak-house cuisine in a space designed by Getty Center architect Richard Meier. Its contemporary lines and cold surfaces recall little of the home comforts of this beloved culinary tradition. And like Meier's design, Puck's fare doesn't dwell much on the past, and a thoroughly modern crab Louis is the closest thing to nostalgia on the menu. Playful dishes like bone marrow flan take center stage before delving into genuine Japanese Kobe beef or a perfect dry-aged hunk of Nebraskan sirloin that proves the Austrian-born superchef understands our quintessentially American love affair. ✉*Regent Beverly Wilshire, 9500 Wilshire Blvd., Beverly Hills* ☎*310/276–8500* ⌂*Reservations essential* ▤*AE, D, DC, MC, V* ☽*Closed Sun. No lunch.*

CENTURY CITY

$$$–$$$$
FRENCH
★

✕**La Cachette.** Owner-chef Jean-François Meteigner, regarded as one of the city's top French chefs (he developed a following while cooking at the revered, now-defunct L'Orangerie), continues to pamper a loyal clientele at La Cachette. Here he combines traditional Gallic fare—foie gras, Provençal bouillabaisse, rack of lamb—with a lighter, more modern cuisine reflected in dishes like seared sea scallops in a harissa–lobster emulsion with couscous. A dressy (well, by L.A. standards) crowd makes sure that this elegant, flower-filled *cachette* (little hiding place) doesn't stay hidden. ✉*10506 Santa Monica Blvd., Century City* ☎*310/470–4992* ⌂*Reservations essential* ▤*AE, D, DC, MC, V* ☽*No lunch weekends.*

HOLLYWOOD

$$–$$$$
AMERICAN

✕**Musso & Frank Grill.** Liver and onions, lamb chops, goulash, shrimp Louis salad, gruff waiters—you'll find all the old favorites here in Hollywood's oldest restaurant. A film-industry hangout since it opened in 1919, Musso & Frank still attracts the working studio set to its maroon faux-leather booths, along with tourists and locals nostalgic for Hollywood's golden era. Great breakfasts are served all day, but the kitchen's famous "flannel cakes" (pancakes) are served only until 3 PM. ✉*6667 Hollywood Blvd., Hollywood* ☎*323/467–7788* ▤*AE, DC, MC, V* ☽*Closed Sun. and Mon.*

¢
AMERICAN
☺

✕**Pink's Hot Dogs.** Orson Welles ate 18 of these hot dogs in one sitting, and you, too, will be tempted to order more than one. The chili dogs are the main draw, but the menu has expanded to include a Martha

Local Chains Worth Stopping For

Cars line up at all hours at **In-N-Out Burger** (many locations), still a family-owned operation (and very possibly America's original drive-thru) whose terrific made-to-order burgers are revered by Angelenos. Satisfy your burger fix by ordering something off the "secret" menu, with variations like "Animal style" (mustard-grilled patty with grilled onions and extra spread) or a "4x4" (four burger patties and four cheese slices for heavy eaters). The company's Web site lists explanations for other popular secret menu items (⊕ www.in-n-out.com).

Tommy's sells a delightfully sloppy chili burger; the original location (✉ 2575 Beverly Blvd., Los Angeles ☎ 213/389–9060) is a no-frills culinary landmark. For rotisserie chicken that will make you forget the Colonel forever, head to **Zankou Chicken** (✉ 5065 Sunset Blvd., Hollywood ☎ 323/665–7845), a small chain noted for its golden crispy-skinned birds, potent garlic sauce, and Armenian specialties. Homesick New Yorkers will appreciate **Jerry's Famous Deli** (✉ 10925 Weyburn Ave., Westwood ☎ 310/208–3354), where the massive menu includes all the classic deli favorites. And **Señor Fish** (✉ 422 E. 1st St., Downtown ☎ 213/625–0566) is known for its healthy Mexican seafood specialties, such as scallop burritos and ceviche tostadas.

Stewart Dog (a 10-inch frank topped with mustard, relish, onions, tomatoes, sauerkraut, bacon, and sour cream). Since 1939 Angelenos and tourists alike have been lining up to plunk down some modest change for one of the greatest guilty pleasures in L.A. Pink's is open until 3 AM on weekends. ✉ 709 N. *La Brea Ave., Beverly–La Brea* ☎ 323/931–4223 ⌕ *Reservations not accepted* ▭ *No credit cards*.

$$
ITALIAN
Fodor's Choice
★

✕ **Pizzeria Mozza.** The other, more casual half of Silverton & Batali's partnership, this casual venue gives newfound eminence to the humble "pizza joint." With traditional Mediterranean items like white anchovies, lardo, squash blossoms, and Gorgonzola, Mozza's pies—thin-crusted delights with golden, blistered edges—are much more Campania than California, and virtually every one is a winner. Utterly simple salads sing with vibrant flavors thanks to superb market-fresh ingredients, and daily specials include crisp duck legs with lentils and *Saba* (a balsamiclike vinegar) or fennel sausage with rapini. Like the menu, the wine list is both interesting and affordable. ✉ 641 N. *Highland Ave., Hollywood* ☎ 323/297–0101 ⌕ *Reservations essential* ▭ *AE, MC, V*.

$$$–$$$$
SEAFOOD
Fodor's Choice
★

✕ **Providence.** Since its opening in 2005, chef-owner Michael Cimarusti has elevated Providence to the ranks of America's finest seafood restaurants. Activity in the elegant dining room, dappled by subtle nautical accents, is smoothly overseen by co-owner–general manager Donato Poto as well-heeled patrons work their way through nine-course tasting menus. Obsessed with quality and freshness, the meticulous chef maintains a network of specialty purveyors, some of whom tip him off to their catch before it even hits the dock. This exquisite seafood then gets the Cimarusti treatment of French technique, traditional American themes, and Asian accents. For instance, you might find an indulgent risotto laced with Santa Barbara sea urchin and Maine lobster, wild salmon from Washington's pristine Quinault River, or big-eye tuna paired with Japanese sword squid, fennel, and oven-dried tomatoes. ✉ *5955 Melrose Ave., Hollywood* ☎ *323/460–4170* ☰ *AE, DC, MC, V* ⊘ *No lunch Mon.–Thurs. and weekends.*

¢–$$ ✗ **Roscoe's House of Chicken 'n Waffles.** The name of this casual eatery
SOUTHERN   may sound a little weird—but don't be put off. Roscoe's is *the* place
�>   for real down-home Southern cooking. Just ask the patrons, who drive from all over L.A. for Roscoe's bargain-price fried chicken, wonderful waffles (which, by the way, turn out to be a great partner for fried chicken), buttery chicken livers, and grits. Although Roscoe's has the intimate feel of a smoky jazz club, those musicians hanging out here are just taking five. ✉ *1514 N. Gower St., Hollywood* ☎ *323/466–7453* ⚴ *Reservations not accepted* ☰ *AE, D, DC, MC, V.*

LOS FELIZ & SILVER LAKE

¢–$$ ✗ **Fred 62.** A tongue-in-cheek take on the American diner created by
ECLECTIC   funky L.A. chef-restaurateur Fred Eric. The usual burgers and shakes
�>   are joined by choices like grilled salmon, Southern-style brisket, and a "Poorest Boy" sandwich (crispy fried chicken, onions, and rémoulade on a French roll). Toasters sit on every table, and breakfasts range from tofu scrambles to "Hunka Hunka Burnin' Love" (pancakes made with peanut butter, chocolate chips, and banana). Like the neighborhood itself, nobody is out of place here, with everybody from button-down businesspeople to tattooed musicians showing up at some point during its 24/7 cycle. ✉ *1850 N. Vermont Ave., Los Feliz* ☎ *323/667–0062* ⚴ *Reservations not accepted* ☰ *AE, DC, MC, V.*

¢   ✗ **Yuca's Hut.** Blink and you'll miss this place, whose reputation far
MEXICAN   exceeds its size (it may be the tiniest place ever to have won a James Beard award). It's known for carne asada, carnitas, and *cochinita pibil* (Yucatán-style roasted pork) tacos and burritos. This is a fast-food restaurant in the finest tradition—independent, family-owned, and sticking to what it does best. The liquor store next door sells lots of Coronas to Hut customers soaking up the sun on the makeshift parking-lot patio. There's no chance of satisfying a late-night craving, though; it closes at 6 PM. ✉ *2056 N. Hillhurst Ave., Los Feliz* ☎ *323/662–1214* ⚴ *Reservations not accepted* ☰ *No credit cards* ⊘ *Closed Sun.*

WEST HOLLYWOOD

$$$$ ✗ **Sona.** Young, intense David Myers—one of the city's most exciting
AMERICAN   and unpredictable chefs—dazzles his fashionable followers here. A
Fodor$Choice   slab of polished granite topped with an exquisite orchid arrangement
★   anchors the sleek dining room. If you're willing to spend the money, the prix-fixe tasting menus ($95 for six courses; $169 for nine) are the way to go, since they allow you to try many of Myers's distinctive dishes. An occasional item is too precious, but the successful dishes win out. Highlights might include seared foie gras paired with beets, kumquats and red wine vinegar ice cream, corn soup with a corn-bacon beignet, tuna au poivre with braised oxtail, and yuzu mousse with edamame

ice cream. ⊠*401 N. La Cienega Blvd., West Hollywood* ☎*310/659–7708* ⌖*Reservations essential* ⊟*AE, D, DC, MC, V* ⊘*Closed Sun. No lunch.*

$$$–$$$$
AMERICAN
★
✕**Lucques.** Formerly silent-film star Harold Lloyd's carriage house, this brick building has morphed into a chic restaurant that has elevated chef/co-owner Suzanne Goin to national prominence. In her veggie-intense contemporary American cooking, Goin uses finesse to balance tradition and invention. Consider the Italian heirloom pumpkin soup with sage and chestnut cream, pancetta-wrapped Alaskan cod with red potatoes, crushed grapes and crème fraîche, and short ribs with horseradish cream. Finish with the likes of acacia honey panna cotta with blood orange granita. ⊠*8474 Melrose Ave., West Hollywood* ☎*323/655–6277* ⌖*Reservations essential* ⊟*AE, MC, V* ⊘*No lunch Sun.*

$$–$$$
FRENCH
Fodor'sChoice
★
✕**Mimosa.** If you're craving a perfect Provençal meal, turn to chef Jean-Pierre Bosc's menu. There's *salade Lyonnaise,* served with a poached egg, a nifty tomato tarte Tatin, probably L.A.'s best bouillabaisse, soulful coq au vin and hearty steak frites. The atmosphere is that of a classic bistro—balanced against a hint of elegance—with mustard walls, cozy banquettes, and crocks of cornichons and olives delivered to every table on arrival. ⊠*8009 Beverly Blvd., West Hollywood* ☎*323/655–8895* ⊟*AE, DC, MC, V* ⊘*Closed Sun. and Mon. No lunch.*

$–$$$
ITALIAN
Fodor'sChoice
★
✕**Angelini Osteria.** You might not guess it from the modest, rather congested dining room, but this is one of L.A.'s most celebrated Italian restaurants. The key is chef-owner Gino Angelini's thoughtful use of superb ingredients, evident in dishes such as a salad of lobster, apples, and pomegranate; and pumpkin tortelli with butter, sage, and asparagus. An awesome lasagna verde, inspired by Angelini's grandmother, is not to be missed. Whole branzino, crusted in sea salt, and boldly flavored rustic specials (e.g., tender veal kidneys, rich oxtail stew) consistently impress. An intelligent selection of mostly Italian wines complements the menu, and desserts like the open-face marmalade tart are baked fresh daily. ⊠*7313 Beverly Blvd., Beverly–La Brea* ☎*323/297–0070* ⊟*AE, MC, V* ⊘*Closed Mon. No lunch weekends.*

$$–$$$$
MEDITERRANEAN
★
✕**Campanile.** Chef-owner Mark Peel has mastered the mix of robust Mediterranean flavors with homey Americana. The 1926 building (which once housed the offices of Charlie Chaplin) exudes a lovely Renaissance charm, and Campanile is one of L.A.'s most acclaimed and beloved restaurants. Appetizers may include butternut squash risotto topped with white truffles, while grilled snapper with Meyer lemon aïoli and prime rib with tapenade are likely to appear as entrées. Thursday night, grilled cheese sandwiches are a huge draw, as the beloved five-and-dime classic is morphed into exotic creations. For an ultimate L.A. experience, come for weekend brunch on the enclosed patio. ⊠*624 S. La Brea Ave., Miracle Mile* ☎*323/938–1447* ⌖*Reservations essential* ⊟*AE, D, DC, MC, V* ⊘*No dinner Sun.*

$$–$$$
MEDITERRANEAN
Fodor'sChoice
★
✕**A.O.C.** Since it opened in 2002, this restaurant and wine bar has revolutionized dining in L.A., pioneering the small-plate format that has now swept the city. The space is dominated by a long, candle-laden bar serving more than 50 wines by the glass. There's also a charcuterie bar, an L.A. rarity. The tapaslike menu is perfectly calibrated for the wine list;

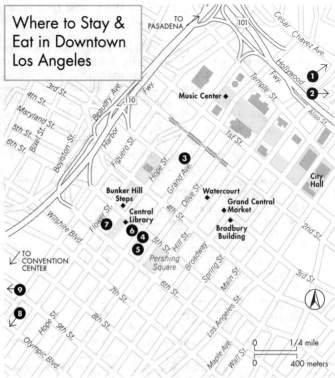

you could pick duck confit, fried oysters with celery root rémoulade, an indulgent slab of pork *rillettes* (a sort of pâté), or just plunge into one of the city's best cheese selections. Named for the acronym for Appellation d'Origine Contrôlée, the regulatory system that ensures the quality of local wines and cheeses in France, A.O.C. upholds the standard of excellence. ⊠*8022 W. 3rd St., south of West Hollywood* ☎*323/653–6359* ⌕*Reservations essential* ⊟*AE, DC, MC, V* ☾*No lunch.*

DOWNTOWN

$$–$$$
AMERICAN
★
✕**Traxx.** Hidden inside historic Union Station, this intimate restaurant is an art deco delight. Its linen-topped tables spill out onto the main concourse. Chef-owner Tara Thomas's menu gussies up popular favorites; for example, crab cakes come with chipotle rémoulade, while pan-roasted Pacific snapper is paired with black rice and jazzed up with a jalapeño vinaigrette. The jacaranda-shaded courtyard is a local secret. A well-stocked bar, occupying what was originally the station's telephone room, is just across the concourse. ⊠*Union Station, 800 N. Alameda St., Downtown* ☎*213/625–1999* ⊟*AE, D, MC, V* ☾*Closed Sun. No lunch Sat.*

¢–$
AMERICAN
✕**Philippe the Original.** L.A.'s oldest restaurant (1908), Philippe claims the French dip sandwich originated here. You can get one made with

☺ beef, pork, ham, lamb, or turkey on a freshly baked roll; the house hot
Fodor'sChoice mustard is as famous as the sandwiches. Its reputation is earned by
★ maintaining traditions, from sawdust on the floor to long communal
tables where customers debate the Dodgers or local politics. The home
cooking—orders are taken at the counter where some of the moth-
erly servers have managed their long lines for decades—includes huge
breakfasts, chili, pickled eggs, and an enormous pie selection. The best
bargain: a cup of java for just 10¢ including tax. ⊠ *1001 N. Alameda
St., Downtown* ☎ *213/628–3781* ⌂ *Reservations not accepted* ⊟ *No
credit cards.*

$$$–$$$$ ✕ **Patina.** In a bold move, chef-owner Joachim Splichal moved his
FRENCH flagship restaurant from Hollywood to downtown's striking Frank
Fodor'sChoice Gehry–designed Walt Disney Concert Hall. His gamble paid off—the
★ contemporary space, surrounded by a rippled "curtain" of rich walnut,
is an elegant, dramatic stage for the acclaimed restaurant's contempo-
rary French cuisine. Specialties include copious amounts of foie gras,
caramelized halibut with mushroom ragoût, olive oil–poached squab
breast with boysenberry gastrique, and a formidable *côte de boeuf* for
two, carved tableside. Finish with a hard-to-match cheese tray (orches-
trated by a genuine *maître fromager*) and sensual desserts. ⊠ *Walt Dis-
ney Concert Hall, 141 S. Grand Ave., Downtown* ☎ *213/972–3331*
⌂ *Reservations essential* ⊟ *AE, D, DC, MC, V No lunch weekends.*

$$$–$$$$ ✕ **Water Grill.** There's a bustling, enticing rhythm here as platters of
SEAFOOD glistening shellfish get whisked from the oyster bar to the cozy can-
★ dlelit booths. Chef David LeFevre's menu shows off his slow-cook-
ing skills. Entrées such as olive oil–poached salmon with a mushroom
vinaigrette and sumac–coated Australian barramundi with calamari-
strewn Israeli couscous and Castelvetrano olives exemplify his light,
sophisticated touch. Excellent desserts and a fine wine list round out
this top-notch dining experience. ⊠ *544 S. Grand Ave., Downtown*
☎ *213/891–0900* ⌂ *Reservations essential* ⊟ *AE, D, DC, MC, V*
⊘ *No lunch weekends.*

COASTAL & WESTERN LOS ANGELES

MALIBU

$$$–$$$$ ✕ **Nobu Malibu.** At famous chef-restaurateur Nobu Matsuhisa's coastal
JAPANESE outpost, the casually chic clientele swarm over morsels of the world's
finest fish. In addition to stellar sushi, Nobu serves many of the same
ingenious specialties offered at his original Matsuhisa in Beverly Hills
or glitzy Nobu in West Hollywood. You'll find exotic species of fish
artfully accented with equally exotic South American peppers, ultra-
tender Kobe beef, and a broth perfumed with rare matsutake mush-
rooms. Elaborate omakase dinners start at $90. ⊠ *3835 Cross Creek
Rd., Malibu* ☎ *310/317–9140* ⌂ *Reservations essential* ⊟ *AE, DC,
MC, V* ⊘ *No lunch.*

SANTA MONICA

$$$–$$$$ ✕ **Wilshire.** The woodsy patio at Wilshire is one of the most coveted
AMERICAN spaces on the L.A. dining circuit—its candlelight, firelight, and gurgling
fountain reel in a hip crowd beneath a cloud of canvas. Chef Christo-

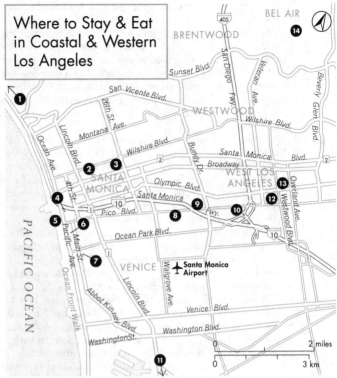

Where to Stay & Eat in Coastal & Western Los Angeles

pher Blobaum is passionate about using organic market-fresh ingredients in dishes like red kuri squash–Asian pear soup with cinnamon cream, a rack of venison with parsnip puree and huckleberry sauce, or Alaskan black cod with roasted cauliflower and white anchovy vinaigrette. The eclectic wine list is first-rate, and there's a lively bar scene here, too. ⊠*2454 Wilshire Blvd., Santa Monica* ☎*310/586–1707* ⌕*Reservations essential* ▤*AE, D, DC, MC, V* ⊘*Closed Sun. No lunch weekends.*

$$$–$$$$　✕**Chinois on Main.** A once-revolutionary outpost in Wolfgang Puck's
ASIAN　　repertoire, this is still one of L.A.'s most crowded—and noisy—restaurants. The jazzy interior is just as loud as the clientele. Although the menu has expanded, the restaurant's happy marriage of Asian and French cuisines shows best in its signature dishes such as Chinois chicken salad, Shanghai lobster with spicy ginger-curry sauce, and Cantonese duck with fresh plum sauce. ⊠*2709 Main St., Santa Monica* ☎*310/392–9025* ⌕*Reservations essential* ▤*AE, D, DC, MC, V* ⊘*No lunch Sat.–Tues.*

$$$$　✕**Mélisse.** In a city where informality reigns, this is one of L.A.'s more
FRENCH　　dressy—but not stuffy—restaurants. A crystal chandelier hangs in the
Fodor'sChoice　dining room, above well-spaced tables topped with flowers and Limo-
★　　ges china. The garden room loosens up with a stone fountain and a retractable roof. Chef-owner Josiah Citrin enriches his modern French

cooking with seasonal California produce. Consider seared sweet corn ravioli in brown butter–truffle froth, lobster Thermidor, venison in savory chocolate sauce, or duck in a Banyuls reduction. The cheese cart is packed with domestic and European selections. ✉ *1104 Wilshire Blvd., Santa Monica* ☎ *310/395–0881* ⚝ *Reservations essential* ☰ *AE, D, DC, MC, V* ⊗ *Closed Sun. and Mon. No lunch.*

$$$$
ITALIAN
Fodor'sChoice
★

✗ **Valentino.** Renowned as one of the country's top Italian restaurants, Valentino has a truly awe-inspiring wine list. With nearly 2,800 labels consuming 130 pages, backed by a cellar overflowing with 100,000 bottles, this restaurant is nothing short of heaven for serious oenophiles. In the 1970s, suave owner Piero Selvaggio introduced L.A. to his exquisite modern Italian cuisine, and he continues to impress guests with dishes like a timballo of wild mushrooms with rich Parmigiano-Reggiano–*saffron fonduta*, squid ink-tinted risotto with Maine lobster, a memorable osso buco, and sautéed branzino with lemon emulsion. A recent addition to this exalted venue is its more casual V-vin bar for wine tasting, crudo, and carpaccio. ✉ *3115 Pico Blvd., Santa Monica* ☎ *310/829–4313* ⚝ *Reservations essential* ☰ *AE, DC, MC, V* ⊗ *Closed Sun. No lunch Sat. and Mon.–Thurs.*

WEST LOS ANGELES

¢
AMERICAN
Fodor'sChoice
★

✗ **The Apple Pan.** A burger-insider haunt since 1947, this unassuming joint with a horseshoe-shaped counter—no tables here—turns out one heck of a good burger topped with Tillamook cheddar, plus a hickory burger with barbecue sauce. You'll also find great fries and, of course, an apple pie indulgent enough to christen the restaurant (although many regulars argue that the banana cream deserves the honor). Be prepared to wait, but the veteran countermen turn the stools at a quick pace. ✉ *10801 W. Pico Blvd., West L.A.* ☎ *310/475–3585* ⚝ *Reservations not accepted* ☰ *No credit cards* ⊗ *Closed Mon.*

$–$$
INDIAN
★

✗ **Bombay Cafe.** Some of the menu items at Bombay Cafe are strictly authentic, others have been lightened up a bit to suit Southern California sensibilities, and a few are truly innovative (e.g., California tandoori salad with lemon-cilantro dressing, green apple-cranberry chutney, ginger margarita). Regulars (and there are many) swear by the chili-laden lamb *frankies* (burritolike snacks sold by vendors on the beaches of Bombay), *sev puri* (wafers topped with onions, potatoes, and chutneys) and Sindhi chicken, a complex poached-then-sautéed recipe with an exotically seasoned crust. ✉ *12021 Pico Blvd., West L.A.* ☎ *310/473–3388* ☰ *MC, V* ⊗ *No lunch weekends.*

$$$–$$$$
JAPANESE
Fodor'sChoice
★

✗ **Mori Sushi.** Only a small fish logo identifies the facade of this restaurant, but many consider it the best sushi bar in L.A. and Morihiro Onodera one of the great sushi masters in America. The austere whitewashed space stands in contrast to the chef's artful presentations of pristine morsels of seafood, all served on ceramic plates he makes himself. Allow him to compose an entire meal for you—this can be an expensive proposition—and he'll send out eye-popping presentations of sushi or sashimi accented with touches of rare sea salts, yuzu, and freshly ground wasabi, as well as intricately conceived salads, housemade tofu, and soups. ✉ *11500 Pico Blvd., West L.A.* ☎ *310/479–3939* ☰ *AE, MC, V* ⊗ *Closed Sun. No lunch Sat.*

4

$–$$$ ✕La Serenata Gourmet. With uncomfortable chairs and crowds from the
MEXICAN nearby Westside Pavilion boosting decibel levels, this branch of the East
★ L.A. original isn't ideal for leisurely conversation. But the restaurant
scores big points for its boldly flavored Mexican cuisine. Pork dishes
and moles are delicious, but seafood is the real star—there are chubby
gorditas (cornmeal pockets stuffed with shrimp), juicy shrimp enchi-
ladas in tomatillo sauce, and simply grilled fish, with cilantro or garlic
sauce, that sings with flavor. If your experience with Mexican food has
been on the Tex-Mex end of the spectrum, come here to broaden your
taste-bud horizons. ✉*10924 W. Pico Blvd., West L.A.* ☎*310/441-
9667* ▭*AE, D, DC, MC, V.*

PASADENA

PASADENA

$$$–$$$$ ✕The Dining Room. Until the arrival of charismatic chef Craig Strong,
AMERICAN there wasn't much to say about this high-price hotel restaurant. But
Fodor'sChoice Strong brought with him global inspirations and a culinary finesse
★ beyond his years. A perfectionist (he insists, for instance, on import-
ing butter from Normandy), Strong continually surprises with dishes
such as lemongrass-scented spicy coconut milk–Dungeness crab soup,
brandade-stuffed squash blossoms, and sautéed duck breast and leg
confit with potato-basil mousseline and huckleberry sauce. The chef
relishes the opportunity to personalize his cuisine, so consider spring-
ing for a customized tasting menu. Langham Hotels, taking over the
property from Ritz-Carlton, promises nothing will change at the res-
taurant. ✉*Langham, Huntington Hotel & Spa, 1401 S. Oak Knoll
Ave., Pasadena* ☎*626/577–2867* ▭*AE, D, DC, MC, V* ☾*Closed Sun.
and Mon. No lunch.*

$–$$$$ ✕Yujean Kang's Gourmet Chinese Cuisine. Forget any and all preconceived
CHINESE notions of what Chinese food should look and taste like—Kang's cui-
Fodor'sChoice sine is nouvelle Chinese. Start with tender slices of veal on a bed of
★ enoki mushrooms, topped with a tangle of quick-fried shoestring
yams; or sea bass with kumquats and passion-fruit sauce. Even famil-
iar dishes, such as the crispy sesame beef, result in nearly revelatory
culinary experiences. And don't shy away from desserts like sweet
bean-curd crepes or delicate mandarin orange cheesecake, which are
elegantly light. ✉*67 N. Raymond Ave., Pasadena* ☎*626/585–0855*
▭*AE, D, DC, MC, V.*

WHERE TO STAY

BEVERLY HILLS, CENTURY CITY, HOLLYWOOD & WEST HOLLYWOOD

BEVERLY HILLS & VICINITY

$$$$ ▥Beverly Hills Hotel. Remarkably still at the top of her game, the "Pink
Palace" continues to attract Hollywood's elite after 95 years. Celebrity
guests favor the private bungalows; most others come for the "royal"
treatment by staff. Standard rooms are also nothing to sniff at, with

original artwork, butler service, Frette linens and duvets, walk-in closets, and huge marble bathrooms. Swiss skin-care company La Prairie runs the hotel's swanky day spa, which specializes in de-aging treatments. The Polo Lounge remains an iconic Hollywood meeting place. Bar Nineteen 12 is a most contemporary addition. Canine guests are also pampered here; 24-hour dog-walking service is available. **Pros:** Multiple recreation choices: pool, spa, and tennis; legendary retro 20-seat Fountain Coffee room. **Cons:** Average and pricey fare at the Polo lounge. ⊠*9641 Sunset Blvd., Beverly Hills* ☎*310/276–2251 or 800/283–8885* ⊕*www.beverlyhillshotel.com* ⇆*204 rooms, 21 bungalows* ♿*In-room: safe, kitchen (some), refrigerator, DVD, VCR, Ethernet. In-hotel: 4 restaurants, room service, bars, tennis courts, pool, gym, spa, concierge, laundry service, public Internet, parking (fee), some pets allowed, no-smoking rooms* ▭*AE, DC, MC, V.*

$$$$
Fodor'sChoice
★
🏨**Beverly Wilshire, a Four Seasons Hotel.** Built in 1928, the Italian Renaissance–style Wilshire wing of this fabled hotel is replete with elegant details: crystal chandeliers, oak paneling, walnut doors, crown moldings, and marble. The contemporary Beverly wing, added in 1971, lacks the Wilshire wing's historic panache. Rodeo Drive beckons outside; a complimentary Rolls-Royce can drive you anywhere within 3 mi of the hotel. Paneled in leather and wood, with soaring ceilings, the Blvd is the hotel's posh dining room. At dinner, Hollywood's elite packs the coolly modern steak house, CUT, featuring steaks and sides by Wolfgang Puck and interiors by architect Richard Meier. Take time to unwind at the hotel's first-rate spa. **Pros:** Chic location; top-notch service; refined vibe. **Cons:** Small lobby; valet parking backs-up at peak times; super-expensive dining choices. ⊠*9500 Wilshire Blvd., Beverly Hills* ☎*310/275–5200 or 800/427–4354* ⊕*www.fourseasons.com/beverly wilshire* ⇆*262 rooms, 137 suites* ♿*In-room: safe, refrigerator, DVD, Ethernet, Wi-Fi. In-hotel: 2 restaurants, room service, bars, pool, gym, spa, concierge, laundry service, public Internet, public Wi-Fi, parking (fee), some pets allowed, no-smoking rooms* ▭*AE, DC, MC, V.*

$$$$
Fodor'sChoice
★
🏨 **Four Seasons Hotel Los Angeles at Beverly Hills.** High hedges and patio gardens make this hotel a secluded retreat that even the hum of traffic can't permeate. It's a favorite of Hollywood's elite, so don't be surprised by a well-known face poolside or in the Windows bar. (Come awards season, expect to spot an Oscar winner or two.) The staff here will make you feel pampered, as will the plush guest rooms, which have beds with Frette linens, soft robes and slippers, and French doors leading to balconies. Extras include 24-hour business services, overnight shoe shine, and a morning newspaper. For a relaxing meal or a healthy smoothie, you can dine poolside on the tropically landscaped terrace. Massages here are among the best. **Pros:** Expert concierge; deferential service; celeb magnet. **Cons:** Small gym; Hollywood scene in bar and restaurant means rarefied prices. ⊠*300 S. Doheny Dr., Los Angeles* ☎*310/273–2222 or 800/332–3442* ⊕*www.fourseasons.com/losangeles* ⇆*187 rooms, 98 suites* ♿*In-room: safe, kitchen (some), refrigerator, DVD, Ethernet, Wi-Fi. In-hotel: 2 restaurants, room service, bar, pool, gym, spa, concierge, laundry service, public Wi-Fi, parking (fee), some pets allowed (fee), no-smoking rooms* ▭*AE, DC, MC, V.*

$$$$
★

Peninsula Beverly Hills. This French Riveria–style palace is a favorite of Hollywood bold-face names, but all kinds of visitors consistently describe their stay as near perfect—though very expensive. Rooms overflow with antiques, artwork, and marble; high-tech room amenities and flat-screen TVs are controlled by a bedside panel. Service is exemplary and always discreet. Soak up the sun by the fifth-floor pool with its fully outfitted cabanas or sip afternoon tea in the living room under ornate chandeliers. Belvedere, the hotel's flower-filled restaurant, is a lunchtime favorite for film business types. A complimentary Rolls-Royce is available for short jaunts in Beverly Hills. **Pros:** Central, walkable Beverly Hills location; stunning flowers; one of the best concierges in the city. **Cons:** Serious bucks or bank account required to stay here; somewhat stuffy. ⊠*9882 S. Santa Monica Blvd., Beverly Hills* ☎*310/551–2888 or 800/462–7899* ⊕*www.beverlyhills.peninsula. com* ⇔*166 rooms, 36 suites, 16 villas* ♿*In-room: safe, refrigerator, DVD, VCR, Ethernet, Wi-Fi. In-hotel: restaurant, room service, bar, pool, gym, spa, concierge, laundry service, concierge, public Wi-Fi, parking (fee), some pets allowed (fee), no-smoking rooms* ▤*AE, D, DC, MC, V.*

$$$
★

The Crescent. Built in 1926 as a dorm for silent film actors, the Crescent is now a sleek boutique hotel within walking distance of the Beverly Hills shopping triangle. Low couches and tables, an indoor-outdoor fireplace, French doors that open to its streetside patio restaurant, boé, and shimmering candlelight at night give the hotel's public areas a welcoming and sophisticated look. Guest rooms are small, but platform beds and built-in furniture maximize the space. Bathrooms are finished in concrete—utilitarian but also coolly cozy. High-tech amenities include flat-screen TVs, in-room iPods, and a library of the latest CDs and DVDs. **Pros:** boé's tasty cuisine and convivial happy hour; the lobby is fashionista-central. **Cons:** Dorm-sized rooms; fee for access to Sports ClubLA gym; no elevator. ⊠*403 N. Crescent Dr., Beverly Hills* ☎*310/247–0505* ⊕*www.crescentbh.com* ⇔*35 rooms* ♿*In-room: refrigerator, Wi-Fi. In-hotel: no elevator, restaurant, room service, bar, laundry service, public Wi-Fi, parking (fee), no-smoking rooms* ▤*AE, D, MC, V.*

HOLLYWOOD & VICINITY

$$$–$$$$

Hollywood Roosevelt Hotel. Think hip bachelor pad when considering the Roosevelt. Poolside cabana rooms have dark-wood furnishings and mirrored walls; rooms in the main building have contemporary platform beds. Although Hollywood's oldest hotel, a renovation and a pair of hot nightspots have breathed new life into this historic spot. Lobby and poolside socializing is nonstop most weekends. Spanish Colonial Revival details include Spanish tiles, painted ceilings, arches, and fountains that evoke early Hollywood glamour. The David Hockney-painted pool adds to the playful vibe. A Metro stop is one block away. **Pros:** In the heart of Hollywood's action; lively social scene; great burgers at hotel's restaurant, 25 Degrees. **Cons:** Noise; attitude; stiff parking charges. ⊠*7000 Hollywood Blvd., Hollywood* ☎*323/466–7000 or 800/950–7667* ⊕*www.hollywoodroosevelt.com* ⇔*305 rooms, 48 suites* ♿*In-room: safe, refrigerator, Wi-Fi. In-hotel: 2 restaurants,* *room service, 3 bars, pool, gym, concierge, laundry service, public Wi-Fi, parking (fee), no-smoking rooms* ⊟*AE, D, DC, MC, V.*

$$$ ⚅ **Renaissance Hollywood Hotel.** Part of the massive Hollywood & High-
★ land shopping and entertainment complex, this 20-story Renaissance is at the center of Hollywood's action. Contemporary art (notably by L.A. favorites Charles and Ray Eames), retro '60s furniture, terrazzo floors, a Zen rock garden, and wood and aluminum accents greet you in the lobby. Rooms are vibrant: chairs are red, table lamps are molded blue plastic. For the ultimate party pad, book the Panorama Suite, with angled floor-to-ceiling windows, vintage Eames furniture, a grand piano, and a sunken Jacuzzi tub with a view. Spa Luce, the hotel's rooftop spa, was added in 2008. **Pros:** Large rooms; blackout shades; Red Line Metro-station adjacent. **Cons:** City hotel = no greenery; large and corporate feeling; very touristy. ⊠*1755 N. Highland Ave., Hollywood* ☎*323/856–1200 or 800/769–4774* ⊕*www.renaissancehollywood. com* ↩*604 rooms, 33 suites* ⌂*In-room: safe, refrigerator, Ethernet. In-hotel: restaurant, room service, bars, pool, gym, concierge, laundry service, executive floor, parking (fee), no-smoking rooms* ⊟*AE, D, DC, MC, V.*

4

$–$$ ⚅ **Farmer's Daughter Hotel.** Tongue-in-cheek country style is the name
★ of the game at this motel: rooms are upholstered in blue gingham with denim bedspreads, and farm tools serve as art. A curving blue wall secludes the interior courtyard and the hotel's clapboard-lined restaurant, Tart. Pancakes here are a local favorite. Rooms are snug but outfitted with whimsical original art and amenities such as CD and DVD players. It's a favorite of *The Price Is Right* hopefuls; the TV show tapes at the CBS studios nearby. **Pros:** Across from the cheap eats of the Farmers Market and The Grove's shopping/entertainment mix. **Cons:** Pricey restaurant; roadside motel-size rooms; shaded pool. ⊠*115 S. Fairfax Ave., Fairfax District,* ☎*323/937–3930 or 800/334–1658* ⊕*www.farmersdaughterhotel.com* ↩*64 rooms, 2 suites* ⌂*In-room: safe, refrigerator, DVD, Ethernet, Wi-Fi. In-hotel: restaurant, room service, pool, concierge, laundry service, public Wi-Fi, parking (fee), no-smoking rooms, some pets allowed (fee)* ⊟*AE, D, DC, MC, V.*

$ ⚅ **Highland Gardens Hotel.** A large, sparkling pool and a lush, if somewhat overgrown, tropical garden set this hotel apart from other budget lodgings. Spacious but basic units have either two queen-size beds, or a king bed with a queen-size sleeper sofa, plus a desk and sitting area with Formica tables. Rooms facing busy Franklin Avenue are noisy; ask for one facing the courtyard. **Pros:** Quick walk to Hollywood and Metro Rail; pet friendly; low price. **Cons:** Late '80s decor; street noise; no elevator. ⊠*7047 Franklin Ave., Hollywood* ☎*323/850–0536 or 800/404–5472* ⊕*www.highlandgardenshotel.com* ↩*70 rooms, 48 suites* ⌂*In-room: kitchen (some), refrigerator, Wi-Fi. In-hotel: no elevator, pool, laundry facilities, public Wi-Fi, parking (no fee), no-smoking rooms, some pets allowed* ⊟*AE, MC, V* ⦿|*CP.*

WEST HOLLYWOOD

$$$$ ⚅ **Chateau Marmont Hotel.** The Chateau's swank exterior disguises its lurid place in Hollywood history—many remember it as the scene of John Belushi's fatal overdose in 1982. Celebs like Johnny Depp and

Lindsay Lohan appreciate the hotel for its secluded cottages, bungalows, and understated suites and penthouses. For those who don't grace the cover of *Vanity Fair,* service can be frosty. The interior is 1920s style, although some of the decor looks dated rather than vintage. The Wi-Fi throughout the hotel means that you can surf the Net while seated on the hotel's scenic, landscaped terrace with drop-dead sunset views. **Pros:** Walking distance to all of Sunset Strip's action; great food and vibe at Bar Marmont; guaranteed celeb spotting. **Cons:** Attitude and then some from staff; ancient elevators. ⊠ *8221 Sunset Blvd., West Hollywood* ☎ *323/656–1010 or 800/242–8328* ⊕ *www.chateaumarmont. com* ⇆ *11 rooms, 63 suites* ⚲ *In-room: safe, refrigerator, DVD, dial-up, Wi-Fi. In-hotel: restaurant, room service, bar, pool, gym, concierge, laundry service, public Wi-Fi, parking (fee), some pets allowed (fee), no-smoking room* ▤ *AE, DC, MC, V.*

$$$$ 🏨 **Mondrian.** An extensive makeover in 2008 added color (from all
★   white) and flat-screen TVs to the Mondrian's highly trafficked suites. The hotel's famed social spots—Asia de Cuba, the Skybar, and pool— stayed the same and remain extremely popular weekends and holidays. More urban resort than business hotel, a spendy attitude pervades and is reinforced via an in-room price list that spells out all costs from candles to bath products, should you decide to take home a souvenir. Bathrooms are compact and tidy; reminiscent of the hotel's previous life as an apartment building. **Pros:** Pool, spa, and nighttime social scene means never having to leave the property. **Cons:** Street noise on Sunset Blvd. side; late-night party scene; inflated prices. ⊠ *8440 Sunset Blvd., West Hollywood* ☎ *323/650–8999 or 800/697–1791* ⊕ *www. mondrianhotel.com* ⇆ *53 rooms, 185 suites* ⚲ *In-room: safe, kitchen, refrigerator, DVD, Ethernet, Wi-Fi. In-hotel: restaurant, room service, bars, pool, gym, spa, concierge, laundry service, public Wi-Fi, parking (fee), no-smoking rooms* ▤ *AE, D, DC, MC, V.*

$$$$ 🏨 **Sunset Marquis Hotel and Villas.** If you're in town to cut your new hit single, you'll appreciate the two on-site recording studios here. Many a rocker has called the Sunset Marquis home—check out their oversize portraits lining the walls of the hotel's exclusive Bar 1200. But even the musically challenged will appreciate this property on a quiet cul-de-sac just off the Sunset Strip. Suites and ultraprivate villas, which are set amid lush gardens, are roomy and plush (ultrasuede bed throws and flat-screen TVs abound). Windows are as soundproof as they come; blackout curtains ensure total serenity. Forty new villas are lavish with extras: kitchens, fireplaces, room-size bathrooms and on-call butlers available to handle everything from unpacking to booking spa appointments. **Pros:** Superior service; discreet setting just off the Strip; clublike atmosphere. **Cons:** Standard suites are somewhat small. ⊠ *1200 N. Alta Loma Rd., West Hollywood* ☎ *310/657–1333 or 800/858–9758* ⊕ *www.sunsetmarquishotel.com* ⇆ *102 suites, 52 villas* ⚲ *In-room: safe, kitchen (some), refrigerator, DVD, VCR, Ethernet, Wi-Fi. In-hotel: 2 restaurants, room service, bars, pools, gym, spa, concierge, laundry service, public Wi-Fi, parking (fee), no-smoking rooms* ▤ *AE, D, DC, MC, V.*

$$ ⊞**The Standard, Hollywood.** Hotelier André Balazs created this playful Sunset Strip hotel out of a former retirement home. The aesthetic is '70s kitsch: pop art, shag carpets, and ultrasuede sectionals fill the lobby, while the rooms have inflatable sofas, beanbag chairs, surfboard tables, and Warhol poppy-print curtains. After a decade of heavy use, rooms show the wear-and-tear, and service issues and staff attitude are commonplace. DJs spin nightly and lobby socializing begins at the front desk and extends to the blue AstroTurfed pool deck outside. **Pros:** Decent on-site 24-hour coffee shop; poolside socializing, live DJs. **Cons:** Extended party scene for twentysomethings; staff big on attitude rather than service. ⊠*8300 Sunset Blvd., West Hollywood* ☎*323/650–9090* ⊕*www.standardhotel.com* ↪*137 rooms, 2 suites* ⚷*In-room: refrigerator, Ethernet. In-hotel: restaurant, room service, bar, pool, concierge, laundry service, public Wi-Fi, parking (fee), some pets allowed* ⊟*AE, D, DC, MC, V.*

DOWNTOWN

$$$$ ⊞**Hilton Checkers Los Angeles.** Opened as the Mayflower Hotel in 1927,
★ Checkers retains much of its original character; its various-size rooms all have charming period details, although they also have contemporary luxuries like pillow-top mattresses, coffeemakers, 24-hour room service, and cordless phones. The rooftop pool deck overlooks the L.A. library and nearby office towers. The plush lobby bar and lounge look like they belong in a private club, with comfortable leather chairs and a large plasma-screen TV. **Pros:** Historic charm; business-friendly; rooftop pool and spa. **Cons:** No on-street parking; some rooms very compact; very urban setting. ⊠*535 S. Grand Ave., Downtown* ☎*213/624–0000 or 800/445–8667* ⊕*www.hiltoncheckers.com* ↪*188 rooms, 9 suites* ⚷*In-room: Ethernet, Wi-Fi. In-hotel: restaurant, room service, bar, pool, gym, spa, concierge, laundry service, public Wi-Fi, parking (fee), no-smoking rooms* ⊟*AE, D, DC, MC, V.*

$$$ ⊞**Millennium Biltmore Hotel.** One of downtown L.A.'s true treasures, the
Fodor'sChoice gilded 1923 beaux arts masterpiece exudes ambience and history. The
★ lobby (formerly the Music Room) was the local headquarters of JFK's presidential campaign, and the ballroom hosted some of the earliest Academy Awards. These days, the Biltmore hosts business types drawn by its central downtown location, ample meeting spaces, and services such as a well-outfitted business center that stays open 24/7. Some of the guest rooms are small by today's standards, but all have classic, formal furnishings, shuttered windows, and marble bathrooms. Bring your bathing suit for the vintage tiled indoor pool and adjacent steam room. **Pros:** Historic character; famed filming location; club-level rooms have many hospitable extras. **Cons:** Pricey valet parking; standard rooms truly compact. ⊠*506 S. Grand Ave. Downtown* ☎*213/624–1011 or 866/866–8086* ⊕*www.millenniumhotels.com* ↪*627 rooms, 56 suites* ⚷*In-room: Ethernet. In-hotel: 3 restaurants, room service, bars, pool, gym, concierge, laundry service, executive floor, public Internet, public Wi-Fi, parking (fee), no-smoking rooms* ⊟*AE, D, DC, MC, V.*

4

$$ ☒ **Figueroa Hotel.** On the outside, it's Spanish Revival; on the inside,
★ this 1926, 12-story hotel is a mix of Southwestern, Mexican, and Mediterranean styles, with earth tones, hand-painted furniture, and wrought-iron beds. You can lounge around the pool and bubbling hot tub surrounded by tropical greenery under the shadow of downtown skyscrapers. (Make it even better with a soothing drink from the back patio bar.) **Pros:** A short walk to Nokia Theatre, LA Live (2009), Convention Center; well-priced; great poolside bar. **Cons:** Somewhat funky room decor; small bathrooms; gentrifying neighborhood. ☒ *939 S. Figueroa St., Downtown* ☎*213/627–8971 or 800/421–9092* ⊕*www. figueroahotel.com* ⇄*285 rooms, 2 suites* ♿*In-room: refrigerator, dial-up, Wi-Fi. In-hotel: restaurant, bars, pool, concierge, laundry facilities, laundry service, public Wi-Fi, parking (fee), no-smoking rooms* ▭*AE, DC, MC, V.*

$$ ☒ **Inn at 657.** Proprietor Patsy Carter runs a homey, welcoming bed-
★ and-breakfast near the University of Southern California. Rooms in this 1904-built Craftsman have down comforters, Oriental silks on the walls, and needlepoint rugs. The vintage dining room table seats 12; conversation is encouraged. You're also welcome to hang out with the hummingbirds in the private garden. All rooms include a hearty breakfast, homemade cookies, and free local phone calls. **Pros:** Vintage home and quiet garden; homemade breakfast; you'll meet the innkeeper. **Cons:** Low-tech stay; you'll have to speak to other guests. ☒ *657 W. 23rd St., Downtown* ☎*213/741–2200 or 800/347–7512* ⊕*www.patsysinn657. com* ⇄*11 rooms* ♿*In-room: refrigerator, VCR, Ethernet, Wi-Fi. In-hotel: no elevator, restaurant, laundry service, public Wi-Fi, parking (no fee), no-smoking rooms* ▭*MC, V* ⎆*BP.*

$–$$ ☒ **The Standard, Downtown L.A.** Built in 1955 as Standard Oil's company
Fodor's Choice headquarters, the building was completely revamped under the sharp
★ eye of owner André Balazs. The large guest rooms are practical and funky: all have orange built-in couches; windows that actually open; and platform beds. Bathrooms have extra-large tubs. The indoor–outdoor rooftop lounge has a preening social scene and stunning setting, but be prepared for some attitude at the door. **Pros:** On-site Rudy's barbershop for grooming; 24/7 coffee shop for dining; rooftop pool and lounge for fun. **Cons:** Party scene weekends and holidays; street noise; hipper-than-thou attitude at the door. ☒ *550 S. Flower St., Downtown* ☎*213/892–8080* ⊕*www.standardhotel.com* ⇄*205 rooms, 2 suites* ♿*In-room: safe, refrigerator, DVD, Ethernet. In-hotel: restaurant, room service, bars, pool, gym, concierge, laundry service, parking (fee), some pets allowed, no-smoking rooms* ▭*AE, D, DC, MC, V.*

COASTAL & WESTERN LOS ANGELES

BEL-AIR

$$$$ ☒ **Hotel Bel-Air.** In a wooded canyon with lush gardens and a swan-filled
Fodor's Choice lake, the Hotel Bel-Air's fairy-tale luxury and seclusion have made it
★ a favorite of discreet celebs and royalty for decades. Bungalow-style rooms feel like fine homes, with country-French, expensively upholstered furniture in silk or chenille; many have hardwood floors. Several

rooms have wood-burning fireplaces (the bell captain will build a fire for you). Eight suites have private outdoor hot tubs. Complimentary tea service greets you upon arrival; enjoy it on the terrace warmed by heated tiles. A pianist plays nightly in the bar. **Pros:** Ultraprivate in-town hideaway; gorgeous restaurant terrace; service par-excellence. **Cons:** Very expensive dining. ✉ *701 Stone Canyon Rd., Bel Air* ☎ *310/472–1211 or 800/648–4097* 🖷 *310/476–5890* ⊕ *www.hotelbelair.com* 💬 *52 rooms, 39 suites* ♿ *In-room: safe, refrigerator, DVD, VCR, Ethernet, Wi-Fi. In-hotel: restaurant, room service, bar, pool, gym, concierge, laundry service, public Internet, public Wi-Fi, parking (no fee), some pets allowed, no-smoking rooms* ▤ *AE, DC, MC, V.*

LOS ANGELES INTERNATIONAL AIRPORT

$$$
★ 🖻 **Sheraton Gateway Hotel.** LAX's coolest-looking hotel is so swank that guests have been known to ask to buy the black-and-white photos hanging behind the front desk. Extras for in-transit visitors include 24-hour room service, a 24-hour fitness center, currency exchange, a business center, and a 24-hour airport shuttle. Rooms are compact but soundproof and have helpful details such as coffeemakers, hooks for hanging garment bags, and oversize work desks. Faux animal-skin headboards and ebonized furniture make the guest rooms feel more sophisticated than corporate. **Pros:** Weekend rates significantly lower; free LAX shuttle; Shula's 347 steak house. **Cons:** Convenient to airport but not much else. ✉ *6101 W. Century Blvd., LAX* ☎ *310/642–1111 or 800/325–3535* ⊕ *www.sheratonlosangeles.com* 💬 *702 rooms, 102 suites* ♿ *In-room: Ethernet, Wi-Fi. In-hotel: 2 restaurants, room service, bar, pool, gym, concierge, laundry service, executive floor, public Internet, public Wi-Fi, airport shuttle, parking (fee), some pets allowed, no-smoking rooms* ▤ *AE, D, DC, MC, V.*

SANTA MONICA

$$$$
★ 🖻 **Hotel Casa del Mar.** In the 1920s it was a posh beach club catering to the city's elite; now the Casa del Mar is one of SoCal's most luxurious and pricey beachfront hotels, with three extravagant two-story penthouses, a raised deck and pool, and an elegant ballroom facing the sand. Guest rooms, designed to evoke the good old days with furnishings like four-poster beds and handsome armoires, are filled with contemporary amenities like flat-screen TVs, iPod docking stations, and supremely comfortable beds with sumptuous white linens. Bathrooms are gorgeous, with sunken whirlpool tubs and glass-enclosed showers. Catch is the hotel's elegant and striking restaurant and sushi bar, specializing in what else? Seafood. **Pros:** Excellent dining by chef Michael Reardon at Catch; lobby socializing; gorgeous beachfront rooms. **Cons:** No room balconies; without a doubt, one of L.A.'s priciest stays. ✉ *1910 Ocean Front Way, Santa Monica* ☎ *310/581–5533 or 800/898–6999* ⊕ *www.hotelcasadelmar.com* 💬 *129 rooms, 4 suites* ♿ *In-room: safe, refrigerator, Ethernet, Wi-Fi. In-hotel: 2 restaurants, room service, bar, pool, gym, spa, concierge, public Wi-Fi, laundry service, parking (fee), some pets allowed, no-smoking rooms* ▤ *AE, D, DC, MC, V.*

$$$$ ⬚ **Le Merigot Beach Hotel & Spa.** Steps from Santa Monica's expansive
★ beach, Le Merigot caters to a corporate clientele (it's a JW Marriott property). Upper floors have panoramic views of the Santa Monica Pier and the Pacific; many rooms have terraces. The contemporary rooms have feather beds and fine linens, and bathrooms come with playful bath toys and votive candles. Expect a seashell (not chocolate) at turndown. A checkerboard slate courtyard, including a pool, cabanas, fountains, and outdoor living room, is the center of activity. You can book a massage at the spa for a true attitude adjustment, or enjoy Cal-French fare at the comfortable Cézanne restaurant. **Pros:** Steps from the beach and pier; welcoming to international travelers; walk to Third Street Promenade. **Cons:** Small shaded pool. ✉*1740 Ocean Ave., Santa Monica* ☎*310/395–9700 or 888/539–7899* ⊕*www.lemerigot hotel.com* ⇆*175 rooms, 15 suites* ♿*In-room: safe, refrigerator, Ethernet. In-hotel: restaurant, room service, bar, pool, gym, spa, beachfront, bicycles, concierge, laundry service, public Internet, public Wi-Fi, parking (fee), some pets allowed (fee), no-smoking rooms* ▭*AE, D, DC, MC, V.*

$$$$ ⬚ **Shutters on the Beach.** Set right on the sand, this gray-shingle inn has
Fodor's Choice become synonymous with in-town escapism. Guest rooms have those
★ namesake shutter doors, pillow-top mattresses, and white built-in cabinets filled with art books and curios. Bathrooms are luxe, each with a whirlpool tub, a raft of bath goodies, and a three-nozzle, glass-walled shower. While the hotel's service gets mixed reviews from some readers, the beachfront location and show-house decor make this one of SoCal's most popular luxury hotels. **Pros:** Romantic; discreet; residential vibe. **Cons:** Service not as good as it should be. ✉*1 Pico Blvd., Santa Monica* ☎*310/458–0030 or 800/334–9000* ⊕*www.shuttersonthebeach.com* ⇆*186 rooms, 12 suites* ♿*In-room: safe, refrigerator, DVD, Ethernet, Wi-Fi. In-hotel: 2 restaurants, room service, bar, pool, gym, spa, beachfront, bicycles, concierge, laundry service, public Wi-Fi, parking (fee), no-smoking rooms* ▭*AE, D, DC, MC, V.*

SAN FERNANDO VALLEY

BURBANK

$$$ ⬚ **Hotel Amarano Burbank.** Close to Burbank's TV and movie studios,
★ the smartly designed Amarano feels like a Beverly Hills boutique hotel. The vibe is residential; the look understated (muted beiges and greens). The lobby is a welcoming living room with glass fireplace and corners for quiet conversation, cocktails or tapas. Feather beds are covered in comfy duvets; thoughtful touches include plush bathrobes and hooks for hanging garment bags. Generous work spaces have state-of-the-art lighting, and bathrooms have granite vanities, makeup mirrors, and shelves for storage. The rooftop sundeck has a brightly striped cabana and view of the nearby hills. **Pros:** Boutique style in a Valley location; rooftop gym; pleasant breakfast room. **Cons:** No pool; summertime temps; Pass Ave. street noise. ✉*322 N. Pass Ave., Burbank* ☎*818/842–8887 or 888/956–1900* ⊕*www.hotelamarano.com* ⇆*91 rooms, 10 suites* ♿*In-room: safe, kitchen (some), refrigerator, DVD, Ethernet, Wi-Fi. In-hotel: restaurant, room service, bar, gym, concierge,*

laundry service, public Wi-Fi, airport shuttle (Burbank), parking (fee), some pets allowed (fee), no-smoking rooms ⊟*AE, D, DC, MC, V.*

PASADENA

$$$$ 🖼 **The Langham, Huntington Hotel & Spa.** An azalea-filled Japanese garden and the unusual Picture Bridge, with murals celebrating California's history, are just two of this grande dame's picturesque attributes. Long a mainstay of Pasadena's social history, the hotel first opened in 1907. The Italianate-style main building, Spanish Revival–style cottages, and lanai building sit on 23 acres fronted by the historic horseshoe garden. In 2008 the hotel was bought by Langham Hotels ending its storied, 15-year stand as Ritz-Carlton. Traditional guest rooms are handsome and sometimes oddly sized; all are in shades of gold and blue. Brocade fabrics are found throughout, as are flat-screen TVs and CD players. The hotel's formal restaurant, the Dining Room, can be counted on for a rarefied contemporary dining experience. Treat yourself and order Chef Craig Strong's multicourse tasting menu. **Pros:** New owners promises updates to the spa, cottages, and restaurants while maintaining the property's many charms. **Cons:** Set in a suburban neighborhood far from local shopping and dining; transition hiccups a possibility. ⊠*1401 S. Oak Knoll Ave., Pasadena* ☎*626/568–3900 or 800/591–7481* ⊕*www.pasadena.langhamhotels.com* 🛏*342 rooms, 38 suites* ⚒*In-room: safe, refrigerator, Ethernet, Wi-Fi. In-hotel: 2 restaurants, room service, bar, tennis courts, pool, gym, spa, bicycles, concierge, laundry service, executive floor, public Internet, public Wi-Fi, parking (fee), some pets allowed (fee), no-smoking rooms* ⊟*AE, D, DC, MC, V.*

Fodor's Choice ★

4

NIGHTLIFE & THE ARTS

Hollywood and West Hollywood, where hip and happening nightspots liberally dot Sunset and Hollywood boulevards, are the epicenter of L.A. nightlife. The city is one of the best places in the world for seeing soon-to-be-famous rockers as well as top jazz, blues, and classical performers. Movie theaters are naturally well represented here, but the worlds of dance, theater, and opera have flourished in the past few years as well.

For a thorough listing of local events, *www.la.com* and *Los Angeles Magazine* are both good sources. The Calendar section of the *Los Angeles Times* (⊕*www.calendarlive.com*) also lists a wide survey of Los Angeles arts events, especially on Thursday and Sunday, as do the more alternative publications, *LA Weekly* and *Citybeat Los Angeles* (both free, and issued every Thursday). Call ahead to confirm that what you want to see is ongoing.

THE ARTS

CONCERT HALLS

Fodor'sChoice Built in 2003 as a grand addition to L.A.'s Music Center, the 2,265-seat
★   **Walt Disney Concert Hall** (⊠*151 S. Grand Ave., Downtown* ☎*323/850–2000*) is now the home of the Los Angeles Philharmonic and the Los Angeles Master Chorale. A sculptural monument of gleaming, curved steel, the theater is part of a complex that includes a public park, gardens, and shops as well as two outdoor amphitheaters for children's and preconcert events. ■TIP➔**In the main hall, the audience completely surrounds the stage, so it's worth checking the seating chart when buying tickets to gauge your view of the performers.** And the acoustics definitely live up to the hype. Also part of the Music Center, the 3,200-seat **Dorothy Chandler Pavilion** (⊠*135 N. Grand Ave., Downtown* ☎*213/972–7211*) is an elegant space with plush red seats and a giant gold curtain. It presents an array of music programs and the L.A. Opera's classics from September through June. Music director Plácido Domingo encourages fresh work. There's also a steady flow of touring ballet and modern ballet companies. In Griffith Park, the open-air auditorium known as the **Greek Theater** (⊠*2700 N. Vermont Ave., Los Feliz* ☎*323/665–1927*), complete with Doric columns, presents big-name performers in its mainly pop-rock-jazz schedule from June through October.

★   Ever since it opened in 1920, in a park surrounded by mountains, trees, and gardens, the **Hollywood Bowl** (⊠*2301 Highland Ave., Hollywood* ☎*323/850–2000* ⊕*www.hollywoodbowl.com*) has been one of the world's largest and most atmospheric outdoor amphitheaters. Its season runs from early July through mid-September; the L.A. Philharmonic spends its summers here. There are performances daily except Monday (and some Sundays); the program ranges from jazz to pop to classical. Concertgoers usually arrive early and bring picnic suppers (picnic tables are available). Additionally, a moderately priced outdoor grill and a more upscale restaurant are among the dining options operated by the Patina Group. ■TIP➔**Be sure to bring a sweater—it gets chilly here in the evening. You might also bring or rent a cushion to apply to the wood seats. Avoid the hassle of parking by taking one of the Park-and-Ride buses, which leave from various locations around town; call the Bowl for information.**

Fodor'sChoice The jewel in the crown of Hollywood & Highland is the **Kodak The-**
★   **atre** (⊠*6801 Hollywood Blvd., Hollywood* ☎*323/308–6363* ⊕*www.kodaktheatre.com*). Created as the permanent host of the Academy Awards, the lavish 3,500-seat theater is also used for music concerts and ballets. Seeing a show here is worthwhile just to witness the gorgeous, crimson-and-gold interior, with its box seating and glittering chandeliers. Fans wishing to view the red carpet parade outside on Oscar day can register for bleacher seats during the month of September at ⊕*www.oscars.org/bleachers*. The one-of-a-kind, 6,300-seat ersatz-Arabic **Shrine Auditorium** (⊠*665 W. Jefferson Blvd., Downtown* ☎*213/748–5116*), built in 1926 as Al Malaikah Temple, hosts touring companies from all over the world, assorted gospel and choral groups, and other musical acts as well as high-profile televised awards shows,

including the Latin Grammys and the Golden Globes.

★ Adjacent to Universal Studios, the 6,250-seat **Gibson Amphitheater** (✉ *100 Universal City Plaza, Universal City* ☎ *818/622–4440*) holds more than 100 performances a year, including the Radio City Christmas Spectacular, star-studded benefit concerts, and all-star shindigs for local radio station KROQ 106.7.

FILM

The **American Cinemathèque Independent Film Series** (✉ *6712 Hollywood Blvd., Hollywood* ☎ *323/466–3456* ⊕ *americancinematheque. com*) screens classics plus recent independent films, sometimes with question-and-answer sessions with the filmmakers. The main venue is the Lloyd E. Rigler Theater, within the 1922 Egyptian Theater, which combines an exterior of pharaoh sculptures and columns with a modern, high-tech design inside. The Cinemathèque also screens movies at the 1940 **Aero Theater** (✉ *1328 Montana Ave., Santa Monica* ☎ *323/466–3456*).

Fodor'sChoice ★ Taking the concept of dinner and a movie to a whole new level, **Cinespace** (✉ *6356 Hollywood Blvd., Hollywood* ☎ *323/817–3456* ⊕ *www. cine-space.com*) screens classics and alternative flicks in its digital theater-restaurant. Comfort food is served during the films, which could be documentaries as easily as they could be old-school faves like *Grease*. The movies are often followed by popular club nights. DJ–provided music and a smoking patio that hovers over bustling Hollywood Boulevard attract indie rockers on Tuesday and hip-hop hell-raisers on weekends.

Fodor'sChoice ★ The **Silent Movie Theatre** (✉ *611 N. Fairfax Ave., Fairfax District* ☎ *323/655–2520* ⊕ *www.silentmovietheatre.com*) is a treasure for both pretalkies and nonsilent films (the artier the better). Live musical accompaniment and shorts precede the films. Each show is made to seem like an event in itself, and it's just about the only theater of its kind. The schedule—which also offers occasional DJ and live music performances—varies, but you can be sure to catch silent screenings every Wednesday.

★ **UCLA** has two fine film series. The programs of the **Billy Wilder Theater** (✉ *10899 Wilshire Blvd., Westwood* ☎ *310/443–7000* ⊕ *www. cinema.ucla.edu*) might cover the works of major directors, documentaries, children's films, horror movies—just about anything. The **School of Film & Television** (⊕ *www.tft.ucla.edu*) uses **the James Bridges**

TICKET SOURCES

In addition to contacting venues directly, try these sources.

Good Time Tickets (☎ *323/464–7383* ⊕ *www.goodtime-tickets. com*) covers events at museums and small theaters, plus some stadium fare.

Razor Gator (☎ *800/542–4466* ⊕ *www.razorgator.com*). Sells harder-to-get tickets.

Theatre League Alliance L.A (⊕ *www.theatrela.org*). Score discounted theater tickets.

Ticketmaster (☎ *213/480–3232, 213/365–3500 fine arts* ⊕ *www. ticketmaster.com*). Still the all-around top dog.

Theater (✉*Melnitz Hall, Sunset Blvd. and Hilgard Ave., Westwood* ☎*310/206–3456*) and has its own program of newer, avant-garde films. Enter the campus at the northeasternmost entrance. Street parking is available on Loring Avenue (a block east of the campus) after 6 PM, or park for a small fee in Lot 3 (go one entrance south to Wyton Drive to pay at the kiosk before 7, after 7 at the lot itself).

MOVIE PALACES The **Arclight** (✉*6360 Sunset Blvd., Hollywood* ☎*323/464–4226*) includes as its centerpiece the geodesic Cinerama Dome, the first theater in the United States designed specifically for the large screen and sound system that went with Cinerama. The complex now includes 14 additional screens, a mall, and a restaurant and bar. The only theater in L.A. to begin movies with greetings and background commentary by theater staff, the Arclight also designates some screenings as "premium," which lets you reserve the best seats for an extra fee. "Over 21" shows let you bring cocktails into designated screening rooms.

Bridge Cinema De Lux (✉*6081 Center Dr., in the Promenade at Howard Hughes Center, West L.A.* ☎*310/568–3375*) comes by its name honestly, with superwide screens, leather recliners, and top-notch food (from wrap sandwiches to pizza) and drink (martinis are their specialty). Sip a cocktail at the bar or order a meal to take into the theater. Regular ticket prices start at $9.75, with higher prices for Directors' Hall seating (reserved seats and even bigger screens).

FodorśChoice ★ **Grauman's Chinese Theatre** (✉*6925 Hollywood Blvd., Hollywood* ☎*323/464–6266*), open since 1927, is perhaps the world's best-known theater, the home of the famous concrete walkway marked by movie stars' hand- and footprints and traditional gala premieres. There are additional, smaller screens at the Mann Chinese Six, in the adjoining Hollywood & Highland Complex. Across the street from Grauman's is the **Pacific's El Capitan** (✉*6838 Hollywood Blvd., Hollywood* ☎*323/467–7674*), an art deco masterpiece meticulously renovated by Disney. First-run movies alternate with Disney revivals, and the theater often presents live stage shows in conjunction with Disney's animated pictures.

THEATER

LA Stage Alliance (⊕*www.lastagealliance.com*) also gives information on what's playing in Los Angeles, albeit with capsules that are either noncommittal or overly enthusiastic. Its LAStageTIX service allows you to buy tickets online the day of the performance at roughly half price.

MAJOR THEATERS Jason Robards and Nick Nolte got their starts at **Geffen Playhouse** (✉*10886 Le Conte Ave., Westwood* ☎*310/208–5454* ⊕*www.geffen playhouse.com*), an acoustically superior, 498-seat theater that showcases new plays in summer—primarily musicals and comedies. Many of the productions here are on their way to or from Broadway.

★ In addition to theater performances, lectures, and children's programs, free summer jazz, dance, cabaret, and occasionally Latin and rock concerts take place at the **John Anson Ford Amphitheatre** (✉*2580 Cahuenga Blvd. E., Hollywood* ☎*323/461–3673* ⊕*www.fordamphitheater.org*), a 1,300-seat outdoor venue in the Hollywood Hills. Winter shows are typically staged at the smaller indoor theater, **Inside the Ford.** There are three theaters in the big downtown complex known as **The Music Center** (⊠*135 N. Grand Ave., Downtown* ☎*213/972–7211* ⊕*www.musiccenter.org*). The 2,140-seat **Ahmanson Theatre** (☎*213/628–2772* ⊕*www.taperahmanson.com*) presents both classics and new plays; the 3,200-seat **Dorothy Chandler Pavilion** shows a smattering of plays between the more prevalent musical performances; and the 760-seat **Mark Taper Forum** (☎*213/628–2772*

> ### JOIN THE STUDIO AUDIENCE
>
> **Audiences Unlimited** (⊠*100 Universal City Plaza, Bldg. 153, Universal City* ☎*818/506–0043* ⊕*www.tvtickets.com*) helps fill seats for television programs (and sometimes for televised award shows). The free tickets are distributed on a first-come, first-served basis. Shows that may be taping or filming include *According to Jim* and *Dr. Phil.* Note: you must be 16 or older to attend a television taping.

⊕*www.taperahmanson.com*) presents new works that often go on to Broadway, such as Tony Kushner's *Caroline, or Change.*

★ The home of the Academy Awards telecast from 1949 to 1959, the **Pantages Theatre** (⊠*6233 Hollywood Blvd., Hollywood* ☎*323/468–1770* ⊕*www.nederlander.com*) is a massive (2,600-seat) and splendid example of high-style Hollywood art deco, presenting large-scale Broadway musicals such as *The Lion King* and *Wicked.* The **Ricardo Montalbán Theatre** (⊠*1615 N. Vine St., Hollywood* ☎*323/463–0089* ⊕*www.nosotros.org*) has an intimate feeling despite its 1,038-seat capacity. It presents plays, concerts, seminars, and workshops with an emphasis on Latin culture. The 1,900-seat, art deco **Wilshire Theatre** (⊠*8440 Wilshire Blvd., Beverly Hills* ☎*323/468–1716* ⊕*www.nederlander.com*) presents Broadway musicals and occasional concerts.

NIGHTLIFE

While the ultimate in velvet-roped vampiness and glamour used to be the Sunset Strip, in the past couple of years the glitz has definitely shifted to Hollywood Boulevard and its surrounding streets. The lines are as long as the skirts are short outside the Hollywood club du jour (which changes so fast, it's often hard to keep track). But the Strip still has plenty going for it, with comedy clubs, hard-rock spots, and restaurants. West Hollywood's Santa Monica Boulevard bustles with gay and lesbian bars and clubs. For less conspicuous—and congested—alternatives, check out the events in downtown L.A.'s performance spaces and galleries. Silver Lake and Echo Park are best for boho bars and live music clubs.

Note that parking, especially after 7 PM, is at a premium in Hollywood. In fact, it's restricted on virtually every side street along the "hot zone" of West Hollywood (Sunset Boulevard from Fairfax to Doheny). Posted signs indicate the restrictions, but these are naturally harder to notice at night. Paying $5 to $10, and at some venues even $15 to $20, for valet or lot parking is often the easiest way to go.

BARS

HOLLYWOOD　The **Beauty Bar** (✉1638 Cahuenga Blvd., Hollywood ☎323/464–
★　　7676) offers manicures and makeovers along with the perfect martinis, but the hotties who flock to this retro salon-bar (the little sister of the Beauty Bars in NYC and San Fran) don't really need the cosmetic care—this is where the edgy beautiful people hang.

★　The casually hip **Three Clubs** (✉1123 N. Vine St., Hollywood ☎323/462–6441) is furtively located in a strip mall, beneath the Bargain Clown Mart discount store. The DJs segue through the many faces and phases of rock-and-roll and dance music. With dark-wood paneling, lamp-lighted tables, and even some sofas, you could be in a giant basement rec room from decades past—no fancy dress required, but fashionable looks suggested.

★　A lovely L.A. tradition is to meet at **Yamashiro** (✉1999 N. Sycamore Ave., Hollywood ☎323/466–5125) for cocktails at sunset. In the elegant restaurant, waitresses glide by in kimonos, and entrées can zoom up to $39; on the terrace, a spectacular hilltop view spreads out before you. ■TIP→**Mandatory valet parking is $3.50, but happy-hour drinks are just a bit more than that.**

WEST　As at so many other nightspots in this neck of the woods, the popu-
HOLLYWOOD　larity and clientele of **Bar Marmont** (✉8171 Sunset Blvd., West Hol-
★　　lywood ☎323/650–0575) bulged—and changed—after word got out it was a favorite of celebrities. Lately, it's gotten a second wind thanks to a strong DJ selection and luscious cocktails. The bar is next to the inimitable hotel Chateau Marmont, which boldface names continue to haunt.

★　The **Rainbow Bar & Grill** (✉9015 Sunset Blvd., West Hollywood ☎310/278–4232), in the heart of the Strip and next door to the legendary Roxy, is a landmark in its own right as *the* drinking spot of the '80s hair-metal scene—and it still attracts a music-industry crowd.

★　A classic Hollywood makeover—formerly a nursing home, this spot in the happening part of Sunset Strip got converted into a smart, brash-looking hotel, the **Standard** (✉8300 Sunset Blvd., West Hollywood ☎323/650–9090), for the young, hip, and connected. (Check out the live model in the lobby's fish tank.) The hotel and especially the bar here is popular with those in the biz.

ECHO PARK &　**Cha Cha Lounge** (✉2375 Glendale Blvd., Silver Lake ☎323/660–7595),
SILVER LAKE　Seattle's coolest rock bar, now aims to repeat its success with this col-
★　orful, red-lighted space. Think part tiki hut, part tacky Tijuana party palace. The tabletops pay homage to the lounge's former performers; they've got portraits of Latin drag queens.

★　The **Echo** (✉1822 Sunset Blvd., Echo Park ☎213/413–8200) sprang from the people behind the Silver Lake rock joint Spaceland. Most evenings this dark and divey space's tiny dance floor and well-worn booths attract artsy local bands and their followers, but things rev up when DJs spin reggae, rock, and funk. Opened in the club's basement in 2007, **the Echoplex** has a different entrance and books bigger national tours and events.

★ **Tiki Ti** (✉ *4427 W. Sunset Blvd., Silver Lake* ☎ *323/669–9381*) is one of the most charming drinking huts in the city. You can spend hours just looking at the Polynesian artifacts strewn all about the place, but be careful—time flies in this tiny tropical bar, and the colorful drinks can be so potent that you may have to stay marooned for a while.

DOWNTOWN
Fodor'sChoice
★

The **Downtown L.A. Standard** (✉ *550 S. Flower St., Downtown* ☎ *213/892–8080*) has a groovy lounge with pink sofas and DJs, as well as an all-white restaurant that looks like something out of *2001: A Space Odyssey*. But it's the rooftop bar, with an amazing view of the city's illuminated skyscrapers, a heated swimming pool, and private, podlike water-bed tents, that's worth waiting in line to get into. And wait you probably will, especially on weekends and in summer.

COMEDY

★ A nightly premier comedy showcase, **Comedy Store** (✉ *8433 Sunset Blvd., West Hollywood* ☎ *323/656–6225*) has been going strong for more than two decades, with three stages (with covers ranging from free to $20) to supply the yuks. Famous comedians occasionally make unannounced appearances.

★ More than a quarter century old, **Groundling Theatre** (✉ *7307 Melrose Ave., Hollywood* ☎ *323/934–9700*) has been a breeding ground for *Saturday Night Live* performers; alumni include Lisa Kudrow and *Curb Your Enthusiasm*'s Cheryl Hines. The primarily sketch and improv comedy shows run Thursday–Sunday, costing $12–$18.50.

Richard Pryor got his start at the **Improv** (✉ *8162 Melrose Ave., West Hollywood* ☎ *323/651–2583*), a renowned establishment showcasing stand-up comedy. Drew Carey's *Totally Improv* is Thursday night on a semiregular basis. Reservations are recommended. Cover is $10–$15, and there's a two-drink minimum.

Fodor'sChoice
★

Look for top stand-ups—and frequent celeb residents, like Bob Saget, or unannounced drop-ins, like Chris Rock—at **Laugh Factory** (✉ *8001 Sunset Blvd., West Hollywood* ☎ *323/656–1336*). The club has shows nightly at 8, plus added shows at 10 and midnight on Friday and Saturday; the cover is $10–$12. New York's **Upright Citizens Brigade** (✉ *5919 Franklin Ave., Hollywood* ☎ *323/908–8702*) marched in with a mix of sketch comedy and wild improvisations skewering pop culture. Members of the L.A. Brigade include VH1 commentator Paul Scheer and *Mad TV*'s Andrew Daly.

DANCE CLUBS

Though the establishments listed below are predominantly dance clubs as opposed to live music venues, there's often some overlap. A given club can vary wildly in genre from night to night, or even on the same night. ■**TIP**→ Gay and promoter-driven theme nights tend to "float" from venue to venue. Call ahead to make sure you don't end up looking for retro

'60s music at an industrial bondage celebration (or vice versa). Covers vary according to the night and the DJs.

★ As a bar, **Boardner's** (⊠*1652 N. Cherokee Ave., Hollywood* ☎*323/769–5001*) has a multidecade history (in the '20s it was a speakeasy), but with the adjoining ballroom, which was added a couple of years ago, it's now a state-of-the-art dance club. DJs may be spinning electronica, funk, or something else depending on the night—at the popular Saturday Goth event "Bar Sinister," patrons must wear black or risk not getting in. The cover here is anywhere from free to $10.

Goa (⊠*1615 Cahuenga Blvd., Hollywood* ☎*323/465–1615* ⊕*www. goasupperclub.com*) is one of Hollywood's most exotic—and exclusive—nightlife oasis. Expect to wait a while under the stars outside, before you're able to mingle amongst them inside.

GAY & LESBIAN CLUBS
Some of the most popular gay and lesbian "clubs" are weekly theme nights at various venues, so read the preceding list of clubs, *LA Weekly* listings, and gay publications such as *Odyssey* in addition to the following recommendations.

★ Nowhere is more gregarious than **Here** (⊠*696 N. Robertson Blvd., West Hollywood* ☎*310/360–8455*), where there are hot DJs and an even hotter clientele. Though it's usually a boys' hangout, you'll find WeHo's wildest ladies' night at Tuesday's Fuse gathering. A long-running gay-gal fave, the **Palms** (⊠*8572 Santa Monica Blvd., West Hollywood* ☎*310/652–6188*) continues to thrive thanks to great DJs spinning dance tunes Wednesday–Sunday. There are also an outdoor patio, pool tables, and an occasional live performance. **Rage** (⊠*8911 Santa Monica Blvd., West Hollywood* ☎*310/652–7055*) is a longtime favorite of the "gym boy" set, with DJs following a different musical theme every night of the week (alternative rock, house, dance remixes, etc.). The cover is free to $10.

ROCK & OTHER LIVE MUSIC
In addition to the venues listed below, many smaller bars book live music, if less frequently or with less publicity.

The landmark formerly known as the Palace is now the **Avalon** (⊠*1735 N. Vine St., Hollywood* ☎*323/462–3000*). The multilevel art deco building opposite Capitol Records has a fabulous sound system, four bars, and a balcony. Big-name rock and pop concerts hit the stage during the week, but on weekends the place becomes a dance club, with the most popular night the DJ-dominated Avaland on Saturday. Upstairs, but with a separate entrance, you'll find celeb hub the **Spider Club,** a Moroccan-style room where celebs and their entourages are frequent visitors. The **Key Club** (⊠*9039 Sunset Blvd., West Hollywood* ☎*310/274–5800*) is a flashy, multitier rock club with four bars presenting current artists of all genres (some on national tours, others local aspirants). After the concerts, there's often dancing with DJs spinning techno and house.

★ The **Knitting Factory** (✉ *7021 Hollywood Blvd., Hollywood* ☎ *323/463–0204*) is the L.A. offshoot of the downtown New York club of the same name. The modern, medium-size room seems all the more spacious for its balcony-level seating and sizable stage. Despite its dubious location on Hollywood Boulevard's tourist strip, it's a great set-up for the arty, big-name performers it presents. There's live music almost every night in the main room and in the smaller Alter-Knit Lounge. Covers are free to $40.

McCabe's Guitar Shop (✉ *3101 Pico Blvd., Santa Monica* ☎ *310/828–4497, 310/828–4403 for concert information*) is rootsy-retro-central, where all things earnest and (preferably) acoustic are welcome—chiefly folk, blues, bluegrass, and rock. It *is* a guitar shop (so no liquor license), with a room full of folding chairs for concert-style presentations. Make reservations well in advance. The **Roxy** (✉ *9009 Sunset Blvd., West Hollywood* ☎ *310/276–2222*), a Sunset Strip fixture for decades, hosts local and touring rock, alternative, blues, and rockabilly bands. Not the comfiest club around, but it's the site of many memorable shows. Neighborhoody and relaxed, **Silver Lake Lounge** (✉ *2906 Sunset Blvd., Silver Lake* ☎ *323/666–2407*) draws a mixed collegiate and boho crowd. The club is very unmainstream "cool," the booking policy an adventurous mix of local and touring alt-rockers. Bands play three to five nights a week; covers vary but are low.

★ The hottest bands of tomorrow, surprises from yesteryear, and unclassifiable bands of today perform at **Spaceland** (✉ *1717 Silver Lake Blvd., Silver Lake* ☎ *323/661–4380* ⊕ *www.clubspaceland.com*), which has a bar, jukebox, and pool table. Monday is always free, with monthlong gigs by the indie fave du jour. Spaceland has a nice selection of beers, some food if you're hungry, and a hip but relaxed interior.

Actor Johnny Depp sold his share of the infamous **Viper Room** (✉ *8852 Sunset Blvd., West Hollywood* ☎ *310/358–1880*) in 2004, but the place continues to rock with a motley live music lineup (Monday, local radio station Indie 103.1 presents new rock), if a less stellar crowd. **Whisky-A-Go-Go** (✉ *8901 Sunset Blvd., West Hollywood* ☎ *310/652–4202*) is the most famous rock-and-roll club on the Strip, where back in the '60s, Johnny Rivers cut hit singles and the Doors, Love, and the Byrds cut their musical eyeteeth. It's still going strong, with up-and-coming alternative, hard rock, and punk bands, though mostly of the unknown variety.

SPORTS & THE OUTDOORS

BEACHES

Los Angeles County beaches (and state beaches operated by the county) have lifeguards on duty year-round, with expanded forces during the summer. Public parking is usually available, though fees can be as much as $8; in some areas, it's possible to find free street and highway parking. Both restrooms and beach access have been brought up to the standards of the Americans with Disabilities Act. Generally, the northernmost beaches are best for surfing, hiking, and fishing, and the wider and sandier southern beaches are better for tanning and relaxing. ■TIP→ **Almost all are great for swimming, but beware: pollution in Santa Monica Bay sometimes approaches dangerous levels, particularly after storms.** Call ahead for beach conditions (☎310/457–9701) or go to www.watchthewater.com for specific beach updates. The following beaches are listed in north–south order:

Leo Carrillo State Beach. On the very edge of Ventura County, this narrow beach is better for exploring than for sunning or swimming (watch that strong undertow!). On your own or with a ranger, venture down at low tide to examine the tide pools among the rocks. Sequit Point, a promontory dividing the northwest and southeast halves of the beach, creates secret coves, sea tunnels, and boulders on which you can perch and fish. Generally, anglers stick to the northwest end of the beach; experienced surfers brave the rocks to the southeast. Campgrounds are set back from the beach; call ahead to reserve campsites. ⊠*35000 PCH, Malibu* ☎*818/880–0350, 800/444–7275 for camping reservations* ⌨*Parking, lifeguard (year-round, except only as needed in winter), restroom, showers, fire pits.*

Fodor'sChoice
★ **Robert H. Meyer Memorial State Beach.** Part of Malibu's most beautiful coastal area, this beach is made up of three minibeaches: El Pescador, La Piedra, and El Matador—all with the same spectacular view. Scramble down the steps to the rocky coves where nude sunbathers sometimes gather—although in recent years, police have been cracking down. "El Mat" has a series of caves, Piedra some nifty rock formations, and Pescador a secluded feel; but they're all picturesque and fairly private. ■TIP→ **One warning: watch the incoming tide and don't get trapped between those otherwise scenic boulders.** ⊠*32350, 32700, and 32900 PCH, Malibu* ☎*818/880–0350* ⌨*Parking, 1 roving lifeguard unit, restrooms.*

Zuma Beach Park. Zuma, 2 mi of white sand usually littered with tanning teenagers, has it all: from fishing and diving to swings for the kids to volleyball courts. Beachgoers looking for quiet or privacy should head elsewhere. Stay alert in the water: the surf is rough and inconsistent. ⊠*30050 PCH, Malibu* ☎*818/880–0350* ⌨*Parking, lifeguard (year-round, except only as needed in winter), restrooms, food concessions, playground.*

Malibu Lagoon State Beach/Surfrider Beach. Steady 3- to 5-foot waves make this beach, just west of Malibu Pier, a surfing paradise. The International Surfing Contest is held here in September—the surf's premium around that time. Water runoff from Malibu Canyon forms a natural lagoon that's a sanctuary for 250 species of birds. Unfortunately, the lagoon is often polluted and algae filled. If you're leery of going into the water, you can bird-watch, play volleyball, or take a walk on one of the nature trails, which are perfect for romantic sunset strolls. ⊠*23200 PCH, Malibu* ☎*310/305–9503* ⌨*Parking, lifeguard (year-round), restrooms, picnic tables.*

Will Rogers State Beach. This clean, sandy, 3-mi beach, with a dozen volleyball nets, gymnastics equipment, and playground equipment for kids, is an all-around favorite. The surf is gentle, perfect for swimmers and beginning surfers. However, it's best to avoid the place after a storm, when untreated water flows from storm drains into the sea. ☒ *15100 PCH, 2 mi north of Santa Monica Pier, Pacific Palisades* ☎ *818/880–0350* ☞ *Parking, lifeguard (year-round, except only as needed in winter), restrooms.*

★ **Santa Monica State Beach.** It's the first beach you'll hit after the Santa Monica Freeway (I–10) runs into the PCH, and it's one of L.A.'s best known. Wide and sandy, Santa Monica is *the* place for sunning and socializing: be prepared for a mob scene on summer weekends, when parking becomes an expensive ordeal. Swimming is fine (with the usual poststorm pollution caveat); for surfing, go elsewhere. For a memorable view, climb up the stairway over the PCH to Palisades Park, at the top of the bluffs. Summer-evening concerts are often held here. ☒ *1642 Promenade, PCH at California Incline, Santa Monica* ☎ *310/305–9503* ☞ *Parking, lifeguard (year-round), restrooms, showers.*

Venice City Beach. The surf and sand of Venice are fine, but the main attraction here is the boardwalk scene, which is a cosmos all its own— with fire-eating street performers, vendors hawking everything from cheap sunglasses and aromatherapy oils, and bicep'ed gym rats lifting weights at legendary Muscle Beach. Go on weekend afternoons for the best people-watching experience. There are also swimming, fishing, surfing, basketball (it's the site of some of L.A.'s most hotly contested pickup games), racquetball, handball, and shuffleboard. You can rent a bike or some in-line skates and hit the Strand bike path. ☒ *West of Pacific Ave., Venice* ☎ *310/577–5700* ☞ *Parking, restrooms, food concessions, showers, playground.*

★ **Redondo Beach.** The Redondo Beach Pier marks the starting point of this wide, sandy, busy beach along a heavily developed shoreline community. Restaurants and shops flourish along the pier, excursion boats and privately owned crafts depart from launching ramps, and a reef formed by a sunken ship creates prime fishing and snorkeling conditions. If you're adventurous, you might try to kayak out to the buoys and hobnob with pelicans and sea lions. A series of free rock and jazz concerts takes place at the pier every summer. ☒ *Torrance Blvd. at Catalina Ave., Redondo Beach* ☎ *310/372–2166* ☞ *Parking, lifeguard (year-round), restrooms, food concessions, showers.*

SPORTS

L.A.'s near-perfect climate allows sports enthusiasts the privilege of being outside year-round. The **City of Los Angeles Department of Recreation and Parks** (☒ *200 N. Main St., Suite 1350* ☎ *888/527-2757* ⊕ *www.cityofla.org/rap*) has information on city parks. For information on county parks contact the **Los Angeles County Department of Parks and Recreation** (☒ *433 S. Vermont Ave.* ☎ *213/738–2961* ⊕ *parks.co.la.ca.us*).

Ticketmaster (☎213/480–3232 ⊕*www.ticketmaster.com*) sells tickets to most sporting events in town.

BASEBALL

You can watch the **Dodgers** take on their National League rivals while you munch on pizza, tacos, or a foot-long "Dodger dog" at one of the game's most comfortable ball parks, **Dodger Stadium** (✉*1000 Elysian Park Ave., exit off I–110, Pasadena Fwy.* ☎*323/224–1448 ticket information* ⊕*www.dodgers.com*). The **Los Angeles Angels of Anaheim** won the World Series in 2002, the first time since the team formed in 1961. For Angels ticket information, contact **Angel Stadium of Anaheim** (✉*2000 Gene Autry Way, Anaheim* ☎*714/663–9000* ⊕*www.angels baseball.com*). Several colleges in the area also have baseball teams worth watching, especially USC, which has been a perennial source of major-league talent.

BASKETBALL

L.A.'s pro basketball teams play at the Staples Center. The **Los Angeles Lakers** (☎*310/426–5000* ⊕*www.nba.com/lakers*) still attract a loyal following that includes celebrity fans like Jack Nicholson, Tyra Banks, and Leonardo DiCaprio. Despite a series of off-the-court conflicts in recent years, the team remains one of the NBA's most successful franchises with 14 NBA championships under its belt. L.A.'s "other" team, the much-maligned but newly revitalized **Clippers** (☎*888/895–8662* ⊕*www.nba.com/clippers*), sells tickets that are generally cheaper and easier to get than those for Lakers games. The **Los Angeles Sparks** (☎*310/426–6031* ⊕*www.wnba.com/sparks*) have built a WNBA dynasty around former USC star Lisa Leslie.

GOLF

The City Parks and Recreation Department lists seven public 18-hole courses in Los Angeles, and L.A. County runs some good ones, too. **Rancho Park Golf Course** (✉*10460 W. Pico Blvd., West L.A.* ☎*310/838–7373*) is one of the most heavily played links in the country. It's a beautifully designed course, but the towering pines present an obstacle for those who slice or hook. There's a two-level driving range, a 9-hole pitch 'n' putt, a snack bar, and a pro shop where you can rent clubs.

★ If you want a scenic course, you've got it in spades at the county-run, par-71 **Los Verdes Golf Course** (✉*7000 W. Los Verdes Dr., Rancho Palos Verdes* ☎*310/377–7370*). You get a cliff-top view of the ocean—time it right and you can watch the sun set behind Catalina Island.

Griffith Park has two splendid 18-hole courses along with a challenging 9-hole course. **Harding Municipal Golf Course** and **Wilson Municipal Golf Course** (✉*4730 Crystal Springs Dr., Los Feliz* ☎*323/663–2555*) are about 1½ mi inside the park entrance, at Riverside Drive and Los Feliz Boulevard. Bridle paths surround the outer fairways, and the San Gabriel Mountains make a scenic background. The 9-hole **Roosevelt Municipal Golf Course** (✉*2650 N. Vermont Ave., Los Feliz* ☎*323/665–2011*) can be reached through the park's Vermont Avenue entrance.

CLOSE UP

Surf City

Nothing captures the laid-back cool of California quite like surfing. Those wanting to sample the surf here should keep a few things in mind before getting wet. First, surfers can be notoriously territorial. Beginners should avoid Palos Verdes and Third Point, at the north end of Malibu Lagoon State Beach, where veterans rule the waves. Once in the water, be as polite and mellow as possible. Give other surfers plenty of space—do *not* cut them off—and avoid swimmers. Beware of rocks and undertows. Surfing calls for caution: that huge piece of flying fiberglass beneath you could kill someone. Also keep in mind that your welcome in the water most likely won't be a shining example of gender equality. Beginning female surfers often get encouragement from local hotshots. A hapless guy, however, should expect a few sneers.

If you're not a strong swimmer, think twice before jumping in; fighting the surf to where the waves break is a strenuous proposition. The best and safest way to learn is by taking a lesson.

A session with **Malibu Ocean Sports** (✉ *29500 PCH* ☎ *310/456–6302*) will keep you on the sand for at least 30 minutes explaining the basics. Lessons start at $100; if you don't catch a wave, you get your money back. **Surf Academy** (✉ *302 19th St., Hermosa Beach* ☎ *310/372–2790* ⊕ *www.surfacademy.org*) teaches at El Segundo (Dockweiler), Santa Monica, and Manhattan Beach, with lessons starting at $45.

Kanoa Aquatics (✉ *302 19th St., Hermosa Beach* ☎ *310/374–1994* ⊕ *www.kanoaaquatics.com*) teaches individuals and groups at Manhat-

tan Beach, Venice, Santa Monica, and Malibu. They also hold highly regarded one- and two-week surf camps for kids ages 5–17. When you hit the surfing hot spots, surf shops with rentals will be in long supply. Competition keeps prices comparable; most rent long and short boards and miniboards (kid-size surfboards) from $20 per day and wet suits from $10 per day (some give discounts for additional days).

Learners should never surf in a busy area; look for somewhere less crowded where you'll catch more waves anyway. Good beaches for beginners are Malibu Lagoon State Beach and Huntington City Beach north of the pier, but you should always check conditions, which change throughout the day, before heading into the water. **L.A. County Lifeguards** (☎ *310/457–9701*) has a prerecorded surf-conditions hotline or go to www.watchthewater.com for beach reports.

4

SHOPPING

AROUND BEVERLY HILLS

N.Y. has Fifth Avenue, but L.A. has famed **Rodeo Drive.** The triangle, between Santa Monica and Wilshire boulevards and Beverly Drive, is one of the city's biggest tourist attractions and is lined with shops featuring the biggest names in fashion. You'll see well-coifed and -heeled ladies toting multiple packages to their Mercedes and paparazzi staking out street corners. While the dress code in L.A. is considerably laid-back, with residents wearing flip-flops year-round, you might find them to be jewel-encrusted on Rodeo. Steep price tags on designer labels make it a "just looking" experience for many residents and tourists alike, but salespeople are used to the ogling and window-shopping. In recent years, more midrange shops have opened up on the strip and surrounding blocks. Keep in mind that some stores are by appointment only. ■TIP→**There are several well-marked, free (for two hours) parking lots around the core shopping area.**

★ **Beverly Center.** This is one of the more traditional malls you'll find in L.A., with eight levels of stores, including Macy's and Bloomingdale's. Fashion is the biggest draw, and there's a little something from everyone, from D&G to H&M, and many shops in the midrange, including Banana Republic, DKNY, Club Monaco, Coach, and Nine West. Look for accessories at Jacqueline Jarrot and separates at Shaya. For a terrific view of the city, head to the top-floor terrace and rooftop food court. Next door is Loehmann's, which offers a huge selection of discounted designer wear. ⊠ *8500 Beverly Blvd., bounded by Beverly, La Cienega, and San Vicente Blvds. and 3rd St., between Beverly Hills and West Hollywood* ☎ *310/854–0071.*

DOWNTOWN

★ **The Fashion District.** Although this 90-block hub of the West Coast fashion industry is mainly a wholesale market, more than 1,000 independent stores sell to the general public (and some wholesalers do so on Saturday, too, when elbow room is scarce). Bonus: bargaining is expected but note that most sales are cash-only and dressing rooms are scarce. **Santee Alley** (between Santee Street and Maple Avenue, from Olympic Boulevard to 11th Street) is known for back-alley deals on knock-offs of designer sunglasses, jewelry, handbags, shoes, and clothing. Be prepared to haggle, and don't lose sight of your wallet. Visit the fashion district's Web site for maps and tips. ⊠ *Roughly between I–10 and 7th St., San Pedro and Main Sts., Downtown* ⊕ *www.fashion district.org.*

The Jewelry District. This area resembles a slice of Manhattan, with the crowded sidewalks, diverse aromas, and haggling bargain hunters. Expect to save 50% to 70% off retail for everything from wedding bands to sparkling belt buckles. The more upscale stores are along Hill Street between 6th and 7th streets. (There's a parking structure next door on Broadway.) ✉*Between Olive St. and Broadway, from 5th to 8th St., Downtown* ⊕*www.lajd.net.*

Fodor's Choice
★ **Olvera Street.** Historic buildings line this redbrick walkway overhung with grape vines. At dozens of clapboard stalls you can browse south-of-the-border goods—leather sandals, bright woven blankets, devotional candles, and the like—as well as cheap toys and tchotchkes. With the musicians and cafés providing background noise, the area is constantly lively. ✉*Between Cesar Chavez Ave. and Arcadia St., Downtown.*

HOLLYWOOD

Local shops may be a mixed bag, but at least you can read the stars below your feet as you browse along Hollywood Boulevard. Lingerie and movie memorabilia stores predominate here, but there are numerous options in the retail-hotel-dining-entertainment complex Hollywood & Highland. Hollywood impersonators (Michael Jackson, Marilyn Monroe, and, er, Chewbacca) join break-dancers and other street entertainers in keeping tourists entertained on Hollywood Boulevard's sidewalks near the Kodak Theater, home to the Oscars. Along La Brea Avenue, you'll find plenty of trendy, quirky, and hip merchandise, from records to furniture and clothing.

Hollywood & Highland. Dozens of stores, a slew of eateries, and the Kodak Theatre fill this outdoor complex, which mimics cinematic glamour. Find designer shops (Coach, Polo, Ralph Lauren, Louis Vuitton) and chain stores (Banana Republic, Planet Funk, Sephora, Virgin Megastore). From the upper levels, there's a camera-perfect view of the famous HOLLYWOOD sign. On the second level, next to the Kodak Theatre, is a **Visitor Information Center** (☎*323/467–6412*) with a multilingual staff, maps, attraction brochures, and information about services. The streets surrounding it provide the setting for the Sunday Hollywood Farmers Market, where you're likely to spot a celebrity or two picking up fresh produce or stopping to eat breakfast from the food vendors. ✉*Hollywood Blvd. and Highland Ave., Hollywood* ☎*323/817–0220.*

LOS FELIZ, SILVER LAKE & ECHO PARK

There's a hipster rock-and-roll vibe to this area, which has grown in recent years to add just the slightest shine to its edge. Come for homegrown, funky galleries, vintage shops, and local designers' boutiques. Shopping areas are concentrated along Vermont Avenue and Hollywood Boulevard in Los Feliz; Sunset Boulevard in both Silver Lake (known as Sunset Junction) and Echo Park; and Echo Park Avenue in Echo Park. ■TIP➔**Keep in mind that things are spread out enough to necessitate a couple of short car trips, and many shops in these neighborhoods don't open until noon but stay open later, so grab dinner or drinks at one of the area's über-cool spots after shopping.**

WEST HOLLYWOOD & MELROSE AVENUE

West Hollywood is prime shopping real estate. And as they say with real estate, it's all about location, location, location. Depending on the street address, West Hollywood has everything from upscale art, design, and antiques store to ladies-who-lunch clothing boutiques to megamusic stores and specialty book vendors. Melrose Avenue, for instance, is part bohemian-punk shopping district (from North Highland to Sweetzer) and part upscale art and design mecca (upper Melrose Avenue and Melrose Place). Discerning locals and celebs haunt the posh boutiques around Sunset Plaza (Sunset Boulevard at Sunset Plaza Drive), on Robertson Boulevard (between Beverly Boulevard and 3rd Street), and along upper Melrose Avenue.

The huge, blue Pacific Design Center, on Melrose at San Vicente Boulevard, is the focal point for this neighborhood's art- and interior design–related stores, including many on nearby Beverly Boulevard. The Beverly–La Brea neighborhood also claims a number of trendy clothing stores. Perched between Beverly Hills and West Hollywood, 3rd Street (between La Cienega and Fairfax) is a magnet for small, friendly designer boutiques. Finally, the Fairfax District, along Fairfax below Melrose, encompasses the flamboyant, historic Farmers Market, at Fairfax Avenue and 3rd Street; the adjacent shopping extravaganza, The Grove; and some excellent galleries around Museum Row at Fairfax Avenue and Wilshire Boulevard.

SANTA MONICA & VENICE

The breezy beachside communities of Santa Monica and Venice are ideal for leisurely shopping. Scads of tourists (and some locals) gravitate to the Third Street Promenade, a popular pedestrians-only strolling–shopping area that is within walking range of the beach and historic Santa Monica Pier. A number of modern furnishings stores are nearby on 4th and 5th streets. Main Street between Pico Boulevard and Rose Avenue offers upscale chain stores, cafés, and some original shops, while Montana Avenue is a great source for distinctive clothing boutiques and child-friendly shopping, especially between 7th and 17th streets. ■TIP➔**Parking in Santa Monica is next to impossible on Wednesday, when some streets are blocked off for the farmers' market, but there are several parking structures with free parking for an hour or two.** In Venice, Abbot Kinney Boulevard is abuzz with midcentury furniture stores, art galleries and boutiques, and cafés.

★ **Third Street Promenade.** Whimsical dinosaur-shaped, ivy-covered fountains and buskers of every stripe set the scene along this pedestrians-only shopping stretch. Stores are mainly the chain variety (Restoration Hardware, Urban Outfitters, Apple), but there are also Quiksilver and Rip Curl outposts for cool surf attire. Movie theaters, bookstores, pubs, and restaurants ensure that virtually every need is covered. ⊠*3rd St. between Broadway and Wilshire Blvd.*

LOS ANGELES ESSENTIALS

BY AIR

It's generally easier to navigate the secondary airports than to get through sprawling LAX, the city's major gateway. Bob Hope Airport in Burbank is closest to downtown L.A., and domestic flights to it can be cheaper than flights to LAX—it's definitely worth checking out. From Long Beach Airport it's equally convenient to go north to central Los Angeles or south to Orange County. Flights to Orange County's John Wayne Airport are often more expensive than those to the other secondary airports. Parking at the smaller airports is cheaper than at LAX.

4

Airport Information **Bob Hope Airport** (*BUR* ☎ *818/840–8830* ⊕ *www.bobhope airport.com*). **John Wayne/Orange County Airport** (*SNA* ☎ *949/252–5006* ⊕ *www.ocair.com*). **Long Beach Airport** (*LGB* ☎ *562/570–2600* ⊕ *www.lgb.org*). **Los Angeles International Airport** (*LAX* ☎ *310/646–5252* ⊕ *www.lawa.org*). **Ontario International Airport** (*ONT* ☎ *909/937–2700* ⊕ *www.lawa.org*).

Shuttles **Prime Time** (☎ *800/733–8267* ⊕ *www.primetimeshuttle.com*). **SuperShuttle** (☎ *323/775–6600, 310/782–6600, or 800/258–3826* ⊕ *www.super shuttle.com*). **Xpress Shuttle** (☎ *800/427–7483* ⊕ *www.expressshuttle.com*).

BY BUS

Inadequate public-transportation systems have been an L.A. problem for decades. That said, many local trips can be made, with time and patience, by bus. In certain cases, it may be your best option; for example, visiting the Getty Center, going to Universal Studios and/or the adjacent CityWalk, or venturing into downtown. The Metropolitan Transit Authority DASH (Downtown Area Short Hop) minibuses cover six different circular routes in Hollywood, Mid-Wilshire, and the downtown area. The buses stop every two blocks or so. The Santa Monica Municipal Bus Line, also known as the Big Blue Bus, is a pleasant and inexpensive way to move around the Westside, where the MTA lines leave off. There's also an express bus to and from downtown L.A., and a shuttle bus, the Tide Shuttle, which runs between Main Street and the Third Street Promenade and stops at hotels along the way. Culver CityBus Lines runs six routes through Culver City.

Bus Information **California Smart Traveler** (☎ *800/266–6883* ⊕ *www.dot. ca.gov/caltrans511*). **Culver CityBus Lines** (☎ *310/253–6500* ⊕ *www.culvercity. org*). **DASH** (☎ *213/626–4455 or 310/808–2273* ⊕ *www.ladottransit.com/dash*). **Greyhound** (☎ *213/629–8405 or 800/231–2222* ⊕ *www.greyhound.com*). **Metropolitan Transit Authority (MTA)** (☎ *213/626–4455* ⊕ *www.mta.net*). **Santa Monica Municipal Bus Line** (☎ *310/451–5444* ⊕ *www.bigbluebus.com*).

BY CAR

Be aware that a number of major streets have similar-sounding names (Beverly Drive and Beverly Boulevard, or numbered streets north to south downtown and east to west in Hollywood, West Hollywood, and Beverly Hills) or exactly the same name (San Vicente Boulevard in West L.A., Brentwood, Santa Monica, and West Hollywood). Also, some smaller streets seem to exist intermittently for miles, so unless you have good directions, you should use major streets rather than try for an alternative that is actually blocked by a dead end or detours, like the side streets off Sunset Boulevard. Try to get clear directions and stick to them.

If you get discombobulated while on the freeway, remember the rule of thumb: even-numbered freeways run east and west, odd-numbered freeways run north and south.

Information **California Highway Patrol** (☎ *323/906–3434 for road conditions, 800/427–7623 in California).* **City of Los Angeles** (⊕ *www.ci.la.ca.us* ⊕ *www. sigalert.com* ⊕ *http://trafficinfo.lacity.org).*

Emergency Services **Freeway Service Patrol** (☎ *213/922–2957 general information).*

CAR RENTALS

Major-chain rates in L.A. begin at $35 a day and $110 a week, plus 8.25% sales tax. Luxury and sport utility vehicles start at $69 a day. Open-top convertibles are a popular choice for L.A. visitors wanting to make the most of the sun. Note that the major agencies offer services for travelers with disabilities, such as hand controls, for little or no extra cost.

Local Agencies **Beverly Hills Budget Car Rental** (☎ *310/274–9173 or 800/227– 7117* ⊕ *www.budgetbeverlyhills.com).* **Beverly Hills Rent-A-Car** (☎ *310/337– 1400 or 800/479–5996* ⊕ *www.bhrentacar.com).* **Enterprise** (☎ *800/736–8222* ⊕ *www.enterprise.com).* **EV Rental Cars** (☎ *877/387–3682* ⊕ *www.evrental. com).* **Midway Car Rental** (☎ *888/682–0166* ⊕ *www.midwaycarrental.com).* **Rent A Wreck** (☎ *800/995–0994* ⊕ *www.rent-a-wreck.com).* **Town Rent A Car** (☎ *310/973–6815 or 323/934–4780).* **@West Rent a Car** (☎ *310/417–9050 or 877/404–0404* ⊕ *www.atwestcarrental.com).*

BY METRO RAIL

Metro Rail covers a limited area of L.A.'s vast expanse, but what there is, is helpful and frequent. The underground Red Line runs from Union Station downtown through Mid-Wilshire, Hollywood, and Universal City on its way to North Hollywood, stopping at the most popular tourist destinations along the way. The light commuter rail Green Line stretches from Redondo Beach to Norwalk, while the partially underground Blue Line goes from downtown to the South Bay (Long Beach/ San Pedro). The Green and Blue lines are not often used by visitors, though the Green is gaining popularity as an alternative, albeit time-consuming, way to reach LAX. The monorail-like Gold Line begins at Union Station and heads northeast to Pasadena and Sierra Madre. The Orange Line, a 14-mi bus corridor, connects the North Hollywood subway station with the western San Fernando Valley.

The Web site is the best way to get info on Metro Rail.

Metro Rail Information **Metropolitan Transit Authority (MTA)** (☎ *800/266–6883 or 213/626–4455* ⊕ *www.mta.net).*

BY TAXI & LIMOUSINE

Don't even try to hail a cab on the street in Los Angeles. Instead, phone one of the many taxi companies. The metered rate is $2.45 per mile, plus a $2.65 per-fare charge. Taxi rides from LAX have an additional $2.50 surcharge. Be aware that distances between sights in L.A. are vast, so cab fares add up quickly. On the other end of the price spectrum, limousines come equipped with everything from a full bar and telephone to a hot tub. If you open any L.A.–area yellow pages, the number of limo companies will astound you. Most charge by the hour, with a three-hour minimum.

Limo Companies **ABC Limousine & Sedan Service** (☎ 818/980–6000 or 888/753–7500). **American Executive** (☎ 213/250–2121 or 800/927–2020). **Black & White Transportation Services** (☎ 800/924–1624). **Chauffeur's Unlimited** (☎ 310/645–8711 or 888/546–6019 ⊕ www.chaufusa.com). **Dav El Limousine Co.** (☎ 310/550–0070 or 800/922–0343 ⊕ www.davel.com). **First Class** (☎ 323/756–4894 or 310/676–9771 ⊕ www.first-classlimo.com). **ITS** (☎ 800/487–4255).

Taxi Companies **Bell Cab** (☎ 888/235–5222 ⊕ www.bellcab.com). **Beverly Hills Cab Co.** (☎ 800/273–6611). **Checker Cab** (☎ 800/300–5007). **Independent Cab Co.** (☎ 800/521–8294 ⊕ www.taxi4u.com). **United Independent Taxi** (☎ 800/411–0303 or 800/822–8294). **Yellow Cab/LA Taxi Co-Op** (☎ 800/200–1085 or 800/200–0011).

BY TRAIN

Union Station in downtown Los Angeles is one of the great American railroad stations. The interior is well kept and includes comfortable seating, a restaurant, and snack bars. As the city's rail hub, it's the place to catch an Amtrak train. Among Amtrak's Southern California routes are 13 daily trips to San Diego and seven to Santa Barbara. Amtrak's luxury *Coast Starlight* travels along the spectacular coastline from Seattle to Los Angeles in just a day and a half (though it's often a little late). The *Sunset Limited* goes to Los Angeles from Florida (via New Orleans and Texas), and the *Southwest Chief* from Chicago. You can make reservations in advance by phone or at the station. As with airlines, you usually get a better deal the farther in advance you book. You must show your ticket and a photo ID before boarding. Smoking is not allowed on Amtrak trains.

Information **Amtrak** (☎ 800/872–7245 ⊕ www.amtrak.com). **Union Station** (✉ 800 N. Alameda St. ☎ 213/683–6979).

VISITOR INFORMATION

Contacts **Beverly Hills Conference and Visitors Bureau** (☎ 310/248–1000 or 800/345–2210 ⊕ www.beverlyhillsbehere.com). **California Office of Tourism** (☎ 916/444–4429 or 800/862–2543 ⊕ gocalif.ca.gov). **Glendale Chamber of Commerce** (☎ 818/240–7870 ⊕ www.glendalechamber.com). **Hollywood Chamber of Commerce Info Center** (☎ 323/469–8311 ⊕ www.hollywoodchamber. net). **L.A. Inc./The Convention and Visitors Bureau** (☎ 213/624–7300 or 800/228–2452 ⊕ www.lacvb.com). **Long Beach Area Convention and Visitors Bureau** (☎ 562/436–3645 ⊕ www.visitlongbeach.com). **Pasadena Convention &**

Visitors Bureau (☏ *626/795-9311* ⊕ *www.pasadenacal.com*). **Redondo Beach Visitors Bureau** (☏ *310/374-2171 or 800/282-0333* ⊕ *www.visitredondo.com*). **Santa Monica Convention & Visitors Bureau** (☏ *310/319-6263 or 800/544-5319* ⊕ *www.santamonica.com*). **Santa Monica Visitor Centers** (☏ *310/393-7593*). **West Hollywood Convention and Visitors Bureau** (☏ *310/289-2525 or 800/368-6020* ⊕ *www.visitwesthollywood.com*).

Channel Islands
National Park

Christy Beach, Santa Cruz Island, Channel Islands National Park

WORD OF MOUTH

"An island always pleases my imagination, even the smallest, as a
small continent and integral portion of the globe."
—Henry David Thoreau

WELCOME TO CHANNEL ISLANDS NATIONAL PARK

TOP REASONS TO GO

★ **Rare flora and fauna:** The Channel Islands are home to 145 species of terrestrial plants and animals found nowhere else on Earth.

★ **Time travel:** With no cars, phones, or services, these undeveloped islands provide a glimpse of what California was like hundreds of years ago. This pristine wilderness is close to the mainland, yet worlds away from hectic modern life.

★ **Underwater adventures:** The incredibly healthy channel waters rank among the top 10 diving destinations on the planet—but you can also visit the kelp forest virtually via an underwater video program.

★ **Marvelous marine mammals:** More than 30 species of seals, sea lions, whales, and other marine mammals ply the park's waters at various times of year.

★ **Sea cave kayaking:** Paddle around otherwise inaccessible portions of the park's 175 mi of gorgeous coastline—including one of the world's largest sea caves.

1 Anacapa. Tiny Anacapa is a 5-mi stretch of three islets, with towering cliffs, caves, natural bridges, and rich kelp forests.

2 San Miguel. Isolated, windswept San Miguel has an ancient caliche forest and hundreds of archaeological sites. More than 30,000 pinnipeds (seals and sea lions) hang out on the island's beaches during certain times of year.

Santa Ynez Peak 4,298 ft

Santa Barbara

Harris Point
Cabrillo Monument
Lester Ranch site
Point Bennett
Tyler Bight
San Miguel Island
Cuyler Harbor
San Miguel Passage
Sandy Point
West Point
Carrington Point
Vail & Vickers Ranch
Torrey Pines
Bechers Bay
Soledad Peak 1,574 ft
East Point
Santa Rosa Island
Johnsons Lee
South Point
Santa Cruz Channel

PACIFIC OCEAN

3 Santa Barbara. Six miles of scenic trails crisscross this tiny island, known for its excellent wildlife viewing and native plants. It's a favorite destination for diving, snorkeling, and kayaking.

GETTING ORIENTED

Channel Islands National Park includes five of the eight Channel Islands and the nautical mile of ocean that surrounds them. The islands range in size from 1-square-mi Santa Barbara to 96-square-mi Santa Cruz. Together they form a magnificent nature preserve with 145 endemic or unique species of plants and animals. Half the park lies underwater, and the surrounding channel waters are teeming with life, including dolphins, whales, seals, sea lions, and seabirds.

4 Santa Cruz. The park's largest island offers some of the best hikes and kayaking opportunities, one of the world's largest and deepest sea caves, and more species of flora and fauna than any other park island.

5 Santa Rosa. Campers love to stay on Santa Rosa, with its myriad hiking opportunities, stunning white-sand beaches, and rare grove of Torrey pines. It's also the only island accessible by plane.

CHANNEL ISLANDS NATIONAL PARK PLANNER

When to Go

Channel Islands National Park records about 620,000 visitors each year, but most never venture beyond the visitor center in Ventura. Still, make your transportation arrangements as soon as possible if you plan to travel to the islands on holidays or summer weekends, when hotels tend to fill up.

The rains usually come from December through March—but this is also the best time to spot gray whales in the channel, and nearby hotels offer considerable discounts. In the late spring, thousands of migratory birds descend on the islands to hatch their young, and wildflowers carpet the slopes. The warm, dry summer months are the best time to go camping, and humpback and blue whales arrive to feed from late June through early fall.

The water temperature is nearly always cool, so bring a wet suit if you plan to spend much time in the ocean, even in the relatively warm months of August and September. Be prepared for fog, high winds, and rough seas any time of the year.

Flora & Fauna

Often called the North American Galapagos, the Channel Islands are home to species found nowhere else on Earth: mammals such as the island fox and the Anacapa deer mouse, birds like the island scrub-jay, and plants like the Santa Barbara live-forever. Other species, such as the Santa Rosa Torrey pine and the island oak, have evolved differently from their counterparts on the mainland.

Getting There & Around

Channel Islands National Park is located in the Santa Barbara Channel, south of Santa Barbara and southwest of Oxnard and Ventura. Transportation to and from the islands is provided by private companies (see Transportation Options box). U.S. Highway 101 and Amtrak trains link all neighboring cities and harbors, providing access to the park. To reach the Channel Islands National Park Visitor Center (on the mainland in Ventura) by car, exit in Ventura at Seaward Boulevard or Victoria Avenue and follow the signs to Ventura Harbor/Spinnaker Drive. In Santa Barbara, exit U.S. Highway 101 at Castillo Street and head south to Cabrillo Boulevard, then turn right for the harbor entrance. If you arrive by train in either Santa Barbara, Ventura, or Oxnard, take a taxi or hop aboard a waterfront shuttle bus.

Anacapa Island is 12 mi (about 1 hour) from Channel Islands Harbor in Oxnard. Santa Cruz Island lies 20 mi (1 to 1½ hours) from the Channel Islands Visitor Center in Ventura Harbor. Santa Rosa Island is 46 mi (2½ to 3 hours) from Ventura; San Miguel is 58 mi (3½ to 4 hours) from the city. It takes 2½ to 3 hours to reach Santa Barbara Island, 55 mi offshore.

AVG. HIGH/LOW TEMPS.

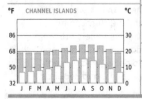

WHAT IT COSTS

¢	$	$$	$$$	$$$$
Camping				
under $10	$10–$17	$18–$35	$36–$50	over $50

Camping prices are for a standard (no hookups, pit toilets, fire grates, picnic tables) campsite per night.

By Cheryl Crabtree

On crystal-clear days the craggy peaks of Channel Islands National Park are easy to see from the mainland, jutting from the Pacific in such sharp detail it seems you could reach out and touch them. The islands really aren't that far away—a high-speed boat will whisk you to the closest ones in less than an hour—yet very few people ever visit them. Those fearless, adventurous types who do will experience one of the most splendid land-and-sea wilderness areas on the planet.

WHAT TO SEE

THE ISLANDS

★ **Anacapa Island.** Although most people think of it as an island, Anacapa is actually comprised of three narrow islets. The tips of these volcanic formations nearly touch but are inaccessible from one another except by boat. All three islets have towering cliffs, isolated sea caves, and natural bridges; Arch Rock, on East Anacapa, is one of the best-known symbols of Channel Islands National Park. Wildlife viewing is the reason most people come to East Anacapa—particularly in summer when seagull chicks are newly hatched and sea lions and seals lounge on the beaches.

The compact **museum** on East Anacapa tells the history of the island, and it houses, among other things, the original lead-crystal Fresnel lens from the island's lighthouse (circa 1937). If you come in summer, you can also learn about the nearby kelp forests by talking with underwater rangers via microphone and camera on Tuesday, Wednesday, and Thursday afternoons at 2; these sessions are broadcast live at the visitor center. Depending on the season and the number of desirable species lurking about there, a limited number of boats travel to Frenchy's Cove, at West Anacapa, where in its pristine tide pools you might see anemones, limpets, barnacles, mussel beds, and colorful marine algae.

The rest of West Anacapa is closed to protect nesting brown pelicans, and trips to Middle Anacapa Island require a ranger escort.

San Miguel Island. The westernmost of the Channel Islands, San Miguel is frequently battered by storms sweeping across the North Pacific. The 15-square-mi island's wild, windswept landscape is lush with vegetation. Point Bennett, at the western tip, offers one of the world's most spectacular wildlife displays when more than 30,000 pinnipeds hit its beach. Explorer Juan Rodríguez Cabrillo was the first European to visit this island; he claimed it for Spain in 1542. Legend holds that Cabrillo died on one of the Channel Islands—no one knows where he's buried, but there's a memorial to him on a bluff above Cuyler Harbor.

Santa Barbara Island. At about 1 square mi, Santa Barbara is the smallest of the Channel Islands. It's also the southernmost island in the chain, nearly 35 mi from the others. Triangular in shape, Santa Barbara's steep cliffs—which offer a perfect nesting spot for the Xantus's murrelet, a rare seabird—are topped by twin peaks. In spring, you can enjoy a brilliant display of yellow coreopsis.

With exhibits on the region's natural history, the small **museum** is a great place to learn about the wildlife on and around the islands. ⊠ *Santa Barbara Island* ☏ *No phone* ☉ *Daily 10–5.*

Santa Cruz Island. Five miles west of Anacapa, 96-square-mi Santa Cruz is the largest of the Channel Islands. The National Park Service manages the easternmost 25% of the island; the rest is owned by the Nature Conservancy, which requires a permit to land. When your boat drops you off on the 70 mi of craggy coastline, you'll find two rugged mountain ranges with peaks soaring to 2,500 feet and deep canyons traversed by streams. This landscape is the habitat of a remarkable variety of flora and fauna—more than 600 types of plants, 140 kinds of land birds, 11 mammal species, five varieties of reptiles, and three amphibian species live here. Bird-watchers may want to look for the endemic scrub-jay, which is found nowhere else in the world.

★ The largest and deepest sea cave in the world, **Painted Cave,** lies along the northwest coast of Santa Cruz. Named for the colorful lichen and algae that cover its walls, Painted Cave is nearly ¼ mi long and 100 feet wide. In spring a waterfall cascades over the entrance. Kayakers may encounter seals or sea lions cruising alongside their boats inside the cave.

Remnants of a dozen Chumash villages can be seen on the island. The largest of these villages, at the eastern end of the island, occupied the area now called **Scorpion Ranch.** The Chumash mined extensive chert deposits on the island for tools to produce shell-bead money, which they traded with people on the mainland. Remnants of the early-1900s ranching era can also be seen in the restored historic buildings, equipment, and adobe ovens that produced bread for the entire island.

Santa Rosa Island. Located between Santa Cruz and San Miguel, Santa Rosa is the second largest of the Channel Islands. The island has a relatively low profile, broken by a central mountain range rising to 1,589

Santa Rosa, Santa Cruz & Anacapa Islands

5

Ventura is approximately 28 miles
Northeast of Prisoners Harbor, Santa Cruz Island

Santa Barbara Channel

Santa Barbara Island is
approximately 52 miles southeast
of Santa Cruz Island

PACIFIC OCEAN

Anacapa Island

Anacapa Passage

Inspiration Point

Light Station & Museum

Summit Peak 936 ft

Smugglers Cove

San Pedro Point

Sandstone Point

Scorpion Ranch

Coche Point

Chinese Harbor

Prisoners Harbor

Main Ranch

Santa Cruz Island

CENTRAL VALLEY

Mount Diablo 2,450 ft

Painted Cave

Morse Point

West Point

Santa Cruz Channel

Skunk Point

East Point

Becher's Bay

Torrey Pines

Carrington Point

Santa Rosa Island

Ford Point

Johnsons Lee

Brockway Point

Vail & Vickers Ranch

Black Mtn 1,298 ft

Soledad Peak 1,574 ft

South Point

Cluster Point

Sandy Point

Santa Miguel Island is
approximately 2.5 miles west
of Santa Rosa Island

5 mi

5 km

0

feet. The coastal areas range from broad sandy beaches to sheer cliffs. The island is home to about 500 species of plants, including the rare Torrey pine. Three unusual mammals—the endemic island fox, spotted skunk, and deer mouse—are among those that make their home here. They hardly compare to the mammoths that once roamed the island; a nearly complete skeleton of a 6-foot-tall pygmy mammoth was unearthed here in 1994. The oldest dated human remains in North America—the Arlington Springs Woman (estimated to be 13,000 BP)–were also discovered here.

The island was once home to the **Vail and Vickers Ranch,** where sheep and cattle were raised from 1901 to 1998. You can see what the operation was like by viewing the historic ranch buildings, barns, equipment, and the wooden pier where cattle were brought onto the island.

VISITOR CENTERS

Channel Islands National Park Robert J. Lagomarsino Visitor Center. The park's main visitor center has a museum, a bookstore, a three-story observation tower with telescopes, and exhibits about the islands. There's also a tide pool where you can see sea stars clinging to rocks, anemones waving their colorful, spiny tentacles, and a brilliant orange garibaldi darting around. The center also has full-size reproductions of a male northern elephant seal and the pygmy mammoth skeleton unearthed on Santa Rosa Island in 1994. Rangers lead various free public programs describing park resources on weekends and holidays at 11 and 3; they can also give you a detailed map and trip-planning packet if you're interested in visiting the actual islands. ✉ *1901 Spinnaker Dr., Ventura* ☎ *805/658–5730* ⊕ *www.nps.gov/chis* ⊙ *Daily 8:30–5.*

> **BRAVING THE ELEMENTS**
>
> High winds can come without notice here, particularly on the outer islands of Santa Rosa and San Miguel. Carry a warm jacket and wear sunscreen, sunglasses, and a wide-brim hat that you can tie on your head.

Outdoors Santa Barbara Visitor Center. The small office in the Santa Barbara Harbor provides maps and other information about Channel Islands National Park, Channel Islands National Marine Sanctuary, and Los Padres National Forest. The same building houses the Santa Barbara Maritime Museum. Volunteers staff the center; call ahead to verify hours. ✉ *113 Harbor Way, Santa Barbara* ☎ *805/884–1475* ⊕ *outdoorsb.noaa.gov* ⊙ *Daily 11–5.*

SPORTS & THE OUTDOORS

DIVING

Some of the best snorkeling and diving in the world can be found in the cool waters surrounding the Channel Islands. In the relatively warm water around Anacapa and eastern Santa Cruz, photographers can get great shots of rarely seen giant black bass swimming among the kelp forests. Here you'll also find a reef covered with red brittle starfish. If

TRANSPORTATION OPTIONS

Channel Islands Aviation. Channel Islands Aviation provides half-day excursions, surf fishing, and camper transportation year-round, flying from Camarillo Airport, about 10 mi east of Oxnard, to an airstrip on Santa Rosa. They will also pick up groups of six or more at Santa Barbara Airport. ✉ *305 Durley Ave., Camarillo* ☎ *805/987–1301* ⊕ *www.flycia.com* 🍽 *$130 per person; $200 per person if camping.*

Island Packers. Sailing from Ventura and Oxnard, Island Packers' two 64-foot high-speed catamarans zip over to Santa Cruz Island—with stops at Anacapa Island—daily in summer, less frequently the rest of the year. Island Packers also visits the other

islands three or four times a month (most frequently in the spring, summer, and fall) and provides transportation for campers. ✉ *3600 S. Harbor Blvd., Oxnard* ☎ *805/642–1393* ✉ *1691 Spinnaker Dr., Ventura* ☎ *805/642–1393* ⊕ *www.island-packers.com* 🍽 *$32–$62.*

Truth Aquatics. Truth Aquatics departs from the Santa Barbara Harbor for single- and multiday scuba trips and multiday hiking excursions to all of the Channel Islands. ✉ *301 W. Cabrillo Blvd., Santa Barbara* ☎ *805/962–1127* ⊕ *www.truthaquatics.com* 🍽 *$100 for scuba day trips; onboard all-inclusive overnight trips average $150 per day.*

you're an experienced diver, you might swim among five species of seals and sea lions, or try your hand at spearing rockfish or halibut near San Miguel and Santa Rosa. The best time to scuba dive is in the summer and fall, when the water is often clear up to a 100-foot depth. ⇨ *Outfitters & Expeditions box for equipment rentals and dive operators.*

HIKING

The terrain on most of the islands ranges from flat to moderately hilly. There are no services (and no public phones; cell-phone reception is dicey) on the islands—you'll have to bring all your own food, water (except on Santa Cruz and Santa Rosa), and supplies. ⇨ *Outfitters & Expeditions box for guided hiking expeditions.*

EASY **Cuyler Harbor Beach.** This easy walk takes you along a 2-mi-long white sand beach on San Miguel. The eastern section is occasionally cut off by high tides. ✉ *San Miguel Campground, San Miguel Island.*

Historic Ranch. This easy ½-mi walk on Santa Cruz Island takes you to a historic ranch where you can see remnants of a cattle ranch. ✉ *Scorpion Beach, Santa Cruz Island.*

♻ **Inspiration Point.** This 1½-mi hike along flat terrain takes in most of East ★ Anacapa; there are great views from Inspiration Point and Cathedral Cove. ✉ *Landing Cove, Anacapa Island.*

Water Canyon. Starting at Santa Rosa Campground, this 2-mi walk along a white-sand beach includes some exceptional beachcombing. Frequent strong winds can turn this easy hike into a fairly strenuous excursion, so be prepared. If you extend your walk into Water Canyon,

OUTFITTERS & EXPEDITIONS

DIVING

Peace Dive Boat. Ventura Harbor-based Peace Dive Boat runs single and multiday live-aboard diving adventures near all the Channel Islands. ✉ *1567 Spinnaker Dr., Ventura* ☎ *866/984–2025 or 805/650–3483* ⊕ *www.peaceboat.com* 🍽 *Day trips start at $100.*

Spectre Dive Boat. The Spectre runs single-day diving trips to Anacapa, Santa Cruz, Santa Rosa, and San Miguel. Fees include three or four dives, air, and food. ✉ *1575 Spinnaker Dr., Suite 105B-75, Ventura* ☎ *866/225–3483 or 805/486–4486* ⊕ *calboatdiving.com* 🍽 *$85–$115.*

Truth Aquatics. Trips to the Channel Islands lasting a day or more can be arranged through this Santa Barbara operator. You live aboard the boats on multiday trips; all meals are provided. ✉ *301 Cabrillo Blvd., Santa Barbara* ☎ *805/962–1127* ⊕ *www. truthaquatics.com* 🍽 *$109–$835.*

KAYAKING

Aquasports. This highly regarded company offers guided one-, two-, and three-day trips to Santa Cruz and one-day trips to Anacapa and Santa Barbara islands for beginner to expert kayakers. Cross-channel passage, instruction, equipment, and guides are included. ✉ *111 Verona Ave., Goleta* ☎ *800/773–2309 or 805/968–7231* ⊕ *www.islandkayak ing.com* 🍽 *$175–$395* ⊙ *Call for times and dates; advance reservations strongly recommended.*

Channel Islands Kayak Center. This company rents kayaks and offers one-day guided kayak and snorkeling trips. Excursions include transportation, equipment, and guides. ✉ *1691 Spinnaker Dr., Ventura* ☎ *805/644–9699* ✉ *3600 Harbor Blvd., Oxnard* ☎ *805/984–5995* ⊕ *www.cikayak. com* 🍽 *$180.*

Paddle Sports. You can take a one-day trip to one of the five islands, or overnight multiday excursions to several islands. All trips include equipment, instruction, and transportation across the channel. ✉ *117B Harbor Way, Santa Barbara* ☎ *805/899–4925* ⊕ *www.kayaksb. com* 🍽 *$195–$700.*

WHALE-WATCHING

Island Packers. Depending on the season, you can take a three-hour tour or an all-day tour from either Ventura or Channel Islands harbors. ✉ *1691 Spinnaker Dr., Ventura* ☎ *805/642–1393* ⊕ *www.island packers.com* 🍽 *$28–$63.*

---

you'll follow animal paths to a lush canyon full of native vegetation. ✉ *Santa Rosa Campground, Santa Rosa Island.*

MODERATE **Cavern Point.** This moderate 2-mi hike takes you to the bluffs northwest
ⓒ of Scorpion harbor on Santa Cruz, where you'll take in magnificent coastal views and see pods of migrating gray whales from December through March. ✉ *Santa Cruz Campground, Santa Barbara Island.*

Elephant Seal Cove. This moderate to strenuous walk takes you across Santa Barbara to a point where you can view magnificent elephant seals from steep cliffs. ✉ *Landing Cove, Santa Barbara Island.*

Fodor'sChoice **Prisoners Harbor.** Taking in quite a bit of Santa Cruz, this moderate to
★ strenuous 3-mi trail to Pelican Cove is one of the best hikes in the park.

You must be accompanied by a ranger or Island Packers staff or secure a permit (call 805/898–1642; allow 15 days to process your application), as the hike takes you through Nature Conservancy property. ⊠ *Prisoners Harbor, Santa Cruz Island.*

Torrey Pines. This moderate 5-mi loop climbs up to Santa Rosa's grove of rare Torrey pines and offers stellar views of Becher's Bay and the channel. ⊠ *Santa Rosa Campground, Santa Rosa Island.*

DIFFICULT **East Point.** This strenuous 12-mi hike along beautiful white-sand beaches yields the opportunity to see rare Torrey pines. Some beaches are closed between March and September, so you'll have to remain on the road for portions of this hike. ⊠ *Santa Rosa Campground, Santa Rosa Island.*

Lester Ranch. This short but strenuous 2-mi hike leads up a spectacular canyon filled with waterfalls and lush native plants. At the end of a steep climb to the top of a peak, you'll be rewarded with views of the historic Lester Ranch and the Cabrillo Monument. (If you plan to hike beyond the Lester Ranch, you'll need a hiking permit; call 805/658–5730.) ⊠ *San Miguel Campground, San Miguel Island.*

Point Bennett. Rangers conduct 15-mi hikes across San Miguel to Point Bennett, where more than 30,000 pinnipeds (four different species of seals and sea lions) can be seen. ⊠ *San Miguel Campground, San Miguel Island.*

KAYAKING

The most remote parts of Channel Islands are accessible only by a sea kayak. Some of the best kayaking in the park can be found on Anacapa, Santa Barbara, and the eastern tip of Santa Cruz. Anacapa has plenty of sea caves, tidal pools, and even natural bridges you can paddle beneath. Brown pelicans, cormorants, and storm petrels nest in Santa Barbara's steep cliffs; you'll find one of the world's largest colonies of Xantus' murrelets here as well, and you can also get up close and personal with seals and sea lions. Santa Cruz has plenty of secluded beaches to explore, as well as seabird nesting sites and seal and sea lion rookeries. You can land at any of the islands, but permits are required for the western side of Santa Cruz. There are no public moorings around the islands, so it's recommended that one person stay aboard the boat at all times. You'll find the best kayaking from July through September or October, when the waters calm down. Santa Barbara Island is an exception; the best months to kayak here are April through June—after that, the southerly swells make smooth kayaking difficult. Outfitters offer tours year-round, but high seas may cause trip cancellations between December and March. The operators listed below hold permits from the National Park Service to conduct kayak tours—if you choose a different company, verify that it holds the proper permits. ⇨ *Outfitters & Expeditions box for kayak rentals and guided tours.*

WHALE-WATCHING

About a third of the world's cetacean species (27 to be exact) can be seen in the Santa Barbara Channel. In July and August, humpback and blue whales feed off the north shore of Santa Rosa. From late

December to April, up to 10,000 gray whales pass through the Santa Barbara Channel on their way from Alaska to Mexico and back again. ⇨ *Outfitters & Expeditions box for whale-watching expeditions.*

EDUCATIONAL OFFERINGS

☾ **Channel Islands Live Dive.** Watch real-time as divers armed with video cameras explore the undersea world of the kelp forest off Anacapa Island; images are transmitted to monitors located on the dock at Landing Cove, in the main visitor center, and via the Internet. You'll see bright red sea stars, spiny sea urchins, and brilliant orange garibaldis. You can even ask the divers questions via interactive lines. ⊠ *Landing Cove, Anacapa Island* ☎ *Free* ⊙ *Memorial Day–Labor Day, Tues.– Thurs. at 2.*

WHERE TO STAY & EAT

ABOUT THE RESTAURANTS

Out on the islands, you won't have any trouble deciding where to dine—there are no restaurants, no snack bars, and in some cases, no potable water. Pack a fancy picnic or a simple sandwich—and don't forget it in your car or hotel room unless you want to starve. If you want to eat a quick meal before or after your island trip, each of the harbors has a number of decent eateries nearby.

ABOUT THE CAMPGROUNDS

Camping is the best way to experience the natural beauty and isolation of Channel Islands National Park. Unrestricted by tour schedules, you'll have plenty of time to explore mountain trails, snorkel in the kelp forests, or kayak into sea caves. Campsites are primitive, with no water (except on Santa Rosa and Santa Cruz) or electricity; enclosed camp stoves must be used. Campfires are not allowed on the islands, and you must carry all your gear and pack out all trash. Campers must arrange transportation to the islands before reserving a campsite (and yes, park personnel do check). You can get specifics on each campground and reserve a campsite ($15 per night) by contacting the **National Park Service Reservation System** (☎ *877/444–6777* ⊕ *www.recreation. gov*) up to six months in advance.

WHERE TO EAT

Picnic Areas. Picnic tables are available on all the islands except San Miguel. You can also picnic on some of the beaches of Santa Cruz, Santa Rosa, and San Miguel; be aware that high winds are always a possibility on Santa Rosa and San Miguel.

WHERE TO STAY

$ 🏕 **Del Norte Campground.** This campground on Santa Cruz, the newest on the islands, offers backpackers sweeping ocean views from its 1,500-foot perch. It's accessed via a 3½-mi hike through a series of canyons and ridges. ✉*Scorpion Beach landing* ☎*877/444–6777* ⊕*www. recreation.gov* ⤳*4 sites* ♿*Pit toilets, picnic tables* ▭*D, MC, V.*

$ 🏕 **East Anacapa Campground.** You'll have to walk ½ mi and ascend more than 150 steps to reach this open, treeless camping area above Cathedral Cove. ✉*East Anacapa landing* ☎*877/444–6777* ⊕*www. recreation.gov* ⤳*7 sites* ♿*Pit toilets, picnic tables, ranger station* ▭*D, MC, V.*

$ 🏕 **San Miguel Campground.** Accessed by a steep 1-mi hike through a lush canyon, this campground is on the site of the Lester Ranch; the Cabrillo Monument is nearby. Be aware that strong winds and thick fog are common on this remote island. ✉*Cuyler Harbor landing* ☎*877/444–6777* ⊕*www.recreation.gov* ⤳*9 sites* ♿*Pit toilets, picnic tables, ranger station* ▭*D, MC, V.*

$ 🏕 **Santa Barbara Campground.** This seldom-visited campground perched on a cliff above Landing Cove is reached via a challenging ½-mi uphill climb. Three-day trips are permitted. ✉*Landing Cove* ☎*877/444–6777* ⊕*www.recreation.gov* ⤳*10 sites* ♿*Pit toilets, picnic tables, ranger station* ▭*D, MC, V.*

$ 🏕 **Santa Cruz Scorpion Campground.** In a grove of eucalyptus trees,
★ this campground is near the historic buildings of Scorpion Ranch. It's accessed via an easy, ½-mi, flat trail from Scorpion Beach landing. ✉*Scorpion Beach landing* ☎*877/444–6777* ⊕*www.recreation.gov* ⤳*25 sites* ♿*Pit toilets, drinking water, picnic tables* ▭*D, MC, V.*

$ 🏕 **Santa Rosa Campground.** Backcountry beach camping for kayakers is available on this island; it's a 1½-mi flat walk to the campground. There's a spectacular view of Santa Cruz Island across the water. ✉*Bechers Bay landing* ☎*877/444–6777* ⊕*www.recreation.gov* ⤳*15 sites* ♿*Drinking water, showers (cold), picnic tables, toilets* ▭*D, MC, V.*

CHANNEL ISLANDS ESSENTIALS

ACCESSIBILITY

The Channel Islands Visitor Center is fully accessible. The islands themselves have few facilities and are not easy to navigate by individuals in wheelchairs or those with limited mobility. Limited wheelchair access is available on Santa Rosa Island via air transportation.

ADMISSION FEES

There is no fee to enter Channel Islands National Park, but there is a $15-per-day fee for staying in one of the campgrounds. The cost of taking a boat to the park varies depending on which operator you choose.

ADMISSION HOURS

The islands are open every day of the year. Channel Islands Visitor Center is closed Thanksgiving and Christmas. Channel Islands National Park is located in the Pacific Time Zone.

EMERGENCIES

In the event of an emergency, contact a park ranger on patrol or call 911.

LOST AND FOUND

The park's lost-and-found is at Channel Islands Visitor Center.

PERMITS

Landing permits are not required to visit Channel Islands. Boaters who want to land on the Nature Conservancy preserve on Santa Cruz Island should call 805/642–0345; allow 15 days to process your application. Private boaters can arrange a hike beyond the ranger station on San Miguel by calling 805/658–5711. (Rangers are available for hikers who land via concession trips.) Anglers require a state fishing license. For details, call the California Department of Fish and Game at 916/653–7664. Twelve Marine Protected Areas (MPAs) with special resource protection regulations surround the islands, so be sure to read the guidelines before you depart. Contact park headquarters for information.

PUBLIC TELEPHONES

Public telephones are available near the Channel Islands Visitor Center. There are no public phones on the islands.

RESTROOMS

Public restrooms are available at the Channel Islands Visitor Center and at the campgrounds on all five islands.

VISITOR INFORMATION

Contacts **Channel Islands Visitor Center** (✉ *1901 Spinnaker Dr., Ventura, CA* ☎ *805/658–5730* ⊕ *www.nps.gov/chis* ⊙ *Daily 8:30–5).*

The Inland Empire

6

Ripening oranges

WORD OF MOUTH

"If you're looking for a skiing vacation, Big Bear gives you the choice of 2 mountains—Snow Summit, which is family-oriented and Bear Mountain, which is dominated by snowboarders."

—Lvk

WELCOME TO THE INLAND EMPIRE

TOP REASONS TO GO

★ **Wine country:** The Temecula Valley is a mélange of rolling hills, faint ocean breezes, old-world-style wineries, and gourmet restaurants.

★ **The Mission Inn:** One of the most unique hotels in America, Riverside's rambling, eclectic Mission Inn has hosted several U.S. presidents.

★ **Apple country:** Oak Glen is Southern California's largest apple-growing region. Attend an old-fashioned hoedown, take a wagon ride, and sample Mile High apple pies and homemade ciders.

★ **Soothing spas:** The lush grounds, bubbling hot springs, and playful mud baths of Glen Ivy are ideal spots to unwind, while Kelly's Spa at the historic Mission Inn provides a Tuscan-style retreat.

★ **Alpine escapes:** Breathe in the clean mountain air, hit the slopes, or cozy up in a rustic cabin at one of four great mountain hideaways in the Inland Empire: Lake Arrowhead, Big Bear, Idyllwild, and Wrightwood.

1 Temecula. Located between San Diego and Corona off the I-15, Southern California's wine country is home to restaurants serving superb California cuisine, great golf courses, and, of course, dozens of wineries.

2 Lake Arrowhead. California's rich and famous have their second homes in this alpine destination, tucked in the San Bernardino Mountains. Here you can take an hour-long cruise on the lake, go shopping at the designer outlets, ice skate on the Olympic rink where Michelle Kwan trained, or enjoy fine food and spa treatments at the Lake Arrowhead Resort.

3 **Mission Inn.** One of the most unique hotels in America is tucked away in the busy, urban city of Riverside, just off I–215. Eight U.S. presidents have stayed at this ornate and majestic resort.

GETTING ORIENTED

Several major freeways provide access to the Inland Empire. Ontario, Corona, and Temecula line up along I–15, and I–215 and State Route 91 lead to Riverside and San Bernardino. The area's popularity as a bedroom community for Los Angeles has created some nasty freeway congestion, so try to avoid driving during rush hour, usually 6 to 8 AM and 4 to 7 PM.

6

Lake Arrowhead

4 **Oak Glen.** Pick a bushel and chow down on some melt-in-your-mouth cider donuts at one of the orchards in this booming apple-growing region.

5 **Glen Ivy Hot Springs.** These natural cool- and warm-water mineral springs—located beneath Temescal Canyon off I–15 in Corona—have been revered for their healing properties since the 1860s.

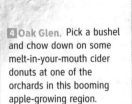

THE INLAND EMPIRE PLANNER

How's the Weather?

The climate varies greatly depending on what part of the Inland Empire you're visiting. Summer temperatures in the mountains and in Temecula, 20 mi from the coast, usually hover around 80°F, though it's not uncommon for Riverside to reach temperatures over 100°F. In winter, temperatures in the mountains and in Temecula usually range from 30°F to 55°F, and in the Riverside area 40°F to 60°F. Most of the ski resorts open when the first natural snow falls (usually in November) and close in mid-March.

About the Restaurants

Inland Empire residents no longer have to travel to their big-sister communities of L.A. or Orange County for a good meal. Downtown Riverside is home to some ambitious restaurants, along with the chains you'll find in most areas. The college towns of Claremont and Redlands are great showcases for creative vegetarian cuisine. In Temecula, the choices expand to wine-country cooking, with many vintners showcasing their products alongside California–French dishes. Your options are limited in the smaller mountain communities; typically each town supports a single upscale restaurant, along with fast-food outlets, steak-and-potatoes family spots, and perhaps an Italian or Mexican eatery. Universally, dining out is casual.

About the Hotels

In the San Gabriel and San Bernardino mountains, most accommodations are B&Bs or rustic cabins, though Lake Arrowhead offers more luxurious resort lodging. Rates for Big Bear lodgings fluctuate widely, depending on the season. When winter snow brings droves of Angelenos to the mountains for skiing, expect to pay sky-high prices for any kind of room. Most establishments require a two-night stay on weekends. In Riverside, you might enjoy a stay at the landmark Mission Inn, a rambling Spanish-style hotel with elaborate courtyards, fountains, and a mixture of ornate Mission revival–, Spanish baroque–, Renaissance revival–, and Asian-architecture styles. In the wine country, lodgings range from chain hotels and motels to golf resorts.

WHAT IT COSTS				
¢	$	$$	$$$	$$$$
Restaurants				
under $10	$10–$15	$16–$22	$23–$30	over $30
Hotels				
under $90	$90–$120	$121–$175	$176–$250	over $250

Restaurant prices are for a main course at dinner, excluding sales tax of 7.75%. Hotel prices are for two people in a standard double room in high season, excluding service charges and 7.75% tax.

Updated by
Amy Wang

FEW PEOPLE THINK OF THE region east of Los Angeles as a worthwhile travel destination. But the Inland Empire, an area often overlooked by vacationers because of its tangled freeways and suburban sprawl, does have its charms. No more than a few hours' drive from metropolitan Los Angeles, you can ski a 7,000-foot mountain overlooking a crystal blue lake or go wine tasting at a vineyard swept by ocean breezes. At the heart of this desert and mountain region is Riverside, the birthplace of California's multimillion-dollar navel-orange industry, established in 1875. The tree that started it all still flourishes on Magnolia Avenue. Today the streets of downtown buzz with people on their way to shop for antiques, eat in exciting restaurants, and listen to live jazz. The scene is completely different northeast of Riverside, in the San Bernardino Mountains. There, Wrightwood, Big Bear Lake, and Lake Arrowhead lie amid prime ski country. To the south, in the San Jacinto Mountains just west of Palm Springs, Idyllwild is a popular year-round getaway with romantic bed-and-breakfasts, fashionable boutiques, and cozy restaurants. In the southernmost reaches of the Inland Empire, on the way from Riverside to San Diego, is the wine-growing region around Temecula, a hip and trendy destination for Southern California singles. This is also prime territory for hot-air ballooning, golfing, fine dining, and—of course—vineyard tours and wine tasting.

6

THE WESTERN INLAND EMPIRE

POMONA, CLAREMONT & THE SAN GABRIEL MOUNTAINS

At the foot of the San Gabriel Mountains, the tree-lined communities of Pomona and Claremont are known for their prestigious colleges: California State Polytechnic University–Pomona and the Claremont colleges. There's not much to do here; the appeal of these towns is simply that they are cute, lively college towns, with pleasant architecture and a few little cafés to kick back in. Turn north into the hills and you'll find Wrightwood, an old-fashioned small town that makes a great base for outdoor adventure.

POMONA

23 mi north of Anaheim on Hwy. 57; 27 mi east of Pasadena on I–210.

The green hills of Pomona, dotted with horses and houses, are perhaps best known as the site of the Los Angeles County Fair and of California State Polytechnic University–Pomona. Named for the Roman goddess of fruit, the city was established in 1938 and has a rich citrus-growing heritage. Today, Pomona is becoming better known for its art galleries and antiques stores.

Don't miss the **Kellogg House** (⊠ *3801 W. Temple Ave.* ☎ *909/869–2280* ⊕ *www.kellogghousepomona.com* ⊠ *Free* ☼ *Oct.–June, open house 1st Sun. of every month, noon–2, otherwise access by group tour only),* which was once the scenic hilltop winter estate of cereal magnate Will Keith Kellogg. The circa-1925 home was designed by Myron Hunt (of Rose Bowl and Huntington Library fame) and has a blend of Islamic, Spanish, and Italian architecture. You can stroll the courtyard and gardens (both open to the public year-round), landscaped by Charles Gibbs Adams of Hearst Castle fame, then head inside for a look at the grand tapestries, hardwood floors, and intricately detailed ceilings.

The classic **Arabian Horse Shows** (⊠*3801 W. Temple Ave.* ☎*909/869–2224* 💲*$3*), started by Kellogg in 1926, are still a tradition on the CSU–Pomona campus. More than 85 of the purebreds still call Kellogg's ranch home, and the university offers exhibitions of the equines in English and Western tack every first Sunday at 2 PM from October through June; tours of the stables are available by appointment only.

Site of the Los Angeles County Fair (ninth-largest in the United States), the **Fairplex** exposition center has a 9,500-seat grandstand, an outdoor exhibit area, and nine exhibit buildings. The venue is the site of open-air markets, antiques shows, and the annual Wines of the World competition. Fairplex houses the **Wally Parks NHRA Motorsports Museum** (☎*909/622–2133* ⊕*www.nhra.com/museum* 💲*$7* ⊗*Wed.–Sun. 10–5*), dedicated to the history of American motor sports. ⊠*1101 W. McKinley Ave.* ☎*909/623–3111* ⊕*www.fairplex.com* ⊗*Call for current show listings and admission prices.*

WHERE TO EAT

$$–$$$ ✕ **Pomona Valley Mining Company.** Perched on a hilltop near an old mining site, this rustic steak-and-seafood restaurant provides a great view of the city at night. The decor reflects the local mining heritage—authentic gold-rush pieces and 1800s memorabilia hang on the walls, and old lanterns are the centerpiece of each table. The food is well prepared, with a special nod to prime rib, and service is friendly. During June book early—this is a favorite spot on prom nights. ⊠*1777 Gillette Rd.* ☎*909/623–3515* ⊕*www.pomonavalleyminingco.com* ▭*AE, D, MC, V* ⊗*No lunch.*

CLAREMONT

4 mi north of Pomona along Gary Ave., then 2 mi east on Foothill Blvd.

Nicknamed "Oxford in the Orange Belt," the seven Claremont colleges are among the most prestigious in California. The campuses are all laid out cheek-by-jowl; as you wander from one leafy street to the next, you won't be able to tell where one college ends and the next begins.

In its heyday, Claremont was the home of the Sunkist cooperative movement. Today, Claremont Village harks back to the 1950s with its main street and hot-rod shows. The downtown district is a beautiful place to visit, with citrus- and oak-lined streets and Victorian, Craftsman, and Spanish-colonial buildings.

College walking tours, a downtown tour, and historic home tours are conducted throughout the year by **Claremont Heritage** (☎*909/621–*

0848). On the first Saturday of each month the organization gives walking tours of the village.

Bert & Rocky's Cream Company (⊠*242 Yale Ave.* ☏*909/625-1852*). **This independent ice-cream store is known for its innovative and simply sinful concoctions. There are more than 175 flavors from which to choose. The champagne and merlot sorbets are hot items, as is the Madagascar vanilla ice cream (paired with a chocolate dessert wine from Rancho Cucamonga winery). And yes, the nonalcoholic varieties are just as heavenly.**

★ Founded in 1927 by Susanna Bixby Bryant, a wealthy landowner and conservationist, **Rancho Santa Ana Botanic Garden** is a living museum and research center dedicated to the conservation of more than 2,800 native-California plant species. Meandering trails, set on 86 acres of ponds and greenery, guide visitors past such fragrant specimens as wild lilacs, big berry manzanita, and four-needled piñon. Countless birds also make their homes here. Before you start your tour, pick up a native-bird field guide at the gift shop. ⊠*1500 N. College Ave.* ☏*909/625-8767* ⊕*www.rsabg.org* ☞*$4 suggested donation* ⊙*Daily 8–5.*

WHERE TO EAT

$ ✕**Caffe Allegro.** This romantic spot in downtown Upland resembles an ★ Italian country villa, complete with candles, worn-looking walls, and an ornate wood bar. Locals rave about the chicken marsala, served on a bed of spinach fettuccine. ⊠*186 N. 2nd Ave., Upland* ☏*909/949– 0805* ▭*AE, D, MC, V.*

NIGHTLIFE

Being a college town, Claremont has lots of bars and cafés, some of which showcase bands. Karaoke and live jazz are popular at the **British Bulldog Pub and Restaurant** (⊠*1667 N. Mountain Ave., Upland* ☏*909/946–6614*). Both college kids and old-timers appreciate the **Buffalo Inn** (⊠*1814 W. Foothill Blvd., Upland* ☏*909/981–5515*), a rustic bar and hamburger joint along historic Route 66. Acoustic musicians sing Jim Croce covers on the patio Tuesday through Sunday.

SPORTS & THE OUTDOORS

SKIING The 10,064-foot mountain's real name is Mt. San Antonio, but **Mt. Baldy Ski Resort**—the oldest ski area in Southern California—takes its name from the treeless slopes. It's known for its steep triple-diamond runs, though the facilities could use some updating. The Mt. Baldy base lies at 6,500 feet, and four chairlifts ascend to 8,600 feet. There are 26 runs; the longest is 2,100 vertical feet. Whenever abundant fresh snow falls, there's a danger of avalanche in out-of-bounds areas. Backcountry skiing is available via shuttle in the spring, and there's a kiddie school ($75, including lift ticket and lunch) on weekends for children ages 5 to 12. Winter or summer, you can take a scenic chairlift ride ($15) to the Top of the Notch restaurant and hiking and moun-

CLAREMONT WEATHER
Be prepared for hot and smoggy conditions; the town is not gifted with SoCal's best climate.

tain-biking trails. ✉*From E. Foothill Blvd., about ½ mi north on N. Claremont Blvd., then 3 mi north on Monte Vista Ave. and 7 mi east on Mount Baldy Rd.* ☎*909/981–3344* ⊕*www.mtbaldy.com* 🎫*Full day $59, half day $39* ⊘*Snow season Nov.–Apr., weekdays 8–4:30, weekends 7:30–4:30; summer season May–Oct., weekends 9–4:30.*

WATER PARK
Ⓒ **Raging Waters,** a tropical-theme water park in San Dimas (10 mi west of Claremont), has 17 chutes and slides with such names as Neptune's Fury, Thunder Rapids, and Dragon's Den. When you're ready for a break, head over to the sandy beach lagoon and relax, or go to the Tropical Bar for a fruit drink or funnel cake. The Tropical Trading Post sells swimsuits, tanning lotion, and sunglasses. Complimentary life jackets are provided for youngsters. Lockers rent for $6 to $8, inner tube rental is free. For a special treat, rent a cabana ($85–$150). Check the Web site for online coupons. Parking is $10. ✉*111 Raging Waters Dr., San Dimas* ☎*909/802–2200* ⊕*www.ragingwaters.com* 🎫*$35* ⊘*Late June–Aug., daily 10–8; 1st 3 wks of June, daily 10–6; May, weekends 10–6; Sept.–mid-Oct., call for hrs.*

ONTARIO

Junction of I–10 and I–15, 6 mi east of Pomona.

Ontario, in the Cucamonga Valley, has a rich agricultural and industrial heritage. The valley's warm climate once supported vineyards that produced Mediterranean-grape varietals such as grenache, mourvedre, and zinfandel. Today almost all of the vineyards have been replaced by housing tracts and shopping malls. But the Inland Empire's major airport is here, so you may well find yourself passing through Ontario.

Ontario's oldest existing business, **Graber Olive House,** opened in 1894 when, at the urging of family and friends, C. C. Graber bottled his meaty, tree-ripened olives and started selling them; they are still sold throughout the United States. Stop by the gourmet shop for a jar, then have a picnic on the shaded grounds. Free tours are conducted year-round; in fall you can watch workers grade, cure, and can the olives. ✉*315 E. 4th St.* ☎*800/996–5483* ⊕*www.graberolives.com* 🎫*Free* ⊘*Daily 9–5:30.*

WHERE TO STAY

$–$$
★ 🏨**Doubletree Hotel Ontario Airport.** A beautifully landscaped courtyard greets you at this exceptional chain, the only full-service hotel in Ontario. Rooms here are spacious and decorated in jewel tones and dark wood; the business center has printers, a copier, and laptop hookups as well as a computer with Internet access. The vineyards are only a few miles away. **Pros:** Well-landscaped grounds; clean, large rooms; good on-site restaurant. **Cons:** Some airport noise; some rooms feel dated. ✉*222 N. Vineyard Ave.* ☎*909/937–0900 or 800/222–8733* ⊕*www.doubletree.com* 🛏*484 rooms, 22 suites* ⅙*In-room: refrigerator, Ethernet, Wi-Fi. In-hotel: 2 restaurants, room service, bars, pool, gym, concierge, laundry service, public Wi-Fi, airport shuttle, some pets allowed, no-smoking rooms* ▤*AE, D, MC, V* ⅞*CP.*

SHOPPING

The gargantuan **Ontario Mills Mall** is California's largest, packing in more than 200 outlet stores, a 30-screen movie theater, and the Improv comedy theater. Also in the mall are three entertainment complexes: Dave & Buster's pool hall–restaurant–arcade, Vans Skate Park, and GameWorks video-game center. Dining options include the kid-friendly jungle-theme Rainforest Cafe (complete with animatronic elephants and simulated thunderstorms), the Cheesecake Factory, and a 1,000-seat food court. ⊠ *1 Mills Circle, 4th St. and I–15* ☎ *909/484–8300* ⊕ *www.ontariomills.com* ⊗ *Mon.–Sat. 10–9:30, Sun. 10–8.*

RANCHO CUCAMONGA

5 mi north of Ontario on I–15.

Once a thriving wine-making area with more than 50,000 acres of wine grapes, Rancho Cucamonga lost most of its pastoral charm after real-estate developers bought up the land for a megamall and affordable housing. It's now a squeaky-clean planned community, but you can still get a taste of the grape here.

At the **Joseph Filippi Winery,** J.P. and Gino Filippi continue the family tradition that was started in 1922. They produce handcrafted wines from cabernet, sangiovese, and zinfandel grapes, among other varieties. You can taste up to five wines for $5, and take the free, guided tour that's given at noon, Wednesday through Sunday. ⊠ *12467 Base Line Rd.* ☎ *909/899–5755* ⊕ *www.josephfilippiwinery.com* ⊠ *Free* ⊗ *Mon.–Sat. 10–6, Sun. 11–5.*

Victoria Gardens feels a lot like downtown Disneyland with its vintage ★ signs, antique lampposts, and colorful California-theme murals along its 12 city blocks. At this shopping, dining, and entertainment complex, such stores as Banana Republic, Abercrombie & Fitch, Williams-Sonoma, and Pottery Barn are flanked by a Macy's and a 12-screen AMC movie theater. After you're finished shopping, grab an ice cream at the Ben & Jerry's shop and linger in the 1920s-style Town Square, a relaxing little park with fountains, grass, and an old-fashioned trolley ($2 per ride). Restaurants such as the Cheesecake Factory, Lucille's Smokehouse Bar-B-Que, P. F. Chang's China Bistro, and the Yard House often have lines out the door. The Victoria Gardens Cultural Center has a library and a 540-seat performing-arts center. ⊠ *12505 N. Main St.* ☎ *909/463–2828 general information, 909/477–2720 Cultural Center* ⊕ *www.victoriagardensie.com* ⊠ *Free* ⊗ *Mon.–Thurs. 10–9, Fri. and Sat. 10–10, Sun. 11–8.*

WHERE TO EAT

$$–$$$ ✕**The Sycamore Inn.** Flickering gas lamps and a glowing fireplace greet ★ you at this rustic inn. Built in 1921, the restaurant stands on the site of a pre-statehood stagecoach stop; it's one of the oldest buildings in town. The specialty of the house is the rack of Colorado lamb, pan seared and roasted with a mustard–bread crumb crust and a red-wine reduction. The wine list is impressive; by the glass, you can choose

from more than 20 vintages from the Central Coast, Napa Valley, and such nearby wineries as Joseph Filippi and Temecula. ⊠*8318 Foothill Blvd.* ☎*909/982–1104* ⊕*www.thesycamoreinn.com* ▤*AE, D, MC, V* ⊘*No lunch.*

¢ ✕ **Vince's Spaghetti House.** A swooping yellow neon arrow points the ★ way to this boisterous family eatery, open since 1945. The restaurant claims to serve more than 15,000 mi of spaghetti every year. The menu is limited, but reliably good. The *mostaccioli* with meat sauce and the meatball sandwiches are excellent choices. ⊠*8241 Foothill Blvd.* ☎*909/981–1003* ⊕*www.vinces-spaghetti.com* ▤*AE, D, MC, V.*

WRIGHTWOOD

39 mi north of Ontario, via I–15, Hwy. 138, and Hwy. 2.

Wrightwood prides itself on having no stoplights, fast-food restaurants, or chain stores. What you will find are old-fashioned candy purveyors, antiques shops, and crafts boutiques. Since Wrightwood has the most accessible roads of all Southland ski-resort communities (no winding roads and jaw-dropping cliffs to deal with), it's popular with day-trippers.

☾ An old stone tower at **Big Pines Visitor Center,** part of Angeles National Forest, marks the highest spot (6,862 feet) along the San Andreas Fault, the unstable crack in the earth's crust that has caused so many California earthquakes. At the visitor center you can get information on camping, fishing, and hiking in the forest; buy souvenirs; and get the National Forest Adventure passes ($5 per vehicle per day) that allow you access to the forest. ⊠*Hwy. 2, 4 mi west of Wrightwood* ☎*760/249–3504* ⊘*Weekends 8:30–4.*

WHERE TO STAY & EAT

$–$$$ ✕ **Blue Ridge Inn.** This rustic 1948 lodge has a bar with a huge fireplace, ★ and a cozy, wood-panel dining room, decorated with flickering lanterns and 19th-century clocks. The food—surf-and-turf specialties, such as grilled Malaysian shrimp and prime rib—is probably the best you'll find in Wrightwood. ⊠*6060 Park Dr.* ☎*760/249–3440* ▤*AE, MC, V* ⊘*Closed Mon. No lunch.*

$–$$ ✕ **Evergreen Café and Raccoon Saloon.** This cozy little coffee shop, adorned with country jars, striped wallpaper, and little white lights, is a favorite of locals. Breakfasts, served all day, are hearty and generous. For lunch, try the grilled chicken sandwich, topped with ortega chilies, tomatoes, jack cheese, onion, and lettuce. For dinner, try the home-style meat loaf, served with soup or salad, rice or potato, vegetables, and toasted garlic bread. ⊠*1269 Evergreen Rd.* ☎*760/249–6393 or 760/249–4277* ▤*MC, V.*

$–$$ ▦ **Pines Motel and Cabins.** This property, steps from Wrightwood's village, has plenty of simple charm. Rooms have knotty-pine walls and lodge-style beds with country quilts. Cabins have living rooms with fireplaces, kitchens, and separate bedrooms; studio suites have dining areas and entertainment centers. Guests also have access to grills and picnic tables. **Pros:** Close to children's park; near shopping village and restaurants. **Cons:** Mediocre beds; some rooms smell smoky. ⊠*6045 Pine St.* ☎*760/249–9974* ➪*10 rooms, 2 cabins, 2 suites* ⓒ*In-room: kitchen (some), refrigerator (some). In-hotel: no elevator* ☐*AE, D, MC, V.*

SPORTS & THE OUTDOORS

HIKING In April, Wrightwood is a major stopping point for hikers traveling the **Pacific Crest Trail** (⊠*Big Pines Visitor Center, Rte. 2, 3 mi west of Wrightwood* ☎*760/249–3504*), which runs 2,600 mi from Mexico to Canada. There's a trailhead near Inspiration Point on Highway 2, 5 mi west of Wrightwood.

SKIING In addition to two mountains, a vertical drop of 8,200 feet, and 220 skiable acres, **Mountain High** (⊠*24510 Hwy. 2* ☎*760/249–5808* ⊕*www. mthigh.com* ✉*$51 eight-hour pass; $46 four-hour pass; $30 night skiing, 5–10*) has 46 trails for skiing and snowboarding. The Point Ticket lets you choose the number of runs you want to take. Snowboarders flock to Mountain High to test their skills at Faultline Terrain Park. There's regular bus service between the mountains. Mountain High North is a tubing park with a moving carpet lift; passes are $34 per day or $18 for two hours (inner tubes are included).

RIVERSIDE AREA

In the late 1700s, Mexican rancheros called this now-suburban region Valle de Paraiso. Citrus-growing here began in 1873, when homesteader Eliza Tibbets planted two navel-orange trees in her yard. The area's biggest draws are the majestic Mission Inn, with its fine restaurants and unique history and architecture, and Glen Ivy Hot Springs.

CORONA

13 mi south of Ontario on I–15.

Corona's Temescal Canyon is named for the dome-shaped mud saunas that the Luiseno Indians built around the artesian hot springs in the early 19th century. Starting in 1860, weary Overland Stage Company passengers stopped to relax in the soothing mineral springs. In 1890 Mr. and Mrs. W. G. Steers turned the springs into a resort whose popularity has yet to fade.

FodorsChoice Presidents Herbert Hoover and Ronald Reagan are among the thou-
★ sands of guests who have soaked their toes at the very relaxing and beautiful **Glen Ivy Hot Springs.** Colorful bougainvillea and birds-of-paradise surround the secluded canyon spa, which offers a full range of facials, manicures, pedicures, body wraps, and massages; some treatments are performed in underground granite spa chambers known collectively as the Grotto, highly recommended by readers. In 2007 the spa added several new pools, renovated its treatment rooms, and opened its Under the Oaks treatment center, a cluster of eight open-air massage rooms surrounded by waterfalls and ancient oak trees. Don't bring your best bikini if you plan to dive into the red clay (brought

Good as Gold

In 1873 a woman named Eliza Tibbets changed the course of California history when she planted two Brazilian navel-orange trees in her Riverside garden.

The trees (which were called Washington Navels in honor of America's first president) flourished in the area's warm climate and rich soil—and before long, Tibbets's garden was producing the sweetest seedless oranges anyone had ever tasted. After winning awards at several major exhibitions, Tibbets realized she could make a profit from her trees. She sold buds to the increasing droves of citrus farmers flocking

to the Inland Empire, and by 1882, almost 250,000 citrus trees had been planted in Riverside alone. California's citrus industry had been born.

Today, Riverside still celebrates its citrus-growing heritage. The downtown Marketplace district contains several restored packing houses, and the Riverside Municipal Museum is home to a permanent exhibit of historic tools and machinery once used in the industry. The University of California at Riverside still remains at the forefront of citrus research; its Citrus Variety Collection includes 900 different fruit trees from around the world.

---

in daily from a local mine) of Club Mud. Children under 16 are not permitted at the spa except on three family days: Memorial Day, July 4, and Labor Day. ⊠ *25000 Glen Ivy Rd., Glen Ivy* ☎ *951/277–3529* ⊕ *www.glenivy.com* ✉ *Mon.–Thurs. $35; Fri.–Sun. $48* ☉ *Apr.–Oct., daily 9:30–6; Nov.–Mar., daily 9:30–5.*

☧ ★ Opened as a produce stand in 1974, **Tom's Farms** has grown to include a hamburger stand, furniture showroom, and health-food store. You can still buy produce here, but the big draw is various attractions for the kiddies: a duck pond, a petting zoo, a children's train, and an old-style carousel. Of interest for adults is the wine-and-cheese shop, which has more than 600 varieties of wine, including many from nearby Temecula Valley; wine tasting ($1 for three samples) takes place daily 11 to 6. On weekends there's a country fair with children's crafts, face painting, a free magic show, and snack booths. ⊠ *23900 Temescal Canyon Rd.* ☎ *951/277–4422* ⊕ *www.tomsfarms.com* ✉ *Free* ☉ *Daily 8–8.*

WHERE TO STAY & EAT

$$–$$$$ ★ ✕ **Napa 29.** A cellar with more than 220 wines from California's Napa Valley and Central Coast is the main draw at this stylish restaurant and specialty-foods shop. Dark wood and white tablecloths are the backdrop for stellar California cuisine, such as cold smoked buffalo and macadamia-crusted sea bass with chardonnay sauce. Live jazz is performed on Friday and Saturday nights. ⊠ *280 Teller St., Suite 130* ☎ *951/273–0529* ▤ *AE, MC, V* ☉ *Closed Mon. No lunch Sat.*

$$ ⌂ **Country Suites By Ayres at Corona West.** This ranch-style hotel, with its leather couches, wrought-iron light fixtures, and courtyard adobe fireplace, harks back to the days of Spanish California. Some rooms have fireplaces. If you feel so inclined, you can mingle with fellow guests over beer, cheese, and crackers during the 5 to 7 PM "social hour." **Pros:**

Close to restaurants and shopping; free breakfasts; comfortable rooms. **Cons:** Located in a busy area. ✉*1900 W. Frontage Rd.* ☎*951/738–9113 or 800/676–1363* 🌐*www.countrysuites.com/coronawest.htm* *114 rooms* *In-room: refrigerator, Ethernet, Wi-Fi. In-hotel: room service, pool, gym, public Wi-Fi* 💳*AE, D, MC, V* *BP.*

RIVERSIDE

14 mi north of Corona on Route 91, 34 mi from Anaheim on Route 91.

By 1882, Riverside was home to more than half of California's citrus groves, making it the state's wealthiest city per capita in 1895. The prosperity produced a downtown area of magnificent architecture, which is well preserved today. Main Street's pedestrian strip is lined with antiques and gift stores, art galleries, salons, and the UCR/California Museum of Photography.

Fodor'sChoice ★ The crown jewel of Riverside is the **Mission Inn,** a remarkable Spanish-revival hotel whose elaborate turrets, clock tower, mission bells, and flying buttresses rise above downtown. The inn was designed in 1902 by Arthur B. Benton and Myron Hunt; the team took its cues from the Spanish missions in San Gabriel and Carmel. You can climb to the top of the Rotunda Wing's five-story spiral stairway or linger awhile in the Courtyard of the Birds, where a tinkling fountain and shady trees invite meditation. You can also peek inside the St. Francis Chapel, where folks such as Bette Davis, Humphrey Bogart, and Richard and Pat Nixon tied the knot before the Mexican cedar altar. The Presidential Lounge, a dark, wood-panel bar, has been patronized by eight U.S. presidents. ✉*3649 Mission Inn Ave.* ☎*951/784–0300 or 800/843–7755* 🌐*www.missioninn.com.*

Fodor'sChoice ★ The Mission Inn also has a luxurious spa, **Kelly's Spa,** a 6,000-square-foot poolside retreat. Warm-tone woods, hand-painted frescoes, Venetian chandeliers, and barrel-vaulted ceilings set the scene for this tranquil Tuscan-style escape, which has six treatment rooms and two private villas. The villas, which run $249 for a half day and $399 for a full day, have outdoor teak rain showers and marble-encased aromatherapy baths, as well as flat-screen TVs. After a round in the eucalyptus-infused steam room, you can grab your white cashmere robe and indulge in your choice of facials, massages, and body polishes. Guests ages 14 to 18 must be accompanied by a parent and must wear swimsuits during treatments. ✉*3649 Mission Inn Ave.* ☎*951/341–6725 or 800/440–5910* 🌐*www.kellysspa.com* ⏲*Daily 7:30 AM–8:30 PM.*

California Citrus State Historic Park. A celebration of California's citrus-growing history, this Victorian-style park occupies 377 well-kept acres of working citrus groves. The grounds, developed in 1880, are perfect for a leisurely afternoon picnic. Work off your lunch on the 2-mi interpretive trail, or check out the park's Craftsman-style bungalows, Victorian banister house, or museum and gift shop. Guided tours are conducted Saturday at 10 AM and by request. On Friday from June through August, free concerts present the bluegrass and jazz of 1900–1930. ✉ *1879 Jackson St.* ☎ *951/780–6222* ⊕ *www.parks.ca.gov* 🎫 *Free* ⊘ *Park Oct.–Mar., daily 8–5, Apr.–Sept., daily 8–7; visitor center Wed. and weekends 10–4.*

The **National Orange Show Festival** (☎ *909/888–6788* ⊕ *www.national orangeshow.com*) held in May, includes orange-crate label exhibits, orange-packing demonstrations, and other citrus-related fun.

WHERE TO STAY & EAT

$–$$$
Fodor's Choice
★

✕ **Mario's Place.** The clientele is as beautiful as the food at this intimate jazz and supper club. The northern Italian cuisine is first-rate, as are the bands that perform Friday and Saturday at 10 PM. Try the pear-and-Gorgonzola wood-fired pizza, followed by the caramelized banana napoleon (made with hazelnut phyllo, vanilla mascarpone, and coffee sauce). ✉ *3646 Mission Inn Ave.* ☎ *951/684–7755* ⊕ *www.marios place.com* ▤ *AE, D, MC, V* ⊘ *Closed Sun. No lunch Mon.–Wed.*

$$$
Fodor's Choice
★

✕🏨 **Mission Inn.** This grand Spanish colonial–era hotel was designated a National Historic Landmark in 1977. Most standard rooms have an early Spanish-California look, with Mission-style artwork and dark wooden headboards. Dining is a rewarding experience, whether you choose the grand Duane's Prime Steak & Seafood ($$–$$$$); Las Campanas ($–$$), where Mexican-style *carnitas* (shredded pork) are served in a pool of *mole negro* (a savory chili-and-chocolate-based sauce); the Mission Inn Restaurant ($–$$), where you can relax next to a bubbling fountain on the Spanish patio; or the Bella Trattoria ($–$$), which serves southern Italian fare like wood-fired pizzas and grilled paninis. ■ TIP→ **Sunday brunch here is excellent, though pricey, say locals.** Pros: Fascinating historical site; clean rooms; great restaurants; on-site spa. Cons: Train noise can be deafening at night. ✉ *3649 Mission Inn Ave., Riverside* ☎ *951/784–0300 or 800/843–7755* ⊕ *www.missioninn.com* 🛏 *211 rooms, 28 suites* �ᐠ *In-room: refrigerator, Ethernet. In-hotel: 3 restaurants, room service, bars, pool, gym, spa, laundry service, public Wi-Fi, airport shuttle, no-smoking rooms* ▤ *AE, D, DC, MC, V.*

NIGHTLIFE & THE ARTS

NIGHTLIFE Savor tapas and sangria at **Cafe Sevilla** (✉ *3252 Mission Inn Ave.* ☎ *951/778–0611*) while enjoying nightly live flamenco, salsa, and rumba music Thursday through Sunday. Dance lessons are offered Thursday nights. On weekend nights, the restaurant plays host to a Latin-Euro Top 40 dance club.

SHOPPING

Some fine boutiques, antiques stores, and specialty shops line pedestrian-only Main Street between 6th and 10th streets. The three-story **Mission Galleria** (✉ *3700 Main St.* ☎ *951/276–8000*) is an antiques mall specializing in vintage furniture, with a café downstairs. **Tiggy-Winkles Gift Shoppe** (✉ *Main and 7th Sts.* ☎ *951/683–0221*) carries toys, designer jewelry, porcelain knickknacks, potpourri, and soaps. The incense-scented **Dragonmarsh** (✉ *3643 University Ave.* ☎ *951/276–1116*) has Renaissance-style jewelry, candles, crystal balls, and swords.

SPORTS & THE OUTDOORS

Golf enthusiasts have eight courses to choose from around Riverside. **Riverside Golf Club** (✉*1011 N. Orange St.* ☎*951/682–3748*) is an 18-hole, par-72 public course with a full-service restaurant and bar. Greens fees: $25–$37. The Harold Heers and Jimmy Powell course at **Indian Hills Golf Club** (✉*5700 Club House Dr.* ☎*951/360–2090* ⊕*www. indianhillsgolf.com*) is a scenic 18-hole, par-70 championship course. Greens fees: $38–$55.

REDLANDS

15 mi northeast of Riverside via I–215 north and I–10 east.

Redlands lies at the center of what once was the largest navel-orange-producing region in the world. The town's main artery, Orange Street, is lined with fancy boutiques, trendy restaurants, and antiques shops. Orange groves are still plentiful throughout the area. You can glimpse Redlands' origins in several fine examples of California Victorian residential architecture.

In 1897 Cornelia A. Hill built **Kimberly Crest House and Gardens** to mimic the châteaux of France's Loire Valley. Surrounded by orange groves, lily ponds, and terraced Italian gardens, the mansion has a French-revival parlor, a mahogany staircase, a glass mosaic fireplace, and a bubbling fountain in the form of Venus rising from the sea. In 1905 the property was purchased by Alfred and Helen Kimberly, founders of the Kimberly-Clark Paper Company. Their daughter, Mary, lived in the house until 1979. Almost all of the home's 22 rooms are in original condition. Guided tours begin at 1 and run every 30 minutes; the last tour is at 3:30. ✉*1325 Prospect Dr.* ☎*909/792–2111* ⊕*www.kimberlycrest. org* ✆*$7* ⊘*Sept.–July, Thurs.–Sun. 1–4.*

☾ To learn more about Southern California's shaky history, head to the **San Bernardino County Museum,** where you can watch a working seismometer or check out a display about the San Andreas Fault. Specializing in the natural and regional history of Southern California, the museum is big on birds, eggs, dinosaurs, and mammals. Afterward, go for a light lunch at the Garden Café, open Tuesday through Sunday 11 to 2. ✉*2024 Orange Tree La.* ☎*909/307–2669* ⊕*www.sbcounty. gov/museum* ✆*$6* ⊘*Tues.–Sun. 9–5.*

After the Franciscan Fathers of Mission San Gabriel built it in 1830, the **Asistencia Mission de San Gabriel** functioned as a mission only for a few years. In 1834 it became part of a Spanish-colonial rancho; later the mission served as a school and a factory and was finally purchased by the county, which restored it in 1937. The landscaped courtyard contains an old Spanish mission bell; one building holds a small museum. ✉*26930 Barton Rd.* ☎*909/793–5402* ⊕*www.sbcounty.gov/museum* ✆*$1* ⊘*Tues.–Sat. 10–3.*

6

WHERE TO EAT

$-$$$ ✕ **Citrone.** This hip and casual downtown bistro has won *Wine Specta-*
Fodor'sChoice   *tor* awards continually since 1998. More than 600 wines are served
★   here, which complement such light California fare as the Citrone Stack
(layered roasted red peppers, red onion, grilled tomato, potato, mush-
rooms, and buffalo mozzarella), or the signature pizza, topped with
feta cheese, onions, and sliced apples. Don't miss the Citrone martini,
made with premium vodka and fresh-squeezed lemons. ✉ *328 Orange
St.* ☎ *909/793–6635* ▭ *AE, MC, V.*

¢–$ ✕ **Royal Falconer.** This stately British-theme pub is a great spot to enjoy a
pint and a traditional English meal of shepherd's pie, fish and chips, or
bangers and mash. There are 20 beers on tap and 30 by the bottle. The
upstairs game room has pool tables and dartboards. ✉ *106 Orange St.*
☎ *909/307–8913* ▭ *AE, MC, V.*

OAK GLEN

★   *17 mi east of Redlands via I–10 and Live Oak Canyon Rd.*

More than 60 varieties of apples are grown in Oak Glen, Southern
California's largest apple-growing region. This rustic village, tucked in
the foothills above Yucaipa, is home to acres of farms, produce stands,
country shops, and homey cafés. The town really comes alive during
the fall harvest (September through December), which is celebrated
with piglet races, live entertainment, and other events.

Start your tour of California's apple country at **Law's Apple Stand, Cider
Mill and Ranch** (✉ *38392 Oak Glen Rd., Oak Glen* ☎ *909/797–3130*
⊕ *www.oakglen.net/lawscidermill.html*), where you can sample differ-
ent apple varieties or mix and match a custom bag. Though it's the
smallest stand in the area, more than 35 varieties of apples are sold
here, as well as fresh cider and apple butter.

Southern California's largest apple grower, **Los Rios Rancho** (✉ *39611
S. Oak Glen Rd., Oak Glen* ☎ *909/797–1005* ⊕ *www.losriosrancho.
com*) is also the most popular. This massive farm has a fantastic coun-
try store where you can stock up on jams, cookbooks, syrups, and can-
died apples. Head into the bakery for a hot tri-tip sandwich (thinly-cut
seasoned beef served hot on a hoagie roll, usually with grilled onions
and bell peppers) and apple streusel pie before going outside to the pic-
nic grounds for lunch. During the fall, you can pick your own apples
and pumpkins, jump on a wagon ride, or enjoy live bluegrass music.
On the grounds of Los Rios Rancho, **The Wildlands Conservancy** is
home to 400 acres of preserved nature trails open weekends 8:30–4:30.
Guided night walks are offered on the third Saturday of each month,
April through December.

Oak Glen's main information center is located at **Mom's Country Orchards**
(✉ *38695 Oak Glen Rd., Oak Glen* ☎ *909/797–4249* ⊕ *www.moms
countryorchards.com*), where you can belly up to the bar and learn
about the nuances of apple tasting, or warm up with a hot cider heated
on an antique stove. Organic produce, dried fruits, homemade honey,

apple butter, and salsa are also specialties here.

Roaming peacocks, emus, and miniature horses wander through the grounds at **Parrish Pioneer Ranch** (⊠*38561 Oak Glen Rd., Oak Glen* ☎*909/797–1753* ⊕*www.parrishranch.com*), the only apple stand in the area that sells hard cider (in addition to the fresh-pressed variety). After browsing the country store and candy shop,

head to the wine bar where you can sample a nice selection of honey meads in addition to fruit wines made with apples, berries, pears, cherries, and rhubarb. Tastings are $1 to $1.50, depending on the variety. The ranch's **Apple Dumplin's Restaurant** (☎*909/797–0037*), housed in the historic stock barn of the Enoch Parrish homestead, serves up rustic American dishes like hearty potato soup and "honey-stung" fried chicken; don't miss their signature apple dumpling for dessert. The barn and neighboring 1876 Parrish house are the oldest stick-frame buildings in San Bernardino County.

Employees dress in period costumes at **Riley's Farm** (⊠*12261 S. Oak Glen Rd., Oak Glen* ☎*909/797–7534* ⊕*www.rileysfarm.com*), one of the most interactive and kid-friendly ranches in apple country. Here, you can hop on a hay ride, take part in a barn dance, pick your own apples, press some cider, or throw a tomahawk while enjoying living-history performances throughout the orchard. The farm offers a wide range of dinner and dancing events throughout the year, including the popular Legend of Sleepy Hollow weekends in October with apple bobbing, square dancing, and pie-eating contests.

California's oldest chestnut tree makes its home at **Snow-Line Orchards** (⊠*39400 Oak Glen Rd., Oak Glen* ☎*909/797–3415* ⊕*www.snow-line.com*). Here, you can watch a vintage 1923 cider press crush and juice apples, sample the flash-pasteurized apple, cherry-apple, and raspberry-apple ciders, or wait your turn in line for a melt-in-your-mouth bite of fresh miniature apple-cider donuts. The grocery store sells a variety of apples and country store items.

For a boutique apple experience check out **Willowbrook Apple Farm** (⊠*12099 S. Oak Glen Rd., Oak Glen* ☎*909/797–9484* ⊕*http://willowbrookapple.tripod.com*), a small family-run farm that specializes in organic raspberries and blackberries and antique Stayman Winesap apples, which are known for their delicious blend of sweet and tart flavors. Open August through November, the farm offers children rides on their 1949 tractor or carrots to feed the resident horse. The shop, decorated in fall decor, sells a wide variety of preserves, apple butter, and cinnamon-sugar apple chips. You can press your own gallon of cider for $14.50.

SAN BERNARDINO MOUNTAINS

The twin resorts of Lake Arrowhead and the always-sunny Big Bear are the recreational center of this area. Though the two are geographically close, they're distinct in appeal—smaller, but similar to Lake Tahoe, say visitors. Lake Arrowhead, with its cool mountain air, trail-threaded woods, and brilliant lake, draws a summertime crowd—a well-heeled one, if the prices in its shops and restaurants are any indication. Big Bear's ski and snowboarding slopes, cross-country trails, and cheerful lodges come alive in winter. Even if you're not interested in the resorts themselves, the Rim of the World Scenic Byway (Highway 18), which connects the two at an elevation of 8,000 feet, is a magnificent drive.

LAKE ARROWHEAD

37 mi northeast of Riverside via I–215 north, to Hwy. 330 north, to Hwy. 18 west.

Lake Arrowhead Village is an alpine community with offices, shops, outlet stores, and eateries that descend the hill to the lake. Outside the village, access to the lake and its beaches is limited to area residents and their guests.

You can take a 45-minute cruise on the *Arrowhead Queen,* operated daily by **LeRoy Sports** (☎909/336–6992) from the waterfront marina in Lake Arrowhead Village. Tickets are available on a first-come, first-served basis and cost $15. Call for departure times.

☾ If you're in the mood to skate, head over to the International-size rink at
★ **Ice Castle,** a former training center for Olympic medalist Michelle Kwan. Skate rentals cost $2 per person. ⊠ *410 Burnt Mill Rd.* ☎*909/337–5283* ⊕*www.icecastle.us* ⊠*$8* ☾*Tues. and Fri. 7:30 PM–9 PM, Sat. 2:30–4:30, Sun. 11–1.*

WHERE TO STAY & EAT

$$–$$$ ✕**Casual Elegance.** Just a few miles outside Arrowhead Village, this inti-
★ mate 1939 house has been charming locals and guests for more than 15 years. Owner-chef Jan Morrison's specialties include the New Zealand rack of lamb with honey-hazelnut crust and a pork tenderloin with Montmorency cherry sauce, but the steaks and seafood are also first-rate. Featured menu items change weekly. Dine by the fireplace for a particularly cozy experience. ⊠*26848 Hwy. 189, Blue Jay* ☎*909/337–8932* ⊟*AE, D, DC, MC, V* ☾*Closed Mon.–Wed. No lunch.*

$–$$ ✕**The Chef's Inn & Tavern.** This romantic lakefront restaurant, which
★ survived Cedar Glen's devastating 2003 wildfires, is a favorite of locals. Once a mountain bordello, the historic building is decorated in the Victorian style with antiques and has a lower-level saloon. Standout dishes such as the sautéed veal jagerschnitzel with wild mushrooms and the chicken cordon bleu stuffed with Westphalian ham and Swiss cheese are accompanied by soup, salad, and vegetables. ⊠*29020 Oak Terr., Cedar Glen* ☎*909/336–4488* ⊟*AE, MC, V.*

¢–$ ✕**Belgian Waffle Works.** This waterfront eatery, just steps from the Arrowhead Queen, is quaint and homey, with country decor and beautiful views of the lake. Don't miss their namesake waffles, crisp on the outside and moist on the inside, topped with fresh berries and cream. Lunch is also delicious, with choices ranging from basic burgers to tuna melts and salads. The restaurant gets crowded during lunch on the weekend, so get there early to snag a table with a view. ✉*28200 Hwy. 189, Bldg. E140, Lake Arrowhead* ☎*909/337–5222* ▤*AE, D, MC, V* ⊘*No dinner Sun.–Thurs.*

$$$ ╳▥ **Lake Arrowhead Resort and Spa.** This lakeside lodge completed a
★ $12-million renovation in 2007. Most rooms have water or forest views with down comforters, granite counters, and LCD TVs. The on-premises Spa of the Pines offers facials, massages, and other body treatments. BIN189 restaurant, with its granite-and-pine decor and private wine-tasting room, serves up a homey menu of international and American specialties including diver scallops in a grape reduction, and braised short ribs with lobster mashed potatoes. In the morning, don't miss the petite house-made donuts set out in the lobby. **Pros:** Beautiful lake views; delicious on-site dining; gorgeous guest rooms. **Cons:** Some rooms have thin walls. ✉*27984 Hwy. 189, Lake Arrowhead Village* ☎*909/336–1511 or 800/800–6792* ⊕*www.lakearrowheadresort.com* ➔*177 rooms, 4 suites, 3 condos* ⬧*In-room: dial-up, Wi-Fi. In-hotel: restaurant, room service, bar, pool, gym, spa, beachfront, children's programs (ages 4–12), public Wi-Fi, no-smoking rooms* ▤*AE, D, DC, MC, V.*

¢–$$$ ▥ **Bracken Fern Manor.** For a unique—albeit spooky—evening, head to this "haunted" English Tudor–style hotel. Mobster Bugsy Siegel opened the property in 1929 as a brothel and private gambling resort; today it's a certified historic landmark, which was completely restored in 1993. Each of the rooms, decorated in florals and English and Belgian antiques, is named for the aspiring actresses who once entertained here. In summer, wine and hors d'oeuvres are offered in the wine cellar, just steps from the secret tunnel used by gangsters in the hotel's heyday. A separate cottage, which sleeps four, includes a fireplace, TV/VCR, kitchenette, and garden patio with barbecue and Jacuzzi. **Pros:** Historic property. **Cons:** Small rooms; no television. ✉*815 Arrowhead Villas Rd., Lake Arrowhead Village* ☎*888/244–5612 or 909/337–8557* ⊕*www.brackenfernmanor.com* ➔*10 rooms* ⬧*In-room: VCR (some). In-hotel: no elevator, no-smoking rooms* ▤*D, MC, V* ▥❶*BP.*

SPORTS & THE OUTDOORS

Waterskiing and wakeboarding lessons are available on Lake Arrowhead in summer at **McKenzie Waterski School** (☎*909/337–3814* ⊕*http:// mckenzieskischool.com*).

Lovely **Lake Gregory** was formed by a dam constructed in 1938. Because the summer water temperature is often quite warm (rare for lakes at this altitude), this is the best swimming lake in the area. It's open in summer only, and there's a nominal charge to swim. You can fish, go on the waterslides, and rent rowboats at Lake Gregory Village. ✉*24171 Lake Dr. off Rim of World Hwy.* ☎*909/338–2233.*

BIG BEAR LAKE

24 mi east of Lake Arrowhead on Hwy. 18 (Rim of the World Hwy.).

The town of Big Bear Lake, on the lake's south shore, has a classic Western Alpine style; you'll spot the occasional chaletlike building here. Big Bear City, at the east end of Big Bear Lake, has restaurants, motels, and a small airport.

From May through October, the paddle wheeler *Big Bear Queen* departs daily at noon, 2, and 4 from **Big Bear Marina** (✉ *500 Paine Rd., Big Bear Lake* ☎ *909/866–3218* ⊕ *www.bigbearmarina.com/queen. html*) for 90-minute tours of the lake; the cost is $15.

☯ Kids will enjoy a cruise on the **Time Bandit Pirate Ship,** which is a small-scale replica of a 17th-century English galleon. The ship, which was featured in Terry Gilliam's 1981 movie, *Time Bandits,* is also the centerpiece attraction at the annual Big Bear Pirate Faire, held in June (⊕ *www.bigbearrenfair.com/pirate*). During the event, Captain John's Harbor in Fawnskin is transformed into a 17th-century Buccaneer Village, complete with ship-to-shore pirate battles, a treasure hunt, and cold grog. ✉ *398 Edgemoor Rd., Big Bear Lake* ☎ *909/878–4040* ⊕ *www.800bigbear.com/water/pirateship* 🎫 *$19* ☉ *Tours daily at 2; call for possible other times.*

☯ **Moonridge Animal Park,** a rescue and rehabilitation center, specializes in animals native to the San Bernardino Mountains. Among its residents are black bears, bald eagles, coyote, beavers, and bobcats. You can catch an educational presentation at noon and feeding tour at 3. ✉ *43285 Goldmine Dr.* ☎ *909/584–1171* ⊕ *www.moonridgezoo.org* 🎫 *$9* ☉ *June–Sept., daily 10–5; Sept.–June, weekdays 10–4, weekends 10–5.*

☯ Take a ride down a twisting bobsled course in winter, or beat the summer heat on a dual waterslide at **Alpine Slide at Magic Mountain.** Miniature golf and go-carts add to the fun. ✉ *800 Wildrose La., ¼ mi west of Big Bear Village* ☎ *909/866–4626* ⊕ *www.alpineslidebigbear.com* 🎫 *$4 single rides, $18 five-ride pass* ☉ *Daily 10–6.*

☯ **Big Bear Discovery Center.** Operated by the forest service, this nature
Fodor'sChoice center is the place to sign up for a canoe ride through Grout Bay,
★ or naturalist-led Discovery Tours, including visits to bald eagle nesting grounds, wildflower fields, and historic gold mines. The popular Bald Eagle Tours, which run January through March, take you to the winter nesting grounds of these magnificent birds. The center also has rotating flora and fauna exhibits, and a nature-oriented gift shop. ✉ *North Shore Dr., Hwy. 38, between Fawnskin and Stanfield Cutoff* ☎ *909/866–3437* ⊕ *www.bigbeardiscoverycenter.com* 🎫 *Free* ☉ *Daily 8:30–4:30.*

WHERE TO STAY & EAT

$$–$$$ ✗**Evergreen International.** This rustic-style steak house has sweeping views of Big Bear Lake. In winter you can stay warm in the comfortable dining room, which has dark paneling and exposed beams; in summer head out to the deck to enjoy a glass of wine while you watch the sun set. Lunch and dinner choices include grilled chicken topped with passion-fruit sauce, pepper-crusted ahi tuna, or prime rib with king crab legs. ⊠*40771 Lakeview Dr.* ☎*909/878–5588* ⊟*MC, V.*

$$–$$$ ✕**Madlon's.** The menu at this gingerbread-style cottage includes sophisticated dishes such as lamb chops with Gorgonzola butter, cream of jalapeño soup, and Asian black-peppercorn filet mignon. Reservations are essential on weekends. ⊠*829 W. Big Bear Blvd., Big Bear City* ☎*909/585–3762* ⊟*D, DC, MC, V* ✕*Closed Tues. No lunch.*

$–$$$ ✕**Mandoline Bistro.** Locals looking to impress out-of-town guests make reservations at this Cal-fusion restaurant, known for its flavorful combinations of Mexican, Thai, Asian, and Island cuisine. The mountain-chic bistro, accented with stark black-and-white linens and antler chandeliers, serves up fusion cuisine like tempura avocados with raspberry rémoulade, roasted duck salad with sweet walnuts and Gorgonzola cheese, or Caribbean salmon with sticky rice and grilled bananas. On Friday and Saturday nights, the Loft Bar offers live jazz. ⊠*40701 Village Dr.* ☎*909/866–4200* ⊟*AE, MC, V* ✕*No lunch Mon. or Tues.*

$$–$$$ ▣**Apples Bed & Breakfast Inn.** Despite its location on a busy road to the
★ ski lifts, the Apples Inn feels remote and peaceful, thanks to the surrounding pine trees. The colorful rooms have names such as Golden Delicious, Royal Gala, and Sweet Bough; all have gas fireplaces, and four have Jacuzzis. A common room has a wood-burning stove, baby grand piano, game table, and library loft. A full breakfast, afternoon refreshments, and evening dessert are included. **Pros:** Large rooms, clean, free snacks and movies, delicious big breakfast. **Cons:** Some traffic noise, sometimes feels very busy. ⊠*42430 Moonridge Rd.* ☎*909/866–0903* ⊕*www.applesbigbear.com* ⊅*13 rooms* △*In-room: no a/c, no phone, DVD, VCR, Wi-Fi. In-hotel: no elevator, public Wi-Fi, no-smoking rooms* ⊟*AE, D, MC, V* ⊙*BP.*

$$–$$$ ▣**Northwoods Resort.** A giant log cabin with the amenities of a resort, Northwoods has a lobby that resembles a 1930s hunting lodge: canoes, antlers, fishing poles, and a grand stone fireplace all decorate the walls. Rooms are large but cozy; some have fireplaces and whirlpool tubs. Stillwells Restaurant, next to the lobby, serves hearty American fare. Ski packages are available. **Pros:** Within walking distance of shops and restaurants; good central Big Bear location. **Cons:** Parts of the hotel are showing their age; rooms can be noisy at night. ⊠*40650 Village Dr.* ☎*909/866–3121 or 800/866–3121* ⊕*www.northwoodsresort.com* ⊅*138 rooms, 9 suites* △*In-room: Ethernet (some), dial-up, Wi-Fi. In-hotel: 2 restaurants, room service, bar, pool, gym, concierge, public Wi-Fi, no-smoking rooms* ⊟*AE, D, DC, MC, V.*

¢–$$$ ▣**Robinhood Resort.** Across the street from the Pine Knot Marina, this family-oriented motel has rooms with fireplaces and some with whirlpool tubs or kitchenettes. Also available are several condos just feet from Snow Summit ski resort and deluxe spa rooms with in-room hot tubs, DVD players, and fireplaces. **Pros:** Short walk from the marina; near shops and restaurants; good on-site restaurant. **Cons:** No a/c in some rooms; parts of motel are showing their age. ⊠*40797 Lakeview Dr.* ☎*909/866–4643 or 800/990–9956* ⊕*www.robinhoodresort.*

6

info ⬎50 rooms, 8 condos ⅏In-room: no a/c (some), kitchen (some), VCR, Wi-Fi (some). In-hotel: no elevator, restaurant, bar, public Wi-Fi, no-smoking rooms ⊟AE, D, MC, V.

SPORTS & THE OUTDOORS

★ You don't have to be a mountain biker to enjoy Bear Mountain's **Scenic Sky Chair**. The lift takes you to the mountain's 8,400-foot peak, where you can lunch at View Haus (¢), a casual outdoor restaurant with breathtaking views of the lake and San Gorgonio mountain. Fare includes barbecued-chicken sandwiches, hot dogs, and burgers, along with cold beer and wine. ⊠*43101 Goldmine Dr.* ☎*909/866–5766* ⊕*www.bigbear mountainresorts.com* ⮞*$10 round-trip* ⊗*Mid-June–early Sept., daily 9–4; early Sept.–mid-June, some weekends, call for hrs.*

Looking for adventure? For $40, you can ride a horse through the snow-covered forest at **Baldwin Lake Stables** (☎*909/585–6482* ⊕*www.baldwin lakestables.com*). If you want to get out on the lake for a day, stop at **Big Bear Parasail and Water Sports** (⊠*439 Pine Knot Ave., Big Bear Lake* ☎*909/866–4359*) for waterskiing, tubing, and parasailing.

Jet Ski, water-ski, fishing boat, and equipment rentals are available from **Big Bear Marina** (⊠*Paine Rd.* ☎*909/866–3218*). **Pine Knot Landing** (⊠*439 Pine Knot* ☎*909/866–2628*) rents fishing boats and sells bait, ice, and snacks.

SKIING **Big Bear Mountain Resorts** is Southern California's largest winter resort.
★ Here you can board more than 200 freestyle terrain features at Bear Mountain's massive snowboard terrain park, then shuttle 1 mi down the road to Snow Summit for its open skiing terrain and special area designed for kids. The megaresort offers 430 skiable acres, 55 runs, and 23 chairlifts, including four high-speed quads. An all-day lift ticket includes admission and shuttle rides at both resorts. On busy winter weekends and holidays it's best to reserve tickets before heading to either mountain. ⊠*Big Bear, 43101 Goldmine Dr., off Moonridge Rd.* ⊠*Snow Summit, 880 Summit Blvd., off Big Bear Blvd.* ☎*909/866–5766* ⊕*www.bigbearmountainresorts.com* ⮞*$51; $64 peak season.*

THE SOUTHERN INLAND EMPIRE

THE SAN JACINTO MOUNTAINS & TEMECULA VALLEY

Life is quieter in the southern portion of the Inland Empire than it is to the north. In this corner of Riverside County, small towns such as Idyllwild and Temecula are oases of the good life for locals and visitors alike.

IDYLLWILD

85 mi south of Big Bear Lake via Hwys. 18, 330, and 30, then I–10 east to Hwy. 243 south; 51 mi southeast of Rte. 60 east and Hwy. 243 south.

Famous as a serene hideaway and artists' colony, the low-key and relaxed community of Idyllwild also has great rock climbing, hiking, and shopping.

At the **Idyllwild Nature Center,** you can learn about the area's Native American history, try your hand at astronomy, and listen to traditional storytellers. Outside there are 3 mi of hiking trails, plus picnic areas. Native-plant lectures and wildflower walks are offered every Memorial Day weekend during the center's Wildflower Show. ⊠25225 Hwy. 243 ☎951/659–3850 ⊕www.idyllwildnaturecenter.com ☜$2 ☉May–Sept., Thurs.–Sun. 9–4:30; Oct.–Apr., Fri.–Sun. 9–4.

WHERE TO STAY & EAT

$-$$$ ★ ✕**Restaurant Gastrognome.** Elegant and dimly lighted, with wood paneling and an often-glowing fireplace, "The Gnome" is where locals go for a romantic dinner with great food, a full bar, and nice ambience. The French onion soup is a standout appetizer; the calamari amandine and Southwest-style grilled pork are excellent entrées. The crème brûlée makes for a sweet finale. ⊠54381 Ridgeview Dr. ☎951/659–5055 ⊕www.gastrognome.com ⊟MC, V.

¢ ✕**Oma's European Bakery and Restaurant.** Three generations of the Solleveld family run this breakfast and lunch spot, tempting early birds with hot *roerei* (a scramble of eggs, onions, and tomatoes) and cinnamon rolls. For lunch, don't miss the Black Forest ham on black bread with German *butterkase* (buttery jack-like cheese), or Oma's wurst platter, stacked high with three European links, red cabbage, or sauerkraut, and German potatoes. ⊠54241 Ridgeview Dr. ☎951/659–2979 ⊟MC, V ☉Closed weekends. No dinner.

$$-$$$ ★ **Strawberry Creek Inn.** This charming B&B nestled among the pines consistently draws raves from readers. Each room boasts Aveda bath products and fluffy white robes. Many rooms have wood-burning fireplaces. In the morning don't miss the German-style French toast, topped with sliced Granny Smith apples, cinnamon sugar, and smoked bratwurst. The cottage is a nice honeymoon spot, equipped with a full kitchen, microwave, fireplace, and deck. **Pros:** Comfortable rooms; gourmet food. **Cons:** Some street noise. ⊠26370 Hwy. 24392549 ☎951/659–3202 or 800/262–8969 ⊕www.strawberrycreekinn.com ◊9 rooms, 1 cottage ♿In-room: refrigerator (some), VCR (some), Wi-Fi. In-hotel: no elevator, public Wi-Fi ⊟D, MC, V �†◎BP.

¢-$$ **Atipahato Lodge.** Perfect for nature lovers, this woodsy retreat is on 5 acres of hilltop that overlook the San Jacinto Wilderness. Each room has pine-panel walls, a vaulted ceiling, and a balcony. Each of two luxury cabins includes a fireplace, Jacuzzi, full kitchen, private deck, CD stereo, cable TV, and VCR. While you're here, check out the nature trail, which passes a springtime stream and waterfall and the Native American Nature Center. **Pros:** Clean rooms; nice views; weekend Continental breakfast. **Cons:** Smallish rooms; not within walking distance of city center. ⌧*25525 Hwy. 243* ☎*888/400–0071* ⊕*www.atipahatolodge. com* ⇆*18 rooms, 2 cabins* ♿*In-room: no a/c (some), kitchen, refrigerator, VCR (some). In hotel: no elevator* ⊟*AE, D, MC, V.*

SPORTS & THE OUTDOORS

FISHING **Lake Fulmor** (⌧*Hwy. 243, 10 mi north of Idyllwild* ☎*951/659–2117)* is stocked with rainbow trout, largemouth bass, catfish, and bluegill. To fish here you'll need a California fishing license and a National Forest Adventure Pass ($5 per vehicle per day). Adventure Passes are available at the **Idyllwild Ranger Station** (⌧*Pine Crest Ave., off Hwy. 243* ☎*951/659–2117).*

HIKING Hike the 2.6-mi Ernie Maxwell Scenic Trail at **Humber Park** (⌧*At top of Fern Valley Rd.* ☎*951/659–2117).* Along the way you'll have views of Little Tahquitz Creek, Marion Mountain, and Suicide Rock. A permit is not required to hike this trail. The **Pacific Crest Trail** is accessible at Highway 74, 1 mi east of Highway 371; or via the Fuller Ridge Trail at Black Mountain Road, 15 mi north of Idyllwild. Permits ($5 per day) are required for camping and day hikes in San Jacinto Wilderness. They are available through the **Idyllwild Ranger Station** (⌧*Pine Crest Ave., off Hwy. 243* ☎*951/659–2117).*

TEMECULA

Fodor'sChoice 43 mi south of Riverside on I–15; 60 mi north of San Diego on I–15;
★ 90 mi southeast of Los Angeles via I–10 and I–15.

In the mood for wine and romance but can't make it to northern California? Temecula, with its rolling green vineyards, comfy country inns, and first-rate restaurants, makes a fine alternative to Napa Valley. There are 20 wineries in the Temecula Valley, with still more being built. The name Temecula comes from a Luiseno Indian word meaning "where the sun shines through the mist," which are ideal conditions for wine growing. Intense afternoon sun and cool nighttime temperatures, complemented by ocean breezes that flow through the Rainbow and Santa Margarita gaps in the coastal range, help grapevines flourish in the area's granitic soil. The Temecula Valley is known for chardonnay, merlot, and sauvignon blanc, but in recent years there has been a trend toward viognier, Syrah, and pinot gris varietals. Most wineries charge a small fee ($5 to $10) for a tasting of several wines. For a map of the area's wineries, visit ⊕*www.temeculawines.org.*

Temecula is more than just vineyards and tasting rooms. For a bit of old-fashioned fun, head to historic **Old Town Temecula** (⌧*Front St., between Rancho California Rd. and Hwy. 79* ☎*951/694–6412),* a turn-of-the-20th-century cluster of storefronts and boardwalks that holds more than 640 antiques stores, boutiques, and art galleries. This is where special events such as the Rod Run, Frontier Days Rodeo, and Fall Car Cruise take place. A farmers' market is held here every Saturday from 8 to noon.

WINERY TOURS

Most of the Temecula wineries are close to each other on Rancho California Road. If you plan to visit several wineries (and taste a lot of wine), catch the **Grapeline Wine Country Shuttle** (✉ *29909 Corte Castille* ☎ *951/693–5463 or 888/894–6379* ⊕ *www.gogrape.com* ✉ *$42*), which operates daily. The Vineyard Picnic Tour, at $88 ($108 Saturday), includes transportation, a wine-making demonstration, free tastings at four wineries, and a gourmet picnic lunch catered by Allie's at Callaway.

Many limousine services offer wine-tasting tours, including **Sterling Rose Limo** (☎ *800/649–6463* ⊕ *www.sterlingroselimo.com*), which offers packages that include four to five tasting tickets and a gourmet picnic lunch or winery restaurant lunch. Per-passenger rates, which start at $96, are cheapest for groups of eight.

Destination Temecula (☎ *877/ 305–0501* ⊕ *www.destem.com*) runs daily four-hour tours of wine country, departing from Old Town Temecula at 11:30. For $89 you're taken around the perimeter of Temecula Valley before stopping for lunch in the barrel room at Frangipani Winery. Tastings at Wilson Creek Winery and La Cereza Winery follow.

☺ If you have the kids along, check out the **Imagination Workshop,** the fictional 7,500-square-foot home of Professor Phineas T. Pennypickle, PhD. This elaborately decorated children's center is filled with secret passageways, machines, wacky contraptions, and time-travel inventions, making it an imaginative way to spend the afternoon. ✉ *42081 Main St.* ☎ *951/308–6376* ⊕ *www.pennypickles.org* ✉ *$4.50* ⊗ *Tues.– Sat. 10–5.*

WINERIES

Baily Vineyard & Winery has grown to include an 8,000-square-foot wine-making facility with 50,000 gallons of wine tanks. Most folks come here for their two noteworthy restaurants, Carol's and Baily's. In the tasting room, browse the gourmet gift shop before sampling the cabernet, Riesling, and Muscat Blanc. ✉ *33440 La Serena Way* ☎ *951/676–9463* ⊕ *www.baily.com* ✉ *Winery free, tastings $5* ⊗ *Sun.–Fri. 11–5, Sat. 10–5.*

Established in 1969, **Callaway Coastal Vineyards** is well known for chardonnays and merlots by winemaker Art Villarreal. Complimentary tours are offered weekdays at 11, 1, and 3, and on weekends 11 to 4 on the hour. ✉ *32720 Rancho California Rd.* ☎ *951/676–4001* ⊕ *www. callawaywinery.com* ✉ *Winery free, tastings $10* ⊗ *Daily 10–5.*

Bringing a bit of French-country elegance to Temecula, **Churon Winery** welcomes you to its tasting room via a winding stone staircase. Try winemaker Marshall Stuart's cabernet sauvignon, Viognier, chenin blanc, and Syrah at the large, dark-wood bar, which has ample seating and doubles as a fine-art gallery. A deli offers gourmet items that you can take outside to the gorgeous patio. ✉ *33233 Rancho California*

Rd. ☎951/694–9070 ⊕*www.innatchuronwinery.com* ✉*Winery free, tastings $10* ⊙*Daily 10–4:30.*

Falkner Winery's big Western-style barn with its wraparound deck over-looking the vineyards is a great spot to enjoy Temecula's cool ocean breezes. Falkner has garnered great word-of-mouth, especially for their red Tuscan Amante. Winemaker Steve Hagata is also known for his Viognier, chardonnay, and Riesling. Packaged snacks, along with a huge variety of gourmet gifts, are available in the shop. Tours are given at 11 AM and 2 PM on weekends. ✉*40620 Calle Contento Rd.* ☎*951/676–8231* ⊕*www.falknerwinery.com* ✉*Winery free, tastings $8, tours $5* ⊙*Daily 10–5.*

Producing consistently delicious sparkling wines, cabernet sauvignons, and gewürztraminers, William Filsinger of **Filsinger Vineyards & Winery** carries on the wine-making traditions of his mother's family, who owned a winery in Germany. His son Eric has joined up as assistant wine-maker. ✉*39050 De Portola Rd.* ☎*951/302–6363* ⊕*www.filsinger winery.com* ✉*Winery free; tastings $3* ⊙*Fri. 11–4, weekends 10–5, Mon.–Thurs. by appointment.*

Barbecues, cigar nights, and tapas parties make **Frangipani Estate Winery** a fun and comfortable stop on Temecula's wine row. Owner and wine-maker Don Frangipani tends to his grapes between pouring splashes of zinfandel, petite sirah, and cabernet sauvignon in the rustic Span-ish–style tasting room. The mood is relaxed and rustic, with olive trees, roaming horses, and rolling hills as your rural backdrop. ✉*39750 De Portola Rd.* ☎*951/699–8845* ⊕*www.frangipaniwinery.com* ✉*Win-ery free, tastings $10* ⊙*Daily 10–5.*

With Mediterranean varietals grown on 11 acres of vineyards in Tem-ecula and in the nearby Cucamonga Valley, **Hart Winery** makes dry reds and the fortified dessert wine Italian Aleatico, named for the rare grape from which it comes. The purple tasting room is decked out with ribbons and medals won by the winery. ✉*41300 Avenida Biona* ☎*951/676–6300* ⊕*www.thehartfamilywinery.com* ✉*Winery free, tastings $5* ⊙*Daily 9–4:30.*

Don't be surprised to come upon a barbecue or equestrian event at **Keyways Vineyard & Winery,** which has an Old West feel. In the tasting room decorated with lanterns and antiques, you can listen to country music while sampling tasty reds such as the zinfandel or cabernet franc. ✉*37338 De Portola Rd.* ☎*951/302–7888* ⊕*www.keywayswinery1. com* ✉*Winery free, tastings $10* ⊙*June–Sept., daily 10–6, Sept.–June, daily 10–5.*

One of the newest vineyards and wineries in Temecula, **Leonesse Cel-lars** is a casual farmhouse-style winery with a stone turret overlooking 20 acres of cabernet sauvignon grapes. The basic tasting includes a chocolate truffle served alongside their port. For a special experience, reserve a VIP tasting for six tastes, a barrel sample, and cheese and chocolate pairing with winemaker Tim Kramer. The on-site restaurant, Block Five, serves up alfresco dishes such as grilled lamb, honey curry chicken with flat bread, or a plate of California cheeses paired with gourmet meats. ✉*38311 DePortola Rd.* ☎*951/302–7601* ⊕*www.leonessecellars.com* ✉*Winery free, tastings $10* ☉*Daily 10–5.*

Maurice Car'rie Vineyard & Winery is housed in an 1800s-style farmhouse. Winemaker Gus Vizgirda works with 16 different varietals, producing wines such as a light and fruity pineapple-flavored sparkling wine. The wines are fairly sweet, but readers rave about the whites. On your way out, stop by the gourmet shop for a chunk of homemade sourdough-and-Brie bread. ✉*34225 Rancho California Rd.* ☎*951/676–1711* ⊕*www.mauriecarriewinery.com* ✉*Tastings $10–$15* ☉*Daily 10–5.*

UP, UP, AND AWAY

If you're in the mood to swoop or float above Temecula's green vineyards and country estates, sign up for a trip with **California Dreamin' Balloon & Biplane Rides** (☎*800/373–3359* ⊕*www.californiadreamin.com*). Balloon trips depart from the company's vineyards at 5:30 AM; the $168 per-person fee includes champagne, coffee, a pastry breakfast, and a souvenir photo.

Temecula holds its annual **Balloon and Wine Festival** (☎*951/676–6713* ⊕*www.tvbwf.com*) each June.

Perched on a hilltop, **Miramonte Winery** is Temecula's hippest, thanks to the vision of owner Cane Vanderhoof, who replanted the vineyard in almost 100% Syrah grapes. Listen to Spanish-guitar recordings while sampling the Opulent Meritage, a supple sauvignon blanc, or the smooth Cinsault rosé. On Friday and Saturday nights from 5 to 8, the winery turns into a hot spot with signature wines ($6 to $8), gourmet meals ($8 to $10), live flamenco music, and dancing that spills out into the vineyards. ✉*33410 Rancho California Rd.* ☎*951/506–5500* ⊕*www.miramontewinery.com* ✉*Winery free, tastings $8* ☉*Tastings daily 11–5.*

★ **Mount Palomar Winery** is generally considered to produce the best wines in Temecula. Winemaker Etienne Cowper trained under Jed Steele of Kendall-Jackson and Villa Mt. Eden fame, and with Andre Tchelistcheff, a mentor of Robert Mondavi and creator (at Beaulieu Vineyards in the 1930s) of California's first world-class cabernets. Mount Palomar was the first winery to introduce Sangiovese grapes to Temecula, and the variety has proven perfectly suited to the region's soil and climate. In a Spanish colonial–style building, the tasting room offers must-tries such as red Meritage, white Cortese, and a cream sherry to die for. If you want to picnic on the grounds, stop by the deli for top-notch potato salad and Italian-style sandwiches. ✉*33820 Rancho California Rd.* ☎*951/676–5047* ⊕*www.mountpalomar.com* ✉*Winery free, tastings $10* ☉*Mon.–Thurs. 10–6, Fri.–Sun. 10–7.*

Palumbo Family Vineyards & Winery occupies a converted garage, but there's something charming about the place. Grab a glass of the Bordeaux-style blend, Tre Fratelli, and enjoy a chat with the owners on the little white deck outside. For $75 per person, Palumbo—who is a chef as well as a winemaker—will prepare a private dinner for 2 to 10 guests; dishes might include a petit filet mignon with a sauce of *cambazola* (a soft blue cheese), with truffle-oil mashed potatoes and baby broccoli with beurre noisette. Palumbo also pours and discusses the wine. ✉*40150 Barksdale Circle* ☎*951/676–7900* ⊕*www.palumbo familyvineyards.com* 🏷*Winery free, tastings $5* ⊙*Fri. noon–5, weekends 10–5, Mon.–Thurs. by appointment.*

★ Lush gardens and 350 acres of vineyards welcome you onto **Ponte Family Estates,** a rustic winery that's a hot spot for tour groups. In the open-beam tasting room, you can sample six different varietals, including cabernet, Syrah (recommended by readers), Viognier, and chardonnay. The open-air marketplace sells artisan ceramics, specialty foods, and wine-country gift baskets. Around lunchtime, the winery's Smokehouse Cafe buzzes with guests who come for the wood-fired Vineyard Pizza, topped with grapes, fresh rosemary, red onion, and aged fontina cheese, or the bacon-wrapped grilled barbecue meat loaf served with rustic fried potato wedges. ✉*35053 Rancho California Rd.* ☎*951/694–8855* ⊕*www.pontewinery.com* 🏷*Winery free; tastings $10 Mon.–Thurs., $12 Fri.–Sun.* ⊙*Daily 10–5.*

At Mediterranean-style **Stuart Cellars,** Marshall and Susan Stuart age their premium wines in French oak for 14 months. In the tasting room, be sure to try the vintage zinfandel port and Tatria, a Bordeaux-style red Meritage. Stuart Cellars' 1998 Vintage Port got a 95 rating by the *Wine Enthusiast,* dubbed "one of the best California Ports on the market." Perched 1,420 feet above Temecula, the grounds are a great spot for a picnic. ✉*33515 Rancho California Rd.* ☎*888/260–0870* ⊕*www.stuartcellars.com* 🏷*Winery free, tastings $10* ⊙*Daily 10–5.*

Fodor'sChoice A rambling French Mediterranean–style stone building houses **Thornton**
★ **Winery,** a producer best known for its sparkling wine. You can taste winemaker Don Reha's outstanding brut reserve and Cuvée Rouge at a table in the lounge, or along with some food at Café Champagne. Readers rave about the pinot blanc. On the weekend, take a free tour of the grounds and the wine cave. Summer smooth-jazz concerts (admission is charged) and elaborate winemaker dinners ($100 to $125) make this a fun place to spend an evening. ✉*32575 Rancho California Rd.* ☎*951/699–0099* ⊕*www.thorntonwine.com* 🏷*Winery free, tastings $10–$17* ⊙*Daily 10–5.*

A small stream winds through flower gardens and vineyards at peaceful, parklike **Wilson Creek Winery & Vineyard.** In the huge tasting room you'll find a little bit of heaven in the "Decadencia" chocolate port and the almond Oh-My-Gosh sparkling wine, much loved by Fodor's readers. ✉*35960 Rancho California Rd.* ☎*951/699–9463* ⊕*www. wilsoncreekwinery.com* 🏷*Winery free, tastings $10* ⊙*Daily 10–5.*

One of the newest kids on the block, the family-operated **Wiens Family Cellars** is run by brothers David, Doug, George, and Jeff. The tasting room is warm and inviting, accented with dark wood open-beamed ceilings and warm taupe walls. During the summer months, the fun spills out onto the patio, where you can listen to live music or enjoy live

Shakespearean theater. For a unique tasting, try the chardonnay-based sparkling cosmopolitan or the tropical Malvasia Bianca, with hints of passion fruit, papaya, and pineapple. There are picnic grounds outside. ✉ *33233 Rancho California Rd.* ☎ *951/694–9892* ⊕ *www.wienscellars. com* 🍷 *Winery free, tastings $10* ⊗ *Daily 10–5.*

WHERE TO STAY & EAT

$$–$$$$
Fodor's Choice
★

✗**Café Champagne.** The spacious patio, with its bubbling fountain, flowering trellises, and views of Thornton Winery's vineyards, is the perfect place to lunch on a sunny day. Inside, the dining room is decked out in French-country style, and the kitchen turns out such dishes as crispy roast duck breast drizzled with ginger-lavender honey sauce. The eclectic menu is complemented by a reasonably priced wine list featuring Italian, French, and California wines—including, of course, Thornton sparklers. ✉ *32575 Rancho California Rd.* ☎ *951/699–0088* ⊕ *www. thorntonwine.com/cafe.html* ▤ *AE, D, MC, V.*

$$–$$$
✗**Baily's Fine Dining and Front Street Bar & Grill.** Locals rave about chef Neftali Torres' well-executed cuisine, which changes weekly according to his creative whims. The menu may include chicken schnitzel drizzled in lemon-caper-wine sauce or sautéed veal medallions with asparagus and béarnaise sauce. The wine list includes more than 100 bottles, most from Temecula Valley. Call ahead to find out about upcoming winemaker dinners. ✉ *28699 Front St.* ☎ *951/676–9567* ⊕ *www.old towndining.com* ▤ *AE, MC, V.*

$$$–$$$$
★

🏨**South Coast Winery Resort and Spa.** Temecula's wine community recently added this luxurious resort. Locals and readers highly recommend its vineyard villas, which are spacious and have marble bathrooms, private patios, and flickering fireplaces. Readers particularly appreciate that there are no common walls between the villas, making their stay quieter than at most resorts. The spa has 13 treatment rooms, featuring such services as Merlot Masks and Grapeseed Body Scrubs. The on-site Vineyard Rose Restaurant serves Asian, European, and Southwest cuisine. **Pros:** Good wine-country location; quiet private villas; beautiful grounds. **Cons:** Service can be hit or miss. ✉ *34843 Rancho California Rd.* ☎ *951/587–9463* ⊕ *www.wineresort.com* ⌨ *76 villas* 🔌 *In-room: safe, refrigerator, Wi-Fi. In-hotel: restaurant, pool, spa, public Wi-Fi, parking (no fee), no-smoking rooms* ▤ *AE, MC, V.*

$$–$$$
★

🏨**Inn at Churon Winery.** You'll feel like royalty when you stay at this château-style winery perched on a hill overlooking manicured gardens and vineyards. Butter-yellow hallways lead to a library nook, where you can relax over a cup of coffee by the fire. Rooms are decorated with French antiques and outfitted with gas-burning fireplaces and marble hot tubs. Each evening a private wine reception is held in the tasting room, with crusty homemade pizza for nibbling. **Pros:** Located on wine-country row; large and comfortable rooms; free breakfast and complimentary wine reception. **Cons:** Restaurant serves breakfast only. ✉ *33233 Rancho California Rd.* ☎ *951/694–9070* ⊕ *www.innatchuron winery.com* ⌨ *16 rooms, 6 suites* 🔌 *In-room: dial-up. In-hotel: restaurant, no-smoking rooms* ▤ *AE, D, DC, MC, V* ⏦*BP.*

6

$$–$$$ 🛏 **Loma Vista Bed and Breakfast.** On the hill just above Baily Vineyard & Winery, this Mission-style home has guest rooms ranging from the luxurious Cabernet Sauvignon suite, with high-beam ceiling, private entrance, fireplace, and tub, to the more budget-minded Champagne room, decked out in art-deco-style furnishings. Some rooms have whirlpool tubs. Champagne breakfast and a wine-and-cheese reception is included with your stay. There's a two-night minimum on weekends. **Pros:** Close to wineries; gracious hosts; good food and complimentary snacks. **Cons:** Not suitable for families with young children. ✉ *33350 La Serena Way* ☎ *909/676–7047* ⊕ *www.lomavistabb.com* 🛏 *9 rooms, 1 suite �delta In-room: no phone* ▤ *MC, V* ❢◯❢*BP*.

SHOPPING

While you're shopping in Old Town, stop by the **Temecula Olive Oil Company** tasting room for a sample of its extra-virgin olive oils, bath products, and Mission, Ascalano, and Italian olives. ✉ *42030 Main St., Suite H* ☎ *866/654–8396* ⊕ *www.temeculaoliveoil.com* ◉ *Daily 9–5*.

SPORTS & THE OUTDOORS

GOLF   Temecula has seven championship golf courses cooled by the valley's ocean breezes.

Redhawk Golf Club (✉ *45100 Redhawk Pkwy.* ☎ *951/302–3850* ⊕ *www.redhawkgolfcourse.com*) has an 18-hole championship course designed by Ron Fream. For a special treat, head to the **Temecula Creek Inn Golf Resort** (✉ *44501 Rainbow Canyon Rd.* ☎ *951/676–2405* ⊕ *www.temeculacreekinn.com*), whose 27-hole course was designed by Ted Robinson and Dick Rossen.

THE INLAND EMPIRE ESSENTIALS

To research prices, get advice from other travelers, and book travel arrangements, visit www.fodors.com.

TRANSPORTATION

BY AIR

Aero Mexico, Alaska, American, Continental, Delta, ExpressJet, JetBlue, Southwest, United, and US Airways serve Ontario International Airport. *See Air Travel in California Essentials for airline phone numbers.*
Contacts **Ontario International Airport** (✉ *Airport Dr., Archibald Ave. exit off I–10, Ontario* ☎ *909/937–2700* ⊕ *www.lawa.org*).

BY BUS

Greyhound serves Claremont, Corona, Fontana, Moreno Valley, Perris, Riverside, San Bernardino, and Temecula. Most stations are open daily during business hours; some are open 24 hours.

The Foothill Transit Bus Line serves Pomona, Claremont, and Montclair, with stops at Cal Poly and the Fairplex. Riverside Transit Authority (RTA) serves Riverside and some outlying communities, as does OmniTrans.

Contacts **Foothill Transit** (☎ *800/743–3463* ⊕ *www.foothilltransit.org*). **Greyhound** (☎ *800/231–2222* ⊕ *www.greyhound.com*). **OmniTrans** (☎ *800/966–6428* ⊕ *www.omnitrans.org*). **Riverside Transit Authority** (☎ *800/800–7821* ⊕ *www.rrta.com*).

CAR TRAVEL

Avoid Highway 91 if possible; it's almost always backed up from Corona through Orange County.

Contact **California Highway Patrol 24-hour road info** (☎ *800/427–7623* ⊕ *www.dot.ca.gov/hq/roadinfo*).

CAR RENTAL Alamo, Avis, Budget, Dollar, Hertz, and National have offices at Ontario International Airport. You can rent from Avis, Budget, or Hertz in Riverside. *See Car Rental in California Essentials for national rental-agency phone numbers.*

BY TRAIN

■ TIP➜ Many locals use the Metrolink to get around, which is clean and quick and generally a much nicer way to travel than by bus.

Metrolink has several Inland Empire stations on its Inter-County, San Bernardino, and Riverside rail lines. The Riverside Line connects downtown Riverside, Pedley, East Ontario, and downtown Pomona with City of Industry and with Union Station in Los Angeles. The Inter-County Rail Line connects San Bernardino, downtown Riverside, Riverside La Sierra, and West Corona with San Juan Capistrano and Orange County. Metrolink's busiest train, the San Bernardino Line, connects Pomona, Claremont, Montclair, and San Bernardino with the San Gabriel Valley and downtown Los Angeles. Bus service extends the reach of train service, to spots including Ontario Airport, the Claremont colleges, and the Fairplex at Pomona. You can buy tickets and passes at the ticket vending machine at each station, or by telephone. A recorded message announces Metrolink schedules 24 hours a day.

Contact **Metrolink** (☎ *800/371–5465* ⊕ *www.metrolinktrains.com*).

CONTACTS & RESOURCES

EMERGENCIES

In an emergency dial 911.

Contacts **Parkview Community Hospital** (✉ *3865 Jackson St., Riverside* ☎ *951/688–2211*). **Rancho Springs Medical Center** (✉ *25500 Medical Center Dr., Murrieta* ☎ *909/696–6000*). **Riverside Community Hospital** (✉ *4445 Magnolia Ave., Riverside* ☎ *951/788–3000*). **St. Bernardine Medical Center** (✉ *2101 N. Waterman Ave., San Bernardino* ☎ *909/883–8711*). **San Bernardino County Sheriff** (☎ *909/955–2444*).

VISITOR INFORMATION

Contacts **Big Bear Lake Resort Association** (✉ *630 Bartlett Rd., Big Bear Lake* ☎ *909/866–7000 or 800/424–4232* ⊕ *www.bigbearinfo.com*). **Claremont Chamber of Commerce** (✉ *205 Yale Ave., Claremont* ☎ *909/624–1681* ⊕ *www.claremontchamber.org*). **Corona Chamber of Commerce** (✉ *904 E. 6th St., Corona* ☎ *951/737–3350* ⊕ *www.coronachamber.org*). **Idyllwild Chamber of Commerce** (✉ *54295 Village Center Dr., Box 304, Idyllwild* ☎ *951/659–3259* or 888/659–3259 ⊕ www.idyllwildchamber.com). **Lake Arrowhead Communities Chamber of Commerce** (⊠ 28200 Hwy. 189, Bldg. F, Suite 290, Box 219, Lake Arrowhead ☎ 909/337–3715 ⊕ www.lakearrowhead.net). **Oak Glen Apple Growers Association** (⊠ 39610 Oak Glen Rd., Yucaipa ☎ 909/797–6833 ⊕ www. oakglen.net). **Ontario Convention & Visitors Authority** (⊠ 2000 Convention Center Way, Ontario ☎ 909/937–3000 ⊕ www.ontariocc.com). **Pomona Chamber of Commerce** (⊠ 401 S. Main St., #210, Pomona ☎ 909/622–1256 ⊕ www. pomonachamber.org). **Redlands Chamber of Commerce** (⊠ 1 E. Redlands Blvd., Redlands ☎ 909/793–2546 ⊕ www.redlandschamber.org). **Riverside Convention and Visitors Bureau** (⊠ 3750 University Ave., #175, Riverside ☎ 888/748–7733 or 951/222–4700 ⊕ www.riversidecb.com). **Temecula Valley Chamber of Commerce** (⊠ 26790 Ynez Ct., Temecula ☎ 951/676–5090 ⊕ www.temecula.org). **Wrightwood Chamber of Commerce** (⊠ Box 416, Wrightwood 92397 ☎ 760/249–4320, 760/249–6822 for recorded information ⊕ www.wrightwoodchamber.com).

Palm Springs & the Southern Desert

World's Biggest Dinosaurs, Cabazon

WORD OF MOUTH

"The Palm Springs Aerial Tramway is the longest span of any gondola in the world and only the second spinning gondola in the world. Most of all it is a great way to see the whole valley and the mountains beyond. A not to be missed attraction."

—Blane

WELCOME TO PALM SPRINGS & THE SOUTHERN DESERT

TOP REASONS TO GO

★ **Fun in the sun:** The Southern Desert has 350 days of sun each year, and—with the exception of summer—the weather's usually perfect for playing one of the area's 100 golf courses.

★ **Spa under the stars:** Many resorts and small hotels now offer after-dark spa services, including outdoor soaks and treatments under the clear, starry sky.

★ **Personal pampering:** The resorts here have it all: beautifully appointed rooms packed with amenities, professional staffs, sublime spas, and delicious dining options.

★ **Divine desert scenery:** You'll probably spend a lot of your time here taking in the gorgeous 360-degree natural panorama, a flat desert floor surrounded by 10,000-foot mountains rising into a brilliant blue sky.

★ **The Hollywood connection:** The Palm Springs area has more celebrity ties than any other resort community. So keep your eyes open— you might catch a glimpse of your favorite star.

1 **Palm Springs.** Just a stone's throw from LA, this Desert resort town is where Hollywood comes to relax (and play).

2 **Palm Desert.** Palm Springs' neighbor has more fantastic shops, restaurants, and golf courses.

3 **Joshua Tree National Park.** This is desert scenery at its best and most abundant. Tiptoe through fields of wildflowers in spring, climb up and around giant boulders, and check out the park's bizarre namesake trees. (⇨ Chapter 8, Joshua Tree National Park.)

4 **Anza-Borrego Desert State Park.** If you're looking for a break from the action, you'll find solace in this 600,000-acre desert landscape.

5 **Salton Sea.** About 400 species of birds frequent the shores of this inland sea, which is also a great place to camp or go boating and fishing.

GETTING ORIENTED

The Palm Springs resort area lies within the Colorado Desert, on the western edge of the Coachella Valley. The area holds seven cities that are strung out along Highway 111, with Palm Springs at the northwestern end of this strip and Indio at the southeastern end. North of Palm Springs, between Interstate 10 and Highway 62, is Desert Hot Springs. Northeast of Palm Springs, the towns of the Morongo Valley lie along Twentynine Palms Highway (Highway 62), which leads to Joshua Tree National Park. Head south on Highway 86 from Indio to reach Anza-Borrego State Park and the Salton Sea. All of the area's attractions are easy day trips from Palm Springs.

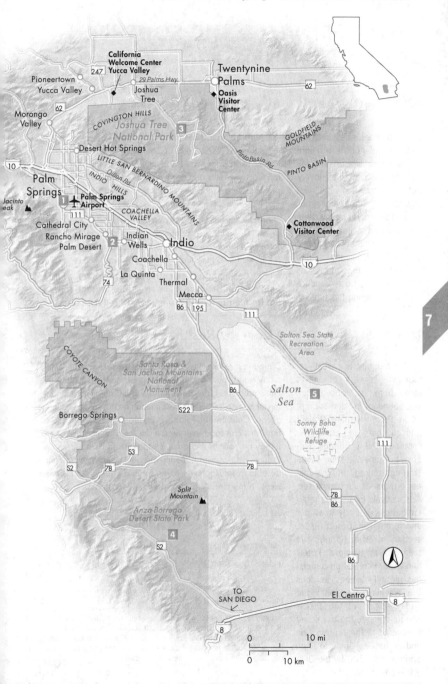

Pioneertown
Yucca Valley
Morongo Valley
California Welcome Center
Yucca Valley
247
29 Palms Hwy.
Joshua Tree
Twentynine Palms
62
Oasis Visitor Center
COVINGTON HILLS
Joshua Tree National Park **3**
GOLDFIELD MOUNTAINS
62
Desert Hot Springs
Pinto Basin Rd.
PINTO BASIN
LITTLE SAN BERNARDINO MOUNTAINS
10
INDIO HILLS
Dillon Rd.
Palm Springs **1**
Palm Springs Airport
COACHELLA VALLEY
Jacinto Peak
111
Cathedral City
Rancho Mirage **2**
Palm Desert
Indian Wells
Indio
Cottonwood Visitor Center
Coachella
La Quinta
74
Thermal
Mecca
86   195
111
10
Salton Sea State Recreation Area
COYOTE CANYON
Santa Rosa & San Jacinto Mountains National Monument
86
Salton Sea **5**
7
Sonny Bono Wildlife Refuge
111
Borrego Springs
S22
S3
S2   78
78
Split Mountain
Anza-Borrego Desert State Park **4**
78
86
S2
86
TO SAN DIEGO
El Centro
8
8
0   10 mi
0   10 km

PALM SPRINGS & THE SOUTHERN DESERT PLANNER

When to Go

Desert weather is best between January and April, the height of the visitor season. The fall months are nearly as lovely, but less crowded and less expensive. During the summer, an increasingly popular time for European visitors, daytime temperatures may rise above 110°F (though evenings cool to the mid-70s); some attractions and restaurants close or reduce their hours during this time.

About the Hotels

You can stay in the desert for as little as $60 or spend more than $1,000 a night. Rates vary widely by season: Hotel/resort prices are frequently 50% less in summer and fall than in winter and early spring. January through May prices soar, and lodgings book up far in advance.

Small boutique hotels and bed-and-breakfasts have historic character and offer good value; they are listed separately below. Discounts are sometimes given for extended stays. Take care when considering budget lodgings; other than reliable chains, they may not be up to par.

■ TIP→ Casino hotels can offer deals on lodging. They hold most of their rooms as amenities for high rollers, but frequently rent the remainder at reduced rates.

Nightlife

Desert nightlife is casual—no brawny bouncers or velvet ropes here. It's concentrated and abundant in Palm Springs, where there are many straight and gay bars and clubs. The Fabulous Palm Springs Follies—a vaudeville-style revue starring retired professional performers—is a must-see. Arts festivals occur on a regular basis, especially in winter and spring. The "Desert Guide" section of *Palm Springs Life* magazine (available at hotels and visitor information centers) has nightlife listings, as does the "Weekender" pullout in the Friday edition of the *Desert Sun* newspaper. The gay scene is covered in the *Bottom Line* and in the *Gay Guide to Palm Springs*, published by the Desert Gay Tourism Guild.

About the Restaurants

Dining in the desert is casual and low-key. Expect to find many good, but not stellar, dining experiences. Celebrity chefs are rare. Fare, once limited to Italian and a smattering of French choices, now includes fresh seafood, contemporary Californian, Asian, vegetarian, and steaks. You can find Mexican food everywhere; in the smaller communities, it may be your best choice. Restaurants that remain open in July and August frequently discount deeply, so you might be able to splurge even if you're on a tight budget. Others close in July and August or offer limited service.

WHAT IT COSTS

	¢	$	$$	$$$	$$$$
Restaurants					
	under $10	$10–$15	$16–$22	$23–$30	over $30
Hotels					
	under $90	$90–$120	$121–$175	$176–$250	over $250

Restaurant prices are for a main course at dinner, excluding sales tax of 7.25%. Hotel prices are for a standard double room in high season, excluding service charges and 9%–13.5% tax. Most hotels add a resort fee of $15 to $30 per day for incidentals. Some charge up to $50 per day for pets (in addition to a security deposit).

Updated by
Bobbi Zane

MANY MILLIONS OF YEARS AGO, the Southern Desert was the bottom of a vast sea. By 10 million years ago, the waters had receded and the climate was hospitable to prehistoric mastodons, zebras, and camels. The first human inhabitants of record were the Agua Caliente, part of the Cahuilla people, who settled in and around the Coachella Valley about 1,000 years ago. Lake Cahuilla dried up about 300 years ago, but by then the Agua Caliente had discovered the area's hot springs and were making use of their healing properties during winter visits to the desert. The springs became a tourist attraction in 1871, when the tribe built a bathhouse (on a site near the current Spa Resort Casino in Palm Springs) to serve passengers on a pioneer stage highway. The Agua Caliente still own about 32,000 acres of desert, 6,700 of which lie within the city limits of Palm Springs.

In the last half of the 19th century, farmers established a date-growing industry at the southern end of the Coachella Valley. By 1900 word had spread about the health benefits of the area's dry climate, inspiring the gentry of the northern United States to winter under the warm desert sun. Growth hit the Coachella Valley in the 1970s, when developers began to construct the fabulous golf courses, country clubs, and residential communities that would draw celebrities, tycoons, and politicians. Communities sprang up south and east of what is now Palm Springs, creating a sprawl of tract houses and strip malls and forcing nature lovers to push farther south into the sparsely settled Anza-Borrego Desert and the Imperial Valley.

7

THE DESERT RESORTS

INCLUDING PALM SPRINGS
Around the desert resorts, privacy is the watchword. Celebrities flock to the desert from Los Angeles, and many communities are walled and guarded. Still, you might spot Hollywood stars, sports personalities, politicians, and other high-profile types in restaurants, out on the town, or on a golf course. For the most part, the desert's social, sports, shopping, and entertainment scenes center on Palm Springs, Palm Desert, and (increasingly) La Quinta.

PALM SPRINGS

90 mi southeast of Los Angeles on I–10.

A tourist destination since the late 19th century, Palm Springs had already caught Hollywood's eye by the time of the Great Depression. It was an ideal hideaway: Celebrities could slip into town, play a few sets of tennis, lounge around the pool, attend a party or two, and, unless things got out of hand, remain safely beyond the reach of gossip columnists. But it took a pair of tennis-playing celebrities to put Palm Springs on the map. In the 1930s actors Charlie Farrell and Ralph Bellamy bought 200 acres of land for $30 an acre and opened the Palm Springs Racquet Club, which soon listed Ginger Rogers, Humphrey Bogart, and Clark Gable among its members.

During its slow, steady growth period from the 1930s to 1970s, the Palm Springs area drew some of the world's most famous architects to design homes for the rich and famous. The collected works, inspired by the mountains and desert sands and notable for the use of glass and indoor–outdoor space, became known as Palm Springs Modernism'. The city lost some of its luster in the 1970s as the wealthy moved to newer down-valley communities. But Palm Springs reinvented itself in the 1990s, restoring the bright and airy old houses and hotels, and cultivating a welcoming atmosphere for well-heeled gay visitors.

You'll find reminders of the city's glamorous past in its unique architecture and renovated hotels; change and progress are evidenced by trendy restaurants and upscale shops. Formerly exclusive Palm Canyon Drive is now a lively avenue filled with coffeehouses, outdoor cafés, and bars.

■TIP➡ Note: Tahquitz Canyon Way marks the division between north and south on major streets (e.g., North and South Palm Canyon Drive).

❶ A trip on the **Palm Springs Aerial Tramway** provides a 360-degree view of the desert through the picture windows of rotating tram cars. The 2½-mi ascent through Chino Canyon, the steepest vertical cable ride in the United States, brings you to an elevation of 8,516 feet in less than 20 minutes. On clear days, which are common, the view stretches 75 mi—from the peak of Mt. San Gorgonio in the north to the Salton Sea in the southeast. At the top, a bit below the summit of Mt. San Jacinto, are several diversions. Mountain Station has an observation deck, two restaurants, a cocktail lounge, apparel and gift shops, picnic facilities, and a theater that screens a worthwhile 22-minute film on the history of the tramway. Take advantage of free guided and self-guided nature walks, or if there's snow on the ground, rent skis, snowshoes, or snow tubes (inner tubes or similar contraptions for sliding down hills). The tramway generally closes for maintenance in mid-September.
■TIP➡ Ride-and-dine packages are available in late afternoon. The tram is a popular attraction; to avoid a two-hour or longer wait, arrive before the first car leaves. ✉*1 Tramway Rd.* ☎*760/325–1391 or 888/515–8726* ⊕*www.pstramway.com* ✎*$22.50, ride-and-dine package $35.50* ☉*Tram cars depart at least every 30 mins from 10 AM weekdays and 8 AM weekends; last car up leaves at 8 PM, last car down leaves Mountain Station at 9:45 PM.*

❷ Stop at the **Palm Springs Visitor Information Center,** near the tramway, for information on sights to see and things to do in the area. ✉*2901 N. Palm Canyon Dr.* ☎*760/778–8418 or 800/347–7746* ⊕*www.palm-springs. org* ☉*Weekdays 9–5.*

❸ A stroll down shop-lined Palm Canyon Drive will take you along the **Palm Springs Starwalk** (✉*Palm Canyon Dr., around Tahquitz Canyon Way, and Tahquitz Canyon Way, between Palm Canyon and Indian Canyon Drs.*), where nearly 200 bronze stars are embedded in the sidewalk (à la Hollywood Walk of Fame). Most of the names, all with a Palm Springs connection, are ones you'll recognize (such as Elvis Pre-

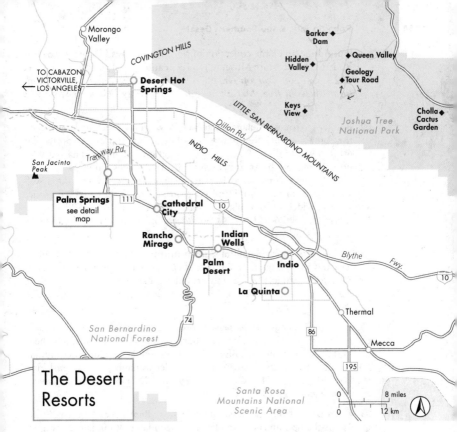

The Desert Resorts

sley, Marilyn Monroe, Lauren Bacall, and Liberace). Others are local celebrities.

4 ★ The **Palm Springs Art Museum** and its grounds hold several wide-ranging collections of contemporary and traditional art displayed in bright, open galleries, with daylight streaming through huge skylights. The permanent collection includes a shimmering display of contemporary studio glass, highlighted by works by Dale Chihuly, Ginny Ruffner, and William Morris. You'll also find handcrafted furniture by the late actor George Montgomery, an array of enormous Native American baskets, and works by artists like Allen Houser, Arlo Namingha, and Fritz Scholder; the museum also displays significant works of 20th-century sculpture by Henry Moore, Marino Marina, Deborah Butterfield, and Mark Di Suvero. The Annenberg Theater presents plays, concerts, lectures, operas, and other cultural events. ⊠ *101 Museum Dr.* ☎ *760/325-7186* ⊕ *www.psmuseum.org* ⊉ *$12.50 Oct.–May, free Thurs. 4–8 during Villagefest* ⊙ *Oct.–May, Tues., Wed., and Fri.–Sun. 10–5, Thurs. noon–8; June–Sept., Wed. and Fri.–Sun. 10–5, Thurs. noon–8.*

5 Three small museums at the **Village Green Heritage Center** illustrate pioneer life in Palm Springs. The **Agua Caliente Cultural Museum** is devoted to the culture and history of the Cahuilla tribe. The McCallum **Adobe** holds the collection of the Palm Springs Historical Society. **Rudy's General Store Museum** is a re-creation of a 1930s general store. ✉ *221 S. Palm Canyon Dr.* ☎ *760/327–2156* ✑ *Agua Caliente Cultural Museum free, McCallum Adobe $2, Rudy's General Store 95¢* ☉ *Call for hrs.*

❻ Ranger-led tours of **Tahquitz Canyon** take you into a secluded canyon on the Agua Caliente Reservation. Within the canyon are a spectacular 60-foot waterfall, rock art, ancient irrigation systems, and native wildlife and plants. Tours are conducted several times daily; participants must be able to navigate 100 steep steps. (You can also take a self-guided tour of the 1.8-mi trail.) A visitor center at the canyon entrance shows a video tour, displays artifacts, and sells maps. ✉ *500 W. Mesquite Ave.* ☎ *760/416–7044* ⊕ *www.tahquitzcanyon.com* ✑ *$12.50* ☉ *Daily 7:30–5.*

❼ Four-acre **Moorten Botanical Garden** nurtures more than 3,000 plant varieties in settings that simulate their original environments. Native American artifacts, rock, and crystal are exhibited. ✉ *1701 S. Palm Canyon Dr.* ☎ *760/327–6555* ✑ *$3* ☉ *Mon., Tues., and Thurs.–Sat. 9–4:30, Sun. 10–4.*

❽ The **Palm Springs Air Museum** showcases 26 World War II aircraft, including a B-17 Flying Fortress bomber, a P-51 Mustang, a Lockheed P-38, and a Grumman TBF Avenger. Cool exhibits include a Grumman Goose into which kids can crawl, model warships, and a Pearl Harbor diorama. ✉ *745 N. Gene Autry Trail* ☎ *760/778–6262* ⊕ *www.air-museum.org* ✑ *$10* ☉ *Daily 10–5.*

❾ For a break from the desert heat, head to **Knott's Soak City.** You'll find 1950s-theme ambience complete with Woodies (antique station wagons from the 1950s), 13 waterslides, a huge wave pool, an arcade, and other fun family attractions. The park also contains the full-service Fitness Point Health Club, where you can take exercise classes—including water aerobics and yoga—use the weight room, or swim; day passes are $11. ✉ *1500 S. Gene Autry Trail* ☎ *760/327–0499, 760/325–8155 Fitness Point Health Club* ⊕ *www.knotts.com* ✑ *$29, after 3 PM $18* ☉ *Mid-May–early Sept., daily; early Sept.–Oct., weekends. Opens at 10 AM, closing times vary.*

❿ The **Indian Canyons** are the ancestral home of the Agua Caliente, part of the Cahuilla people. You can see remnants of their ancient life, including rock art, house pits and foundations, irrigation ditches, bedrock mortars, pictographs, and stone houses and shelters built atop high cliff walls. Short, easy walks

---

ACCESSIBLE WILDERNESS

Mount San Jacinto State Park. The park, accessible by hiking or via the Palm Springs Aerial Tramway, has primitive camping and picnic areas and 54 mi of hiking trails. The Nordic Ski Center rents cross-country ski equipment. You must get a free permit, available only via the Internet, before coming for day or overnight wilderness hiking or camping. ✉ *Mountain Station* ☎ *951/659-2607* ⊕ *www.parks.ca.gov* ✑ *Free.*

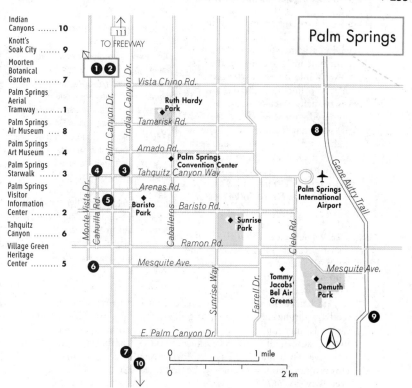

Palm Springs

through the canyons reveal palm oases, waterfalls, and spring wild-flowers. Tree-shaded picnic areas are abundant. The attraction includes three canyons open for touring: Palm Canyon, noted for its stand of Washingtonia palms; Murray Canyon, home of Peninsula bighorn sheep and a herd of wild ponies; and Andreas Canyon, where a stand of fan palms contrasts with sharp rock formations. Ranger-led hikes to Palm and Andreas canyons are offered daily for an additional charge. The trading post at the entrance to Palm Canyon has hiking maps and refreshments, as well as Native American art, jewelry, and weavings. ⊠*38520 S. Palm Canyon Dr.* ☎*760/323–6018* ⊕*www.indian-canyons. com* ⊠*$8, ranger hikes $3* ☉*Oct.–June, daily 8–5; July–Sept., Fri.–Sun. 8–5.*

WHERE TO EAT

$$$$ ✕ **Europa.** Housed inside the Villa Royale Inn, this intimate restaurant provides both indoor and garden dining—and artfully prepared cuisine. Popular menu items include rack of lamb with tapenade of dates and olives, duck confit with Grand Marnier, and salmon in parchment with wild mushrooms. ⊠*1620 Indian Trail* ☎*760/327–2314* ⊠*Reservations essential* ⊟*AE, D, DC, MC, V* ☉*Closed Mon. No lunch.*

$$$$ ✕ **The Falls Prime Steak House.** A mile-long martini menu lures a chic, moneyed crowd to this steak house with an inside waterfall tucked into

an upstairs corner overlooking the Palm Canyon Drive action. Reserve well in advance for one of the outdoor balcony tables to get the best view. While this eatery specializes in aged prime beef, there is a small vegan menu. Steaks and chops are prepared your way with a selection of sides that includes seven-cheese mac and cheese and steamed asparagus with hollandaise sauce. Hang around late to savor the action at the Martini Dome bar. ✉ *155 S. Palm Canyon Dr.* ☎ *760/416–8664* ⚑ *Reservations essential* 🖃 *AE, MC, V* ☻ *No lunch.*

$$$$ ✗**Le Vallauris.** Le Vallauris, in the
★ historic Roberson House, is popular with ladies who lunch, all of whom get a hug from the maître d'. The menu changes daily, and each day it's handwritten on a white board. Lunch entrées may include perfectly rare tuna niçoise salad, or grilled whitefish with Dijon mustard sauce. Dinner might bring a sublime smoked salmon, sautéed calves' liver roasted quail with orange sauce, or rack of lamb. Service is beyond attentive. The restaurant has a lovely tree-shaded garden. On cool winter evenings, request a table by the fireplace. ✉ *385 W. Tahquitz Canyon Way* ☎ *760/325–5059* ⚑ *Reservations essential* 🖃 *AE, D, DC, MC, V* ☻ *Closed July and Aug.*

$$$ ✗**Copley's on Palm Canyon.** Chef Manion Copley is cooking up the most innovative cuisine in the desert, drawing fans region-wide. Start with such appetizers as roasted beet and warm goat cheese salad or perfectly grilled charred prawns and scallops. Oh My Lobster Pot Pie is the biggest hit on an entrée menu that features unusual seafood. And save room for Copley's sweet and savory servings of herb ice cream. The rustic, casual eatery is in a hacienda that was once owned by Cary Grant. Service is pleasant and friendly. ✉ *621 N. Palm Canyon Dr.* ☎ *760/327–9555* 🖃 *AE, D, DC, MC, V* ☻ *Closed Mon. No lunch.*

$$$ ✗**Matchbox Vintage Pizza Bistro.** The name says pizza, but this bistro offers much more: you'll find interesting salads topped with sweet and tangy calamari or grilled tuna, and a selection of sandwiches with fillings like crab cakes or portobello mushrooms. The pizzas are made just about any way you'd like—even with fresh berries and mascarpone for dessert. This is the place to go for cocktails, small plates, and cigars after work. The bistro has an upstairs location in Marcado Plaza, and overlooks the nightly action on Palm Canyon Drive. ✉ *155 S. Palm Canyon Dr.* ☎ *760/778–6000* 🖃 *AE, D, DC, MC, V* ☻ *No lunch.*

$$$ ✗**Purple Palm.** The hottest tables in Palm Springs are those that surround
★ the pool at the Colony Palms Hotel, where the hip and elite pay homage to Purple Gang mobster Al Wertheimer, who reportedly built the hotel

---

SINATRA & THE DESERT

Old Blue Eyes probably had more haunts in the Palm Springs area than any other celebrity. He owned two homes here, one of them a mid-century modern jewel built in 1947 (Twin Palms Estate at 1148 E. Alejo Rd.) and called the landscape home for more than 50 years. He frequented Melvyn's Restaurant and Lounge at the Ingleside Hotel (200 W. Ramon Rd.)—ask Melvyn to tell you about Sinatra's pre-wedding dinner with Barbara Marx in 1976—as well as Riccio's (1900 E. Palm Canyon Dr.) and Lord Fletcher's (70-385 Hwy. 111).

in the mid-1930s. Now it's a casual, convivial place that offers a tantalizing menu designed by executive chef James Corwell, who earned his toque cooking at the Greystone Restaurant in Napa Valley. Start with some Miyagi oyster shooters or steamed Carlsbad mussels. Seafood dishes dominate the main courses, but you can also have roast saddle of Colorado lamb, Jidori chicken with Muscat grapes, or Muscovy duckling. An impressive wine list roams the globe. ⊠ *572 N. Indian Canyon Dr.* ☎ *800/557–2187* ⬥ *Reservations essential* ▤ *AE, D, DC, MC, V.*

$$ ✕**Wang's in the Desert.** Locals flock to Wang's for its lovely Asian setting, complete with koi pond, indoor garden, and original art on the walls. The menu's well-chosen selection of Chinese and Asian-influence entrées includes spicy kung pao chicken, tangerine shrimp, and jalapeño pork chops. Most people dine family-style here, sharing entrées, appetizers, and sides. ⊠ *424 S. Indian Canyon Dr.* ☎ *760/325–9264* ▤ *AE, D, DC, MC, V* ⊘ *No lunch.*

¢ ✕**Peabody's Café Bar & Coffee.** The place to go for a cup of joe and people-watching, Peabody's has been a Palm Canyon Drive institution for years. By day Peabody's serves lunch, including salads and hot and cold sandwiches. By night the place becomes a popular bar (open until 2 AM Thursday through Saturday). ⊠ *134 S. Palm Canyon Dr.* ☎ *760/322–1877* ▤ *DC, MC, V* ⊘ *Closed mid-July–mid-Aug. No dinner.*

> **TRIBAL WEALTH**
>
> The Agua Caliente band of Cahuilla Indians owns nearly half the land in the Palm Springs area. Wanting to encourage the railroad to bring their trains through the desert, Congress granted half the land to the railroad and the other half to the Native Americans. The Cahuilla were granted all the even-numbered one-square-mi sections—but they were unable to develop the land for years due to litigation. The resulting patchwork of developed and vacant land can still be seen today (though the Cahuilla are making up for lost time by opening new hotels and casinos).

WHERE TO STAY

HOTELS & RESORTS

$$$$

★

▦**The Parker Palm Springs.** A cacophony of color, flashing lights, and over-the-top contemporary art assembled by New York designer Jonathan Adler, this is the hippest hotel in the desert, appealing to a young L.A.-based clientele. When you arrive, a greeter will whisk you from your car to your room to complete registration; the stroll takes you through a brilliant desert garden. You may find relaxation around the pools, if nowhere else—pulsating music fills the air throughout the resort. Rooms have textured sisal floor coverings, exotic woven fabrics in bright reds and browns, and leather seating. All have private balconies or patios (with hammocks) that are secluded behind tall shrubs. The clubby restaurant, Mister Parker's ($$$$), will delight any well-heeled carnivore. **Pros:** Fun in the sun; celebrity clientele; pure indulgence at the Palm Springs Yacht Club Spa. **Cons:** Pricey drinks and wine; confused service; long walks in the hot sun to get anywhere. ⊠ *4200 E. Palm Canyon Dr.* ☎ *760/770–5000 or 800/543–4300* ⊕ *www.theparker palmsprings.com* ↪ *133 rooms, 12 suites* ⬧ *In-room: safe, refrigerator, DVD, Wi-Fi. In-hotel: 2 restaurants, room service, bar, tennis* *courts, pools, gym, spa, bicycles, laundry service, concierge, parking (no fee), no-smoking rooms* ⊟*AE, D, DC, MC, V.*

$$$$ 🖼 **Smoke Tree Ranch.** A world apart from Palm Springs' pulsating urban
★ village, the area's most exclusive resort occupies 400 pristine desert acres, surrounded by mountains and quiet desert vistas. A laid-back genteel retreat since the mid-1930s for some of the world's foremost families, including Walt Disney, it still provides a quietly luxurious experience reminiscent of the Old West. A collection of simple cottages, renovated in 2007, is spread among manicured desert gardens and shaded by smoke trees. Most have fireplaces and private patios. A large rambling ranch house right out of an old western movie, with gleaming paneled walls and picture windows, holds a dining room where three meals are served daily. Two optional meal plans are offered: full American plan at $78 per day per person, and breakfast plan at $15 per day per person. There is a dress code at dinner. **Pros:** Priceless privacy; simple luxury; home of classy Jose Higuera Tennis Academy. **Cons:** No glitz or glamour; limited entertainment options; family atmosphere. ⊠*1800 S. Sunrise Way* ☎*760/327–1221 or 800/787–3922* ⊕*www.smoketreeranch. com* ➪*55 cottages* ♿*In-room: refrigerator, DVD, Wi-Fi. In-hotel: restaurant, bar, tennis courts, pool, gym, bicycles, no elevator, concierge, children's programs (ages 5–12), laundry facilities, public Internet, public Wi-Fi, airport shuttle, parking (no fee), some pets allowed, no-smoking rooms* ⊟*AE, D, MC, V* ⊗*Closed Apr.–late Oct.*

$$$$ 🖼 **The Viceroy Palm Springs.** The first thing that strikes you at the Vice-
★ roy is its bright, sunny white-and-yellow ambience, reminiscent of a sun-filled desert day. Guest rooms for two and villas for three or more (some with fireplaces and private patios) are spread out over 4 tree-shaded acres, where secluded nooks and blue-and-white-striped cabanas beg chic bikini-clad guests to hole up with a good book and a glass of the inn's delicious iced tea. The tranquil inn, just a short walk from Palm Canyon Drive, is home to the stylish eatery Citron ($$$$), which is decorated with larger-than-life-size photos of Marilyn Monroe and Clark Gable. The inn is exceptionally canine friendly—they even offer dog-walking and spa services. **Pros:** Hot restaurant; gardens. **Cons:** Uneven service. ⊠*415 S. Belardo Rd., 92262* ☎*760/320–4117 or 800/327–3687* ⊕*www.viceroypalmsprings.com* ➪*43 rooms, 16 suites* ♿*In-room: safe, kitchen (some), refrigerator, Wi-Fi, Ethernet. In-hotel: restaurant, room service, bar, pools, gym, spa, bicycles, no elevator, public Internet, parking (fee), some pets allowed, no-smoking rooms* ⊟*AE, D, MC, V.*

$$$ 🖼 **Spa Resort Casino.** Part of a complex that includes a spa and a casino across the street, this hotel, owned and operated by the Agua Caliente, is adjacent to a mineral-water spring used by generations of Native Americans. (The spa uses the healing Taking of the Waters treatments that draw locals on a regular basis.) Public areas and rooms are simply decorated in soothing desert colors—aqua, coral, and sand. The hotel attracts a mature crowd, many of whom enjoy sunning around the expansive pool or indulging in basic spa treatments. **Pros:** Value; natural hot springs spa; slots 24/7. **Cons:** Basic rooms; lots of group tours; popular with the Centrum set. ⊠*100 N. Indian Canyon Dr.,*

☎760/325–1461 or 800/854–1279 ⊕*www.sparesortcasino.com* ↩*206 rooms, 22 suites* ₺*In-room: refrigerator, Ethernet, Wi-Fi. In-hotel: restaurant, room service, bars, golf, pools, gym, spa, laundry service, concierge, public Wi-Fi, parking (no fee), no-smoking rooms* ▤*AE, D, DC, MC, V.*

$$ 🏨**Colony Palms Hotel.** Detroit's Purple mobster gang, Hollywood's starlets and leading men, and Sea Biscuit all cast a long shadow over the Colony Palms. The hotel has been the hip place to go since the 1930s, when gangster Al Wertheimer built it to front his casino, bar, and brothel. It became the Howard Hotel, owned by Hollywood luminaries Robert Leeds and Andrea Howard (who also owned the race horse). They hosted young Frank Sinatra, Elizabeth Taylor, and Liberace. Fast forward to now. The hotel is still hot with a nice youthful vibe. The rooms, created by A-list designer Martyn Lawrence Bullard, are quasi-Moroccan with brilliantly colored mosaic tiles and fabrics, rich woods, and black-and-white vintage movie star photos everywhere. Mature gardens throughout the property provide privacy, even though rooms open to a central courtyard holding the pool. When you go, ask to visit the speakeasy beneath the bar. **Pros:** Glam with a swagger; attentive staff; all that history. **Cons:** High noise level outside; not for families with young children. ✉*572 N. Indian Canyon Dr., Palm Springs* ☎*760/969–1800 or 800/577–2187* ⊕*www.colonypalmshotel.com* ↩*43 rooms, 3 suites, 8 casitas* ₺*In-room: safe, refrigerators, Ethernet, dial-up, Wi-Fi. In-hotel: restaurant, room service, bar, pool, gym, spa, bicycles, laundry service, concierge, public Wi-Fi, parking (no fee), some pets allowed, no-smoking rooms* ▤*AE, D, DC, MC, V.*

¢ 🏨**Vagabond Inn.** Rooms are smallish at this centrally located motel, but they're clean, comfortable, and a good value. Continental breakfast and daily newspaper are included in the price. **Pros:** Quiet; inexpensive; breakfast included. **Cons:** Limited amenities, facilities, and service. ✉*1699 S. Palm Canyon Dr.* ☎*760/325–7211 or 800/522–1555* ⊕*www.vagabondinn.com* ↩*117 rooms* ₺*In-room: refrigerator, Ethernet, dial-up. In-hotel: pool, public Internet, parking (no fee), some pets allowed, no-smoking rooms* ▤*AE, D, DC, MC, V* ⦿*CP.*

SMALL HOTELS
& BED-AND-
BREAKFASTS

$$$$
★

🏨**Movie Colony Hotel.** This intimate hotel, designed in 1935 by Albert Frey, evokes mid-century minimalist charm. Its sparkling, white, two-story buildings, flanked with balconies and porthole windows, evoke the image of a luxury yacht. Rooms are elegantly appointed with soft desert colors accented by bright reds and yellows; many features, including tiny showers, are authentic to the period. A cool vibe prevails in late afternoon, as sophisticated young guests share experiences during the wine hour and again over morning coffee and a sumptuous Continental breakfast served in the flower-decked courtyard. **Pros:** Architectural icon; Dean Martinis at happy hour; cruiser bikes. **Cons:** Close quarters; off the beaten path; staff is not available 24 hours. ✉*726 N. Indian Canyon Dr.* ☎*760/320–6340 or 888/953–5700* ⊕*www.moviecolony hotel.com* ↩*13 rooms, 3 suites* ₺*In-room: refrigerator, DVD, Ethernet (some), dial-up, Wi-Fi (some). In-hotel: bar, pools, bicycles, no elevator, public Wi-Fi, parking (no fee), no kids under 21, no-smoking rooms* ▤*AE, MC, V* ⦿*CP.*

$$$$
★   🏨**Willows Historic Palm Springs Inn.** This luxurious hillside B&B is within walking distance of many village attractions. An opulent Mediterranean-style mansion built in the 1920s, it has gleaming hardwood and slate floors, stone fireplaces, frescoed ceilings, hand-painted tiles, iron balconies, antiques throughout, and a 50-foot waterfall that splashes into a pool outside the dining room. There's even a private hillside garden planted with native flora, which has one of the best views in the area. Guest rooms are decorated to recall the movies of Hollywood's golden era. **Pros:** Luxurious, sublime service; little touches like pouches of cookies and trail mix in rooms. **Cons:** Noisy hardwood floors; pricey. ⊠*412 W. Tahquitz Canyon Way* ☎*760/320–0771 or 800/966–9597* ⊕*www. thewillowspalmsprings.com* ↩*8 rooms* ♿*In-room: refrigerator, DVD, VCR, dial-up, Wi-Fi. In-hotel: room service, pool, no elevator, concierge, parking (no fee), no-smoking rooms* ☰*AE, D, DC, MC, V* ⚏*BP.*

$$$ 🏨**Calla Lily Inn.** This tranquil palm-shaded oasis one block from Palm Canyon Drive has spacious rooms decorated in a vaguely tropical style. Furnishings are contemporary wicker, and an image of a calla lily adorns every room. Rooms surround the pool. **Pros:** Lush tropical gardens; gracious hosts; within walking distance of everything. **Cons:** Small property; rooms are close to the pool. ⊠*350 S. Belardo Rd.* ☎*760/323–3654 or 888/888–5787* ⊕*www.callalilypalmsprings.com* ↩*9 rooms* ♿*In-room: kitchens (some), refrigerator, DVD, VCR, Ethernet, Wi-Fi. In-hotel: pool, no elevator, parking (free), no-smoking rooms* ☰*D, MC, V.*

$$$ 🏨**East Canyon Resort & Spa.** This classy resort, which serves a primarily gay clientele, is the only one in the desert with an in-house spa exclusively for men. Large rooms, each individually decorated, surround a sparkling pool; they have carefully coordinated dark colors, Frette linens, and ample bathrooms. The clubroom has a giant TV, plus a library well stocked with videos and books. The vibe here is social, presided over by the resort's gracious hosts. **Pros:** Elegant laid-back feel; attentive service. **Cons:** Spa is for men only. ⊠*288 E. Camino Monte Vista* ☎*760/320–1928 or 877/324–6835* ⊕*www.eastcanyonps.com* ↩*15 rooms, 1 suite* ♿*In-room: refrigerator, DVD, VCR, Wi-Fi. In-hotel: pool, spa, no elevator, concierge, public Wi-Fi, parking (no fee), no-smoking rooms* ☰*AE, MC, V* ⚏*CP.*

$$$ 🏨**Orbit In Hotel.** Step back to 1957 at this hip inn, located on a quiet back street downtown. The architectural roots here date back to the late 1940s and '50s—nearly flat roofs, wide overhangs, glass everywhere—with the ambience to match. Rooms are appointed with mid-century modern furnishings by such designers as Eames, Noguchi, and Breuer. Some have private patios; all have a few Melmac dishes tucked here and there. There's an outside shower, vintage cruiser bikes, books, games, and videos available for guest use. A lively atmosphere prevails poolside, where a complimentary breakfast is served daily. **Pros:** Saltwater pool; in-room spa services; Orbitini cocktail hour. **Cons:** Best for couples; not to everyone's taste; staff not available 24 hours. ⊠*562 W. Arenas Rd.* ☎*760/323–3585 or 877/996–7248* ⊕*www.orbitin. com* ↩*9 rooms* ♿*In-room: safes, kitchen (some), refrigerator, DVD, Ethernet, Wi-Fi. In-hotel: pools, bicycles, no elevator, public Internet,*

public Wi-Fi, parking (no fee), no-smoking rooms ⊟*AE, D, MC, V* ⍟*CP.*

$$ ⌕**Casitas Laquita.** This collection of Spanish-style bungalows occupying more than an acre caters mainly to lesbians. Rooms, decorated with a Southwestern theme, have handcrafted furnishings; many have fireplaces. Expansive, colorful gardens are great places to curl up with a good mystery. The innkeepers regularly host informal social activities. **Pros:** Large rooms; women only; social activities. **Cons:** Women only; older buildings; limited amenities. ⊠*450 E. Palm Canyon Dr.,* ☎*760/416–9999 or 877/203–3410* ⊕*www.casitaslaquita.com* ⏎*15 rooms* ⌂*In-room: kitchen, Wi-Fi. In-hotel: pool, no elevator, public Internet, no-smoking rooms* ⊟*MC, V* ⍟*CP.*

NIGHTLIFE & THE ARTS

NIGHTLIFE **Hair of the Dog English Pub** (⊠*238 N. Palm Canyon Dr.* ☎*760/323–9890*) is a friendly bar popular with a young crowd that likes to tip back English ales and ciders. **Village Pub** (⊠*266 S. Palm Canyon Dr.* ☎*760/323–3265*) is a popular but loud sports bar with friendly service that caters to a young crowd. **Zelda's** (⊠*169 N. Indian Canyon Dr.* ☎*760/325–2375*) has two rooms, one featuring Latin sounds and another with Top 40 dance music and a male dance revue. It's closed Sunday and Monday.

Casino Morongo (⊠*Cabazon off-ramp, Interstate 10* ☎*800/252–4499*), about 20 minutes west of Palm Springs, has 2,000 slot machines plus Vegas-style shows. The classy **Spa Resort Casino** (⊠*401 E. Amado Rd.* ☎*888/999–1995*) holds 1,000 slot machines, black-jack tables, a high-limit room, four restaurants, two bars, and a lounge with entertainment.

GAY & LESBIAN **Oasis** (⊠*611 S. Palm Canyon Dr.* ☎*760/416–0950*) is a multitier dance club catering to a mixed gay clientele. **Hunter's Video Bar** (⊠*302 E. Arenas Rd.* ☎*760/323–0700*) is a popular bar with dancing that draws a young crowd. **Toucans** (⊠*2100 N. Palm Canyon Dr.* ☎*760/416–7584*), a friendly place with a tropical jungle in a rain-forest setting, serves festive drinks.

In late March, when the world's finest female golfers hit the links for the Annual LPGA Kraft Nabisco Championship in Rancho Mirage, thousands of lesbians converge on Palm Springs for a four-day party popularly known as **Dinah Shore Weekend–Palm Springs** (⊕*www.clubskirts. com*). The **White Party** (☎*323/944–0051 for tickets* ⊕*www.jeffrey sanker.com*), held on Easter weekend, draws tens of thousands of gay men from around the country to the Palm Springs area for a round of parties and gala events.

THE ARTS At the Palm Springs Art Museum, the **Annenberg Theater** (⊠*101 Museum Dr.* ☎*760/325–4490* ⊕*www.psmuseum.org*) is the site of Broadway shows, opera, lectures, Sunday-afternoon chamber concerts, and other events. In mid-January the **Palm Springs International Film Festival** (☎*760/322–2930 or 800/898-7256* ⊕*www.psfilmfest.org*) brings stars and more than 150 feature films from 25 countries, plus panel discussions, short films, and documentaries, to the McCallum and other venues.

7

The Spanish-style **Historic Plaza Theatre** (⊠*128 S. Palm Canyon Dr.* ☎*760/327–0225*) opened in 1936 with a glittering premiere of the MGM film *Camille*. In the '40s and '50s, it presented some of Hollywood's biggest stars, including Bob Hope, Bing Crosby, and Frank Sinatra. Today it plays host to the hottest ticket in the desert, the **Fabulous Palm Springs Follies** (⊕*www.palmspringsfollies.com*), which mounts 10 weekly sell-out performances November through May. The vaudeville-style revue, about half of which focuses on mid-century nostalgia, stars extravagantly costumed, retired (but very fit) showgirls, singers, and dancers. Acts scheduled for a 2009 tribute to Route 66 include Freda Payne, Susan Anton, and John Davidson. Tickets are $59 to $92. In addition to the follies, the theater is home to a January film festival and is favored by fans of old-time radio even in the off-season.

SPORTS & THE OUTDOORS

BICYCLING Many hotels and resorts have bicycles available for guest use. **Big Wheel Tours** (☎*760/802–2236* ⊕*www.bwbtours.com*) rents cruisers, performance road bikes, and mountain bikes in Palm Springs and offers road tours to La Quinta Loop, Joshua Tree National Park, and the San Andreas fault. Off-road tours are also available. The company doesn't have a retail outlet but will pick up and deliver bikes to your hotel and supply you with area maps. **Palm Springs Recreation Division** (⊠*401 S. Pavilion Way* ☎*760/323–8272* ☉ *Weekdays 7:30–6*) can provide you with maps of city bike trails.

GOLF Palm Springs is host to more than 100 golf tournaments annually. The Palm Springs Desert Resorts Convention and Visitors Bureau **Events Hotline** (☎*760/770–1992*) lists dates and locations. **Palm Springs TeeTimes** can match golfers with courses and arrange tee times. If you know which course you want to play, you can book tee times online (⊕*www. palmspringsteetimes.com*).

Indian Canyons Golf Resort (⊠*1097 E. Murray Canyon Dr.* ☎*760/327–6550* ⊕*www.indiancanyonsgolf.com*), an 18-hole course designed by Casey O'Callaghan and Amy Alcott and operated by the Aqua Caliente tribe, is located at the base of the mountains. **Tahquitz Creek Palm Springs Golf Resort** (⊠*1885 Golf Club Dr.* ☎*760/328–1005* ⊕*www. tahquitzgolfresort.com*) has two 18-hole, par-72 courses and a 50-space driving range. Greens fees, including cart, run $65 to $110, depending on the course and day of the week. **Tommy Jacobs' Bel Air Greens Country Club** (⊠*1001 S. El Cielo Rd.* ☎*760/322–6062*) has a 9-hole executive course. The greens fee is $20 ($10 for replay).

SPAS Taking the Waters at the **Spa Resort Casino** (⊠*100 N. Indian Canyon Dr.* ☎*760/778–1772* ⊕*www.sparesortcasino.com*) is an indulgent pleasure. You can spend a full day enjoying a five-step, wet-and-dry treatment program that includes a mineral bath, steam, sauna, and eucalyptus inhalation. The program allows you to take fitness classes and use the gym and, for an extra charge, add massage or body treatments. During the week, the spa admission rate is $40 for a full day, less for hotel guests or if you combine it with a treatment; on weekends you cannot purchase a day pass without booking a treatment.

TENNIS **Demuth Park** (⊠*4375 Mesquite Ave.* ☎*760/323–8272*) has four lighted courts. **Plaza Racquet Club Tennis Center** (⊠*1300 Baristo Rd.* ☎*760/323–8997*), which has nine lighted courts, offers lessons and clinics. **Ruth Hardy Park** (⊠*Tamarisk Rd. and Avenida Caballeros* ☎*No phone*) has eight lighted courts.

SHOPPING

The main **North Palm Canyon Drive shopping district** (⊠*Between Alejo and Ramon Rds.*) is the commercial core of Palm Springs. Anchoring the center of the drive is the Palm Springs Mall, with about 35 boutiques. **Villagefest** (⊠*Palm Canyon Dr., between Tahquitz Canyon Way and Baristo Rd.* ☎*760/327–3781* ⊕*www.palmspringsvillagefest.com*) fills the drive with street musicians, a farmers' market, and stalls with food, crafts, art, and antiques. It's a great place for celebrity spotting.

Extending north of the main shopping area, the **Uptown Heritage Galleries & Antiques District** (⊠*N. Palm Canyon Dr., between Amado Rd. and Tachevah Dr.* ☎*760/318–7227* ⊕*www.palmcanyondrive.org*) is a loose-knit collection of consignment and secondhand shops, galleries, and restaurants whose theme is decidedly retro. Many shops and galleries offer mid-century modern furniture and decorator items, and others carry consignment clothing and estate jewelry.

East Palm Canyon Drive can be a source of great bargains. **Estate Sale Co.** (⊠*4185 E. Palm Canyon Dr.* ☎*760/321–7628*) is the biggest consignment store in the desert, with a warehouse of furniture, fine art, china and crystal, accessories, jewelry, movie memorabilia, and exercise equipment. Prices are set to keep merchandise moving. It's closed Monday and Tuesday.

About 20 mi west of Palm Springs at the Cabazon exit of I–10 lies **Desert Hills Premium Outlets** (⊠*48400 Seminole Rd., Cabazon* ☎*951/849–6641* ⊕*www.premiumoutlets.com*), an outlet center with more than 130 brand-name discount fashion shops, among them Versace, Giorgio Armani, Gucci, and Prada.

At the Cabazon exit of I–10, **Hadley's Fruit Orchards** (⊠*48–980 Seminole Dr., Cabazon* ☎*800/854–5655* ⊕*www.hadleyfruitorchards.com*) sells dried fruit, nuts, date shakes, and wines.

CATHEDRAL CITY

2 mi southeast of Palm Springs on Hwy. 111.

One of the fastest-growing communities in the desert, Cathedral City is more residential than tourist oriented. However, the city has a number of good restaurants and entertainment venues with moderate prices.

Pickford Salon, a small museum inside the Mary Pickford Theater, showcases the life of the famed actress. On display is a selection of personal items contributed by family members, including her 1976 Oscar for contributions to the film industry, a gown she wore in the 1927 film *Dorothy Vernon of Haddon Hall,* and dinnerware from Pickfair. One of the two biographical video presentations was produced by Mary herself. ✉*36-850 Pickfair St.* ☎*760/328–7100* 🎫*Free* ☉*Daily 10:30 AM–midnight.*

⟳ At **Boomers Camelot Park** you can play miniature golf, drive bumper boats, climb a rock wall, drive a go-kart, swing in the batting cages, test your skill in an arcade, and play video games. ✉*67–700 E. Palm Canyon Dr.* ☎*760/770–7522* 🎫*$5–$8 per activity, $28 day passes* ☉*Mon.–Thurs. 11–10, Fri.–Sun. 11–11.*

WHERE TO EAT

$$$ ✕**Trilussa.** Locals gather at this San Francisco–style storefront restaurant for delicious food, big drinks, and a friendly welcome. The congenial bar is busy during the happy hour (Monday to Thursday), after which diners drift to their nicely spaced tables indoors and out. The long menu changes daily, but staples include homemade pasta, risotto, veal, and fish. All come with an Italian accent. ✉ *68718 Hwy. 111* ☎*760/ 328–2300* ▤*AE, D, DC, MC, V.*

NIGHTLIFE

At **Buddy Greco's Dinner Club** (✉*68805 E. Palm Canyon Dr.* ☎*760/883– 5812* ⊕*www.buddygreco.com* 🎫*$45 without dinner*), longtime entertainer Buddy Greco serves up two hours of vintage Vegas songs and personal reminiscences from the Rat Pack era in an intimate setting, Wednesday through Sunday. Vocalist Lezlie Anders pays tribute to Peggy Lee.

DESERT HOT SPRINGS

9 mi north of Palm Springs on Gene Autry Trail.

Desert Hot Springs' famous hot mineral waters, thought by some to have curative powers, bubble up at temperatures of 90°F to 148°F and flow into the wells of more than 40 hotel spas.

WHERE TO STAY

$$$ 🏨**The Spring.** This laid-back single-story inn, tucked into a hillside with a lovely desert view, caters to guests seeking quiet and personal service. Simply furnished rooms have modern decor; most open onto the pool and colorful flower gardens. In addition to the typical wraps, scrubs, and massages, the inn's spa menu offers treatments like the Splurge Back Facial, the 90-minute Spring Buff, and the Cranial Dreamwork massage. Spa packages, which include two nights' accommodations, Continental breakfast, and four hours of treatment, start at $549. **Pros:** European massage, colorful gardens, refrigerators stocked to order. **Cons:** Far from everything, dinner not available, adults only. ✉*12699 Reposo Way* ☎*760/251–6700 or 877/200–2110* ⊕*www.the-spring. com* ⌨*12 rooms* ⟳*In-room: no phone, kitchen (some), refrigerator, no TV, Wi-Fi. In-hotel: pool, spa, no elevator public Wi-Fi, no kids under 18, no-smoking rooms* ▤*AE, D, DC, MC, V.*

RANCHO MIRAGE

4 mi southeast of Cathedral City on Hwy. 111.

Much of the scenery in exclusive Rancho Mirage is concealed behind the walls of gated communities and country clubs. The rich and famous live in estates and patronize elegant resorts and expensive restaurants. The city's golf courses host many high-profile tournaments. When the excesses of the luxe life become too much, the area's residents can check themselves into the Betty Ford Center, the famous drug-and-alcohol rehab center.

You'll find some of the swankiest resorts in the desert here—including a luxurious new Ritz-Carlton that, at this writing, was slated to open in spring 2009—plus great golf, and plenty of peace and quiet.

The **Children's Discovery Museum of the Desert** contains instructive hands-on exhibits—a miniature rock-climbing area, a magnetic sculpture wall, make-it-and-take-it-apart projects, a rope maze—and an area for toddlers. Kids can paint a VW Bug, work as chefs in the museum's pizza parlor, and build pies out of arts and crafts supplies. ✉*71–701 Gerald Ford Dr.* ☎*760/321–0602* ⊕*www.cdmod.org* ✉*$8* ⊘*Jan.–Apr., Mon.–Sat. 10–5; May–Dec., Tues.–Sat. 10–5, Sun. noon–5.*

WHERE TO STAY & EAT

$$$ ✕**Shame on the Moon.** Old-fashioned ambience complete with big booths, friendly service, an eclectic menu, and modest prices makes this one of the most popular restaurants in the desert. Entrées, which come with soup or salad, include baked salmon with a horseradish crust, chicken and wild mushroom balsamico, and roasted vegetable lasagna. Portions leave you plenty to take home. ✉*69-950 Frank Sinatra Dr.* ☎*760/324–5515* ⚏*Reservations essential* ▤*AE, MC, V* ⊘*No lunch.*

$–$$$ ✕**Las Casuelas Nuevas.** Hundreds of artifacts from Guadalajara, Mexico, lend festive charm to this casual restaurant, which has an expansive garden patio. Tamales and shellfish dishes are among the specialties. A special tequila menu lists dozens of aged and reserve selections, served by the shot or incorporated into one of the eatery's margaritas. ✉*70-050 Hwy. 111* ☎*760/328–8844* ⚏*Reservations essential* ▤*AE, D, DC, MC, V.*

$$$$ ▦**Rancho Las Palmas Resort & Spa.** Fresh from a $30 million renovation that upgraded the entire 240-acre property, the Rancho is ready to welcome back well-heeled guests. Rooms, in two-story Spanish-style buildings that surround courtyards, gardens, and the property's golf course, were completely redone in light colors in 2007. French doors lead to balconies or patios where you can take in the mountain views. The new spa has 26 treatment rooms as well as a private courtyard with a sanctuary pool. Kids and their parents will love Splashtopia, a huge water feature holding rides, two water slides, a sandy beach, and lazy river for floating. **Pros:** Ted Robinson–designed golf course; fitness trails for hiking and jogging; great views from all rooms. **Cons:** Grounds are quite spread out; rooms are close to the golf course; lots of kids. ✉*41-000 Bob Hope Dr.,* ☎*760/568–2727 or 800/423–1195*

⊕*www.rancholaspalmas.com* ⊲444 *rooms* ♿*In-room: safe, refrigerator, Ethernet, Wi-Fi. In-hotel: 5 restaurants, room service, bar, golf course, tennis courts, pools, gym, spa, no elevator, children's programs (ages 5–12), laundry service, concierge, public Internet, public Wi-Fi, parking (no fee), some pets allowed, no-smoking rooms* ▤*AE, D, DC, MC, V.*

$$$$ 🏨**Westin Mission Hills Resort.** A sprawling resort on 360 acres, the Wes-
♿ tin is surrounded by fairways, putting greens, and a collection of time-
share accommodations. Rooms, in two-story buildings amid patios
and fountains, have a stylish Arts-and-Crafts look with sleek, dark,
mahogany furnishings accented with sand-color upholstery and crisp
white linens. All have private patios or balconies. In the cool early
morning, enjoy a walk or jog on the property's many paths, which
wind past bougainvillea-covered walls, beds planted with blue salvia
and pink petunias, families of ducks, and a koi pond. There's also
a lagoon-style swimming pool with a waterslide that's several stories
high. **Pros:** Gorgeous grounds; first-class golf facilities; excellent for
families. **Cons:** Lots of dogs; rooms are very spread out. ✉*71333
Dinah Shore Dr.* ☎*760/328–5955 or 800/544–0287* ⊕*www.westin.
com* ⊲*472 rooms, 30 suites* ♿*In-room: safe, refrigerator (some), Ethernet, dial-up. In-hotel: no elevator, restaurants, room service, bar, golf
courses, tennis courts, pools, gym, spa, concierge, children's programs
(ages 5–12), parking (no fee), some pets allowed, no-smoking rooms*
▤*AE, D, DC, MC, V.*

NIGHTLIFE

The elegant and surprisingly quiet **Agua Caliente Casino** (✉*32-250 Bob
Hope Dr.* ☎*760/321–2000*) contains 1,800 slot machines, 48 table
games, a high-limit room, and a no-smoking area. The Cahuilla Showroom presents such headliners as the Smothers Brothers and Carrot
Top as well as live boxing, and there are six restaurants and a food
court.

SPORTS & THE OUTDOORS

The best female golfers in the world compete in the LPGA **Kraft Nabisco
Championship** (✉*Mission Hills Country Club* ☎*760/324–4546* ⊕*www.
kncgolf.com*) held in late March.

★ Of the two golf courses at the **Westin Mission Hills Resort Golf Club** (✉*71-
501 Dinah Shore Dr.* ☎*760/328–3198* ⊕*www.troongolf.com*), the
18-hole, par-70 Pete Dye course is especially noteworthy. The club
plays host to a number of major tournaments, is a member of the Troon
Golf Institute, and has several teaching facilities, including the Westin
Mission Hills Resort Golf Academy and the Golf Digest Golf School.
Greens fees are $165 during peak season, including a mandatory cart;
off-season promotional packages sometimes run as low as $35.

SHOPPING

The **River at Rancho Mirage** (✉*71-800 Hwy. 111* ☎*760/341–2711*) is a
shopping-dining-entertainment complex with a collection of 20 high-
end shops. Bang & Olufsen, Borders Books & Music, Cohiba Cigar
Lounge, Tulip Hill Winery tasting room, and other shops front a faux

river with cascading waterfalls. The complex includes a 12-screen cinema, an outdoor amphitheater, and seven restaurants, including Flemings Prime Steakhouse and P.F. Chang's.

PALM DESERT

2 mi southeast of Rancho Mirage on Hwy. 111.

Palm Desert is a thriving retail and business community, with some of the desert's most popular restaurants, private and public golf courses, and premium shopping.

★ West of and parallel to Highway 111, **El Paseo** (⊠ *Between Monterey and Portola Aves.* ☎ *877/735–7273* ⊕ *www.elpaseo.com*) is a mile-long Mediterranean-style avenue with fountains and courtyards, French and Italian fashion boutiques, shoe salons, jewelry stores, children's shops, 28 restaurants, and nearly 30 art galleries. The pretty strip is a pleasant place to stroll, window-shop, people-watch, and exercise your credit cards. Each January, the **Palm Desert Golf Cart Parade** (☎ *760/346–6111* ⊕ *www.golfcartparade.com*) celebrates golf with a procession of 100 carts disguised as floats buzzing up and down El Paseo.

☾ Come eyeball-to-eyeball with wolves, coyotes, mountain lions, chee-
★ tahs, bighorn sheep, golden eagles, warthogs, and owls at the **Living Desert.** Easy to challenging scenic trails traverse 1,200 acres of desert preserve populated with plants of the Mojave, Colorado, and Sonoran deserts in 11 habitats. But in recent years, the park has expanded its vision to Africa. At the 3-acre African Wa TuTu village, there's a traditional marketplace as well as camels, leopards, hyenas, and other African animals. Children can pet African domestic animals, including goats and guinea fowl, in a petting kraal. Gecko Gulch Children's Play Land has crawl-through underground tunnels and climb-on snake sculptures. Yet another exhibit demonstrates the path of the San Andreas Fault across the Coachella Valley. The Tennity Amphitheater stages daily wildlife shows, and "Wildlights," an evening light show, takes place during the winter holidays. ■ TIP→ **A garden center sells native desert flora, much of which is unavailable elsewhere.** ⊠ *47-900 Portola Ave.* ☎ *760/346–5694* ⊕ *www.livingdesert.org* ✉ *Mid-June–Aug. $8.75, Sept.–mid-June $12* ⊙ *Mid-June–Aug., daily 8–1:30; Sept.–mid-June, daily 9–5.*

The **Santa Rosa Mountains/San Jacinto National Monument,** administered by the Bureau of Land Management, protects Peninsula bighorn sheep and other wildlife on 272,000 acres of desert habitat. For an introduction to the site, stop by the visitor center—staffed by knowledgeable volunteers—for a look at exhibits illustrating the natural history of the desert. A landscaped garden displays native plants and frames a sweeping view. ⊠ *51-500 Hwy. 74* ☎ *760/862–9984* ⊕ *www.ca.blm.gov/palmsprings* ✉ *Free* ⊙ *Daily 9–4.*

7

WHERE TO STAY & EAT

$$$$ ✗**Cuistot.** The creation of chef-owner Bernard Dervieux, Cuistot is a big, bright, airy reproduction of a rustic French farmhouse on El Paseo's west end. The menu lists rabbit bourguignon with mushrooms and pancetta, along with such signature dishes as skillet-roasted veal chop with mushrooms and roasted garlic, fresh Dover sole with hazelnut-lemon sauce, and handmade vegetable ravioli with white truffle oil. ⊠*72-595 El Paseo* ☎*760/340–1000* ⚑*Reservations essential* ☐*AE, D, MC, V* ✆*Closed Mon. and July and Aug. No lunch Sun.*

> ### GREEN PALM DESERT
>
> The City of Palm Desert has a plan to reduce energy consumption by 30% over the next five years. The most ambitious plan of its kind in California, it involves incentives to install efficient pool pumps, air-conditioners, refrigeration, and lighting. The city has also banned drive-through restaurants and made golf carts legal on city streets. For concrete evidence of the city's commitment to going green, visit the recently opened visitor center, built with recycled materials such as seeds and tires.

$$–$$$$ ✗**Palmie.** Its humble location in the back of a shopping center gives nary a hint of the subtle creations prepared at this gem of a French restaurant. The two-cheese soufflé is one of several mouthwatering appetizers. Equally impressive are the duck cassoulet, duck fillets served with pear slices in red wine, and Palmie's signature dish: a perfectly crafted fish stew in a thin yet rich buttercream broth. ⊠*44-491 Town Center Way* ☎*760/341–3200* ☐*AE, DC, MC, V* ✆*Closed Sun. and July and Aug.*

$$–$$$$ ✗**Café des Beaux Arts.** This café brings a little bit of Paris to the desert, with sidewalk dining, colorful flower boxes, and a bistro menu of French and Californian favorites, such as a broiled portobello mushroom with duck confit served with a sherry sauce, and ravioli stuffed with lobster. Leisurely dining is encouraged, which allows more time to savor the well-chosen French and domestic wines. ⊠*73-640 El Paseo* ☎*760/346–0669* ☐*AE, D, DC, MC, V* ✆*Closed July and Aug.*

$$ ✗**Daily Grill.** This combination upscale coffee shop and bar serves good salads (the niçoise is particularly scrumptious), a fine gazpacho, zesty pasta dishes, and various blue-plate specials. The sidewalk terrace invites people-watching, and the weekend brunches are festive. ⊠*73-061 El Paseo* ☎*760/779–9911* ☐*AE, D, DC, MC, V.*

$$$$ ▦**J. W. Marriott's Desert Springs Resort and Spa.** This sprawling convention-oriented hotel set on 450 landscaped acres has a dramatic U-shaped design. The building wraps around the desert's largest private lake, into which an indoor, stair-stepped waterfall flows. Rooms in the main building wrap around the lobby; some have lake or Santa Rosa Mountains views, balconies, and oversize bathrooms. It's a long walk from the lobby to the rooms; if you're driving, you might want to request a room close to the parking lot. **Pros:** Gondola rides to restaurants; caters to families; business services. **Cons:** Crowded in season; rooms and facilities are spread out. ⊠*74-855 Country Club Dr.* ☎*760/341–2211 or 800/331–3112* ⊕*www.desertspringsresort. com* ⇱*833 rooms, 51 suites* ⚲*In-room: safe, refrigerator, Ethernet,*

dial-up. In-hotel: restaurants, room service, bars, golf courses, tennis courts, pools, gym, spa, concierge, children's programs (ages 4–12), laundry service, concierge, public Wi-Fi, parking (fee), no-smoking rooms ⊟*AE, D, DC, MC, V.*

THE ARTS

McCallum Theatre (⊠*73-000 Fred Waring Dr.* ☎*760/340–2787* ⊕*www. mccallumtheatre.com*), the principal cultural venue in the desert, presents film, classical and popular music, opera, ballet, and theater.

SPORTS & THE OUTDOORS

BALLOONING **Fantasy Balloon Flights** (⊠*74-181 Parosella St.* ☎*760/568–0997* ⊕*www. fantasyballoonflights.com*) operates sunrise excursions over the southern end of the Coachella Valley. Flights ($170 per person) run from an hour to an hour and a half, followed by a traditional champagne toast.

BICYCLING **Big Wheel Bike Tours** (☎*760/779–1837* ⊕*www.bwbtours.com*) delivers rental mountain, three-speed, and tandem bikes to area hotels. The company also conducts full- and half-day escorted on- and off-road bike tours throughout the area, starting at about $75 per person.

GOLF **Desert Willow Golf Resort** (⊠*38-500 Portola Ave.* ☎*760/346–7060* ⊕*www.desertwillow.com*), one of the newest golf resorts in the desert, has been praised for its environmentally smart design, which features pesticide-free and water-thrifty turf grasses. The clubhouse holds a display of contemporary art, including an original blown glass chandelier by Dale Chihuly. The public course, managed by the City of Palm Desert, has two challenging 18-hole links. The greens fee is $175, including cart.

INDIAN WELLS

5 mi east of Palm Desert on Hwy. 111.

For the most part a quiet residential community, Indian Wells is the site of golf and tennis tournaments throughout the year, including the Pacific Life Open tennis tournament. The city has three hotels that share access to city-owned championship golf and tennis facilities.

WHERE TO STAY & EAT

$$$$ ✕**Sirocco.** This family-run restaurant in the Renaissance Esmeralda hotel is one of the best in the desert, a local choice for special occasions or entertaining important clients. "If you don't see what you want on the menu, just ask for it," urges chef-owner Livio Massignani, who offers to set up customized tasting menus from the extensive Italian list that includes Dungeness crab cakes, aged prime beef carpaccio, lamb marsala, and stuffed veal chop. An extensive wine list offers a wide selection of hard-to-find Italian vintages and selections from the best California wineries. The dining room has floor-to-ceiling windows that reveal a view of water fountains against a golf course background. ⊠*44-400 Indian Wells La.* ☎*760/773–4444* ⌖*Reservations essential* ⊟*AE, D, DC, M, V* ⊗*No lunch.*

$$$$ ⊡ **Hyatt Grand Champions Resort.** This stark-white resort on 34 acres is one of the grandest in the desert. Standard rooms, large even by local standards, come with furnished patios or balconies and separate living and sleeping areas; they're decorated in warm desert golds and greens. Private villas have secluded garden courtyards with outdoor whirlpool tubs, living rooms with

> **FROM DATES TO DOLLARS**
>
> Originally a community of date farmers, Indian Wells residents now have an annual median income of $114,500 per family, making this 15-square-mi city one of the wealthiest in the country.

fireplaces, dining rooms, and private butlers who attend to your every whim. The pool area is a kind of garden water park, surrounded by palms and private cabanas. Despite all of its resorty trappings, the Hyatt actually caters to business travelers, not vacationers. **Pros:** Spacious rooms; excellent business services. **Cons:** Big and impersonal; spread out over many acres; noisy public areas. ⊠*44-600 Indian Wells La.* ☎*760/341–1000 or 800/552–4386* ⊕*www.grandchampions.hyatt. com* ⇋*426 rooms, 54 suites* △*In-room: safe, refrigerator, Ethernet, Wi-Fi. In-hotel: 4 restaurants, room service, bars, golf courses, tennis courts, pools, gym, spa, bicycles, concierge, executive floor, children's programs (ages 3–12), laundry service, public Internet, public Wi-Fi, parking (no fee), no-smoking rooms* ⊟*AE, D, DC, MC, V.*

$$$$ ⊡ **Miramonte Resort & Spa.** A warm bit of Tuscany against a backdrop ★ of the Santa Rosa Mountains characterizes the smallest, most intimate, and opulent of the Indian Wells hotels. Guest rooms, with opulent appointments (especially in the bathrooms) are in red-roofed villas on 11 acres of bougainvillea-filled gardens. Many have private patios or balconies with views of perfectly manicured, brilliantly colored gardens. Reading nooks and hammocks are tucked into secluded corners. The resort holds one of the best spas in the desert: although small, The Well offers guests intimate indulgence and relaxation in relaxation suites, mud bars, and river benches. Guests may use facilities at the Indian Wells Golf and Tennis Center. **Pros:** Romantic intimacy; gorgeous gardens; discreet service. **Cons:** Adult oriented; limited resort facilities on site. ⊠*45-000 Indian Wells La.92210* ☎*760/341–2200* ⊕*www.miramonteresort.com* ⇋*215 rooms* △*In-room: safes, refrigerators, DVD (some), Ethernet, Wi-Fi. In-hotel: 2 restaurants, room service, bars, golf course, tennis courts, pools, gym, spa, bicycles, laundry service, concierge, public Wi-Fi, parking (no fee), some pets allowed, no smoking rooms* ⊟*AE, D, DC, M, V.*

$$$$ ⊡ **Renaissance Esmeralda Resort and Spa.** The centerpiece of this luxuri- ☾ ous resort is an eight-story atrium lobby, to which most rooms open. There's soothing water everywhere...pools, ponds, lakes, fountains, and streams. Rooms are bright and airy, with ample balconies affording pool or mountain views. They're decorated in dark wood and sand tones, furnished with work desks, chaise longues, and oversize marble bathrooms with clear glass showers. Although the hotel is popular with business travelers, it's also very family-friendly. One of the pools has a sandy beach that kids love. **Pros:** Balcony views; adjacent to golf-tennis

complex. **Cons:** Higher noise level in rooms surrounding pool; somewhat impersonal ambience. ⊠*44-400 Indian Wells La.* ☎*760/773–4444 or 800/214-5540* ⊕*www.marriotthotels.com* ⇔*538 rooms, 22 suites* ⚷*In-room: safe, refrigerators, Ethernet, Wi-Fi. In-hotel: 5 restaurants, room service, bars, golf courses, tennis courts, pools, gym, spa, bicycles, children's programs (ages 5–12), laundry service, concierge, public Internet, public Wi-Fi, parking (no fee), some pets allowed, no-smoking rooms* ☰*AE, D, DC, MC, V.*

SPORTS & THE OUTDOORS

GOLF Next door to the Hyatt Grand Champions Resort, the **Golf Resort at Indian Wells** (⊠*44-500 Indian Wells La.* ☎*760/346–4653*) has two 18-hole Ted Robinson–designed championship courses: the 6,500-yard West Course and the 6,700-yard East Course. A public course, it has been named one of the country's top 10 resorts by *Golf Magazine.* Monday through Thursday the greens fee is $145; Friday through Sunday it's $155 (fees may be deeply discounted in summer). The resort also offers instruction through the Indian Wells Golf School.

TENNIS The **Pacific Life Open** (☎*800/999–1585 for tickets* ⊕*www.pacificlife open.com*) tennis tournament draws 200 of the world's top players to the Indian Wells Tennis Garden for two weeks in March. With more than 16,000 seats, the stadium is the second largest in the nation.

LA QUINTA

4 mi south of Indian Wells via Washington St.

The desert became a Hollywood hideout in the 1920s, when La Quinta Hotel (now La Quinta Resort) opened, introducing the Coachella Valley's first golf course. The opening of Old Town La Quinta in 2004 changed the once-quiet atmosphere of this community. A popular attraction, the complex holds dining spots, shops, and galleries.

WHERE TO STAY & EAT

$$$$ ✕**Arnold Palmer's.** From the photos on the walls to the trophy-filled display cases to the putting green for diners awaiting a table, Arnie's image fills this restaurant. It's a big, clubby place where families gather for birthdays and Sunday dinners, and the service is attentive and knowledgeable. Don't eat too many of the addictive house-made potato chips with blue cheese sauce before you dive into the barbecued pork ribs, fillet with béarnaise sauce, or signature seared scallops. And save room for the splendid desserts, which range from root-beer floats to grasshopper ice-cream sandwiches. There's entertainment nightly. ⊠*78-164 Ave. 52* ☎*760/771–4653* ⚖*Reservations essential* ☰*AE, D, MC, V* ☽*No lunch.*

$$$ ✕**Hog's Breath Inn.** Clint Eastwood watches over this replica of his Hog's Breath restaurant in Carmel, his presence felt in the larger-than-life photos that fill the walls of its bright dining room. The menu lists a large selection of American comfort food ranging from barbecued baby back ribs to beef brisket to the Dirty Harry dinner: chopped sirloin with capers and mashed potatoes. ⊠*78-065 Main St.* ☎*760/564–5556 or 866/464–7888* ☰*AE, D, DC, MC, V.*

$$$$ **La Quinta Resort and Club.** Opened in 1926 (and now a member of the Waldorf-Astoria Collection), the desert's oldest resort is a lush green oasis. Broad expanses of lawn separate the adobe casitas that house some rooms; other rooms, decorated in early-California style with wrought iron, tile, and dark woods, are in newer two-story units surrounding individual swimming pools and hot tubs amid brilliant gardens. Fireplaces, stocked refrigerators, and fruit-laden orange trees contribute to a luxurious ambience. A premium is placed on privacy, which accounts for La Quinta's continuing popularity with Hollywood celebrities. You can play on the championship golf courses either at La Quinta or at the adjacent PGA West. **Pros:** Individual swimming pools; beautiful gardens; best golf courses in the desert. **Cons:** A party atmosphere sometimes prevails; must walk long distances to get around the property ⌧ *49-499 Eisenhower Dr.* ☏ *760/564–4111 or 800/598–3828* ⊕ *www.laquintaresort.com* ⤴ *640 rooms, 244 suites* ⌂ *In-room: safe (some), refrigerator (some), dial-up, Wi-Fi (some). In-hotel: 7 restaurants, room service, bar, golf courses, tennis courts, pools, gym, spa, no elevator, children's programs (ages 4–12), concierge, parking (no fee), some pets allowed, no-smoking rooms* ▤ *AE, D, DC, MC, V.*

> ### THE FIRST CELEBRITY HOTEL
>
> Frank Capra probably started the trend when he booked a casita at the then-new, very remote La Quinta Hotel (now Resort) to write the script for the movie *It Happened One Night*. The movie went on to earn an Academy Award, and Capra continued to book that room whenever he had some writing to do. A long line of Hollywood stars followed Capra's example over the years; the current list includes Oprah Winfrey, Adam Sandler, and Christina Aguilera.

THE ARTS

La Quinta Arts Festival (☏ *760/564-1244* ⊕ *www.lqaf.com*), normally held in mid-March at the La Quinta Civic Center, showcases painting, sculpture, photography, drawing, and printmaking. The show is accompanied by entertainment and food.

SPORTS & THE OUTDOORS

★ **PGA West** (⌧ *49-499 Eisenhower Dr.* ☏ *760/564–5729 for tee times* ⊕ *www.pgawest.com*) operates three 18-hole, par-72 championship courses and provides instruction and golf clinics. Greens fees (which include a mandatory cart) range from $50 on weekdays in summer to $235 on weekends in February and March. Bookings are accepted 30 days in advance, but prices are lower when you book close to the date you need.

INDIO

5 mi east of Indian Wells on Hwy. 111.

Indio is the home of the date shake, which is exactly what it sounds like: a delicious, extremely thick milk shake made with dates. The city and surrounding countryside generate 95% of the dates grown and harvested in the United States. If you take a hot-air balloon ride, you will likely drift over the tops of date palm trees.

☺ Displays at the **Coachella Valley Museum and Cultural Center**, in a former farmhouse, explain how dates are harvested and how the desert is irrigated for date farming. On the grounds you'll find a restored 1909 schoolhouse and displays depicting Native American and pioneer life. ✉ *82-616 Miles Ave.* ☎ *760/342-6651* 🏷 *$3* ☙ *Oct.–May, Fri. and Sat. 10–4, Sun. 1–4.*

> **ROCKIN' AT COACHELLA**
>
> The Coachella Valley Music and Arts Festival, one of the biggest parties in SoCal, draws hundreds of thousands of rock music fans to Indio for three days of live concerts and dancing. Hundreds of bands show up, including headliners such as Jack Johnson, the Raconteurs, Portishead, Roger Waters, and My Morning Jacket. Everybody camps at the Polo Grounds. Visit www.coachella.com for details and tickets.

You take a walking tour of the 175-acre palm arboretum and orchard at **Oasis Date Gardens.** On the tour you learn how dates are pollinated, grown, sorted, stored, and packed for shipping. ✉ *59-111 Hwy. 111, Thermal* ☎ *800/827-8017* ⊕ *http://oasisdategardens.com* 🏷 *Free* ☙ *Walking tours daily 10:30 and 2:30.*

☺ Indio celebrates its raison d'être each February at the **National Date Festival and Riverside County Fair.** The midmonth festivities include an Arabian Nights pageant, camel and ostrich races, and exhibits of local dates. Admission includes camel rides. ✉ *Riverside County Fairgrounds, 46-350 Arabia St.* ☎ *800/811-3247* ⊕ *www.datefest.org* 🏷 *$8.*

WHERE TO STAY & EAT

$ ✕ **Ciro's Ristorante and Pizzeria.** This popular casual restaurant has been serving pizza and pasta since the 1970s. The menu lists some unusual pizzas, such as cashew with three cheeses. Daily pasta specials vary but might include red- or white-clam sauce or scallops with parsley and red wine. ✉ *81-963 Hwy. 111* ☎ *760/347-6503* ⊕ *www.cirospasta.com* 🖃 *AE, D, MC, V* ☙ *No lunch Sun.*

$$–$$$ 🏨 **Fantasy Springs Resort Casino.** This family-oriented resort casino, ☺ operated by the Cabazon Band of Mission Indians, is the tallest building in the Coachella Valley, affording mountain views from most rooms and the rooftop bar. Rooms are appointed in dark-wood Arts-and-Crafts style. Many have balconies overlooking the pool area, which has not only a free-form pool with a sandy beach at one end but also fountains and waterfalls adjacent to a grassy area where families can picnic. The casino provides Las Vegas–style gaming. The hip Pom restaurant opened in 2008. **Pros:** Big-name entertainment; great views from the rooftop bar; bowling alley. **Cons:** In the middle of nowhere; average service. ✉ *84-245 Indio Springs Pkwy.* ☎ *760/342-5000 or 800/827-2946* ⊕ *www.fantasyspringsresort.com* 🛏 *240 rooms, 11 suites* ☙ *In-room: safe, refrigerator (some), DVD (some), Ethernet, Wi-Fi. In-hotel: 5 restaurants, room service, bars, golf, pools, gym, concierge, parking (no fee), no-smoking rooms* 🖃 *AE, D, MC, V.*

ALONG TWENTYNINE PALMS HIGHWAY

The towns of Yucca Valley and Twentynine Palms punctuate Twentynine Palms Highway (Highway 62)—the northern highway from the desert resorts to Joshua Tree National Park (⇨ *Chapter 8, Joshua Tree National Park*)—and provide visitor information, lodging, and other services to park goers.

YUCCA VALLEY

30 mi northeast of Palm Springs on Hwy. 62, Twentynine Palms Hwy.

One of the fastest-growing cities in the high desert, Yucca Valley is emerging as a bedroom community for people who work as far away as Ontario, 85 mi to the west. In this sprawling suburb you can shop for necessities, get your car serviced, and chow down at the fast-food outlets.

The **Hi-Desert Nature Museum** has a small live animal display containing creatures that make their homes in Joshua Tree, including scorpions, snakes, ground squirrels, and chuckwallas, a type of lizard. There's also a collection of rocks, minerals, and fossils from the Paleozoic era, a Native American collection, and a children's room. ✉ *57-116 Twentynine Palms Hwy.* ☎ *760/369–7212* ⊕ *www.yucca-valley.org* ✉ *Free* ☉ *Tues.–Sun. 10–5.*

In 1946 Roy Rogers, Gene Autry, the Sons of the Pioneers (the music group for whom the town is named), and Russ Hayden built **Pioneertown** (✉ *Pioneertown Rd., 4 mi north of Yucca Valley* ⊕ *www.pioneertown. com*), an 1880s-style Wild West movie set complete with hitching posts, saloon, and an OK Corral. Today 250 people call the place home, even as film crews continue shooting. You can stroll past wooden and adobe storefronts and feel like you're back in the Old West. The new owners of Pappy & Harriet's have started building an outdoor concert venue for about 500 people and have started booking popular bands and singers. Gunfights are staged April through October, Saturday at 1 and 2 and Sunday at 2:30.

WHERE TO STAY & EAT

$ ✕ **Pappy & Harriet's Pioneertown Palace.** Smack in the middle of a Western-movie-set town is this Western-movie-set saloon where you can have dinner, dance to live country-and-western music, or just relax with a drink at the bar. The food ranges from Tex-Mex to Santa Maria barbecue to steak and burgers—no surprises but plenty of fun. ■TIP➔ **Pappy & Harriet's may be in the middle of nowhere, but you'll need reservations for dinner on weekends.** ✉ *53688 Pioneertown Rd., Pioneertown* ☎ *760/365–5956* ⊕ *www.pappyandharriets.com* ☐ *AE, D, MC, V* ☉ *Closed Tues. and Wed.*

¢ ✕ **Park Rock Café.** If you're on your way to the national park on Highway 62, stop in the town of Joshua Tree (not to be confused with the park) to fill up on a hearty breakfast bagel sandwich and order a bag lunch to take with you. The café creates some hearty sandwiches, such as chicken Parmesan. Outside dining is pleasant here. ✉*6554 Park Blvd., Joshua Tree* ☎*760/366–3622* ▭*MC, V* ☉*No dinner Sun.–Thurs.*

$$ ⊡ **Best Western Yucca Valley Hotel & Suites.** This new hotel, opened in 2008, is a welcome addition to the slim pickings in the Joshua Tree NP area. Rooms are spacious, nicely appointed, and decorated in soft desert colors. There are two sections: one is exclusively extended-stay while the other is for short-term guests. Continental breakfast, served in the parlor, is included in the price. **Pros:** Convenient to Joshua Tree NP; brand new. **Cons:** Location on busy highway; limited service. ✉*56525 Twentynine Palms Hwy. 92284* ☎*760/365–3555* ⊕*www. bestwestern.com* ↩*95 rooms* ⚙*In-room: safe, kitchens (some), refrigerators, Ethernet, Wi-Fi. In hotel: pool, gym, laundry facilities, public Internet, public Wi-Fi, parking, no-smoking rooms* ▭*AE, D, DC, M, V* |○|*CP.*

¢ ⊡ **Pioneertown Motel.** Built in 1946 as a bunkhouse for Western film stars shooting in Pioneertown, this motel sticks close to its roots. The clean rooms are named for the stars who stayed in them while filming in Pioneertown in the 1950s and 1960s—Gene Autry, Gail Davis, and Barbara Stanwyck—and are as simply furnished as they would have been back then. Hiking trails outside the motel lead into the desert. Bring your horse—there are corrals for visiting animals. **Pros:** Western movie time warp; great stargazing; horses welcome. **Cons:** No frills; small rooms; hot in summer. ✉*5040 Curtis Rd., Pioneertown* ☎*760/365–4879* ⊕*www.pioneertownmotel.com* ↩*20 rooms* ⚙*In-room: no phone, kitchen (some), refrigerator, Wi-Fi. In-hotel: no elevator, public Wi-Fi, some pets allowed, no-smoking rooms* ▭*MC, V.*

TWENTYNINE PALMS

24 mi east of Yucca Valley on Hwy. 62, Twentynine Palms Hwy.

The main gateway town to Joshua Tree National Park (⇨*Chapter 8, Joshua Tree National Park*), Twentynine Palms is also the location of the U.S. Marine Air Ground Task Force Training Center. You can find services, supplies, and lodgings in town.

The history and current life of Twentynine Palms is depicted in **Oasis of Murals,** a collection of 20 murals painted on the sides of buildings. If you drive around town, you can't miss the murals, but you can also pick up a free map from the **Action Council for 29 Palms** (✉*6455B Mesquite Ave.* ☎*760/361–2286* ⊕*www.oasisofmurals. com*). **29 Palms Art Gallery** (✉*74055 Cottonwood Dr.* ☎*760/367–7819* ⊕*www.29palmsartgallery.com* ☉ *Wed.–Sun. noon–3*) features work by local painters, sculptors, and jewelry makers who find inspiration in the desert landscape.

WHERE TO STAY & EAT

$$ ✕⊡ **29 Palms Inn.** The funky 29 Palms is the lodging closest to the entrance to Joshua Tree National Park. The collection of adobe and wood-frame cottages, some dating back to the 1920s and 1930s, is scattered over 70 acres of grounds that are popular with birds and

bird-watchers year-round. Innkeeper Jane Smith's warm, personal service more than makes up for the cottages' rustic qualities. Ranging from pasta to seafood, the contemporary fare at the inn's convivial restaurant ($$) is more sophisticated than its Old West appearance might suggest. **Pros:** Gracious hospitality; exceptional bird-watching; popular with artists. **Cons:** Rustic accommodations; limited amenities. ✉73-950 Inn Ave. ☎760/367–3505 ⊕*www.29palmsinn.com* ⇌*18 rooms, 5 suites* ♿*In-room: no a/c (some), no phone. In hotel: restaurant, pool, no elevator, public Wi-Fi, parking, some pets allowed, no-smoking rooms* ⊟*AE, D, DC, MC, V* ⦿*CP.*

$$ ✪ **Roughley Manor.** To the wealthy pioneer who erected the stone man-
★ sion now occupied by this B&B, expense was no object. A 50-foot-long planked maple floor is the pride of the great room, the carpentry on the walls throughout is intricate, and huge stone fireplaces warm the house on the rare cold night. Original fixtures still gleam in the bathrooms, and bedrooms hold pencil and canopy beds and some fireplaces. The innkeepers serve afternoon tea and evening dessert. An acre of gardens shaded by Washingtonia palms surrounds the house. **Pros:** Elegant rooms and public spaces; good stargazing in the gazebo; great horned owls on property. **Cons:** Somewhat isolated location; three-story main building doesn't have an elevator. ✉74-744 Joe Davis Rd. ☎760/367–3238 ⊕*www.roughleymanor.com* ⇌*2 suites, 7 cottages* ♿*In-room: no phone, kitchen (some), refrigerator. In-hotel: pool, no elevator, some pets allowed, no-smoking rooms* ⊟*DC, MC, V* ⦿*BP.*

ANZA-BORREGO DESERT

Largely uninhabited, the Anza-Borrego Desert is popular with those who love solitude, silence, space, starry nights, light, and sweeping vistas. The desert lies south of the Palm Springs area, stretching along the western shore of the Salton Sea down toward Interstate 8 along the Mexican border. Isolated from the rest of California by mile-high mountains to the north and west, most of this desert falls within the borders of Anza-Borrego Desert State Park, which at more than 600,000 acres is the largest state park in the contiguous United States. This is a place where you can escape the cares of the human world.

For thousands of years Native Americans of the Cahuilla and Kumeyaay people inhabited this area, spending their winters on the warm desert floor and their summers in the mountains. The first Europeans—a party led by Spanish explorer Juan Baptiste de Anza—crossed this desert in 1776. Anza, for whom the desert is named, made the trip through here twice. Roadside signs along highways 86, 78, and S2 mark the route of the Anza expedition, which spent Christmas Eve 1776 in what is now Anza-Borrego Desert State Park. Seventy-five years later thousands of immigrants on their way to the goldfields up north crossed the desert on the Southern Immigrant Trail, remnants of which remain along Highway S2. Permanent settlers arrived early in the 20th century, and by the 1930s the first adobe resort cottage had been built.

BORREGO SPRINGS

59 mi south of Indio via Hwys. 86 and S22.

The permanent population of Borrego Springs, set squarely in the middle of Anza-Borrego Desert State Park, hovers around 2,500. Long a quiet town, it's emerging as a laid-back destination for desert lovers. September through June, when temperatures stay in the 80s and 90s, you can engage in outdoor activities such as hiking, nature study, golf, tennis, horseback riding, and mountain biking. If winter rains cooperate, Borrego Springs puts on some of the best wildflower displays in the low desert. In some years the desert floor is carpeted with color: yellow dandelions and sunflowers, pink primrose, purple sand verbena, and blue phacelia. The bloom generally runs from late February through April. For current information on wildflowers around Borrego Springs, call Anza-Borrego Desert State Park's wildflower hotline (☎ 760/767–4684).

Flowers aren't the only thing popping up from the earth in Borrego Springs. At **SkyArt** (✉ *Borrego Springs Rd. from Christmas Circle to Henderson Canyon* ☎ *760/767–5555* ⊕ *www.galletameadows.com* ✉ *Free*) camels, llamas, sabre-toothed tigers, tortoises, and monumental gomphotherium (a sort of ancient elephant) appear to roam the earth again. These life-size bronze figures are of prehistoric animals whose fossils can be found in the Borrego Badlands. The collection, currently seven sets of animals and growing, is the project of a wealthy Borrego Springs resident who is installing the works of art on property he owns for the entertainment of locals and visitors. Maps are available from Borrego Springs Chamber of Commerce.

★ One of the richest living natural-history museums in the nation, **Anza-Borrego Desert State Park** is a vast, nearly uninhabited wilderness where you can step through a field of wildflowers, cool off in a palm-shaded oasis, count zillions of stars in the black night sky, and listen to coyotes howl at dusk. The landscape, largely undisturbed by humans, reveals a rich natural history. There's evidence of a vast inland sea in the piles of oyster beds near Split Mountain and of the power of natural forces such as earthquakes and flash floods. In addition, recent scientific work has confirmed that the Borrego Badlands, with more than 6,000 meters of exposed fossil-bearing sediments is likely the richest such deposit in North America, telling the story of 7 million years of climate change, upheaval, and prehistoric animals. They've found evidence of saber-tooth cats, flamingos, zebras, and the largest flying bird in the Northern Hemisphere beneath the now-parched sand. Today the desert's most treasured inhabitants are the herds of elusive and endangered native bighorn sheep, or *borego,* for which the park is named. Among the strange desert plants you may observe are the gnarly elephant trees. As these are endangered, rangers don't encourage visitors to seek out the secluded grove at Fish Creek, but there are a few examples at the visitor center garden. After a wet winter you can see a short-lived but stunning display of cacti, succulents, and desert wildflowers in bloom.

Anza-Borrego Desert State Park is unusually accessible to visitors. Admission to the park is free, and few areas are off-limits. Unlike most parks in the country, Anza-Borrego lets you camp anywhere; just follow the trails and pitch a tent wherever you like. There are more than 500 mi of dirt roads, two huge wilderness areas, and 110 mi of riding and hiking trails. Many of the park's sites can be seen from paved roads, but some require driving on dirt roads, for which rangers recommend you use a four-wheel-drive vehicle. When you do leave the pavement, carry the appropriate supplies: a cell phone (which may be unreliable in some areas), a shovel and other tools, flares, blankets, and plenty of water. The canyons are susceptible to flash flooding, so inquire about weather conditions (even on sunny days) before entering.

To get oriented and obtain information on weather and wildlife conditions, stop by the **Visitors Information Center.** Designed to keep cool during the desert's blazing hot summers, the center is built underground, beneath a demonstration desert garden. A nature trail here takes you through a garden containing examples of most of the native flora and a little pupfish pond. ■TIP→ **Borrego resorts and restaurants have Wi-Fi, but the service is spotty at best. If you need to talk to someone in the area, it's best to find a phone with a land line.** ⊠ *200 Palm Canyon Dr., Hwy. S22* ☎ *760/767–5311, 760/767–4684 wildflower hotline* ⊕ *www.parks.ca.gov* ≤ *Free* ⊙ *June–Sept., weekends and holidays 9–5; Oct.–May, daily 9–5.*

At **Borrego Palm Canyon** (⊠ *Palm Canyon Dr., Hwy. S22, about 1 mi west of the Visitors Information Center*), a 1½-mi trail leads to one of the few native palm groves in North America. There are more than 1,000 native fan palms in the grove, and a stream and waterfall greet you at trail's end. The moderate hike is the most popular in the park.

Yaqui Well Nature Trail (⊠ *Hwy. 78, across from Tamarisk Campground*) takes you along a path to a desert water hole where birds and wildlife are abundant. It's also a good place to look for wildflowers in spring.

Coyote Canyon (⊠ *Off DiGiorgio Rd., 4½ mi north of Borrego Springs*) has a year-round stream and lush plant life, making it one of the best places to see and photograph spring wildflowers. Portions of the canyon road follow a section of the old Anza Trail. The canyon is closed between June 15 and September 15 to allow native bighorn sheep undisturbed use of the water. The dirt road that gives access to the canyon may be sandy enough to require a four-wheel-drive vehicle.

The late-afternoon vista of the Borrego badlands from **Font's Point** (⊠ *Off Borrego Salton Seaway, Hwy. S22, 13 mi east of Borrego Springs*) is one of the most breathtaking views seen in the desert, especially when the setting sun casts a golden glow in high relief on the eroded mountain slopes. The road from the Font's Point turnoff can be rough enough to make using a four-wheel-drive vehicle advisable; inquire about its condition at the visitor center before starting out. Even if you can't make it out on the paved road, you can see some of the view from the highway.

Narrows Earth Trail (⊠ *Off Hwy. 78, 13 mi west of Borrego Springs*) is a short walk off the road east of Tamarisk Grove campground. Along the way you can see evidence of the many geologic processes involved in forming the canyons of the desert, such as a contact zone between two earthquake faults, and sedimentary layers of metamorphic and igneous rock.

Geology students from all over the world visit the Fish Creek area of Anza-Borrego to explore a canyon known as **Split Mountain** (⊠ *Split Mountain Rd., 9 mi south of Hwy. 78, at Ocotillo Wells*). The narrow gorge with 600-foot walls was formed by an ancient stream. Fossils in this area indicate that a sea once covered the desert floor.

The easy, mostly flat **Pictograph/Smuggler's Canyon Trail** (⊠ *Blair Valley, Hwy. S2, 6 mi southeast of Hwy. 78, at Scissors Crossing intersection*) traverses a boulder-strewn trail. At the end is a collection of rocks covered with muted red and yellow pictographs painted within the last hundred years or so by Native Americans. Walk about ½ mi beyond the pictures to reach Smuggler's Canyon, where an overlook provides views of the Vallecito Valley. The hike is 2 to 3 mi round-trip.

Just a few steps off the paved road, **Carrizo Badlands Overlook** (⊠ *Off Hwy. S2, 40 mi south of Scissors Crossing [intersection of Hwys. S2 and 78]*) offers a view of eroded and twisted sedimentary rock that obscures the fossils of the mastodons, saber-tooths, zebras, and camels that roamed this region a million years ago. The route to the overlook through Earthquake Valley and Blair Valley parallels the Southern Emigrant Trail.

WHERE TO STAY & EAT

$$$ ✕**The Arches.** Set right on the edge of the Borrego Springs Golf Course, with both indoor and outdoor seating, this is one of the most pleasant dining options in the area. There's indoor and outdoor seating, and the offerings are surprisingly good: try the chicken potpie for dinner. The Arches is open for breakfast as well. ⊠ *1112 Tilting T Dr.* ☎ *760/767–5700* ⊟ *AE, MC, V* ☉ *Summer hrs vary; call ahead.*

$$$ ✕**Krazy Coyote Bar & Grill.** Dine inside in the cozy bar or outside by the pool at this restaurant at the Palms at Indianhead. Either way you'll hear Bing Crosby and Peggy Lee softly crooning '50s songs in the background as you enjoy well-prepared crab cakes, beef Wellington, or prime rib. ⊠ *2220 Hoberg Rd.* ☎ *760/767–7788* ⊟ *AE, D, DC, MC, V* ☉ *No lunch. Closed summer.*

$$ ✕**Red Ocotillo.** This locally popular eatery tucked into a Quonset hut at the airport serves up a selection of comfort-food favorites all day long: eggs Benedict for breakfast, sandwiches and burgers for lunch, and chicken-fried steak and three-cheese pasta for dinner. ⊠ *818 Palm Canyon Dr.* ☎ *760/767–7400* ⊟ *AE, D, DC, MC, V.*

$$$$ ✕⊡ **La Casa del Zorro.** This serene resort pampers guests with spectacu-
★ lar desert scenery, luxurious accommodations, and gracious service. A few hundred yards away from your room is a quiet desert garden, where you can walk and find yourself surrounded by ocotillo and cholla. Accommodations range from ample standard rooms to private

casitas with their own pools or private outdoor hot tubs. Most rooms have original art on the walls, minibars, fireplaces, and extra-large bathrooms. Guests have access to the private Montesoro golf course. The elegant restaurant ($$$$) has excellent service, fireside dining, and a good Sunday brunch. La Casa schedules wine, music, and astronomy weekends throughout the year. In summer, prices are deeply discounted. **Pros:** Pristine exercise pool; casitas with secluded outdoor hot tubs; abundant pampering. **Cons:** Very expensive; limited nightlife; lots of business travelers. ⊠*3845 Yaqui Pass Rd.* ☎*760/767–5323 or 800/824–1884* ⊕*www.lacasadelzorro.com* ⌧*44 rooms, 19 1- to 4-bedroom casitas* ⋔*In-room: Kitchens (some), refrigerators (some), DVD (some), VCR (some), Ethernet, dial-up, Wi-Fi. In-hotel: 2 restaurants, room service, bar, tennis courts, pools, gym, spa, bicycles, laundry service, concierge, public Wi-Fi, airport shuttle, parking (no fee), some pets allowed, no-smoking rooms* ▤*AE, D, MC, V.*

$ ▦**Borrego Springs Resort and Country Club.** This quiet resort is a good value compared to other Borrego Springs lodgings. Large rooms in a collection of two-story buildings surrounding the swimming pool are nicely kept and appointed with simple oak furnishings. All have shaded balconies or patios with pleasant desert views. In spring, desert gardens surrounding the property burst into colorful bloom. **Pros:** Golf and tennis on site; most rooms have good desert views. **Cons:** Limited amenities; average service. ⊠*1112 Tilting T Dr.* ☎*760/767–5700 or 888/826–7734* ⊕*www.borregospringsresort.com* ⌧*66 rooms, 34 suites* ⋔*In-room: kitchen (some), refrigerator, Wi-Fi (some). In-hotel: 2 restaurants, bar, golf courses, tennis courts, pools, gym, laundry facilities, public Wi-Fi, parking (no fee), some pets allowed (fee), no-smoking rooms* ▤*AE, D, MC, V* ⓘ⚬*CP.*

SPORTS & THE OUTDOORS

The 27 holes of golf at **Borrego Springs Resort and Country Club** (⊠*1112 Tilting T Dr.* ☎*760/767–3330* ⊕*www.borregospringsresort.com*) are open to the public. Three 9-hole courses, with natural desert landscaping and mature date palms, can be played individually or in any combination. Greens fees are $65 to $75, depending on the course and the day of the week, and include a cart. **Roadrunner Club** (⊠*1010 Palm Canyon Dr.* ☎*760/767–0004* ⊕*www.roadrunnerclub.com*) has an 18-hole golf course. The greens fee is $20.

You can select from a variety of equine encounters at **Smoketree Institute and Ranch** (☎*760/767–5850* ⊕*www.smoketreearabianranch.com*), which gives desert horseback rides on Arabian or quarter horses, pony rides for kids, and a nonriding human-to-horse communication experience similar to horse-whispering.

SALTON SEA

★ *30 mi southeast of Indio via Hwy. 86 on western shore and via Hwy. 111 on eastern shore; 29 mi east of Borrego Springs via Hwy. S22.*

The Salton Sea, barely 100 years old, is the product of both natural and artificial forces. The sea occupies the Salton Basin, a remnant of prehistoric Lake Cahuilla. Over the centuries the Colorado River flooded the basin and the water drained into the Gulf of California. In 1905 a flood once again filled the Salton Basin, but the exit to the gulf was blocked by sediment. The floodwaters remained in the basin, creating a saline lake 228 feet below sea level, about 35 mi long and 15 mi wide, with a surface area of nearly 380 square mi. The sea, which lies along the Pacific Flyway, supports 400 species of birds. Four sport fish inhabit the Salton Sea: corvina, sargo, Gulf croaker, and tilapia. Fishing, boating, camping, and bird-watching are popular activities year-round.

♻ On the north shore of the sea, the huge **Salton Sea State Recreation Area** draws thousands each year to its playgrounds, hiking trails, fishing spots, boat launches, and swimming areas. The Headquarters Visitor Center contains exhibits and shows a short film on the history of the Salton Sea. Summer is the best time for fishing here. ✉ *100-225 State Park Rd., North Shore* ☎ *760/393-3052* ⊕ *www.parks.ca.gov* ☒ *$6* ⊗ *Park daily 8–sunset; visitor center Oct.–Apr., daily 8–sunset, May–Sept., weekends 8–sunset.*

The 1,785-acre **Sonny Bono National Wildlife Refuge,** on the Pacific Flyway, is a wonderful spot for viewing migratory birds. You might see eared grebes, burrowing owls, great blue herons, ospreys, yellow-footed gulls, white and brown pelicans, and snow geese heading south from Canada. Facilities include a visitor center with bird displays, self-guided trails, observation platforms, and interpretive exhibits. Fishing and waterfowl hunting are permitted in season in designated areas. ✉ *906 W. Sinclair Rd., Calipatria* ☎ *760/348-5278* ⊕ *www.fws.gov/ saltonsea* ☒ *Free* ⊗ *Sept.–June daily sunrise–sunset, visitor center weekdays 7–3:30; June–Sept., weekends 8–4:30.*

PALM SPRINGS & THE SOUTHERN DESERT ESSENTIALS

To research prices, get advice from other travelers, and book travel arrangements, visit ⊕ *www.fodors.com.*

TRANSPORTATION

BY AIR

Palm Springs International Airport is the major airport serving California's southern desert. Alaska, American, Continental, Delta, United, and US Airways all fly to Palm Springs year-round. A Valley Cabousine has taxis serving the Palm Springs airport. *See By Air in California Essentials for airline phone numbers.*

Information **Palm Springs International Airport** (☎ *760/318–3800* ⊕ *www. palmspringsairport.com*). **A Valley Cabousine** (☎ *760/340–5845*).

BY BUS

Greyhound provides service to the Palm Springs depot. SunBus, operated by the SunLine Transit Agency, serves the entire Coachella Valley, from Desert Hot Springs to Mecca.

Information **Greyhound** (☎ *800/231–2222* ⊕ *www.greyhound.com*). **Palm Springs Depot** (✉ *311 N. Indian Canyon Dr.*). **SunLine Transit** (☎ *800/347–8628* ⊕ *www.sunline.org*).

BY CAR

The desert resort communities occupy a 20-mi stretch between I–10 to the east and Palm Canyon Drive (Highway 111) to the west. The area is about a two-hour drive east of Los Angeles and a three-hour drive northeast of San Diego. It can take twice as long to make the trip from Los Angeles to the desert on winter weekends because of heavy traffic. From Los Angeles take the San Bernardino Freeway (I–10) east to Highway 111. From San Diego I–15 heading north connects with the Pomona Freeway (Highway 60), leading to the San Bernardino Freeway (I–10) east.

To reach Borrego Springs from Los Angeles, take I–10 east past the desert resorts area to Highway 86 south, and follow it to the Borrego Salton Seaway (Highway S22). Drive west on S22 to Borrego Springs. You can reach the Borrego area from San Diego via I–8 to Highway 79 through Cuyamaca State Park. This will take you to Highway 78 in Julian, which you follow east to Yaqui Pass Road (S3) into Borrego Springs.

BY TAXI

A Valley Cabousine serves Palm Desert and goes to the Palm Springs airport. Mirage Taxi serves the Coachella Valley and the Los Angeles and Ontario International airports. Fares in the Coachella Valley run about $2.25 per mi and up to $290 one-way to LAX.

Taxi Companies **A Valley Cabousine** (☎ *760/340–5845*). **Mirage Taxi** (☎ *760/322–2008*).

TRAIN TRAVEL

The Amtrak *Sunset Limited,* which runs between Florida and Los Angeles, stops in Palm Springs and Indio.

Information **Amtrak** (☎ *800/872–7245* ⊕ *www.amtrakcalifornia.com*).

CONTACTS & RESOURCES

EMERGENCIES

In an emergency dial 911.

Never travel alone in the desert. Let someone know your trip route, destination, and estimated time and date of return. Before setting out, make sure your vehicle is in good condition. Carry a jack, tools, and towrope or chain. Fill up your tank whenever you see a gas pump. Stay on main roads, and watch out for wild burros, horses, and range cattle.

Drink at least a gallon of water a day (three gallons if you're hiking or otherwise exerting yourself). Dress in layered clothing and wear comfortable, sturdy shoes and a hat. Keep snacks, sunscreen, and a first-aid kit on hand. If you suddenly have a headache or feel dizzy or nauseous, you could be suffering from dehydration. Get out of the sun immediately and drink plenty of water. Dampen your clothing to lower your body temperature.

Do not enter mine tunnels or shafts. Avoid canyons during rainstorms. Never place your hands or feet where you can't see them. Rattlesnakes, scorpions, and black widow spiders may be hiding there.

Contacts **Borrego Medical Center** (⊠ *4343 Yaqui Pass Rd., Borrego Springs* ☎ *760/767–5051*). **Desert Regional Medical Center** (⊠ *1150 N. Indian Canyon Dr., Palm Springs* ☎ *760/323–6511*).

TOUR OPTIONS

Desert Adventures takes to the wilds with two- to four-hour red Jeep tours ($109 to $159) on private land along the canyons and palm oases of the San Andreas earthquake fault. Their other public tours include Indian Cultural Adventure, Pioneer Adventure, and Joshua Tree National Park. Groups are small and guides are knowledgeable. Departures are from Palm Springs and La Quinta; hotel pickups are available. Elite Land Tours gives three- to five-hour luxurious treks via Hummer and helicopter, led by knowledgeable guides who take you to the San Andreas Fault, Joshua Tree National Park, Indian Canyons, Pioneertown, Old Indian Pueblo in Desert Hot Springs, and the Salton Sea. Tours include hotel pickup, lunch, snacks, and beverages.

Three thousand windmills churn mightily on the slopes surrounding Palm Springs, generating electricity used by Southern California residents. Each windmill stands more than 150 feet high. Eco-Adventure Tours conducts 1½-hour tours among the giant rotors, towers, and blades in what NASA declares is one of the most consistently windy places on earth. Palm Springs Celebrity Tours conducts 2½-hour tours that cover Palm Springs–area history, points of interest, and celebrity homes. Desert Safari Guides conducts tours of various lengths through the Indian Canyons, moonlight hiking in the Palm Springs area, and daytime excursions to Joshua Tree National Park. Transportation from most area hotels is included.

The city of Palm Desert offers four self-guided tours of its 150-piece Art in Public Places collection. Each tour is walkable or drivable: The El Paseo tour features sculptures installed along the grassy median strip that runs the length of the street; the Fred Waring Corridor Tour includes sculptures of bighorn sheep, komodo dragons, and mountain lions along the street named for the bandleader; the City Tour encompasses several large pieces of art ringing the Desert Willow Golf Resort; and the Civic Center Park walk includes a massive water feature and plantings of 68 varieties of roses. Maps are available at Palm Desert Visitor Center.

Palm Springs holds one of the largest collections of homes and public buildings designed by the famed Desert Moderne architects of the

1950s, Albert Frey, Richard Neutra, and William F. Cody. You can see many of these beauties on tours assembled by the cities of Palm Springs and Palm Desert; the Palm Springs Visitor Center also offers three-hour tours to these mid-century landmarks (you can also pick up a copy of *Palm Springs: Brief History and Architectural Guide* here). If you'd rather go it alone, pick up a map and guide to more than 40 distinctive mid-century buildings at the Palm Desert Visitor Center.

Contacts **Desert Adventures** (✉ *74-794 Lennon Pl., Suite A, Palm Desert* ☎ *760/340-2345* ⊕ *www.red-jeep.com*). **Desert Safari Guides** (✉ *Box 8394, Palm Springs 92263* ☎ *760/325-4453 or 888/324-4453* ⊕ *www.palmspringshiking.com*). **Elite Land Tours** (✉ *555 S. Sunrise Way, Suite 200, Palm Springs* ☎ *760/318-1200* ⊕ *www.elitelandtours.com*). **Eco-Adventure Tours** (✉ *62-950 20th Ave., North Palm Springs* ☎ *760/251-1997* ⊕ *www.windmilltours.com*). **Palm Desert Visitor Center** (✉ *72-567 Hwy. 111, Palm Desert* ☎ *760/568-1441* ⊕ *www.palm-desert. org*). **Palm Springs Celebrity Tours** (✉ *4751 E. Palm Canyon Dr., Palm Springs* ☎ *760/770-2700*). **Palm Springs Visitor Center** (✉ *2901 N. Palm Canyon Dr., Palm Springs* ☎ *760/318-6118* ⊕ *www.palm-springs.org*).

VISITOR INFORMATION

Contacts **Borrego Springs Chamber of Commerce** (✉ *786 Palm Canyon Dr., Borrego Springs* ☎ *760/767-5555 or 800/559-5524* ⊕ *www.borregosprings.org*). **Palm Springs Desert Resorts Convention and Visitors Authority** (✉ *70-100 Hwy. 111, Rancho Mirage* ☎ *760/770-9000 or 800/967-3767* ⊕ *www.giveinto thedesert.com*). **Palm Springs Visitor Information Center** (✉ *2901 N. Palm Canyon Dr., Palm Springs* ☎ *800/347-7746* ⊕ *www.palm-springs.org*). **Twentynine Chamber and Visitor Bureau** (✉ *73666 Civic Center Dr., Suite D, Twentynine Palms* ☎ *760/367-3445*).

Joshua Tree National Park

WORD OF MOUTH

"Take your time here, too, and let the desert take hold of you. Joshua Tree National Park provides a haven from everyday routines, space for self-discovery, a refuge for the human spirit, and a sense of place in the greater scheme of things."

—Ed Zahniser, National Park Service

WELCOME TO JOSHUA TREE NATIONAL PARK

TOP REASONS TO GO

★ **Rock climbing:** Joshua Tree is a world-class site with challenges for climbers of just about every skill level.

★ **Peace and quiet:** Savor the solitude of one of the last great wildernesses in America.

★ **Stargazing:** You'll be mesmerized by the Milky Way flowing across the dark night sky. For spectacular natural fireworks, visit in mid-August during the Perseid meteor shower and watch shooting stars streak overhead.

★ **Wildflowers:** In spring, the hillsides explode in a patchwork of yellow, blue, pink, and white.

★ **Sunsets:** Twilight is a special time here, especially during the winter, when the setting sun casts a golden glow on the mountains.

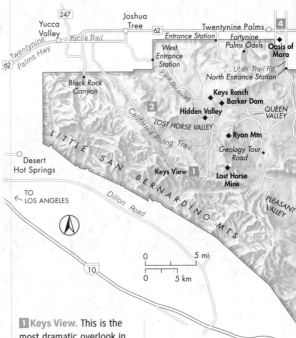

1 Keys View. This is the most dramatic overlook in the park—on clear days you can see the Signal Mountains in Mexico.

2 Hidden Valley. Crawl between the big rocks and you'll understand why this boulder-strewn area was once a cattle rustlers' hideout.

3 Cholla Cactus Gardens. Come here in the late afternoon, when the spiky stalks of the bigelow (jumping) cholla cactus is backlit against an intense blue sky.

4 Oasis of Mara. Walk the nature trail around this desert oasis, which the first settlers, the Serrano, dubbed "the place of little springs and much grass."

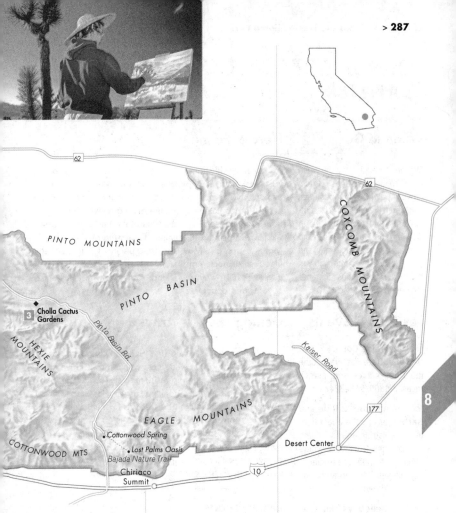

PINTO MOUNTAINS

COXCOMB MOUNTAINS

62

62

PINTO BASIN

Pinto Basin Rd.

◆ Cholla Cactus
3 Gardens

HEXIE MOUNTAINS

Kaiser Road

EAGLE MOUNTAINS

177

8

● Cottonwood Spring

COTTONWOOD MTS

● Lost Palms Oasis
Bajada Nature Trail

Desert Center

Chiriaco
Summit

10

GETTING ORIENTED

Dagger-like tufts grace the branches of the namesake of Joshua Tree National Park in southeastern California, where the arid Mojave Desert meets the sparsely vegetated Colorado Desert (part of the Sonoran Desert, which lies within California and Northern Mexico). Passenger cars are fine for paved areas, but you'll need four-wheel drive for many of the rugged backcountry roadways. At the park's most popular sites, parking is limited. Joshua Tree does not have public transportation.

Rock climbng

JOSHUA TREE NATIONAL PARK PLANNER

When to Go

October through May, is when most of Joshua Tree's visitors arrive. Daytime temperatures range from the mid-70s in December and January to mid-90s in October and May. Lows can dip to near freezing in mid-winter, and you may even encounter snow at the higher elevations. Summer temperatures can reach 110°F.

Flora & Fauna

Joshua Tree will shatter your notions of the desert as a vast wasteland. Life flourishes in this land of little rain, as flora and fauna have adapted to heat and drought. In most areas you'll be walking among native Joshua trees, ocotillos, and yuccas. One of the best spring desert wildflower displays in Southern California blooms here in March, April, and May. You'll see plenty of animals—reptiles such as nocturnal sidewinders, birds like golden eagles or burrowing owls, and occasionally mammals like coyotes and bobcats.

Festivals & Events

FEB. Riverside County Fair & National Date Festival. Come Indio for camel and ostrich races. ☎ 800/811–3247.

MAY Pony Express Ride and Barbecue. This reenactment of the historic mail delivery service runs from Twentynine Palms or Joshua Tree (depending on year) to Pioneertown. ☎ 760/365–6323.

OCT. Pioneer Days. Outhouse races, beard contests, and arm-wrestling mark this annual celebration in Twentynine Palms. ☎ 760/367–3445.

Getting There & Around

A rarity these days, Joshua Tree National Park is an isolated island of pristine wilderness within a short drive of 11 million Southern California residents. Most visitors, in fact, make the two-hour drive from the Los Angeles area to enjoy a weekend of solitude in 585,000 acres of untouched desert. The urban sprawl of Palm Springs is 45 mi away, but gateway towns Joshua Tree and Twentynine Palms are just north of the park. You can see the park's highlights in about a day, but you'll need to spend two or three days here to truly experience the quiet beauty of the desert.

Great Reads

If you want a general introduction to hiking in Joshua Tree, try **On Foot in Joshua Tree,** by Patty Furbush, which lists more than 90 trails in the park.

AVG. HIGH/LOW TEMPS.

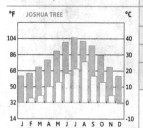

°F	JOSHUA TREE	°C
104		40
86		30
68		20
50		10
32		0
14		-10
	J F M A M J J A S O N D	

WHAT IT COSTS

	¢	$	$$	$$$	$$$$
Camping					
	under $10	$10–$17	$18–$35	$36–$50	over $50

Camping prices are for a standard (no hookups, pit toilets, fire grates, picnic tables) campsite per night.

By Bobbi Zane

Ruggedly beautiful desert scenery attracts nearly 2 million visitors each year to Joshua Tree National Park, one of the last great wildernesses in the continental United States. Its mountains support mounds of enormous boulders and jagged rock; natural cactus gardens and lush oases shaded by tall fan palms mark the meeting place of the Mojave (high) and Sonora (low) deserts. Extensive stands of Joshua trees give the park its name; the plants (really shrubs) reminded early white settlers of the biblical Joshua, with their thick, stubby branches representing the prophet raising his arms toward heaven.

The park stands at 1,239 square mi, most of it roadless wilderness. Elevation in some areas of the park exceeds 5,000 feet, and light snowfalls and cold, strong north winds are common in winter. There are no services within the park and little water, so you should carry at least a gallon of water per person per day. Apply sunscreen liberally at any time of the year.

SCENIC DRIVES

Geology Tour Road. Some of the park's most fascinating landscapes can be observed from this 18-mi dirt road. Parts of the journey are rough, so make sure you have a 4x4. Sights to see include a 100-year-old stone dam called Squaw Tank, defunct mines, and a large plain with an abundance of Joshua trees. There are 16 stops along the way, so give yourself about two hours to make the round-trip. ⊠ *South of Park Blvd., west of Jumbo Rocks.*

★ **Park Boulevard.** Traversing the most scenic portions of Joshua Tree, this well-paved road connects the north and west entrances in the park's high desert section. Along with some sweeping desert views, you'll see jumbles of splendid boulder formations, extensive stands of Joshua trees, and Hidden Valley and Barker Dam, remnants of the area's wild and woolly past. From the Oasis Visitor Center, drive south. After about 5 mi, the road forks; turn right and head west toward Jumbo Rocks (clearly marked with a road sign).

WHAT TO SEE

HISTORIC SITES

Barker Dam. Built around 1900 by ranchers and miners to hold water for cattle and mining operations, the dam now collects rainwater and is used by elusive bighorn sheep and other wildlife. ⊠ *Barker Dam Rd., off Park Blvd., 14 mi south of West Entrance.*

Hidden Valley. This legendary cattle-rustlers hideout is set among big boulders, which kids love to scramble over and around. ⊠ *Park Blvd., 14 mi south of West Entrance.*

★ **Keys Ranch.** This 150-acre ranch once belonged to William and Frances Keys and illustrates one of the area's most successful attempts at homesteading. The couple raised five children under extreme desert conditions. Most of the original buildings, including the house, school, store, and workshop, have been restored to the way it was when William died in 1969. The only way to see the ranch is on one of the 60-minute, ranger-led walking tours, offered weekdays between October and May. ⊠ *2 mi north of Barker Dam Rd.* ☎ *760/367–5555* ⊛ *Reservations essential* ⊠ *$5* ⊙ *Oct.–May, tours weekdays at 10 and 1.*

Lost Horse Mine. This historic mine illustrates the gold prospecting and mining activities that took place here in the late 1800s. The site is accessed via a fairly strenuous 2-mi hike. ⊠ *Keys View Rd., about 15 mi south of West Entrance.*

SCENIC STOPS

Cholla Cactus Garden. This stand of bigelow cholla (sometimes called jumping cholla, since its hooked spines seem to jump at you) is best seen and photographed in late afternoon, when the backlit spiky stalks stand out against a colorful sky. ⊠ *Pinto Basin Rd., 20 mi north of Cottonwood Visitor Center.*

Cottonwood Spring Oasis. Noted for its abundant birdlife, this is an example of the palm-shaded oases that were a welcome sight to prospectors traveling through the area. The remains of an *arrastra,* a primitive type of gold mill, can be found nearby. Bighorn sheep frequent this area in winter. Take the 1-mi paved trail that begins at sites 13A and 13B of the Cottonwood Campground. ⊠ *Cottonwood Visitor Center.*

Fortynine Palms Oasis. Sights within the oasis include stands of fan palms, interesting petroglyphs, and evidence of fires built by early Native Americans. Since animals frequent this area, you may spot a coyote, bobcat, or roadrunner. ⊠ *End of Canyon Rd., 4 mi west of Twentynine Palms.*

★ **Keys View.** At 5,185 feet, this point affords a sweeping view of the Coachella Valley, the mountains of the San Bernardino National Forest, and—on a rare clear day—Signal Mountain in Mexico. Sunrise and sunset are magical times, when the light throws rocks and trees into high relief before bathing the hills in brilliant shades of red, orange, and gold. ⊠ *Keys View Rd., 21 mi south of West Entrance.*

> **LOOK, DON'T TOUCH–REALLY**
>
> Some cactus needles, like those on the cholla, can become embedded in your skin with just the slightest touch. If you do get zapped, use tweezers to gently pull it out.

Lost Palms Oasis. More than 100 palms comprise the largest group of the exotic plants in the park. A spring bubbles from between the rocks but disappears into the sandy, boulder-strewn canyon. As you hike along the 4-mi trail, you might spot bighorn sheep. ⊠ *Cottonwood Visitor Center.*

Ocotillo Patch. Stop here for a roadside exhibit on the dramatic display made by the red-tipped succulent after even the shortest rain shower. ⊠ *Pinto Basin Rd., about 3 mi east of Cholla Cactus Gardens.*

VISITOR CENTERS

Cottonwood Visitor Center. Exhibits in this small center, staffed by rangers and volunteers, illustrate the region's natural history. ⊠ *Pinto Basin Rd.* ☎ *No phone* ⊕ *www.nps.gov/jotr* ☉ *Daily 8–4.*

Joshua Tree Visitor Center. This visitor center, opened in summer 2006, holds exhibits illustrating park geology, cultural and historic sites, and hiking and rock-climbing activities. There's also a small bookstore. ⊠ *6554 Park Blvd.* ☎ *760/367–5500* ⊕ *www.nps.gov/jotr* ☉ *Daily 8–5.*

Oasis Visitor Center. Exhibits here illustrate how Joshua Tree was formed, reveal the differences between the two types of desert within the park, and demonstrate how plants and animals eke out an existence in this arid climate. Take the ½-mi nature walk through the nearby Oasis of Mara, which is alive with cottonwood trees, palm trees, and mesquite shrubs. ⊠ *74485 National Park Dr., Twentynine Palms* ☎ *760/367–5500* ⊕ *www.nps.gov/jotr* ☉ *Daily 8–5.*

SPORTS & THE OUTDOORS

BICYCLING

Mountain biking is a great way to see Joshua Tree. With newer routes opened in backcountry areas, there are plenty of trails waiting to be explored. Keep in mind that all except Thermal Canyon are also open to horseback riding.

Black Eagle Mountain Road. This dead-end, 9-mi road peppered with defunct mines runs along the edge of a former lake bed, then crosses a number of dry washes before navigating several of Eagle Mountain's canyons. ⊠ *Off Pinto Basin Rd., 6½ mi north of Cottonwood Visitor Center.*

Covington Flats. This 4-mi trail leads you past some of the park's most impressive Joshua trees as well as pinyon pines, junipers, and areas of lush desert vegetation. It's tough going toward the end, but once you reach 5,516-foot Eureka Peak, you'll have great views of Palm Springs, the Morongo Basin, and the surrounding mountains. ⊠ *Covington Flats picnic area, La Contenta Rd., 10 mi south of Rte. 62.*

Old Dale Road. The first 11 mi of this 23-mi route run across Pinto Basin to the Old Dale Mining District, where several side roads head off toward dusty old shafts. Here you'll find Mission Well, dug to provide water for the area's mines and mills. The vegetation is remarkably varied, including tiny yellow chinchweed and desert willows. ⊠ *Off Pinto Basin Rd., 7 mi north of Cottonwood Visitor Center.*

Pinkham Canyon Road. This challenging 20-mi trail follows Smoke Tree Wash, then descends into Pinkham Canyon. Be careful—the route crosses some soft sand. ⊠ *Starts at Cottonwood Visitor Center.*

Queen Valley. This 13.4-mi network of mostly level dirt roads winds through one of the park's most impressive groves of Joshua trees. Bike racks at the Barker Dam and Hidden Valley trailheads allow you to park your ride and go hiking. ⊠ *Hidden Valley Campground.*

Thermal Canyon Bike Trail. This newly opened 10-mi trail—intended for mountain bikers who want a wilderness experience—follows a rigorous route along Berdoo Canyon Road through a rugged portion of the Cottonwood Mountains; the views are lovely. ⊠ *Off Geology Tour Rd.*

OUTFITTERS &   **Big Wheel Tours.** Based in Palm Desert, Big Wheel offers Jeep, bike,
EXPEDITIONS   and hike excursions through the park. ⊠ *Box 4185, Palm Desert* ☎ *760/779–1837* ⊕ *www.bwbtours.com* ⊠ *$95–$149 per person.*

BIRD-WATCHING

Birding is a popular pastime in Joshua Tree. During the fall migration, which runs from mid-September through mid-October, there are several reliable sighting areas. At Barker Dam you might spot white-throated swifts, several types of swallows, or red-tailed hawks. Lucy's warbler, lesser goldfinches, and Anna's hummingbirds cruise around Cottonwood Spring, a serene tree-shaded setting where you'll likely see the largest concentrations of birds in the park. At Black Rock Canyon and Covington Flats, you're likely to see LaConter's thrashers, ruby crowned kinglets, and warbling vireos. Rufus hummingbirds, Pacific slope flycatchers, and various warblers are frequent visitors to Indian Cove.

HIKING

There are more than 50 mi of hiking trails in Joshua Tree, ranging from ¼-mi treks to 35-mi journeys. Many cross each other, so you can design your own desert maze. Remember that drinking water is hard to come by—you won't find water in the park except at the entrances. Bring along at least a gallon per person for all but the shortest hikes, more if the weather is hot. Before striking out on a hike or apparent

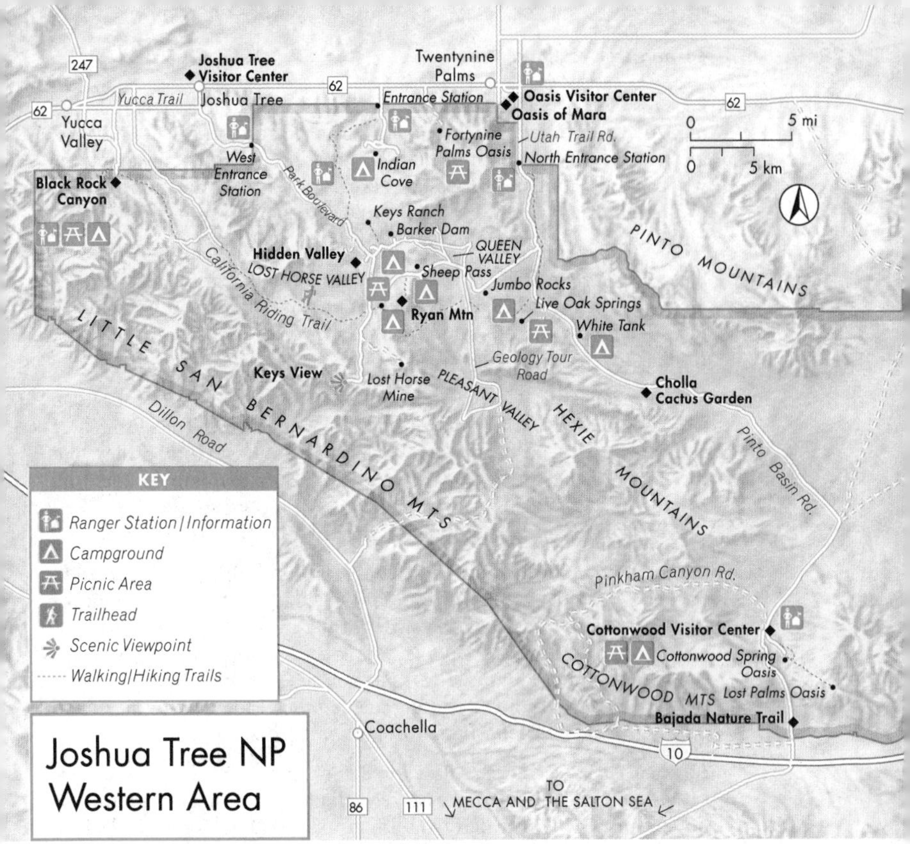
247
62
Joshua Tree Visitor Center
Twentynine Palms
Yucca Trail
Joshua Tree
Entrance Station
Oasis Visitor Center
Oasis of Mara
Yucca Valley
Fortynine Palms Oasis
Utah Trail Rd.
North Entrance Station
0 5 mi
0 5 km
West Entrance Station
Indian Cove
Black Rock Canyon
Park Boulevard
Keys Ranch
Barker Dam
PINTO MOUNTAINS
QUEEN VALLEY
Hidden Valley
LOST HORSE VALLEY
Sheep Pass
California Riding Trail
Jumbo Rocks
Live Oak Springs
Ryan Mtn
White Tank
LITTLE SAN BERNARDINO MTS
Geology Tour Road
Keys View
Lost Horse Mine
PLEASANT VALLEY
HEXIE MOUNTAINS
Cholla Cactus Garden
Dillon Road
Pinto Basin Rd.
KEY
Ranger Station/Information
Campground
Picnic Area
Trailhead
Scenic Viewpoint
Walking/Hiking Trails
Pinkham Canyon Rd.
Cottonwood Visitor Center
Cottonwood Spring Oasis
COTTONWOOD MTS
Lost Palms Oasis
Bajada Nature Trail
Coachella
10
86
111
TO MECCA AND THE SALTON SEA
Joshua Tree NP Western Area

nature trail, check out the signage. Hiking trails are marked with a hiking figure; similar signs without the hiking figure identify rock-climbing routes.

EASY **Bajada All Access.** Learn all about what plants do to survive in the desert on this easy, wheelchair accessible ¼-mi loop. ✉ *South of Cottonwood Visitor Center, ½ mi from park entrance.*

Cap Rock. This ½-mi wheelchair accessible loop—named after a boulder that sits atop a huge rock formation like a cap—winds through fascinating rock formations and has signs that explain the geology of the Mojave Desert. ✉ *Junction of Park Blvd. and Keys View Rd.*

Indian Cove Trail. Look for lizards and roadrunners along this ½-mi loop that follows a desert wash. This easy trail has signs with interesting facts about these and other animals of the Mojave Desert. ✉ *West end of Indian Cove Campground.*

Skull Rock Trail. The ¼-mi loop guides hikers through boulder piles, desert washes, and a rocky alley. It's named for what is perhaps the park's most famous rock formation, which resembles a human head. ✉ *Jumbo Rocks Campground.*

MODERATE   **California Riding and Hiking Trail.** This well-traveled route stretches for 35 mi between the Black Rock Canyon Entrance and the North Entrance. No need to hike the entire trail, however. Start at any point along the way, including where it crosses major roads near Ryan Campground or Belle Campground, for hikes from 4 to 11 mi. ⊠ *Trailheads at Covington Flats, Keys View, and Squaw Tank.*

High View Nature Trail. This 1.3-mi loop climbs nearly to the top of 4,500-foot Summit Peak. The views of nearby Mt. San Gorgonio make the moderately steep journey worth the effort. ⊠ *½ mi west of Black Rock Canyon Campground.*

Fodor'sChoice   **Ryan Mountain Trail.** The payoff for hiking to the top of 5,461-foot Ryan
★   Mountain is one of the best panoramic views of Joshua Tree. From here you can see Mt. San Jacinto, Mt. San Gorgonio, Lost Horse Valley, and the Pinto Basin. You'll need two to three hours to complete the 3-mi round-trip. ⊠ *Ryan Mountain parking area, 16 mi southeast of West Entrance or Sheep Pass, 16 mi southwest of Oasis Visitor Center.*

DIFFICULT   **Boy Scout Trail.** The moderately strenuous 16-mi trail, suitable for backpackers, runs through the westernmost edge of the Wonderland of Rocks, passing through a forest of Joshua trees, past granite towers, and around willow-lined pools. Completing the round-trip journey requires camping along the way, so you may want to hike only part of the trail or have a car waiting at the other end. ⊠ *Between Quail Springs Picnic Area and Indian Cove Campground.*

Fortynine Palms Oasis Trail. Allow three hours for this moderately strenuous 3-mi trek. The trail makes a steep climb into the hills, then it drops down into a canyon where you'll find an oasis lined with fan palms. There's plenty of evidence of Native Americans in this area, from traces of cooking fires to rocks carved with petroglyphs. ⊠ *End of Canyon Rd., 4 mi west of Twentynine Palms.*

Lost Horse Mine Trail. This fairly strenuous 4-mi round-trip hike follows a former mining road to a well-preserved mill that was used in the 1890s to crush gold-encrusted rock mined from the nearby mountain. The operation was one of the area's most successful, and the mine's cyanide settling tanks and stone buildings are the area's best preserved. From the mill area, a short but steep 10-minute side trip takes you to the top of a 5,278-foot peak with great views of the valley. ⊠ *1¼ mi east of Keys View Rd.*

Lost Palms Oasis Trail. Allow four to six hours for the moderately strenuous, 7½-mi round-trip, which leads to the most impressive oasis in the park. You'll find more than 100 fan palms and an abundance of wildflowers here. ⊠ *Cottonwood Spring Oasis.*

★   **Mastodon Peak Trail.** Some boulder scrambling is required on this 3-mi hike up 3,371-foot Mastodon Peak, but the journey rewards you with stunning views of the Salton Sea. The trail passes through a region where gold was mined from 1919 to 1932, so be on the lookout for open mines. The peak draws its name from a large rock formation that early miners believed looked like the head of a prehistoric behemoth. ⊠*Cottonwood Spring Oasis.*

OUTFITTERS & EXPEDITIONS

Joshua Tree Hiking Adventures. Joshua Tree Hiking Adventures leads easy to moderate to strenuous hikes, depending on your needs, to park destinations such as Quail Mountain, Pinto Mountain, Lost Horse Peak, and the remote Wonderland of Rocks; they also offer custom trips. Most hikes are three to six hours. ⊠*Box 1088, Joshua Tree* ☎*760/366–7985* ⊕*www.joshua treehike.com* ▨*$55–$240 per person depending upon number in party and duration* ☼*Daily.*

ROCK CLIMBING

FodorsChoice ★

With an abundance of weathered igneous boulder outcroppings, Joshua Tree is one of the nation's top winter climbing destinations and offers a full menu of climbing experiences—from bouldering for beginners in the Wonderland of Rocks to multiple-pitch climbs at Echo Rock and Saddle Rock. The best-known climb in the park is Hidden Valley's Sports Challenge Rock. A map inside the *Joshua Tree Guide* shows locations of selected wilderness and nonwilderness climbs.

OUTFITTERS & EXPEDITIONS

Backcountry Found conducts two-day backpacking/rock-climbing excursions. Climbing gear, instructions, group camping, and most meals are included. They also offer custom-designed trips. ⊠*221 Noe St. #200, San Francisco* ☎*415/710–8158* ▨*$750 per person* ☼*Apr. and Nov.*

Joshua Tree Rock Climbing School offers several programs, from one-day introductory classes to multiday programs for experienced climbers. The school provides all needed equipment. Beginning classes are limited to six people age 10 or older (children under 13 must be accompanied by parent). ▱*Box 3034, Joshua Tree, 92252* ☎*760/366–4745 or 800/890–4745* ⊕*www.joshuatreerockclimbing.com* ▨*$120 for beginner class* ☼*Aug.–June.*

Vertical Adventures Rock Climbing School trains about 1,000 climbers each year in Joshua Tree National Park. Classes meet at a designated location in the park, and all equipment is provided. ☎*800/514–8785* ⊕*www.verticaladventures.com* ▨*$125 per person for one-day class* ☼*Sept.–June.*

GUIDED TOURS

Desert Adventures. Red Jeep tours combine excursions on roads less traveled with hikes and nature walks. ⊠ *74794 Lennon Pl., Suite A, Palm Desert* ☎ *888/440–5337* ⊕ *www.red-jeep.com* ▨ *$150 per person* ☼ *Daily in fall, winter, spring.*

Elite Land Tours. This luxury outfitter conducts half-day Hummer tours through the park's backcountry and evening excursions that utilize night-vision equipment. ⊠ *555 S. Sunrise Way, Suite 200, Palm Springs* ☎ *760/318–1200* ⊕ *www.elitelandtours.com* ▨ *$150 per person* ☼ *Daily.*

8

WHERE TO STAY & EAT

ABOUT THE CAMPGROUNDS

Joshua Tree's campgrounds, set at elevations from 3,000 to 4,500 feet, have only primitive facilities; few have drinking water. With the exception of Black Rock and Indian Cove campgrounds—which accept reservations up to five months in advance (☎800/365–2267)—campsites are on a first-come, first-served basis. During the busy fall and spring weekends, plan to arrive early in the day to ensure a site, or if you have an organized group, reserve one of the group sites in advance. Temperatures can drop at night during any part of the year—bring a sweater or light jacket. If you plan to camp in late winter or early spring, be prepared for the gusty Santa Ana winds that may sweep through the park. Backcountry camping is permitted in certain wilderness areas of Joshua Tree. You must sign in at a backcountry register board if you plan to stay overnight. For more information, stop at the visitor centers or ranger stations.

PICNIC AREAS

Black Rock Canyon. Set among Joshua trees, pinyon pines, and junipers, this popular picnic area has barbecue grills and drinking water. It's one of the few with flush toilets. ⊠ *End of Joshua Lane at the Black Rock Canyon Campground.*

Cottonwood Spring. Shady trees make this a pleasant place to picnic. It has drinking water and restrooms with flush toilets. ⊠ *On Pinto Basin Rd., adjacent to visitor center.*

Covington Flats. This is a great place to get away from crowds. There's just one table, and it's surrounded by flat open desert dotted here and there by Joshua trees. ⊠ *La Contenta Rd., 10 mi from Rte. 62.*

Hidden Valley. Set among huge rock formations, with picnic tables shaded by dense trees, this is one of the most pleasant places in the park to stop for lunch. ⊠ *Park Blvd., 14 mi south of the West Entrance.*

Indian Cove. The view here is rock formations that draw thousands of climbers to the park each year. This isolated area is reached via Twentynine Palms Highway. ⊠ *End of Indian Cove Rd.*

Live Oak Springs. Tucked among piles of boulders, this picnic area in the midst of interesting rock formations is near a stand of Joshua trees. ⊠ *Park Blvd., east of Jumbo Rocks.*

CAMPGROUNDS & RV PARKS

$$–$$$ ⛺ **Sheep Pass Campground.** At 4,500 feet, Sheep Pass is the highest campground in the park. It's also the smallest—it has only six sites, all designated for groups. The campsites, set among boulders and relatively dense vegetation, are fairly private. ⊠ *Park Blvd., 16 mi from Oasis of Mara* ☎760/367–5500, 877/444–6777 *for reservations* ⊕*www. recreation.gov* ⇄31 *group sites* ⛁*Pit toilets, fire pits, picnic tables* ⚓*Reservations essential* ⊟*D, MC, V* ☉*Year-round.*

$ ⛺ **Black Rock Canyon Campground.** Set among juniper bushes, cholla cacti, and other desert shrubs, Black Rock Canyon is one of the prettiest campgrounds in Joshua Tree. South of Yucca Valley, it's the closest campground to most of the desert communities. Located on the California Riding and Hiking Trail, it has facilities for horses and mules. ⊠*Joshua Lane, south of Hwy. 62 and Hwy. 247* ☎*760/367–5500, 877/444–6777 for reservations* ⊕*www.recreation.gov* ⚑*100 sites* ⚭*Flush toilets, dump station, drinking water, fire pits, picnic tables, ranger station* ▤*D, MC, V* ☙*Year-round.*

$ △**Cottonwood Campground.** In spring this campground, the southernmost one in the park (and therefore often the last to fill up), is surrounded by some of the desert's finest wildflowers. Reservations are not accepted. ⊠*Pinto Basin Rd., 32 mi south of North Entrance Station* ☎*760/367–5500* ⊕*www.recreation.gov* ⚑*62 sites, 3 group sites* ⚭*Flush toilets, dump station, fire pits, picnic tables, ranger station* ▤*D, MC, V* ☙*Year-round.*

$ △**Indian Cove Campground.** This is a very sought-after spot for rock climbers, primarily because it lies among the 50 square mi of rugged terrain at the Wonderland of Rocks. Popular climbs near the campground include Pixie Rock, Feudal Wall, and Corral Wall. Call ahead to reserve one of the 13 group sites. ⊠*Indian Cove Rd., south of Hwy. 62* ☎*760/367–5500, 877/444–6777 for reservations* ⊕*www.recreation. gov* ⚑*101 sites, 13 group sites* ⚭*Pit toilets, fire pits, picnic tables* ⚭*Reservations essential* ▤*D, MC, V* ☙*Year-round.*

¢ △**Belle Campground.** This small campground is popular with families, as there are a number of boulders kids can scramble over and around. Campsites here are small and not recommended for recreational vehicles. First come, first served. ⊠*9 mi south of Oasis of Mara* ☎*760/367–5500* ⊕*www.nps.gov/jotr* ⚑*18 sites* ⚭*Pit toilets, fire pits, picnic tables* ☙*Year-round.*

¢ △**Hidden Valley Campground.** This campground is a favorite with rock climbers, who make their way up valley formations that have names like the Blob, Old Woman, and Chimney Rock. RVs are permitted, but there are no hookups. First come, first served. ⊠*Off Park Blvd., 20 mi southwest of Oasis of Mara* ☎*760/367–5500* ⊕*www.nps.gov/ jotr* ⚑*39 sites* ⚭*Pit toilets, fire pits, picnic tables* ⚭*Reservations not accepted* ☙*Year-round.*

¢ △**Jumbo Rocks.** Each campsite at this well-regarded campground tucked among giant boulders has a bit of privacy. It's a good home base for visiting many of Joshua Tree's attractions, including Geology Tour Road. ⊠*Park Blvd., 11 mi from Oasis of Mara* ☎*760/367–5500* ⊕*www.nps.gov/jotr* ⚑*125 sites* ⚭*Pit toilets, fire pits, picnic tables* ⚭*Reservations not accepted* ☙*Year-round.*

¢ △**Ryan Campground.** At the foot of Ryan Mountain, this primitive campground is east of the turnoff leading to Keys View and Lost Horse Mine. Although there are no facilities for them, horses are permitted here. ⊠*16 mi south of West Entrance* ☎*760/367–5500, 760/367–5540 to reserve horse camp* ⊕*www.nps.gov/jotr* ⚑*31 sites* ⚭*Pit toilets, fire pits, picnic tables* ⚭*Reservations not accepted* ☙*Year-round.*

¢ △**White Tank.** This small, quiet campground is popular with families because a nearby trail leads to a natural arch. Campsites are small and not recommended for RVs or trailers. ⊠*Pinto Basin Rd., 11 mi*

8

south of Oasis of Mara   ☎*760/367–5500* ⊕*www.nps.gov/jotr* ⟳*15 sites* ♿*Pit toilets, fire pits, picnic tables* 🏕*Reservations not accepted* ⊙*Year-round.*

JOSHUA TREE ESSENTIALS

ACCESSIBILITY
Black Rock Canyon and Jumbo Rocks campgrounds each have one accessible campsite. Nature trails at Oasis of Mara, Bajada, Keys View, and Cap Rock are accessible. Some trails at roadside viewpoints can be negotiated by those with limited mobility.

ADMISSION FEES
$15 per car, $5 per person on foot. The Joshua Tree Pass, good for one year, is $30.

ADMISSION HOURS
The park is open every day, around the clock. Oasis Visitor Center is open daily 8–5; Cottonwood Visitor Center, daily 8–4; Joshua Tree Visitor Center, daily 8–5; park 24 hours. The park is in the Pacific time zone.

EMERGENCIES
Emergency assistance within Joshua Tree is limited. Emergency-only phones are at Intersection Rock at the entrance to Hidden Valley Campground and Indian Cove Campground; call San Bernardino Dispatch at (909) 383–5651, or dial 911.

LOST AND FOUND
Report any lost or found items at any of the park's visitor centers.

PERMITS
Free permits—available at all visitor centers—are required for rock climbing.

PUBLIC TELEPHONES
Pay phones are at Oasis Visitor Center and Black Rock Canyon Campground. There are no telephones in the interior of the park, and cell phones don't work in most areas.

VISITOR INFORMATION
Contacts **Joshua Tree National Park** ✉ *74485 National Park Dr., Twentynine Palms* ☎ *760/367–5500* 📠 *760/367–6392* ⊕ *www.nps.gov/jotr.*

Death Valley National Park

Sand dunes, Death Valley

WORD OF MOUTH

"This valley we call Death isn't really that different from much of the rest of the desert West. It's just a little deeper, a little hotter, and a little drier. What sets it apart more than anything else is the mind's eye. For it is a land of illusion, a place in the mind, a shimmering mirage of riches and mystery and death. These illusions have distorted its landscape and contorted its history."

—Richard E. Lingenfelter, *Death Valley & The Amargosa: A Land of Illusion*

WELCOME TO DEATH VALLEY

TOP REASONS TO GO

★ **Weird science:** Death Valley's Racetrack is home to moving boulders, an unexplained phenomenon that has scientists baffled.

★ **Lowest spot on the continent:** Stand on the lowest spot on the continent at Badwater, 282 feet below sea level.

★ **Wildflower explosion:** During the spring, this desert landscape is ablaze with greenery and colorful flowers, especially south of Badwater and north of Ashford Mill.

★ **Ghost towns:** Death Valley is renowned for its Wild West heritage and is home to dozens of crumbling settlements including Ballarat, Cerro Gordo, Chloride City, Greenwater, Harrisburg, Keeler, Leadfield, Panamint City, Rhyolite, and Skidoo.

★ **Natural wonders:** From canyons to sand dunes to salt flats and dry lake beds, Death Valley serves up plenty of geological treasures.

1 Central Death Valley. Furnace Creek sits in the heart of Death Valley—if you only have a short time in the park, this is where you'll want to start. You can visit gorgeous Golden Canyon, Zabriskie Point, the Salt Creek Interpretive Trail, and Artist's Drive, among other popular points of interest.

2 Northern Death Valley. For more action, stay in Beatty, Nevada, where you can gamble in the casino by night and play in the park by day. Be sure to stop by Rhyolite Ghost Town on Highway 374 before entering the park and exploring Moorish Scotty's Castle, colorful Titus Canyon, crumbling Keane Wonder Mine, and jaw-dropping Ubehebe Crater.

3 Southern Death Valley. This is a desolate area, but there are plenty of sights that help convey Death Valley's rich history. Don't miss the Dublin Gulch Caves, or the famous Amargosa Opera House, where aging ballerina Marta Beckett still wows the crowds.

Mule Train

4 Western Death Valley. Panamint Springs Resort is a nice place to grab a meal and get your bearings before moving on to quaint Darwin Falls, smooth, rolling sand dunes, beehive-shaped Wildrose Charcoal Kilns, and historic Stovepipe Wells Village. On the way in, stop at Cerro Gordo Ghost Town, where you can view restored buildings dating back to 1867.

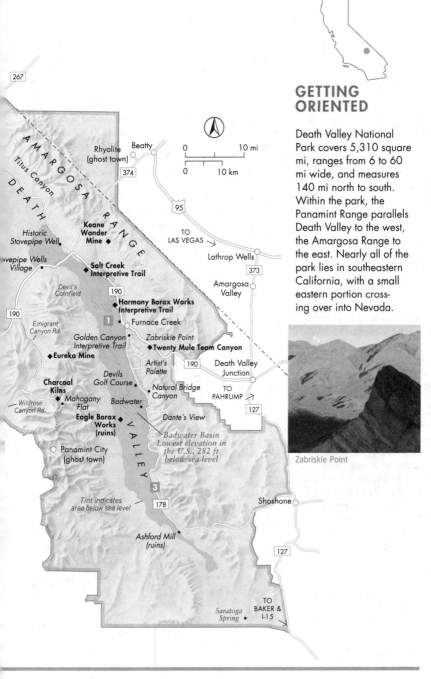

GETTING ORIENTED

Death Valley National Park covers 5,310 square mi, ranges from 6 to 60 mi wide, and measures 140 mi north to south. Within the park, the Panamint Range parallels Death Valley to the west, the Amargosa Range to the east. Nearly all of the park lies in southeastern California, with a small eastern portion crossing over into Nevada.

Zabriskie Point

9

Map labels

267

Rhyolite (ghost town)
Beatty
374
95
0   10 mi
0   10 km

TO LAS VEGAS

Lathrop Wells
373
Amargosa Valley

AMARGOSA RANGE
Titus Canyon
DEATH

Historic Stovepipe Well
Keane Wonder Mine
vepipe Wells Village
Salt Creek Interpretive Trail
Devil's Cornfield
190
Harmony Borax Works Interpretive Trail
190
Emigrant Canyon Rd.
1
Furnace Creek
Golden Canyon Interpretive Trail
Zabriskie Point
Eureka Mine
Twenty Mule Team Canyon
Artist's Palette
190
Death Valley Junction
Devils Golf Course
Charcoal Kilns
Natural Bridge Canyon
TO PAHRUMP
Wildrose Canyon Rd.
Mahogany Flat
Badwater
127
Eagle Borax Works (ruins)
Dante's View
VALLEY
Panamint City (ghost town)
Badwater Basin
Lowest elevation in the U.S., 282 ft below sea level

Tint indicates area below sea level
178
3
Shoshone

Ashford Mill (ruins)
127

Saratoga Spring
TO BAKER & I-15

DEATH VALLEY NATIONAL PARK PLANNER

When to Go

Most of the park's 1 million annual visitors still come between late fall and early spring, taking advantage of moderate temperatures and the lack of rainfall. During these cooler months you will need to book a room in advance, but don't worry: the park never feels crowded. If you visit during summer, believe everything you've ever heard about desert heat—it can be brutal. The dry air wicks moisture from the body without causing a sweat, so remember to drink plenty of water. Bring sunglasses, a hat, and sufficient clothing to block the sun's rays and the wind. Because there's little vegetation to soak up the rain and keep soil together, flash floods are common; sections of roadway can be flooded or washed away. The wettest month of the year is February, when the park receives an average of 3/10-inch of rain. You can check the park's daily weather report online at www.nps.gov/deva/planyourvisit/weather.htm.

AVG. HIGH/LOW TEMPS.

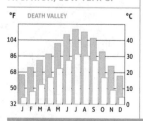

Flora & Fauna

There's a general misconception that Death Valley National Park consists of mile upon endless mile of flat desert sands, scattered cacti, and an occasional cow skull. Many people don't realize that across the valley floor from Badwater—the lowest point in the Western Hemisphere—Telescope Peak towers 11,049 feet above sea level. The extreme topography of Death Valley is a lesson in geology. Two hundred million years ago seas covered the area, depositing layers of sediment and fossils. Between 3.5 million and 5 million years ago faults in the Earth's crust and volcanic activity pushed and folded the ground, causing mountain ranges to rise and the valley floor to drop. The valley was then filled periodically by lakes, which eroded the surrounding rocks into fantastic formations and deposited the salts that now cover the floor of the basin.

Most animal life in Death Valley (58 mammal, 37 reptile, 347 bird, and 6 amphibian species) is found near the limited sources of water. The bighorn sheep spend most of their time in the secluded upper reaches of the park's rugged canyons and ridges. Coyotes can often be seen lazing in the shade next to the golf course and have been known to run onto the fairways to steal a golf ball. The only native fish in the park is the pupfish, which grows to slightly longer than 1 inch. In winter, when the water is cold, the fish lie dormant in the bottom mud, becoming active again in spring. Because they are wary of large moving shapes, you must stand quietly over a pool at Salt Creek to see them.

Botanists say there are more than 1,000 species of plants here (21 exist nowhere else in the world), though many annual plants lie dormant as seeds for all but a few months in spring, when rains trigger a bloom. The rest congregate around limited sources of water. Most of the low-elevation vegetation grows around the oases at Furnace Creek and Scotty's Castle, where oleanders, palms, and salt cedar grow. At higher elevations you will find pinyon, juniper, and bristlecone pine.

Getting There & Around

It can take more than three hours to cross from one side of the park to another. If you're driving from Los Angeles, enter through the western portion along Highway 395; enter from the north at Beatty, Nevada, or via the central entrance at Death Valley Junction if you're coming from Las Vegas. Travelers from Orange County, San Diego, and the Inland Empire should access the park via I–15 north at Baker.

Distances can be deceiving within the park: what seems close can be very far away. Much of the park can be toured on regularly scheduled bus tours, but these often don't allow time for hikes to sites not seen from the road, such as Salt Creek, Golden Canyon, and Natural Bridge. The best option is to drive to a number of the sites, get out of the car, and walk.

When driving in Death Valley, reliable maps are a must, as signage is often limited or, in some places, nonexistent. Other important accessories include a compass, a mobile phone (though these don't always work in remote areas), and extra food and water (3 gallons per person per day is recommended, plus additional radiator water). If you're able to take a four-wheel-drive vehicle, bring it: many of Death Valley's most spectacular canyons are otherwise inaccessible. Be aware of possible winter closures or driving restrictions due to snow.

The **California State Department of Transportation Hotline** (☎916/445–7623 or 800/427–7623 ⊕www. dot.ca.gov) has updates on Death Valley road conditions. The **California Highway Patrol** (☎760/256–1727 near Barstow, 760/872–5900 near Bishop ⊕http://www.cad. chp.ca.gov/) offers the latest traffic incident information.

WHAT IT COSTS

	¢	$	$$	$$$	$$$$
Restaurants					
	under $8	$8–$12	$13–$20	$21–$30	over $30
Hotels					
	under $50	$50–$100	$101–$150	$151–$200	over $200
Camping					
	under $10	$10–$17	$18–$35	$36–$50	over $50

Festivals & Seasonal Events

MAR. Diaz Lake Trout Derby. The first Saturday of the month, you can take a shot at the "big one" in this fully stocked lake at 3,700 feet above sea level. Admission is free. ☎760/876-4444.

APR. Shoshone Desert Art Show. Admission is free for this annual arts-and-crafts show and sale weekend. ☎760/852–4254 or 775/727–5460.

MAY Bishop Mule Days. Headline entertainment includes top country music stars, steer roping, barbecues, country dances, and the longest-running nonmotorized parade in the United States. Admission is free. ☎760/872-4263 ⊕www. muledays.org.

SEPT. Lone Pine Film Festival. Every Columbus Day weekend, this sleepy little town pays tribute to its Hollywood history with a three-day festival of tours, films, lectures, and Old West celebrity guests. ☎760/876-9103 ⊕www.lonepinefilmfestival.org.

NOV. Death Valley 49er Encampment Days. Originally a centennial celebration held in 1949 to honor the area's first European visitors, this event annually draws thousands of people to the park from around the world. The weeklong celebration includes art shows, organized seminars and walks, demonstrations, and dances. ⊕www.deathvalley49ers.org.

9

By Veronica Hill

The desert is no Disneyland. With its scorching summer heat and vast, sparsely populated tracts of land, it's not often at the top of the list when most people assemble their "must-see" list of California attractions. But the natural riches of Death Valley—the largest national park outside Alaska—are overwhelming: rolling waves of sand dunes, black cinder cones thrusting up hundreds of feet from a blistered desert floor, riotous sheets of wildflowers, bizarrely shaped Joshua trees basking in the orange glow of a sunset, and a silence that is both dramatic and startling.

SCENIC DRIVE

★ **Artist's Drive.** This 9-mi, one-way route skirts the foothills of the Black Mountains and provides colorful views of the changing landscape. Once inside the palette, the huge expanses of the valley are replaced by the intimate, small-scale natural beauty of pigments created by volcanic deposits. It's a quiet, lonely drive. Reach by heading north off Badwater Road.

WHAT TO SEE

HISTORIC SITES

Charcoal Kilns. Ten stone kilns, each 30 feet high and 25 feet wide, stand as if on parade in a line up a mountain. The kilns, built by Chinese laborers in 1879, were used to burn wood from pinyon pines to turn it into charcoal. The charcoal was then transported over the mountains into Death Valley, where it was used to extract lead and silver from the ore mined there. If you hike nearby Wildrose Peak, you will be rewarded with terrific views of the kilns. ⊠ *Wildrose Canyon Rd., 37 mi south of Stovepipe Wells.*

Harmony Borax Works Museum. Constructed in 1883, one of the oldest buildings in Death Valley houses the Borax Museum, 2 mi south of the borax works. Originally a miners' bunkhouse, the building once stood in Twenty Mule Team Canyon. Now it displays mining machinery and historical exhibits. The adjacent structure is the original mule-team barn. ⊠ *Harmony Borax Works Rd., west of Hwy. 190, 2 mi north of Furnace Creek* ◷ *Daily 10–5:00.*

Fodor'sChoice **Keane Wonder Mine.** The tram towers and cables from the old mill used
★ to process gold from Keane Wonder Mine are still here, leading up to the crumbling mine, which is a steep 1-mi hike up the mountain. A nearby path leads north to Keane Wonder Spring. ⊠ *Access road off Beatty Cutoff Rd., 17½ mi north of Furnace Creek.*

☾ **Scotty's Castle.** This Moorish-style mansion, begun in 1924 and never
★ completed, takes its name from Walter Scott, better known as Death Valley Scotty. An ex-cowboy, prospector, and performer in Buffalo Bill's Wild West Show, Scotty always told people the castle was his, financed by gold from a secret mine. In reality, there was no mine, and the house belonged to a Chicago millionaire named Albert Johnson, whom Scott had finagled into investing in the fictitious mine. The house still contains works of art, imported carpets, handmade European furniture, and a tremendous pipe organ. Costumed rangers re-create life at the castle circa 1939. Try to arrive for the first tour of the day to avoid a wait, which can be up to two hours. Check out the Underground Mysteries Tour, which takes you through a ¼-mile tunnel in the castle basement. ⊠ *Scotty's Castle Rd. (Hwy. 267), 53 mi north of Furnace Creek* ☎ *760/786–2392* ⊕ *www.nps.gov/deva* ⊠ *$11* ◷ *Daily 7–5, tours daily 9–5.*

SCENIC STOPS

★ **Artist's Palette.** So called for the brilliant colors of its volcanic deposits, this is one of the most magnificent sights in Death Valley. Artist's Drive, the approach to the area, is one way heading north off Badwater Road, so if you're visiting Badwater, come here on the way back. The drive winds through foothills of sedimentary and volcanic rocks. ⊠ *11 mi south of Furnace Creek, off Badwater Rd.*

Badwater. This shallow sodium chloride pool lies in an expanse of desolate salt flats. At 282 feet below sea level, Badwater is the lowest spot on land in the Western Hemisphere—and also one of the hottest. ⊠ *Badwater Rd., 19 mi south of Furnace Creek.*

Fodor'sChoice **Dante's View.** This lookout is more than 5,000 feet up in the Black
★ Mountains. In the dry desert air you can see across most of 110-mi-wide Death Valley. The view is astounding: you can see the highest and lowest spots in the contiguous United States from the same vantage point. The tiny blackish patch far below is Badwater, at 282 feet below sea level; on the western horizon is Mt. Whitney, which rises to 14,496 feet. ⊠ *Dante's View Rd. off Hwy. 190, 35 mi from Badwater, 20 mi south of Twenty Mule Team Canyon.*

DEATH VALLEY IN ONE DAY

If you begin the day in Furnace Creek, you can see many different sights without doing much driving. Bring plenty of water with you, and some food in case you get hungry in a remote location. Get up early and drive the 20 mi on Badwater Road to **Badwater,** which looks out on the lowest point in the Western Hemisphere and is a dramatic place to watch the sunrise. Returning north, stop at Natural Bridge, a medium-size conglomerate rock formation that has been hollowed at its base to form a span across the canyon, and then at the **Devil's Golf Course,** so named because of the large pinnacles of salt present here. Detour to the right onto **Artist's Drive,** a 9-mi one-way, northbound route that passes **Artist's Palette.** The reds, yellows, oranges, and greens come from minerals in the rocks and the earth. Four miles north of Artist's Drive you will come to the **Golden Canyon Interpretive Trail,** a 2-mi round-trip that winds through a canyon with colorful rock walls. Just before Furnace Creek, take Highway 190 3 mi east to **Zabriskie Point,** overlooking dramatic, furrowed red-brown hills and the **Twenty Mule Team Canyon.** Return to Furnace Creek, where you can have lunch and visit the museum at the Furnace Creek Visitor Center. Heading north from Furnace Creek, pull off the highway and take a look at the **Harmony Borax Works.**

Darwin Falls. Named for Dr. Darwin French, who explored this desert wilderness in 1860, the 80-foot Darwin Falls are a unique sight in the arid, unforgiving desert. This rocky landscape, accented with trees and moss, pours down into a cool plunge pool. (Swimming is not permitted.) ⊠ *Hwy. 190, 1 mi west of Panamint Springs. Exit south on the signed dirt road and travel 2½ mi to the parking area.*

Devil's Golf Course. Thousands of miniature salt pinnacles carved into surreal shapes by the desert wind dot this wildly varied landscape. The salt was pushed up to the earth's surface by pressure created as underground salt- and water-bearing gravel crystallized. In some spots, perfectly round holes descend into the ground. ⊠ *Badwater Rd., 13 mi south of Furnace Creek. Turn right onto dirt road and drive 1 mi.*

Golden Canyon. Just South of Furnace Creek, these glimmering mountains are perhaps best known for their role in the original *Star Wars.* The canyon is also a fine hiking spot, with gorgeous views of the Panamint Mountains, ancient dry lake beds, and alluvial fans. ⊠ *From the Furnace Creek Visitor Center, drive 2 mi south on Hwy. 190, then 2 mi south on Hwy. 178 to the parking area. The lot has an informational kiosk with trail guides.*

★ **Racetrack.** Getting here involves a 27-mi journey over rough and almost nonexistent dirt road, but the trip is well worth the reward. Where else in the world do rocks move on their own? This phenomenon has baffled scientists for years. No one has actually seen the rocks in motion, but theory has it that when it rains, the hard-packed lake bed becomes slippery enough that gusty winds push the rocks along—sometimes for several hundred yards. When the mud dries, a telltale trail remains. The trek to the Racetrack can be made in a passenger vehicle, but high clearance is suggested. ⊠*From Ubehebe Crater, 27 mi west on the dirt rd.*

Sand Dunes at Mesquite Flat. These dunes, made up of minute pieces of quartz and other rock, are ever-changing products of the wind-rippled hills, with curving crests and a sun-bleached hue. The dunes are the most photographed destination in the park, and you can see them at their best at sunrise and sunset. There are no trails, you can roam where you please. Keep your eyes open for animal tracks—you may even spot a coyote or fox. Bring plenty of water, and note where you parked your car: it's easy to become disoriented in this ocean of sand. If you lose your bearings, climb to the top of a dune and scan the horizon for the parking lot. ⊠*19 mi north of Hwy. 190, northeast of Stovepipe Wells Village.*

Stovepipe Wells Village. This tiny 1926 town, the first resort in Death Valley, takes its name from the stovepipe that an early prospector left to indicate where he found water. The area contains a motel, restaurant, grocery store, campgrounds, and landing strip. Off Highway 190, on a 3-mi gravel road immediately southwest, are the multicolor walls of **Mosaic Canyon.** ⊠*Hwy. 190, 2 mi from Sand Dunes, 77 mi east of Lone Pine.*

★ **Titus Canyon.** Titus Canyon is a popular 28-mi drive from Beatty south along Scotty's Castle Road. Along the way you'll pass Leadville Ghost Town, petroglyphs at Klare Spring, and spectacular limestone and dolomite narrows at the end of the canyon. Toward the end, a section of gravel road will lead you into the mouth of the canyon. ⊠*Access road off Scotty's Castle Rd., 33 mi northwest of Furnace Creek.*

Twenty Mule Team Canyon. This canyon was named for the 20-mule teams that, between 1883 and 1889, carried 10-ton loads of borax through the burning desert. At places along the loop road off Highway 190 the soft rock walls reach high on both sides, making it seem like you're on an amusement-park ride. Remains of prospectors' tunnels are visible here, along with some brilliant rock formations. ⊠*20 Mule Team Rd., off Hwy. 190, 4 mi south of Furnace Creek, 20 mi west of Death Valley Junction.*

Ubehebe Crater. At 500 feet deep and ½ mi across, this crater resulted from underground steam and gas explosions about 3,000 years ago. Volcanic ash spreads out over most of the area, and the cinders lie as deep as 150 feet, near the crater's rim. You'll get superb views of the valley from here, and you can take a fairly easy hike around the west side of the rim to Little Hebe Crater, one of a smaller cluster of craters to the south and west. ⊠*N. Death Valley Hwy., 8 mi northwest of Scotty's Castle.*

★ **Zabriskie Point.** Although only about 710 feet in elevation, this is one of Death Valley National Park's most scenic spots, overlooking a striking panorama of wrinkled, multicolor hills. It's a great place to watch the sunrise. ⊠*Hwy. 190, 5 mi south of Furnace Creek.*

9

VISITOR CENTERS

Furnace Creek Visitor Center and Museum. The exhibits and artifacts here provide a broad overview of how Death Valley formed; you can pick up maps at the bookstore run by the Death Valley Natural History Association. This is also the place to sign up for ranger-led walks (available November through April) or check out a live presentation about the valley's cultural and natural history. The center offers a 15-minute slide show about the park continuously. ⊠ *Hwy. 190, 30 mi northwest of Death Valley Junction* ☎ *760/786–3200* ⊕ *www.nps.gov/deva* ☉ *Daily 8–5 winter, 9–5 summer.*

Scotty's Castle Visitor Center and Museum. If you visit Death Valley, you'll likely make a stop here at the main ticket center for Scotty's Castle living-history tours. Here you'll also find a nice display of exhibits, books, self-guided tour pamphlets, and displays about the castle's creators, Death Valley Scotty and Albert M. Johnson. Buy sandwiches or souvenirs before heading back out to the park. ⊠ *Rte. 267, 53 mi northwest of Furnace Creek and 45 mi northwest of Stovepipe Wells Village* ☎ *760/786–2392* ⊕ *www.nps.gov/deva* ☉ *Daily 9–4:30 summer, 9–5 winter.*

SPORTS & THE OUTDOORS

BICYCLING

There are no bike rentals in the park, but mountain biking is permitted on any of the back roads open to public vehicles. A free flier with suggested bike routes is at the Furnace Creek Visitor Center. Bicycle Path, a 4-mi round-trip trek from the visitor center to Mustard Canyon, is a good place to start, as is Desolation Canyon, an easy 2-mi round-trip trail 4 mi south of Badwater Road. For a better workout, try the 10-mi round-trip journey to Big Four Mine, starting 4½ mi east of Panamint Springs. ⇨ *Outfitters & Expeditions box for bicycle tours.*

BIRD-WATCHING

Approximately 347 bird species have been identified in Death Valley. The best place to see the park's birds is along the Salt Creek Interpretive Trail, where you can spot ravens, common snipes, killdeer, spotted sandpipers, and great blue herons. Along the fairways at Furnace Creek Golf Club, you can see kingfishers, peregrine falcons, hawks, Canada geese, yellow warblers, and the occasional golden eagle—just remember to stay off the greens. Scotty's Castle attracts wintering birds from around the globe, who are attracted to its running water, shady trees, and shrubs. Other good spots to find birds are at Saratoga Springs, Mesquite Springs, Travertine Springs, and Grimshaw Lake near Tecopa. You can download a complete park bird checklist, divided by season, at www.nps.gov/deva/Birdlist.htm. Rangers at Furnace Creek Visitor Center often lead birding walks through Salt Creek between November and March.

OUTFITTERS & EXPEDITIONS

Reserve well in advance for all tours.

BICYCLING

Mountain bike into the heart of Death Valley during a six-day adventure through the national park with **Spirit of the Mojave Mountain Biking Tour** (*Escape Adventures* ☎ *800/596–2953 or 702/838–6966*). The 110-mi journey includes accommodations (both camping and inns). Tours are $995 per person; bikes, tents, sleeping bags, helmets, and other gear may be rented for an additional price. Tours are available February–April and October only.

FOUR-WHEELING

The 10-hour **Death Valley SUV Tour** (*Death Valley Tours* ☎ *800/719–3768*) departs from Las Vegas and takes you on a fully narrated whirl through Death Valley in a four-wheel-drive Jeep. Tours ($205 per person) depart Monday and Wednesday at 7 AM and include free pickup from designated hotels. Bottled water and snacks are provided, and camera rentals, tripods, and film are available for an additional fee.

HIKING

Available during the spring months, **Death Valley National Park and Red Rock Canyon Hiking Tour** (*Death Valley Tours* ☎ *800/719–3768* ⊕ *www.deathvalleytours.net*) is a six-day adventure that begins in Las Vegas. All transportation, permits, park fees, meals, snacks, beverages, first aid, and camping gear is included in the fee. Tours are $1,230 per person.

Join an experienced guide and spend six days exploring Death Valley's most popular sights with **Death Valley National Park and Red Rock Hiker** (*Escape Adventures* ☎ *800/596–2953 or 702/838–6966* ⊕ *www.escapeadventures.com*). The tour ($995), offered October and February–April, also spends two days in Red Rock Canyon National Conservation Area. For an additional fee, you can rent hiking shoes, tents, sleeping bags, trekking poles, water bottles, and more. The price includes a night in the Furnace Creek Inn.

HORSEBACK & CARRIAGE RIDES

Set off on a one- or two-hour guided horseback or carriage ride ($10–$60) from **Furnace Creek Ranch** (⊠ *Hwy. 190, Furnace Creek* ☎ *760/786–2345 Ext. 339*). The rides traverse trails with views of the surrounding mountains, where multicolor volcanic rock and alluvial fans form a background for date palms and other vegetation. Evening carriage rides take passengers around the golf course and Furnace Creek Ranch. Cocktail rides, with champagne, margaritas, and hot spiced wine, are available. It's open October–May only.

MOTORCYCLE TOURS

Sign up for a guided **Death Valley Dualsport Tour** (*Adventure Motorcycle (AdMo) Tours* ☎ *760/249–1105*). The four-day tour ($1,530) through Death Valley on a rented Suzuki DR-Z400S (or your own) bike covers about 400 mi of terrain through Death Valley National Park. The tours, which run October–May, include bike rental, gasoline, snacks, hotel accommodations for three nights, and a professional tour guide. To join, you should have a motorcycle driver's license, health insurance, and protective gear.

9

FOUR-WHEELING

Maps and SUV guidebooks for four-wheel-drive and other backcountry roads (including the popular Cottonwood/Marble canyons, Racetrack, Eureka Dunes, Saratoga Springs, Warm Springs Canyon) are offered at the Furnace Creek Visitor Center. Remember: never travel alone and be sure to pack plenty of water and snacks. Driving off established roads is strictly prohibited in the park. ⇨ *Outfitters & Expeditions box for guided four-wheeling expeditions.*

Butte Valley. This 21-mi road in the southwest part of the park climbs from 200 feet below sea level to an elevation of 4,000 feet. The geological formations along the drive reveal the development of Death Valley. ✉ *Trailhead on Warm Spring Canyon Rd., 50 mi south of Furnace Creek Visitor Center.*

Hunter Mountain. From Teakettle Junction to the park boundary, this 20-mi road climbs from 4,100 feet to 7,200 feet, winding through a pinyon-and-juniper forest. This route may be closed or muddy in winter and spring. ✉ *Trailhead 28 mi southwest of Scotty's Castle.*

Warm Springs Canyon. This route takes you past Warm Springs talc mine and through Butte Valley, over Mengel Pass and toward **Geologists Cabin,** a charming and cheery little cabin where you can spend the night (if nobody else beats you to it!). The cabin, which sits under a cottonwood tree, has a fireplace, table and chairs, and a sink. Farther up the road, the cabins at Mengel's Home and Russell Camp are also open for public use. Keep the historic cabins clean and restock any items that you use. ✉ *Warm Springs Canyon Rd., off Hwy. 190/Badwater Rd.*

HIKING

Plan to hike before or after midday, when the sun is hottest. Carry plenty of water, wear protective clothing, and keep an eye out for tarantulas, black widows, scorpions, snakes, and other potentially dangerous creatures. Some of the best trails are unmarked; ask locals for directions. ⇨ *Outfitters & Expeditions box for guided expeditions.*

EASY **Darwin Falls.** This lovely 2-mi round-trip hike rewards you with a refreshing waterfall surrounded by thick vegetation and a rocky gorge. No swimming or bathing is allowed, but it's a beautiful place for a picnic. Adventurous hikers can scramble higher toward more rewarding views of the falls. ✉ *Access the 2-mi graded dirt road and parking area off Hwy. 190, 1 mi west of Panamint Springs Resort.*

Fodor'sChoice
★

★ **Natural Bridge Canyon.** The somewhat rough 2-mi access road has interesting geological features in addition to the bridge itself. It's ½ mi round-trip. ✉ *Access road off Badwater Rd., 15 mi south of Furnace Creek.*

Salt Creek Interpretive Trail. This trail, a ½-mi boardwalk circuit, loops through a spring-fed wash. The nearby hills are brown and gray, but the floor of the wash is alive with aquatic plants such as pickerelweed and salt grass. The stream and ponds here are among the few places in the park to see the rare pupfish, the only native fish species in Death Valley. Animals such as bobcats, fox, coyotes, and snakes visit

Darwin Falls Trail

Parking

Darwin Falls Trail

4WD Road

Big Falls   Last Falls

Darwin
Falls

First Narrows

Parking

DARWIN CANYON

4WD Road

the spring, and you may also see ravens, common snipes, killdeer, and great blue herons. ⊠ *Off Hwy. 190, 14 mi north of Furnace Creek.*

★ **Titus Canyon.** The narrow floor of Titus Canyon is made of hard-packed gravel and dirt, and it's a constant, moderate uphill walk. Klare Spring and some petroglyphs are 5½ mi from the mouth of the canyon, but you can get a feeling for the area on a shorter walk.

MODERATE **Fall Canyon.** This is a 3½-mi one-way hike from the Titus canyon parking area. First, walk ½ mi north along the base of the mountains to a large wash, then go 2½ mi up the canyon to a 35-foot dry fall. You can continue by climbing around to the falls on the south side. ⊠ *Access road off Scotty's Castle Rd., 33 mi northwest of Furnace Creek.*

☾ **Mosaic Canyon.** A gradual uphill trail (4 mi round-trip) winds through the smoothly polished walls of this narrow canyon. There are dry falls to climb at the upper end. ⊠ *Access road off Hwy. 190, ½ mi west of Stovepipe Wells Village.*

DIFFICULT **Keane Wonder Mine.** Allow two hours for the 2-mi round-trip trail that
Fodor'sChoice follows an out-of-service aerial tramway to this mine. The way is steep,
★ but the views of the valley are spectacular. Do not enter the tunnels or hike beyond the top of the tramway—it's dangerous. The trailhead is 2

mi down an unpaved and bumpy access road. ⊠ *Access road off Beatty Cutoff Rd., 17½ mi north of Furnace Creek.*

Telescope Peak Trail. The 14-mi round-trip begins at Mahogany Flat Campground. The steep trail winds through pinyon, juniper, and bristlecone pines, with excellent views of Death Valley and Panamint Valley. Ice axes and crampons may be necessary in winter—check at the Furnace Creek Visitor Center. It takes a minimum of eight hours to hike to the top of the 11,049-foot peak and then return. Getting to the peak is a strenuous endeavor; take plenty of water and only attempt it in fall unless you're an experienced hiker. ⊠ *Off Wildrose Rd., south of Charcoal Kilns.*

EDUCATIONAL OFFERINGS

GUIDED TOURS

Death Valley Adventure Tours. This 11-hour luxury motor coach tour of the park passes through its most famous landmarks. Tours include lunch and hotel pickup from designated Las Vegas–area hotels. ☎ *800/719–3768 Death Valley Tours, 800/566–5868 or 702/233–1627 Look Tours* 🖾 *$195–$207* ☉ *Tues., Fri., and Sun. at 7 AM.*

Furnace Creek Visitor Center tours. This center has the most tour options, including the Harmony Borax Walk and guided hikes to Mosaic Canyon, and Golden Canyon. Less strenuous options include wildflower walks, birding walks, geology walks, and Furnace Creek Inn historical tour. ⊠ *Furnace Creek Visitor Center, Rte. 190, 30 mi northwest of Death Valley Junction* ☎ *760/786–3200.*

Gadabout Tours. Take multiday trips through Death Valley from Ontario, California. ⊠ *Sheraton Ontario Airport, 428 N. Vineyard Ave., Ontario* ⌖ *700 E. Tahquitz Canyon Way, Palm Springs, 92262* ☎ *760/325–5556 or 800/952–5068* ⊕ *www.gadabouttours.com.*

RANGER PROGRAMS

ↄ **Junior Ranger Program.** Children can join this program at either of the two visitor centers, where they can pick up a workbook and complete up to 15 projects (based on their age) to earn a souvenir badge.

ARTS & ENTERTAINMENT

ENTERTAINMENT

Marta Becket's Amargosa Opera House. An artist and dancer from New York, Becket first visited the former railway town of Amargosa while on tour in 1964. Three years later she returned to town and bought a boarded-up theater that sat amid a group of rundown mock–Spanish colonial buildings. To compensate for the sparse audiences in the early days, Becket painted a Renaissance-era Spanish crowd on the walls and ceiling, turning the theater into a trompe l'oeil masterpiece. Now in her late 70s, Becket performs her blend of ballet, mime, and 19th-century melodrama to sellout crowds. After the show you can meet her in the adjacent gallery, where she sells her paintings and autographs her books. There are no performances mid-May through October. Reservations are required. ⊠*Rte. 127, Death Valley Junction* ☎*760/852–4441* 🖃*$15* ☉*Nov.–May (through Mother's Day weekend).*

WHERE TO STAY & EAT

ABOUT THE RESTAURANTS

If you're looking for a special evening out in Death Valley, head to the Furnace Creek Dining Room, where you'll be spoiled with fine wines and gourmet fare such as rattlesnake empanadas or a juicy New York steak. It's also a great spot to start the day with a hearty gourmet breakfast. Most other spots within the park are mom-and-pop type places with basic American fare.

ABOUT THE HOTELS

It's difficult to find lodging anywhere in Death Valley that doesn't have breathtaking views of the park and surrounding mountains. Most accommodations, aside from Furnace Creek Inn, are homey and rustic. Rooms fill up quickly during the fall and spring seasons, and reservations are required about three months in advance for the prime weekends.

The western side of Death Valley, along the eastern Sierras, is a gorgeous setting, though it's quite a distance from Furnace Creek. Here, you can stay in the historic Dow Villa Motel, where John Wayne spent many a night, or head farther south to the ghost towns of Randsburg or Cerro Gordo for a true Wild West experience. *For information on hotels outside the park,* ⇨*Chapter 10, The Mojave Desert.*

ABOUT THE CAMPGROUNDS

You may build fires in the fire grates that are available at all campgrounds except Sunset and Emigrant. Fires may be restricted during summer at Thorndike, Mahogany Flat, and Wildrose (check with rangers about current conditions). Wood gathering is prohibited at all campgrounds. A limited supply of firewood is available at general stores in Furnace Creek and Stovepipe Wells, but since prices are high and supplies limited, you're better off bringing your own if you intend to camp.

Backcountry camping is allowed in areas that are at least 2 mi from maintained campgrounds and the main paved or unpaved roads, and ¼ mi from water sources. You will need a high-clearance or a 4x4 vehicle to reach these locations. For your own safety, fill out a backcountry registration form so the rangers will know where to find you.

WHERE TO EAT

$$$ ✕**Inn Dining Room.** Fireplaces, beamed ceilings, and spectacular views
Fodor'sChoice provide a visual feast to match the inn's ambitious menu. Dishes may
★ include such desert-theme items as rattlesnake empanadas and crispy cactus, and simpler fare such as cumin-lime shrimp, lamb, and New York strip steak. An evening dress code (no jeans, T-shirts, or shorts) is

enforced. Afternoon tea is an inn tradition since 1927. Breakfast and Sunday brunch are also served. ⊠*Furnace Creek Inn Resort, Hwy. 190, Furnace Creek* ☎760/786–3385 ⊕*www.furnacecreekresort. com* ⚑*Reservations essential* ⊟*AE, D, DC, MC, V* ⊘*Closed mid-May–mid-Oct.*

$$$ ✕**Wrangler Buffet and Steakhouse.** This casual, family-style restaurant has a buffet for breakfast and lunch, and steak house favorites for dinner. It's slightly more formal than the other restaurant at the Furnace Creek Resort, the Forty-Niner Cafe. ⊠*Furnace Creek Ranch, Hwy. 190, Furnace Creek* ☎760/786–2345 ⊕*www.furnacecreekresort.com* ⊟*AE, D, DC, MC, V* ⊘*No buffet lunch Nov. 25–Dec. 22, but the coffee shop still serves lunch.*

$$–$$$ ✕**Panamint Springs Resort Restaurant.** This is a great place for steak and a beer, or pasta and a salad. In summer, evening meals are served outdoors on the porch, which has spectacular views of Panamint Valley. Breakfast and lunch are also served. ⊠*Hwy. 190, 31 mi west of Stovepipe Wells* ☎775/482–7680 ⚑*Reservations essential* ⊟*AE, D, MC, V.*

$$–$$$ ✕**Toll Road Restaurant.** There are wagon wheels in the yard and Old West artifacts on the interior walls at this restaurant in the Stovepipe Wells Village hotel. A stone fireplace heats the dining room. A full menu, with steaks, chicken, fish, and pasta, is served year-round; breakfast and dinner buffets are laid out during summer. ⊠*Hwy. 190, Stovepipe Wells* ☎760/786–2387 ⊟*AE, D, DC, MC, V*

¢–$$ ✕**Forty-Niner Cafe.** This casual coffee shop serves typical American fare for breakfast, lunch, and dinner. The restaurant is done up in a rustic mining style with whitewashed pine walls, vintage map-covered tables, and prospector-branded chairs. Past menus and old photographs decorate the walls. ⊠*Furnace Creek Ranch, Hwy. 190, Furnace Creek* ☎760/786–2345 ⊕*www.furnacecreekresort.com* ⊟*AE, D, DC, MC, V.*

¢–$ ✕**19th Hole.** Overlooking the world's lowest golf course (214 feet below sea level), this open-air spot serves hamburgers, hot dogs, chicken, and sandwiches. There is drive-through service for golfers in carts. ⊠*Furnace Creek Golf Club, Hwy. 190, Furnace Creek* ☎760/786–2345 ⊟*AE, D, DC, MC, V* ⊘*Closed June–Sept. No dinner.*

WHERE TO STAY

During the busy season (November–March) you should make reservations for lodgings within the park at least one month in advance.

$$$$ ✕▥ **Furnace Creek Inn.** Built in 1927, this adobe-brick-and-stone lodge
Fodor's Choice is nestled in one of the park's greenest oases. A warm mineral stream
★ gurgles across the property, and its 85°F waters feed into a swimming pool. The rooms are decorated in earth tones, with old-style furnishings. The top-notch Furnace Creek Inn Dining Room ($$$) serves desert-theme dishes such as rattlesnake empanadas and crispy cactus, as well as less exotic fare such as cumin-lime shrimp, lamb, and New York strip steak. Afternoon tea has been a tradition since 1927. ⊠*Furnace Creek Village, near intersection of Hwy. 190 and Badwater Rd.* ⌂*Box 1, Death Valley, 92328* ☎760/786–2345 ☐760/786–2514 ⊕*www.*

furnacecreekresort.com 📶 *66 rooms* ⚙ *In-room: dial-up. In-hotel: restaurant, room service, bar, tennis courts, pool* ⊟ *AE, D, DC, MC, V* ⊘ *Closed mid-May–mid-Oct.*

$$–$$$ ✕🏨 **Furnace Creek Ranch.** Originally crew headquarters for the Pacific Coast Borax Company, the four buildings here have motel-type rooms that are good for families. The best ones overlook the green lawns of the resort and the surrounding mountains. The property is adjacent to a golf course with its own team of pros, and also has a general store and a campground. The family-style Wrangler Steak House and Forty-Niner Cafe *(⇨above)* serve American fare in simple surroundings. ⊠ *Hwy. 190, Furnace Creek* 🏠 *Box 1, Death Valley, 92328* ☎ *760/786–2345 or 800/236–7916* 🖷 *760/786–2514* ⊕ *www.furnacecreekresort.com* 📶 *224 rooms* ⚙ *In-room: dial-up. In-hotel: restaurant, room service, bar, tennis courts, pool* ⊟ *AE, D, DC, MC, V.*

$–$$ 🏨 **Stovepipe Wells Village.** If you prefer quiet nights and an unfettered view of the night sky and nearby sand dunes, this property is for you. No telephones break the silence here, and only the deluxe rooms have televisions and some refrigerators. Rooms are simple yet comfortable and provide wide-open desert vistas. The Toll Road Restaurant *(⇨above)* serves American breakfast, lunch, and dinner favorites, from omelets and sandwiches to burgers and steaks. RV campsites with full hookups ($28) are available on a first-come, first-served basis. ⊠ *Hwy. 190, Stovepipe Wells* 🏠 *Box 559, Death Valley, 92328* ☎ *760/786–2387* 🖷 *760/786–2389* ⊕ *www.stovepipewells.com* 📶 *83 rooms* ⚙ *In-room: no phone (some), refrigerator (some). In-hotel: restaurant, bar, pool, no elevator, no-smoking rooms, some pets allowed* ⊟ *AE, D, MC, V.*

$ 🏨 **Panamint Springs Resort.** Ten miles inside the west entrance of the park, this low-key resort overlooks the sand dunes and peculiar geological formations of the Panamint Valley. It's a modest mom-and-pop-style operation with a wraparound porch and rustic furnishings. One room has a king-size bed, and two of the rooms accommodate up to six people. A pay phone, a gas pump, and a grocery store are on the premises. The resort uses satellite telephones to link to the outside world, so it is sometimes difficult to reach the property via phone. ⊠ *Hwy. 190, 28 mi west of Stovepipe Wells* 🏠 *Box 395, Ridgecrest, 93556* ☎ *775/482–7680* ⊕ *www.deathvalley.com* 🖷 *775/482–7682* 📶 *14 rooms, 1 cabin* ⚙ *In-room: no a/c (some), no phone, no TV. In-hotel: restaurant, bar, no-smoking rooms, some pets allowed* ⊟ *AE, D, MC, V.*

CAMPGROUNDS **$$** 🏕 **Furnace Creek.** This campground, 196 feet below sea level, has some shaded tent sites. Pay showers, a laundry, and a swimming pool are at nearby Furnace Creek Ranch. Reservations are accepted for stays between mid-October and mid-April; at other times sites are available on a first-come, first-served basis. Two group campsites can accommodate 40 people each. ⊠ *Hwy. 190, Furnace Creek* ☎ *877/444–6777 reservations* ⊕ *www.recreation.gov* 📶 *135 tent/RV sites* ⚙ *Flush toilets, dump station, drinking water, fire grates, picnic tables, public telephone, ranger station* ⊟ *AE, DC, MC, V, credit cards accepted for reservations only, otherwise, no credit cards.*

9

$–$$ △Panamint Springs Resort. Part of a complex that includes a motel and cabin, this campground is surrounded by cottonwoods. The daily fee includes use of the showers and restrooms. ⊠ *Hwy. 190, 28 mi west of Stovepipe Wells* ☎ *775/482–7680* ⊅ *12 full-hookup RV sites, 26 tent sites, 25 water-only sites* ⟳ *Flush toilets, full hookups, partial hookups (water), dump station, drinking water, showers, fire grates, picnic tables, public telephone, general store, service station (gas only)* ⊟ *AE, D, MC, V.*

$–$$ △Stovepipe Wells Village. This is the second-largest campground in the park. Like Sunset, this area is little more than a giant parking lot, but pay showers and laundry facilities are available at the adjacent motel. RV sites are open year-round. ⊠ *Hwy. 190, Stovepipe Wells* ☎ *760/786–2387* ⊅ *190 tent sites, 14 RV sites with full hookups* ⟳ *Flush toilets, dump station, drinking water, public telephone, general store, swimming (pool)* ⟳ *Reservations not accepted* ⊟ *No credit cards* ⊗ *Mid-Oct.–mid-Apr.*

$ △Mesquite Springs. There are tent and RV spaces here, some of them shaded, but no RV hookups. No generators are allowed. Since Mesquite Springs is the only campground on the north end of the park, it attracts younger campers intent on getting away from the crowds. ⊠ *Access road 2 mi south of Scotty's Castle* ☎ *No phone* ⊅ *30 tent/RV sites* ⟳ *Flush toilets, dump station, drinking water, fire grates, picnic tables* ⟳ *Reservations not accepted* ⊟ *No credit cards.*

$ △Sunset Campground. Hookups are not available here, but you can walk across the street to the showers, laundry facilities, and swimming pool at Furnace Creek Ranch. Many of Sunset's denizens are senior citizens who migrate to Death Valley each winter to play golf and tennis or just to enjoy the mild, dry climate. No fires are allowed. ⊠ *Sunset Campground Rd., 1 mi north of Furnace Creek* ☎ *760/786–2331* ⊕ *www.nps.gov/deva* ⊅ *256 tent/RV sites* ⟳ *Flush toilets, dump station, drinking water, public telephone, play area, ranger station* ⟳ *Reservations not accepted* ⊟ *No credit cards* ⊗ *Mid-Oct.–mid-Apr.*

$ △Texas Spring. This campsite south of the Furnace Creek Visitor
★ Center has good facilities and is a few dollars cheaper than Furnace Creek. No generators are allowed. Not all sites may be available for RV use. ⊠ *Off Hwy 190, south of the Furnace Creek Visitor Center* ☎ *800/365–2267* ⊅ *92 tent/RV sites* ⟳ *Flush toilets, dump station, drinking water, fire grates, picnic tables* ⟳ *Reservations not accepted* ⊟ *No credit cards* ⊗ *Mid-Oct.–mid-Apr.*

¢ △Mahogany Flat. If you have a four-wheel-drive vehicle and want to
★ scale Telescope Peak, the park's highest mountain, you might want to sleep at one of the few shaded spots in Death Valley, at a cool 8,133 feet. It's the most scenic campground, set among pinyon pines and junipers, with a view of the valley. ⊠ *Off Wildrose Rd., south of Charcoal Kilns* ☎ *No phone* ⊅ *10 tent sites* ⟳ *Pit toilets, fire grates, picnic tables* ⟳ *Reservations not accepted* ⊟ *No credit cards* ⊗ *Mar.–Nov.*

¢ △Thorndike. Folks who visit the park in summer often travel to this alpine campground high in the Panamint Mountains. During certain road conditions, you may need a four-wheel-drive vehicle to access the road. ⊠ ½ *mi east of Charcoal Kilns* ☎ *No phone* ⊅ *6 tent/RV* sites ♿ *Pit toilets, fire grates, picnic tables* ♨ *Reservations not accepted* ▭ *No credit cards* ⊙ *Mar.–Nov.*

¢   ⚠ **Wildrose.** Since it's on a paved road at a lower elevation (4,100 feet) than nearby Mahogany Flat, Wildrose is less likely to be closed because of snow in winter. The view here is not as spectacular as that from Mahogany Flat, but it does overlook the northern end of the valley. ✉ *Wildrose Canyon Road, 37 mi south of Stovepipe Wells* ☏ *No phone* ⬑ *23 tent/RV sites* ♿ *Pit toilets, drinking water (Apr.–Nov. only), fire grates, picnic tables* ♨ *Reservations not accepted* ▭ *No credit cards.*

DEATH VALLEY ESSENTIALS

ACCESSIBILITY

All of Death Valley's visitor centers, contact stations, and museums are accessible to all visitors. The campgrounds at Furnace Creek, Sunset, and Stovepipe Wells have wheelchair-accessible sites. The grounds at Scotty's Castle are accessible to the mobility impaired and the guided tour of the main house has provisions for a wheelchair lift to the upper floors. Highway 190, Badwater Road, Scotty's Castle Road, and paved roads to Dante's View and Wildrose provide access to the major scenic viewpoints and historic points of interest.

ADMISSION FEES

The entrance fee is $20 per vehicle and $10 for those entering on foot, bus, bike, or motorcycle. The payment, valid for seven consecutive days, is collected at the park's entrance stations and at the visitor center at Furnace Creek. (If you enter the park on Highway 190, there is no entrance station; remember to stop by the visitor center to pay the fee.)

ADMISSION HOURS

Most facilities within the park remain open year-round, daily 8–5.

ATMS/BANKS

Contacts **Furnace Creek Ranch Registration Office** (✉ *Hwy. 190, north of the Furnace Creek Visitor Center*). **Stovepipe Wells Village** (✉ *Hwy. 190, 23 mi northwest of Furnace Creek*).

AUTOMOBILE SERVICE STATIONS

Contacts **Furnace Creek Gas Station** (✉ *Hwy. 190, Furnace Creek* ☏ *760/786–2232*). **Scotty's Castle Gas Station** (✉ *Scotty's Castle, Hwy. 190, 53 mi northwest of Furnace Creek* ☏ *760/786–2325*). **Stovepipe Wells Gas Station** (✉ *Hwy. 190, Stovepipe Wells* ☏ *760/786–2578*).

EMERGENCIES

For all emergencies, call 911. Note that cell phones don't work in many parts of the park.

LOST AND FOUND

The park's lost-and-found is at the Furnace Creek Visitor Center.

9

PERMITS

If you're planning an overnight visit to the backcountry, complete a registration form at the Furnace Creek Visitor Center. Backcountry camping is allowed in areas that are at least 2 mi from maintained campgrounds and the main paved or unpaved roads, and ¼ mi from water sources. Most abandoned mining areas are restricted to day use. Ask at the visitor centers for other restrictions and current road conditions.

PUBLIC TELEPHONES

You'll find public telephones at Furnace Creek Visitor Center and Stovepipe Wells ranger station, as well as at the park's gas stations and lodgings.

RESTROOMS

Flush toilets are available at many of the campgrounds throughout the park and at Scotty's Castle. There are public restrooms at Furnace Creek Visitor Center and Stovepipe Wells ranger station.

VISITOR INFORMATION

Contacts **Death Valley National Park** (☐ *Box 579, Death Valley, 92328* ☎*760/786-3200, 760/786-3225 TDD* 🖷*760/786-3283* ⊕*www.nps.gov/deva*). **Death Valley Natural History Association** (☐ *Box 188, Death Valley, 92328* ☎ *800/478-8564*).

The Mojave Desert

WITH OWENS VALLEY

Lone Pine Peak, Mount Whitney

WORD OF MOUTH

"We loved the Mojave Desert Drive through Kelso—an old railway transit stop with great atmosphere, and the sand dunes and volcanic areas along the way. We met a group of twenty or so cowboys, proper cowboys with horses and lassos and big hats, waiting for their HELICOPTER to find a burro in the dunes."

—Carrabella

WELCOME TO THE MOJAVE DESERT

TOP REASONS TO GO

★ **Nostalgia:** Old neon signs, historic motels, and restored Harvey House rail stations abound across this desert landscape. Don't miss some of the classic eateries along the way, including Bagdad Café in Newberry Springs, Emma Jean's Hollandburger Cafe in Victorville, and Summit Inn on the Cajon Pass.

★ **Death Valley wonders:** Visit this strange landscape to tour some of the most breathtaking desert terrain in the world (⇨ *Chapter 9, Death Valley National Park*).

★ **Great ghost towns:** California's gold rush brought miners to the Mojave, and each of the towns they left behind has its own unique charms.

★ **Cool down in Sierra country:** Head up Highway 395 toward Bishop to visit the High Sierras, home to majestic Mt. Whitney.

★ **Explore ancient history:** The Mojave Desert is home to rare petroglyphs, some dating back almost 16,000 years.

1 Death Valley National Park. This arid desert landscape is one of the hottest, lowest, and driest places in North America. Here, among the beautiful canyons and wide-open spaces, you'll find some quirky bits of Americana, including the elaborate Scotty's Castle and eclectic Amargosa Opera House. (⇨ *Chapter 9, Death Valley National Park*)

2 Calico Ghost Town. Though Walter Knott of Knott's Berry Farm fame restored this silver/borax mining camp into a squeaky-clean amusement park in the 1950s, the one-time boomtown still boasts many original buildings.

3 Petroglyph Canyons. You'll need an advanced and somewhat lengthy application to get on the property, but this tour of Renegade Canyon is well worth it. Along the 1½-mi hike, you'll see some of America's finest aboriginal drawings of sheep, cats, mountain lions, and deer—some up to 16,000 years old.

4 **World's Tallest Thermometer.** If you're heading through the Mojave on your way to Las Vegas or Death Valley, stop in Baker for a quick bite to eat and a photo op with this kitschy piece of Americana, built in 1991.

5 **Mojave National Preserve.** Approximately 1.4 million acres make up this desert playground, located between I-10 and I-40. Here, you can explore the old Mojave Road; check out cool cave formations of Mitchell Caverns; wander through Hole-in-the-Wall, an old hangout of Butch Cassidy gang member Bob Holliman; or tour the splendidly restored Kelso Depot.

The Mojave Desert, once part of an ancient inland sea, is one of largest swaths of open land in Southern California. Its boundaries to the south include the San Gabriel and San Bernardino mountain ranges; the areas of Palmdale and Ridgecrest to the west; the areas of Death Valley and Primm, Nevada, to the north; and Needles to the east. The area is instantly distinguishable by its wide-open sandy spaces, peppered with creosote bushes, Joshua trees, and abandoned homesteads. You can access the Mojave via Interstate 40 or 14, Highway 395, and Highway 95.

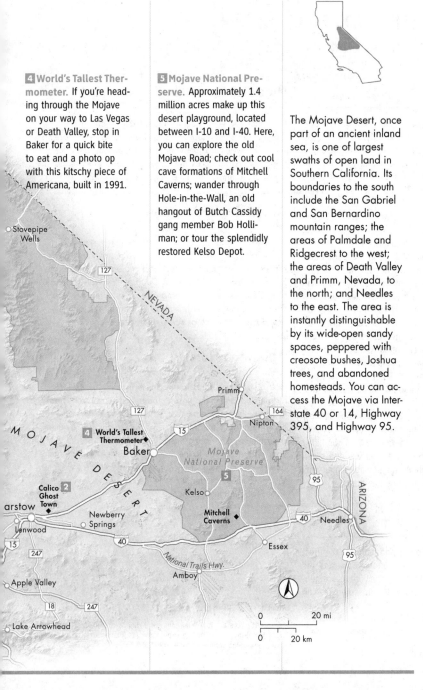

10

THE MOJAVE DESERT PLANNER

Warnings

Believe everything you've ever heard about desert heat: it can be brutal. You need sunglasses, sunblock, a hat, clothing that blocks the sun's rays and the wind, and plenty of water. Because this region is vast and the weather is unpredictable, you'll also need to make careful driving plans. Facilities such as gas stations and supermarkets are few, so be sure to fill your gas tank whenever you can and check your vehicle's fluids and tire pressure frequently. Shut off your car's air-conditioning on steep grades to avoid engine overheating. At the start of each day load the car with three gallons of water per person, plus additional radiator water, and a cooler stocked with extra food. Be sure to bring reliable maps; signage can be limited or nonexistent. It's a good idea to have a compass and a cell phone (though the signal may fade in remote areas).

Timing

Spring and fall are the best seasons to tour the desert and Owens Valley. Winters are generally mild, but summers can be cruel. If you're on a budget, keep in mind that room rates drop as the temperatures rise.

Hours of Operation

Early morning is the best time to visit sights and avoid crowds, but some museums and visitor centers don't open until 10. If you schedule your town arrivals for late afternoon, you can drop by the visitor centers just before closing hours to line up an itinerary for the next day.

About the Restaurants

Throughout the desert and the eastern Sierra, dining is a simple affair. Owens Valley is home to many mom-and-pop eateries, as well as a few fast-food chains. The restaurants in Death Valley (⇨ Chapter 9, Death Valley National Park) range from coffee shops to upscale cafés. In the Mojave there are chain establishments in Ridgecrest, Victorville, and Barstow, as well as some ethnic eateries.

About the Hotels

Hotel chains and roadside motels make up most of the lodging options in the desert. The tourist season runs from late May through September, when many travelers are heading out of California on I–15. Reservations are never a problem: you're almost always guaranteed a room. But if your plans take you to the most luxurious resort in the entire desert—the Furnace Creek Inn, in Death Valley (⇨ Chapter 9, Death Valley National Park)—be sure to book in advance for the winter season.

WHAT IT COSTS				
¢	$	$$	$$$	$$$$
Restaurants				
under $10	$10–$15	$16–$22	$23–$30	over $30
Hotels				
under $90	$90–$120	$121–$175	$176–$250	over $250

Restaurant prices are for a main course at dinner, excluding sales tax of 7.75%. Hotel prices are for two people in a standard double room in high season, excluding service charges and 7.25% tax.

Updated by
Amy Wang

DUST AND DESOLATION, TUMBLEWEEDS AND rattlesnakes, barren landscapes—these are the bleak images that come to mind when most people hear the word *desert*. But east of the Sierra Nevada, where the land quickly flattens and the rain seldom falls, the desert is anything but a wasteland. The topography here is extreme; whereas Death Valley (⇨ *Chapter 9, Death Valley National Park*) drops to almost 300 feet below sea level and contains the lowest (and hottest) spot in the Western Hemisphere, the Mojave Desert, which lies to the south, has elevations ranging from 3,000 to 5,000 feet. These remote regions (which are known, respectively, as low desert and high desert) possess a singular beauty found nowhere else in California: there are vast open spaces populated with spiky Joshua trees, undulating sand dunes, faulted mountains, and dramatic rock formations. Owens Valley is where the desert meets the mountains; its 80-mi width separates the depths of Death Valley from Mt. Whitney, the highest mountain in the continental United States. Exploring the wonders of Death Valley in the morning and then heading to the Sierra to cool off in the afternoon is an amazing study in contrasts.

> ### NOT SOUVENIRS
>
> You may spot fossils at some of the archaeological sites in the desert. If you do, leave them where they are; it's against the law to remove them.

THE WESTERN MOJAVE

PALMDALE

60 mi north of Los Angeles on Hwy. 14.

Before calling itself the aerospace capital of the world, the desert town of Palmdale was an agricultural community. Swiss and German descendants, moving west from Nebraska, first settled here in 1886. Most residents made their living as farmers, growing alfalfa, pears, and apples. After World War II, with the creation of Edwards Air Force Base and U.S. Air Force Plant 42, the area turned into a center for aerospace and defense, with such big companies as McDonnell Douglas, Rockwell, Northrop, and Lockheed establishing factories here. Today, it's one of the fastest-growing cities in Southern California.

10

A mile from the San Andreas Fault, the namesake of the **Devil's Punchbowl Natural Area** is a natural bowl-shaped depression in the earth, framed by 300-foot rock walls. At the bottom is a stream, which you can reach via a 1-mi hike; at the top an interpretive center has displays of native flora and fauna, including live animals such as snakes, lizards, and birds of prey. ⊠28000 *Devil's Punchbowl Rd., south of Hwy. 138, Pearblossom* ☎661/944–2743 ⊠*Free* ⊗*Park daily sunrise–sunset, center daily 8–4.*

The Benedictine monastery **St. Andrew's Abbey** stands on 760 acres of lush greenery and natural springs. A big draw here is the property's ceramics studio, established in 1969; St. Andrew's Ceramics sells hand-

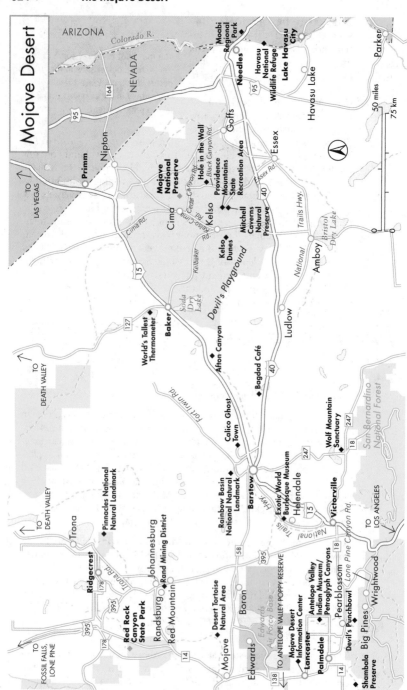

Mojave Desert

ARIZONA

Colorado R.

NEVADA

TO LAS VEGAS →

Primm

Nipton

164

95

Moabi Regional Park

Needles

Havasu National Wildlife Refuge

Lake Havasu City

Parker

Havasu Lake

Goffs

Hole in the Wall

Black Canyon Rd.

Mojave National Preserve

Cima

Cedar Canyon Rd.

Providence Mountains State Recreation Area

Essex

Essex Rd.

Kelso

Kelso-Cima Rd.

Mitchell Caverns Natural Preserve

40

Kelbaker Rd.

Cima Rd.

15

Kelso Dunes

National Trails Hwy.

Amboy

Bristol Dry Lake

Soda Dry Lake

Devil's Playground

Ludlow

127

World's Tallest Thermometer

Baker

TO DEATH VALLEY ↑

Afton Canyon

Bagdad Café

40

50 miles

75 km

Fort Irwin Rd.

Calico Ghost Town

247

Wolf Mountain Sanctuary

18

San Bernardino National Forest

TO DEATH VALLEY ↑

Pinnacles National Natural Landmark

Trona

Rainbow Basin National Natural Landmark

Barstow

Exotic World Burlesque Museum

Helendale

15

Victorville

247

TO LOS ANGELES →

National Trails Hwy.

Ridgecrest

178

Trona Rd.

Johannesburg

Rand Mining District

Randsburg

Red Mountain

395

Desert Tortoise Natural Area

58

395

18

Lone Pine Canyon Rd.

FOSSIL FALLS, LONE PINE ↑

178

Red Rock Canyon State Park

Boron

Antelope Valley Indian Museum/ Petroglyph Canyons

Pearblossom

Wrightwood

14

Mojave

Edwards Air Force Base

TO ANTELOPE VALLEY POPPY RESERVE

Mojave Desert Information Center

Lancaster

Palmdale

Devil's Punchbowl

Big Pines

Shambala Preserve

138

14

TO LOS ANGELES

made tile saints, angels, and plaques designed by Father Maur van Doorslaer, a monk from Sint Andries in Bruges, Belgium, whose work is collected across the United States and Canada. Don't miss the abbey's fall festival, where you can sample tasty dishes and enjoy entertainment that includes singing nuns and dancing monks. ⊠*31101 N. Valyermo Rd., south of Hwy. 138, Valyermo* ☎*888/454–5411, 661/944–1047 ceramics studio* ⊕*www.saintsandangels.org* ⌚*Free* ⊙ *Weekdays 9– 12:30 and 1:30–4:30, weekends 9–11:45 and 12:30–4:30.*

Adventure-seekers will enjoy flying over the scenic San Gabriel mountain pines, across the jagged San Andreas Fault, and over the sandy soil of El Mirage Dry Lake at **Great Western Soaring School,** the only place near Los Angeles that offers sailplane rides (no engines!). You'll be accompanied by an FAA-certified instructor, who will teach you the basics of airspeed control, straight flight, and turns before letting you handle the craft on your own. Basic flights range from $96 to $176. Advance reservations are required. ⊠*32810 165th St. E, Llano* ☎*661/944–9449* ⊕*www.greatwesternsoaring.com* ⊙*Fri.–Mon. 10– 6, Tues.–Thurs. by appointment.*

You can take ultralight (very small two-seater planes that can be flown without a pilot's license) lessons at the **Brian Ranch Airport,** which offers 15-minute ($40), half-hour ($60), and hour-long ($95) rides across the Mojave. The airport is also known for its annual "World's Smallest Air Show" every Memorial Day weekend, which draws aviation enthusiasts from around the country. ⊠*34180 Largo Vista Rd., Llano* ☎*661/261–3216* ⊕*www.brianranch.com.*

The closest you'll get to an African safari near Los Angeles is **Shambala Preserve,** an 80-acre wildlife preserve run by actress Tippi Hedren. Afternoon safaris, held once a month by advance reservation only, get you up to a foot away from 70 rescued wildcats and an African elephant. ⊠*6867 Soledad Canyon, Acton* ☎*661/268–0380* ⊕*www. shambala.org* ⌚*$40 minimum donation.*

WHERE TO STAY

$$ ⊞**Best Western John Jay Inn & Suites.** Antique furnishings decorate the rooms and suites at this full-service hotel. Each room has a large desk with ergonomic chair. Suites have balconies, fireplaces, wet bars, and Jacuzzis. Buffet breakfast and a *USA Today* newspaper are included in your room rate. **Pros:** Clean; good rates; spacious rooms. **Cons:** No on-site restaurant. ⊠*600 W. Palmdale Blvd.* ☎*661/575–9322* ⊕*www. bestwestern.com* ⇴*45 rooms, 18 suites* ⌂*In-room: refrigerator, Ethernet, Wi-Fi. In-hotel: pool, gym, laundry service, public Wi-Fi, no-smoking rooms* ▭*AE, D, DC, MC, V* ⊶*CP.*

10

LANCASTER

8 mi north of Palmdale via Hwy. 14.

Lancaster was founded in 1876, when the Southern Pacific Railroad arrived. Before that it was inhabited by Native American tribes: Kawaiisu, Kitanemuk, Serrano, Tataviam, and Chemehuevi. Descendants of some of these tribes still live in the surrounding mountains. Points of interest around Lancaster are far from the downtown area, some in neighboring communities.

**OFF THE
BEATEN
PATH**

Desert Tortoise Natural Area. Between mid-March and mid-June, this natural habitat of the elusive desert tortoise blazes with desert candles, primroses, lupine, and other wildflowers. Get there bright and early to spot the state reptile, while it grazes on fresh flowers and grass shoots. It's also a great spot to see desert kit fox, red-tailed hawks, cactus wrens, and Mojave rattlesnakes. ⊠*8 mi northeast of California City via Randsburg Mojave Rd.* ☎*951/683–3872* ⊕*www.tortoise-tracks. org* ⊠*Free* ☉*Daily.*

★ California's state flower, the California poppy, can be spotted just about anywhere in the state, but the densest concentration is in the **Antelope Valley Poppy Reserve.** Seven miles of trails lead you through 1,745 acres of hills carpeted with poppies and other wildflowers as far as the eye can see. Peak blooming time is usually March through May, though you're free to hike the grounds year-round. The visitor center has books and information about the reserve and other desert areas. Many trails are wheelchair- and stroller-accessible. ⊠*Ave. I, between 110th and 170th Sts.* W ☎*661/724–1180 or 661/942–0662* ⊕*www.parks.ca.gov* ⊠*$5 per vehicle* ☉ *Visitor center mid-Mar.–mid-May, daily 9–5.*

Ⓒ Thirteen species of wildcats, from the weasel-size jaguarundi to leopards, tigers, and jaguars, inhabit the **Exotic Feline Breeding Compound & Feline Conservation Center.** You can see the cats (behind barrier fences) in the parklike public zoo and research center. The center's biggest achievement has been the successful breeding of the rare Amur leopard, whose native habitat is remote border areas between Russia and China. ⊠*Off Mojave-Tropico Rd., Rosamond,* ⊹*4½ mi west of Hwy. 14 via Rosamond Blvd., 10 mi north of Lancaster* ☎*661/256–3793, 661/256–3332 recorded information* ⊕*www.cathouse-fcc.org* ⊠*$5* ☉*Thurs.–Tues. 10–4.*

A winery in the middle of the desert? Only in California could you find a place like **Antelope Valley Winery and Buffalo Company.** Industry scoffing hasn't stopped Cecil W. McLester, a graduate of UC Davis's renowned wine-making and viticulture program, from crafting a decent batch of wines, including the award-winning AV Burgundy (a house red) and Paloma Blanca (a Riesling-style blend of French Colombard, chenin blanc, and muscat grapes). The winery is also home to the Antelope Valley Buffalo Company, a producer of fine buffalo steaks, patties, and jerky, made from its roaming herd in the Leona Valley. ⊠*42041 20th St.* W ☎*661/722–0145* ⊕*www.avwinery.com* ⊠ *Winery free, 6-wine tasting $6* ☉ *Wed.–Sun. 11–6.*

RED ROCK CANYON STATE PARK

48 mi north of Lancaster via Hwy. 14; 17 mi west of U.S. 395 via Red Rock–Randsburg Rd.

A geological feast for the eyes with its layers of pink, white, red, and brown rock, Red Rock Canyon State Park is also a region of fascinating biological diversity—the ecosystems of the Sierra Nevada, the Mojave Desert, and the Basin Range all converge here. Entering the park from the south on Red Rock–Randsburg Road, you pass through a steep-walled gorge to a wide bowl tinted pink by volcanic ash. Native Americans known as the Old People lived here some 20,000 years ago; later, Mojave Indians roamed the land for centuries. Gold-rush fever hit the region in the mid-1800s, and you can still see remains of mining operations in the park. In the 20th century, Hollywood invaded the canyon, shooting westerns, TV shows, commercials, music videos, and movies such as *Jurassic Park* here. Be sure to check out the Red Cliffs Preserve on Highway 14, across from the entrance to the Red Rock campground. ✉*Ranger station: Abbott Dr. off Hwy. 14* ☎*661/942–0662* ⊕*www.parks.ca.gov* 🎫*$5 per vehicle* ✆*Visitor center Fri.–Sun. 10–4.*

> **LIQUID REFRESHMENT**
>
> After driving through the hot desert, you'll surely appreciate a cold one at **Indian Wells Brewing Company** (✉*2565 N. Hwy. 14, Inyokern, 2 mi west of Hwy. 395* ☎*760/377–5989* ⊕*www.mojave-red.com* ✆*Daily 9:30–5*), where master brewer Rick Lovett lovingly crafts his Desert Pale Ale, Eastern Sierra Lager, Mojave Gold, and Sidewinder Missile Ales. If you have the kids along, grab a six-pack of his specialty root beer, black cherry, orange, or cream sodas. The large gift shop carries bottled beer to go, as well as beef jerky, beer-infused barbecue sauces, and souvenirs.

RIDGECREST

28 mi northeast of Red Rock Canyon State Park via Hwy. 14; 77 mi south of Lone Pine via U.S. 395.

A military town that serves the U.S. Naval Weapons Center to its north, Ridgecrest has dozens of stores, restaurants, and hotels. It's a good base for exploring the northwestern Mojave, because it's the last big city you'll hit along U.S. 395 before you enter the desert.

The **Maturango Museum,** which also serves as a visitor information center, has pamphlets and books about the region. Small but informative exhibits detail the natural and cultural history of the northern Mojave. The museum runs wildflower tours in March and April. ✉*100 E. Las Flores Ave.* ☎*760/375–6900* ⊕*www.maturango.org* 🎫*$5* ✆*Daily 10–5.*

Fodor'sChoice ★ Guided tours conducted by the Maturango Museum are the only way to see **Petroglyph Canyons,** among the desert's most amazing spectacles. The two canyons, commonly called Big Petroglyph and Little Petroglyph, are in the Coso Mountain Range on the million-acre U.S. Naval Weapons Center at China Lake. Each of the canyons holds a superlative con-

10

centration of ancient rock art, the largest of its kind in the Northern Hemisphere. Thousands of well-preserved images of animals and humans—some more than 16,000 years old—are scratched or pecked into dark basaltic rocks. The tour takes you through 3 mi of sandy washes and boulders, so wear comfortable walking shoes. ■TIP→**At an elevation of 5,000 feet, weather conditions can be quite extreme, so dress in layers and bring plenty of drinking water (none is available at the site) and snacks.** Children under 10 are not allowed on the tour. The military requires everyone to produce a valid driver's license, social security number, passport, and vehicle registration before the trip (nondrivers must provide a birth certificate). ⊠*Tours depart from Maturango Museum* ☎*760/375–6900* ⊕*www.maturango.org* ⊠*$35* ☉*Museum daily 10–5. Tours Feb.–June and Sept. or Oct.–early Dec.; call for tour times.*

> **FORMER BOOMTOWNS**
>
> The towns of Randsburg, Red Mountain, and Johannesburg make up the **Rand Mining District** (⊠*U.S. 395, 20 mi south of Ridgecrest*), which first boomed with the discovery of gold in the Rand Mountains in 1895. Rich tungsten ore, used in World War I to make steel alloy, was discovered in 1907, and silver was found in 1919. The boom has gone bust, but the area still has a few residents, a dozen antiques shops, and plenty of character. Johannesburg is overlooked by an archetypal Old West cemetery in the hills above town.

☺ Rounded up by the Bureau of Land Management on public lands throughout the Southwest, the animals at the **Wild Horse and Burro Corrals** are available for adoption. You can bring along an apple or carrot to feed the horses, but the burros are usually too wild to approach. Individual and group tours are available. ⊠*Off Hwy. 178, 3 mi east of Ridgecrest* ☎*760/384–5765* ⊕*www.blm.gov* ⊠*Free* ☉*Weekdays 7:30–4.*

It's worth the effort (especially for sci-fi buffs, who will recognize the landscape from the film *Star Trek V*) to seek out **Trona Pinnacles National Natural Landmark.** These fantastic-looking formations of calcium carbonate, known as tufa, were formed underwater along fault lines in the bed of what is now Searles Dry Lake. A ½-mi trail winds around this surreal landscape of more than 500 spires, some of which stand as tall as 140 feet. Wear sturdy shoes—tufa cuts like coral. The best road to the area can be impassable after a rainstorm. ⊠*5 mi south of Hwy. 178, 18 mi east of Ridgecrest* ☎*760/384–5400 Ridgecrest BLM office* ⊕*www.blm.gov/ca/st/en/fo/ridgecrest/trona.3.html.*

WHERE TO STAY & EAT

$$ ✕▥ **Carriage Inn.** All the rooms at this large hotel are roomy and well kept, but the poolside cabanas are a bit cozier. The hotel has a long list of amenities, some of which are definitely not standard: a mister cools off sunbathers during the hot summer months. Café Potpourri serves a mix of American, Italian, and Southwestern specials. Charlie's Pub & Grill ($) serves burgers and sandwiches, which go nicely with the custom home-brewed ale from Indian Wells Valley Brewery. **Pros:**

Quiet location; full complimentary breakfast; nice outdoor pool. **Cons:** Old decor; some rooms could use an update. ✉ *901 N. China Lake Blvd., 93555* ☎*760/446–7910 or 800/772–8527* ⊕*www.carriageinn. biz* ⇲*152 rooms, 8 suites, 2 cabanas* ⌂*In-room: dial-up, Wi-Fi. In-hotel: no elevator, 2 restaurants, room service, bar, pool, gym, public Wi-Fi, no-smoking rooms* ☰*AE, D, DC, MC, V* ⏐◎⏐*MAP*.

$ ✕❑ **Heritage Inn and Suites.** This well-appointed and popular establishment is geared to business travelers, but the staff is equally attentive to tourists' concerns. Victoria's Restaurant ($), with an American-casual menu, is a favorite fine-dining spot for locals. **Pros:** Spacious rooms; full complimentary breakfast. **Cons:** Some walls are thin. ✉*1050 N. Norma St.* ☎*760/446–6543 or 800/843–0693* ⊕*www.heritage innsuites.com* ⇲*82 rooms, 44 suites* ⌂*In-room: refrigerator, dial-up. In-hotel: restaurant, room service, bar, pool, gym, laundry facilities, public Wi-Fi, airport shuttle, some pets allowed, no-smoking rooms* ☰*AE, D, DC, MC, V* ⏐◎⏐*BP*.

THE EASTERN MOJAVE

VICTORVILLE

87 mi south of Ridgecrest on U.S. 395. Turn east onto Bear Valley Rd. and travel 2 mi to town center.

At the southwest corner of the Mojave is the sprawling town of Victorville, a town rich in Route 66 heritage. Victorville was named for Santa Fe Railroad pioneer Jacob Nash Victor, who drove the first locomotive through the Cajon Pass here in 1885. Once home to Native Americans, the town later became a rest stop for Mormons and missionaries. In 1941 George Air Force Base (which now serves as an airport and storage area) brought scores of military families to the area, many of whom have stayed on to raise families of their own. February is one of the best times to visit, when the city holds its annual Roy Rogers and Dale Evans Western Film Festival and Adelanto Grand Prix, the largest motorcycle and quad off-road event in the country.

10

Fans of the Mother Road can visit the **California Route 66 Museum,** whose exhibits chronicle the history of America's most famous highway. At the museum you can pick up a book that details a self-guided tour of the old Sagebrush Route from Oro Grande to Helendale. The road passes Route 66 icons such as Potapov's Gas and Service Station (where the words BILL'S SERVICE are still legible) and the once-rowdy Sagebrush Inn, now a private residence. ✉*16825 D St., Rte. 66* ☎*760/951–0436* ⊕*www.califrt66museum.org* ✉*Free* ⏱*Thurs., Fri., and Mon. 10–4, Sun. 11–3.*

Forested **Silverwood Lake State Recreation Area** lies at the base of the San Bernardino Mountains, 10 mi east of Cajon Pass. One of the desert's most popular boating and fishing areas, 1,000-acre Silverwood Lake also has a beach with a lifeguard. You can fish for trout, largemouth bass, crappie, and catfish; hike and bike the trails; or come in winter to count bald eagles, which nest in the tall Jeffrey pines by the shore. Campgrounds accommodate tents and RVs. At the marina, you can rent pontoon and fishing boats as well as paddleboats, kayaks, and Waver-unners. Campfire programs are offered in summer, and public Wi-Fi is available in the park. ⊠*14651 Cedar Cir., Hesperia* ☎*760/389–2303* ⊕*www.parks.ca.gov* ⊒*$8 per car, $8 per boat* ☉*May–Sept., daily 6 AM–9 PM; Oct.–Apr., daily 7–7.*

WHERE TO EAT

¢–$ ✕**Emma Jean's Hollandburger Cafe.** This circa-1940s diner sits right on
★   U.S. Historic Route 66 and is favored by locals for its generous portions and old-fashioned home cooking. Try the biscuits and gravy, chicken-fried steak, or the famous Trucker's Sandwich, chock-full of roast beef, bacon, chilies, and cheese. ⊠*17143 D St.* ☎*760/243–9938* ⊟*AE, MC, V* ☉*Closed Sun. No dinner.*

¢–$ ✕**Summit Inn.** Elvis Presley is one of many famous customers who passed through this kitschy diner perched atop the Cajon Pass. Open since 1951, the restaurant is filled with Route 66 novelty items, a gift shop, and vintage jukebox, which plays oldies from the 1960s. The food isn't anything special, but the funky decor and historic significance make it worth a stop. ⊠*6000 Mariposa Rd., Oak Hills* ☎*760/949–8688* ⊟*MC, V.*

BARSTOW

32 mi northeast of Victorville on I–15.

In 1886, when a subsidiary of the Atchison, Topeka, and Santa Fe Railway began construction of a depot and hotel here, Barstow was born. Today outlet stores, chain restaurants, and motels define the landscape, though old-time neon signs light up the town's main street.

When the sun sets in the Mojave, check out a bit of surviving Americana at the **Skyline Drive-In Theatre,** where you can watch the latest Hollywood flicks among the Joshua trees and starry night sky in good old-fashioned stereo FM sound. ⊠*31175 Old Hwy. 58* ☎*760/256–3333* ⊒*$6* ☉*Shows daily at 7:30.*

The **California Welcome Center** has exhibits about desert ecology, wildflowers, and wildlife, as well as general visitor information for the state of California. ⊠*2796 Tanger Way* ☎*760/253–4782* ⊕*www.visitcwc. com* ☉*Daily 9–6.*

★   The earliest-known Americans fashioned the artifacts buried in the walls and floors of the pits at **Calico Early Man Archaeological Site.** Nearly 12,000 stone tools—used for scraping, cutting, and gouging—have been excavated here. The apparent age of some of these items (said to be as much as 200,000 years old) contradicts the dominant archaeological theory that humans populated North America only 13,000 years ago. Noted archaeologist Louis Leakey was so impressed with the Calico site that he became its director in 1963 and served in that capacity until his death in 1972. His old camp is now a visitor center and museum. The only way into the site is by guided tour (call ahead, as scheduled tours sometimes don't take place). ⊠ *Off I–15, Minneola Rd. exit, 15 mi northeast of Barstow* ☎ *760/254–2248* ⊕ *www.blm.gov/ca/st/en/fo/ barstow/calico.html* ▨ *$5* ☺ *Visitor center Wed. 12:30–4:30, Thurs.– Sun. 9–4:30; tours Wed. 1:30 and 3:30, Thurs.–Sun. 9:30, 11:30, 1:30, and 3:30.*

☺ Fodor's Choice ★ **Calico Ghost Town** was once a wild and wealthy mining town. In 1881 prospectors found a rich deposit of silver in the area, and by 1886 more than $85 million worth of silver, gold, and other precious metals had been harvested from the surrounding hills. Once the price of silver fell, though, the town slipped into decline. Many buildings here are authentic, but the restoration has created a theme-park version of the 1880s. You can stroll the wooden sidewalks of Main Street, browse shops filled with Western goods, roam the tunnels of Maggie's Mine, and take a ride on the Calico-Odessa Railroad. Festivals in March, May, October, and November celebrate Calico's Wild West theme. ⊠ *Ghost Town Rd., 3 mi north of I–15, 5 mi east of Barstow* ☎ *760/254–2122* ⊕ *www.calicotown.com* ▨ *$6* ☺ *Daily 9–5.*

A Spanish-named spot meaning "house of the desert," the **Casa Del Desierto Harvey House** was one of many hotel and restaurant depots opened by Santa Fe railroad guru Fred Harvey in the early 20th century. The location where Judy Garland's film *The Harvey Girls* was shot, the building is now completely restored. Inside the Casa Del Desierto is the Route 66 Mother Road Museum and Gift Shop. ⊠ *681 N. 1st Ave.* ☎ *760/255–1890* ⊕ *www.route66museum.org* ▨ *Free* ☺ *Apr.– Oct., Fri.–Sun. 10–4; Mar.–Nov., Fri.–Sun. 11–4. Guided tours by appointment.*

☺ Stop by the **Desert Discovery Center** to see exhibits of fossils, plants, and local animals. The main attraction here is Old Woman, the second-largest iron meteorite ever found in the United States. It was discovered in 1976 about 50 mi from Barstow in the Old Woman Mountains. The center also has visitor information for the Mojave Desert. ⊠ *831 Barstow Rd.* ☎ *760/252–6060* ⊕ *www.discoverytrails.org* ▨ *Free* ☺ *Tues.–Sat. 11–4.*

One of the world's largest natural Native American art galleries, **Inscription Canyon,** north of Barstow in the Black Mountains, has nearly 10,000 petroglyphs and pictographs of bighorn sheep and other Mojave wildlife. ⊠ *EF373, off Copper City Rd., 10 mi west of Fort Irwin Rd.* ☎ *760/252–6000* ☺ *Weekdays 7:45–4:30.*

★ So many science-fiction movies set on Mars have been filmed at **Rainbow Basin National Natural Landmark,** 8 mi north of Barstow, that you may feel like you're visiting the Red Planet. Huge slabs of red, orange, white, and green stone tilt at crazy angles like ships about to capsize; hike the washes, and you'll likely see the fossilized remains of creatures (such as mastodons and bear-dogs), which roamed the basin up to 16 million years ago. You can camp here, at Owl Canyon Campground, on the east side of Rainbow Basin. Part of the drive to the basin is on dirt roads. ⊠ *Fossil Bed Rd., 3 mi west of Fort Irwin Rd.* ☎ *760/252– 6000* ⊕ *www.blm.gov/ca/Barstow/basin.html.*

10

🔅 If you're a railroad buff, then you'll love the **Western American Rail Museum.** It houses memorabilia from Barstow's early railroad days, as well as interactive and historic displays on railroad history. Be sure to check out the old locomotives and cabooses for a truly nostalgic experience. ✉ *685 N. 1st St.* ☎ *760/256–9276* ⊕ *www.barstowrailmuseum. org* 🗺 *Free* ⊗ *Fri.–Sun. 11–4.*

🔅 If you've seen Jodie Foster's movie *Contact,* about intelligent signals from outer space, then you'll probably enjoy visiting the **Goldstone Deep Space Communications Complex** on the Fort Irwin Military Base near Barstow. By appointment, the staff offers guided tours of the 53-square-mi complex, including its large antennas, which search for signs of otherworldly life. Start out at the Goldstone Museum, with its exhibits dedicated to current missions, past missions, and Deep Space Network history, or take the kids into the hands-on room for a lesson about the universe. ✉ *35 mi north of Barstow on Ft. Irwin Military Base* ☎ *760/255–8687 or 760/255–8688* ⊕ *http://deepspace.jpl.nasa.gov/dsn/features/goldstone-tours.html* 🗺 *Free* ⊗ *Guided tours by appointment only.*

WHERE TO STAY & EAT

$–$$$$ ✕ **Idle Spurs Steakhouse.** Since the 1950s this roadside ranch has been a
★ Barstow dining staple. Covered in cacti outside and Christmas lights inside, it's a colorful, cheerful place with a big wooden bar. The menu features prime cuts of meat, ribs, and lobster, and there's a great microbrew list. ✉ *690 Hwy. 58* ☎ *760/256–8888* ⊕ *www.idlespurssteak house.com* ☰ *AE, D, MC, V* ⊗ *No lunch weekends.*

¢–$ ✕ **Bagdad Café.** Tourists from all over the world flock to the site where
★ the 1988 film of the same name was shot. Built in the 1940s, this Route 66 eatery serves a home-style menu of burgers, chicken-fried steak, and seafood. An old Airstream trailer from the movie sits outside the café. ✉ *46548 National Trails Hwy., Newberry Springs* ☎ *760/257–3101* ⊕ *www.bagdadcafeusa.com* ☰ *AE, MC, V.*

¢–$ ✕ **Slash X Ranch Cafe.** If you have a craving for cold beer, burgers, and chili-cheese fries, look no further than this Wild West watering hole, a Barstow favorite since 1954. Named for the cattle ranch that preceded it, the café lures a mix of visitors and locals, who relish its rowdy atmosphere, hearty portions, and friendly service. Shuffleboard tables and horseshoe pits add to the fun. ✉ *28040 Barstow Rd.* ☎ *760/252–1197* ⊕ *www.slashxranchcafe.com* ☰ *AE, D, MC, V* ⊗ *Closed weekdays.*

¢–$ 🏨 **Ramada Inn.** Though this large property is slightly more expensive than others lining Main Street, it also has more amenities (which is why it tends to attract business travelers). The modern rooms have a desert theme and are decorated in browns and pinks that evoke the surrounding landscape. **Pros:** Clean, large rooms. **Cons:** Some rooms feel dated; occasional nighttime train noise. ✉ *1511 E. Main St. 92311* ☎ *760/256–5673* ⊕ *www.ramada.com* ⇌ *148 rooms* ♿ *In-room: Ethernet (some), dial-up, Wi-Fi. In-hotel: restaurant, room service, pool, laundry service, public Wi-Fi, some pets allowed, no-smoking rooms* ☰ *AE, D, DC, MC, V* 🍽 *BP.*

BAKER

63 mi northeast of Barstow on I–15; 84 mi south of Death Valley Junction via Hwy. 127.

The small town of Baker is Death Valley's gateway to the western Mojave. There are several gas stations and restaurants (most of them fast-food outlets), a few motels, and one general store (which has the distinction of selling the most winning Lotto tickets in California).

■ TIP➡ While you're driving through the Mojave, tune in to the Highway Stations (98.1 FM near Barstow, 98.9 FM near Essex, and 99.7 FM near Baker)

for the latest Mojave traffic and weather. The stations cover 40,000 square mi of the desert, making it an important source of information on the area. Traffic can be especially troublesome Friday through Sunday, when scores of harried Angelenos head to Las Vegas for a bit of R&R.

You can't help but notice Baker's 134-foot-tall **thermometer** (⊠ *72157 Baker Blvd.*), whose height in feet pays homage to the record-high U.S. temperature: 134°F, recorded in Death Valley on July 10, 1913.

AFTON CANYON

Because of its colorful, steep walls, **Afton Canyon** (⊠ *Off Afton Canyon Rd., 36 mi northeast of Barstow via I–15*) is often called the Grand Canyon of the Mojave. It was carved over thousands of years by the rushing waters of the Mojave River, which makes one of its few aboveground appearances here. The dirt road that leads to the canyon is ungraded in spots, so you are best off driving it in an all-terrain vehicle.

PRIMM, NV

52 mi northeast of Baker, via I–15; 118 mi east of Death Valley, via Hwy. 160 and I–15; 114 mi north of Barstow, via I–15.

Amid the rugged beauty of the Mojave's landscapes, this bustling mecca for gamblers and theme-park lovers has sprung up on the border between California and southern Nevada. The casino resorts here are the first to greet you on the lonely stretch of road connecting Los Angeles with Las Vegas—and increasingly, visitors are simply stopping and spending their gambling vacations here.

10

One of Primm's greatest claims to fame is its 24-hour **Bonnie and Clyde Gangster Exhibit.** Here, you'll find the bullet-riddled Ford car in which the 1930s duo perished in a hailstorm of gunfire in Louisiana on May 3, 1934. There are also other Bonnie and Clyde memorabilia, such as newspaper clippings and items owned by the couple, and a restored 1931 armored Lincoln belonging to gangsters Al Capone and Dutch Schultz. The exhibits are free to view in the rotunda connecting Primm Valley Resort and Casino with the Fashion Outlet Mall. ⊠ *32100 Las Vegas Blvd. S.* ☎ *702/874–1400 Ext. 7073.*

Though there are plenty of family-friendly activities in Primm (such as shopping at the mall, hitting the waterslide at Whiskey Pete's, or the amusement park at Buffalo Bill's), guests under 21 are not allowed on the casino floors, and children under 13 may not be left unattended.

Each of the casinos has a video arcade, which may provide some solace for the teenage set.

WHERE TO STAY & EAT

¢–$$ ✕⬚ **Buffalo Bill's Resort and Casino.** Decorated in the style of a Western frontier town, this hotel is the biggest and most popular in Primm. Its buffalo-shaped swimming pool and a large amusement park—which features several roller coasters and other rides—make the property a hit with families. The casino itself is enormous (46,000 square feet), and rooms here are bright and cheery and decorated with lodge-style furniture. Among the resort's several restaurants, Tony Roma's ($–$$$) is a favorite. **Pros:** On-site restaurants and shops; casino. **Cons:** Roller coaster noise at night; basic rooms seem a little worn. ⊠*31700 Las Vegas Blvd. S.* ☎*702/386–7867, 800/386–7867* ⊕*www.primmvalley resorts.com* ⟳*1,193 rooms, 49 suites* ⌖*In-room: kitchen (some), refrigerator (some), dial-up, Wi-Fi. In-hotel: 8 restaurants, bars, pool, concierge, no-smoking rooms* ▭*AE, D, DC, MC, V.*

¢–$$ ✕⬚ **Primm Valley Resort and Casino.** This elegant resort, which evokes a 1930s country club, is conveniently near the Primm Valley Conference Center. Rooms are decorated in warm tones, with dark-wood furniture. If you feel like splurging, check into one of the 640-square-foot Jacuzzi suites. GP's ($–$$$), one of the on-site restaurants, is the fanciest in town, and popular for its aged prime rib and veal cordon bleu. **Pros:** On-site restaurants and shops; casino. **Cons:** Basic rooms seem a little worn. ⊠*31900 Las Vegas Blvd. S.* ☎*702/386–7867 or 800/386–7867* ⊕*www.primmvalleyresorts.com* ⟳*592 rooms, 31 suites* ⌖*In-room: kitchen (some), refrigerator (some), dial-up, Wi-Fi. In-hotel: 3 restaurants, room service, bars, pool, no-smoking rooms* ▭*AE, D, DC, MC, V.*

¢–$$ ✕⬚ **Whiskey Pete's Hotel and Casino.** Opened in 1977, this castle-inspired property is the oldest of the three casinos in Primm. Rooms are decorated in mahogany and have Spanish tile floors; each of the 725-square-foot Jacuzzi suites has a four-person hot tub in the living room and a full bar. If you're visiting in summer, the tropical-theme pool with its shade trees and waterslide is a cool retreat. The Silver Spur Steakhouse ($–$$) serves excellent prime rib and chateaubriand. **Pros:** Nice pool; cheap rooms. **Cons:** Rooms feel a bit worn and dated. ⊠*100 W. Primm Blvd.* ☎*702/386–7867 or 800/386–7867* ⊕*www.primmvalleyresorts. com* ⟳*765 rooms, 12 suites* ⌖*In-room: kitchen (some), refrigerator (some), dial-up, Wi-Fi. In-hotel: 4 restaurants, room service, bars, pool, gym, no-smoking rooms* ▭*AE, D, DC, MC, V.*

SPORTS & THE OUTDOORS

All hotel guests have privileges at the **Primm Valley Golf Club** (☎*888/847–2757*), which has two 18-hole courses designed by Tom Fazio that rank among the top 100 in the nation. Two putting greens and a pro shop complete the club, which is 4 mi south of Primm Valley Resort.

MOJAVE NATIONAL PRESERVE

Between I–15 and I–40, roughly east of Baker and Ludlow to the California/Nevada border.

The 1.4 million acres of the Mojave National Preserve hold a surprising abundance of plant and animal life—especially considering their elevation (nearly 8,000 feet in some areas). There are traces of human history here as well, including abandoned army posts and vestiges of mining and ranching towns. The town of Cima still has a small functioning store.

Created millions of years ago by volcanic activity, **Hole-in-the-Wall** formed when gases were trapped between layers of deposited ash, rock, and lava; the gas bubbles left holes in the solidified material. The area was named by Bob Hollimon, a member of the Butch Cassidy gang, because it reminded him of his former hideout in Wyoming. To hike the canyon, you first must make your way down Rings Trail, a narrow 200-foot vertical chute. To make the rather strenuous descent you must grasp a series of metal rings embedded in the rock. The trail drops you into Banshee Canyon, where you are surrounded by steep, pockmarked walls and small caverns. You can explore the length of the canyon, but climbing the walls is not recommended, as the rock is soft and crumbles easily. Keep your eyes open for native lizards such as the chuckwalla. The Hole-in-the-Wall ranger station has docents who can answer questions about the area. ⊠ *Black Canyon Rd., 9 mi north of Mitchell Caverns* ☎ *760/928–2572* ⊕ *www.nps.gov/moja* ☉ *Fri.–Sun. 9–4.*

★ As you enter the preserve from the south, you'll pass miles of open scrub brush, Joshua trees, and beautiful red-black cinder cones before encountering the **Kelso Dunes** (⊠ *Kelbaker Rd., 90 mi east of I–15 and 14 mi north of I–40* ☎ *760/928–2572 or 760/252–6100* ⊕ *www.nps.gov/moja*). These perfect, pristine slopes of gold-white sand cover 70 square mi, often reaching heights of 500 to 600 feet. You can reach them via a ½-mi walk from the main parking area. When you reach the top of a dune, kick a little bit of sand down the lee side and listen to the sand "sing." North of the dunes, in the town of Kelso, is the Mission revival–style **Kelso Depot Information Center,** flanked by three swaying palm trees. The building, which dates to 1923, is the main stopping point for Mojave National Preserve. The Depot's Beanery restaurant features the same historic menu that refueled weary passengers and rail workers. Primitive campsites are available at no charge near the dunes' main parking area.

⚬ The National Park Service administers most of the Mojave preserve, but ★ **Providence Mountains State Recreation Area** is under the jurisdiction of the California Department of Parks. The visitor center has views of mountain peaks, dunes, buttes, crags, and desert valleys. At **Mitchell Caverns Natural Preserve** (⊠ *$5*) you have a rare opportunity to see all three types of cave formations—dripstone, flowstone, and erratics—in one place. The year-round 65°F temperature provides a break from the desert heat. Tours, the only way to see the caverns, are given daily at 1:30. Reservations must be made by mail and at least three weeks in advance; call first to check availability. ⊠ *Essex Rd., 16 mi north of I–40* ☎ *760/928–2586* ⊕ *www.parks.ca.gov* ☉ *Visitor center May–Sept., weekends 9–4.*

10

NEEDLES

I–40, 150 mi east of Barstow.

On Route 66 and the Colorado River, Needles is a good base for exploring many desert attractions, including Mojave National Preserve. Founded in 1883, the town of Needles, named for the jagged mountain peaks that overlook the city, served as a stop along the Santa Fe Railroad. One of its crown jewels was the elegant El Garces Harvey House Train Depot, which at this writing was being restored. Today, Needles is a thriving community and a popular getaway for California residents who want to enjoy the river a little closer to home.

Don't miss the historic 1908 **El Garces Harvey House Train Depot** (⊠ *900 Front St.* ☎ *760/326–5678*), one of the many restaurant-boardinghouses built by the Fred Harvey company.

Mystic Maze (⊠ *Park Moabi Rd., off I–40, 11 mi southeast of Needles* ☎ *760/326–5678*) is an unexplained geological site of spiritual significance to Pipa Aha Macav (Fort Mojave) Indians. The maze consists of several rows of rocks and mounds of dirt in different patterns.

☾ In 1941, after the construction of Parker Dam, President Franklin D.
Fodor'sChoice Roosevelt set aside **Havasu National Wildlife Refuge,** a 24-mi stretch of
★ land along the Colorado River between Needles and Lake Havasu City. Best seen by boat, this beautiful waterway is punctuated with isolated coves, sandy beaches, and Topock Marsh, a favorite nesting site of herons, egrets, and other waterbirds. You can see wonderful petroglyphs on the rocky red canyon cliffs of Topock Gorge. The park has 11 access points, including boat launches at Catfish Paradise, Five Mile Landing, and Pintail Slough. There's camping below Castle Rock. ⊠ *Off I–40, 13 mi southeast of Needles* ☎ *760/326–3853* ⊕ *www.fws. gov/southwest/refuges/arizona/havasu.*

Moabi Regional Park, on the banks of the Colorado River, is a good place for swimming, boating, picnicking, horseback riding, and fishing. Bass, bluegill, and trout are plentiful in the river. There are 600 campsites with full amenities, including RV hookups, laundry and showers, and grills. ⊠ *Park Moabi Rd., off I–40, 11 mi southeast of Needles* ☎ *760/326–3831* ⊕ *www.moabi.com* ☜ *Day use $10, camping $15–$35.*

WHERE TO STAY & EAT

¢–$$ ✕ **River City Pizza.** It's slim pickin's in Needles when it comes to finding good grub, but this little pizza place is a local favorite. The restaurant is clean and simple, and the walls are covered with vibrant hand-painted scenes of Route 66 and the Colorado River. Try the Teriyaki Chicken Pizza with a mug of cold lager or a glass of wine. ⊠ *819 Broadway* ☎ *760/326–9191* ⊟ *AE, D, MC, V.*

¢–$$ ⊡ **Best Western Colorado River Inn.** The country-western style rooms at this reliable chain are spartan, but they're decorated in rich colors. The property is right off Interstate 40. Expect the standard Best Western amenities, including free local calls and complimentary coffee in the lobby each morning. **Pros:** Good rates; clean rooms. **Cons:** Occasional nighttime train noise. ⊠*2371 Needles Hwy.* ☎*760/326–4552 or 800/780–7234* ⊕*www.bestwestern.com* ⇆*63 rooms* ⌂*In-room: refrigerator (some), Ethernet (some), dial-up, Wi-Fi. In-hotel: no elevator, pool, laundry facilities, public Wi-Fi, some pets allowed, no-smoking rooms* ⊟*AE, DC, MC, V* ⃝*BP.*

¢ ⊞**Fender's River Road Resort.** This funky little 1960s-era motel is one of the best-kept secrets in Needles. The rooms are clean and well kept, many decorated with such whimsical accents as fish and stars. On a calm section of the Colorado River, this resort caters to families and has a grassy play area shaded with trees and an area with grills and picnic tables. Camping is $44 a night. **Pros:** On the river; clean rooms. **Cons:** Bare-bones amenities. ⊠*3396 Needles Hwy.,* ☎*760/326–3423* ⊕*www.fendersriverroadresort.com* ⇆*10 rooms, 27 campsites with full hookups* ⌂*In-room: kitchen, refrigerator. In-hotel: no elevator, beachfront, laundry facilities* ⊟*D, MC, V.*

LAKE HAVASU CITY, AZ

Hwy. 95, 43 mi southeast of Needles in Arizona.

In summer Angelenos throng to Lake Havasu. This wide spot in the Colorado River, which has backed up behind Parker Dam, is accessed from its eastern shore in Arizona. Here you can swim; zip around on a Jet Ski; paddle a kayak; fish for trout, bass, or bluegill; or boat beneath the London Bridge, one of the desert's oddest sights. During sunset the views are breathtaking.

Once home to the Mohave Indians, this riverfront community (which means "blue water") was settled in the 1930s with the construction of Parker Dam.

WHERE TO EAT

$–$$$ ✕**Shugrue's.** This lakefront restaurant, a favorite of locals and tour-
★ ists, serves up beautiful views of London Bridge and the English Village. Heavy on fresh seafood, steak, and lobster, the restaurant is also known for such specials as Bombay chicken and shrimp, served with spicy yogurt sauce and mango chutney. ⊠*1425 McCulloch Blvd.* ☎*928/453–1400* ⊕*www.shugrues.com/lhc* ⊟*AE, D, DC, V.*

SPORTS & THE OUTDOORS

☾ Docked at the London Bridge, the *Dixie Bell* (☎*928/453–6776* ⊡*$15*) offers a leisurely way to spend an afternoon. The two-story, old-fashioned paddle-wheel boat, with air-conditioning and a cocktail lounge, takes guests on a one-hour narrated tour around the island. Tours are given daily

10

LONDON, ARIZONA?

What really put this town on the map was the piece-by-piece reconstruction in 1971 of **London Bridge** by town founder Robert P. McCulloch. Today the circa-1831 bridge, designed by John Rennie, connects the city to a small island and is the center of a town including numerous restaurants, hotels, RV parks, and a reconstructed English village. ☎*928/855–4115* ⊕*www.havasuchamber.com* ⊡*Free* ⊙*Daily 24 hrs.*

at noon and 1:30. Right on the beach, **London Bridge Watercraft Tours & Rentals** (⊠*1534 Beachcomber Blvd., Crazy Horse Campground* ☏*928/453–8883* ⊕*www.londonbridgewatercraft.com*) rents personal watercraft such as Jet Skis and Sea-Doos.

OWENS VALLEY

Along U.S. 395 east of the Sierra Nevada.

Lying in the shadow of the eastern Sierra Nevada, the Owens Valley stretches along U.S. 395 from the Mono–Inyo county line, in the north, to the town of Olancha, in the south. This stretch of highway is dotted with tiny towns, some containing only a mini-mart and a gas station. If you're traveling from Yosemite National Park to Death Valley National Park or are headed from Lake Tahoe or Mammoth to the desert, U.S. 395 is your corridor.

LONE PINE

30 mi west of Panamint Valley via Hwy. 190.

Mt. Whitney towers majestically over this tiny community, which supplied nearby gold- and silver-mining outposts in the 1860s. In more recent decades—especially the 1950s and '60s—the town has been touched by Hollywood glamour: more than 300 movies, TV shows, and commercials have been filmed here. The Lone Pine Film Festival now takes place here every October.

Drop by the Lone Pine Visitor Center for a map of the **Alabama Hills** and take a drive up Whitney Portal Road (turn west at the light) to this wonderland of granite boulders. Erosion has worn the rocks smooth; some have been chiseled to leave arches and other formations. The hills have become a popular location for rock climbing. There are three campgrounds among the rocks, each with a stream for fishing. ⊠ *Whitney Portal Rd., 4½ mi west of Lone Pine.*

★ Straddling the border of Sequoia National Park and Inyo National Forest–John Muir Wilderness, **Mt. Whitney** (14,496 feet) is the highest mountain in the continental United States. A favorite game for travelers passing through Lone Pine is trying to guess which peak is Mt. Whitney. Almost no one gets it right because Mt. Whitney is hidden behind other mountains. There is no road that ascends the peak, but you can catch a glimpse of the mountain by driving curvy Whitney Portal Road west from Lone Pine into the mountains. The pavement ends at the trailhead to the top of the mountain, which is also the start of the 211-mi John Muir Trail from Mt. Whitney to Yosemite National Park. At the portal, a restaurant (known for its pancakes) and a small store mostly cater to hikers and campers staying at Whitney Portal Campground. You can see a waterfall from the parking lot and go fishing in a small trout pond. The portal area is closed from mid-October to early May; the road closes when snow conditions require.

WHERE TO STAY & EAT

$–$$$ ✕**Seasons Restaurant.** This inviting, country-style diner serves all kinds of upscale American fare. For a special treat, try the medallions of Cervena venison, smothered in port wine, dried cranberries, and toasted walnuts; finish with the Baileys Irish Cream cheesecake or the lemon crème brûlée for dessert. Children's items include a mini–sirloin steak. ✉ *206 S. Main St.* ☎ *760/876–8927* 🍽 *AE, D, MC, V* ⊘ *No lunch.*

¢–$ ✕**Mt. Whitney Restaurant.** A boisterous family-friendly restaurant with a game room and 50-inch television, this place is especially popular during *Monday Night Football.* The best burgers in town are here—you can choose from the usual beef or branch out with ostrich, venison, or buffalo burgers. There's a gift shop on the premises. ✉ *227 S. Main St.* ☎ *760/876–5751* 🍽 *D, MC, V.*

¢–$$ 🏨**Dow Villa Motel and Hotel.** John Wayne slept here, and you can, too. Built in 1923 to cater to the film industry, Dow Villa is in the center of Lone Pine. Some rooms have views of the mountains; both buildings are within walking distance of just about everything in town. There are in-room coffeemakers and whirlpool tubs, though some of the guest rooms share bathrooms. Pets are allowed only in the motel rooms. Many units have an Old West feel, and are decorated with antique furniture and pictures of John Wayne or Mt. Whitney. **Pros:** Historic property; nice views. **Cons:** Feels a bit dated. ✉ *310 S. Main St.* ☎ *760/876–5521 or 800/824–9317* ⊕ *www.dowvillamotel.com* 🛏 *91 rooms* ⚒ *In-room: refrigerator, VCR, Ethernet (some), dial-up, Wi-Fi. In-hotel: pool, no elevator, public Wi-Fi, no-smoking rooms* 🍽 *AE, D, DC, MC, V.*

MANZANAR NATIONAL HISTORIC SITE

U.S. 395, 11 mi north of Lone Pine.

A reminder of an ugly episode in U.S. history, the remnants of the Manzanar War Relocation Center have been designated the Manzanar National Historic Site. This is where some 10,000 Japanese-Americans were confined behind barbed-wire fences between 1942 and 1945. Manzanar was the first of 10 such internment camps erected by the federal government following Japan's attack on Pearl Harbor in 1941. In the name of national security, American citizens of Japanese descent were forcibly relocated to these camps, many of them losing their homes, businesses, and most of their possessions in the process. Today not much remains of Manzanar but a guard post, the auditorium, and some concrete foundations. But you can stop at the entrance station, pick up a brochure, and drive the one-way dirt road past the ruins to a small cemetery, where a monument stands as a reminder of what took place here. Signs mark where structures such as the barracks, a hospital, school, and fire station once stood. An 8,000-square-foot interpretive center, opened in 2004, has exhibits and a 15-minute film. ⊞ *Manzanar Information, c/o Superintendent: Death Valley National Park, Death Valley, 92398* ☎ *760/878–2932* ⊕ *www.nps.gov/manz* 🎫 *Free* ⊘ *Park daily dawn–dusk. Center Apr.–Nov., daily 9–5:30; Nov.–Apr., daily 9–4:30.*

10

CERRO GORDO GHOST TOWN

★ *20 mi east of Lone Pine.*

Discovered by Mexican miner Pablo Flores in 1865, Cerro Gordo was California's biggest producer of silver and lead, raking in almost $13 million before it shut down in 1959. Today it's a ghost town, home to many original buildings, including the circa-1871 American Hotel, the fully restored 1904 bunkhouse, the 1868 Belshaw House, a bullet-riddled saloon, and Union Mine and General Store, which now serves as a museum and outlook point over the majestic Sierra mountains and Owens Dry Lake. The Sarsaparilla Saloon inside the hotel serves up its own Cerro Gordo Freighting Company Root Beer, bottled in nearby Indian Wells (proceeds go back to restoring and maintaining the ghost town). You'll have to time your visit for summer (usually early June through mid-November), as its 8,300-foot elevation means that the steep road into the town is impassable in winter. A four-wheel-drive vehicle is recommended at all times. A day pass is $5 per person, which includes a tour if arranged in advance. Guests are forbidden to take artifacts from the area or explore nearby mines. ⌂ *Box 221, Keeler, 93530* ☎ *760/876–5030* ⊕ *www.cerrogordo.us.*

INDEPENDENCE

U.S. 395, 5 mi north of Manzanar National Historic Site.

Named for a military outpost that was established near here in 1862, Independence is small and sleepy. But the town has some wonderful historic buildings and is certainly worth a stop on your way from the Sierra Nevada to Death Valley.

♻ As you approach Independence from the north, you'll pass the **Mt. Whitney Fish Hatchery,** a delightful place for a family picnic. Bring some dimes for the machines filled with fish food; the hatchery's lakes are full of hefty, always-hungry breeder trout. Built in 1915, the hatchery was one of the first trout farms in California, and today it produces fish that stock lakes throughout the state. ⊠ *Fish Hatchery Rd., 1 mi north of Independence* ☎ *760/878–2272* ☑ *Free* ⊙ *Daily 9–4.*

The **Eastern California Museum** provides a glimpse of Inyo County's history. Highlights include a fine collection of Paiute and Shoshone Indian basketry and a yard full of agricultural implements used by early area miners and farmers. ⊠ *155 N. Grant St.* ☎ *760/878–0364* ⊕ *www.inyocounty.us/ecmuseum* ☑ *Donations accepted* ⊙ *Wed.–Mon. 10–5.*

WHERE TO STAY

¢–$$ ⊞ **Winnedumah Hotel Bed & Breakfast.** This 1927 B&B has the best—and most famous—digs in town: celebrities such as Roy Rogers, John Wayne, and Bing Crosby all stayed here while filming nearby. Outfitted in an eclectic mix of Wild West chic and modern bric-a-brac, the rooms are simple yet comfortable. There are also hostel rooms. Breakfast is usually a hearty affair of bacon, eggs, waffles, and fresh fruit. **Pros:** Historic property; clean rooms. **Cons:** No television. ⊠ *211 N. Edwards*

St. 93526 ☎760/878–2040 ⊕*www.winnedumah.com* ↩*24 rooms,
14 with bath* ♿*In-room: no phone (some), no TV, Wi-Fi. In-hotel: no
elevator, public Wi-Fi, some pets allowed, no-smoking rooms* ▭*AE,
D, DC, MC, V* ⦿*BP.*

**EN
ROUTE**

Traveling north from Independence on U.S. 395, turn onto Highway
168 and follow the signs 31 mi to the **Ancient Bristlecone Pine Forest.** Here
you can see some of the oldest living trees on earth, some of which date
back more than 40 centuries. These rare, gnarled pines in the White
Mountains can grow only in harsh, frigid conditions above 9,000 feet.
At the **Schulman Grove Visitor Center** (☎760/873–2500 ⊕*www.fs.fed.
us/r5/inyo/about*), open from 8 to 4:30 weekdays, late May through
October, you can learn about the bristlecone and take a walk to the
4,700-year-old Methuselah tree. Admission to the forest is $3.

BISHOP

U.S. 395, 43 mi north of Independence.

One of the biggest towns along U.S. 395, Bishop has views of the
Sierra Nevada and the White and Inyo mountains. First settled by the
Northern Paiute Indians, the area was named in 1861 for cattle rancher
Samuel Bishop, who established a camp here. Paiute and Shoshone
people reside on four reservations in the area.

One of Bishop's biggest draws is its **Mule Days Celebration** each Memorial Day weekend. More than 40,000 tourists and RVers pack into
this lazy town for the longest nonmotorized parade in the world, mule
races, a rodeo, and good old-fashioned country-and-western concerts.
☎760/872–4263 ⊕*www.muledays.org.*

The **Laws Railroad Museum** is a complex of historic buildings and train
cars from the Carson and Colorado Railroad Company, which set up
a narrow-gauge railroad yard here in 1883. Among the exhibits are a
self-propelled car from the Death Valley Railroad and a full village of
rescued buildings, including a post office, an 1883 train depot, the 1909
North Inyo Schoolhouse, and a restored 1900 ranch house. ⊠*U.S. 6, 3
mi north of U.S. 395* ☎760/873–5950 ⊕*www.lawsmuseum.org* ▭*$5
suggested donation* ⊘*Daily 10–4.*

10

WHERE TO STAY & EAT

¢–$$$ ✕**Whiskey Creek.** Since 1924, this Wild West–style saloon, restaurant,
★ and gift shop has been serving crisp salads, warm soups, and juicy
barbecued steaks to locals and tourists. Warm days are perfect for sit-
ting on the shaded deck and enjoying one of the many available micro-
brews. ⊠*524 N. Main St.* ☎760/873–7174 ▭*AE, MC, V.*

¢ ✕**Erick Schat's Bakkerÿ.** A popular stop for motorists traveling to and
from Mammoth Lakes, this shop is chock-full of delicious pastries,
cookies, rolls, and other baked goods. But the biggest draw is the
sheepherder bread, a hand-shaped and stone hearth–baked sourdough
that was introduced during the gold rush by immigrant Basque sheep-
herders in 1907. In addition to the bakery, Schat's has a gift shop and a

sandwich bar. ⊠*763 N. Main St.* ☎*760/873–7156* ⊕*www.erickschats bakery.com* ☰*AE, MC, V.*

$–$$ 🏨**Best Western Creekside Inn.** One of the nicest spots to stay in Bishop, this clean and comfortable mountain-style hotel is a good base from which to explore the town or go skiing and trout fishing nearby. Rooms are elegantly furnished with cherrywood armoires and beds; the ranch-style lobby has a wonderfully large brick hearth. In summer you can sit on the patio near a trickling creek. **Pros:** Nice pool; spacious and modern rooms. **Cons:** Pets not allowed. ⊠*725 N. Main St. 93514* ☎*760/872–3044 or 800/273–3550* ⊕*www.bestwestern.com* 🛏*89 rooms* ♿*In-room: refrigerators (some), kitchen (some), dial-up, Wi-Fi. In-hotel: pool, public Wi-Fi, no-smoking rooms* ☰*AE, MC, V* 🍴*CP.*

SPORTS & THE OUTDOORS

Sierra Mountain Center (⊠*174 W. Line St.* ☎*760/873–8526* ⊕*www. sierramountaincenter.com*) provides instruction and guided hiking, skiing, snowshoeing, rock-climbing, and mountain-biking trips for all levels of expertise.

FISHING   The Owens Valley is trout country; its glistening alpine lakes and streams are brimming with feisty rainbow, brown, brook, and golden trout. Popular spots include Owens River, the Owens River gorge, and Pleasant Valley Reservoir. Although you can fish year-round here, some fishing is catch-and-release. Bishop is the site of fishing derbies throughout the year, including the popular Blake Jones Blind Bogey Trout Derby, in March. Whether you want to take a fly-fishing class or a guided wade trip, **Brock's Flyfishing Specialists and Tackle Experts** (⊠*100 N. Main St.* ☎*760/872–3581 or 888/619–3581* ⊕*www.brocksflyfish.com*) is a valuable resource.

HORSE   The **Rock Creek Pack Station** (🏷*Box 248, 93516* ☎*760/935–4493 in*
PACKING   *summer, 760/872–8331 in winter* ⊕*www.rockcreekpackstation.com*) outfit runs 3- to 24-day horse-packing trips in the High Sierra, including Mt. Whitney, Yosemite National Park, and other parts of the John Muir Wilderness. One expedition tracks wild mustangs through Inyo National Forest; another is an old-fashioned horse drive between the Owens Valley and the High Sierra.

THE MOJAVE ESSENTIALS

To research prices, get advice from other travelers, and book travel arrangements, visit ⊕*www.fodors.com.*

TRANSPORTATION

AIRPORTS & TRANSFERS

Inyokern Airport, near Ridgecrest, is served by United Express from Los Angeles. McCarran International Airport, in Las Vegas, is served by dozens of major airlines and is about as close as Inyokern Airport to Furnace Creek in Death Valley National Park. Needles Airport serves small, private planes, as does Furnace Creek's 3,000-foot airstrip in Death Valley. See Air Travel in California Essentials for airline phone numbers.

Contacts **Inyokern Airport** (⊠ *Inyokern Rd., Hwy. 178, 9 mi west of Ridgecrest, Inyokern* ☎ *760/377–5844* ⊕ *www.inyokernairport.com*). **McCarran International Airport** (⊠ *5757 Wayne Newton Blvd., Las Vegas, NV* ☎ *702/261–5733* ⊕ *www.mc carran.com*). **Needles Airport** (⊠ *711 Airport Rd., Needles* ☎ *760/326–5263*).

BY BUS

Greyhound serves Baker, Barstow, Ridgecrest, and Victorville. Victor Valley Transit serves Victorville, Hesperia, Phelan, Adelanto, and other nearby areas.

Contacts **Greyhound** (☎ *800/231–2222* ⊕ *www.greyhound.com*). **Victor Valley Transit** (☎ *760/948–3030* ⊕ *www.vvta.org*).

BY CAR

The major north–south route through the western Mojave is U.S. 395, which intersects with I–15 between Cajon Pass and Victorville. U.S. 395 travels north into the Owens Valley, passing such dusty little stops as Lone Pine, Independence, Big Pine, and Bishop. Farther west, Highway 14 runs north–south between Inyokern (near Ridgecrest) and Palmdale. Two major east–west routes travel through the Mojave: to the north, I–15 between Barstow and Las Vegas, Nevada; to the south, I–40 between Barstow and Needles. At the intersection of the two interstates, in Barstow, I–15 veers south toward Victorville and Los Angeles, and I–40 gives way to Highway 58 toward Bakersfield.

Contact **California Highway Patrol 24-hour road info** (☎ *800/427–7623* ⊕ *www.dot.ca.gov/hq/roadinfo*).

BY TRAIN

Amtrak makes stops in Victorville, Barstow, and Needles, but the stations are not staffed and do not have phone numbers, so you'll have to purchase your tickets in advance and handle your own baggage. You can travel west to connect with the *Coast Starlight* in Los Angeles or the *Pacific Surfliner* in Fullerton. The *Southwest Chief* stops twice a day at the above cities on its route from Los Angeles to Chicago and back. The Barstow station is served daily by Amtrak California motor coaches that travel between San Joaquin, Bakersfield, and Las Vegas.

Contact **Amtrak** (☎ *800/872–7245* ⊕ *www.amtrakcalifornia.com*).

10

CONTACTS & RESOURCES

EMERGENCIES

In an emergency dial 911.

Never travel alone in the desert. Let someone know your trip route, destination, and estimated time of return. Before setting out, make sure your vehicle is in good condition. Carry a jack, tools, and towrope or chain. Fill up your tank whenever you see a gas pump. Stay on main roads, and watch out for wild burros, horses, and cattle.

Drink at least a gallon of water a day (three gallons if you're hiking or otherwise exerting yourself). Dress in layered clothing and wear comfortable, sturdy shoes and a hat. Keep snacks, sunscreen, and a first-aid kit on hand. If you have a headache or feel dizzy or nauseous, you could be suffering from dehydration. Get out of the sun immediately and drink plenty of water. Dampen your clothing to lower your body temperature.

Do not enter mine tunnels or shafts. The structures may be unstable, and there may be hidden dangers such as pockets of bad air. Avoid canyons during rainstorms. Floodwaters can quickly fill up dry riverbeds and cover or wash away roads. Never place your hands or feet where you can't see them. Rattlesnakes, scorpions, and black widow spiders may be hiding there.

Contacts **BLM Rangers** (☎ 760/255–8700). **Community Hospital** (✉ Barstow ☎ 760/256–1761). **Northern Inyo Hospital** (✉ 150 Pioneer La., Bishop ☎ 760/873–5811). **San Bernardino County Sheriff** (☎ 760/256–1796 in Barstow, 760/733–4448 in Baker).

TOUR OPTIONS

The Mojave Group of the Sierra Club regularly organizes field trips to interesting spots, and the San Gorgonio Sierra Club chapter also conducts desert excursions.

Contact **Sierra Club** (✉ 3345 Wilshire Blvd., Suite 508, Los Angeles ☎ 213/387–4287, 951/684–6203 for San Gorgonio chapter ⊕ www.sierraclub.com).

VISITOR INFORMATION

Contacts **Barstow Area Chamber of Commerce and Visitors Bureau** (✉ 681 N. 1st Ave., Barstow ☎ 760/256–8617 ⊕ www.barstowchamber.com). **Big Pine Chamber of Commerce** (✉ 128 S. Main St., Big Pine ☎ 760/938–2114). **Bishop Chamber of Commerce** (✉ 690 N. Main St., Bishop ☎ 760/873–8405 ⊕ www.bishopvisitor.com). **Bureau of Land Management** (✉ California Desert District Office, 6221 Box Springs Blvd., Riverside ☎ 909/697–5200 ⊕ www.ca.blm.gov). **California Welcome Center** (✉ 2796 Tanger Way, Barstow ☎ 760/253–4782 ⊕ www.visitcwc.com). **Desert Discovery Center** (✉ 831 Barstow Rd., Barstow ☎ 760/252–6060). **Independence Chamber of Commerce** (✉ 139 N. Edwards, Independence ☎ 760/878–0084 ⊕ www.independence-ca.com). **Lone Pine Chamber of Commerce** (✉ 126 S. Main St., Lone Pine ☎ 760/876–4444 or 877/253–8981 ⊕ www.lonepinechamber.org). **Needles Chamber of Commerce** (✉ 100 G St., Needles ☎ 760/326–2050 ⊕ www.needleschamber.com). **Ridgecrest Area Convention and Visitors Bureau** (✉ 100 W. California Ave., Ridgecrest ☎ 760/375–8202 or 800/847–4830 ⊕ www.visitdeserts.com). **San Bernardino County Regional Parks Department** (✉ 777 E. Rialto Ave., San Bernardino ☎ 909/387–2594 ⊕ www.co.san-bernardino.ca.us/parks). **Victorville Chamber of Commerce** (✉ 14174 Green Tree Blvd., Victorville ☎ 760/245–6506 ⊕ www.vvchamber.com).

The Southern Sierra

AROUND SEQUOIA, KINGS CANYON & YOSEMITE NATIONAL PARKS

Bodie State Historic Park

WORD OF MOUTH

"Mono Lake is well worth exploring. Go to the nature center (the turn is just north of town, a bit past the Mono Inn) and walk the boardwalk to the water's edge. Signs note the changing levels of the lake over the years—it is finally on its way to recovery. You will see an amazing number of birds on the water from the observation platform."

—Enzian

WELCOME TO THE SOUTHERN SIERRA

TOP REASONS TO GO

★ **Quite a sight:** Even though these mountain towns and attractions lie outside Yosemite and Sequoia and Kings Canyon National Parks (⇨ *Chapter 12, Yosemite National Park and chapter 13, Sequoia and Kings Canyon National Parks*), the scenery will still enchant you.

★ **Mammoth undertaking:** The town of Mammoth Lakes, which this decade has enjoyed an upscale construction boom, is eastern California's most exciting resort area.

★ **Old-world charm:** Tucked in the hills south of Oakhurst, the elegant Château du Sureau will make you feel as if you've stepped into a fairy tale.

★ **Go with the flow:** Three Rivers, the gateway to Sequoia National Park, is the launching pad for white-water trips down the Kaweah River.

★ **Rock on:** The bizarre geological formations at Devil's Postpile National Monument resemble clumps of cooked spaghetti.

1 Mammoth Lakes. Remote but stunning, this mountain town is one of California's fastest-growing tourist destinations. It's packed with upscale hotels, restaurants, golf courses, and ski resorts, with more on the way in the next few years. In the not-so-distant future, this out-of-the-way Sierra town is expected to have a Vail-like atmosphere.

2 Three Rivers. Most motorists sigh with relief when they arrive in Three Rivers via Highway 198, the hot Central Valley behind them and two of the nation's most underrated national parks, Sequoia and Kings Canyon, just ahead. Overnighting here is a good budget move.

3 Oakhurst. About an hour's drive south of Yosemite, this bustling little town is a good place to stock up on gas and picnic supplies—and a good place to spend at least one night in less-expensive accommodations.

4 Fish Camp. Smaller than Oakhurst but just 4 mi from Yosemite, this woodsy hamlet offers something that kids may find more entertaining than waterfalls and scenic overlooks: the Yosemite Mountain Sugar Pine Railroad.

5 El Portal. Pack the car with provisions here so that you don't have to pay through the nose in Yosemite. Fourteen miles west of the national park on Highway 140, this no-frills town serves a purely pragmatic purpose.

11

GETTING ORIENTED

The transition between the Central Valley and the rugged Southern Sierra may be the most dramatic in California sightseeing; as you head into the mountains, your temptation to stop the car and gawk will increase with every foot gained in elevation. While you should spend most of your time here in the national parks (⇨ Chapter 12, Yosemite National Park, and chapter 13, Sequoia and Kings Canyon National Parks), be sure to check out some of the mountain towns on the parks' fringes—in addition to being great places to stock up on supplies, they have a variety of worthy attractions, restaurants, and lodging options.

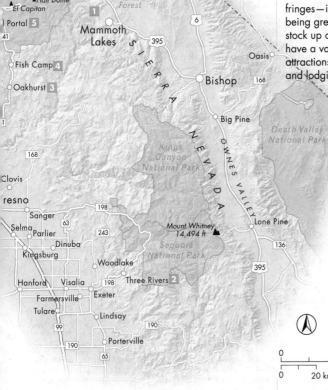

THE SOUTHERN SIERRA PLANNER

Skiing & Boarding

Famous for its incredible snow-pack—some of the deepest anywhere on the North American continent—the Sierra Nevada has something for every winter-sports fan. But Mammoth Mountain Ski Area is the star of the Southern Sierra winter-sports scene. One of the biggest and best ski resorts in the western United States, Mammoth offers terrain to suit downhill skiers' every taste and ability level, plus great facilities for snowboarders.

Hiking

Hiking is the primary outdoor activity in the Sierra Nevada. Whether you walk the paved loops that pass by major attractions in the national parks or head off the beaten path into the backcountry, a hike through groves and meadows or alongside streams and waterfalls will allow you to see, smell, and feel nature up close. No matter which trail you decide to take, always carry lots of water and a pocket-size emergency rain poncho for unexpected summer thunderstorms.

About the Restaurants

Most small towns in the Sierra Nevada have at least one restaurant; with few exceptions, dress is casual. You'll most likely be spending a lot of time in the car while you're exploring the area, so pick up snacks and drinks to keep with you. With picnic supplies on hand, you'll be able to enjoy an impromptu meal under giant trees.

About the Hotels

If you're planning to stay on the Sierra's western side, book your hotel in advance—especially in summer. Otherwise, you may end up driving pretty far to find a place to sleep. Thanks to the surge in hotel development in Mammoth Lakes, making an advance reservation is not as critical on the Sierra's less-traveled eastern side. Wherever you visit, however, be prepared to for sticker shock—rural and rustic does not mean inexpensive here.

Booking a Room

If you'd like assistance booking your lodgings, try the following agencies: **Mammoth Lakes Visitors Bureau Lodging Referral** (☎760/934-2712 or 888/466-2666 ⊕www.visitmammoth.com). **Mammoth Reservations** (☎800/223-3032 ⊕www.mammothreservations.com). **Three Rivers Reservation Center** (☎866/561-0410 or 559/561-0410 ⊕www.rescentre.com).

WHAT IT COSTS				
¢	$	$$	$$$	$$$$
Restaurants				
under $10	$10–$15	$16–$22	$23–$30	over $30
Hotels				
under $90	$90–$120	$121–$175	$176–$250	over $250

Restaurant prices are for a main course at dinner, excluding sales tax of 7.25%–7.75% (depending on location). Hotel prices are for two people in a standard double room in high season, excluding service charges and 9%–10% tax.

11

Updated by
Reed Parsell

VAST GRANITE PEAKS AND GIANT sequoias are among the mind-boggling natural wonders of the Southern Sierra, many of which are protected in three national parks (Yosemite, Sequoia, and Kings Canyon; ⇨ *Chapters 12 and 13*). Outside the parks, pristine lakes, superb skiing, rolling hills, and small towns complete the picture of the Southern Sierra. Heading up Highway 395, on the Sierra's eastern side, you'll be rewarded with outstanding vistas of dramatic mountain peaks, including Mt. Whitney, the highest point in the contiguous United States, and Mono Lake, a vast but slowly vanishing expanse of deep blue—one of the most-photographed natural attractions in California.

THREE RIVERS

200 mi north of Los Angeles via I–5 to Hwy. 99 to Hwy. 198; 8 mi south of Ash Mountain/Foothills entrance to Sequoia National Park on Hwy. 198.

In the foothills of the Sierra along the Kaweah River, this sparsely populated, serpentine hamlet serves as the main gateway town to Sequoia and Kings Canyon national parks (⇨ *Chapter 13, Sequoia and Kings Canyon National Parks)*. Its livelihood depends largely on tourism from the parks, courtesy of two markets, a few service stations, banks, a post office, and several lodgings, which are good spots to find a room when park accommodations are full.

WHERE TO STAY & EAT

$$–$$$ ✕**Gateway Restaurant and Lodge.** The patio of this raucous roadhouse overlooks the roaring Kaweah River as it plunges out of the high country, and though the food is nothing special, the location makes up for it. Standouts include baby back ribs and eggplant parmigiana; there's also a cocktail lounge, and guest rooms are available for overnight visitors. Breakfast isn't served weekdays; dinner reservations are essential on weekends. ⊠*45978 Sierra Dr.* ☎*559/561–4133* ▤*AE, D, MC, V.*

¢ ✕**We Three Bakery.** This friendly, popular-with-the-locals spot packs lunches for trips into the nearby national parks; they're also open for breakfast. ⊠*43688 Sierra Dr.* ⊕*www.wethreerestaurant.com* ☎*559/561–4761* ▤*MC, V.*

¢–$$ ⌂**Buckeye Tree Lodge.** Every room at this two-story motel has a patio facing a sun-dappled grassy lawn, right on the banks of the Kaweah River. Accommodations are simple and well kept, and the lodge sits a mere quarter mile from the park gate. Book well in advance for the summer. The jointly owned Sequoia Village Inn, across the highway, was extensively renovated in 2006 and is another good option (☎*559/561–3652)*; accommodation options there are cottages, cabins, and chalets. **Pros:** Scenic setting, clean, popular. **Cons:** Could use an update. ⊠*46000 Sierra Dr., Hwy. 198* ☎*559/561–5900* ⊕*www. buckeyetree.com* ⇆*11 rooms, 1 cottage* ⌂*In-room: VCR, Wi-Fi. In-hotel: no elevator, pool, some pets allowed, no-smoking rooms* ▤*AE, D, DC, MC, V* ⍟*CP.*

Kaweah White Water Adventures (☎*559/561–1000 or 800/229–8658* ⊕*www.kaweah-whitewater.com*) guides two-hour and full-day rafting trips in spring and early summer, with some Class III rapids; longer trips may include some Class IV.

For hourly horseback rides or riding lessons, contact **Wood 'n' Horse Training Stables** (✉*42846 N. Fork Dr.* ☎*559/561–4268*).

SOUTH OF YOSEMITE

FROM OAKHURST TO EL PORTAL

OAKHURST

40 mi north of Fresno and 23 mi south of Yosemite National Park's south entrance on Hwy. 41.

Motels, restaurants, gas stations, and small businesses line both sides of Highway 41 as it cuts through Oakhurst. This is the last sizable community before Yosemite and a good spot to find provisions. There are two major grocery stores near the intersection of highways 41 and 49. Three miles north of town, then 6 mi east, honky-tonky Bass Lake is a popular spot in summer with motorboaters, Jet Skiers, and families looking to cool off in the reservoir.

WHERE TO STAY & EAT

$$$$
Fodor'sChoice
★

✕ **Erna's Elderberry House.** Austrian-born Erna Kubin-Clanin, the grande dame of Château du Sureau, has created a culinary oasis, stunning for its elegance, gorgeous setting, and impeccable service. Crimson walls and dark beams accent the dining room's high ceilings, and arched windows reflect the glow of candles. The seasonal six-course prix-fixe dinner can be paired with superb wines, a must-do for oenophiles. When the waitstaff places all the plates on the table in perfect synchronicity, you know this will be a meal to remember. Pre-meal drinks are served in the former wine cellar. ✉*48688 Victoria La.* ☎*559/683–6800* ⊕*www.elderberryhouse.com* ⌘*Reservations essential* ▭*AE, D, MC, V* ☾*No lunch Mon.–Sat.*

¢–$$

✕ **Yosemite Fork Mountain House.** Bypass Oakhurst's greasy spoons and instead head to this family restaurant, 3 mi north of the Highway 49/ Highway 41 intersection, with an open-beam ceiling and a canoe in the rafters. Portions are huge. Expect standard American fare: bacon and eggs at breakfast, sandwiches at lunch, and pastas and steaks at dinner. ✉*Hwy. 41, at Bass Lake turnoff* ☎*559/683–5191* ⌘*Reservations not accepted* ▭*D, MC, V.*

$$$$
Fodor'sChoice
★

▦ **Château du Sureau.** This romantic inn, adjacent to Erna's Elderberry House, is straight out of one of Grimm's fairy tales. From the moment you drive through the wrought-iron gates and up to the enchanting castle, you feel pampered. Every room is impeccably styled with European antiques, sumptuous fabrics, fresh-cut flowers, and oversize soaking tubs. Fall asleep by the glow of a crackling fire amid feather-light goose-down pillows and Italian linens, awaken to a hearty European breakfast in the dining room, then relax with a game of chess in the grand salon beneath an exquisite mural—or play chess on the giant board amid tall pine trees off the impeccably landscaped garden trail. Cable TV is available by request only. In 2006 the Château added a stunning spa. **Pros:** Luxurious; spectacular property. **Cons:** You'll need to take out a second mortgage to stay here. ⊠ *48688 Victoria La.* ☎ *559/683–6860* ⊕ *www.elderberryhouse.com* ⟿ *10 rooms, 1 villa* ⚷ *In-room: dial-up, Wi-Fi. In-hotel: no elevator, restaurant, bar, pool, spa, laundry service, no kids under 8, no-smoking rooms* ⊟ *AE, MC, V* ⍠ *BP.*

FISH CAMP

57 mi north of Fresno and 4 mi south of Yosemite National Park's south entrance.

As you climb in elevation along Highway 41 northbound, you see nothing but trees until you get to the small settlement of Fish Camp, where there's a post office and general store, but no gasoline (for gas, head 10 mi north to Wawona, in the park, or 17 mi south to Oakhurst).

The **Yosemite Mountain Sugar Pine Railroad** has a narrow-gauge steam train that chugs through the forest. It follows 4 mi of the route the Madera Sugar Pine Lumber Company cut through the forest in 1899 to harvest timber. The steam train, as well as Jenny railcars, run year-round on fluctuating schedules; call for details. On Saturday (and Wednesday in summer), the Moonlight Special dinner excursion (reservations essential) includes a picnic with toe-tappin' music by the Sugar Pine Singers, followed by a sunset steam-train ride. ⊠ *56001 Hwy. 41* ☎ *559/683–7273* ⊕ *www.ymsprr.com* ⊠ *$17.50 steam train; Jenny railcar $13.50; Moonlight Special $46* ⟟ *Mar.–Oct., daily.*

WHERE TO STAY & EAT

$$$$ ✕◫ **Tenaya Lodge.** One of the region's largest hotels, the Tenaya Lodge
★ is ideal for people who enjoy wilderness treks by day but prefer creature comforts at night. The hulking prefab buildings and giant parking lot look out of place in the woods, but inside, the rooms have all the amenities of a modern, full-service hotel. The ample regular rooms are decorated in pleasant earth tones, deluxe rooms have minibars and other extras, and the suites have balconies. Off-season rates can be as low as $100. The Sierra Restaurant ($$–$$$$), with its high ceilings and giant fireplace, serves Continental cuisine. The more casual Jack-alopes Bar and Grill ($–$$) has burgers, salads, and sandwiches. **Pros:** Rustic setting with modern comforts; good off-season deals. **Cons:** So big it can seem impersonal; pricey during summer; few dining options. ⊠ *1122 Hwy. 41* ⌁ *Box 159, 93623* ☎ *559/683–6555 or 888/514–2167* ⊕ *www.tenayalodge.com* ⟿ *244 rooms, 6 suites* ⚷ *In-room: refrigerator, dial-up, Wi-Fi. In-hotel: 2 restaurants, room service, bar, pool, gym, bicycles, concierge, children's programs (ages 5–12), laundry service, no-smoking rooms* ⊟ *AE, D, DC, MC, V.*

$$–$$$ ✕◫ **Narrow Gauge Inn.** All of the rooms at this well-tended, family-
★ owned property have balconies (some shared) and great views of the

surrounding woods and mountains. For maximum atmosphere, book a room overlooking the brook; for quiet, choose a lower-level room on the edge of the forest. All of the recently renovated rooms are comfortably furnished with old-fashioned accents. Reserve way ahead. The restaurant ($$–$$$$; open Apr.–Oct., Wed.–Sun.), which is festooned with moose, bison, and other wildlife trophies, specializes in steaks and American fare, and merits a special trip. **Pros:** Close to Yosemite's south entrance; well-appointed, wonderful balconies. **Cons:** Rooms can feel a bit dark; dining options are limited (especially for vegetarians). ⌂ *48571 Hwy. 41* ☎ *559/683–7720 or 888/644–9050* ⊕ *www. narrowgaugeinn.com* ⌫ *26 rooms, 1 suite* ⌂ *In-room: no a/c (some), dial-up, Wi-Fi (some). In-hotel: no elevator, restaurant, bar, pool, some pets allowed, no-smoking rooms* ⊟ *D, MC, V* ⎮◯⎮*CP.*

EL PORTAL

14 mi west of Yosemite Valley on Hwy. 140.

The market in town is a good place to pick up provisions before you get to Yosemite. There's also a post office and a gas station, but not much else.

WHERE TO STAY

$$$ **Yosemite View Lodge.** The Yosemite View Lodge's motel-like design aesthetic is ameliorated by its location right on the banks of the boulder-strewn Merced River and its proximity to the park entrance 2 mi east. Many rooms have whirlpool baths, fireplaces, kitchenettes, and balconies or decks. The motel complex is on the public bus route to the park, near fishing and river rafting. Ask for a river-view room. The lodge's sister property, the Cedar Lodge, sits 6 mi farther west and has similar-looking, less expensive rooms without river views. **Pros:** Huge spa baths; great views; friendly service. **Cons:** Air-conditioning is inconsistent; restaurant can get crowded; can be pricey. ⌂ *11136 Hwy. 140* ☎ *209/379–2681 or 888/742–4371* ⊕ *www.yosemiteresorts.us* ⌫ *335 rooms* ⌂ *In-room: kitchen (some). In-hotel: restaurant, bar, pools, laundry facilities, some pets allowed, no-smoking rooms* ⊟ *AE, MC, V.*

MAMMOTH AREA

A jewel in the vast eastern Sierra Nevada, the Mammoth Lakes area lies just east of the Sierra crest, on the back side of Yosemite (⇨ *Chapter 12, Yosemite National Park)* and the Ansel Adams Wilderness. It's a place of rugged beauty, where giant sawtooth mountains drop into the vast deserts of the Great Basin. In winter, 11,053-foot-high Mammoth Mountain provides the finest skiing and snowboarding in California— sometimes as late as June or even July. Once the snows melt, Mammoth transforms itself into a warm-weather playground, with fishing, mountain biking, golfing, hiking, and horseback riding. Nine deep-blue lakes are spread through the Mammoth Lakes Basin, and another 100 lakes dot the surrounding countryside. Crater-pocked Mammoth Mountain hasn't had a major eruption for 50,000 years, but the region is alive with hot springs, mud pots, fumaroles, and steam vents.

MAMMOTH LAKES

30 mi south of eastern edge of Yosemite National Park on U.S. 395.

Much of the architecture in Mammoth Lakes (elevation 7,800 feet) is of the faux-alpine variety. You'll find increasingly sophisticated dining and lodging options here. International real-estate developers joined forces with Mammoth Mountain Ski Area and have worked hard to transform the once sleepy town into a chic ski destination. The Mammoth Mountain Village *(below)* is the epicenter of all the recent development. Winter is high season at Mammoth; in summer room rates plummet. Highway 203 heads west from U.S. 395, becoming Main Street as it passes through the town of Mammoth Lakes, and later Minaret Road (which makes a right turn) as it continues west to the Mammoth Mountain ski area and Devils Postpile National Monument.

The lakes of the **Mammoth Lakes Basin,** reached by Lake Mary Road off Highway 203 southwest of town, are popular for fishing and boating in summer. First comes Twin Lakes, at the far end of which is Twin Falls, where water cascades 300 feet over a shelf of volcanic rock. Also popular are Lake Mary, the largest lake in the basin; Lake Mamie; and Lake George. Horseshoe Lake is the only lake in which you can swim.

The glacier-carved sawtooth spires of the Minarets, the remains of an ancient lava flow, are best viewed from the **Minaret Vista,** off Highway 203 west of Mammoth Lakes.

Even if you don't ski, ride the **Panorama Gondola** to see Mammoth Mountain, the aptly named dormant volcano that gives Mammoth Lakes its name. Gondolas serve skiers in winter and mountain bikers and sightseers in summer. The high-speed, eight-passenger gondolas whisk you from the chalet to the summit, where you can read about the area's volcanic history and take in top-of-the-world views. Standing high above the tree line atop this dormant volcano, you can look west 150 mi across the state to the Coastal Range; to the east are the highest peaks of Nevada and the Great Basin beyond. You won't find a better view of the Sierra High Country without climbing. Remember, though, that the air is thin at the 11,053-foot summit; carry water, and don't overexert yourself. The boarding area is at the Main Lodge. ⊠ *Off Hwy. 203* ☎ *760/934–2571 Ext. 2400 information, Ext. 3850 gondola station* ⊠ *$18 in summer* ⊙ *July 4–Oct., daily 9–4:30; Nov.–July 3, daily 8:30–4.*

Fodor'sChoice ★

The overwhelming popularity of Mammoth Mountain has generated a real-estate boom, and a huge new complex of shops, restaurants, and luxury accommodations, called the **Village at Mammoth,** has become the town's tourist center. Parking can be tricky. There's a lot across the street on Minaret Road; pay attention to time limits.

WHERE TO STAY & EAT

$$$–$$$$ ✕**Restaurant LuLu.** LuLu imports the sunny, sensual, and assertive fla-
★ vors of Provençale cooking—think olive tapenade, aioli, and lemony
vinaigrettes—to Mammoth Lakes. At this outpost of the famous San
Francisco restaurant, the formula remains the same: small plates of
southern French cooking served family-style in a spare, modern, and
sexy dining room. Standouts include rotisserie meats, succulent roasted
mussels, homemade gnocchi, and a fantastic wine list, with 50 vintages
available in 2-ounce pours. Outside, the sidewalk café includes a fire pit
where kids will love do-it-themselves s'mores. LuLu's only drawback is
price, but if you can swing it, it's worth every penny. The waiters wear
jeans, so you can, too. ⊠ *Village at Mammoth, 1111 Forest Trail, Unit
201* ☎ *760/924–8781* ⌲ *Reservations essential* ▭ *AE, D, MC, V.*

$$–$$$$ ✕**Restaurant at Convict Lake.** Tucked in a tiny valley ringed by mile-
★ high peaks, Convict Lake is one of the most spectacular spots in the
eastern Sierra. Thank heaven the food lives up to the view. The chef's
specialties include beef Wellington, rack of lamb, and pan-seared local
trout, all beautifully prepared. The woodsy room has a vaulted knotty-
pine ceiling and a copper-chimney fireplace that roars on cold nights.
Natural light abounds there in the daytime, but if it's summer, opt
instead for outdoor dining under the white-barked aspens. Service is so
good that if you forget your glasses, the waiter will provide a pair. The
wine list is exceptional for its reasonably priced European and California varietals. ⊠ *2 mi off U.S. 395, 4 mi south of Mammoth Lakes*
☎ *760/934–3803* ⌲ *Reservations essential* ▭ *AE, D, MC, V* ⊘ *No
lunch early Sept.–July 4.*

$$$ ✕**Petra's Bistro & Wine Bar.** Other restaurateurs speak highly of Petra's as
the most convivial restaurant in town. Its lovely ambience—quiet, dark,
and warm—complements the carefully prepared meat main dishes and
seasonal sides, and the more than two dozen California wines from
behind the bar. The service is top-notch. Downstairs, the Clocktower
Cellar bar provides a late-night, rowdy alternative—or chaser. ⊠ *6080
Minaret Rd.,* ☎ *760/934–3500* ⌲ *Reservations essential* ▭ *AE, D,
DC, MC, V* ⊘ *No lunch.*

$–$$ ✕**The Stove.** A longtime family favorite for down-to-earth, folksy
☯ cooking, the Stove is the kind of place you take the family to fill up
before a long car ride. The omelets, pancakes, huevos rancheros, and
meat loaf won't win any awards, but they're tasty. The room is cute,
with gingham curtains and pinewood booths, and service is friendly.
Breakfast and lunch are the best bets here. ⊠ *644 Old Mammoth Rd.*
☎ *760/934–2821* ⌲ *Reservations not accepted* ▭ *AE, MC, V.*

¢–$$ ✕**Burgers.** Don't even think about coming to this bustling restau-
☯ rant unless you're hungry. Burgers is known, appropriately enough,
for its burgers and sandwiches, and everything comes in mountain-
ous portions. At lunch try the sourdough patty melt, at dinner the
pork ribs; salads are great all day. The seasoned french fries are deli-
cious. ⊠ *6118 Minaret Rd., across from the Village.* ☎ *760/934–6622*
▭ *MC, V* ⊘ *Closed 2 wks in May and 4–6 wks in Oct.–Nov.*

¢–$ ✕**Side Door Café.** Half wine bar, half café, this is a laid-back spot for
an easy lunch or a long, lingering afternoon. The café serves grilled

panini sandwiches, sweet and savory crepes, and espresso. At the wine bar, order cheese plates and charcuterie platters, designed to pair with the 25 wines (fewer in summertime) available by the glass. If you're lucky, a winemaker will show up and hold court at the bar. ⊠ *Village at Mammoth, 1111 Forest Trail, Unit 229* ☎*760/934–5200* ⊟*AE, D, MC, V.*

$$$–$$$$ ✕⟨⟩ **Double Eagle Resort and Spa.** You won't find a better spa retreat in the eastern Sierra than the Double Eagle. Dwarfed by towering, craggy peaks, the resort is in a spectacularly beautiful spot along a creek, near June Lake, 20 minutes north of Mammoth Lakes. Accommodations are in comfortable knotty-pine two-bedroom cabins that sleep up to six, or in cabin suites with efficiency kitchens; all come fully equipped with modern amenities. If you don't want to cook, the Eagles Landing Restaurant serves three meals a day, but the quality is erratic. Spa services and treatments are available for nonguests by reservation. The small, uncrowded June Mountain Ski Area is 1½ mi away. **Pros:** Pretty setting; generous breakfast; good for families. **Cons:** Expensive. ⊠*5587 Hwy. 158, Box 736, June Lake* ☎*760/648–7004 or 877/648–7004* ⊕*www. doubleeagleresort.com* ⇆*16 2-bedroom cabins, 16 cabin suites, 1 3-bedroom cabin* ⟨⟩*In-room: no a/c, kitchen (some), refrigerator, VCR, dial-up. In-hotel: restaurant, bar, pool, gym, spa, some pets allowed, no-smoking rooms* ⊟*AE, D, MC, V.*

¢–$$$$
Fodor's Choice
★
✕⟨⟩ **Tamarack Lodge Resort & Lakefront Restaurant.** Tucked away on the edge of the John Muir Wilderness Area, where cross-country ski trails loop through the woods, this original 1924 lodge looks like something out of a snow globe, and the lake it borders is serenely beautiful. Rooms in the charming main lodge have spartan furnishings, and in old-fashioned style, some share a bathroom. For more privacy, opt for one of the cabins, which range from rustic to downright cushy; many have fireplaces, kitchens, or wood-burning stoves. In warm months, fishing, canoeing, hiking, and mountain biking are right outside. The small and romantic Lakefront Restaurant ($$$) serves outstanding contemporary French-inspired dinners, with an emphasis on game, in a candlelit dining room. Reservations are essential. **Pros:** Rustic but not run-down; tons of nearby outdoor activities. **Cons:** Thin walls; some main lodge rooms have shared bathrooms. ⊠*Lake Mary Rd., off Hwy. 203* ⟨⟩*Box 69, 93546* ☎*760/934–2442 or 800/626–6684* ⊕*www.tamaracklodge. com* ⇆*11 rooms, 35 cabins* ⟨⟩*In-room: no a/c, kitchen (in all cabins), no TV. In-hotel: no elevator, restaurant, bar, public Wi-Fi, no-smoking rooms* ⊟*AE, MC, V.*

$$$$ ⟨⟩ **Village at Mammoth.** At the epicenter of Mammoth's burgeoning dining and nightlife scene, this cluster of four-story timber-and-stone condo buildings nods to Alpine style, with exposed timbers and peaked roofs. Units have gas fireplaces, kitchens or kitchenettes, daily maid service, high-speed Internet access, DVD players, slate-tile bathroom floors, and comfortable furnishings. The decor is a bit sterile, but there are high-end details like granite counters. And you won't have to drive anywhere: the buildings are connected by a ground-floor pedestrian mall, with shops, restaurants, bars, and—best of all—a gondola (November through mid-April only) that whisks you right from the Village to the mountain. **Pros:** Central location; clean; big rooms; lots of good restaurants nearby. **Cons:** Pricey; can be noisy outside. ✉*100 Canyon Blvd.* ☐*Box 3459, 93546* ☎*760/934–1982 or 800/626–6684* ⊕*www.mammothmountain.com* ➪*277 units* ⚘*In-room: no a/c, kitchen (some), Ethernet, dial-up. In-hotel: pool, gym, laundry facilities, parking (no fee), no-smoking rooms* ▭*AE, MC, V.*

$$–$$$$ ▦**Juniper Springs Lodge.** Tops for slope-side comfort, these condominium-style units have full kitchens and ski-in ski-out access to the mountain. Extras include gas fireplaces, balconies, and stereos with CD players; the heated outdoor pool—surrounded by a heated deck—is open year-round. If you like to be near nightlife, you'll do better at the Village, but if you don't mind having to drive to go out for the evening, this is a great spot. In summer fewer people stay here, although package deals and lower prices provide incentive. Skiers: the lifts on this side of the mountain close in mid-April; for springtime ski-in ski-out access, stay at the Mammoth Mountain Inn. **Pros:** Bargain during summer; direct access to the slopes; good views. **Cons:** No nightlife within walking distance; no a/c; some complaints about service. ✉*4000 Meridian Blvd.* ☐*Box 2129, 93546* ☎*760/924–1102 or 800/626–6684* ⊕*www.mammothmountain.com* ➪*10 studios, 99 1-bedrooms, 92 2-bedrooms, 3 3-bedrooms* ⚘*In-room: no a/c, kitchen, refrigerator, VCR, Ethernet, dial-up. In-hotel: restaurant, room service, bar, golf course, pool, bicycles, concierge, laundry facilities, no-smoking rooms* ▭*AE, MC, V.*

$$–$$$$ ▦**Mammoth Mountain Inn.** If you want to be within walking distance of the Mammoth Mountain Main Lodge, this is the place. In summer the proximity to the gondola means you can hike and mountain bike to your heart's delight. The accommodations, which vary in size, include standard hotel rooms and condo units. The inn, ski lodge, and other summit facilities are likely to be razed and rebuilt within a decade, bringing more of a 21st-century ski resort feel to what's been a quaint 1950s-born resort. Meanwhile, the inn has done a respectable job with continual refurbishing. **Pros:** Great location; big rooms; a traditional place to stay. **Cons:** Can be crowded in ski season; won't be around for many more years. ✉*Minaret Rd., 4 mi west of Mammoth Lakes* ☐*Box 353, 93546* ☎*760/934–2581 or 800/626–6684* ⊕*www.mammothmountain.com* ➪*124 rooms, 91 condos* ⚘*In-room: no a/c, kitchen (some), refrigerator (some), Ethernet, dial-up (some). In-hotel: Wi-Fi, 2 restaurants, bar, year-round outdoor pool, laundry facilities, no-smoking rooms* ▭*AE, MC, V.*

$–$$ ▦**Alpenhof Lodge.** The owners of the Alpenhof lucked out when developers built the fancy-schmancy Village at Mammoth right across the street from their mom-and-pop motel. The place remains a simple, mid-budget motel, with basic comforts and a few niceties like attractive pine furniture. Rooms are dark and the foam pillows thin, but the damask bedspreads are pretty and the low-pile carpeting clean, and best of all you can walk to restaurants and shops. Downstairs there's a lively, fun pub; if you want quiet, request a room that's not above it. Some rooms have fireplaces and kitchens. In winter the Village Gondola is across the street, a major plus for skiers. **Pros:** Convenient for skiers; good price. **Cons:** Could use an update; rooms above the pub can be noisy. ✉*6080 Minaret Rd., Box 1157* ☎*760/934–6330 or 800/828–0371* ⊕*www.alpenhof-lodge.com* 🛏*54 rooms, 3 cabins* &*In-room: no a/c, kitchen (some), refrigerator (some). In-hotel: restaurant, bar, pool, laundry facilities, no-smoking rooms* ▤*AE, D, MC, V.*

SPORTS & THE OUTDOORS

For information on winter conditions around Mammoth, call the **Snow Report** (☎*760/934–7669 or 888/766–9778*). The **U.S. Forest Service ranger station** (☎*760/924–5500*) can provide general information year-round.

BICYCLING **Mammoth Mountain Bike Park** (✉*Mammoth Mountain Ski Area* ☎*760/934–3706* ⊕*www.mammothmountain.com*) opens when the snow melts, usually by July, with 70-plus mi of single-track trails—from mellow to super-challenging. Chairlifts and shuttles provide trail access, and rentals are available. Various shops around town also rent bikes and provide trail maps, if you don't want to ascend the mountain.

FISHING Crowley Lake is the top trout-fishing spot in the area; Convict Lake, June Lake, and the lakes of the Mammoth Basin are other prime spots. One of the best trout rivers is the San Joaquin, near Devils Postpile. Hot Creek, a designated Wild Trout Stream, is renowned for fly-fishing (catch-and-release only). The fishing season runs from the last Saturday in April until the end of October. To maximize your time on the water, get tips from local anglers, or better yet, book a guided fishing trip with **Sierra Drifters Guide Service** (☎*760/935–4250* ⊕*www.sierradrifters.com*).

Kittredge Sports (✉*3218 Main St., at Forest Trail* ☎*760/934–7566* ⊕*www.kittredgesports.com*) rents rods and reels and also conducts guided trips.

GOLF Because it's nestled right up against the forest, you might see deer and bears on the fairways on the picture-perfect 18-hole **Sierra Star Golf Course** (✉*2001 Sierra Star Pkwy.* ☎*760/924–2200* ⊕*www.mammothmountain.com*), California's highest-elevation golf course (take it slow!). Greens fees run $84 to $129.

The 9-hole course at **Snowcreek Resort** (✉*Old Mammoth Rd.* ☎*760/934–6633* ⊕*www.snowcreekresort.com*) sits in a meadow with drop-dead gorgeous, wide-open vistas of the mountains. Nine-hole play costs $35 and includes a cart; 18 holes run $55.

MAMMOTH MUSIC

The summertime **Mammoth Lakes Jazz Jubilee** (☎*760/934–2478 or 877/686–5299* ⊕*www.mammothjazz.org*) takes place in 10 venues, most with dance floors. For one long weekend every summer, Mammoth Lakes holds **Bluesapalooza and Festival of Beers** (☎*760/934–0606 or 800/367–6572* ⊕*www.mammothbluesbrewfest.com*), a blues-and-beer festival—with emphasis on the beer. Concerts occur throughout the year on Mammoth Mountain; contact **Mammoth Mountain Music** (☎*760/934–0606* ⊕*www.mammothevents.com*) for listings.

HIKING

Hiking in Mammoth is stellar, especially along the trails that wind through the pristine alpine scenery around the Lakes Basin. Carry lots of water; and remember, you're above 8,000-foot elevation, and the air is thin. Stop at the **U.S. Forest Service ranger station** (⊠*Hwy. 203* ☎*760/924–5500* ⊕*www.fs.fed.us/r5/inyo*), on your right just before the town of Mammoth Lakes, for a Mammoth area trail map and permits for backpacking in wilderness areas.

HORSEBACK
RIDING

Stables around Mammoth are typically open from June through September. **Mammoth Lakes Pack Outfit** (⊠*Lake Mary Rd., between Twin Lakes and Lake Mary* ☎*760/934–2434 or 888/475–8747* ⊕*www. mammothpack.com*) runs day and overnight horseback trips, or will shuttle you to the high country. **McGee Creek Pack Station** (☎*760/935– 4324 or 800/854–7407* ⊕*www.mcgeecreekpackstation.com*) customizes pack trips or will shuttle you to camp alone. Operated by the folks at McGee Creek, **Sierra Meadows Ranch** (⊠*Sherwin Creek Rd., off Old Mammoth Rd.* ☎*760/934–6161*) conducts horseback and wagon rides that range from one-hour to all-day excursions.

HOT-AIR
BALLOONING

The balloons of **Mammoth Balloon Adventures** (☎*760/937–8787* ⊕*www. mammothballoonadventures.com*) glide over the countryside in the morning from spring until fall, weather permitting.

SKIING

June Mountain Ski Area. In their rush to Mammoth Mountain, most people overlook June Mountain, a compact, low-key resort 20 mi north of Mammoth. Snowboarders especially dig it. Two freestyle terrain areas are for both skiers and boarders, including a huge 16-foot-wall super pipe. Best of all, there's rarely a line for the lifts—if you want to avoid the crowds but must ski on a weekend, this is the place. And in a storm, June is better protected from wind and blowing snow than Mammoth Mountain. (If it starts to storm, you can use your Mammoth ticket at June.) Expect all the usual services, including a rental-and-repair shop, ski school, and sports shop, but the food quality is better at Mammoth. Lift tickets run $64, with discounts for multiple days. ⊠*3819 Hwy. 158, off June Lake Loop, June Lake* ☎*760/648–7733 or 888/586– 3686* ⊕*www.junemountain.com* ⟳*35 trails on 500 acres, rated 35% beginner, 45% intermediate, 20% advanced. Longest run 2½ mi, base 7,510 feet, summit 10,174 feet. Lifts: 7.*

Fodor'sChoice
★

Mammoth Mountain Ski Area. If you ski only one mountain in California, make it Mammoth. One of the West's largest and best ski areas, Mammoth has more than 3,500 acres of skiable terrain and a 3,100-foot vertical drop. The views from the 11,053-foot summit are some of the most stunning in the Sierra. Below, you'll find a 6½-mi-wide swath of groomed boulevards and canyons, as well as pockets of tree-skiing and a dozen vast bowls. Snowboarders are everywhere on the slopes; there are three outstanding freestyle terrain parks of varying technical difficulty, with jumps, rails, tabletops, and giant super pipes (this is the location of several international snowboarding competitions). Mammoth's season begins in November and often lingers into May. Lift tickets cost $65. Lessons and equipment are available, and there's a children's ski and snowboard school. Mammoth runs free shuttle-bus routes around town and to the ski area, and the Village Gondola runs from the Village complex to Canyon Lodge. However, only overnight guests are allowed to park at the Village for more than a few hours. Warning: The main lodge is dark and dated, unsuited in most every way for the crush of ski season. Within a decade, it's likely to be replaced. ⊠*Minaret Rd., west of Mammoth Lakes* ☎*760/934–2571, 800/626–6684, 760/934–0687 shuttle* ⚡*150 trails on 3,500 acres, rated 30% beginner, 40% intermediate, 30% advanced. Longest run 3 mi, base 7,953 feet, summit 11,053 feet. Lifts: 27, including 9 high-speed and 2 gondolas.*

Trails at **Tamarack Cross Country Ski Center** (⊠*Lake Mary Rd., off Hwy. 203* ☎*760/934–5293 or 760/934–2442* ⊕*www.tamaracklodge.com*), adjacent to Tamarack Lodge, meander around several lakes. Rentals are available.

Mammoth Sporting Goods (⊠*1 Sierra Center Mall, Old Mammoth Rd.* ☎*760/934–3239* ⊕*www.mammothsportinggoods.com*) rents good skis for intermediates, and sells equipment, clothing, and accessories. Advanced skiers should rent from **Kittredge Sports** (⊠*3218 Main St.* ☎*760/934–7566* ⊕*www.kittredgesports.com*).

★ When the U.S. Ski Team visits Mammoth and needs their boots adjusted, they head to **Footloose** (⊠*3043 Main St.* ☎*760/934–2400* ⊕*www.footloosesports.com*), the best place in town—and possibly all California—for ski-boot rentals and sales, as well as custom insoles (ask for Kevin or Corty).

EAST OF YOSEMITE NATIONAL PARK

FROM LEE VINING TO BRIDGEPORT

LEE VINING

20 mi east of Tuolumne Meadows via Hwy. 120 to U.S. 395; 30 mi north of Mammoth Lakes on U.S. 395.

Tiny Lee Vining is known primarily as the eastern gateway to Yosemite National Park (summer only; ⇨*chapter 12*) and the location of vast and desolate Mono Lake. Pick up supplies at the general store year-round, or stop here for lunch or dinner before or after a drive through the high country. In winter the town is all but deserted, except for the ice climbers who come to scale frozen waterfalls. You can meet these hearty souls at Nicely's restaurant, where the climbers congregate for breakfast around 8 on winter mornings.

If you want to try your hand at the ice climbing, contact **Sierra Mountain Guides** (☎*760/648–1122 or 877/423–2546* ⊕*www.themountain guide.com*).

★ Eerie tufa towers—calcium carbonate formations that often resemble castle turrets—rise from impressive **Mono Lake.** Since the 1940s, the city of Los Angeles has diverted water from streams that feed the lake, lowering its water level and exposing the tufa. Court victories by environmentalists in the 1990s forced a reduction of the diversions, and the lake has since risen about 9 feet. From April through August, millions of migratory birds nest in and around Mono Lake. The best place to view the tufa is at the south end of the lake along the mile-long **South Tufa Trail**. To reach it, drive 5 mi south from Lee Vining on U.S. 395, then 5 mi east on Highway 120. There's a $3 fee. You can swim (or float) in the salty water at Navy Beach near the South Tufa Trail or take a kayak or canoe trip for close-up views of the tufa (check with rangers for boating restrictions during bird-nesting season). You can rent kayaks in Mammoth Lakes. The sensational **Scenic Area Visitor Center** (⊠ *U. S. 395* ☎ *760/647–3044*) is open daily from June through September (Sunday–Thursday 8–5, Friday and Saturday 8–7), and the rest of the year Thursday–Monday 9–4. Its hilltop, sweeping views of Mono Lake, along with its interactive exhibits inside, make this one of California's best visitor centers. Rangers and naturalists lead walking tours of the tufa daily in summer and on weekends (sometimes on cross-country skis) in winter. In town, the Mono Lake Committee Information Center & Bookstore (⊠ *U.S. 395 and Third St.* ☎ *760/647–6595* ⊕ *www. monolake.org*) has more information about this beautiful area.

EN ROUTE Heading south from Lee Vining, U.S. 395 intersects the **June Lake Loop** (⊠ *Hwy. 158 W*). This gorgeous 17-mi drive follows an old glacial canyon past Grant, June, Gull, and other lakes before reconnecting with U.S. 395 on its way to Mammoth Lakes. The loop is especially colorful in fall.

WHERE TO STAY & EAT

$–$$ ✕ **Tioga Gas Mart & Whoa Nelli Deli.** Near the eastern entrance to Yosem-
★ ite, Whoa Nelli serves some of Mono County's best food, including lobster taquitos, pizzas, and enormous slices of multilayered cakes. But what makes it special is that it's in a gas station—possibly the only one in America where you can order cocktails (a pitcher of mango margaritas, anyone?)—and outside there's a full-size trapeze where you can take lessons (by reservation).This wacky spot is well off the noisy road, and has plenty of shaded outdoor tables with views of Mono Lake; bands play here on summer evenings, and locals love it, too. ⊠ *Hwy. 120 and U.S. 395* ☎ *760/647–1088* ☐ *AE, MC, V* ⊗ *Closed mid-Nov.–mid-Apr.*

$ ⌂ **Lake View Lodge.** Lovely landscaping, which includes several inviting and shaded places to sit, is what sets this clean motel apart from its handful of competitors in town. It's also up and off the highway by a few hundred feet, which means it's peaceful as well as pretty. Open morning and early afternoon, a stand-alone coffee shop adds to the appeal. The cottages lack the main building's lake views; some have kitchens and can sleep up to six. **Pros:** Attractive, clean; friendly staff. **Cons:** Could use updating. ⊠ *51285 U.S. 395 93541* ☎ *760/647–6543 or 800/990–6614* ⊕ *www.lakeviewlodgeyosemite.com* ⌖ *76 rooms, 12 cottages* ⌂ *In-room: no a/c, refrigerators (some), microwaves (some), Wi-Fi. In-hotel: no elevator, no-smoking rooms* ☐ *AE, D, MC, V.*

BODIE STATE HISTORIC PARK

23 mi northeast of Lee Vining via U.S. 395 to Hwy. 270 (last 3 mi are unpaved).

Fodor'sChoice ★

Old shacks and shops, abandoned mine shafts, a Methodist church, the mining village of Rattlesnake Gulch, and the remains of a small China-town are among the sights at fascinating **Bodie Ghost Town.** The town, at an elevation of 8,200 feet, boomed from about 1878 to 1881, as gold prospectors, having worked the best of the western Sierra mines, headed to the high desert on the eastern slopes. Bodie was a mean place—the booze flowed freely, shootings were commonplace, and licentiousness reigned. Evidence of the town's wild past survives today at an excel-lent museum, and you can tour an old stamp mill and a ridge that contains many mine sites. Bodie, unlike Calico in Southern Califor-nia near Barstow, is a genuine ghost town, its status proudly stated as "arrested decay." No food, drink, or lodging is available in Bodie. Though the park stays open in winter, snow may close Highway 270. Still, it's a fantastic time to visit: rent cross-country skis in Mammoth Lakes, drive north, ski in, and have the park to yourself. ✉*Museum: Main and Green Sts.* ☎*760/647–6445* ⊕*www.bodie.net* ☂*Park $3, museum free* ☉*Park: late May–early Sept., daily 8–7; early Sept.–late May, daily 8–4. Museum: late May–early Sept., daily 9–6; early Sept.– late May, hrs vary.*

SOUTHERN SIERRA ESSENTIALS

To research prices, get advice from other travelers, and book travel arrangements, visit www.fodors.com.

TRANSPORTATION

BY AIR

Fresno Yosemite International Airport (FYI) is the nearest airport to Sequoia and Kings Canyon national parks. Alaska, Allegiant, Ameri-can, Continental, Delta, Frontier, Hawaiian, Horizon, Mexicana, Northwest, United Express, and US Airways fly here. The closest major airport to Mammoth Lakes is in Reno. See chapter 22, Lake Tahoe, for details on the Reno airport.

Contacts **Fresno Yosemite International Airport** (✉ *5175 E. Clinton Ave., Fresno* ☎ *559/621–4500 or 559/498–4095* ⊕ *www.flyfresno.org*).

BY BUS

Greyhound serves Fresno, Merced, and Visalia from many California cities. VIA Adventures runs five daily buses from Merced to Yosemite Valley; buses also depart daily from Mariposa. The 2½-hour ride from Merced costs $25 round-trip, which includes admission to the park.

Contacts **Greyhound** (☎ *800/231–2222* ⊕ *www.greyhound.com*). **VIA Adven-tures** (☎ *888/727–5287 or 209/384–1315* ⊕ *www.via-adventures.com*).

BY CAR

From San Francisco, Interstate 80 and Interstate 580 are the fastest routes toward the central Sierra Nevada, but avoid driving these routes during weekday rush hours. Through the Central Valley, Interstate 5 and Highway 99 are the fastest north–south routes, but the latter is narrower and has heavy farm-truck traffic. To get to Kings Canyon, plan on a six-hour drive. Two major routes, Highways 180 and 198, intersect with Highway 99 (Highway 180 is closed east of Grant Grove in winter). To get to Yosemite, plan on driving five hours. Enter the park either on Highway 140, which is the best route in inclement weather, or on Highway 120, which is the fastest route when the roads are clear. To get to Mammoth Lakes in summer and early fall (or whenever snows aren't blocking Tioga Road), you can travel via Highway 120 (to U.S. 395 south) through the Yosemite high country; the quickest route in winter is Interstate 80 to U.S. 50 to Highway 207 (Kingsbury Grade) to U.S. 395 south; either route takes about seven hours.

Keep your tank full. Distances between gas stations can be long, and there's no fuel available in Yosemite Valley, Sequoia, or Kings Canyon. If you're traveling from October through April, rain on the coast can mean heavy snow in the mountains. Carry tire chains, and know how to put them on (on Interstate 80 and U.S. 50 you can pay a chain installer $20 to do it for you, but on other routes you'll have to do it yourself). Alternatively, you can rent a four-wheel-drive vehicle with snow tires. Always check road conditions before you leave. Traffic in national parks in summer can be heavy, and there are sometimes travel restrictions.

Contacts **California Road Conditions** (☎ *800/427-7623* ⊕ *www.dot.ca.gov/hq/ roadinfo*). **Sequoia–Kings Canyon Road and Weather Information** (☎ *559/565-3341*). **Yosemite Area Road and Weather Conditions** (☎ *209/372-0200*).

CONTACTS & RESOURCES

EMERGENCIES

In an emergency dial 911.

Emergency Services **Mammoth Hospital** (✉ *85 Sierra Park Rd., Mammoth Lakes* ☎ *760/934-3311* ⊕ *www.mammothhospital.com*). **Yosemite Medical Clinic** (✉ *Ahwahnee Rd., north of Northside Dr.* ☎ *209/372-4637*).

VISITOR INFORMATION

Contacts **Bridgeport Chamber of Commerce** (✉ *Box 541, Bridgeport, 93517* ☎ *760/932-7500* ⊕ *www.bridgeportcalifornia.com*). **DNC Parks & Resorts at Yosemite** (✉ *Box 578, Yosemite National Park, 95389* ☎ *209/372-1000* ⊕ *www. yosemitepark.com*). **Lee Vining Chamber of Commerce** (✉ *Box 29, Lee Vining, 93541* ☎ *760/647-6629* ⊕ *www.monolake.org/chamber*). **Mammoth Lakes Visitors Bureau** (✉ *Along Hwy. 203, Main St., near Sawmill Cutoff Rd., Box 48, Mammoth Lake,s 93546* ☎ *760/934-2712 or 888/466-2666* ⊕ *www.visitmammoth.com*). **Mono Lake** (✉ *Box 49, Lee Vining, 93541* ☎ *760/647-3044* ⊕ *www.monolake. org*). **Yosemite Sierra Visitors Bureau** (✉ *41969 Hwy. 41, Box 1998, Oakhurst, 93644* ☎ *559/683-4636* ⊕ *www.yosemitethisyear.com*).

Yosemite National Park

Half Dome, Yosemite National Park

WORD OF MOUTH

"Awful in stern, immovable majesty, how softly these rocks are adorned, and how fine and reassuring the company they keep: their feet among beautiful groves and meadows, their brows in the sky, a thousand flowers leaning confidingly against their feet, bathed in floods of water, floods of light, while the snow and waterfalls, the winds and avalanches and clouds shine and sing and wreathe about them as the years go by."

—John Muir, *The Yosemite*

WELCOME TO YOSEMITE

TOP REASONS TO GO

★ **Feel the earth move:** An easy stroll brings you to the base of Yosemite Falls, America's highest, where thundering springtime waters shake the ground.

★ **Tunnel to heaven:** Winding down into Yosemite Valley, Wawona Road passes through a mountainside and emerges before one of the park's most heart-stopping vistas.

★ **Touch the sky:** Watch clouds scudding across the bright blue dome that arches above the High Sierra's Tuolumne Meadows, a wide-open alpine valley ringed by 10,000-foot granite peaks.

★ **Walk away from it all:** Early or late in the day, leave the crowds behind and take a forest hike on a few of Yosemite's 800 mi of trails.

★ **Powder your nose:** Winter's hush floats into Yosemite on snowflakes. Wade into a fluffy drift, lift your face to the sky, and listen to the trees.

1 Yosemite Valley. In the southern third of the park, east of the High Sierra, beats Yosemite's heart. This is where you'll find the park's most famous sights and biggest crowds.

2 Wawona and Mariposa Grove. The park's southeastern tip holds Wawona, with its grand old hotel and pioneer history center, and the Mariposa Grove of Big Trees, filled with giant sequoias. These are closest to the South Entrance, 35 mi (a 1½-hour drive) south of Yosemite Village.

3 Glacier Point. Take in the entire valley with one glance from Glacier Point, south of the valley, about 16 hilly, twisting miles east of Wawona Road (Route 41). November–May, Glacier Point Road is only open between Wawona Road and Badger Pass Ski Area, where you can play in the snow.

4 Tuolumne Meadows. The highlight of east-central Yosemite is this wildflower-strewn valley with hiking trails, nestled between sharp, rocky peaks. It's a two-hour drive northeast of Yosemite Valley along Tioga Road (closed November–May).

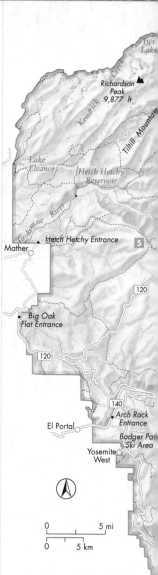

12

5 **Hetch Hetchy.** The most remote, least-visited part of Yosemite accessible by automobile, this glacial valley is dominated by a reservoir and veined with wilderness trails. It's near the park's western boundary, about half an hour's drive north of Big Oak Flat Entrance.

Except for its southwestern quadrant and a narrow strip across its midsection, Yosemite—a park the size of Rhode Island—is wild country seen only by backpackers and horsepackers. Most visitors spend their time along the park's southwestern border, between Wawona and Big Oak Flat Entrance; a bit farther east in Yosemite Valley and Badger Pass Ski Area; and along the east–west corridor of Tioga Road, which spans the park north of Yosemite Valley and bisects Tuolumne Meadows.

YOSEMITE NATIONAL PARK PLANNER

When to Go

During extremely busy periods, you may experience delays at the entrance gates. If you can only make it to Yosemite in the warmest months, try to visit midweek.

In winter, heavy snows occasionally cause road closures, and tire chains or four-wheel drive may be required on the roads that remain open. Tioga Road is closed from late October through the end of May or middle of June, depending on the snowmelt. The road to Glacier Point beyond the turnoff for Badger Pass is closed after the first major snowfall—usually in late October—through May; Mariposa Grove Road is typically closed for a shorter period in winter.

The ideal time to visit is from mid-April through Memorial Day and from mid-September through October.

The chart below is for Yosemite Valley. In the high country, temperatures are cooler—by as much as 10°F–20°F in Tuolumne Meadows—and precipitation is greater.

AVG HIGH/LOW TEMPS

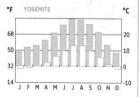

Flora & Fauna

Dense stands of incense cedar and Douglas fir—as well as ponderosa, Jeffrey, lodgepole, and sugar pines—cover much of the park, but the stellar standout, quite literally, is the *Sequoia sempervirens*, the giant sequoia. Sequoias grow only along the west slope of the Sierra Nevada between 4,500 and 7,000 feet in elevation. Starting from a seed the size of a rolled-oat flake, each of these ancient monuments assumes remarkable proportions in adulthood; you can see them in the Mariposa Grove of Big Trees. In late May the Valley's dogwood trees bloom with white, starlike flowers. Wildflowers, such as black-eyed Susan, bull thistle, cow parsnip, lupine, and meadow goldenrod, peak in June in the Valley and in July at higher elevations. Yosemite's waterfalls are at their most spectacular in May and June. By summer's end, some falls, including the mighty Yosemite Falls, dry up. They begin flowing again in late fall, and in winter they may be hung dramatically with ice. Visit the park during a full moon, and you can stroll in the evening without a flashlight and still make out the silhouettes of the giant granite monoliths and ribbons of falling water. Regardless of the season, sunset casts a brilliant orange light onto Half Dome, a stunning sight.

The most visible animals in the park are the mule deer, the only kind of deer in Yosemite. Though sightings of bighorn sheep are infrequent in the park itself, you can sometimes see them on the eastern side of the Sierra Crest, just off Route 120 in Lee Vining Canyon. The American black bear, which often has a brown, cinnamon, or blond coat, is the only species of bear in Yosemite (the California grizzlies were hunted to extinction in the 1920s), though few people ever see them. Watch for the blue Steller's jay along trails, in campgrounds, and around public buildings. Golden eagles are sometimes seen soaring above the Valley.

Getting There & Around

To get to Yosemite, take Route 120 east to the Big Oak Flat entrance or west to the Tioga Pass entrance (summer to late fall only); Route 140 east to the Arch Rock entrance; or Route 41 to the South entrance. Yosemite Valley is about 200 mi from San Francisco; the park is about 300 mi from Reno or Los Angeles, and about 500 mi from Las Vegas.

When it's crowded, some roads are closed to private vehicles; the road to Happy Isles and the Mist Trail is only accessible by shuttle. You can avoid traffic jams by leaving your car at any of the designated lots and taking the free hybrid diesel-electric shuttle bus. Shuttles serve eastern Yosemite Valley between Camp 4 and Happy Isles year-round, every day. From May to September, shuttles run from 7 AM to 10 PM; the rest of the year, shuttles run from 9 AM to 10 PM. In summer, shuttles also operate between the visitor center and El Capitan, between Wawona and the Mariposa Grove, and between the Tioga Pass entrance and Olmstead Point. In winter, a shuttle runs between Yosemite Valley and Badger Pass Ski Area. For more information on shuttles within the park, visit ⊕ *www.nps.gov/yose/trip/shuttle.htm* or call ☎ *209/372-1240.*

There are few gas stations within Yosemite, so fuel up before you reach the park. From late fall until early spring, the weather is unpredictable, and driving can be treacherous. You should carry chains; they are often mandatory on Sierra roads in snowstorms. Pick chains up before you arrive—if you buy them in the Valley, you'll pay twice the normal price. For information about road conditions, call ☎ *800/427-7623* or *209/372-0200* from within California or go to ⊕ *www.dot.ca.gov.*

WHAT IT COSTS				
¢	$	$$	$$$	$$$$
Restaurants				
under $8	$8–$12	$13–$20	$21–$30	over $30
Hotels				
under $50	$50–$100	$101–$150	$151–$200	over $200
Camping				
under $10	$10–$17	$18–$35	$36–$50	over $50

Restaurant prices are per person for a main course at dinner. Hotel prices are per night for two people in a standard double room in high season, excluding taxes and service charges. Camping prices are for a standard (no hookups, pit toilets, fire grates, picnic tables) campsite per night.

Bears

The Sierra Nevada are home to thousands of bears, and you should take all necessary precautions to keep yourself—and the bears—safe. Bears that acquire a taste for human food can become very aggressive and destructive and often must be destroyed by rangers. The national parks' campgrounds and some campgrounds outside the parks provide food-storage boxes that can keep bears from pilfering your edibles (portable canisters for backpackers can be rented in most park stores). It's imperative that you move all food, coolers, and items with a scent (including toiletries, toothpaste, chewing gum, and air fresheners) from your car (including the trunk) to the storage box at your campsite; day-trippers should lock food in bear boxes provided at parking lots. If you don't, a bear may break into your car by literally peeling off the door or ripping open the trunk, or it may ransack your tent. The familiar tactic of hanging your food from high tree limbs is not an effective deterrent, as bears can easily scale trees. In the Southern Sierra, bear canisters are the only effective and proven method for preventing bears from getting human food.

12

By Constance Jones

You can lose your perspective in Yosemite. This is a land where everything is big. Really big. There are big rocks, big trees, and big waterfalls. The park has been so extravagantly praised and so beautifully photographed that some people wonder if the reality can possibly measure up. For almost everyone it does: here, you will remember what *breathtaking* really means.

With 1,189 square mi of parkland—94.5% of it undeveloped wilderness accessible only to the backpacker and horseback rider—Yosemite is a nature lover's wonderland. The western boundary dips as low as 2,000 feet in the chaparral-covered foothills; the eastern boundary rises to 13,000 feet at points along the Sierra Crest. Yosemite Valley has many of the park's most famous sites and is easy to reach, but take the time to explore the high country above the Valley and you'll see a different side of the park; the fragile and unique alpine terrain is arresting. Wander through this world of wind-warped trees, scurrying animals, and bighorn sheep, and you'll come away with a distinct sense of peace and solitude.

The Miwok, the last of several Native American peoples to inhabit the Yosemite area (they were forced out by gold miners in 1851), named the Yosemite Valley *Ahwahnee,* which is thought to mean "the place of the gaping mouth." Abraham Lincoln established Yosemite Valley and the Mariposa Grove of Giant Sequoias as public land in 1864, when he deeded the land to the state of California. This grant was the first of its kind in America, and it laid the foundation for the establishment of national and state parks. The high country above the Valley, however, was not protected. John Muir, concerned about the destructive effects of over-grazing on subalpine meadows, rallied together a team of dedicated supporters and lobbied for expanded protection of lands surrounding Yosemite Valley. As a result of their efforts, Yosemite National Park was established by Congress on October 1, 1890.

SCENIC DRIVES

Route 41. From the South entrance station, curvy Route 41 provides great views and stopover points en route to the Valley. Just past the gate, an offshoot to the right leads to the Mariposa Grove of Big Trees (it's closed once there's snow on the ground). A few miles north on Route 41 is Wawona, where you can stop for lunch. Drive another 15 mi, and you'll come to the turnoff for Glacier Point. Farther along on Route 41, you'll pass through a tunnel, after which you can pull off the road and park. "Tunnel View" is one of the most famous views of Yosemite Valley, with El Capitan on the left, Bridalveil Fall on the right, and Half Dome as a backdrop. Continue another 5 mi on Route 41 until you reach Yosemite Valley. From beginning to end, drive time alone is about an hour; with stops it will take a minimum of three hours to complete this tour.

Tioga Road. In summer, a drive up Tioga Road (Route 120) to the high country will reward you with gorgeous alpine scenery, including crystal-blue lakes, grassy meadows dotted with wildflowers, and high-alpine peaks. Keep a sharp eye out for the neon colors of rock climbers, who seem to defy gravity on the cliffs. Wildflowers peak in July and August. The one-way trip to Tioga Pass takes approximately 1½ hours.

WHAT TO SEE

Yosemite is so large that you can think of it as five different parks. Yosemite Valley, famous for waterfalls and cliffs, and Wawona, where the giant sequoias stand, are open all year. Hetch Hetchy, home of less-used backcountry trails, closes after the first big snow and reopens in May or June. The subalpine high country, Tuolumne Meadows, is open for summer hiking and camping; in winter it's accessible only via cross-country skis or snowshoes. Badger Pass Ski Area is open in winter only.

HISTORIC SITES

★ **Ahwahnee Hotel.** Built in 1927, this stately lodge of granite and concrete beams stained to look like redwood is a perfect man-made complement to Yosemite's natural majesty. Even if you aren't a guest, take time to visit the immense parlors with walk-in hearths and priceless, antique Native American rugs and baskets. The dining room, its high ceiling interlaced with massive sugar-pine beams, is extraordinary. Dinner is formal; breakfast and lunch are more casual. ⊠*Ahwahnee Rd., about ¾ mi east of Yosemite Valley Visitor Center, Yosemite Village* ☎*801/559–5000, lodging reservations; 209/372–1407, dining reservations.*

Ahwahneechee Village. Tucked behind the Valley Visitor Center, a short loop trail of about 100 yards circles through a re-creation of an Ahwahneechee Native American village as it might have appeared in 1872, 21 years after the Native Americans' first contact with Europeans. Markers explain the lifestyle of Yosemite's first residents. Allow

GREAT ITINERARIES

YOSEMITE IN ONE DAY

Your first stop as you enter the Yosemite from the west is the graceful 620-foot cascade of **Bridalveil Fall.** As you continue east, you'll spot 3,593-foot **El Capitan,** the world's largest granite monolith, across the Valley. Follow signs to **Yosemite Village,** and stop in at the **Valley Visitor Center** to pick up maps and brochures. Behind the center, walk through a small, re-created **Ahwahneechee village.** For more Native American lore, take a quick peek at the **Yosemite Museum** next door, where there's an impressive collection of baskets. If you're a photography buff, the nearby **Ansel Adams Gallery** is a must-see. Next, amble over to **Sentinel Bridge,** walk to its center, and take in the best view of **Half Dome,** with its reflection in the Merced River. Before you leave the Village, stop at the Village Store or a snack bar to pick up provisions for a picnic lunch.

Return to your car, drive over Sentinel Bridge, turn left, and continue on Southside Drive toward **Curry Village.** Hardy hikers may want to go straight to the day-use lot, walk to the end of the shuttle-bus road, and climb the moderately steep trail to the footbridge overlooking 317-foot **Vernal Fall** (1½ mi round-trip; allow 1½ hours). Looping back toward Yosemite Village, follow signs to the **Ahwahnee Hotel.**

Back on the main road heading west, drive to **Yosemite Falls,** the highest waterfall in North America. If you have time at the end of the day, drive up to **Glacier Point** for a sunset view of the Valley and the surrounding peaks.

YOSEMITE IN THREE DAYS

If you have three days, start at the **Valley Visitor Center.** Head west for a short hike to **Yosemite Falls.** Afterward, continue driving west for a valley view of giant, granite **El Capitan.** Continue west on North-side Drive, and follow signs for **Route 41 (Wawona Road);** head south. At the Chinquapin junction, make a left turn onto Glacier Point Road (summer only). From **Glacier Point,** you'll get a phenomenal bird's-eye view of the entire Valley, including **Half Dome, Vernal Fall,** and **Nevada Fall.** If you want to avoid the busloads of tourists at Glacier Point, stop at **Sentinel Dome** instead.

On Day 2, head south on Route 41 and visit the **Mariposa Grove of Big Trees** and the **Pioneer Yosemite History Center.** Stop at the historic **Wawona Hotel** and have lunch. Return to Yosemite Valley on Route 41, stopping at the **Tunnel View** pullout to take in the breathtaking panorama of the Valley, with the afternoon sun lighting up the peaks. Back in the Valley, stop at **Bridalveil Falls** on the right side of the road. Then head to the **Ahwahnee Hotel.**

On the third day, have breakfast near the Valley Visitor Center in **Yosemite Village,** then see the **Ansel Adams Gallery,** the re-created **Ahwahneechee Village,** and the **Yosemite Museum.** Pick up light provisions before hiking to **Vernal Fall** or **Nevada Fall.** Picnic on the trail or in the Valley, then visit **Tuolumne Meadows,** 55 mi east of the Valley on **Tioga Road (Route 120)** (summer only).

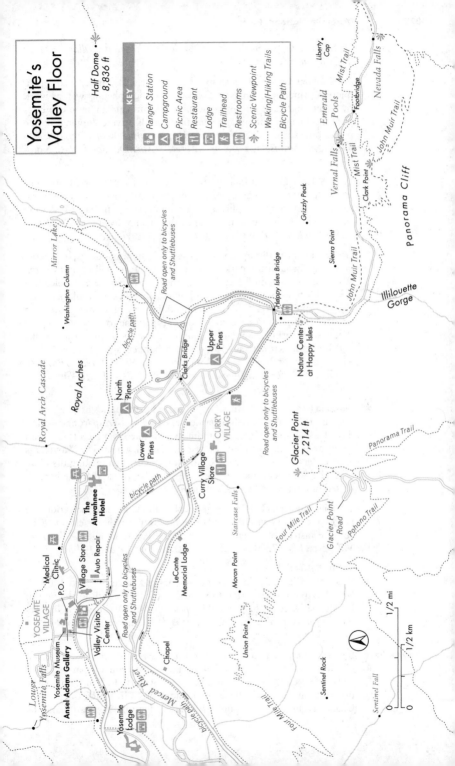

Yosemite's Valley Floor

KEY

🏠	Ranger Station
🔺	Campground
🧺	Picnic Area
🍴	Restaurant
🏨	Lodge
🥾	Trailhead
🚻	Restrooms
🌟	Scenic Viewpoint
......	Walking/Hiking Trails
------	Bicycle Path

Half Dome 8,836 ft

Liberty Cap

Mist Trail

Nevada Falls

Emerald Pools

Footbridge

Vernal Falls

Mist Trail

John Muir Trail

Clark Point

Panorama Cliff

Grizzly Peak

Sierra Point

John Muir Trail

Illilouette Gorge

Mirror Lake

Washington Column

Road open only to bicycles and Shuttlebuses

bicycle path

Royal Arch Cascade

Royal Arches

North Pines

Clarks Bridge

Upper Pines

Happy Isles Bridge

Nature Center at Happy Isles

Lower Pines

Glacier Point 7,214 ft

Panorama Trail

CURRY VILLAGE

Curry Village Store

Road open only to bicycles and Shuttlebuses

Staircase Falls

The Ahwahnee Hotel

bicycle path

LeConte Memorial Lodge

Four Mile Trail

Glacier Point Road

Pohono Trail

Medical Clinic

Village Store

Auto Repair

P.O.

YOSEMITE VILLAGE

Valley Visitor Center

Chapel

Moran Point

Union Point

Yosemite Museum

Ansel Adams Gallery

Lower Yosemite Falls

Road open only to bicycles and Shuttlebuses

bicycle path

Merced River

Yosemite Lodge

Sentinel Rock

Sentinel Fall

Four Mile Trail

0   1/2 mi

0   1/2 km

30 minutes to see it all. ⊠*Northside Dr., Yosemite Village* ⊑*Free* ⊗*Daily sunrise–sunset.*

Ansel Adams Gallery. This shop displays and sells original and reproduction prints by the master Yosemite photographer, as well as work by other landscape photographers. Its elegant camera shop conducts photography workshops and sometimes holds private showings of fine prints on Saturdays. ⊠*Northside Dr., Yosemite Village* ☎*209/372–4413* ⊕*www.anseladams.com* ⊑*Free* ⊗*Apr.–Oct., daily 9–6; Nov.–Mar., daily 9–5.*

Curry Village. Opened in 1899 by David and Jenny Curry, Curry Village offers tented lodgings for a modest price. There are also several stores, an evening campfire program in summer, and an ice-skating rink in winter. If you want to rent rafts or bicycles, this is the place. ⊠*Southside Dr., about ½ mi east of Yosemite Village.*

Pioneer Yosemite History Center. Yosemite's first buildings, relocated here from around the park, make up this historic collection near the Wawona Hotel—you'll even enter on the covered bridge that welcomed the park's first tourists. There's a homesteader's cabin, a blacksmith's shop, a bakery, and a U.S. Cavalry headquarters, all from the late 19th or early 20th centuries. Costumed docents play the roles of the pioneers Wednesday through Sunday in summer; ask about ranger-led walks and horse-drawn carriage rides, which happen sporadically. ⊠*Rte. 41, Wawona* ☎*209/375–9531 or 209/379–2646* ⊑*Free* ⊗*Building interiors are open mid-June–Labor Day, Wed. 2–5, Thurs.–Sun. 10–1 and 2–5.*

★ **Wawona Hotel.** In the southern tip of Yosemite, the park's first lodge was built in 1879. With a whitewashed exterior and wraparound verandas, this National Historic Landmark is a fine example of Victorian resort architecture—a blend of rusticity and elegance. The Wawona is an excellent place to stay or to stop for lunch when making the drive from the South entrance to the Valley, but be aware that the hotel is closed in January. ⊠*Rte. 41, Wawona* ☎*209/375–6556.*

Yosemite Museum. This museum's collection and demonstrations in beadwork, basket weaving, and other traditional activities elucidate the cultural history of Yosemite's Miwok and Paiute people. ⊠*Yosemite Village* ☎*209/372–0281* ⊑*Free* ⊗*Daily 9–noon and 1–4:30.*

SCENIC STOPS

★ **El Capitan.** Rising 3,593 feet—more than 350 stories—above the Valley, El Capitan is the largest exposed-granite monolith in the world. It's almost twice the height of the Rock of Gibraltar. Look for climbers scaling the vertical face. ⊠*Off Northside Dr., about 4 mi west of the Valley Visitor Center.*

Fodor's Choice   **Glacier Point.** A Yosemite hot spot for its sweeping, bird's-eye views, ★   Glacier Point looms 3,214 feet above the Valley. From the parking area, walk a few hundred yards and you'll see waterfalls, Half Dome, and other mountain peaks. It's a tremendous place to watch the sun set. Glacier Point is also a popular hiking destination. You can make the strenuous hike up, or take a bus ($20) to the top and hike down. The bus runs June through October, weather permitting; call 209/372–1240 for schedules. ⊠ *Glacier Point Rd., 16 mi northeast of Rte. 41.*

★ **Half Dome.** Though you may have seen it on countless postcards and calendars, it's still arresting to see Half Dome, the Valley's most recognizable formation, which tops out at an elevation of 8,842 feet. The afternoon sun lights its face with orange and yellow shades that are reflected in the Merced River; stand on the Sentinel Bridge at sunset for the best view.

Hetch Hetchy Reservoir. The Hetch Hetchy Reservoir, which supplies water and hydroelectric power to San Francisco, is about 40 mi from Yosemite Valley. Some say John Muir died of heartbreak when this grand valley was dammed and flooded beneath 300 feet of water in 1913. Almost from the start, environmental groups such as the Sierra Club have lobbied the government to drain the reservoir; in 2006 the State of California issued a report stating that restoration of the valley is feasible. ⊠ *Hetch Hetchy Rd., about 15 mi north of the Big Oak Flat entrance station.*

High Country. The above–tree line, high-alpine region east of the Valley—land of alpenglow and top-of-the-world vistas—is often missed by crowds who come to gawk at the Valley's more publicized splendors. If you've never seen Sierra high country, go. If you've already been there, you know why it's not to be missed. Summer wildflowers, which usually spring up mid-July through August, carpet the meadows and mountainsides with pink, purple, blue, red, yellow, and orange. On foot or on horseback are the best ways to get here. For information on trails and backcountry permits, check with the visitor center.

★ **Mariposa Grove of Big Trees.** Mariposa is Yosemite's largest grove of giant sequoias. The Grizzly Giant, the oldest tree here, is estimated to be 2,700 years old. You can visit the trees on foot or, in summer, on a one-hour tram tour. If the road to the grove is closed in summer—which happens when Yosemite is crowded—park in Wawona and take the free shuttle (9–4:30) to the parking lot. The access road to the grove may also be closed by snow for extended periods from November to mid-May; you can still usually walk, snowshoe, or ski in. ⊠ *Rte. 41, 2 mi north of the South entrance station.*

Sentinel Dome. The view from here is similar to that from Glacier Point, except you can't see the Valley floor. A 1.1-mi path climbs to the viewpoint from the parking lot. The trail is long and steep enough to keep the crowds away, but it's not overly rugged. ⊠ *Glacier Point Rd., off Rte. 41.*

★ **Tuolumne Meadows.** The largest subalpine meadow in the Sierra, at 8,600 feet, is a popular way station for backpack trips along the Sierra-scribing Pacific Crest and John Muir trails. No wonder: the cracklingly clear air and dramatic sky above the river-scored valley can make even the most jaded heart soar. The colorful wildflowers peak in mid-July and August. Tioga Road provides easy access to the high country, but

Q & A WITH RANGER SCOTT GEDIMAN

What's your favorite thing to do in the park?

I really enjoy hiking in Yosemite; in my opinion there's no better way to see the park. My favorite is the classic hike up the Mist Trail to Vernal Fall. I've done it literally hundreds of times—I've got family photos of my folks pushing me up the trail in a stroller. If you can only take one hike in Yosemite, do this one, especially in spring and summer.

Which time of year is best for visiting Yosemite?

The spring is wonderful, with the waterfalls going full blast and the meadows so green. The fall colors are beautiful, too. But in winter, the weather is great. The most stunning time in the valley is when a winter storm clears and there are incredible blue skies above the granite rocks, and the snow. There's a feeling you get seeing Half Dome with snow on it, or doing a winter hike on the Four-Mile Trail, Yosemite Falls Trail, or the Glacier Point trails.

What's there to do here in winter?

There's the ice-skating rink at Curry Village, and up at Badger Pass there's a wonderful ski school that specializes in teaching kids. There's cross-country skiing on groomed tracks along Glacier Point Road. Snowshoeing is really catching on. It's fun, it's easy, families can do it. You don't need special skills or a bunch of gear to go hiking through the snow; just put some snowshoes on your sneakers or hiking boots, and you're off. Every morning from about mid-December to mid-March, park rangers lead free snowshoe walks from Badger Pass. We talk about winter ecology and adaptations animals make, or we hike up to the old Badger Summit for some fantastic views.

What about summer?

There's a misperception that the crowds are unmanageable, but it's not true. It's very easy to get away from the crowds in the Valley. One easy way is to hike the Valley Loop Trail, which a lot of people don't even know about. It goes all around the valley perimeter. Five minutes from Yosemite Lodge, and you won't see anybody.

How crowded does the Valley really get?

At the busiest time, probably Memorial Day Weekend, there can be as many as 25,000 people in the park at one time, many of them in the Valley. The biggest mistake people make in summer is to drive everywhere. It's frustrating because of the traffic, and it takes longer even than walking. Park your car in the day-use lot or leave it at your hotel, and take the free shuttle around. The shuttle goes to all the popular spots in the Valley.

the highway closes when snow starts to fall, usually in mid-October. ⊠ *Tioga Rd. (Rte. 120), about 8 mi west of the Tioga Pass entrance station.*

WATERFALLS When the snow starts to melt (usually peaking in May), almost every rocky lip or narrow gorge becomes a spillway for streaming snowmelt churning down to meet the Merced River. But even in drier months, the waterfalls can be breathtaking. If you choose to hike any of the trails to or up the falls, be sure to wear shoes with good, no-slip soles; the rocks can be extremely slick. Stay on trails at all times.

Bridalveil Fall, a filmy fall of 620 feet that is often diverted as much as 20 feet one way or the other by the breeze, is the first marvelous view of Yosemite Valley you will see if you come in via Route 41.

Climb Mist Trail from Happy Isles for an up-close view of 594-foot **Nevada Fall,** the first major fall as the Merced River plunges out of the high country toward the eastern end of Yosemite Valley. If you don't want to hike, you can see it—distantly—from Glacier Point.

At 1,612 feet, **Ribbon Fall** is the highest single fall in North America. It's also the first valley waterfall to dry up in summer; the rainwater and melted snow that create the slender fall evaporate quickly at this height. Look just west of El Capitan from the Valley floor for the best view of the fall from the base of Bridalveil Fall.

Fern-covered black rocks frame 317-foot **Vernal Fall,** and rainbows play in the spray at its base. Take Mist Trail from Happy Isles to see it—or, if you'd rather not hike, go to Glacier Point for a distant view.

Fodor'sChoice **Yosemite Falls**—which form the highest waterfall in North America and ★ the fifth-highest in the world—are actually three falls, one on top of another. The water from the top descends a total of 2,425 feet, and when the falls run hard, you can hear them thunder all across the Valley. When they dry up, as often happens in late summer, the Valley seems naked without the wavering tower of spray. To view the falls up close, head to their base on the trail from Camp 4.

VISITOR CENTERS

Le Conte Memorial Lodge. A cute stone cottage from the outside and a dramatic mini-cathedral on the inside, the Valley's first visitor center is now operated by the Sierra Club. You can browse its substantial library, small children's library, and environmental exhibits, and attend evening programs. It's across from Housekeeping Camp. ⊠ *Southside Dr., about ½ mi west of Curry Village* ⊙ *Memorial Day–Labor Day, Wed.–Sun. 10–4.*

Nature Center at Happy Isles. Named after the pair of little islands in the Merced River where it enters Yosemite Valley, this family-oriented center has books, dioramas, and interactive exhibits on the park, with special attention paid to recent natural phenomena, such as recurring rock slides. ⊠ *Off Southside Dr., about ¾ mi east of Curry Village* 🎫 *Free* ⊙ *Mid-May–Oct., 10–noon and 12:30–4.*

Valley Visitor Center. The museum here is state-of-the-art, with interactive and high-tech exhibits. Be sure to stop by and learn a little about the park; you can also pick up maps, guides, and information from park rangers. ⊠ *Yosemite Village* ☎ *209/372–0299* ⊕ *www.yosemite park.com* 🖃 *Free* ☽ *Memorial Day–Labor Day, daily 8–6; Labor Day–Memorial Day, daily 9–5.*

Wilderness Center. The staff at the Wilderness Center in Yosemite Village provides free wilderness permits for overnight camping, maps, and advice to hikers heading into the backcountry. When the center is closed, go to the Valley Visitor Center next door. ⊠ *Yosemite Village* ☽ *Memorial Day–Labor Day, daily 7:30 AM –6 PM.*

SPORTS & THE OUTDOORS

BICYCLING

There may be no more enjoyable way to see Yosemite Valley than to ride a bike beneath its lofty granite monoliths. The eastern valley has 12 mi of paved, flat bicycle paths across meadows and through woods, with bike racks at convenient stopping points. For a greater challenge, you can ride on 196 mi of paved park roads—but bicycles are not allowed on hiking trails or in the backcountry. Kids under 18 must wear a helmet. *For information on renting equipment,* ⇨ *Outfitters & Expeditions box.*

BIRD-WATCHING

More than 200 bird species have been spotted in the park, including the sage sparrow, pygmy owl, blue grouse, and mountain bluebird. Park rangers lead free bird-watching walks in Yosemite Valley and Tuolomne one day each week in summer; check at a visitor center or information station for times and locations. *For information on tours,* ⇨ *Outfitters & Expeditions box.*

FISHING

The waters in Yosemite are not stocked; trout, mostly brown and rainbow, live here but are not plentiful. Yosemite's fishing season begins on the last Saturday in April and ends on November 15. Some waterways are off-limits at certain times; be sure to inquire at the visitor center about regulations.

A California fishing license is required; licenses run $11.30 for one day, $17.60 for two days, and $34.90 for 10 days. Full season licenses cost $30.70 for state residents, and a whopping $82.45 for nonresidents.

Buy your license in season at Yosemite Village Sport Shop (☎ 209/372–1286) or at the Wawona Store (☎ 209/375–6574). You can also obtain a license by writing the **California Department of Fish and Game.** ⊠ *1416 9th St., Sacramento* ☎ *916/227–2245* ⊕ *www.dfg.ca.gov. For information on tours,* ⇨ *Outfitters & Expeditions box.*

GOLF

Wawona Golf course is one of the country's few organic golf courses; it's also an Audubon Cooperative sanctuary for birds. You can play a round or take a lesson from the pro here.

Wawona Golf Course. The 9-hole, par-35 course at Wawona has different tee positions per side, providing 18 holes at par 70. The pro shop rents out electric golf carts, rents and sells other equipment, and sells golf clothing. ⊠ *Rte. 41, Wawona* ☎ *209/375–6572 Wawona Golf Shop* ⊕ *www.yosemitepark.com* ☒ *$18.50–$29.50* ⊗ *Mid-Apr.–Oct., daily.*

HIKING

For information on tours, ⇨ *Outfitters & Expeditions box.*

EASY **"A Changing Yosemite" Interpretive Trail.** This self-guided, wheelchair- and stroller-accessible walk begins about 75 yards in front of the Valley Visitor Center, where you can pick up an informative pamphlet that explains the continually changing geology visible along the walk. The trail follows the road, then circles through Cook's Meadow on a paved path. ⊠ *Across from the Valley Visitor Center.*

★ **Yosemite Falls Trail.** This is the highest waterfall in North America. The upper fall (1,430 feet), the middle cascades (675 feet), and the lower fall (320 feet) combine for a total of 2,425 feet and, when viewed from the valley, appear as a single waterfall. The ¼-mi trail leads from the parking lot to the base of the falls. Upper Yosemite Fall Trail, a strenuous 3½-mi climb rising 2,700 feet, takes you above the top of the falls. ⊠ *Northside Dr. at Camp 4.*

MODERATE **Mist Trail.** You'll walk through rainbows when you visit 317-foot Vernal
★ Fall. The hike to the bridge at the base of the fall is moderately strenuous and less than 1 mi long. It's another steep (and often wet) ¾-mi grind up to the top. From there, you can continue 2 mi to the top of Nevada Fall, a 594-foot cascade as the Merced River plunges out of the high country. The trail is open late spring to early fall, depending on snowmelt. ⊠ *Happy Isles.*

★ **Panorama Trail.** Starting at Glacier Point, the trail circles 8½ mi down through forest, past the secluded Illilouette Falls, to the top of Nevada Fall, where it connects with Mist Trail and the John Muir Trail. You'll pass Nevada, then Vernal Fall on your way down to the Valley floor for a total elevation loss of 3,200 feet. Arrange to take the early-morning hiker bus to Glacier Point, and allow a full day for this hike. ⊠ *Glacier Point.*

DIFFICULT **Chilnualna Falls Trail.** This Wawona-area trail runs 4 mi one way to the top of the falls, then leads into the backcountry, connecting with miles of other trails. This is one of the park's most inspiring and secluded—albeit strenuous—trails. Past the tumbling cascade, and up through forests, you'll emerge before a panoramic vista at the top. ⊠ *Chilnualna Falls Rd., off Rte. 41, Wawona.*

12

OUTFITTERS & EXPEDITIONS

BICYCLING

Yosemite Bike Rentals. You can rent bikes by the hour ($7.50) or by day ($24.50) from either Yosemite Lodge or Curry Village bike stands. Bikes with child trailers, baby-jogger strollers, and wheelchairs are also available. ✉ *Yosemite Lodge or Curry Village* ☎ *209/372–1208* ⊕ *www.yosemitepark.com* ✉ *$7.50 (hour)/$24 (day)* ⊙ *Apr.–Oct.*

BIRD-WATCHING

Birding Seminars. The Yosemite Association sponsors one- to four-day seminars for beginner and intermediate birders. ☎ *209/379–2321* ⊕ *www.yosemite.org* ✉ *$82–$254* ⊙ *Apr.–Aug.*

FISHING

Southern Yosemite Mountain Guides (☎ *800/231–4575* ⊕ *www. symg.com*) offers fly-fishing lessons and day- and weekend trips deep in Yosemite's backcountry.

HIKING & BACKPACKING

The staff at the **Wilderness Center** (✉ *Yosemite Village* ⊙ *Yosemite Wilderness Reservations, Box 545, Yosemite, 95389* ☎ *209/372–0740* ⊕ *www.nps.gov/yose*) provides free wilderness permits, which are required for overnight camping (advance reservations are available for $5 and are highly recommended for popular trailheads from May through September and on weekends). They also provide maps and advice to hikers heading into the backcountry.

Yosemite Mountaineering School and Guide Service (✉ *Yosemite Mountain Shop, Curry Village* ☎ *209/372–8344* ⊕ *www.yosemite park.com*) can take you on guided two-hour to full-day treks from April through November.

HORSEBACK RIDING

Tuolumne Meadows Stables (✉ *Off Tioga Rd., about 2 mi east of Tuolumne Meadows Visitor Center* ☎ *209/372–8427* ⊕ *www. yosemitepark.com*) runs two-, four-, and eight-hour trips—which cost $53, $69, and $96, respectively—and High Sierra four- to six-day camping treks on mules, which begin at $625. Reservations are essential.

Wawona Stables (✉ *Rte. 41, Wawona* ☎ *209/375–6502*) has two- and five-hour rides, starting at $53 (reservations essential).

You can tour the valley and the start of the high country on two-hour, four-hour, and all-day rides at **Yosemite Valley Stables** (✉ *At entrance to North Pines Campground, 100 yards northeast of Curry Village* ☎ *209/372–8348* ⊕ *www. yosemitepark.com*). You must reserve in advance for the $53, $69, and $96 trips.

RAFTING

The per-person rental fee at **Curry Village Raft Stand** covers the raft (4- to 6-person), two paddles, and life jackets, plus a shuttle to the launch point on Sentinel Beach. ✉ *South side of Southside Dr., Curry Village* ☎ *209/372–8319* ⊕ *www. yosemitepark.com* ✉ *$20.50* ⊙ *Late May–July.*

12

ROCK CLIMBING

The one-day basic lesson at **Yosemite Mountaineering School and Guide Service** includes some bouldering and rappelling, and three or four 60-foot climbs. Climbers must be at least 10 (kids under 12 must be accompanied by a parent or guardian) and in reasonably good physical condition. Intermediate and advanced classes include instruction in belays, self-rescue, summer snow climbing, and free climbing. ✉ *Yosemite Mountain Shop, Curry Village* ☎ *209/372-8344* ⊕ *www.yosemitepark.com* 🖅 *$80-$190* 🕘 *Apr.–Nov.*

SKIING & SNOWSHOEING

California's first ski resort, **Badger Pass Ski Area** (✉ *Badger Pass Rd., off Glacier Point Rd., 18 mi from Yosemite Valley* ☎ *209/372-8430* ✍ *35% beginner, 50% intermediate, 15% advanced. Longest run 3/10 mi, base 7,200 feet, summit, 8,000 feet. Lifts: 5*) has 10 downhill runs, 90 mi of groomed cross-country trails, and two excellent ski schools. Free shuttle buses from Yosemite Valley operate during ski season (December–early April, weather permitting). Lift tickets are $38, downhill equipment rents for $24, and snowboard rental with boots is $35.

The gentle slopes of Badger Pass make **Yosemite Ski School** (☎ *209/372-8430*) an ideal spot for children and beginners to learn downhill skiing or snowboarding for as little as $28 for a group lesson.

The highlight of Yosemite's cross-country skiing center is a 21-mi loop from Badger Pass to Glacier Point. You can rent cross-country skis for $21.50 per day at the **Cross-Country Ski School** (☎ *209/372-8444*),

which also rents snowshoes ($19.50 per day), telemarking equipment ($29), and skate-skis ($24).

Yosemite Mountaineering School (✉ *Badger Pass Ski Area* ☎ *209/372-8344* ⊕ *www.yosemitepark.com*) conducts snowshoeing, cross-country skiing, telemarking, and skate-skiing classes starting at $30.

Four-Mile Trail. You can take the hiker bus up to Glacier Point ($15), and then descend from there, zigzagging through the forest to the Valley floor, where you can catch a free shuttle back to your starting hiker-bus stop. If you decide to hike up Four-Mile Trail and back down again, allow about six hours for the challenging 9½-mi round-trip (the original 4-mi-long trail was lengthened to make it less steep). The Valley floor trailhead is on Southside Drive near Sentinel Beach, and the elevation change is 3,220 feet. ⊠ *Glacier Point.*

Fodor's Choice ★ **John Muir Trail to Half Dome.** Ardent and courageous trekkers can continue on from the top of Nevada Fall, off Mist Trail, to the top of Half Dome. Some hikers attempt this entire 10- to 12-hour, 16¾-mi round-trip trek from Happy Isles in one day; if you're planning to do this, remember that the 4,800-foot elevation gain and the 8,842-foot altitude will cause shortness of breath. Another option is to hike to a campground in Little Yosemite Valley near the top of Nevada Fall the first day, then climb to the top of Half Dome and hike out the next day; it's highly recommended that you get your wilderness permit reservations at least a month in advance. Be sure to wear hiking boots and bring gloves. The last pitch up the back of Half Dome is very steep—the only way to climb this sheer rock face is to pull yourself up using the steel cable handrails, which are in place only from late spring to early fall. Those who brave the ascent will be rewarded with an unbeatable view of Yosemite Valley below and the high country beyond. Before heading out, check conditions with rangers, and don't attempt the final ascent if there are any storm clouds overhead. ⊠ *Happy Isles.*

HORSEBACK RIDING

Reservations for guided trail rides must be made in advance at the hotel tour desks or by phone. For overnight saddle trips, which use mules, call ☎ 801/559–5000 on or after September 15 to request a lottery application for the following year. Scenic trail rides range from two hours to a full day; six-day High Sierra saddle trips are also available. *For information on tours,* ⇨ *Outfitters & Expeditions box.*

ICE-SKATING

Winter visitors have skated at the outdoor **Curry Village ice-skating rink** for decades, and there's no mystery why: it's a kick to glide across the ice while soaking up views of Half Dome and Glacier Point. ⊠ *South side of Southside Dr., Curry Village* ☎ *209/372–8319* ⌸ *$6.50 per 2½ hrs, $3.25 skate rental* ☉ *Mid-Nov.–mid-Mar. afternoons and evenings daily, morning sessions weekends.*

RAFTING

Rafting is permitted only on designated areas of the Middle and South Forks of the Merced River. Check with the Valley Visitor Center for closures and other restrictions. *For information on equipment,* ⇨ *Outfitters & Expeditions box.*

ROCK CLIMBING

Fodor'sChoice The granite canyon walls of Yosemite Valley are world-renowned for
★ rock climbing. El Capitan, with its 3,593-foot vertical face, is the most
famous and difficult, but there are many other options here for all skill
levels. *For information on classes, ⇨ Outfitters & Expeditions box.*

12

SKIING & SNOWSHOEING

The beauty of Yosemite under a blanket of snow has long inspired
poets and artists, as well as ordinary folks. Skiing and snowshoeing
activities in the park center on Badger Pass Ski Area, California's oldest snow-sports resort, which is about 40 minutes away from the valley
on Glacier Point Road. Here you can rent equipment, take a lesson,
have lunch, join a guided excursion, and take the free shuttle back to
the valley after a drink in the lounge. *For information on lessons and
equipment, ⇨ Outfitters & Expeditions box.*

SWIMMING

The pools at Curry Village and Yosemite Lodge are open to nonguests.
Several swimming holes with small sandy beaches can be found in midsummer along the Merced River at the eastern end of Yosemite Valley. Find gentle waters to swim; currents are often stronger than they
appear, and temperatures are chilling. To conserve riparian habitats,
step into the river at sandy beaches and other obvious entry points.
Do not attempt to swim above or near waterfalls or rapids; fatalities
have occurred.

Nonguests can swim in the pool at **Curry Village** (☎ *209/372–8324
⊕ www.yosemitepark.com*) for $5. The pool is open late May–early
September.

The pool at **Yosemite Lodge** (☎ *209/372–1274 ⊕ www.yosemitepark.
com*), open late May-mid-September, is available to nonguests for $5.

EDUCATIONAL OFFERINGS

CLASSES & SEMINARS

Art Classes. Professional artists conduct workshops in watercolor, etch-
ing, drawing, and other mediums. Bring your own materials or purchase the basics at the Art Activity Center, next to the Village Store.
Call to verify scheduling. On the Web site, look for Activities, then Fun
Park Activities. ⊠ *Art Activity Center, Yosemite Village* ☎ *209/372–
1442 ⊕ www.yosemitepark.com* ✉ *Free* ⊙ *Early Apr.–early Oct.,
Mon.–Sat. 10–2.*

Yosemite Outdoor Adventures. Naturalists, scientists, and park rangers
lead multihour to multiday educational outings on topics from wood-
peckers to fire management to pastel painting. Most sessions take place
spring through fall, but a few focus on winter phenomena. ⊠ *Various
locations* ☎ *209/379–2321 ⊕ www.yosemite.org* ✉ *$82–$465.*

RANGER PROGRAMS

Junior Ranger Program. Children 3–13 can participate in the informal, self-guided Little Cub and Junior Ranger programs. A park activity handbook ($5) is available at the Valley Visitor Center or the Nature Center at Happy Isles; once your child has completed the book, a ranger will present him or her with a certificate and a badge. ⊠ *Valley Visitor Center or the Nature Center at Happy Isles* ☎ *209/372–0299.*

Ranger-Led Programs. Rangers lead walks and hikes and give informative and entertaining talks on a range of topics at different locations several times a day from spring through fall. The schedule is reduced in winter, but most days you can usually find a ranger program somewhere in the park. In the evenings at Yosemite Lodge and Curry Village, lectures by rangers, slide shows, and documentary films present unique perspectives on Yosemite. On summer weekends, Camp Curry and Tuolumne Meadows Campground host sing-along campfire programs. There's usually at least one ranger-led activity each night in the Valley; schedules and locations are posted on bulletin boards throughout the park and published in *Yosemite Today.*

TOURS

★ **Ansel Adams Photo Walks.** Photography enthusiasts shouldn't miss these two-hour guided camera walks offered by professional photographers. Some walks are hosted by the Ansel Adams Gallery, others by Delaware North Corporation; meeting points vary. All are free, but participation is limited—call up to 10 days in advance or visit the gallery. In-depth information about the walks can be found at www.anseladams.com. ☎ *209/372–4413 or 800/568–7398* ⊕ *www.yosemitepark.com* ⊡ *Free* ⚲ *Reservations essential.*

Big Trees Tram Tour. This open-air tram tour of the Mariposa Grove of Big Trees takes one hour. The trip does not include transportation from the Valley to the Grove, so plan to drive or take the shuttle. ☎ *209/372–1240* ⊡ *$16* ⊗ *Usually June–Oct., depending on snowfall.*

Glacier Point Tour. This four-hour trip takes you from Yosemite Valley (you're picked up from your hotel) to the Glacier Point vista, 3,214 feet above the Valley floor. ☎ *209/372–1240* ⊡ *$32.50* ⚲ *Reservations essential* ⊗ *June–Oct.*

Grand Tour. For a full-day tour of the Mariposa Grove and Glacier Point, try the Grand Tour. The tour stops for lunch at the historic Wawona Hotel, but the meal is not included in the tour price. ☎ *209/372–1240* ⊡ *$62 ($7 additional for lunch)* ⚲ *Reservations essential* ⊗ *June–Thanksgiving.*

Moonlight Tour. A late-evening version of the Valley Floor Tour takes place on moonlit nights, depending on weather conditions. ☎ *209/372–1240* ⊡ *$22.00* ⊗ *Apr.–Sept.*

Tuolumne Meadows Tour. For a full day's outing to the high country, opt for this ride up Tioga Road to Tuolumne Meadows. You'll stop at several overlooks, and you can connect with another shuttle at Tuolumne Lodge. This service is mostly for hikers and backpackers who want to

YOSEMITE IN BLACK & WHITE:

THE WORK OF ANSEL ADAMS

What John Muir did for Yosemite with words, Ansel Adams did with photographs. His photographs have inspired millions of people to visit Yosemite, and his persistent activism has helped to ensure the park's conservation.

Born in 1902, Adams first came to the valley when he was 14, photographing it with a Box Brownie camera. He later said his first visit "was a culmination of experience so intense as to be almost painful. From that day in 1916 my life has been colored and modulated by the great earth gesture of the Sierra." By 1919 he was working in the valley, as custodian of LeConte Memorial Lodge, the Sierra Club headquarters in Yosemite National Park.

Adams had harbored dreams of a career as a concert pianist, but the park sealed his fate as a photographer in 1928, the day he shot "Monolith: The Face of Half Dome," which remains one of his most famous works. Adams also married Virginia Best in 1928, in her father's studio in the valley (now the Ansel Adams Gallery).

As his photographic career took off, Yosemite began to sear itself into the American consciousness. David Brower, first executive director of the Sierra Club, later said of Adams' impact, "That Ansel Adams came to be recognized as one of the great photographers of this century is a tribute to the places that informed him."

In 1934, Adams was elected to the Sierra Club's board of directors; he would serve until 1971. As a representative of the conservation group, he combined his work with the club's mission, showing his photographs of the Sierra to influential officials such as Secretary of the Interior Harold L. Ickes, who showed them to President Franklin Delano Roosevelt. The images were a key factor in the establishment of Kings Canyon National Park.

In 1968, the Department of the Interior granted Adams its highest honor, the Conservation Service Award, and in 1980 he received the Presidential Medal of Freedom in recognition of his conservation work. Until his death in 1984, Adams continued not only to record Yosemite's majesty on film but to urge the federal government and park managers to do right by the park.

In one of his many public pleas on behalf of Yosemite, Adams said, "Yosemite Valley itself is one of the great shrines of the world and—belonging to all our people—must be both protected and appropriately accessible." As an artist and an activist, Adams never gave up on his dream of keeping Yosemite wild yet within reach of every visitor who wants to experience that wildness.

12

reach high-country trailheads, but anyone can ride. ☎*209/372–1240* ✉*$23* ⛺*Reservations essential* ⊙*July–Labor Day.*

Valley Floor Tour. Take a 26-mi, two-hour tour of the Valley's highlights, with narration on area history, geology, and plant and animal life. Tour vehicles are either trams or enclosed motor coaches, depending on weather conditions. ☎*209/372–1240* ✉*$22* ⊙*Year-round.*

WHERE TO STAY & EAT

ABOUT THE RESTAURANTS

For the most part, food service in Yosemite is geared toward handling a large number of visitors—that is, it's often fast, plain, and sometimes not very good. The three notable exceptions are the full-service dining rooms at the Ahwanee and Wawona and at Yosemite Lodge at the Falls, which strive to present imaginative American dishes prepared with fresh—often local and organic—ingredients. Spring through fall, it's a good idea to make dinner reservations. All food concessions are run by the Delaware North Corporation.

ABOUT THE HOTELS

Lodgings in Yosemite range from canvas tent-cabins without heat or bath to luxury suites with room service. All have lovely, if not spectacular, settings, though those in the valley are far from peaceful in summer. In season, rooms of any description are expensive and hard to come by; if you can, make your reservations a year in advance—the day your chosen dates open for booking. All lodging concessions, except Redwoods Guest Cottages, are run by Delaware North Corporation.

ABOUT THE CAMPGROUNDS

Camping in Yosemite is the most popular lodging choice; it's relatively inexpensive, and it can be a great outdoor experience. The park has lots of camping sites (nearly 2,000 in summer, 400 year-round), and though none have RV hookups, they fill up quickly, especially in the Valley. Near the park are a number of appealing, readily accessible campgrounds for tents and RVs. Most get very busy in fine weather, and many don't accept reservations.

All campgrounds listed here are front-country spots you can reach with a car. The park's backcountry and the surrounding wilderness have some unforgettable campsites that can be reached only via long and often difficult hikes or horseback rides. Delaware North Corporation operates five High Sierra Camps with comfortable, furnished tent cabins in the remote reaches of Yosemite; rates include breakfast and dinner service. The park concessionaire books the extremely popular backcountry camps by lottery each December for the following late June to early September season. Phone ☎*559/253–5674* for more information.

Overnight hiking is restricted in Yosemite's backcountry to limit human impact on natural areas, and you'll need a wilderness permit to camp there. It's a good idea to make reservations for wilderness permits, especially if you visit May through September. (Note that making a request for a reservation does not guarantee you'll get one.) You can reserve two days to 24 weeks in advance by calling ☎209/372–0740, logging on to ⊕*www.nps.gov/yose/wilderness*, or by writing to Wilderness Permits, Box 545, Yosemite, 95389. Include your name, address, daytime phone, the number of people in your party, trip date, alternative dates, starting and ending trailheads, and a brief itinerary. There's a $5-per-person processing fee for reservations; permits are free if obtained in person at wilderness permit offices at Big Oak Flat, Hetch Hetchy, Tuolumne, Wawona, the Wilderness Center, and Yosemite Valley in summer; fall through spring, visit the Valley Visitor Center.

12

WHERE TO EAT

In addition to the dining options listed here, you'll find fast-food grills and cafeterias, plus temporary snack bars, hamburger stands, and pizza joints lining park roads in summer. Many dining facilities in the park are open summer only.

$$$–$$$$
Fodor'sChoice
★
✕**Ahwahnee Hotel Dining Room.** This is the most dramatic dining room in Yosemite, if not California. The massive room has a 34-foot ceiling supported by immense sugar-pine beams, and floor-to-ceiling windows. In the evening, everything glows with candlelight. Specialties on the often-changing menu highlight sustainable, organic produce and include salmon, duckling, and prime rib. Collared shirts and long pants (no jeans) are required for men at dinner; dresses, skirts, or pants for women. ⊠*Ahwahnee Hotel, Ahwahnee Rd., about ¾ mi east of Yosemite Valley Visitor Center, Yosemite Village* ☎209/372–1407 ⚏*Reservations essential* ▤AE, D, DC, MC, V.

$$–$$$
★
✕**Mountain Room.** Though remarkably good, the food becomes secondary when you see Yosemite Falls through this dining room's wall of windows—almost every table has a view. The chef makes a point of using locally sourced, organic ingredients, so you can be assured of fresh salad and veggies here. Grilled trout and salmon, steak, pasta, and several children's dishes are also on the menu. ⊠*Yosemite Lodge, Northside Dr. about ¾ mi west of the visitor center, Yosemite Village* ☎209/372–1281 ⚏*Reservations essential* ▤AE, D, DC, MC, V ◷*No lunch.*

$$–$$$
✕**Tuolumne Meadows Lodge.** Adjacent to the Tuolumne River under a giant tent canopy, this restaurant serves hearty American fare at breakfast and dinner. ⊠*Tioga Rd. (Rte. 120)* ☎209/372–8413 ⚏*Reservations essential* ▤AE, D, DC, MC, V ◷*No lunch. Closed late Sept.–Memorial Day.*

$$–$$$
★
✕**Wawona Hotel Dining Room.** Watch deer graze on the meadow while you dine in the romantic, candlelit dining room of the whitewashed Wawona Hotel, which dates from the late 1800s. The American-style cuisine favors fresh California ingredients and flavors; trout is a menu staple. There's also a Sunday brunch Easter through Thanksgiving, and a barbecue on the lawn Saturday evenings in summer. A jacket is required at dinner. ⊠*Wawona Hotel, Rte. 41, Wawona* ☎209/375–1425 ⚏*Reservations essential* ▤AE, D, DC, MC, V ◷*Closed Jan. and Feb.*

$-$$ ✕**Pavillion Buffet.** Come to this Curry Village restaurant for a hot, cafeteria-style meal. Bring your tray outside to the deck, and take in the views of the Valley's granite walls. ✉*Curry Village* ☎*209/372–8333* ▤*AE, D, DC, MC, V* ⊘*No lunch. Closed weekdays Dec.–early-Mar.*

$-$$ ✕**White Wolf Lodge.** This high-country historic lodge's casual, rustic dining room fills up at breakfast and dinner. The short menu offers good, creative meat-and-potato meals. Takeout is offered at lunchtime. ✉*Tioga Rd. (Rte. 120), 45 minutes west of Tuolumne Meadows and 30 minutes east of Crane Flat* ☎*209/372–8416* ⚠*Reservations essential* ▤*AE, D, DC, MC, V* ⊘*Closed mid-Sept.–mid-June.*

¢–$$ ✕**Food Court at Yosemite Lodge.** Fast and convenient, the food court serves simple fare, ranging from hamburgers and pizzas to pastas, carved roasted meats, and salads at lunch and dinner. There's also a selection of beer and wine. At breakfast, you can get pancakes and eggs made any way you like. An espresso and smoothie bar near the entrance keeps longer hours. ✉*Yosemite Lodge, about ¾ mi west of the visitor center, Yosemite Village* ☎*209/372–1265* ▤*AE, D, DC, MC, V.*

¢–$ ✕**Tuolumne Meadows Grill.** Serving continuously throughout the day until 5 or 6 PM, this fast-food grill cooks up breakfast, lunch, and snacks. Stop in for a quick meal before exploring the Meadows. ✉*Tioga Rd. (Rte. 120), 1½ mi east of Tuolumne Meadows Visitor Center* ☎*209/372–8426* ▤*AE, D, DC, MC, V* ⊘*Closed Oct.–Memorial Day.*

¢–$ ✕**The Village Grill.** This family-friendly eatery in Yosemite Village serves hamburgers and grilled sandwiches from a counter. Take your tray out to the deck and enjoy your meal under the trees. ✉*100 yards east of Yosemite Valley Visitor Center, Yosemite Village* ☎*209/372–1207* ▤*AE, D, DC, MC, V* ⊘*No breakfast, no dinner after 5 PM. Closed Oct.–May.*

PICNIC AREAS   Ready-made picnic lunches are available at Ahwahnee and Wawona with advance notice. Otherwise, stop at the Food Court at Yosemite Lodge for a pre-packaged salad or sandwich, or at grocery stores in the village to pick up supplies. There are 13 designated picnic areas around the park; restrooms and grills or fire grates are available only at those in the valley. Outside the valley, there are picnic areas at Cascades Falls, Glacier Point, Lembert Dome, Mariposa Grove, Wawona, Tenaya Lake, and Yosemite Creek.

Cathedral Beach is on Southside Drive underneath spire-like Cathedral Rocks. There are usually fewer people here than at the eastern end of the valley. No drinking water.

Tucked behind the Ahwahnee Hotel, **Church Bowl** nearly abuts the granite walls below the Royal Arches. If you're walking from the village with your supplies, this is the shortest trek to a picnic area. No drinking water.

At the western end of the valley on Northside Drive, the **El Capitan** picnic area has great views straight up the giant granite wall above. No drinking water.

On Southside Drive, **Sentinel Beach** is right alongside a running creek and the Merced River. The area is usually crowded in season. No drinking water.

East of Sentinel Beach on Southside Drive, **Swinging Bridge** is the name of a little wooden footbridge that crosses the Merced River, just past the picnic area. No drinking water.

Right next to Sentinel Beach on Southside Drive, **Yellow Pine** is named for the towering trees that cluster on the banks of the Merced River. No drinking water. No restroom.

WHERE TO STAY

Reserve your room or cabin in Yosemite as far in advance as possible—you can make a reservation up to a year before your arrival (within minutes after the reservation office makes a date available, the Ahwahnee, Yosemite Lodge, and Wawona Hotel often sell out their weekends, holiday periods, and all days between May and September). Almost all reservations for lodging in Yosemite are made through the concessionaire, **Delaware North Corporation.** ⊠*6771 N. Palm Ave., Fresno* ☎*801/559–5000* ⊕*www.yosemitepark.com.*

$$$–$$$$ The Redwoods In Yosemite. The only lodging in the park not operated by Delaware North Corporation, this collection of individually owned cabins and homes in the Wawona area is a great alternative to the overcrowded Valley. Fully furnished cabins range from small, romantic one-bedroom units to bright, resort-like, six-bedroom houses with decks overlooking the river. Most have fireplaces, TVs, and phones. All have unlimited, free long-distance service. The property rarely fills up, even in summer, so it's a good choice for last-minute lodging; there's a two-night minimum in the off-season and a three-night minimum in summer. ⊠*8038 Chilnualna Falls Rd., off Rte. 41, Wawona* ☎*866/931–1229* 🖷*209/375–6400* ⊕*www.redwoodsinyosemite.com* 🛏*125 units* ♿*In-room: no a/c (some), no phone (some), kitchen, VCR (some), no TV (some). In-hotel: no-smoking rooms, some pets allowed* 🗏*AE, D, MC, V.*

$–$$ Curry Village. Opened in 1899 as a place where travelers could enjoy the beauty of Yosemite for a modest price, Curry Village has plain accommodations: standard motel rooms, cabins, and tent cabins, which have rough wood frames, canvas walls, and roofs. The tent cabins are a step up from camping, with linens and blankets provided (maid service upon request). Some have heat. Most of the cabins share shower and toilet facilities. ⊠*South side of Southside Dr., Yosemite Valley* 🕾*Delaware North Reservations, 6771 N. Palm Ave., Fresno, 93704* ☎*801/559–5000* ⊕*www.yosemitepark.com* 🛏*18 rooms; 183 cabins, 103 with bath; 427 tent cabins* ♿*In-room: no a/c, no phone, no TV. In-hotel: 3 restaurants, bar, pool, bicycles, no elevator, no-smoking rooms* 🗏*AE, D, DC, MC, V.*

$–$$ White Wolf Lodge. Set in a subalpine meadow, this tiny lodge offers rustic accommodations in tent cabins that share nearby baths or in wooden cabins with baths. This is an excellent base camp for hiking the backcountry. Breakfast and dinner are served in the snug, white main building. ⊠ *Off Tioga Rd. (Rte. 120), 45 minutes west of Tuolumne Meadows and 30 minutes east of Crane Flat* ⊕*Delaware North Reservations, 6771 N. Palm Ave., Fresno, 93704* ☎*801/559–5000* ⤳*24 tent cabins, 4 cabins* ⌂*In-room: no a/c, no phone, no TV. In-hotel: restaurant, no elevator* ⊟*AE, D, DC, MC, V* ⊗*Closed mid-Sept.–early June.*

$$$$
Fodor's Choice
★

✕⌨ **The Ahwahnee.** This grand 1920s-era mountain lodge, a National Historic Landmark, is constructed of rocks and sugar-pine logs. Guest rooms have Native American design motifs; public spaces are decorated with art deco detailing, oriental rugs, and elaborate iron- and woodwork. Some luxury hotel amenities, including turndown service and guest bathrobes, are standard here. The Dining Room ($$$–$$$$, reservations essential) is by far the most impressive restaurant in the park, and one of the most beautiful rooms in California. If you stay in a cottage room, be aware that each cottage has multiple guest rooms. Each of the cushy cottages contains two nonadjoining guest rooms with en suite bath. ⊠ *Ahwahnee Rd. north of Northside Dr., Yosemite Village, 95389* ⊕*Delaware North Reservations, 6771 N. Palm Ave., Fresno, 93704* ☎*801/559–5000* ⊕*www.yosemitepark.com* ⤳*99 lodge rooms, 24 cottage rooms* ⌂*In-room: no a/c (some), refrigerator, Wi-Fi. In-hotel: restaurant, room service, bar, tennis court, pool, concierge* ⊟*AE, D, DC, MC, V.*

$$–$$$

✕⌨ **Wawona Hotel.** This 1879 National Historic Landmark sits at Yosemite's southern end, near the Mariposa Grove of Big Trees. It's an old-fashioned New England–style estate, with whitewashed buildings, wraparound verandas, and pleasant, no-frills rooms decorated with period pieces. About half the rooms share bathrooms; those that do come equipped with robes. The romantic, candlelit dining room ($$–$$$) lies across the lobby from the cozy Victorian parlor, which has a fireplace, board games, and a piano, where a pianist plays ragtime most evenings. ⊠*Hwy. 41, Wawona* ⊕*Delaware North Reservations, 6771 N. Palm Ave., Fresno, 93704* ☎*801/559–5000* ⊕*www.yosemitepark. com* ⤳*104 rooms, 50 with bath* ⌂*In-room: no a/c, no phone, no TV. In-hotel: restaurant, bar, golf course, tennis court, pool, no elevator* ⊟*AE, D, DC, MC, V* ⊗*Closed early Jan.–late Mar.*

$$–$$$

✕⌨ **Yosemite Lodge at the Falls.** This lodge near Yosemite Falls, which dates from 1915, looks like a 1960s motel-resort complex, with numerous brown, two-story buildings tucked beneath the trees around large parking lots. Motel-style rooms have two double beds, and larger rooms also have dressing areas and patios or balconies. A few have views of the falls. Of the lodge's eateries, the Mountain Room Restaurant ($$–$$$) is the most formal. The cafeteria-style Food Court (¢–$) serves three meals a day. Many park tours depart from the main building. ⊠*Northside Dr. about ¾ mi west of the visitor center, Yosemite Village* ⊕*Delaware North Reservations, 6771 N. Palm Ave., Fresno, 93704* ☎*801/559–5000* ⊕*www.yosemitepark.com* ⤳*245 rooms* ⌂*In-room: no a/c, Wi-Fi. In-hotel: 2 restaurants, bar, pool, bicycles, no elevator, no-smoking rooms* ⊟*AE, D, DC, MC, V.*

CAMPGROUNDS & RV PARKS Reservations are required at most of Yosemite's campgrounds, especially in summer. You can reserve a site up to five months in advance. Unless otherwise noted, book your site through the central National Park Service reservations office. **National Park Reservation Service.** ⌂ *Box 1600, Cumberland, MD 21502* ☎ *877/444–6777* ⊕ *www.recreation. gov* ⊟ *D, MC, V* ⊘ *Mar.–Oct., daily 10 AM–midnight; Nov.–Feb., daily 10–10 (EST).*

$$$$ **Housekeeping Camp.** Set along the Merced River, these three-sided concrete units with canvas roofs may look a bit rustic, but they're good for travelers with RVs or those without a tent who want to camp. You can cook here on gas stoves rented from the front desk, or you can use the fire pits. Toilets and showers are in a central building, and there is a camp store for provisions. ⌂ *Southside Dr., ½ mi west of Curry Village* ⌂ *Delaware North Reservations, 6771 N. Palm Ave., Fresno, 93704* ☎ *801/559–5000 reservations* ⊕ *www.yosemitepark.com* ⬳ *266 units* ⌂ *Laundry facilities, no a/c, no phone, no TV* ⊟ *AE, D, DC, MC, V* ⊘ *May–Sept.*

$$ **Crane Flat.** This camp on Yosemite's western boundary, south of Hodgdon Meadow, is just 17 mi from the valley but far from its bustle. Two groves of sequoias are nearby. Half of the sites are first-come, first-served. ⌂ *From Big Oak Flat entrance on Hwy. 120, drive 10 mi east to campground entrance on right* ☎ *877/444–6777 or 209/379–2123* ⊕ *www.recreation.gov* ⬳ *166 sites (tent or RV)* ⌂ *Flush toilets, drinking water, bear boxes, fire pits, picnic tables, general store, ranger station* ⌂ *Reservations essential* ⊟ *AE, D, MC, V* ⊘ *June–Sept.*

$$ **Hodgdon Meadow.** On the park's western boundary, at an elevation of about 4,900 feet, the vegetation here is similar to that in the valley—but there's no river and no development. Reservations are essential. ⌂ *From Big Oak Flat entrance on Hwy. 120, immediately turn left to campground* ☎ *877/444–6777 or 209/379–2123* ⊕ *www.recreation. gov* ⬳ *105 sites (tent or RV)* ⌂ *Flush toilets, drinking water, bear boxes, grills, picnic tables, ranger station* ⊟ *AE, D, MC, V* ⊘ *May–Sept.*

$$ **Lower Pines.** This moderate-size campground sits directly along the Merced River; it's a short walk to the trailheads for the Mirror Lake and Mist trails. Expect small sites and lots of people. ⌂ *At east end of valley* ☎ *877/444–6777 or 209/372–8502* ⊕ *www.recreation.gov* ⬳ *60 sites (tent or RV)* ⌂ *Flush toilets, drinking water, bear boxes, fire grates, picnic tables, public telephone, ranger station, swimming (river)* ⌂ *Reservations essential* ⊟ *AE, D, MC, V* ⊘ *Mar.–Oct.*

$$ **North Pines.** Set along the Merced River at an elevation of 4,000 feet, this campground is near many trailheads. Sites are close together, and there is little privacy. ⌂ *At east end of valley, near Curry Village* ☎ *877/444–6777 or 209/372–8502* ⊕ *www.recreation.gov* ⬳ *80 sites (tent or RV)* ⌂ *Flush toilets, drinking water, showers, bear boxes, fire grates, picnic tables, ranger station, swimming (river)* ⌂ *Reservations essential* ⊟ *AE, D, MC, V* ⊘ *Apr.–Sept.*

$$ **Tuolumne Meadows.** In a wooded area at 8,600 feet, just south of its **Fodor'sChoice** namesake meadow, this is one of the most spectacular and sought-after ★ campgrounds in Yosemite. Hot showers can be used at the Tuolumne Meadows Lodge—though only at certain strictly regulated times. Half the sites are first-come, first-served, so arrive early or make reservations. The campground is open July–September. ⊠*Hwy. 120, 46 mi east of Big Oak Flat entrance station* ☎*209/379-2123 or 877/444-6777* ⊕*www.recreation.gov* ⟿*304 sites (tent or RV)* ⚹*Flush toilets, dump station, drinking water, bear boxes, fire grates, picnic tables, public telephone, general store, ranger station* ▤*AE, D, MC, V* ⊙*July–Sept.*

$$ 🏕**Upper Pines.** This is the valley's largest campground, and the closest one to the trailheads. Expect large crowds in the summer—and little privacy. ⊠*At east end of valley, near Curry Village* ☎*877/444-6777* ⊕*www.recreation.gov* ⟿*238 sites (tent or RV)* ⚹*Flush toilets, dump station, drinking water, bear boxes, fire grates, picnic tables, public telephone, ranger station, swimming (river)* ⚏*Reservations essential* ▤*AE, D, MC, V* ⊙*Year-round.*

$$ 🏕**Wawona.** Near the Mariposa Grove, just downstream from a popular fishing spot, this year-round campground (reservations essential May–September) has larger, less densely packed sites than campgrounds in the valley, located right by the river. The downside is that it's an hour's drive to the valley's major attractions. ⊠*Hwy. 41, 1 mi north of Wawona* ☎ *877/444-6777* ⊕*www.recreation.gov* ⟿*93 sites (tent or RV)* ⚹*Flush toilets, dump station, drinking water, bear boxes, fire grates, picnic tables, ranger station, swimming (river)* ▤*AE, D, MC, V* ⊙*Year-round.*

$ 🏕**Bridalveil Creek.** This campground sits among lodgepole pines at 7,200 feet, above the valley on Glacier Point Road. From here, you can easily drive to Glacier Point's magnificent valley views. Fall evenings can be quite cold. ⊠*From Hwy. 41 in Wawona, go north to Glacier Point Rd. and turn right; entrance to campground is 25 mi ahead on right side* ⊕*www.nps.gov/yose* ⟿*110 sites (tent or RV)* ⚹*Flush toilets, drinking water, bear boxes, grills, picnic tables, public telephone* ⚏*Reservations not accepted* ▤*AE, D, MC, V* ⊙*July–early Sept.*

$ 🏕**Porcupine Flat.** Sixteen miles west of Tuolumne Meadows, this campground sits at 8,100 feet. Sites are close together, but if you want to be in the high country and Tuolumne Meadows is full, this is a good bet. There is no water available. ⊠*16 mi west of Tuolumne Meadows on Hwy. 120* ⊕*www.nps.gov/yose* ⟿*52 sites (tent or RV up to 24 feet)* ⚹*Pit toilets, bear boxes, fire pits, picnic tables* ⚏*Reservations not accepted* ▤*AE, D, MC, V* ⊙*July–Sept.*

$ 🏕**Tamarack Flat.** This rather primitive campground sits in a forested area at an elevation of 6,300 feet, with lodgepole pines, red firs, and some cedars. There's no water. ⊠*From Big Oak Flat entrance station, turn left on Tioga Rd. (Hwy. 120); 3 mi ahead turn right to enter campground, 2½ mi from Tioga Rd.* ⊕*www.nps.gov/yose* ⟿*52 tent sites* ⚹*Pit toilets, bear boxes, fire grates, picnic tables* ⚏*Reservations not accepted* ▤*No credit cards* ⊙*June–early Sept.*

$ 🏕**White Wolf.** Set in the beautiful high country at 8,000 feet, this is a
★ prime spot for hikers. RVs up to 27 feet long are permitted. ⊠*From Big Oak Flat entrance, go 15 mi east on Tioga Road (Hwy. 120); campground is on left* ⊕*www.nps.gov/yose* ⟿*74 sites (tent or RV)* ⚹*Flush toilets, drinking water, bear boxes, fire grates, picnic tables, public tele-*

phone, ranger station ⚲*Reservations not accepted* ▭*No credit cards* ☉*July–early Sept.*

$ 🏕**Yosemite Creek.** This secluded campground, set at 7,600 feet on a dirt road, is not suitable for large RVs. It's a good jumping-off point for spectacular hikes to the rim of the valley and to the top of Yosemite Falls. There is no water available. ✉*From Big Oak Flat entrance station, turn left onto Tioga Rd. (Hwy. 120) and continue 30 mi to the posted turnoff on right; drive 5 mi to campground* ⊕*www.nps.gov/ yose* ⟿*75 sites (tent or RV)* ⚲*Pit toilets, bear boxes, fire grates, picnic tables, public telephone* ⚲*Reservations not accepted* ▭*No credit cards* ☉*July–early Sept.*

¢ 🏕**Camp 4.** Formerly known as Sunnyside Walk-In, this is the only valley campground available on a first-come, first-served basis—and the only one west of Yosemite Lodge. Open year-round, it is a favorite for rock climbers and solo campers; it fills quickly and is typically sold out by 9 AM daily spring through fall. This is a tents-only campground. ✉*Base of Yosemite Falls Trail, just west of Yosemite Lodge on Northside Dr., Yosemite Village* ☎*209/372–8502* ⊕*www.nps. gov/yose* ⟿*35 sites* ⚲*Flush toilets, drinking water, bear boxes, fire grates, picnic tables, public telephone, ranger station* ▭*AE, D, MC, V* ☉*Year-round.*

YOSEMITE ESSENTIALS

ACCESSIBILITY

Yosemite's facilities are continually being upgraded to make them more accessible. Many of the Valley floor trails—particularly at Lower Yosemite Falls, Bridalveil Falls, and Mirror Lake—are wheelchair accessible, though some assistance may be required. The Valley Visitor Center is fully accessible, as are the shuttle buses around the Valley. A sign-language interpreter is available for ranger programs if you call ahead. For complete details, pick up the park's accessibility brochure at any visitor center or entrance, read it at ⊕*www.nps.gov/yose/access*, or call the public information office at ☎209/372–0200. Visitors with respiratory difficulties should take note of the park's high elevations—the Valley floor is approximately 4,000 feet above sea level, but Tuolumne Meadows and parts of the high country hover around 10,000 feet.

ADMISSION FEES

The vehicle admission fee is $20 per car and is valid for seven days. Individuals arriving by bus, or on foot, bicycle, motorcycle, or horseback pay $10 for a seven-day pass.

ADMISSION HOURS

The park is open daily, 24 hours a day. All entrances are open at all hours, except for Hetch Hetchy Entrance, open roughly dawn to dusk. Yosemite is in the Pacific time zone.

EMERGENCIES

In an emergency, call 911. You can also call the Yosemite Medical Clinic dispatch in Yosemite Village at 209/379–1997. The clinic provides 24-hour emergency care.

LOST AND FOUND

To inquire about items lost or found in Yosemite's restaurants, hotels, lounges, shuttles, or tour buses, call Delaware North Corporation at 209/372–4357 or e-mail yoselost@dncinc.com. For items lost or found in other areas of the park, contact the National Park Service at 209/379–1001 or e-mail yose_web_manager@nps.gov.

PERMITS

If you plan to camp in the backcountry, you must have a wilderness permit. Availability of permits, which are free, depends upon trailhead quotas. It's best to make a reservation, especially if you will be visiting May through September. You can reserve two days to 24 weeks in advance by phone, mail, or e-mail; a $5-per-person processing fee is charged if and when your reservations are confirmed. In your request, include your name, address, daytime phone, the number of people in your party, trip date, alternative dates, starting and ending trailheads, and a brief itinerary. Without a reservation, you may still get a free permit on a first-come, first-served basis at wilderness permit offices at Big Oak Flat, Hetch Hetchy, Tuolumne, Wawona, the Wilderness Center, and Yosemite Valley in summer; fall through spring, visit the Valley Visitor Center.

Contacts **Wilderness Permits** (Box 545, Yosemite, 95389 ☎ 209/372–0740 ⊕ www.nps.gov/yose/wilderness/permits.htm).

PUBLIC TELEPHONES

There are public telephones at park entrance stations, visitor centers, all restaurants and lodging facilities in the park, gas stations, and in Yosemite Village.

RESTROOMS

Public restrooms are at visitor centers; all restaurants and lodging facilities in the park; at the Village Store, the Vernal Falls footbridge, Yosemite Falls, Tuolumne Meadows, and Glacier Point; and at the Swinging Bridge, Cathedral Beach, Sentinel Beach, Church Bowl, and El Capitan picnic areas.

VISITOR INFORMATION

Contacts **Yosemite National Park** (Information Office, Box 577, Yosemite National Park, 95389 ☎ 209/372–0200 ⊕ www.nps.gov/yose).

Sequoia and Kings Canyon National Parks

Isosceles and Columbine Peak, Dusty Basin, Kings Canyon National Park

WORD OF MOUTH

"Who of all the dwellers of the plains and prairies and fertile home forests of round-headed oak and maple, hickory and elm, ever dreamed that earth could bear such growths—trees that the familiar pines and firs seem to know nothing about, lonely, silent, serene, with a physiognomy almost godlike; and so old, thousands of them still living had already counted their years by tens of centuries when Columbus set sail from Spain."

—John Muir, *Our National Parks*

WELCOME TO SEQUOIA AND KINGS CANYON

TOP REASONS TO GO

★ **Gentle giants:** You'll feel small—in a good way—walking among some of the world's largest living things in Sequoia's Giant Forest and Kings Canyon's Grant Grove.

★ **Because it's there:** You can't even glimpse it from the main part of Sequoia, but the sight of majestic Mt. Whitney is worth the trek to the eastern face of the High Sierra.

★ **Underground exploration:** Far older even than the giant sequoias, the gleaming limestone formations in Crystal Cave will draw you along dark, marble passages.

★ **A grander-than-Grand Canyon:** Drive the twisting Kings Canyon Scenic Byway down into the jagged, granite Kings River Canyon, deeper in parts than the Grand Canyon.

★ **Regal solitude:** To spend a day or two hiking in a subalpine world of your own, pick one of the 11 trailheads at Mineral King.

1 Giant Forest–Lodgepole Village. The most heavily visited area of Sequoia lies at the base of the "thumb" portion of Kings Canyon National Park and contains major sights such as Giant Forest, General Sherman Tree, Crystal Cave, and Moro Rock.

2 Grant Grove Village–Redwood Canyon. The "thumb" of Kings Canyon National Park is its busiest section, where Grant Grove, General Grant Tree, Panoramic Point, and Big Stump are the main attractions.

3 Kings River Canyon–Cedar Grove Village. Most visitors to the huge, high-country portion of Kings Canyon National Park don't go farther than Roads End, a few miles east of Cedar Grove on the canyon floor. Here, the river runs through Zumwalt Meadow, surrounded by magnificent granite formations.

Climbing Bubbs Creek wall

4 Mineral King. In the southeast section of Sequoia, the highest road-accessible part of the park is a good place to hike, camp, and soak up the unspoiled grandeur of the Sierra Nevada.

5 Mt. Whitney. The highest peak in the Lower 48 stands on the eastern edge of Sequoia; to get there from Giant Forest you must either backpack eight days through the mountains or drive nearly 400 mi around the park to its other side.

GETTING ORIENTED

The two parks comprise 865,952 acres, mostly on the western flank of the Sierra. A map of the adjacent parks looks vaguely like a mitten, with the palm of Sequoia National Park south of the north-pointing, skinny thumb and long fingers of Kings Canyon National Park. Between the western thumb and eastern fingers, north of Sequoia, lies part of Sequoia National Forest, which includes Giant Sequoia National Monument.

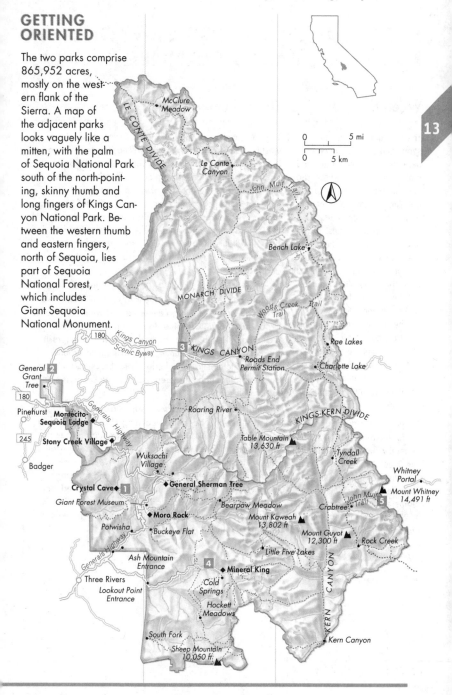

13

0 — 5 mi
0 — 5 km

McClure Meadow

LE CONTE DIVIDE

Le Conte Canyon

John Muir Trail

Bench Lake

MONARCH DIVIDE

Woods Creek Trail

180 Kings Canyon Scenic Byway

3 KINGS CANYON

Rae Lakes

Roads End Permit Station

Charlotte Lake

General Grant Tree 2

180

Pinehurst Montecito-Sequoia Lodge

245 Stony Creek Village

Generals Highway

Roaring River

KINGS-KERN DIVIDE

Badger

Table Mountain 13,630 ft

Tyndall Creek

Wuksachi Village

Whitney Portal

Crystal Cave 1 General Sherman Tree

Mount Whitney 14,491 ft

Giant Forest Museum

Moro Rock

Bearpaw Meadow

Crabtree 5

John Muir Trail

Potwisha Buckeye Flat

Mount Kaweah 13,802 ft

Mount Guyot 12,300 ft

Rock Creek

Generals Highway

Ash Mountain Entrance

Little Five Lakes

KERN CANYON

Three Rivers Lookout Point Entrance

4 Mineral King

Cold Springs

Hockett Meadows

South Fork

Sheep Mountain 10,050 ft

Kern Canyon

SEQUOIA AND KINGS CANYON NATIONAL PARKS PLANNER

When to Go

The best times to visit are late spring and early fall, when temperatures are moderate and crowds thin. Summertime can draw hordes of tourists to see the giant sequoias, and the few, narrow roads mean congestion at peak holiday times. If you must visit in summer, go during the week. By contrast, in wintertime you may feel as though you have the parks all to yourself. But because of heavy snows, sections of the main park roads can be closed without warning, and low-hanging clouds can move in and obscure mountains and valleys for days. Check road and weather conditions before venturing out mid-November to late April.

Temperatures in the chart below are for the midlevel elevations, generally between 4,000 and 7,000 feet. At higher elevations, temperatures drop and precipitation rises; at lower elevations, temperatures rise—by as much as 20°F in summer—and annual precipitation drops.

AVG. HIGH/LOW TEMPS (°F)

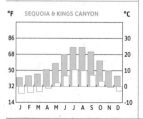

Flora & Fauna

The parks can be divided into three distinct zones. In the west (1,500–4,500 feet) are the rolling, lower-elevation foothills, covered with shrubby chaparral vegetation or golden grasslands dotted with oaks. Chamise, red-barked manzanita, and the occasional yucca plant grow here. Fields of white popcorn flower cover the hillsides in spring, and the yellow fiddleneck flourishes. In summer, intense heat and absence of rain cause the hills to turn golden brown. Wildlife includes the California ground squirrel, noisy blue-and-gray scrub jay, black bears, coyotes, skunks, and gray fox.

At middle elevation (5,000–9,000 feet), where the giant sequoia belt resides, rock formations mix with meadows and huge stands of evergreens—red and white fir, incense cedar, and ponderosa pines to name a few. Wildflowers, including yellow blazing star and red Indian paintbrush, bloom in spring and summer. Golden-mantled ground squirrels, Steller's jays, mule deer, and black bears (most active in fall) inhabit the area, as does the Douglas squirrel, or chickaree.

The high alpine section of the parks is extremely rugged, with a string of rocky peaks reaching above 13,000 feet to Mt. Whitney's 14,494 feet. Fierce weather and scarcity of soil make vegetation and wildlife sparse. Foxtail and whitebark pines have gnarled and twisted trunks, the result of high wind, heavy snowfall, and freezing temperatures. In summer you can see yellow-bellied marmots, pikas, weasels, mountain chickadees, and Clark's nutcrackers. Leopard lilies and shooting stars grow near streams and meadows.

Getting There & Around

Sequoia is 36 mi east of Visalia on Route 198; Kings Canyon is 53 mi east of Fresno on Route 180. There is no automobile entrance on the eastern side of the Sierra. Routes 180 and 198 are connected by Generals Highway, a paved two-lane road that's open year-round. Ongoing improvements to Generals Highway can cause delays of up to an hour at peak times, and the road is extremely narrow and steep from Route 198 to Giant Forest. Keep an eye on your engine temperature gauge, as the incline and congestion can cause vehicles to overheat.

Do not travel beyond Potwisha Campground with an RV longer than 22 feet on Route 198; take straighter, easier Route 180 instead. Maximum vehicle length on Generals Highway is 40 feet, or 50 feet combined length for vehicles with trailers.

Snowstorms are common late October–April. Unless you have four-wheel drive with snow tires, always carry chains and know how to apply them to the tires on the drive axle. Generals Highway between Lodgepole and Grant Grove is sometimes closed by snow. The Mineral King Road from Route 198 into southern Sequoia National Park is closed 2 mi below Atwell Mill either on November 1 or after the first heavy snow. The Buckeye Flat–Middle Fork Trailhead Road is closed mid-October–mid-April when the Buckeye Flat Campground closes. The lower Crystal Cave Road is closed when the cave closes in November. Its upper 2 mi, as well as the Panoramic Point and Moro Rock–Crescent Meadow roads, are closed with the first heavy snow. Because of the danger of rockfall, the portion of Kings Canyon Scenic Byway east of Grant Grove closes in winter. For current conditions, call the park at 559/565–3341 Ext. 4.

WHAT IT COSTS				
¢	$	$$	$$$	$$$$
Restaurants				
under $8	$8–$12	$13–$20	$21–$30	over $30
Hotels				
under $50	$50–$100	$101–$150	$151–$200	over $200
Camping				
under $10	$10–$17	$18–$35	$36–$50	over $50

Restaurant prices are per person for a main course at dinner. Hotel prices are per night for two people in a standard double room in high season, excluding taxes and service charges. Camping prices are for a standard campsite per night.

Festivals & Events

DEC. Annual Trek to the Tree. On the second Sunday, thousands of Christmas carolers, many of whom arrive en masse from Sanger, gather at the base of General Grant Tree, the nation's official Christmas tree. ☎559/565–4307.

MAR. Blossom Days Festival. The first Saturday of March, communities along Fresno County's Blossom Trail celebrate the flowering of the area's many orchards, citrus groves, and vineyards. You can drive the 62-mi trail any time of year, but peak blossom season is late February–mid-March. ☎559/262–4271 ⊕www.driveblossomtrail.com.

APR. Jazzaffair. Held just south of the parks in the town of Three Rivers, a festival of mostly swing jazz takes place at several locations, with shuttle buses between sites. The festival is usually the second weekend of the month. ☎559/561–4592 or 559/561–3105 ⊕www.jazzaffair.info.

MAY Woodlake Rodeo. A weekend-long event thrown by the Woodlake Lions, this rodeo draws large crowds to Woodlake (near Three Rivers) on Mother's Day weekend. ☎559/564–8555 ⊕www.woodlakelionsrodeo.com.

SEPT. Celebrate Sequoias Festival. On the second Saturday of the month, rangers guide field trips to the lesser known groves of Sequoia National Park. ☎559/565–4307 Grant Grove Visitor Center.

13

By Constance Jones

The silent giants of Sequoia and Kings Canyon, surrounded by vast granite canyons and towering snowcapped peaks, strike awe in most everyone who sees them. No less than famed naturalist John Muir proclaimed the sequoia tree "the most beautiful and majestic on earth." The largest living things on the planet, *Sequoiadendron giganteum* trees are not as tall as the coast redwoods (*Sequoia sempervirens*), but they're more massive and, on average, older. Exhibits at the visitor centers explain why they can live so long and grow so big, as well as the special relationship between these trees and fire (their thick, fibrous bark helps protect them from flames and insects, and their seeds can't germinate until they first explode out of a burning pinecone).

Sequoia and Kings Canyon share a boundary and are administered together. They encompass 1,353 square mi, rivaled only by Yosemite in rugged Sierra beauty. The topography ranges from the western foothills at an elevation of 1,500 feet to the towering peaks of the Great Western Divide and the Sierra Crest. The Kings River cuts a swath through the backcountry and over the years has formed a granite canyon that, in places, towers nearly 4,000 feet above the canyon floor. From Junction Overlook, on the drive to Cedar Grove, you can see the 8,200-foot drop from Spanish Mountain to the Kings River, as well as the confluence of the Middle and South forks of the Kings River. Mt. Whitney, the highest point in the contiguous United States, is the crown jewel of the eastern side.

EXPLORING SEQUOIA NATIONAL PARK

SCENIC DRIVES

★ **Generals Highway.** Connecting the two parks from Grant Grove to Giant Forest and the foothills to the south, this narrow, twisting road runs past Stony Creek, Lost Grove, Little Baldy, General Sherman Tree, Amphitheater Point, and Foothills Visitor Center. Stop to see the Giant Forest Museum, which focuses entirely on the ecology of the sequoia. Also stop at the Lodgepole Visitor Center, which has excellent exhibits and audiovisual programs describing the Sierra Nevada and the natural history of the area. Under normal conditions it takes two hours to complete the drive one way, but when parks are crowded in summer, traffic can slow to a crawl in some areas.

Mineral King Road. Accessible from Memorial Day weekend through October (weather permitting), this small, winding, rough, steep road begins outside the park south of the Ash Mountain entrance, off Route 198. Trailers and RVs are prohibited. The exciting 25-mi drive ascends approximately 6,000 feet to a subalpine valley, where there are a ranger station and limited facilities. Bring a picnic lunch. Many backpackers use this as a trailhead, and you can take a fine day hike from here as well. Allow 90 minutes for the one-way drive.

WHAT TO SEE

SCENIC STOPS

Auto Log. At one time, cars drove right on top of this giant fallen sequoia. Now it's a great place to pose for pictures. ⊠ *Moro Rock–Crescent Meadow Rd., 1 mi south of Giant Forest.*

Crescent Meadow. Walk on fallen logs and trails through spectacular fields of summertime wildflowers. ⊠ *End of Moro Rock–Crescent Meadow Rd., 2.6-mi east off Generals Hwy.*

★ **Crystal Cave.** Ten thousand feet of passageways in this marble cave were created from limestone that metamorphosed under tremendous heat and pressure. Formations are relatively undisturbed. The standard tour is 50 minutes in length. In summer, Sequoia Natural History Association offers a four- to six-hour "wild cave" tour (reservations required) and a 90-minute discovery tour, a less-structured excursion with fewer people. Tickets are not available at the cave; purchase them by 2:30 PM, and at least 90 minutes in advance, from the Lodgepole or Foothills visitor center. ⊠ *Crystal Cave Rd., 6 mi west off Generals Hwy.* ☎ *559/565–3759* ⊕ *www.sequoiahistory.org* 🎫 *$11* 🕐 *Mid-May–mid-Oct., daily, call for schedule.*

★ **General Sherman Tree.** This, the world's largest living tree, is estimated to be about 2,100 years old. ⊠ *Generals Hwy. (Rte. 198), 2 mi south of Lodgepole Visitor Center.*

Mineral King. This subalpine valley sits at 7,800 feet at the end of a steep, winding road. The trip from the park's entrance can take up to two hours. This is the highest point to which you can drive in the park. ✉ *End of Mineral King Rd., 25 mi east of Generals Hwy. (Rte. 198), east of Three Rivers.*

★ **Moro Rock.** Climb the steep 400-step staircase 300 feet to the top of this granite dome for spectacular views of the Great Western Divide and the western regions of the park. To the southwest you look down the Kaweah River to Three Rivers, Lake Kaweah, and—on clear days—the Central Valley and the Coast Range. To the northeast are views of the High Sierra. Thousands of feet below lies the middle fork of the Kaweah River. ✉ *Moro Rock–Crescent Meadow Rd., 2 mi east off Generals Hwy. (Rte. 198) to parking area.*

> ## SEQUOIA SIGHTSEEING TOURS
>
> The only licensed tour operator in either park offers daily interpretive sightseeing tours in a 10-passenger van with a friendly, knowledgeable guide. Reservations are essential. They also offer private tours of Kings Canyon. ☎ *559/561–4489* ⊕ *www.sequoiatours.com.*

Tunnel Log. You can drive your car through this tunnel carved in a fallen sequoia. There's a bypass for larger vehicles. (There is no upright drive-through sequoia tree in the park. There used to be one in Yosemite, but it fell in 1969.) ✉ *Moro Rock–Crescent Meadow Rd., 2 mi east of Generals Hwy. (Rte. 198).*

VISITOR CENTERS

★ **Beetle Rock Family Nature Center.** At Beetle Rock Education Center, across the road from Giant Forest Museum, the National Park Service operates a nature center with interactive exhibits with science-oriented games and activities. ✉ *Generals Hwy., 4 mi south of Lodgepole Visitor Center* ☎ *559/565–4251* ✉ *Free* ☉ *Late June–Aug., daily 10–4.*

Foothills Visitor Center. Exhibits focusing on the foothills and resource issues facing the parks are on display here. You can also pick up books, maps, and a list of ranger-led walks, and get wilderness permits. ✉ *Generals Hwy. (Rte. 198), 1 mi north of the Ash Mountain entrance* ☎ *559/565–3135* ☉ *Daily 8–4:30.*

★ **Giant Forest Museum.** You'll find outstanding exhibits on the ecology of the giant sequoia at the park's premier museum. Though housed in a historic building, it's entirely wheelchair accessible. ✉ *Generals Hwy., 4 mi south of Lodgepole Visitor Center* ☎ *559/565–4480* ✉ *Free* ☉ *Daily 9–4:30.*

Lodgepole Visitor Center. The center has exhibits on the early years of the park and a slide program on geology and forest life. Books and maps are sold here. ✉ *Generals Hwy. (Rte. 198), 21 mi north of Ash Mountain entrance* ☎ *559/565–4436* ☉ *Mid-May–Oct., daily 9–4:30; Nov.–May, weekends only 10–4.*

Mineral King Ranger Station. The small visitor center here houses a few exhibits on the history of the area; wilderness permits and some books and maps are available. ✉ *End of Mineral King Rd., 25 mi east of*

East Fork entrance ☎ *559/565–3768* ⊙ *Late May–early Sept., daily call for hours.*

SPORTS & THE OUTDOORS

BIRD-WATCHING

Not seen in most parts of the United States, the white-headed woodpecker and the pileated woodpecker are common in most mid-elevation areas here. There are also many hawks and owls, including the renowned spotted owl. Species are diverse in both parks due to the changes in elevation, and range from warblers, kingbirds, thrushes, and sparrows in the foothills to goshawk, blue grouse, red-breasted nuthatch, and brown creeper at the highest elevations. Ranger-led bird-watching tours are held on a sporadic basis. Call the parks at 559/565–3341 for information.

Contact the **Sequoia Natural History Association** (⌂ *HCR 89, Box 10, 93271* ☎ *559/565–3759* ⊕ *www.sequoiahistory.org*) for information on bird-watching in the southern Sierra.

CROSS-COUNTRY SKIING

For a one-of-a-kind experience, cut through the groves of mammoth sequoias in Giant Forest. Some of the Crescent Meadow trails (⇨ *Hiking, below*) are suitable for skiing as well. None of the trails is groomed. You can park at Giant Forest. Note that roads can be precarious in bad weather. Some advanced trails begin at Wolverton.

Pear Lake Ski Hut. Primitive lodging is available at this backcountry hut, reached by a steep and extremely difficult 7-mi trail from Wolverton. Only expert skiers should attempt this trek. Space is limited; make reservations well in advance. ⊠ *Trailhead at end of Wolverton Rd., 1½ mi northeast off Generals Hwy. (Rte. 198)* ☎ *559/565–3759* 💲 *$26* ⊙ *Late Dec.–late Apr.*

Wuksachi Lodge. Rent skis and snowshoes here. Depending on snowfall amounts, there may also be instruction available. Reservations are recommended. Marked trails cut through Giant Forest, which sits 5 mi south of the lodge. ⊠ *Off Generals Hwy. (Rte. 198), 2 mi north of Lodgepole* ☎ *559/565–4070* 💲 *$15–$20 ski rental* ⊙ *Nov.–May (unless no snow), daily 9–4.*

FISHING

There's limited trout fishing, bagging minimal hauls, in the creeks and rivers from late April to mid-November. The Kaweah River is a popular spot; check at visitor centers for open and closed waters. Some of the park's secluded backcountry lakes have good fishing. A California fishing license is $12.60 for one day, $19.45 for two days, $38.86 for 10 days (discounts are available for state residents) and is required for persons 16 and older. For park regulations, closures, and restrictions, call the parks at 559/565–3341 or stop at a park visitor center. Licenses and fishing tackle are usually available in Lodgepole.

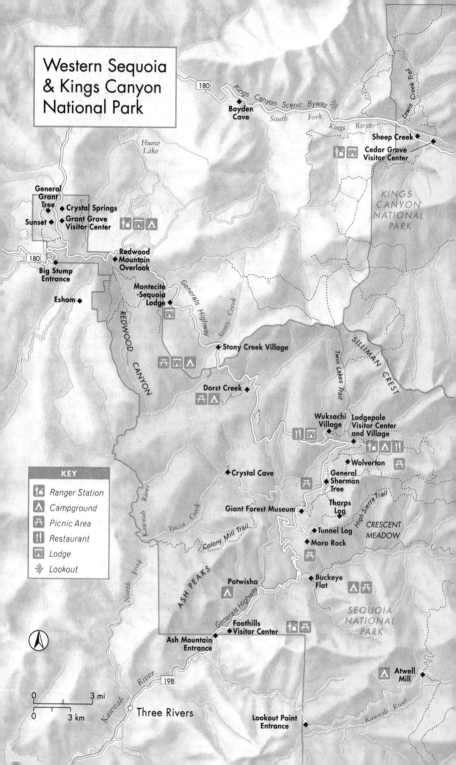

Western Sequoia & Kings Canyon National Park

Boyden Cave

Kings Canyon Scenic Byway

South Fork Kings River

Lewis Creek Trail

Sheep Creek

Cedar Grove Visitor Center

Hune Lake

KINGS CANYON NATIONAL PARK

General Grant Tree

Crystal Springs

Grant Grove Visitor Center

Sunset

180

Big Stump Entrance

Redwood Mountain Overlook

Eshom

Montecito-Sequoia Lodge

Generals Highway

Stony Creek

REDWOOD CANYON

Stony Creek Village

SILLIMAN CREST

Dorst Creek

Twin Lakes Trail

Wuksachi Village

Lodgepole Visitor Center and Village

Wolverton

Crystal Cave

General Sherman Tree

Giant Forest Museum

Tharps Log

High Sierra Trail

CRESCENT MEADOW

Tunnel Log

Moro Rock

Kaweah River

Yucca Creek

Colony Mill Trail

ASH PEAKS

Potwisha

Buckeye Flat

SEQUOIA NATIONAL PARK

North Fork

Generals Highway

Foothills Visitor Center

Ash Mountain Entrance

Atwell Mill

198

Kaweah River

Three Rivers

Lookout Point Entrance

Kaweah River

KEY

🧍 Ranger Station
△ Campground
🏕 Picnic Area
🍴 Restaurant
🏠 Lodge
↘ Lookout

0 ——— 3 mi
0 ——— 3 km

Among many other functions, the **California Department of Fish and Game** (☎916/928–5805 ⊕www.dfg.ca.gov) supplies fishing licenses.

HIKING

The best way to see the park is to hike it. The grandeur and majesty of the Sierra is best seen up close. Carry a hiking map—available at any visitor center—and plenty of water. Check with rangers for current trail conditions, and be aware of rapidly changing weather. As a rule of thumb, plan on trekking 1 MPH. For books about hikes in Sequoia National Park, contact the **Sequoia Natural History Association** (⊠47050 Generals Hwy., Three Rivers ☎559/565–3759 ⊕www. sequoiahistory.org).

13

EASY **Big Trees Trail.** The Giant Forest is known for its trails through sequoia groves. You can get the best views of the big trees from the meadows, where flowers are in full bloom by June or July. The .7-mi trail—the park's only wheelchair-accessible trail—circles Round Meadow. ⊠Off Generals Hwy. (Rte. 198), near the Giant Forest Museum.

★ **Congress Trail.** This easy 2-mi trail is a paved loop that begins near General Sherman Tree and winds through the heart of the sequoia forest. Watch for the groups of trees known as the House and Senate, and the individual trees called the President and McKinley. ⊠Off Generals Hwy. (Rte. 198), 2 mi north of Giant Forest.

Fodor'sChoice **Crescent Meadow Trails.** John Muir reportedly called Crescent Meadow
★ the "gem of the Sierra." Brilliant wildflowers bloom here by midsummer, and a 1.8-mi trail loops around the meadow. A 1.6-mi trail begins at Crescent Meadow and leads to Tharp's Log, a cabin built from a fire-hollowed sequoia. ⊠End of Moro Rock–Crescent Meadow Rd., 2.6 mi east off Generals Hwy. (Rte. 198).

Muir Grove Trail. An easy 2-mi hike with some distant views brings you to a sequoia grove where you might well find some solitude. Give yourself a couple of hours to make the round-trip. ⊠Dorst Creek Campground, Generals Hwy. (Rte. 198), 8 mi north of Lodgepole Visitor Center.

MODERATE **Little Baldy Trail.** Climbing 700 vertical feet in 1.75 mi of switchbacking, this trail ends at a granite dome with a great view of the peaks of the Mineral King area and the Great Western Divide. The walk to the summit and back takes about four hours. ⊠Little Baldy Saddle, Generals Hwy. (Rte. 198), 11 mi north of Giant Forest.

Tokopah Falls Trail. This moderate trail follows the Marble Fork of the Kaweah River for 1¾ mi one way and dead-ends below the impressive granite cliffs and cascading waterfall of Tokopah Canyon. It takes 2½ to 4 hours to make the 3½-mi round-trip journey. The trail passes through a mixed-conifer forest. ⊠Off Generals Hwy. (Rte. 198), ¼ mi north of Lodgepole Campground.

DIFFICULT **Marble Falls Trail.** The 3.7-mi, moderately strenuous hike to Marble Falls crosses through the rugged foothills before reaching the cascading water. Plan on three to four hours one way. ⊠Off the dirt road across from the concrete ditch near site 17 at Potwisha Campground, off Generals Hwy. (Rte. 198).

Mineral King Trails. Many trails to the high country begin at Mineral King. At 7,800 feet, this is the highest point to which one can drive in either of the parks, and the Great Western Divide runs right above this area. Get a map and provisions, and check with rangers about conditions. ⊠ *Trailhead at end of Mineral King Rd., 25 mi east of Generals Hwy. (Rte. 198).*

HORSEBACK RIDING

Scheduled trips take you through redwood forests, flowering meadows, across the Sierra, or even up to Mt. Whitney. Costs per person range from $25 for a one-hour guided ride to around $200 per day for fully guided trips for which the packers do all the cooking and camp chores.

Grant Grove Stables (⇨ *Exploring Kings Canyon, below*) is the stable to choose if you want a short ride.

Horse Corral Pack Station. Hourly, half-day, full-day, or overnight trips through Sequoia are available for beginning and advanced riders. ⊠ *Off Big Meadows Rd., 12 mi east of Generals Hwy. (Rte. 198) between Sequoia and Kings Canyon national parks* ☎ *559/565–3404 in summer, 559/564–6429 in winter* ⊕ *www.horsecorralpackers.com* ☞ *$35–$185 day trips* ⊙ *May–Sept.*

Mineral King Pack Station. Day and overnight tours in the high-mountain area around Mineral King are available here. ⊠ *End of Mineral King Rd., 25 mi east of East Fork entrance* ☎ *559/561–3039 in summer, 520/855–5885 in winter* ⊕ *mineralking.tripod.com* ☞ *$25–$75 day trips* ⊙ *July–late Sept. or early Oct.*

SNOWSHOEING

You can rent snowshoes at the Giant Forest Museum or Wuksachi Lodge and strike out on your own, or you can join a guided group on Saturdays and holidays.

Snowshoers may stay at the Pear Lake Ski Hut (⇨ *Cross-country Skiing, above*). You can rent snowshoes for $15–$20 at the Wuksachi Lodge (☎ *559/565–4070*), 2 mi north of Lodgepole. Rangers lead snowshoe walks around Giant Forest and Wuksachi Lodge, conditions permitting, on Saturdays and holidays. Snowshoes are provided for a $1 donation. Make reservations and check schedules at Giant Forest Museum (☎ *559/565–4480*) or Wuksachi Lodge.

SWIMMING

Drowning is the number-one cause of death in both Sequoia and Kings Canyon parks. Though it is sometimes safe to swim in the parks' rivers in the late summer and early fall, it is extremely dangerous to do so in the spring and early summer, when the snowmelt from the high country causes swift currents and icy temperatures. Stand clear of the water when the rivers are running, and stay off wet rocks to avoid falling in. Check with rangers if you're unsure about conditions or to learn the safest locations to wade in the water.

EXPLORING KINGS CANYON NATIONAL PARK

SCENIC DRIVES

★ **Kings Canyon Scenic Byway.** Winding alongside the powerful Kings River (the byway along Route 180, east of Grant Grove), drive below the towering granite cliffs and past two tumbling waterfalls in the Kings River Canyon. One mile past the Cedar Grove Village turnoff, the U-shaped canyon becomes broader, and you can see evidence of its glacial past and the effects of wind and water on the granite. Four miles farther is Grand Sentinel Viewpoint, where you can see the 3,500-foot-tall granite monolith and some of the most interesting rock formations in the canyon. The drive dead-ends in the canyon, so you must double back. It's about one hour each way.

WHAT TO SEE

HISTORIC SITES

★ **Fallen Monarch.** No matter how tall you are, you could theoretically walk through the entire 100-foot length of this burned-out, fallen sequoia near the General Grant Tree. (In order to protect it, access to the log's interior is prohibited indefinitely.) Early explorers, cattle ranchers, and Native Americans used the log for shelter, and soldiers who began patrolling the area in the late 1880s used it to stable their horses. ☒ *Trailhead 1 mi north of Grant Grove Visitor Center.*

Gamlin Cabin. Built as a summer cabin in 1867, this building was used primarily for storage. Listed on the National Register of Historic Places, the cabin was returned to an area close to its original site in 1931 and was rehabilitated in 1981. The roof and lower timber are giant sequoia. ☒ *Trailhead 1 mi north of Grant Grove Visitor Center.*

Knapp's Cabin. During the Roaring '20s wealthy Santa Barbara business-man George Knapp commissioned extravagant fishing expeditions into the Kings River Canyon. To store quantities of gear, he built a small cabin, which still stands. ☒ *Kings Canyon Scenic Byway, 2 mi east of Cedar Grove Village turnoff.*

SCENIC STOPS

Canyon View. The glacial history of the Kings River Canyon is evident from this viewpoint. Note the canyon's giant "U" shape, which sparked John Muir to compare it to Yosemite to the north. ☒ *Kings Canyon Scenic Byway (Rte. 180), 1 mi east of the Cedar Grove turnoff.*

General Grant Tree. The nation's Christmas tree, this is also the world's third-largest living tree. ☒ *Trailhead 1 mi north of Grant Grove Visitor Center.*

★ **Redwood Mountain Grove.** This is the largest grove of giant sequoias in the world. As you head south through Kings Canyon toward Sequoia on Generals Highway, several paved turnouts allow you to look out over the treetops. The grove itself is accessible only on foot or by horse-back, but the drive to the trailhead, on a twisting, rutted dirt road

13

Kings Canyon's Cedar Grove Area

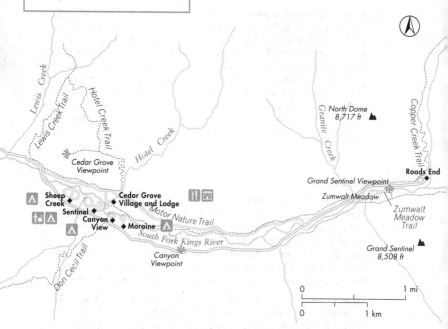

down a steep gorge, is dramatic in itself. ⊠ *Drive 5 mi south of Grant Grove on Generals Hwy. (Rte. 198), then turn right at Quail Flat; follow it 1½ mi to the Redwood Canyon trailhead.*

VISITOR CENTERS

Cedar Grove Visitor Center. This tiny, historic log ranger station provides information and sells books and maps. ⊠ *Kings Canyon Scenic Byway, 30 mi east of park entrance* ☎ *559/565–3793* ⊙ *Spring–fall, daily 9–5.*

Grant Grove Visitor Center. A film and extensive exhibits on the park's sequoia and human history provide an engaging introduction to Kings Canyon. Books, maps, and wilderness permits are for sale. ⊠ *Generals Hwy. (Rte. 198), 3 mi northeast of Rte. 180, Big Stump entrance* ☎ *559/565–4307* ⊙ *Summer, daily 8–6; winter, daily 8–5.*

Road's End Permit Station. If you're planning to hike the Kings Canyon backcountry, you can pick up a permit and information on the backcountry here. You can also rent or buy bear canisters, a must for backcountry campers. When the station is closed, you can still complete a self-service permit form. ⊠ *5 mi east of Cedar Grove Visitor Center, at the end of Kings Canyon Scenic Byway* ⊙ *Late May–late Sept., daily 7–3* ☎ *No phone.*

SPORTS & THE OUTDOORS

BIRD-WATCHING

For information on bird-watching in Sequoia and Kings Canyon national parks, ⇨ Sports & the Outdoors in Sequoia National Park.

CROSS-COUNTRY SKIING

Roads to Grant Grove are easily accessible during heavy snowfall, making the trails here a good choice over Sequoia's Giant Forest when harsh weather hits.

Grant Grove Ski Touring Center. The Grant Grove Market doubles as the ski-touring center, where you can rent cross-country skis. Start here for a number of marked trails, including the Panoramic Point and General Grant Tree trails *(⇨ Hiking, below).* ⊠ *Grant Grove Market, Generals Hwy. (Rte. 198), 3 mi northeast of Rte. 180, Big Stump entrance* ☎ *559/335–5500 Ext. 309* ⊠ *$6–$11* ⊙ *Daily 8 AM–9 PM.*

FISHING

There is limited trout fishing in the park from late April to mid-November, and catches are minor. Still, Kings River is a popular spot. Some of the park's backcountry lakes have good fishing. Licenses ($19.45 for two days, $38.85 for 10 days, less for state residents) are required for those over 16, and are available, along with fishing tackle, in Grant Grove (open year-round) and Cedar Grove.

Fishing licenses are issued by the **California Department of Fish and Game** (☎ *916/928–5805* ⊕ *www.dfg.ca.gov*).

HIKING

You can enjoy many of Kings Canyon's sights from your car, but you'll miss out on the more visceral experiences of hearing the birds in the trees and your footsteps crunching on pine needles as you pass through the forest. The giant gorge of the Kings River Canyon and the sweeping vistas of some of the highest mountains in the United States are best seen on foot. Carry a hiking map—available at any visitor center—and plenty of water. Check with rangers for current trail conditions, and be aware of rapidly changing weather.

EASY **Big Stump Trail.** A walk along this 1-mi trail graphically demonstrates the toll heavy logging takes on the wilderness. ⊠ *Trailhead near Rte. 180, Big Stump entrance.*

General Grant Tree Trail. One of the shortest trails in the parks is the one that leads to General Grant Tree, the third-largest living tree in the world. The trail is only .3 mi, but it passes Gamlin Cabin and Fallen Monarch. It's paved and fairly level. ⊠ *Trailhead off Generals Hwy. (Rte. 198), 1 mi northwest of Grant Grove Visitor Center.*

Roaring River Falls Walk. Take a shady five-minute walk to this forceful waterfall that rushes through a narrow granite chute. The trail is paved and mostly accessible. ⊠ *Trailhead 3 mi east of Cedar Grove Village turnoff from Kings Canyon Scenic Byway.*

13

Fodor's Choice
★ **Zumwalt Meadow Trail.** Walk beneath high granite walls and along the meandering Kings River, en route to the lush Zumwalt Meadow. The 1.5-mi trail involves a little rock-hopping but is otherwise easy. ⊠ *Trailhead 4½ mi east of Cedar Grove Village turnoff from Kings Canyon Scenic Byway.*

MODERATE
★ **Big Baldy.** This hike climbs 600 feet and 2 mi up to the 8,209-feet summit of Big Baldy. Your reward is the view of Redwood Canyon. The round-trip hike is 4 mi. ⊠ *Trailhead 8 mi south of Grant Grove on Generals Hwy. (Rte. 198).*

Mist Falls Trail. This sandy trail follows the glaciated South Fork Canyon through forest and chaparral, past several rapids and cascades, to one of the largest waterfalls in the two parks. Nine miles round-trip, the hike is relatively flat, but climbs 600 feet in the last mile. It takes four to five hours to complete. ⊠ *Trailhead at end of Kings Canyon Scenic Byway, 5½ mi east of Cedar Grove Village.*

Panoramic Point Trail. While in Grant Grove take the time to walk up to Panoramic Point. Trailers and RVs are not permitted on the steep and narrow road. A steep ¼-mi walk from the parking lot leads to a viewpoint where you can see the High Sierra from Mt. Goddard in northern Kings Canyon National Park to Eagle Scout Peak in Sequoia. ⊠ *End of Panoramic Point Rd., 2.3 mi from Grant Grove Village.*

★ **Redwood Canyon Trail.** Whether you hike the perimeter of two adjoining loops or take only one of them, this 6- or 10-mi trek in Redwood Canyon leads through the world's largest grove of sequoias. Take in the cascades, the quiet pools of Redwood Creek, and the mixed conifer forest on a day hike or overnight backpacking trip. ⊠ *Drive 5 mi south of Grant Grove on Generals Hwy. (Rte. 198), then turn right at Quail Flat; follow it 1½ mi to the Redwood Canyon trailhead.*

DIFFICULT
Buena Vista Peak. For a 360-degree view of Redwood Canyon and the High Sierra, make the 2-mi ascent to Buena Vista. ⊠ *Trailhead off Generals Hwy. (Rte. 198), south of Kings Canyon Overlook, 7 mi southeast of Grant Grove.*

Don Cecil Trail. This trail climbs the cool north-facing slope of the Kings River Canyon, passes Sheep Creek Cascade and provides several good views of the canyon and the 11,000-foot Monarch Divide. The trail leads to Lookout Peak, which affords an incredible panorama of the park's backcountry. It's a strenuous, all-day hike—13 mi round-trip—and climbs 4,000 feet. ⊠ *Trailhead off Kings Canyon Scenic Byway, across from parking lot, .2 mi west of Cedar Grove Village.*

★ **Hotel Creek Trail.** For gorgeous canyon views, take this trail from the canyon floor at Cedar Grove up a series of switchbacks until it splits. Follow the route left through chaparral to the forested ridge and rocky outcrop known as Cedar Grove Overlook, where you can see the Kings River Canyon stretching below. This strenuous 5-mi round-trip hike gains 1,200 feet and takes three to four hours to complete. For a longer hike, return via Lewis Creek Trail for an 8-mi loop. ⊠ *Trailhead at Cedar Grove pack station, 1 mi east of Cedar Grove Village.*

HORSEBACK RIDING

One-day destinations by horseback out of Cedar Grove include Mist Falls and Upper Bubb's Creek. In the backcountry, many equestrians head for Volcanic Lakes or Granite Basin, ascending trails that reach elevations of 10,000 feet. Costs per person range from $25 for a one-hour guided ride to around $200 per day for fully guided trips for which the packers do all the cooking and camp chores.

Cedar Grove Pack Station. Take a day or overnight trip along the Kings River Canyon. Popular routes include the Rae Lakes Loop and Monarch Divide. ⊠*Kings Canyon Scenic Byway, 1 mi east of Cedar Grove Village* ☎*559/565–3464 in summer, 559/337–3231 off-season* ✉*Call for prices* ⊗*May–Oct.*

Grant Grove Stables. A one- or two-hour trip through Grant Grove is a good way to get a taste of horseback riding in Kings Canyon. ⊠*Rte. 180, ½ mi north of Grant Grove Visitor Center, near Grant Grove Village* ☎*559/335–9292* ✉*$40–$60* ⊗*June–Labor Day, daily 8–6.*

SNOWSHOEING

Snowshoeing is good around Grant Grove, where you can take naturalist-guided snowshoe walks on Saturdays and holidays mid-December through mid-March as conditions permit.

Grant Grove Market. If you prefer to take a self-guided walk, you can rent snowshoes here. ⊠*Generals Hwy. (Rte. 198), 3 mi northeast of Rte. 180, Big Stump entrance* ☎*559/335–5500 Ext. 309* ⊗*Daily 9–7.*

Grant Grove Visitor Center. For a $1 donation, the visitor center rents out snowshoes for ranger-led walks. ⊠*Generals Hwy. (Rte. 198), 3 mi northeast of Rte. 180, Big Stump entrance* ☎*559/565–4307* ⊗*Daily 9:30–4:30.*

SWIMMING

Swimming in the parks is generally quite dangerous. *For more information,* ⇨ *Swimming in Sequoia National Park.*

WHERE TO STAY & EAT

ABOUT THE RESTAURANTS

In the parks, fare is extremely humble except at the Wuksachi Lodge Dining Room; it's the only restaurant in the area where you really need reservations, but even there you can wear jeans and order a burger.

ABOUT THE HOTELS

Except for Wuksachi Lodge in Sequoia, in-park accommodations are no-frills. You'll nonetheless pay a premium to stay in the parks, but it is well worth it to spare yourself the long drive from even the lodgings closest by.

ABOUT THE CAMPGROUNDS

The campgrounds within Sequoia and Kings Canyon afford pretty settings for a relaxed getaway. Many do not accept reservations or cash, and none has full-service bells and whistles (or even RV hookups), but there are plenty of options that don't require you to hike in. Those around Lodgepole and Grant Grove get quite busy in summer with vacationing families, while Cedar Grove sites attract a younger, crunchier set. Permits are required for backcountry camping.

WHERE TO EAT

IN SEQUOIA

$-$$$ ✕**Wuksachi Village Dining Room.** In the high-ceiling dining room at ★ Sequoia's only upscale restaurant, huge windows run the length of the room, providing a view of the surrounding trees. The dinner menu lists everything from sandwiches and burgers to steaks and pasta. Breakfast and lunch are also served. ⊠ *Wuksachi Village* ☎ *559/565–4070* ⌂ *Reservations essential* ☰*AE, D, DC, MC, V.*

$ ✕**Wolverton Barbecue.** All-you-can-eat barbecue ribs and chicken, hot dogs and hamburgers, and lots of sides and desserts are whipped up outdoors overlooking Wolverton Meadow Friday through Sunday evenings. After the meal is a ranger talk, campfire sing-along, or living-history demonstration. Buy tickets at Wuksachi Lodge or Lodgepole Market. ⊠ *Wolverton Rd., 1½ mi northeast off Generals Hwy. (Rte. 198)* ☎ *559/565–4070* ☰*AE, D, DC, MC, V* ⊘*No lunch. Closed Mon.–Thurs. and Sept.–mid-June.*

¢ ✕**Lodgepole Market and Snack Bar.** Visit the market for prepackaged sandwiches and salads to go or to assemble the components of a picnic. In summer, there's a deli for sandwiches and a snack bar for breakfast, pizza, and hamburgers. ⊠ *Next to Lodgepole Visitor Center* ☎ *559/565–3301* ☰*AE, D, DC, MC, V* ⊘*Closed Sept.–Apr.*

PICNIC AREAS **Crescent Meadow.** This area near Moro Rock has vistas over the meadows. Tables are under the giant sequoia, off the parking area. There are restrooms and drinking water. Fires are not allowed. ⊠*End of Moro Rock–Crescent Rd., 2.6 mi east off Generals Hwy. (Rte. 198).*

Foothills Picnic Area. Near the parking lot at the southern entrance of the park, this small area has tables on grass. Drinking water and restrooms are available. ⊠*Near Foothills Visitor Center.*

Halstead Meadow. Tables are at the edge of the meadow at this area off the main road and a short walk from parking. Grills and restrooms are provided, but there's no drinking water. The Dorst Campground is nearby. ⊠*Generals Hwy. (Rte. 198), 4 mi north of Lodgepole junction.*

Hospital Rock. Native Americans once ground acorns into meal at this site; outdoor exhibits tell the story. Tables are on grass a short distance from the parking lot. Grills, drinking water, and restrooms are available. The Buckeye Flat Campground is nearby. ⊠*Generals Hwy. (Rte. 198), 6 mi north of Ash Mountain entrance.*

Pinewood Picnic Area. Picnic in Giant Forest, among the giant sequoia trees. Drinking water, restrooms, and grills are provided. ⊠*Generals Hwy. (Rte. 198), 2 mi north of Giant Forest Museum, halfway between Giant Forest Museum and General Sherman Tree.*

Wolverton Meadow. At a major trailhead to the backcountry, this is a great place to stop for lunch before a hike. The area sits in a mixed-conifer forest adjacent to parking. Drinking water, grills, and restrooms are available. ☒ *Wolverton Rd., 1½ mi northeast off Generals Hwy. (Rte. 198).*

IN KINGS CANYON

$–$$$ ✕**Grant Grove Restaurant.** Come here year-round for simple family-style dining. The restaurant serves full breakfasts, and hot entrées and sandwiches for lunch and dinner. Take-out service is available. ☒ *Grant Grove Village* ☎ *559/335–5500* ▭ *AE, D, MC, V.*

¢–$$ ✕**Cedar Grove Restaurant.** This snack bar with counter service serves eggs at breakfast, sandwiches and hamburgers at lunch and dinner, and in the evening also has several specials like chicken-fried steak. Take your tray onto the deck overlooking the Kings River. ☒ *Cedar Grove Village* ☎ *559/565–0100* ▭ *AE, D, MC, V* ☺ *Closed Oct.–May.*

¢–$ ✕**Cedar Grove Market.** You can pick up sandwiches and salads to go at this market, as well as a range of grocery items. It's open daily 8–7. ☒ *Cedar Grove Village* ☎ *559/565–0100* ▭ *AE, D, MC, V* ☺ *Closed late Oct.–mid-Apr.*

PICNIC AREAS **Big Stump.** At the edge of a logged sequoia grove, some trees still stand at this site. Near the park's entrance, the area is paved and next to the road. It's the only picnic area in either park that is plowed in the wintertime. Restrooms, grills, and drinking water are available, and the area is entirely accessible. ☒ *Rte. 180, just inside park, Big Stump entrance.*

Columbine. This grassy picnic area near the sequoias is relatively level. Tables, restrooms, drinking water, and grills are available. ☒ *Grant Tree Rd., just off Generals Hwy. (Rte. 198), ½ mi northwest of Grant Grove Visitor Center.*

Grizzly Falls. A short walk from the parking area leads to a grassy picnic spot near the bottom of a canyon. The area is not level. Tables and restrooms are available, grills and water are not. ☒ *Off Rte. 180, 2½ mi west of Cedar Grove entrance.*

WHERE TO STAY

IN SEQUOIA

$$$–$$$$ 🏠**Wuksachi Lodge.** These cedar-and-stone lodge buildings, which blend
FodorsChoice with the landscape, house comfortable rooms with modern ameni-
★ ties. The village is 7,200 feet above sea level; many of the rooms have spectacular views of the surrounding mountains. ☒ *Wuksachi Village 93262* ☎ *559/565–4070 front desk, 559/253–2199, 888/252–5757 reservations* ☒ *559/456–0542* ⊕ *www.visitsequoia.com* ➩ *102 rooms* ⌂ *In-room: no a/c, refrigerator, dial-up, Wi-Fi. In-hotel: restaurant, bar, no-smoking rooms* ▭ *AE, D, DC, MC, V.*

$–$$$ 🏠**Silver City Resort.** High on the Mineral King Road, this resort pro-
☺ vides an excellent alternative to the crowded properties at the parks' lower elevations. Lodgings range from modern Swiss-style chalets to traditional rustic alpine cabins with woodstoves and central bathing facilities. There is a small general store, a bakery serving homemade pies, and a modestly priced restaurant on-site, though the latter serves Thursday through Monday only. Some cabins share a central shower

and bath. ⊠*Mineral King Rd., 20 mi east of Hwy. 198,* ☎*559/561–3223 or 805/528–2730* ⊕*www.silvercityresort.com* ⟿*13 units, 8 with shared bath* ☖*In-room: no a/c, no phone (some), kitchen, refrigerator (some), no TV, dial-up (some). In-hotel: restaurant, no-smoking rooms* ☰*MC, V* ☉*Closed Nov.–May.*

CAMPGROUNDS

$$ 🏕 **Buckeye Flat Campground.** This tents-only campground at the southern end of Sequoia National Park is smaller than campgrounds elsewhere in the park. Because of its low elevation (2,800 feet), it scorches in summer. ⊠*Generals Hwy., 6 mi north of Foothills Visitor Center* ☎*559/565–3341* ⟿*28 tent sites* ☖*Flush toilets, drinking water, bear boxes, fire grates, picnic tables* ⚠*Reservations not accepted* ☰*No credit cards* ☉*Open daily.*

$$ 🏕 **Dorst Creek Campground.** This large campground is at 6,700 feet. Use the bear boxes: this is a popular area for the furry creatures to raid. Reservations, made by mail or through the Web site, are essential in summer. There are accessible sites here. ⊠*Generals Hwy. (Rte. 198), 8 mi north of Lodgepole Visitor Center, near Kings Canyon border* ☎*877/444–6777* ⊕*www.recreation.gov* ⟿*204 tent and RV sites* ☖*Flush toilets, dump station, drinking water, bear boxes, fire grates, picnic tables, public telephone* ☰*D, MC, V* ☉*Memorial Day–Labor Day.*

$$ 🏕 **Lodgepole Campground.** The largest Lodgepole-area campground is also the noisiest, though things do quiet down at night. Restrooms are nearby. Lodgepole and Dorst (7 mi to the west) are the two campgrounds within Sequoia that accept reservations (essential up to five months in advance for stays between mid-May and mid-October). ⊠*Off Generals Hwy. beyond Lodgepole Village* ☎*877/444–6777* ⊕*www.recreation.gov* ⟿*214 tent and RV sites* ☖*Flush toilets, dump station (summer only), drinking water, guest laundry (summer only), showers (summer only), bear boxes, fire grates, picnic tables, public telephone, general store* ☰*D, MC, V* ☉*Year-round.*

$$ 🏕 **Potwisha Campground.** On the Marble Fork of the Kaweah River, this midsize campground with attractive surroundings sits at 2,100 feet—which means it gets no snow in winter and is hotter in summer than campgrounds at higher elevations. RVs up to 30 feet long can camp here. ⊠*Generals Hwy., 4 mi north of Foothills Visitor Center* ☎*559/565–3341* ⟿*42 tent and RV sites* ☖*Flush toilets, dump station, drinking water, bear boxes, fire grates, picnic tables, public telephone* ⚠*Reservations not accepted* ☰*No credit cards* ☉*Year-round.*

$ 🏕 **Atwell Mill Campground.** At 6,650 feet, this tents-only campground is just south of the Western Divide. There are telephones and a general store is ½ mi away at the Silver City Resort. Reservations are not accepted. ⊠*Mineral King Rd., 20 mi east of Hwy. 198* ☎*559/565–3341* ⟿*21 tent sites* ☖*Pit toilets, drinking water, showers, bear boxes, fire grates, picnic tables* ☰*No credit cards* ☉*Memorial Day–Oct.*

$ 🏕 **Cold Springs Campground.** Near the end of Mineral King Road, this tents-only campground sits up high at 7,500 feet. You can hike to the spectacular high country from here. ⊠*At end of Mineral King Rd.* ☎*559/565–3341* ⟿*40 tent sites* ☖*Pit toilets, drinking water, bear* *boxes, picnic tables, ranger station* ⚑*Reservations not accepted* ▭*No credit cards* ◷*May–Oct.*

IN KINGS CANYON

$$ ✕▥ **Cedar Grove Lodge.** This lodge manages to deliver peace and quiet because the hard-core hiking types who stay here go to bed early. It's not particularly attractive or clean, but it's the only accommodation out in Kings River Canyon. Book far in advance—the lodge has only 21 rooms. Each has two queen-size beds, and three have kitchenettes and patios. You can order trout, hamburgers, hot dogs, and sandwiches at the snack bar (¢–$) and take them to one of the picnic tables along the river's edge. ⊠*Kings Canyon Scenic Byway* ☎*Sequoia Kings Canyon Park Services Co., 5755 E. Kings Canyon Rd., Suite 101, Fresno, 93727* ☎*559/335–5500 or 866/522–6966* 🖷*559/335–5507* ⊕*www.sequoia-kingscanyon.com* ⇆*21 rooms* ♿*In-room: no phone, kitchen (some), no TV. In-hotel: laundry facilities, no-smoking rooms* ▭*AE, D, MC, V* ◷*Closed Oct.–May.*

$–$$ ✕▥ **Grant Grove Cabins.** Some of the wood-panel cabins here have heaters, electric lights, and private baths, but most have woodstoves, battery lamps, and shared baths. Those who don't mind roughing it might opt for the tent cabins. The Grant Grove Restaurant (¢–$$), a family-style coffee shop, serves American standards for breakfast, lunch, and dinner. In winter, only the cabins that have private baths remain open. ⊠*Kings Canyon Scenic Byway in Grant Grove Village* ☎*Sequoia Kings Canyon Park Services Co., 5755 E. Kings Canyon Rd., Suite 101, Fresno, 93727* ☎*559/335–5500 or 866/522–6966* 🖷*559/335–5507* ⊕*www.sequoia-kingscanyon.com* ⇆*36 cabins, 9 with bath; 19 tents* ♿*In-room: no a/c, no phone, no TV. In-hotel: restaurant* ▭*AE, D, MC, V.*

$$$ ▥ **John Muir Lodge.** This modern, timber-sided lodge is nestled in a wooded area near Grant Grove Village. The rooms and suites all have queen beds and private baths, and there's a comfortable common room with low-pile carpeting and a stone fireplace where you can play cards and board games. The inexpensive, family-style Grant Grove Restaurant is a three-minute walk away. Though it's little more than a good motel, this is the finest place to stay in Grant Grove. ⊠*Kings Canyon Scenic Byway, ¼ mi north of Grant Grove Village* ☎*Sequoia Kings Canyon Park Services Co., 5755 E. Kings Canyon Rd., Suite 101, Fresno, 93727* ☎*559/335–5500 or 866/522–6966* 🖷*559/335–5507* ⊕*www.sequoia-kingscanyon.com* ⇆*30 rooms, 6 suites* ♿*In-room: no a/c, no TV* ▭*AE, D, MC, V.*

CAMPGROUNDS
$$ ⚑ **Azalea Campground.** Of the three campgrounds in the Grant Grove area (the others are Sunset and Crystal Springs), Azalea is the only one open year-round. It sits at 6,500 feet amid giant sequoias, yet is close to restaurants, stores, and other facilities. Some sites at Azalea are wheelchair accessible. The campground can accommodate RVs up to 30 feet. ⊠*Kings Canyon Scenic Byway, ¼ mi north of Grant Grove Village* ☎*559/565–3341* ⇆*113 tent and RV sites* ♿*Flush toilets, drinking water, showers, bear boxes, fire grates, picnic tables, public telephone, general store* ▭*No credit cards* ◷*Year-round.*

$$ ⚠**Canyon View Campground.** One of four sites near Cedar Grove, this campground is near the start of the Don Cecil Trail, which leads to Lookout Point. The elevation of the camp is 4,600 feet along the Kings River. There are no accessible sites. ⊠ *Off Kings Canyon Scenic Byway, ½ mi east of Cedar Grove Village* ☎*No phone* ↩*37 tent sites* ♿*Flush toilets, drinking water, bear boxes, fire grates, picnic tables, public telephone* ♿*Reservations not accepted* ▤*No credit cards* ☉*Late May– late Sept., as needed.*

$$ ⚠**Crystal Springs Campground.** Near the Grant Grove Village and the towering sequoias, this camp is at 6,500 feet. There are accessible sites here. ⊠ *Off Generals Hwy. (Rte. 198), ¼ mi north of Grant Grove Visitor Center* ☎*No phone* ↩*62 tent and RV sites* ♿*Flush toilets, drinking water, bear boxes, fire grates, picnic tables, public telephone* ♿*Reservations not accepted* ▤*No credit cards* ☉*Memorial Day– Labor Day.*

$$ ⚠**Moraine Campground.** Close to the Kings River and a short walk from Cedar Grove Village, this camp is set at 4,600 feet along the Kings River. There are no accessible sites. ⊠ *Off Kings Canyon Scenic Byway, ¾ mi west of Cedar Grove Village* ☎*No phone* ↩*120 tent and RV sites* ♿*Flush toilets, drinking water, bear boxes, fire grates, picnic tables, public telephone* ♿*Reservations not accepted* ▤*No credit cards* ☉*Late May–late Sept., as needed.*

$$ ⚠**Sentinel Campground.** Of the three campgrounds in the Cedar Grove area (the other two are Sheep Creek and Canyon View, both open June–September only), Sentinel is open the latest. At 4,600 feet and within walking distance of Cedar Grove Village, it fills up fast in the summer. Some sites are wheelchair accessible, and the campground can accommodate RVs up to 30 feet. Nearby, there are laundry facilities, a restaurant, a general store, and a ranger station. ⊠*Kings Canyon Scenic Byway, ¼-mi west of Cedar Grove Village* ☎*559/565–3341* ↩*82 tent and RV sites* ♿*Flush toilets, drinking water, bear boxes, fire grates, picnic tables, public telephone* ♿*Reservations not accepted* ▤*No credit cards* ☉*May–Oct.*

$$ ⚠**Sheep Creek Campground.** The camp, like the adjacent Cedar Grove, FodorśChoice is at 4,600 feet along the Kings River. ⊠ *Off Kings Canyon Scenic* ★ *Byway, 1 mi west of Cedar Grove Village* ☎*No phone* ↩*111 tent and RV sites* ♿*Flush toilets, drinking water, bear boxes, fire grates, picnic tables, public telephone* ♿*Reservations not accepted* ▤*No credit cards* ☉*Late May–late Sept.*

$$ ⚠**Sunset Campground.** Many of the easiest trails through Grant Grove are adjacent to this large camp, near the giant sequoias at 6,500 feet. ⊠*Off Generals Hwy. (Rte. 198), near Grant Grove Visitor Center* ☎*No phone* ↩*200 tent and RV sites* ♿*Flush toilets, drinking water, bear boxes, fire grates, picnic tables, public telephone* ♿*Reservations not accepted* ▤*No credit cards* ☉*Memorial Day–late Sept.*

SEQUOIA & KINGS CANYON ESSENTIALS

ACCESSIBILITY

All of the visitor centers, the Giant Forest Museum, and Big Trees Trail are wheelchair-accessible, as are some short ranger-led walks and talks. General Sherman Tree can be reached via a paved, level trail near a parking area. None of the caves is accessible and wilderness areas must be reached by horseback or on foot. Some picnic tables are extended to accommodate wheelchairs. Many of the major sites are in the 6,000-foot range, and thin air at high elevations can cause respiratory distress for people with breathing difficulties. Carry oxygen if necessary. Contact the park's main number for more information.

ADMISSION FEES

The vehicle admission fee is $20 and valid for seven days in both parks. Those who enter by bus, on foot, bicycle, motorcycle, or horse pay $10 for a seven-day pass. Senior citizens who are U.S. residents over the age of 62 pay $10 for a lifetime pass, and permanently disabled U.S. residents are admitted free.

ADMISSION HOURS

The parks are open daily 24 hours. Sequoia and Kings Canyon National Parks are in the Pacific time zone.

EMERGENCIES

Call 911 from any telephone within the park in an emergency. Rangers at the Cedar Grove, Foothills, Grant Grove, and Lodgepole visitor centers and the Mineral King ranger station are trained in first aid. National park rangers have legal jurisdiction within park boundaries: contact a ranger station or visitor center for police matters. For non-emergencies, call the parks' main number, *559/565–3341.*

LOST AND FOUND

Report lost items or turn in found items at any visitor center or ranger station. Items are held at a central location and are handled by park rangers. For more information, call park headquarters at *559/565–3341.*

PERMITS

If you plan to camp in the backcountry, your group must have a backcountry camping permit, which costs $15 for hikers or $30 for stock users (horseback riders, etc.). One permit covers the entire group. Availability of permits depends upon trailhead quotas. Advance reservations are accepted by mail, fax, or e-mail for the $15 fee, from March to early September. Without a reservation, you may still get a permit on a first-come, first-served basis starting at 1 PM the day before you plan to hike. For more information on backcountry camping or travel with pack animals (horses, mules, burros, or llamas), contact the Wilderness Permit Office.

Contacts **Wilderness Permit Office** (☎ *530/565-3766*). **Wilderness Permit Reservations** (✉ *HCR 89 Box 60, Three Rivers, 93271* ☎ *559/575-3766* 📠 *559/565-4239*).

PUBLIC TELEPHONES

Public telephones may be found at the park entrance stations, visitor centers, ranger stations, some trailheads, and at all restaurants and lodging facilities in the park.

RESTROOMS

Public restrooms may be found at all visitor centers and campgrounds. Additional locations include Big Stump, Columbine, Grizzly Falls, Hospital Rock, Wolverton, Crescent Meadow, Giant Forest Museum, and Crystal Cave.

VISITOR INFORMATION

Contacts **Delaware North Park Services** (*Box 89, Sequoia National Park, 93262* 🕾 *866/807–3598* ⊕ *www.visitsequoia.com*). This concessionaire operates the lodgings and visitor services in Sequoia and some in Kings Canyon. **Sequoia and Kings Canyon National Parks** (✉ *47050 Generals Hwy. [Rte. 198], Three Rivers, 93271–9651* 🕾 *559/565–3341* ⊕ *www.nps.gov/seki*). **Sequoia Natural History Association** (*HCR 89 Box 10, Three Rivers, 93271* 🕾 *559/565–3759* ⊕ *www.sequoiahistory.org*). The SNHA operates Crystal Cave and the Pear Lake Ski Hut and provides educational materials and programs. **U.S. Forest Service, Sequoia National Forest** (✉ *900 W. Grand Ave., Porterville, 93527* 🕾 *559/784–1500* ⊕ *www.fs.fed.us/r5/sequoia*). **Kings Canyon Park Services** (*Box 909, Kings Canyon National Park, 93633* 🕾 *559/335–5500 or 866/522–6966* ⊕ *www.sequoia-kingscanyon.com*). Some park services, including lodging, are operated by this company.

The Central Valley

HIGHWAY 99 FROM BAKERSFIELD TO LODI

Fresno

WORD OF MOUTH

"A trip through the Forestiere Underground Gardens is a near-magical experience. The tunnels, the exotic trees, the grottoes—it's amazing to think someone actually lived here."

—marie606

WELCOME TO THE CENTRAL VALLEY

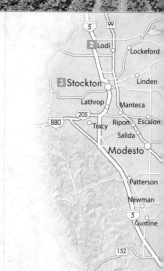

TOP REASONS TO GO

★ **Down under:** Forestiere Underground Gardens is not the flashiest tourist attraction in California, but it is one of the strangest—and it's oddly inspirational.

★ **Grape escape:** In the past decade, Lodi's wineries have grown enough in stature for the charming little town to become a must-sip destination.

★ **Port with authority:** Stockton has long been a hub for merchandise that is being transferred from roadway to waterway—or vice versa. Watch some of that commotion in commerce from the riverfront downtown area.

★ **Go with the flow:** White-water rafting will get your blood pumping, and maybe your clothes wet, on the Stanislaus River near Oakdale.

★ **Hee haw!:** Kick up your heels and break out your drawl at Buck Owens' Crystal Palace in Bakersfield, a city some believe is the heart of country music.

1 Fresno. This flat, dusty city of 480,000 is the urban heart of the Central Valley. Fresno has a small but varied core of interesting attractions: a sprawling park with a rain forest, an underground garden, and an impressive metropolitan museum.

2 Lodi. This town of about 60,000 residents—many of whom commute to Sacramento or the Bay Area—has a compact and pleasant downtown, but its most appealing attractions are on the outskirts. The wineries in this region are not crowded but worthy of visitors from afar.

3 Stockton. For several seasons, the University of the Pacific's football team once had Amos Alonzo Stagg as its coach—the man who invented the huddle. The school no longer has a team, but its campus is pretty and the nearby Haggin Museum has a fine collection of 19th-century California landscapes.

Harvesting an orange grove in Fresno

4 Bakersfield. Merle Haggard was born here and Buck Owens called it home for more than a half century. But, although Bakersfield has a worldwide reputation for its country-music scene, the town's fortunes have turned on the region's oil production, and lately business has been bad. Driving about downtown is a bit like seeing a ghost town in the making—which some might find interesting.

5 Hanford. Take a stroll among the restored buildings of Courthouse Square, wander down China Alley, or tour the town in a restored 1930s Studebaker fire truck.

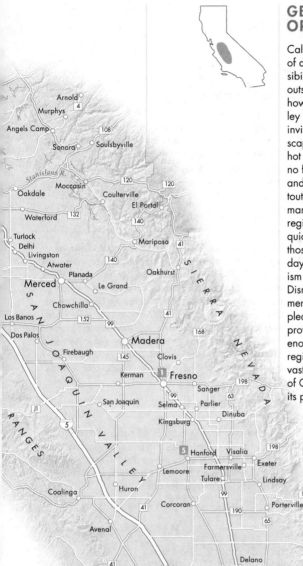

14

GETTING ORIENTED

California has a diversity of delicious vacation possibilities. Among its many outstanding regions, however, the Central Valley is arguably the least inviting. This flat landscape, sometimes blistery hot and smelly, contains no famous attractions and cannot honestly be touted as a can't-miss. For many vacationers, it is a region to drive through as quickly as possible. For those who have an extra day or two, whose tourism tastes don't demand Disneyland-level excitement, it can represent a pleasant diversion and provide insights into an enormous agricultural region. The valley is the vast geographical center of California, if not quite its proverbial heart.

THE CENTRAL VALLEY PLANNER

Exploring the Central Valley

The 225-mi Central Valley cuts through Kern, Tulare, Kings, Fresno, Madera, Merced, Stanislaus, and San Joaquin counties. It's bounded on the east by the mighty Sierra Nevada and on the west by the smaller coastal ranges. Interstate 5 runs south–north through the valley, as does Highway 99.

When to Go

Spring, when wildflowers are in bloom and the scent of fruit blossoms is in the air, and fall, when the air is brisk and leaves turn red and gold, are the best times to visit. Many of the valley's biggest festivals take place during these seasons. (If you suffer from allergies, though, beware of spring, when stone-fruit trees blossom.) Summer, when temperatures often top 100°F, can be oppressive. June through August, though, are great months to visit area water parks and lakes or to take in the air-conditioned museums. Many attractions close in winter, which can get dreary. Thick, ground-hugging fog is a common driving hazard November through February.

Tour Options

Central Valley Tours provides general and customized tours of the Fresno area and the valley, with special emphasis on the fruit harvests and Blossom Trail.

Contacts Central Valley Tours (☎ *559/276–4479* ⊕ *www.angelfire.com/poetry/inc/valleytours.html*).

About the Restaurants

Fast-food places and chain restaurants dominate valley highways, but away from the main drag, independent and family-owned eateries will awaken your taste buds. Many bistros and fine restaurants take advantage of the local produce and locally raised meats that are the cornerstone of California cuisine. Even simple restaurants produce hearty, tasty fare that often reflects the valley's ethnic mix. Some of the nation's best Mexican restaurants call the valley home. Chinese, Italian, Armenian, and Basque restaurants also are abundant; many serve massive, several-course meals.

About the Hotels

The Central Valley has many chain motels and hotels, but independently owned hotels and bed-and-breakfasts also can be found. There's a large selection of upscale lodgings, Victorian-style B&Bs, and places that are simply utilitarian but clean and comfortable.

WHAT IT COSTS				
¢	$	$$	$$$	$$$$
Restaurants				
under $10	$10–$15	$16–$22	$23–$30	over $30
Hotels				
under $90	$90–$120	$121–$175	$176–$250	over $250

Restaurant prices are for a main course at dinner, excluding sales tax of 7%–10% (depending on location). Hotel prices are for two people in a standard double room in high season, excluding service charges and 8%–13% tax.

Updated by
Reed Parsell

AMONG THE WORLD'S MOST FERTILE working lands, the Central Valley is important due to the scale of its food production, but, to be honest, it lacks substantial appeal for visitors. For most people, the Central Valley is simply a place to pass through on the way to greater attractions in the north, south, east, or west. For those willing to invest a little effort, however, California's heartland can be rewarding.

The agriculturally rich area is home to a diversity of wildlife. Many telephone posts are crowned by a hawk or kestrel hunting the land below. Vineyards, especially in the northern valley around Lodi, and almond orchards whose white blossoms make February a brighter month are pleasant sights out motorists' windows. In the towns, historical societies display artifacts of the valley's eccentric past; concert halls and restored theaters showcase samplings of contemporary culture; and museums provide a blend of both. Restaurants can be very good, whether they be fancy or mom-and-pop. For fruit lovers, roadside stands can be treasure troves. Country-music enthusiasts will find a lot to appreciate on the radio and on stages, especially in the Bakersfield area. Summer nights spent at one of the valley's minor-league baseball parks—Bakersfield, Fresno, Modesto, Stockton, and Visalia have teams—can be a relaxing experience. Whether on back roads or main streets, people are not only friendly but proud to help outsiders explore the Central Valley.

14

SOUTHERN CENTRAL VALLEY

BAKERSFIELD & KERNVILLE

BAKERSFIELD

110 mi north of Los Angeles on I–5 and Hwy. 99; 110 mi west of Ridgecrest via Hwy. 14 south and Hwy. 58 west.

Bakersfield's founder, Colonel Thomas Baker, arrived with the discovery of gold in the nearby Kern River valley in 1851. Now Kern County's biggest city (it has a population of 328,000, which includes the largest Basque community in the United States), Bakersfield probably is best known as Nashville West, a country-music haven and hometown of performers Buck Owens (who died in 2006) and Merle Haggard. It also has its own symphony orchestra and two good museums.

☾ The 16-acre **Kern County Museum and Lori Brock Children's Discovery Center**
★ form one of the Central Valley's top museum complexes. The indoor-outdoor Kern County Museum is set up as an open-air, walk-through historic village with more than 55 restored or re-created buildings dating from the 1860s to the 1940s. "Black Gold: The Oil Experience," a permanent exhibit, shows how oil is created, discovered, extracted, and transformed for various uses. The Lori Brock Children's Discovery Center, for ages 8 and younger, has hands-on displays and an indoor playground. ✉*3801 Chester Ave.* ☎*661/852–5000* ⊕*www.kcmuseum. org* ⊞*$8* ⊙*Mon.–Sat. 10–5, Sun. noon–5.*

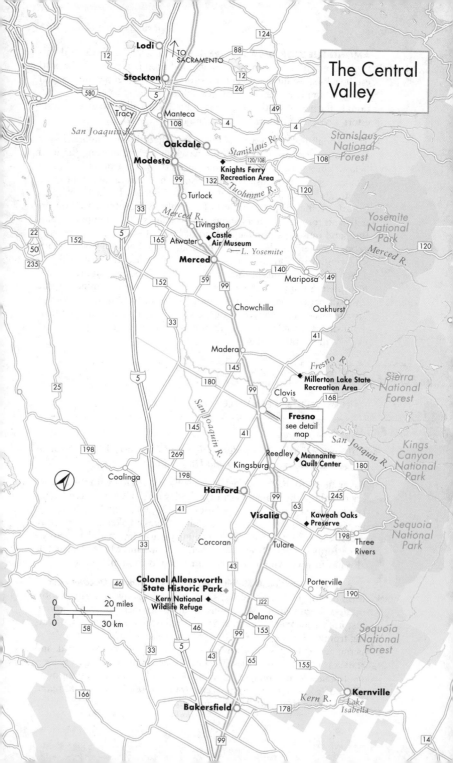

The Central Valley

124

Lodi
TO SACRAMENTO
88
12
Stockton
12
26
580
49
Tracy
Manteca
108
4
San Joaquin R.
4
Oakdale
Stanislaus
National
Forest
Modesto
Stanislaus R.
120/108
108
99
132
Knights Ferry
Recreation Area
Tuolumne R.
120
33
Turlock
Merced R.
Livingston
Yosemite
National
Park
22
152
165
Atwater
Castle
Air Museum
50
L. Yosemite
Merced R.
120
235
Merced
140
59
99
152
Mariposa
49
33
Chowchilla
Oakhurst
Madera
41
145
Fresno R.
180
Millerton Lake State
Recreation Area
Sierra
National
Forest
25
5
99
Clovis
168
145
Fresno
see detail
map
San Joaquin R.
Kings
Canyon
National
Park
198
41
Reedley
Mennonite
Quilt Center
180
269
Kingsburg
198
Coalinga
Hanford
99
63
245
41
Visalia
Kaweah Oaks
Preserve
Sequoia
National
Park
33
Corcoran
Tulare
198
Three
Rivers
43
Colonel Allensworth
State Historic Park
Porterville
190
46
Kern National
Wildlife Refuge
J22
0   20 miles
Delano
0   30 km
46
99
155
58
33
43
65
155
5
166
Kernville
Kern R.
Lake
Isabella
Bakersfield
178
99
14

San Joaquin R.

☺ At the **California Living Museum,** a
★ combination zoo, botanical garden, and natural-history museum,
the emphasis is on the zoo. All animal and plant species displayed are
native to the state. Within the reptile house lives every species of rattlesnake found in California. The
landscaped grounds—in the hills
about a 20-minute drive northeast
of Bakersfield—also shelter captive bald eagles, tortoises, coyotes,
black bears, and foxes. ✉ *10500
Alfred Harrell Hwy. Hwy. 178
east, then 3½ mi northwest on Alfred Harrell Hwy.* ☎ *661/872–2256*
⊕ *www.calmzoo.org* ✆ *$7* ☯ *Daily 9–5.*

14

WHERE TO EAT

$-$$$ ✕**Uricchio's Trattoria.** This downtown restaurant draws everyone from
office workers to oil barons—all attracted by the tasty food and casual
atmosphere. *Panini* (Italian pressed sandwiches, served at lunch only),
pasta, and Italian-style chicken dishes dominate the menu; the chicken
piccata outsells all other offerings. Reservations are recommended.
✉ *1400 17th St.* ☎ *661/326–8870* ▭ *AE, D, DC, MC, V* ☯ *Closed
Sun. No lunch Sat.*

$ ✕**Jake's Original Tex Mex Cafe.** Don't let the cafeteria-style service fool
you; this is probably the best lunch place in Bakersfield. The chicken
burritos and the chili fries (with meaty chili ladled on top) are superb,
the coleslaw draws raves, too; for dessert, try the Texas sheet cake. It's
open for dinner, too. ✉ *1710 Oak St.* ☎ *661/322–6380* ✍ *Reserva-
tions not accepted* ▭ *AE, D, MC, V* ☯ *Closed Sun.*

NIGHTLIFE & THE ARTS

★ **Buck Owens' Crystal Palace** (✉ *2800 Buck Owens Blvd.* ☎ *661/328–
7560* ⊕ *www.buckowens.com*) is a combination nightclub, restaurant,
souvenir store, and showcase of country-music memorabilia. Country-
and-western singers perform here, as Owens did countless times before
his death in March 2006. A dance floor beckons customers who can
still twirl after sampling the menu of steaks, burgers, nachos, and gooey
desserts. Entertainment is free on most weeknights; on Friday and Sat-
urday nights, there's a cover charge (usually $8 to $15) for some of the
more well-known entertainers.

KERNVILLE

50 mi northeast of Bakersfield, via Hwys. 178 and 155.

The wild and scenic Kern River, which flows through Kernville en route
from Mt. Whitney to Bakersfield, delivers some of the most exciting
white-water rafting in the state. Kernville (population 1,700) rests in
a mountain valley on both banks of the river and also at the northern
tip of Lake Isabella (a dammed portion of the river used as a reser-

voir and for recreation). By far the most scenic town described in this chapter, Kernville has lodgings, restaurants, and antiques shops. The main streets are lined with Old West–style buildings, reflecting Kernville's heritage as a rough-and-tumble gold-mining town once known as Whiskey Flat. (Present-day Kernville dates from the 1950s, when it was moved upriver to make room for Lake Isabella.) The road from Bakersfield includes stretches where the rushing river is on one side and granite cliffs are on the other.

WHERE TO STAY & EAT

$–$$ ✕ **That's Italian.** For northern Italian cuisine in a typical trattoria, this is the spot. Try the braised lamb shanks in a Chianti wine sauce or the linguine with clams, mussels, calamari, and shrimp in a white-wine clam sauce. ⊠ *9 Big Blue Rd.* ☎ *760/376–6020* ⊟ *AE, D, MC, V.*

$$–$$$$ ▥ **Whispering Pines Lodge Bed & Breakfast.** Perched on the banks of the Kern River, this 8-acre property gives you a variety of overnight options. Units are motel-style or in duplex bungalows and all have fireplaces, coffeemakers, and king-size beds. Some have full kitchens, queen-size sleepers, and whirlpool tubs. **Pros:** Rustic setting; big breakfasts; great views; very clean. **Cons:** Bungalows are pricey. ⊠ *13745 Sierra Way,* ☎ *760/376–3733 or 877/241–4100* ⊕ *www.kernvalley.com/whispering pines* ⇩ *17 rooms* ⋄ *In-room: kitchen (some), refrigerator (some). In-hotel: pool, no elevator* ⊟ *AE, D, MC, V* ⋈ *BP.*

SPORTS & THE OUTDOORS

BOATING &   The Lower Kern River, which extends from Lake Isabella to Bakersfield
WINDSURFING   and beyond, is open for fishing year-round. Catches include rainbow trout, catfish, smallmouth bass, crappie, and bluegill. Lake Isabella is popular with anglers, water-skiers, sailors, and windsurfers. Its shoreline marinas have boats for rent, bait and tackle, and moorings. **North Fork Marina** (☎ *760/376–1812*) is in Wofford Heights, on the lake's north shore. **French Gulch Marina** (☎ *760/379–8774*) is near the dam on Lake Isabella's west shore.

WHITE-WATER   The three sections of the Kern River—known as the Lower Kern, Upper
RAFTING   Kern, and the Forks—add up to nearly 50 mi of white water, ranging from Class I (easy) to Class V (expert). The Lower and Upper Kern are the most popular and accessible sections. Organized trips can last from one hour (for as little as $35) to more than two days. Rafting season usually runs from late spring until the end of summer. **Kern River Tours** (☎ *800/844–7238* ⊕ *www.kernrivertours.com*) leads several rafting tours from half-day trips to three days of navigating Class V rapids, and also arranges for mountain-bike trips.

Mountain & River Adventures (☎ *760/376–6553 or 800/861–6553* ⊕ *www. mtnriver.com*) gives calm-water kayaking tours as well as white-water rafting trips, plus leads mountain bike excursions and has a campground. In the wintertime, M&R has snowshoe and cross-country ski rentals. Half-day Class II and III white-water rafting trips are emphasized at the recently expanded **Sierra South** (☎ *760/376–3745 or 800/457–2082* ⊕ *www.sierrasouth.com*), which also offers kayaking classes and calm-water excursions.

MID-CENTRAL VALLEY

FROM VISALIA TO FRESNO

COLONEL ALLENSWORTH STATE HISTORIC PARK

★ *45 mi north of Bakersfield on Hwy. 43.*

A former slave who became the country's highest-ranking black military officer of his time founded Allensworth—the only California town settled, governed, and financed by African-Americans—in 1908. After enjoying early prosperity, the town was plagued by hardships and eventually was deserted. Its scattering of rebuilt buildings reflect the few years in which it thrived. Festivities each October commemorate the town's rededication. ✉ *4129 Palmer Ave.* ☎ *661/849–3433* ⊕ *www. cal-parks.ca.gov* 🏷 *$4 per car* ⊘ *Daily sunrise–sunset, visitor center open on request, buildings open by appointment.*

14

VISALIA

40 mi north of Colonel Allensworth State Historic Park on Hwy. 99 and east on Hwy. 198; 75 mi north of Bakersfield via Hwy. 99 north and Hwy. 198 east.

Visalia's combination of a reliable agricultural economy and civic pride has yielded perhaps the most vibrant downtown in the Central Valley. A clear day's view of the Sierra from Main Street is spectacular, if sadly rare due to smog and dust, and even Sunday night can find the streets busy with pedestrians.

Founded in 1852, the town contains many historic homes; ask for a free guide at the **visitor center** (✉ *220 N. Santa Fe St.* ☎ *559/734–5876* ⊘ *Mon. 10–5, Tues.–Fri. 8:30–5).*

The **Chinese Cultural Center,** housed in a pagoda-style building, mounts exhibits about Asian art and culture. ✉ *500 S. Akers Rd., at Hwy. 198* ☎ *559/625–4545* 🏷 *Free* ⊘ *Wed.–Sun. 11–6.*

☙ In oak-shaded **Mooney Grove Park** you can picnic alongside duck ponds, rent a boat for a ride around the lagoon, and view a replica of the famous *End of the Trail* statue. The original, designed by James Earl Fraser for the 1915 Panama-Pacific International Exposition, is now in the Cowboy Hall of Fame in Oklahoma. ✉ *27000 S. Mooney Blvd., 5 mi south of downtown* ☎ *559/733–6291* 🏷 *$6 per car, free in winter (dates vary)* ⊘ *Late May–early Sept., weekdays 8–7, weekends 8 AM–9 PM; early Sept.–Oct. and Mar.–late May, Mon., Thurs., and Fri. 8–5, weekends 8–7; Nov.–Feb., Thurs.–Mon. 8–5.*

The indoor-outdoor **Tulare County Museum** contains several re-created environments from the pioneer era. Also on display are Yokuts tribal artifacts (basketry, arrowheads, clamshell-necklace currency) as well as saddles, guns, dolls, quilts, and gowns. A $1.45 million replacement building is expected to open in 2009. ✉ *Mooney Grove Park, 27000 S.*

Mooney Blvd., 5 mi south of downtown ☎559/733–6616 ✉*Free with park entrance fee of $6* ☉ *Weekdays 10–4, weekends 1–4.*

Trails at the 324-acre **Kaweah Oaks Preserve**, a wildlife sanctuary off the main road to Sequoia National Park (⇨ *Chapter 13*), lead past majestic valley oak, sycamore, cottonwood, and willow trees. Among the 134 bird species you might spot are hawks, hummingbirds, and great blue herons. Lizards, coyotes, and cottontails also live here. ✉*Follow Hwy. 198 for 7 mi east of Visalia, turn north on Rd. 182, and proceed ½ mi to gate on left side* ☎559/738–0211 ∰*www.sequoiariverlands.org* ✉*Free* ☉ *Daily sunrise–sunset.*

WHERE TO STAY & EAT

$$–$$$$ ✕**The Vintage Press.** Built in 1966, the Vintage Press is the best restau-
Fodor'sChoice   rant in the Central Valley. Cut-glass doors and bar fixtures decorate the
★   artfully designed rooms. The California–Continental cuisine includes dishes such as crispy veal sweetbreads with a port-wine sauce, and a bacon-wrapped filet mignon stuffed with mushrooms. The chocolate Grand Marnier cake is a standout among the homemade desserts and ice creams. The wine list has more than 900 selections. ✉*216 N. Willis St.* ☎559/733–3033 ∰*www.thevintagepress.com* ▤*AE, DC, MC, V.*

¢–$$$ ✕**Henry Salazar's.** Traditional Mexican food with a contemporary twist is served at this restaurant that uses fresh ingredients from local farms. Bring your appetite if you expect to finish the Burrito Fantastico, a large flour tortilla stuffed with your choice of meat, beans, and chili sauce, and smothered with melted Monterey Jack cheese. Another signature dish is grilled salmon with lemon-butter sauce. Colorfully painted walls, soft reflections from candles in wall niches, and color-coordinated tablecloths and napkins make the atmosphere cozy and restful. ✉*123 W. Main St.* ☎559/741–7060 ▤*AE, D, MC, V.*

HANFORD

★   *20 mi west of Visalia on Hwy. 198; 43 mi north of Colonel Allensworth State Historic Park on Hwy. 43.*

Founded in 1877 as a Southern Pacific Railroad stop, Hanford had one of California's largest Chinatowns—the Chinese came to help build the railroads and stayed on to farm.

You can take a self-guided walking tour with the help of a free brochure, or take a driving tour in a restored 1930s Studebaker fire truck ($35 for up to 15 people) through the **Hanford Conference & Visitor's Agency** (☎559/582–5024 ∰*www.visithanford.com*). One tour explores the restored buildings of Courthouse Square, whose art-deco Hanford Auditorium is a visual standout; another heads to narrow China Alley. If you have specific interests, a tour can also be designed for you.

The **Hanford Carnegie Museum** displays fashions, furnishings, toys, and military artifacts that tell the region's story. The living-history museum is inside the former Carnegie Library, a Romanesque building dating from 1905. ✉*109 E. 8th St.* ☎559/584–1367 ✉*$1* ☉ *Tues.–Fri. noon–3, Sat. noon–4.*

A first-floor museum in the 1893 **Taoist Temple** displays photos, furnishings, and kitchenware from Hanford's once-bustling Chinatown. The second-floor temple, largely unchanged for a century, contains altars, carvings, and ceremonial staves. You can visit as part of a guided tour at noon on the first Saturday of the month, or by appointment. ⊠*12 China Alley* ☎*559/582–4508* ☜*Free; donations welcome.*

WHERE TO STAY & EAT

$–$$$ ✕**The Purple Potato.** This modern, colorful restaurant has become what locals say is the best restaurant in town. The broad menu, which includes steaks, pasta, and poultry, draws raves for its shrimp scampi and pan-seared scallops. The wine list is extensive. ⊠*A few blocks west of downtown, 601 W. 7th St.* ☎*559/587–4568* ☰*AE, D, MC, V* ☉*No lunch weekends.*

¢–$ ✕**La Fiesta.** Mexican-American families, farmworkers, and farmers all eat here, polishing off traditional Mexican dishes such as enchiladas and tacos. The Fiesta Special—for two or more—includes nachos, garlic shrimp, shrimp in a spicy red sauce, clams, and two pieces of top sirloin. ⊠*106 N. Green St.* ☎*559/583–8775* ☰*AE, D, MC, V.*

¢–$$ ☷**Irwin Street Inn.** This inn is one of the few lodgings in the valley that
★ warrants a detour. Four tree-shaded, restored Victorian homes have been converted into spacious accommodations with comfortable rooms and suites. Most have antique armoires, dark-wood detailing, lead-glass windows, and four-poster beds; bathrooms have old-fashioned tubs, brass fixtures, and marble basins. **Pros:** Big rooms and bathrooms; funky decor; very unlike chain hotels. **Cons:** Mattresses can be uncomfortable; not much to do in town. ⊠*522 N. Irwin St.* ☎*559/583–8000* ➥*24 rooms, 3 suites* ♿*In-hotel: no elevator, restaurant, pool* ☰*AE, D, DC, MC, V* ❢*CP.*

14

FRESNO

35 mi north of Hanford via Hwys. 43 and 99 north.

Sprawling Fresno, with more than 480,000 people, is the center of the richest agricultural county in the United States. Cotton, grapes, and tomatoes are among the major crops; poultry and milk are also important. About 75 ethnic groups, including Armenians, Laotians, and Indians, call Fresno home. The city has a vibrant arts scene, several public parks, and an abundance of low-price restaurants. The Tower District—with its chic restaurants, coffeehouses, and boutiques—is the trendy spot. Pulitzer Prize–winning playwright and novelist William

BLOSSOM TRAIL

This 62-mi self-guided driving tour takes in Fresno-area orchards, citrus groves, and vineyards during spring blossom season. Pick up a route map at the **Fresno City & County Convention and Visitors Bureau** (⊠*848 M St., Fresno* ☎*559/233–0836 or 800/788–0836* ⊕*www.fresnocvb.org*). The Blossom Trail passes through small towns and past rivers, lakes, and canals. The most colorful and aromatic time to go is from late February to mid-March, when almond, plum, apple, orange, lemon, apricot, and peach blossoms shower the landscape with shades of white, pink, and red.

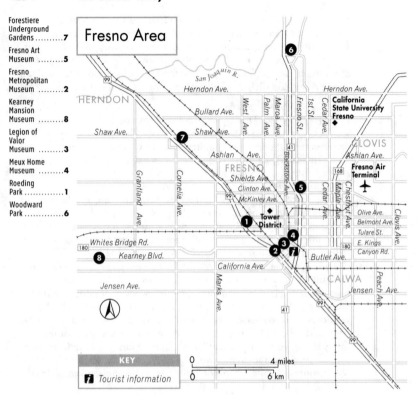

Fresno Area

Saroyan (*The Time of Your Life, The Human Comedy*) was born here in 1908.

❶ Tree-shaded **Roeding Park** is a place of respite on hot summer days; it has picnic areas, playgrounds, tennis courts, horseshoe pits, and a zoo. The most striking exhibit at **Chaffee Zoological Gardens** (☎*559/498–2671* ⊕*www.chaffeezoo.org* ᴬ*$7* ⊙*Feb.–Oct., daily 9–4; Nov.–Jan., daily 10–3*) is the tropical rain forest, where you'll encounter exotic birds along the paths and bridges. Elsewhere on the grounds you'll find tigers, grizzly bears, sea lions, tule elk, camels, elephants, and hooting siamangs. Also here are a high-tech reptile house and a petting zoo. A train, little race cars, paddleboats, and other rides for kids are among the amusements that operate March through November at **Playland** (☎*559/233–3980* ⊙*Wed.–Fri. 11–5, weekends 10–6*). Children can explore attractions with fairy-tale themes at Rotary **Storyland** (☎*559/264–2235* ⊙*Weekdays 11–5, weekends 10–6*), which is also open March through November. ⊠*Olive and Belmont Aves.* ☎*559/498–1551* ᴬ*$1 per vehicle at park entrance, Playland rides require tokens, Storyland $4.*

❷ The **Fresno Metropolitan Museum,** whose delayed renovation project was expected to be completed by late 2008, mounts art, history, and hands-on science exhibits, many of them quite innovative. The William Saroyan History Gallery presents a riveting introduction in words and pictures to the author's life and times. ✉ *1515 Van Ness Ave.* ☎ *559/441–1444* ⊕ *www.fresnomet.org* 🎫 *$8* ⏱ *Tues., Wed., and Fri.–Sun. 11–5.*

❸ The **Legion of Valor Museum** is a real find for military-history buffs of all ages. It has German bayonets and daggers, a Japanese Namby pistol, a Gatling gun, and an extensive collection of Japanese, German, and American uniforms. The staff is extremely enthusiastic. ✉ *2425 Fresno St.* ☎ *559/498–0510* ⊕ *www.legionofvalor.com* 🎫 *Free* ⏱ *Mon.– Sat. 10–3.*

❹ Inside a restored 1889 Victorian, the **Meux Home Museum** displays furnishings typical of early Fresno. Guided tours proceed from the front parlor to the backyard carriage house. ✉ *Tulare and R Sts.* ☎ *559/233–8007* ⊕ *www.meux.mus.ca.us* 🎫 *$5* ⏱ *Fri.–Sun. noon–3:30.*

❺ The **Fresno Art Museum** exhibits American, Mexican, and French art; highlights of the permanent collection include pre-Columbian works and graphic art from the postimpressionist period. The 152-seat Bonner Auditorium is the site of lectures, films, and concerts. ✉ *Radio Park, 2233 N. 1st St.* ☎ *559/441–4221* ⊕ *www.fresnoartmuseum.org* 🎫 *$4; free Sun.* ⏱ *Tues., Wed., and Fri.–Sun. 11–5, Thurs. 11–8.*

❻ ★ **Woodward Park,** the Central Valley's largest urban park with 300 acres of jogging trails, picnic areas, and playgrounds in the northern reaches of the city, is especially pretty in spring, when plum and cherry trees, magnolias, and camellias bloom. Outdoor concerts take place in summer. The **Shinzen Friendship Garden** has a teahouse, a koi pond, arched bridges, a waterfall, and Japanese art. ✉ *Audubon Dr. and Friant Rd.* ☎ *559/621–2900* 🎫 *$3 per car Feb.–Oct.; additional $3 for Shinzen Garden* ⏱ *Apr.–Oct., daily 7 AM–10 PM; Nov.–Mar., daily 7–7.*

❼ ☾ ★ Sicilian immigrant Baldasare Forestiere spent four decades (1906–46) carving out the **Forestiere Underground Gardens,** a subterranean realm of rooms, tunnels, grottoes, alcoves, and arched passageways that once extended for more than 10 acres between Highway 99 and busy, mall-pocked Shaw Avenue. Only a fraction of Forestiere's prodigious output is on view, but you can tour his underground living quarters, including bedrooms (one with a fireplace), the kitchen, living room, and bath, as well as a fishpond and auto tunnel. Skylights allow exotic full-grown fruit trees, including one that bears seven kinds of citrus as a result of grafting, to flourish more than 20 feet belowground. The gardens were extensively renovated in 2007. ✉ *5021 W. Shaw Ave., 2 blocks east of Hwy. 99* ☎ *559/271–0734* ⊕ *www.undergroundgardens.info* 🎫 *$10* ⏱ *Tours weekends 11–2 year-round; also Fridays during the summer. Call for other tour times.*

❽ The drive along palm-lined Kearney Boulevard is one of the best reasons to visit the **Kearney Mansion Museum,** which stands in shaded 225-acre **Kearney Park.** The century-old home of M. Theo Kearney, Fresno's onetime "raisin king," is accessible only by taking a guided 45-minute

14

tour. ✉*7160 W. Kearney Blvd., 6 mi west of Fresno* 📞*559/441–0862* 🎫*Museum $5; park $4 (waived for museum visitors)* 🕐*Park 7 AM–10 PM; museum tours Fri.–Sun. at 1, 2, and 3.*

WHERE TO STAY & EAT

$–$$$ ✕**Tahoe Joe's.** This restaurant is known for its steaks—rib eye, strip, or filet mignon. Other selections include the slow-roasted prime rib, center-cut pork chops, and chicken breast served with a whiskey-peppercorn sauce. The baked potato that accompanies almost every dish is loaded table-side with your choice of butter, sour cream, chives, and bacon bits. Tahoe Joe's has two Fresno locations. ✉*7006 N. Cedar Ave.* 📞*559/299–9740* ✉*2700 W. Shaw Ave.* 📞*559/277–8028* 🌐*www.tahoejoes.com* ⚓*Reservations not accepted* 💳*AE, D, MC, V* 🕐*No lunch.*

$–$$ ✕**La Rocca's Ristorante Italiano.** The sauces that top these pasta and meat dishes will make your taste buds sing. The rich tomato sauce, which comes with or without meat, is fresh and tangy. The marsala sauce—served on either chicken or veal—is rich but not overpowering. Typical red-sauce dishes such as spaghetti, rigatoni, and lasagna are offered here, but you'll also be happily surprised with more adventurous offerings such as the bow-tie pasta with cream, peas, bacon, tomato sauce, and olive oil. Pizzas also are served. ✉*6735 N. First St.* 📞*559/431–1278* 💳*AE, MC, V* 🕐*No lunch weekends.*

$$ 🏨**Piccadilly Inn Shaw.** This two-story property has 7½ attractively landscaped acres and a big swimming pool. The sizable rooms have king- and queen-size beds, robes, ironing boards, and coffeemakers; some have fireplaces and wireless Internet access. **Pros:** Big rooms; nice pool; best lodging option in town. **Cons:** Some visitors complain of a smell; some rooms are showing wear; neighborhood is somewhat sketchy. ✉*2305 W. Shaw Ave.* 📞*559/226–3850* 📠*559/226–2448* 🌐*www.piccadillyinn.com* ⤴*194 rooms, 5 suites* ♿*In-room: refrigerator, dial-up, Wi-Fi. In-hotel: restaurant, pool, gym, laundry facilities, laundry service, no-smoking rooms* 💳*AE, D, DC, MC, V.*

NIGHTLIFE & THE ARTS

The **Tower Theatre for the Performing Arts** (✉*815 E. Olive Ave.* 📞*559/485–9050* 🌐*www.towertheatrefresno.org*) has given its name to the trendy Tower District of theaters, clubs, restaurants, and cafés. The restored 1930s art-deco movie house presents theater, ballet, concerts, and other cultural events year-round.

SPORTS & THE OUTDOORS

Kings River Expeditions (✉*211 N. Van Ness Ave.* 📞*559/233–4881 or 800/846–3674* 🌐*www.kingsriver.com*) arranges one- and two-day whitewater rafting trips on the Kings River. **Wild Water Adventures** (✉*11413 E. Shaw Ave., Clovis* 📞*559/299–9453 or 800/564–9453* 🌐*www.wild*

OLD TOWN CLOVIS

Old Town Clovis (✉*Upper Clovis Ave., Clovis*) is an area of restored brick buildings with numerous antiques shops and art galleries (along with restaurants and saloons). Be warned, though—not much here is open on Sunday. To get here, head east on Fresno's Herndon Avenue about 10 mi, and then turn right onto Clovis Avenue.

water.net ✉*$26, $17 after 3* PM), a 52-acre water park about 10 mi east of Fresno, is open from late May to early September.

NORTH CENTRAL VALLEY

FROM MERCED TO LODI

MERCED

50 mi north of Fresno on Hwy. 99.

Thanks to a branch of the University of California opening in 2005 and an aggressive community redevelopment plan, the downtown of county seat Merced is coming back to life. The transformation is not yet complete, but there are promising signs: a brewpub, several boutiques, a multiplex, the restoration of numerous historic buildings, and foot traffic won back from outlying strip malls.

Even if you don't go inside, be sure to swing by the **Merced County Courthouse Museum.** The three-story former courthouse, built in 1875, is a striking example of Victorian Italianate style. The upper two floors are a museum of early Merced history. Highlights include ornate restored courtrooms and an 1870 Chinese temple with carved redwood altars. ✉*21st and N Sts.* ☎*209/723–2401* ⊕*www.mercedmuseum.org* ✉*Free* ⊙ *Wed.–Sun. 1–4.*

The **Merced Multicultural Arts Center** displays paintings, sculpture, and photography. The Big Valley Arts & Culture Festival, which celebrates the area's ethnic diversity and children's creativity, is held here in late September or early October. ✉*645 W. Main St.* ☎*209/388–1090* ⊕*www.artsmerced.org* ✉*Free* ⊙ *Weekdays 9–5, Sat. 10–2.*

WHERE TO STAY & EAT

$$–$$$ ✕**The Branding Iron.** Beef is what this restaurant is all about. It's a favorite among farmers and ranchers looking for a place to refuel as they travel through cattle country. Try the juicy cut of prime rib paired with potato and Parmesan-cheese bread. California cattle brands decorate the walls, and when the weather is nice, cooling breezes refresh diners on the outdoor patio. ✉*640 W. 16th St.* ☎*209/722–1822* ⊕*www.thebrandingiron-merced.com* ▤*AE, MC, V* ⊙*No lunch weekends.*

$–$$$ ✕**DeAngelo's.** This restaurant isn't just the best in Merced—it's one ★ of the best in the Central Valley. Chef Vincent DeAngelo, a graduate of the Culinary Institute of America, brings his considerable skill to everything from basic ravioli to calamari steak topped with two prawns. Half the restaurant is occupied by a new bar-bistro with its own menu, which includes brick-oven pizza. The delicious crusty bread comes from the Golden Sheath bakery, in Watsonville. ✉*350 W. Main St.* ☎*209/383–3020* ⊕*www.deangelosrestaurant.com* ▤*AE, D, MC, V* ⊙*No lunch weekends.*

$$ ▦**Hooper House Bear Creek Inn.** This 1931 neocolonial home stands regally at the corner of M Street. The immaculately landscaped 1½-acre property has fruit trees and grapevines, and the house is appointed in

14

well-chosen antiques and big, soft beds. Breakfast (which can be served in your room) is hearty and imaginative, featuring locally grown foods such as fried sweet potatoes and black walnuts. Across the street is a walking–bicycling trail that runs for a few miles beside the creek. **Pros:** Historic charm; friendly staff; good breakfast. **Cons:** Front rooms can be noisy. ⊠*575 W. N. Bear Creek Dr., at M St.,* ☎*209/723–3991* ⊕*www.hooperhouse.com* ⌁*3 rooms, 1 cottage* ⌂*In-room: dial-up. In-hotel: no elevator, no-smoking rooms* ☰*AE, D, MC, V* ⏧*BP.*

SPORTS & THE OUTDOORS

At **Lake Yosemite Regional Park** (⊠*N. Lake Rd. off Yosemite Ave., 5 mi northeast of Merced* ☎*209/385–7426* ⛁*$6 per car late May–early Sept.*), you can boat, swim, windsurf, water-ski, and fish on a 387-acre reservoir. Paddleboat rentals and picnic areas are available.

MODESTO

38 mi north of Merced on Hwy. 99.

Modesto, a gateway to Yosemite and the southern reaches of the Gold Country, was founded in 1870 to serve the Central Pacific Railroad. The frontier town was originally to be named Ralston, after a railroad baron, but as the story goes, he modestly declined—thus the name Modesto. The Stanislaus County seat, a tree-lined city of 207,000, is perhaps best known as the site of the annual Modesto Invitational Track Meet and Relays and birthplace of film producer-director George Lucas, creator of the *Star Wars* film series.

The **Modesto Arch** (⊠*9th and I Sts.*) bears the city's motto: WATER, WEALTH, CONTENTMENT, HEALTH.

The prosperity that water brought to Modesto has attracted people from all over the world. The city holds a well-attended **International Heritage Festival** (☎*209/521–3852*) in early October that celebrates the cultures, crafts, and cuisines of many nationalities.

You can witness the everyday abundance of the Modesto area at the **Blue Diamond Growers Store** (⊠*4800 Sisk Rd.* ☎*209/545–3222*), which offers free samples, shows a film about almond growing, and sells many roasts and flavors of almonds, as well as other nuts.

★ A rancher and banker built the 1883 **McHenry Mansion**, the city's sole surviving original Victorian home. The Italianate mansion has been decorated to reflect Modesto life in the late 19th century. Its period-appropriate wallpaper is especially impressive. ⊠*15th and I Sts.* ☎*209/577–5341* ⊕*www.mchenrymuseum.org* ⛁*Free* ☉*Sun.–Thurs. 12:30–4.*

The **McHenry Museum** is a repository of early Modesto and Stanislaus County memorabilia, including re-creations of an old-time dentist's office, a blacksmith's shop, a one-room schoolhouse, an extensive doll collection, and a general store stocked with period goods such as hair crimpers and corsets. ⊠*14th and I Sts.* ☎*209/577–5366* ⊕*www.mchenrymuseum.org* ⛁*Free* ☉*Tues.–Sun. noon–4.*

WHERE TO STAY & EAT

$$$-$$$$ ✕**Hazel's Elegant Dining.** Hazel's is *the* special-occasion restaurant in Modesto. The seven-course dinners include Continental entrées served with appetizer, soup, salad, pasta, and dessert. Members of the Gallo family, which owns much vineyard land in the Central Valley, eat here often, perhaps because the wine cellar's offerings are so comprehensive. ⊠*431 12th St.* ☎*209/578–3463* ⊕*www.hazelsmodesto.com* ▤*AE, D, DC, MC, V* ⊘*Closed Sun. and Mon. No lunch Sat.*

$$-$$$ ✕**Tresetti's World Caffe.** An intimate setting with white tablecloths and contemporary art draws diners to this eatery—part wineshop (with 500-plus selections), part restaurant—with a seasonally changing menu. For a small supplemental fee, the staff will uncork any wine you select from the shop. The Cajun-style crab cakes, served for lunch year-round, are outstanding. ⊠*927 11th St.* ☎*209/572–2990* ⊕*www. tresetti.com* ▤*AE, D, DC, MC, V* ⊘*Closed Sun.*

$-$$ ✕**Hero's Sports Lounge & Pizza Co.** Modesto's renowned microbrewery makes Hero's (formerly St. Stan's) beers. The 14 on tap include the delicious Whistle Stop pale ale and Red Sky ale. The restaurant is casual and serves good corned-beef sandwiches loaded with sauerkraut as well as a tasty beer-sausage nibbler. ⊠*821 L St.* ☎*209/524–2337* ▤*AE, MC, V* ⊘*Closed Sun.*

¢ ⌹**Best Western Town House Lodge.** The downtown location is the primary draw for this hotel. The county's historical library is across the street, and the McHenry Mansion and the McHenry Museum are nearby. All rooms come equipped with a coffeemaker, hair dryer, and iron. **Pros:** Perfect location, recently renovated. **Cons:** Staff's knowledge of town is sometimes limited. ⊠*909 16th St.* ☎*209/524–7261 or 800/772–7261* ⊕*www.bestwesterncalifornia.com* ⇆*59 rooms* ⌂*In-room: refrigerator, Wi-Fi. In-hotel: pool, parking (no fee), no-smoking rooms* ▤*AE, D, DC, MC, V* ⦿|*CP.*

OAKDALE

15 mi northeast of Modesto on Hwy. 108.

Oakdale is a bit off the beaten path from Modesto.

You can sample the wares at **Oakdale Cheese & Specialties** (⊠*10040 Hwy. 120* ☎*209/848–3139* ⊕*www.oakdalecheese.com*), which has tastings (try the aged Gouda) and cheese-making tours. There's a picnic area and a petting zoo.

If you're in Oakdale—formerly home of a Hershey's chocolate factory—the third weekend in May, check out the **Oakdale Chocolate Festival** (☎*209/847–2244* ◖*$4*), which attracts 50,000 to 60,000 people each year. The event's main attraction is Chocolate Avenue, where vendors proffer cakes, cookies, ice cream, fudge, and cheesecake.

☾ The featured attraction at the **Knights Ferry Recreation Area** is the 355-
★ foot-long Knights Ferry covered bridge. The beautiful and haunting structure, built in 1863, crosses the Stanislaus River near the ruins of an old gristmill. The park has picnic and barbecue areas along the

riverbanks, as well as three campgrounds accessible only by boat. You can hike, fish, canoe, and raft on 4 mi of rapids. ⊠*Corps of Engineers Park, 17968 Covered Bridge Rd., Knights Ferry, 12 mi east of Oakdale via Hwy. 108* ☎*209/881–3517* 🖼*Free* ☺*Daily dawn–dusk.*

SPORTS & THE OUTDOORS

Rafting on the Stanislaus River is a popular activity near Oakdale. **River Journey** (⊠*14842 Orange Blossom Rd.* ☎*209/847–4671 or 800/292–2938* ⊕*www.riverjourney.com*) will take you out for a few hours of fun. To satisfy your white-water or flat-water cravings, contact **Sunshine River Adventures** (☎*209/848–4800 or 800/829–7238* ⊕*www.raftadventure.com*).

> ## ASPARAGUS FEST
>
> If you're here in late April, don't miss the **Stockton Asparagus Festival** (☎*209/644-3740* ⊕*www.asparagusfest.com*), at the Downtown Stockton Waterfront. The highlight of the festival is the food, with more than 500 vendor booths; organizers try to prove that almost any dish can be made with asparagus.

STOCKTON

29 mi north of Modesto on Hwy. 99.

California's first inland port—connected since 1933 to San Francisco via a 60-mi-long deepwater channel—is wedged between I–5 and Highway 99, on the eastern end of the Sacramento River delta. Stockton, founded during the gold rush as a way station for miners traveling from San Francisco to the Mother Lode and now a city of 290,000, is where many of the valley's agricultural products begin their journey to other parts of the world. In recent years, the city has made significant strides in sprucing up its riverfront area downtown, including a spiffy minor-league baseball park for the Stockton Ports.

★ The **Haggin Museum,** in pretty Victory Park, has one of the Central Valley's finest art collections. Highlights include landscapes by Albert Bierstadt and Thomas Moran, a still life by Paul Gauguin, a Native American gallery, and an Egyptian mummy. ⊠*1201 N. Pershing Ave.* ☎*209/940–6300* ⊕*www.hagginmuseum.org* 🖼*$5* ☺*Wed.–Sun. 1:30–5; open until 9 on 1st and 3rd Thurs.*

WHERE TO EAT

$$$–$$$$ ✕**Le Bistro.** This upscale restaurant serves modern interpretations of classic French cuisine—steak tartare, Grand Marnier soufflé—and a recent change in chefs has enlivened the dishes. ⊠*Marina Center Mall, 3121 W. Benjamin Holt Dr., off I–5, behind Lyon's* ☎*209/951–0885* ⊟*AE, D, DC, MC, V* ☺*No lunch weekends.*

¢–$ ✕**On Lock Sam.** This Stockton landmark (it's been operating since 1898) is in a modern pagoda-style building with framed Chinese prints on the walls, a garden outside one window, and a sparkling bar area. One touch of old-time Chinatown remains: a few booths have curtains that can be drawn for complete privacy. The Cantonese food is among the best in the valley. ✉*333 S. Sutter St.* ☎*209/466–4561* ▭*AE, D, MC, V.*

SPORTS & THE OUTDOORS

Several companies rent houseboats (of various sizes, usually for three, four, or seven days) on the Sacramento River delta waterways near Stockton. **Herman & Helen's Marina** (✉*15135 W. 8 Mile Rd.* ☎*209/951–4634*) rents houseboats with hot tubs and fireplaces. **Paradise Point Marina** (✉*8095 Rio Blanco Rd.* ☎*209/952–1000*) rents a variety of watercraft, including patio boats.

LODI

14

13 mi north of Stockton and 34 mi south of Sacramento on Hwy. 99.

Founded on agriculture, Lodi was once the watermelon capital of the country. Today it's surrounded by fields of asparagus, pumpkins, beans, safflowers, sunflowers, kiwis, melons, squashes, peaches, and cherries. It also has become a wine-grape capital of sorts, producing zinfandel, merlot, cabernet sauvignon, chardonnay, and sauvignon blanc grapes. For years California wineries have built their reputations on the juice of grapes grown around Lodi. Now the area that includes Lodi, Lockeford, and Woodbridge is a wine destination in itself, boasting about 40 wineries, many offering tours and tastings. Lodi still retains an old rural charm, despite its population of nearly 70,000. You can stroll downtown or visit a wildlife refuge, all the while benefiting from a Sacramento River delta breeze that keeps this microclimate cooler in summer than anyplace else in the area.

☺ The 258-acre **Micke Grove Regional Park,** an oak-shaded county park 5 mi north of Stockton off Highway 99, includes a Japanese tea garden, picnic areas, children's play areas, softball fields, an agricultural museum, and a water-play feature. (Micke Grove Golf Links, an 18-hole course, is next to the park.) Geckos and frogs, black-and-white ruffed lemurs, and hissing cockroaches found only on Madagascar inhabit "An Island Lost in Time," an exhibit at the **Micke Grove Zoo** (☎*209/953–8840* ⊕*www.mgzoo.com* ✑*$2* ⊘*Daily 10–5*). California sea lions, Chinese alligators and a walk-through Mediterranean aviary are among the highlights of this compact facility. Most rides and attractions at the park's **Fun Town at Micke Grove** (☎*209/369–7330* ⊘*Mid-May–Labor Day, daily 11–dusk*), a family-oriented amusement park, are geared to children. ✉*11793 N. Micke Grove Rd.* ☎*209/953–8800* ✑*Parking $3 weekdays, $5 weekends and holidays.*

Stop by the **Lodi Wine & Visitor Center** (✉*2545 W. Turner Rd.* ☎*209/365–0621*) to see exhibits on Lodi's viticultural history, pick up a map of area wineries, and even buy wine.

★ One of the standout wineries in the area is **Jessie's Grove** (✉*1973 W. Turner Rd.* ☎*209/368–0880* ⊕*www.jgwinery.com* ⊘*Daily 11–5*), a wooded horse ranch and vineyard that has been in the same family since 1863. In addition to producing outstanding old-vine zinfandels, it presents blues concerts on various Saturdays June through October.

At the **Woodbridge Winery** (✉*5950 E. Woodbridge Rd., Acampo* ☎*209/365–8139* ⊕*www.woodbridgewines.com* ⊘*Tues.–Sun. 10:30–4:30*), you can take a free 30-minute tour of the vineyard and barrel room. The label's legendary founder, Robert Mondavi, died in 2008 at age 94.

At its homey facility, kid-friendly **Phillips Farms Michael-David Winery** (✉*4580 W. Hwy. 12* ☎*209/368–7384* ⊕*www.lodivineyards.com*) offers tastings from its affordable Michael-David vineyard. You can also cut flowers from the garden, pet the animals, eat breakfast or lunch at the café, and buy Phillips' and other local produce.

Vino Piazza (✉*12470 Locke Rd., Lockeford* ☎*209/727–9770* ⊕*www. vinopiazza.com*) is a sort of winery village, with 10 independent wineries, each with production facilities and separate tasting rooms. An on-site restaurant, theater group, and frequent special events make this a fun, all-in-one destination.

WHERE TO STAY & EAT

$$–$$$$ ✕**Rosewood Bar & Grill.** In downtown Lodi, Rosewood offers fine dining without formality. Operated by the folks at Wine & Roses Hotel and Restaurant, this low-key spot serves American fare with a twist, such as meat loaf wrapped in bacon, and daily seafood specials. The bar has a full-service menu, and live music on Friday and Saturday. ✉*28 S. School St.* ☎*209/369–0470* ⊕*www.rosewoodbarandgrill.com* ▭*AE, D, DC, MC, V* ⊘*No lunch*.

$ ✕**Habanero Hots.** If your mouth can handle the heat promised by the restaurant's name, try the tamales. If you want to take it easy on your taste buds, stick with the rest of the menu. ✉*1024 E. Victor Rd.* ☎*209/369–3791* ⊕*www.habanerohots.com* ▭*AE, MC, V.*

$$$–$$$$ ✕🏨 **Wine & Roses Hotel and Restaurant.** Set on 7 acres amid a tapestry of
★ informal gardens, this hotel has cultivated a sense of refinement typically associated with Napa or Carmel. Rooms are decorated in rich earth tones, and linens are imported from Italy. Some rooms have fireplaces; all have coffeemakers, irons, and hair dryers. Some of the bathrooms even have TVs. The restaurant ($$$–$$$$) is *the* place to eat in Lodi. The Sunday champagne brunch buffet includes ham, prime rib, and made-to-order crepes and omelets. Afterward, consider heading to the spa for a facial or herbal body scrub. **Pros:** Luxurious; relaxing; quiet. **Cons:** Expensive; isolated; some guests have said the walls are thin. ✉*2505 W. Turner Rd.* ☎*209/334–6988* ⊕*www.winerose.com* ↪*47 rooms, 4 suites* ⌂*In-room: refrigerator, dial-up, Wi-Fi. In-hotel: restaurant, room service, bar, spa, laundry service, no-smoking rooms* ▭*AE, D, DC, MC, V* ⊙*CP.*

$$–$$$ 🏨 **The Inn at Locke House.** Built in 1865, this B&B was a pioneer doctor's
★ family home and is on the National Register of Historic Places. Airy rooms with garden views are filled with Locke family antique furnishings, and all have fireplaces and private bathrooms. The centerpiece of the three-level Water Tower Suite is a queen canopy bed; it also has a deck and a private sitting room at the top of the tower. Refreshments are served in the parlor, where there's also an old pump organ. Breakfasts made with local organic products are served in the carriage-

way. **Pros:** Friendly; quiet; lovely. **Cons:** Remote; can be hard to find. ✉19960 N. Elliott Rd., Lockeford ☎209/727–5715 ⊕www.theinnat lockehouse.com ⇔4 rooms, 1 suite ♨In-room: Wi-Fi, no TV. In-hotel: no elevator, no-smoking rooms ☐AE, D, DC, MC, V ⑩BP.

SPORTS & THE OUTDOORS

Even locals need respite from the heat of Central Valley summers, and **Lodi Lake Park** (✉1101 W. Turner Rd. ☎209/333–6742 ✉$5) is where they find it. The banks, shaded by grand old elms and oaks, are much cooler than other spots in town. Swimming, bird-watching, and picnicking are possibilities, as is renting a kayak, canoe, or pedal boat ($2 to $4 per half hour, Tuesday through Sunday, late May through early September only).

THE CENTRAL VALLEY ESSENTIALS

To research prices, get advice from other travelers, and book travel arrangements, visit www.fodors.com.

TRANSPORTATION

BY AIR

Fresno Yosemite International Airport is serviced by Alaska, Allegiant, American and American Eagle, Delta, ExpressJet, Horizon, Mexicana, Skywest, United, United Express, and US Airways. Kern County Airport at Meadows Field is serviced by Delta, ExpressJet, United Express, and US Airways. United Express flies from Los Angeles and San Francisco to Modesto City Airport, and US Airways flies from Las Vegas to Visalia Municipal Airport. *See Air Travel in California Essentials for airline phone numbers.*

Contacts **Fresno Yosemite International Airport** (✉4995 E. Clinton Way, Fresno ☎559/621–4500 ⊕www.fresno.gov/flyfresno). **Kern County Airport at Meadows Field** (✉1401 Skyway Dr., Bakersfield ☎661/391–1800 ⊕www.meadowsfield. com). **Modesto City Airport** (✉617 Airport Way, Modesto ☎209/577–5319 ⊕www.modairport.com). **Visalia Municipal Airport** (✉9501 W. Airport Dr., Visalia ☎559/713–4201 ⊕www.flyvisalia.com).

BY BUS

Greyhound provides service between major valley cities. Orange Belt Stages provides bus service, including Amtrak connections, to many valley locations.

Contacts **Greyhound** (☎800/231–2222 ⊕www.greyhound.com). **Orange Belt Stages** (☎800/266–7433 ⊕www.orangebelt.com).

BY CAR

Highway 99 is the main route between the valley's major cities and towns. I–5 runs roughly parallel to it to the west but misses the major population centers; its main use is for quick access from San Francisco or Los Angeles. Major roads that connect I–5 with Highway 99 are Highways 58 (to Bakersfield), 198 (to Hanford and Visalia), 152 (to

Chowchilla, via Los Banos), 140 (to Merced), 132 (to Modesto), and 120 (to Manteca). For road conditions, call the California Department of Transportation hotline.

Contacts **California Department of Transportation** (☎ *800/266–6883 or 916/445–1534*).

BY TRAIN

Amtrak's daily *San Joaquin* travels among Bakersfield, San Jose, and Oakland, stopping in Hanford, Fresno, Madera, Merced, Modesto, and Stockton.

Contacts **Amtrak** (☎ *800/872-7245* ⊕ *www.amtrakcalifornia.com*).

CONTACTS & RESOURCES

EMERGENCIES

In an emergency dial 911.

Hospitals **Bakersfield Memorial Hospital** (✉ *420 34th St., Bakersfield* ☎ *661/327-4647*). **St. Joseph's Medical Center** (✉ *1800 N. California St., Stockton* ☎ *209/467-6700*). **University Medical Center** (✉ *445 S. Cedar Ave., Fresno* ☎ *559/459-4000*).

VISITOR INFORMATION

Contacts **Fresno City & County Convention and Visitors Bureau** (✉ *848 M St., Fresno* ☎ *559/445-8300 or 800/788-0836* ⊕ *www.fresnocvb.org*). **Greater Bakersfield Convention & Visitors Bureau** (✉ *515 Truxton Ave., Bakersfield* ☎ *661/325-5051 or 866/425-7353* ⊕ *www.bakersfieldcvb.org*). **Hanford Visitor Agency** (✉ *200 Santa Fe Ave., Suite D, Hanford* ☎ *559/582-5024* ⊕ *www. visithanford.com*). **Kern County Board of Trade** (✉ *2101 Oak St., Bakersfield* ☎ *661/500-5376 or 800/500-5376* ⊕ *www.visitkern.com*). **Lodi Conference and Visitors Bureau** (✉ *2545 W. Turner Dr., Lodi* ☎ *209/365-1195 or 800/798-1810* ⊕ *www.visitlodi.com*). **Merced Conference and Visitors Bureau** (✉ *710 W. 16th St., Merced* ☎ *209/384-2791 or 800/446-5353* ⊕ *www.yosemite-gateway.org*). **Modesto Convention and Visitors Bureau** (✉ *1150 9th St., Suite C, Modesto* ☎ *209/526-5588 or 888/640-8467* ⊕ *www.visitmodesto.com*). **Stockton Visitors Bureau** (✉ *46 W. Fremont St., Stockton* ☎ *209/547-2770 or 888/778-6258* ⊕ *www.visitstockton.org*). **Visalia Chamber of Commerce and Visitors Bureau** (✉ *220 N. Santa Fe St., Visalia* ☎ *559/334-0141* ⊕ *www.visaliachamber.org*).

The Central Coast

Santa Barbara

WORD OF MOUTH

"The drive from Cambria to Carmel is one of the most spectacular things one ever can experience. Many people enjoy stopping frequently and hiking or, in my case, taking photos. So I would not plan on blasting up Highway 1."

—youngtom2910

WELCOME TO THE CENTRAL COAST

TOP REASONS TO GO

★ **Incredible nature:** Much of the Central Coast looks as wild and wonderful as it did centuries ago; the area is home to Channel Islands National Park (⇨ *Chapter 5*), two national marine sanctuaries, state parks and beaches, and the vast and rugged Los Padres National Forest.

★ **Edible bounty:** Land and sea provide enough fresh regional foods to satisfy even the savviest of foodies—grapes, strawberries, seafood, olive oil . . . the list goes on and on. Get your fill at countless farmers' markets, wineries, and restaurants.

★ **Outdoor activities:** Kick back and revel in the casual California lifestyle. Surf, golf, kayak, hike, play tennis—or just hang out and enjoy the gorgeous scenery.

★ **Small-town charm, big-city culture:** Small, friendly, uncrowded towns offer an amazing array of cultural amenities. With all the art and history museums, theater, music, and festivals, you might start thinking you're in L.A. or San Francisco.

1 Ventura and Ojai. Ventura is an up-and-coming city with a thriving arts community, miles of beaches, and a vibrant harbor—the gateway to the Channel Islands (⇨ *Chapter 5, Channel Islands National Park*). Eleven miles inland, tiny, artsy Ojai plays host to folks who want to golf, meditate, and commune with tony peers in an idyllic mountain setting.

2 Santa Barbara County. Down-home surfers rub elbows with Hollywood celebrities in sunny, well-scrubbed Santa Barbara, 95 mi north of Los Angeles. Its Spanish–Mexican heritage is reflected in the architectural style of its mission, courthouse, and many homes and public buildings. Wineries, ranches, and small villages dominate the quintessentially Californian landscape in the more rural north county.

Santa Barbara

3 Channel Islands National Park. Home to 145 species of plants and animals found nowhere else on Earth, this relatively undiscovered gem of a park encompasses five islands and a mile of surrounding ocean. (⇨ *Chapter 5, Channel Islands National Park*).

4 San Luis Obispo County. San Luis Obispo, a friendly college town, serves as hub of a burgeoning wine region that stretches nearly 100 mi from Pismo Beach north to Paso Robles; the 230-plus wineries here have earned reputations for high-quality vintages that rival those of northern California.

5 The Big Sur Coastline. Rugged cliffs meet the Pacific for more than 60 mi—one of the most scenic and dramatic drives in the world.

Coast near Big Sur.

GETTING ORIENTED

The Central Coast region begins about 60 mi north of Los Angeles, near the seaside city of Ventura. From there the coastline stretches north about 200 mi, winding through the small cities of Santa Barbara and San Luis Obispo, then north through the small towns of Morro Bay and Cambria to Carmel. The drive through this region, especially the section of Highway 1 from San Simeon to Big Sur, is one of the most scenic in the state.

15

San Lucas

101

G18

San Miguel

aso Robles

46

Templeton 41

Cayucos

Atascadero

58

Morro Bay

1

Los Osos

San Luis Obispo 4

Pismo Beach

Avila Beach

Arroyo Grande

Grover Beach

Nipomo 166

Guadalupe

1

Santa Maria

Orcutt

101

Los Olivos

Lompoc 246

Santa Ynez

S A N   R A F A E L   M T S.

Buellton

Solvang 154

1

101

Goleta

Montecito

Mira Monte

Ojai

2 Santa Barbara

Carpinteria

Oak View

1

3 TO CHANNEL ISLANDS

101

Santa Paula

Ventura

126

Oxnard

0   20 mi

0   30 km

THE CENTRAL COAST PLANNER

When to Go

The Central Coast climate is usually mild throughout the year. If you like to sunbathe and swim in warmer (though still nippy) ocean waters, July and August are the best months to visit. Be aware that this is also high season. Fog often rolls in all along the coastal areas in early summer; you'll need a jacket, especially after sunset, close to the shore. The rains usually come from December through March. From April to early June and in the early fall the weather is almost as fine as in high season, and the pace is less hectic.

Getting Around

Driving is the easiest way to experience the Central Coast. A car gives you the flexibility to stop at scenic vista points along Highway 1, take detours through wine country, and drive to rural lakes and mountains. Traveling north through Ventura County to San Luis Obispo (note that from just south of Ventura up to San Luis Obispo, U.S. 101 and Highway 1 are the same road), you can take in the rolling hills, peaceful valleys, and rugged mountains that stretch for miles along the shore. Amtrak trains link major cities throughout the region.

About the Hotels

There are plenty of lodging options throughout the Central Coast—but expect to pay top dollar for any rooms along the shore, especially in summer. Moderately priced hotels and motels do exist—most just a short drive inland from their higher-price counterparts. Make your reservations as early as possible and take advantage of midweek specials to get the best rates. It's common for hotels to require minimum stays on holidays and some weekends, especially in summer, and to double their rates during festivals and other events.

About the Restaurants

The cuisine in Ventura and Santa Barbara is every bit as eclectic as it is in California's bigger cities; fresh seafood is a standout. The region from Solvang to Big Sur is far enough off the Interstate to ensure that nearly every restaurant or café has its own personality—from chic to down-home and funky. A foodie renaissance has overtaken the Santa Ynez Valley, San Luis Obispo, Cambria, and Paso Robles, spawning dozens of new restaurants touting nouveau cuisine made with fresh organic produce and meats.

Dining attire on the Central Coast is generally casual, though slightly dressy casual wear is the custom at pricier restaurants.

WHAT IT COSTS				
¢	$	$$	$$$	$$$$
Restaurants				
under $10	$10–$15	$16–$22	$23–$30	over $30
Hotels				
under $90	$90–$120	$121–$175	$176–$250	over $250

Restaurant prices are for a main course at dinner, excluding sales tax of 7.25%–7.75% (depending on location). Hotel prices are for two people in a standard double room in high season, excluding service charges and 9%–10% tax.

Updated
by Cheryl
Crabtree

BALMY WEATHER, GLORIOUS BEACHES, CRYSTAL-CLEAR air, and serene landscapes have lured people to the Central Coast since prehistoric times. It's an ideal place to relax, slow down, and appreciate the good things in life. Along the Pacific coast, the scenic variety is stunning—everything from dramatic cliffs and grass-tufted bluffs to wildlife estuaries and miles of dunes. Offshore, a pristine national park and a vast marine sanctuary protect the wild, wonderful underwater resources of this incredible corner of the planet. But not all of the Central Coast's top attractions are natural: the small cities of Ventura, Santa Barbara, and San Luis Obispo are filled with sparkling examples of Spanish-Mediterranean architecture, bustling shopping districts, and first-rate restaurants showcasing regional foods and wines.

VENTURA COUNTY

15

VENTURA

60 mi north of Los Angeles on U.S. 101.

Like Los Angeles, the city of Ventura enjoys gorgeous weather and sun-kissed beaches—but without the smog and congestion. The city is filled with classic California buildings, farmers' and fish markets, art galleries, and shops. The miles of beautiful beaches attract both athletes—bodysurfers and boogie boarders, runners and bikers—and those who'd rather doze beneath a rented umbrella all day. Ventura Harbor is home to the Channel Islands National Park Visitor Center and myriad fishing boats, restaurants, and water-activity centers where you can rent boats and take harbor cruises. Foodies can get their fix here, too; dozens of upscale cafés and wine and tapas bars have opened in recent years. Ventura is also a magnet for arts and antiques buffs who come to browse the dozens of galleries and shops in the downtown area.

You can pick up culinary, antiques, and shopping guides downtown at the **visitor center** (⊠ *101 S. California St.* ☎ *805/648–2075 or 800/333–2989* ⊕ *www.ventura-usa.com*) run by the Ventura Visitors and Convention Bureau.

More than three millennia of human history in the Ventura region is charted in the archaeological exhibits at the small **Albinger Archaeological Museum.** Some of the relics on display date back to 1600 BC. ⊠ *113 E. Main St.* ☎ *805/648–5823* 🖃 *Free* 🕙 *June–Aug., Wed.–Sun. 10–4; Sept.–May, Wed.–Fri. 10–2, weekends 10–4.*

🌣 Lunker largemouth bass, rainbow trout, crappie, redears, and channel catfish live in the waters at **Lake Casitas Recreation Area,** an impoundment of the Ventura River. The lake is one of the country's best bass-fishing areas, and anglers come from all over the United States to test their luck. The park, nestled below the Santa Ynez Mountains' Laguna Ridge, is also a beautiful spot for pitching a tent or having a picnic. The Casitas Water Adventure, which has two water playgrounds and a lazy river for tubing and floating, is a great place to take kids in summer ($12 for an all-day pass; $5 from 5 to 7 PM). The park is 13 mi northwest of Ventura. ✉11311 Santa Ana Rd., off Hwy. 33 ☎805/649–2233, 805/649–1122 campground reservations ⊕www. lakecasitas.info ✉$8 per vehicle, $7 per boat ☉Daily.

The ninth of the 21 California missions, **Mission San Buenaventura** was established in 1782 but burned to the ground in the 1790s. It was rebuilt and rededicated in 1809. A self-guided tour takes you through a small museum, a quiet courtyard, and a chapel with 250-year-old paintings. ✉211 E. Main St. ☎805/643–4318 ⊕www.sanbuena venturamission.org ✉$2 ☉Weekdays 10–5, Sat. 9–5, Sun. 10–4.

WHERE TO STAY & EAT

$$$ ✗ **71 Palm Restaurant.** This elegant restaurant occupies a 1910 house, and it still has touches that make it feel like a home: lace curtains, wood floors, a dining patio for good weather, and a fireplace that's often crackling in winter. A standout appetizer is the homemade country pâté with cornichons; for dinner, try the grilled salmon on a potato pancake, or the New Zealand rack of lamb Provençal. ✉71 N. Palm St. ☎805/653–7222 ⊟AE, D, DC, MC, V ☉Closed Sun.

$$ ✗ **Jonathan's at Peirano's.** The main dining room here has a gazebo where you can eat surrounded by plants and local art. The menu has dishes from Spain, Portugal, France, Italy, Greece, and Morocco. Standouts are the Basque-style chicken, the penne checca pasta, and the halibut with almonds. The owners also run an evening tapas bar next door, which serves exotic martinis. ✉204 E. Main St. ☎805/648–4853 ⊟AE, D, DC, MC, V ☉No lunch.

$ ✗ **Andria's Seafood.** At this casual, family-oriented restaurant in Ventura Harbor, the specialties are fresh fish-and-chips—said to rival England's best—and homemade clam chowder. After placing your order at the counter, you can sit outside on the patio with a view of the harbor and marina. ✉1449 Spinnaker Dr., Suite A ☎805/654–0546 ⊟MC, V.

$ ✗ **Busy Bee Cafe.** A local favorite for decades, this classic 1950s diner has a jukebox on every table and serves hearty burgers and American comfort food (think meat loaf and mashed potatoes, pot roast, and Cobb salad). For breakfast, tuck into a huge breakfast omelet; for a snack or dessert, be sure to order a shake or hot fudge sundae from the soda fountain. ✉478 E. Main St. ☎805/643–4864 ⊟MC, V.

$$$ ▦ **Pierpont Inn.** Back in 1910, Josephine Pierpont-Ginn built the original Pierpont Inn on a hill overlooking Ventura Beach. Today's renovated complex, which includes an Arts-and-Crafts lobby and English Tudor cottages set amid gardens and gazebos, reflects much of the hotel's

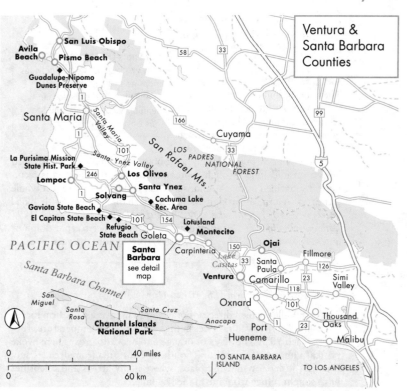

Ventura &
Santa Barbara
Counties

San Luis Obispo
Avila Beach
Pismo Beach
Guadalupe-Nipomo Dunes Preserve
Santa Maria
Santa Maria Valley
La Purisima Mission State Hist. Park
Lompoc
Los Olivos
Santa Ynez Valley
Santa Ynez
Solvang
Gaviota State Beach
El Capitan State Beach
Refugio State Beach
Goleta
Santa Barbara see detail map
Carpinteria
Montecito
Lotusland
Cachuma Lake Rec. Area
San Rafael Mts.
LOS PADRES NATIONAL FOREST
Cuyama
Ojai
Fillmore
Santa Paula
Lake Casitas
Ventura
Camarillo
Simi Valley
Oxnard
Thousand Oaks
Port Hueneme
Malibu
Anacapa
PACIFIC OCEAN
Santa Barbara Channel
San Miguel
Santa Rosa
Santa Cruz
Channel Islands National Park

0 ——— 40 miles
0 ——— 60 km

TO SANTA BARBARA ISLAND
TO LOS ANGELES

original elegance. For a fee you can work out at the neighboring Pierpont Racquet Club, which has indoor and outdoor pools, 15 tennis courts, racquetball courts, spa services, aerobics, and child care. The inn's restaurant has great views of the ocean and harbor. **Pros:** Near the beach; lush gardens; Tempur-Pedic mattresses and pillows. **Cons:** Near the freeway and train tracks; difficult to walk downtown from here. ⊠ *550 Sanjon Rd.* ☎ *805/643–6144 or 800/285–4667* ⊕ *www.pierpontinn.com* ⬧ *65 rooms, 9 suites, 2 cottages* ⌂ *In-room: no a/c (some), refrigerator (some), Ethernet, Wi-Fi. In-hotel: restaurant, bar, no-smoking rooms* ⊟ *AE, D, DC, MC, V* ⊚ *CP.*

$$–$$$ 🏨 **Holiday Inn Express Ventura Harbor.** A favorite among travelers to the Channel Islands, this quiet, comfortable lodge sits right at the Ventura Harbor entrance. A major renovation in 2006 transformed the guest quarters into spacious, sophisticated retreats with flat-screen TVs and puffy duvets. The south side of the hotel overlooks the marinas; ask for an upper-floor harborside room or suite for the best views. **Pros:** Quiet at night; easy access to harbor restaurants and activities; on shuttle bus route to city attractions. **Cons:** Busy area on weekends; five-minute drive to downtown sights. ⊠ *1080 Navigator Dr. 93001* ☎ *805/856–9533 or 800/315–2621* ⊕ *www.hiexpress.com* ⬧ *68 rooms, 23 suites* ⌂ *In-room: no a/c, kitchen (some), Ethernet.*

In-hotel: pool, gym, laundry service, public Wi-Fi, no-smoking rooms ☰*AE, D, DC, MC, V* ⦿|*BP.*

SPORTS & THE OUTDOORS

The most popular outdoor activities in Ventura are beach-going and whale-watching. California gray whales migrate offshore through the Santa Barbara Channel from late December through March; giant blue and humpback whales feed here from mid-June through September. In fact, the channel is teeming with marine life year-round, so tours include more than just whale sightings. A cruise through the Santa Barbara Channel with **Island Packers** (✉*1691 Spinnaker Dr., Ventura Harbor* ☎*805/642–1393* ⊕*www.islandpackers.com*) will give you the chance to spot dolphins and seals—and sometimes even whales—throughout the year.

> ### HOTEL HELP
>
> **Hot Spots** (☎*800/793–7666* ⊕*www.hotspotsusa.com*) provides room reservations and tourist information for destinations in Ventura, Santa Barbara, and San Luis Obispo counties.

OJAI

15 mi north of Ventura, U.S. 101 to Hwy. 33.

The Ojai Valley, which director Frank Capra used as a backdrop for his 1936 film *Lost Horizon,* sizzles in the summer when temperatures routinely reach 90°F. The acres of orange and avocado groves here evoke postcard images of agricultural Southern California from decades ago. This is a lush, slow-moving place, where many artists and celebrities have sought refuge from life in the fast lane.

The town can be easily explored on foot; you can also hop on the **Ojai Valley Trolley** (⊕*www.ojaitrolley.com* ✑*50¢*), which rides on two routes around Ojai and neighboring Miramonte between 7:15 and 5:40 on weekdays, 9 and 5 on weekends. If you tell the driver you're a visitor, you'll get an informal guided tour.

Maps and tourist information are available at the **Ojai Valley Chamber of Commerce** (✉*201 S. Signal St.* ☎*805/646–8126* ⊕*www.ojaichamber. org* ☉*Weekdays 9–4*).

The work of local artists is displayed in the Spanish-style shopping arcade along **Ojai Avenue** *(Hwy. 150).* Organic and specialty growers sell their produce on Sunday from 10 to 2 (9 to 1 in summer) at the farmers' market behind the arcade.

The **Ojai Center for the Arts** (✉*113 S. Montgomery St.* ☎*805/646–0117*) exhibits artwork and presents theater and dance performances.

The **Ojai Valley Museum** (✉*130 W. Ojai Ave.* ☎*805/640–1390*) has exhibits on the valley's history and many Native American artifacts.

The 18-mi **Ojai Valley Trail** (✉*Parallel to Hwy. 33, from Soule Park in Ojai to ocean in Ventura* ☎*805/654–3951* ⊕*www.ojaichamber.org*) is open to pedestrians, bikers, joggers, equestrians, and nonmotorized vehicles. You can access it anywhere along its route.

WHERE TO STAY & EAT

$$$ ✕**The Ranch House.** This elegant yet laid-back eatery—said to be the best
★ in town—has been around for decades, attracting celebrities and locals
alike. Main dishes such as rack of lamb in an oyster-and-mushroom
cream sauce, and grilled diver scallops with curried sweet-corn sauce
are not to be missed. The verdant patio is a wonderful place to have
Sunday brunch. ⊠*500 S. Lomita Ave.* ☎*805/646–2360* ▤*AE, D,
DC, MC, V* ⊗*Closed Mon. No lunch.*

$$$ ✕**Suzanne's Cuisine.** Peppered filet mignon, linguine with steamed clams,
and grilled salmon with caramelized-citrus glaze are among the offerings
at this European-style restaurant. Game, seafood, and vegetarian dishes
dominate the dinner menu, and salads and soups star at lunchtime. All
the breads and desserts are made on the premises. ⊠*502 W. Ojai Ave.*
☎*805/640–1961* ▤*AE, MC, V* ⊗*Closed Tues. and 1st 2 wks in Jan.*

$$ ✕**Azu.** Delectable tapas, a full bar, slick furnishings, and piped jazz
music lure diners to this popular, artsy European bistro. You can also
order soups, salads, and traditional bistro fare such as veal shanks,
paella, and cassoulet. Save room for the homemade gelato. Live music
is sometimes performed after 9 PM, and brunch is served on Sunday.
⊠*457 E. Ojai Ave.* ☎*805/640–7987* ▤*AE, D, MC, V.*

$ ✕**Boccali's.** Edging a ranch, citrus groves, and a seasonal garden that
provides much of the produce for menu items, family-run Boccali's has
attracted droves of loyal fans to its modest but cheery restaurant since
1986. In the warmer months, you can dine alfresco in the oak-shaded
patio and lawn area and sometimes listen to live music. Best known
for their hand-rolled pizzas and homestyle pastas (don't miss the egg-
plant lasagna), Boccali's also serves a seasonal strawberry shortcake
that some patrons drive many miles to savor every year. ⊠ *3277 Ojai
Ave., about 2 mi east of downtown* ☎ *805/646–6116* ▤*No credit
cards accepted* ⊗*No lunch Mon. and Tues.*

$$$$ ▥**Ojai Valley Inn & Spa.** This outdoorsy, golf-oriented resort and spa is
★ set on beautifully landscaped grounds, with hillside views in nearly all
directions. Nearby is the inn's 800-acre ranch, where you can take rid-
ing lessons and go on guided trail rides. In 2005 the resort completed
a $70 million renovation. Two restaurants, a ballroom, and 100 guest
rooms were added; all existing rooms and suites were refurbished to
reflect the Spanish-colonial architecture of the original 1923 resort.
If you're a history buff, ask for a room in the original 80-year-old
adobe building. The four restaurants tout "Ojai regional cuisine,"
which incorporates locally grown produce and fresh seasonal meats
and seafood. **Pros:** Gorgeous grounds; exceptional outdoor activities;
romantic yet kid-friendly. **Cons:** Expensive; staff isn't always attentive.
⊠*905 Country Club Rd.* ☎*805/646–1111 or 800/422–6524* ⊕*www.
ojairesort.com* ⊃*231 rooms, 77 suites* ⚿*In-room: refrigerator, Eth-
ernet. In-hotel: 4 restaurants, bar, golf course, tennis courts, pools,
spa, bicycles, children's programs (ages 5–12), public Wi-Fi, some pets
allowed, no-smoking rooms* ▤*AE, D, DC, MC, V.*

$$$–$$$$ ▥**Su Nido.** Just a short walk from downtown Ojai sights and restau-
rants, this posh Spanish hacienda–style inn is nested in a quiet neigh-
borhood a few blocks from Libbey Park. One- and two-bedroom suites,

15

each named after a bird, ring a cobblestone courtyard with fountains and olive trees. All suites have spacious living rooms, private patios, and either kitchens or kitchenettes, fireplaces, and featherbeds. **Pros:** Walking distance from downtown; homey feel. **Cons:** No pool; can get hot during summer. ☒*301 N. Montgomery St.* ☎*805/646–7080 or 866/646–7080* ⊕*www.sunidoinn.com* ☞*9 suites* ⚲*In-room: kitchen, refrigerator, DVD, Wi-Fi. In-hotel: no elevator, no-smoking rooms* ▤*AE, D, MC, V.*

$$$ ⊞ **Oaks at Ojai.** Rejuvenation is the name of the game at this comfortable spa resort. You can work out all day or just lounge by the pool. The fitness package is a great value and includes lodging; use of the spa facilities; a choice of 16 daily exercise classes, hikes, and fitness activities; and three nutritionally balanced, low-calorie meals a day, plus snacks and beverages. Nonguests can eat here, too, but it's mainly for the fitness-conscious. Cell-phone use is not allowed in public areas. Bringing kids under age 16 is discouraged. **Pros:** Great place to get fit; peaceful retreat; healthy meals. **Cons:** Rooms are basic; sits on the main highway through town. ☒*122 E. Ojai Ave.* ☎*805/646–5573 or 800/753–6257* ⊕*www.oaksspa.com* ☞*46 rooms* ⚲*In-hotel: no elevator, restaurant, pool, gym, spa, public Wi-Fi, no-smoking rooms* ▤*AE, D, MC, V* ⦿*FAP* ☞*2-night minimum stay.*

$–$$ ⊞ **The Blue Iguana Inn & Cottages.** Artists run this Southwestern-style hotel, and their work (which is for sale) decorates the rooms. The small, cozy main inn is about 2 mi west of downtown. Its sister property, the Emerald Iguana Inn, consists of eight more art-nouveau cottages closer to downtown Ojai. Suites and cottages all have kitchenettes. **Pros:** Colorful art everywhere; secluded property; breakfast delivered to each room. **Cons:** Two miles from the heart of Ojai; sits on the main highway to Ventura; small. ☒*11794 N. Ventura Ave., Hwy. 33* ☎*805/646–5277* ⊕*www.blueiguanainn.com* ☞*4 rooms, 7 suites, 8 cottages* ⚲*In-room: kitchen (some), refrigerator, VCR (some), Wi-Fi. In-hotel: pool, no elevator, some pets allowed, no-smoking rooms* ▤*AE, D, DC, MC, V.*

THE ARTS

On Wednesday evenings in summer, all-American music played by the Ojai Band draws crowds to **Libbey Park** (☒*Ojai Ave.* ☎*805/646– 8430* ✉*Free*) in downtown Ojai. Since 1947, the **Ojai Music Festival** (☎*805/646–2094* ⊕*www.ojaifestival.org*) has attracted internationally known progressive and traditional musicians for outdoor concerts in Libbey Park for a weekend in late May or early June.

SANTA BARBARA

27 mi northwest of Ventura and 29 mi west of Ojai on U.S. 101.

Santa Barbara has long been an oasis for Los Angelenos seeking respite from hectic big-city life. The attractions begin at the ocean and end in the foothills of the Santa Ynez Mountains. A few miles up the coast—but still very much a part of Santa Barbara—is the exclusive residential district of Hope Ranch. Santa Barbara is on a jog in the coastline, so the ocean is actually to the south, instead of the west; for this reason, directions can be confusing. "Up" the coast toward San Francisco is west, "down" toward Los Angeles is east, and the mountains are north. A car is handy but not essential if you're planning to stay in town. The beaches and downtown are easily explored by bicycle or on foot. You can also hop aboard one of the electric shuttles that cruise the downtown and waterfront every 8 to 15 minutes (25¢ each way) and connect with local buses such as Line 22, which goes to major visitor sights (⊕*www.sbmtd.gov*).

Visit **Santa Barbara Car Free** (⊕*www.santabarbaracarfree.org*) for bike route and walking-tour maps and car-free vacation packages with substantial lodging discounts.

A motorized San Francisco–style cable car operated by **Santa Barbara Trolley Co.** (☎*805/965–0353* ⊕*www.sbtrolley.com*) makes 90-minute runs from 10 to 4 past major hotels, shopping areas, and attractions. Get off whenever you like, and pick up another trolley when you're ready to move on (they come every hour). The trolley departs from and returns to Stearns Wharf. The fare is $19 for the day.

Land and Sea Tours (⊠ State St. at Stearns Wharf ☎*805/683–7600* ⊕*www. out2seeSB.com* ⊠*$25* ☉ *Tours May–Oct., daily noon, 2, and 4; Nov.– Apr., daily noon and 2*) takes visitors on narrated, 90-minute land-and-sea adventures in an amphibious 49-passenger vehicle, nicknamed the Land Shark. Tours begin with a drive through the city and continue with a plunge into the harbor for a cruise to the wharf.

FROM THE OCEAN TO THE MOUNTAINS

Santa Barbara's waterfront is beautiful, with palm-studded promenades and plenty of sand. In the few miles between the beaches and the hills are downtown, the old mission, and the botanic gardens.

For maps and visitor information, drop by the **Santa Barbara Chamber of Commerce Visitor Information Center** (⊠*1 Garden St., at Cabrillo Blvd.* ☎*805/965–3021* ⊕*www.sbchamber.org*).

WHAT TO SEE

⑮ Andree Clark Bird Refuge. This peaceful lagoon and gardens sit north of East Beach. Bike trails and footpaths, punctuated by signs identifying native and migratory birds, skirt the lagoon. ⊠*1400 E. Cabrillo Blvd.* ⊠*Free.*

❸ Carriage and Western Art Museum. The country's largest collection of old horse-drawn vehicles—painstakingly restored—is exhibited here. Everything from polished hearses to police buggies to old stagecoaches and circus vehicles is on display. In August the Old Spanish Days Fiesta borrows many of the vehicles for a jaunt about town. This is one of the city's true hidden gems, a wonderful place to help history come alive— especially for children. Docents lead tours the third Sunday of every month from 1 to 4 PM. ⊠*129 Castillo St.* ☎*805/962–2353* ⊕*www. carriagemuseum.org* ⊠*Free* ☉ *Weekdays 9–3.*

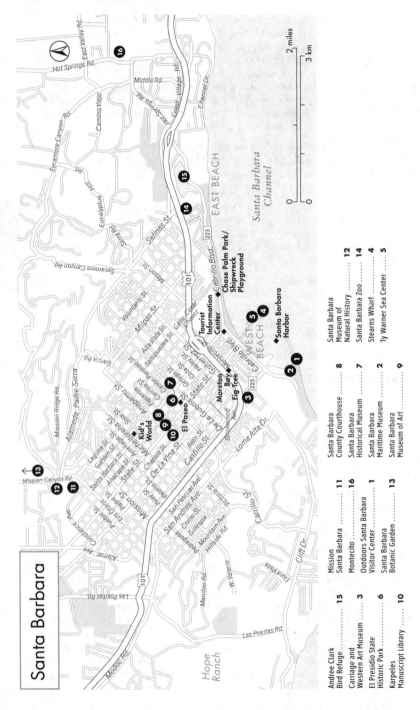

Santa Barbara

6 **El Presidio State Historic Park.**
★ Founded in 1782, El Presidio was one of four military strongholds established by the Spanish along the coast of California. The park encompasses much of the original site in the heart of downtown. El Cuartel, the adobe guardhouse, is the oldest building in Santa Barbara and the second oldest in California. ⊠ *123 E. Canon Perdido St.* ☎ *805/965–0093* ⊕ *www.sbthp. org* ⊠ *$5* ⊗ *Daily 10:30–4:30.*

10 **Karpeles Manuscript Library.** Ancient political tracts and old Disney cartoons are among the holdings at this facility, which also houses one of the world's largest privately owned collections of rare manu-

> ### SANTA BARBARA STYLE
>
> Why does downtown Santa Barbara look so scrubbed and uniform? After a 1925 earthquake, which demolished many buildings, the city seized a golden opportunity to create a Spanish–Mediterranean look. It established an architectural board of review, which, along with city commissions, created strict architectural codes for the downtown district: red tile roofs, earth-tone facades, arches, wrought-iron embellishments, and limited height restrictions (about four stories).

scripts. Fifty display cases contain a sampling of the archive's million-plus documents. ⊠ *21 W. Anapamu St.* ☎ *805/962–5322* ⊕ *www. karpeles.com* ⊠ *Free* ⊗ *Daily 10–4.*

11 **Mission Santa Barbara.** Widely referred to as the "Queen of Missions,"
Fodor's Choice this is one of the most beautiful and frequently photographed build-
★ ings in coastal California. The architecture, which was originally built in 1786, evolved from adobe-brick buildings with thatch roofs to more permanent edifices as its population burgeoned. An earthquake in 1812 destroyed the third church built on the site. Its replacement, the present structure, is still a functioning Catholic church. The building is surrounded by cacti, palms, and other succulents. ⊠ *2201 Laguna St.* ☎ *805/682–4149* ⊕ *www.sbmission.org* ⊠ *$4* ⊗ *Daily 9–5.*

16 **Montecito.** Since the late 1800s the tree-studded hills and valleys of this town have attracted the rich and famous (Hollywood icons, business tycoons, dot-commers who divested before the crash, and old-money families who installed themselves here years ago). Shady roads wind through the community, which consists mostly of gated estates. Swank boutiques line Coast Village Road, where well-heeled residents such as Oprah Winfrey and John Cleese sometimes browse for truffle oil, picture frames, and designer sweats. Residents also hang out in the Upper Village, a chic shopping area with restaurants and cafés at the intersection of San Ysidro and East Valley roads. Montecito is just about 3 mi east of Santa Barbara.

Fodor's Choice The 37-acre Montecito estate called **Lotusland** (☎ *805/969–9990* ⊕ *www.*
★ *lotusland.org* ⊠ *$35*) once belonged to Polish opera singer Ganna Walska. Many of the exotic trees and other subtropical flora were planted in 1882 by horticulturist R. Kinton Stevens. On the two-hour guided tour (the only option for visiting), you'll see an outdoor theater, a topiary garden, a huge collection of rare cycads (an unusual plant genus

that has been around since the time of the dinosaurs), and a lotus pond. Tours are conducted mid-February through mid-November, Wednesday through Saturday at 10 and 1:30. Reservations are required. Children under 10 are not allowed, except on family tours, offered on Thursday and the second Saturday of each month.

> **BEST VIEWS**
>
> Drive along Alameda Padre Serra, a hillside road that begins near the mission and continues to Montecito, to feast your eyes on spectacular views of the city and the Santa Barbara Channel.

❶ Outdoors Santa Barbara Visitor Center. The small office provides maps and other information about Channel Islands National Park, Channel Islands National Marine Sanctuary, and Los Padres National Forest. The same building houses the Santa Barbara Maritime Museum. ✉*113 Harbor Way* ☎*805/884–1475* ⊕*www.outdoorsb.noaa.gov* ✉*Free* ☉*Daily 11–5.*

❸ Santa Barbara Botanic Garden. Scenic trails meander through the garden's 78 acres of native plants. The Mission Dam, built in 1806, stands just beyond the redwood grove and above the restored aqueduct that once carried water to Mission Santa Barbara. An ethnobotanical display demonstrates how Native Americans used plants to create baskets, clothing, and structures. ✉*1212 Mission Canyon Rd.* ☎*805/682–4726* ⊕*www.sbbg.org* ✉*$8* ☉*Mar.–Oct., daily 9–6; Nov.–Feb., daily 9–5. Guided tours daily at 2, additional tour on weekends at 11.*

❽ Santa Barbara County Courthouse. Hand-painted tiles and a spiral stair-
★ case infuse the courthouse with the grandeur of a Moorish palace. This magnificent building was completed in 1929, part of a rebuilding process after a 1925 earthquake destroyed many downtown structures. At the time, Santa Barbara was also in the midst of a cultural awakening, and the trend was toward an architectural style appropriate to the area's climate and history. The result is the harmonious Mediterranean–Spanish look of much of the downtown area, especially the municipal buildings. An elevator rises to an arched observation area in the court-house tower that provides a panoramic view of the city. The murals in the ceremonial chambers on the courthouse's second floor were painted by an artist who did backdrops for some of Cecil B. DeMille's films. ✉*1100 block of Anacapa St.* ☎*805/962–6464* ⊕*www.santabarbara courthouse.org* ☉*Weekdays 8–4:45, weekends 10–4:30. Free guided tours Mon., Tues., and Fri. at 10:30, Mon.–Sat. at 2.*

NEED A BREAK? ☕
Both children and adults can enjoy themselves at Kids' World (✉*Garden St. at Micheltorena St.*), a public playground with a complex, castle-shaped maze of fanciful climbing structures, slides, and tunnels built by Santa Barbara parents.

❼ Santa Barbara Historical Museum. The historical society's museum exhibits decorative and fine arts, furniture, costumes, and documents from the town's past. Adjacent to it is the Gledhill Library, a collection of books, photographs, maps, and manuscripts. ✉*136 E. De La Guerra*

St. 🕿805/966–1601 ⊕www.santabarbaramuseum.com 🖃Museum by donation; library $2–$5 per hr for research ⊗Museum Tues.–Sat. 10–5, Sun. noon–5; library Tues.–Fri. 10–4, 1st Sat. of month 10–1. Free guided tours Wed. and weekends at 1:30.

② **Santa Barbara Maritime Museum.** California's seafaring history is the focus at this museum. High-tech, hands-on exhibits, such as a sportfishing activity that lets you catch a "big one" and a local surfing history retrospective, opened in 2008, make this a fun stop for families. ✉113 Harbor Way 🕿805/962–8404 ⊕www.sbmm.org 🖃$7 ⊗June–Aug., Thurs.–Tues. 10–6; Sept.–May, Thurs.–Tues. 10–5.

⑨ **Santa Barbara Museum of Art.** The highlights of this museum's permanent collection include ancient sculpture, Asian art, impressionist paintings, contemporary Latin American art, and American works in several media. ✉1130 State St. 🕿805/963–4364 ⊕www.sbma.net 🖃$9, free on Sun. ⊗Tues.–Sun. 11–5. Free guided tours Tues.–Sun. at noon and 1.

⑫ **Santa Barbara Museum of Natural History.** The gigantic skeleton of a blue whale greets you at the entrance of this complex. The major draws include the planetarium, space lab, and a gem and mineral display. A room of dioramas illustrates Chumash Indian history and culture. Startlingly alive-looking stuffed specimens, complete with nests and eggs, roost in the bird diversity room. Many exhibits have interactive components. Outdoors you can stroll on nature trails that wind through the serene oak-studded grounds. Admission is free on the third Sunday of each month. ✉2559 Puesta del Sol Rd. 🕿805/682–4711 ⊕www.sbnature.org 🖃$10 ⊗Daily 10–5.

⑭ **Santa Barbara Zoo.** The grounds of this smallish zoo are so gorgeous people book their weddings here long in advance. The palm-studded lawns on a hilltop overlooking the beach are perfect spots for family picnics. The natural settings of the zoo shelter elephants, gorillas, exotic birds, and big cats such as the rare snow leopard, a thick-furred, high-altitude dweller from Asia. For small children, there's a scenic railroad and barnyard petting zoo. ✉500 Niños Dr. 🕿805/962–5339 main line, 805/962–6310 information ⊕www.santabarbarazoo.org 🖃Zoo $11, parking $4 ⊗Daily 10–5.

NEED A BREAK?

The antique carousel, large playground with a nautical theme, picnic areas, and snack bar make the scenic waterfront Chase Palm Park and Shipwreck Playground (✉Cabrillo Blvd., between Garden St. and Calle Cesar Chavez) a favorite destination for kids and parents.

④ **Stearns Wharf.** Built in 1872, historic Stearns Wharf is Santa Barbara's most visited landmark. Expansive views of the mountains, cityscape, and harbor unfold from every vantage point on the three-block-long pier. Although it's a nice walk from the Cabrillo Boulevard parking areas, you can also park on the pier and then wander through the shops or stop for a meal at one of the wharf's restaurants. ✉Cabrillo Blvd., at foot of State St. 🕿805/897–2683 or 805/564–5531.

15

⑤ Ty Warner Sea Center. A branch of the Santa Barbara Museum of Natural History, the Sea Center specializes in Santa Barbara Channel marine life and conservation. In 2005 it reopened in a new $6.5 million facility bearing the name of Ty Warner, Beanie Baby mogul and local resident, whose hefty donation helped the center complete the final stages of construction. The new Sea Center is small compared to aquariums in Monterey and Long Beach, but it's a fascinating, hands-on marine science laboratory that lets you participate in experiments, projects, and exhibits, including touch tanks. Haul up and analyze water samples, learn to identify marine mammals, and check out amazing creatures in the tide-pool lab and animal nursery. The two-story glass walls open to stunning ocean, mountain, and city views. ⊠ *211 Stearns Wharf* ☎ *805/962–2526* ⊕ *www.sbnature.org* ☞ *$8* ☉ *Daily 10–5.*

WHERE TO STAY & EAT

$$$$ ✕ **The Stonehouse.** Part of the San Ysidro Ranch resort, this elegantly rustic restaurant, which reopened in 2007 following the resort's $150-million remodel, is housed in a century-old granite farmhouse. Executive chef John Trotta harvests herbs and veggies from the onsite garden, then adds them to an array of top-quality local ingredients to create outstanding regional cuisine. The menu changes constantly but typically includes favorites such as crab cake with mango relish appetizer and Parmesan-crusted halibut. Dine on the radiant-heated ocean-view deck with stone fireplace, next to a fountain under a canopy of loquat trees, or in the romantic, candlelit dining room overlooking a creek. The Plow & Angel pub, downstairs, offers more casual bistro fare. ⊠ *900 San Ysidro La., Montecito* ☎ *805/969–4100* ☞ *Reservations essential* ⊟ *AE, DC, MC, V* ☉ *No lunch.*

$$$$ ✕ **Wine Cask.** Seared peppercorn ahi tuna and grilled filet mignon are among the most popular entrées at this slick restaurant, which has a beautiful wooden interior and Santa Barbara's most extensive wine list. In fine weather, couples seek out the romantic outdoor patio. ⊠ *813 Anacapa St.* ☎ *805/966–9463* ☞ *Reservations essential* ⊟ *AE, DC, MC, V.*

$$$ ✕ **Bouchon.** This upscale restaurant showcases fine local wines, produce, and such regional specialties as fresh Pacific ahi tuna and organic pork chops. The mood is intimate and the wine selection huge. ⊠ *9 W. Victoria St.* ☎ *805/730–1160* ⊟ *AE, DC, MC, V* ☉ *No lunch.*

$$$ ✕ **Olio e Limone.** Sophisticated Italian cuisine (with an emphasis on Sicily) is served at this restaurant near the Arlington Center for the Performing Arts. The juicy veal chop is a popular dish, but surprises abound here; be sure to try unusual dishes such as ribbon pasta with quail and sausage in a mushroom ragout, duck ravioli, or swordfish with Sicilian ratatouille. Tables are placed a bit close together, so this may not be the best spot for intimate conversations. ⊠ *17 W. Victoria St.* ☎ *805/899–2699* ⊟ *AE, D, DC, MC, V* ☉ *No lunch Sun.*

$$$ ✕ **Palace Grill.** Mardi Gras energy, team-style service, lively music, and great food have made the Palace a Santa Barbara icon. Acclaimed for its Cajun and creole dishes such as blackened redfish and jambalaya with dirty rice, the Palace also serves Caribbean fare, including a delicious coconut-shrimp dish. If you're spice-phobic, you can choose

pasta, soft-shell crab, or filet mignon. Be prepared to wait as long as 45 minutes for a table on Friday and Saturday nights, when reservations are taken for a 5:30 seating only. ⊠*8 E. Cota St.* ☏*805/963–5000* ⊟*AE, MC, V.*

$$ ✕**Arigato Sushi.** You might have to wait 45 minutes for a table at this trendy, two-story restaurant and sushi bar—locals line up early for the hip, casual atmosphere and wildly creative combination rolls. Fans of authentic Japanese food sometimes disagree about the quality of the seafood, but all dishes are fresh and artfully presented. The menu includes traditional dishes as well as innovative creations such as sushi pizza on seaweed and Hawaiian sashimi salad. ⊠*1225 State St.* ☏*805/965–6074* ⚄*Reservations not accepted* ⊟*AE, MC, V* ⊘*No lunch.*

$$ ✕**Brophy Bros.** The outdoor tables at this casual harborside restaurant have perfect views of the marina and mountains. The staff serves enormous, exceptionally fresh fish dishes—don't miss the seafood salad and chowder—and provides you with a pager if there's a long wait for a table. You can stroll along the waterfront until the beep lets you know your table's ready. This place is hugely popular, so it can be crowded and loud, especially on weekend evenings. ⊠*119 Harbor Way* ☏*805/966–4418* ⊟*AE, MC, V.*

$$ ✕**Roy.** Owner-chef Leroy Gandy serves a $25 fixed-price dinner (some selections are $20, some $30)—a real bargain—that includes a small salad, fresh soup, homemade organic bread, and a selection from a rotating list of contemporary American main courses. If you're lucky, the entrée choices might include grilled local fish with a mandarin beurre blanc or bacon-wrapped filet mignon. You can also choose from an à la carte menu of inexpensive appetizers and entrées, plus local wines. Half a block from State Street in the heart of downtown, Roy is a favorite spot for late-night dining (it's open until midnight and has a full bar). ⊠*7 W. Carrillo St.* ☏*805/966–5636* ⊟*AE, D, DC, MC, V* ⊘*No lunch.*

$ ✕**The Taj Cafe.** Traditional village-style Indian cooking and exotic decor—fabrics, curtains, and artwork are all imported from the East—make for a deliciously different dining experience here. The chef uses organic spices to create a host of lean, healthful dishes, such as tandoori entrées, curries, masalas, vegetarian dishes, and Frankies (Bombay-style burritos). Can't decide? Try the Taj Special, with samples of various tandoori dishes, or one of the many combination plates. ⊠*905 State St.* ☏*805/564–8280* ⊟*AE, D, MC, V.*

$ ✕**Zen Yai Thai Cuisine.** As the shingle above the tiny storefront amid lower State Street's club scene states, the food here is "reminiscent of things Thai." That might drive away diners seeking absolute authenticity, but every day a trendy flock of fans packs the room for delectable dishes made from fresh local ingredients. Reserve a table or be prepared for a wait. ⊠*425 State St.* ☏*805/957–1102* ⊟*AE, MC, V* ⊘*No lunch Mon. and weekends.*

¢ ✕**La Super-Rica.** Praised by Julia Child, this food stand with a patio on ★ the east side of town serves some of the spiciest and most authentic Mexican dishes between Los Angeles and San Francisco. Fans drive for miles to fill up on the soft tacos served with yummy spicy or mild sauces and legendary beans. Three specials are offered each day. Portions are on the small side; order several dishes and share. ⊠*622 N. Milpas St., at Alphonse St.* ☎*805/963–4940* ⊟*No credit cards.* ⊘*Closed Wed.*

$$$$ ✕⌷**Canary Hotel.** The only full-service hotel in the heart of downtown, the Canary blends the feel of a casual beach getaway with tony urban sophistication. It first opened as the Hotel Andalucia in 2004. New owners revamped it in 2008 to match swank sisters Shutters on the Beach and Casa del Mar in Santa Monica. Moroccan rugs, African masks, dark wood floors, and seagrass color schemes create an exotic mood throughout. Homey touches in the light-filled rooms include walnut four-poster beds, yoga mats, candles, and binoculars to take along while touring the town. The Perch, a sixth-floor guests-only rooftop lounge, has a pool and stunning views. The Coast restaurant ($$$) on the lobby floor serves upscale comfort food centered around fresh local ingredients. **Pros:** Easy stroll to museums, shopping, dining; friendly, attentive service; adjacent fitness center (fee). **Cons:** Across from main bus transit center; some rooms feel cramped. ⊠*31 W. Carrillo St.* ☎*805/884–0300 or 877/468–3515* ⊕*www.canarysantabarbara.com* ↩*77 rooms, 20 suites* ⌂*In-room: safe, refrigerator, DVD, Ethernet, Wi-Fi. In-hotel: restaurant, room service, bar, pool, concierge, laundry service, public Internet, public Wi-Fi, parking (fee), some pets allowed, no-smoking rooms* ⊟*AE, D, DC, MC, V.*

$$$$ ✕⌷**Four Seasons Resort The Biltmore Santa Barbara.** Surrounded by lush,
★ perfectly manicured gardens and across from the beach, Santa Barbara's grande dame has long been a favorite for quiet, California-style luxury. The sumptuous 10,000-square-foot spa, which includes 11 treatment rooms, near the resort's pool and gardens, is an oasis for rejuvenation. Dining is upscale casual at the ocean-view Bella Vista Restaurant ($$$–$$$$), where the seasonal California-contemporary menu changes monthly. **Pros:** First-class resort; historic Santa Barbara character; personal service; steps from the beach. **Cons:** Back rooms are close to train tracks; expensive. ⊠*1260 Channel Dr.* ☎*805/969–2261 or 800/332–3442* ⊕*www.fourseasons.com/santabarbara* ↩*181 rooms, 26 suites* ⌂*In-room: DVD, Ethernet, Wi-Fi. In-hotel: restaurant, room service, bar, tennis courts, pool, gym, spa, concierge, children's programs (ages 5–12), some pets allowed, no-smoking rooms* ⊟*AE, D, DC, MC, V.*

$$$$ ✕⌷**San Ysidro Ranch.** At this romantic hideaway on an historic property
★ in the Montecito foothills—where John and Jackie Kennedy spent their honeymoon and Oprah sends her out-of-town guests—guest cottages are scattered among groves of orange trees and flower beds. All have down comforters and fireplaces; most have private outdoor spas, and one has its own pool. Seventeen miles of hiking trails crisscross 500 acres of open space surrounding the property. The Stonehouse Restaurant ($$–$$$$; *see above*) and Plow & Angel Bistro ($–$$$) are Santa Barbara institutions. The hotel completed a $150 million restoration in 2007. **Pros:** Ultimate privacy; surrounded by nature; celebrity hangout; pet-friendly. **Cons:** Very expensive; too remote for some. ⊠*900 San Ysidro La., Montecito* ☎*805/565–1700 or 800/368–6788* ⊕*www.sanysidroranch.com* ↩*23 rooms, 4 suites, 14 cottages* ⌂*In-*

*room: refrigerator, DVD, Ethernet, Wi-Fi. In-hotel: no elevator, 2 res-
taurants, room service, bar, pool, gym, some pets allowed, no-smoking
rooms ⊟AE, MC, V ☞2-day minimum stay on weekends, 3 days on
holiday weekends.*

$$$$ ☷ **Inn of the Spanish Garden.** A half block from the Presidio in the heart
of downtown, this elegant Spanish-Mediterranean retreat celebrates
Santa Barbara style, from tile floors, wrought-iron balconies, and
exotic plants to original art by famed local *plein air* artists. The luxury
rooms have private balconies or patios, fireplaces, Frette linens, and
deep soaking tubs. In the evening, you can order a glass of wine and
relax in the candlelighted courtyard. This inn is a good choice if you
want to park your car for most of your stay and walk to theaters, restaurants, and shuttle buses. **Pros:** Walking distance from downtown;
classic Spanish-Mediterranean style; caring staff. **Cons:** Far from the
beach; not much here for kids. ✉*915 Garden St.* ☎*805/564–4700
or 866/564–4700 ⊕www.spanishgardeninn.com ☞23 rooms ♿In-
room: VCR, Ethernet, Wi-Fi. In-hotel: bar, pool, gym, concierge, laundry service, parking (no fee), no-smoking rooms ⊟AE, D, DC, MC,
V ⏏CP.*

$$$$ ☷ **Simpson House Inn.** If you're a fan of traditional B&Bs, this property,
★   with its beautifully appointed Victorian main house and acre of lush
gardens, is for you. If privacy and luxury are your priority, choose
one of the elegant cottages or a room in the century-old barn; each
has a wood-burning fireplace, luxurious bedding, and state-of-the-art
electronics (several even have whirlpool baths). In-room massages and
other spa services are available. Room rates include use of a downtown
athletic club. **Pros:** Impeccable landscaping; walking distance from
everything downtown; ranked among the nation's top B&Bs. **Cons:**
Some rooms in the main building are small; 2-night minimum stay on
weekends. ✉*121 E. Arrellaga St.* ☎*805/963–7067 or 800/676–1280
⊕www.simpsonhouseinn.com ☞11 rooms, 4 cottages ♿In-room:
refrigerator (some), DVD, Wi-Fi. In-hotel: no elevator, bicycles, no-
smoking rooms ⊟AE, D, MC, V ⏏BP.*

$$ ☷ **Franciscan Inn.** Part of this Spanish-Mediterranean motel, a block
from the harbor and West Beach, dates back to the 1920s. The friendly
staff and range of cheery, spacious country-theme rooms, from sin-
gles to mini- and family suites, make this a good choice for families.
Pros: Walking distance from waterfront and harbor; family-friendly;
great value. **Cons:** Busy lobby; pool can be crowded. ✉*109 Bath St.*
☎*805/963–8845 or 800/663–5288 ⊕www.franciscaninn.com ☞48
rooms, 5 suites ♿In-room: kitchen (some), refrigerator (some), VCR,
dial-up, Wi-Fi. In-hotel: no elevator, pool, laundry facilities, no-smok-
ing rooms ⊟AE, DC, MC, V ⏏CP.*

$-$$ ☷ **Motel 6 Santa Barbara Beach.** A half block from East Beach amid
fancier hotels sits this basic but comfortable motel, which was the first
Motel 6 in existence. It's an incredible bargain for the location and
fills quickly; book months in advance if possible. Kids 17 and under
stay free. Sister properties in Goleta and in Carpinteria, 12 mi south
of Santa Barbara and 1 mi from the beach, offer equally comfortable
rooms at even lower rates. **Pros:** Less than a minute's walk from the zoo

and beach; friendly staff; clean and comfortable. **Cons:** No frills; motel-style rooms; no breakfast. ✉*443 Corona Del Mar Dr.* ☎*805/564–1392 or 800/466–8356* ⊕*www.motel6.com* ⬅*51 rooms* ⎙*In-room: refrigerator (some), Wi-Fi. In-hotel: no elevator, pool, public Wi-Fi, some pets allowed, no-smoking rooms* ⊟*AE, D, DC, MC, V.*

NIGHTLIFE & THE ARTS

Most major hotels present entertainment nightly during the summer season and on weekends all year. Much of the town's bar, club, and live music scene centers around lower State Street (between the 300 and 800 blocks). The thriving arts district, with theaters, restaurants, and cafés, starts around the 900 block of State Street and continues north to the Arlington Center for the Performing Arts, in the 1300 block. Santa Barbara supports a professional symphony and a chamber orchestra. The proximity to the University of California at Santa Barbara assures an endless stream of visiting artists and performers. To see what's scheduled around town, pick up a copy of the free weekly *Santa Barbara Independent* newspaper or visit their Web site, *www.independent.com.*

NIGHTLIFE   Rich leather couches, a crackling fire in chilly weather, a cigar balcony, and pool tables draw a fancy Gen-X crowd to **Blue Agave** (✉*20 E. Cota St.* ☎*805/899–4694*) for good food and designer martinis. All types of people hang out at **Dargan's** (✉*18 E. Ortega St.* ☎*805/568–0702*), a lively pub with four pool tables, a great selection of draft beer and Irish whiskeys, and a full menu of traditional Irish dishes. The **James Joyce** (✉*513 State St.* ☎*805/962–2688*), which sometimes plays host to folk and rock performers, is a good place to have a few beers and while away an evening.

Call ahead to reserve an outdoor table at **Indochine** (✉*434 State St.* ☎*805/962–0154*), a sleek Thai-style nightclub filled with Southeast Asian furniture and art, open Wednesday through Sunday nights. **Joe's Cafe** (✉*536 State St.* ☎*805/966–4638*), where steins of beer accompany hearty bar food, is a fun, if occasionally rowdy, collegiate scene. The bartenders at **Left at Albuquerque** (✉*700 State St.* ☎*805/564–5040*) pour 141 types of tequila, making the Southwestern-style bar one of Santa Barbara's less sedate nightspots. A slick sports bar attached to an upscale steak house owned by the maker of Lucky Brand Dungarees, **Lucky's** (✉*1279 Coast Village Rd., Montecito* ☎*805/565–7540*) attracts a flock of hip, fashionably dressed patrons hoping to see and be seen.

SOhO (✉*1221 State St.* ☎*805/962–7776*)—a hip restaurant, bar, and music club—schedules an eclectic mix of live music groups, from jazz to blues to rock, every night of the week.

THE ARTS   **Arlington Center for the Performing Arts** (✉*1317 State St.* ☎*805/963–4408*), a Moorish-style auditorium, is the home of the Santa Barbara Symphony. **Center Stage Theatre** (✉*700 block of State St., 2nd fl. of Paseo Nuevo* ☎*805/963–0408*) presents plays, music, dance, and readings. **Ensemble Theatre Company** (✉*914 Santa Barbara St.* ☎*805/962–8606*) stages plays by authors ranging from Henrik Ibsen and David Mamet to rising contemporary dramatists. Originally opened in 1924, the landmark **Granada Theatre** (✉*1214 State St.* ☏ *805/899–3000 general info, 805/899–2222 box office*) reopened to great fanfare in 2008 following a $50 million restoration and modernization. The **Lobero Theatre** (✉*33 E. Canon Perdido St.* ☏*805/963–0761*), a state landmark, hosts community theater groups and touring professionals. In Montecito, the **Music Academy of the West** (✉*1070 Fairway Rd.* ☏*805/969–4726, box office 805/969–8787*) showcases orchestral, chamber, and operatic works every summer.

> ### BIRTHPLACE OF THE ENVIRONMENTAL MOVEMENT
>
> In 1969, 200,000 gallons of crude oil spilled into the Santa Barbara Channel, causing an immediate outcry from residents, particularly in the UCSB community. The day after the spill, Get Oil Out (GOO) was established; the group helped lead the successful fight for legislation to limit and regulate offshore drilling in California. The Santa Barbara spill also spawned Earth Day, which is still celebrated in communities across the nation today.

15

SPORTS & THE OUTDOORS

BEACHES Santa Barbara's beaches don't have the big surf of the shoreline farther south, but they also don't have the crowds. You can usually find a solitary spot to swim or sunbathe. In June and July, fog often hugs the coast until about noon. The wide swath of sand at the east end of Cabrillo Boulevard on the harbor front is a great spot for people-watching. **East Beach** (✉*1118 Cabrillo Blvd.* ☏*805/897–2680*) has sand volleyball courts, summertime lifeguard and sports competitions, and arts-and-crafts shows on Sunday and holidays. You can use showers, a weight room, and lockers (bring your own towel) and rent umbrellas and boogie boards at the Cabrillo Bathhouse. Next door, there's an elaborate jungle-gym play area for kids. The usually gentle surf at **Arroyo Burro County Beach** (✉*Cliff Dr., at Las Positas Rd.*) makes it ideal for families with young children.

BICYCLING The level, two-lane, 3-mi **Cabrillo Bike Lane** passes the Santa Barbara Zoo, the Andree Clark Bird Refuge, beaches, and the harbor. There are restaurants along the way, and you can stop for a picnic along the palm-lined path looking out on the Pacific. **Wheel Fun Rentals** (✉*23 E. Cabrillo Blvd.* ☏*805/966–2282*) has bikes, quadricycles, and skates; a second outlet around the block rents small electric cars and scooters.

BOATS & CHARTERS **Captain Don's** (✉*Stearns Wharf* ☏*805/969–5217*) operates whale-watching and pirate-theme harbor cruises aboard the 40-foot *Harbour Queen* and the *Speed Twin*, a high-speed catamaran. **Santa Barbara Sailing Center** (✉*Santa Barbara Harbor launching ramp* ☏*805/962–2826 or 800/350–9090*) offers sailing instruction, rents and charters sailboats, and organizes dinner and sunset champagne cruises, island excursions, and whale-watching trips. **Sea Landing** (✉*Cabrillo Blvd., at Bath St. and the breakwater in the Santa Barbara Harbor* ☏*805/965–3564*) operates surface and deep-sea fishing charters year-round. From Sea Landing, the *Condor Express* (☏*805/963–3564*), a 75-foot high-speed catamaran, whisks up to 149 passengers toward the Channel

Islands on dinner cruises, whale-watching excursions, and pelagic-bird trips. **Truth Aquatics** (☎ *805/962–1127*) departs from Sea Landing in the Santa Barbara Harbor to ferry passengers on excursions to the National Marine Sanctuary and Channel Islands National Park. Their three dive boats also take scuba divers on single-day and multiday trips.

GOLF Like Pebble Beach, the 18-hole, par-72 **Sandpiper Golf Club** (✉ *7925 Hollister Ave., 14 mi north of downtown on Hwy. 101* ☎ *805/968—1541*) sits on the ocean bluffs and combines stunning views with a challenging game. Greens fees are $129–$149; a cart (optional) is $16. **Santa Barbara Golf Club** (✉ *Las Positas Rd. and McCaw Ave.* ☎ *805/687–7087*) has an 18-hole, par-70 course. The greens fees are $40–$50; a cart (optional) costs $26 per person.

TENNIS Many hotels in Santa Barbara have courts. The **City of Santa Barbara Parks and Recreation Department** (☎ *805/564–5418*) operates public courts with lighted play until 9 PM weekdays. You can purchase day permits ($6) at the courts, or call the department. **Las Positas Municipal Courts** (✉ *1002 Las Positas Rd.*) has six lighted hard courts open daily. The 12 hard courts at the **Municipal Tennis Center** (✉ *1414 Park Pl., near Salinas St. and U.S. 101*) include an enclosed stadium court and three lighted courts open daily. **Pershing Park** (✉ *100 Castillo St., near Cabrillo Blvd.*) has eight lighted courts available for public play after 5 PM weekdays and all day on weekends and Santa Barbara City College holidays.

SHOPPING

SHOPPING **State Street,** roughly between Cabrillo Boulevard and Sola Street, is
AREAS the commercial hub of Santa Barbara and a shopper's paradise. Chic malls, quirky storefronts, antiques emporia, elegant boutiques, and funky thrift shops abound here. **Paseo Nuevo** (✉ *700 and 800 blocks of State St.*), an open-air mall anchored by chains such as Nordstrom and Macy's, also contains a few local institutions such as the children's clothier This Little Piggy. You can do your shopping on foot or by a battery-powered trolley (25¢) that runs between the waterfront and the 1300 block.

Shops, art galleries, and studios share the courtyard and gardens of **El Paseo** (✉ *Canon Perdido St., between State and Anacapa Sts.*), a historic arcade. Antiques and gift shops are clustered in restored Victorian buildings on **Brinkerhoff Avenue** (✉ *2 blocks west of State St., at West Cota St.*). Serious antiques hunters can head a few miles south of Santa Barbara to the beach town of **Summerland,** which is full of shops and markets.

CLOTHING **The Beach House** (✉ *10 State St.* ☎ *805/963–1281*) carries surf clothing, gear, and collectibles; it's also the home of Santa Barbara Surf Shop and the exclusive local dealer of Surfboards by Yater. The complete line of **Big Dog Sportswear** (✉ *6 E. Yanonali St.* ☎ *805/963–8728*) is sold at the Santa Barbara–based company's flagship store. Established in the early 2000s, the original **Blue Bee** (✉ *911½ State St.* ☎ *805/897–1137*) boutique and its chic line of California clothes and accessories quickly morphed into an empire that now includes seven specialty shops peddling designer jeans, shoes, jewelry, and clothing for men, women, and kids; most occupy individual spaces in the La Arcada shopping plaza at State and Figueroa streets, across from the Santa Barbara Museum of Art. **Pierre Lafond–Wendy Foster** (⊠ *833 State St.* ☎*805/966–2276*) is a casual-chic clothing store for women. **Territory Ahead** (⊠ *Main store: 515 State St.* ⊠ *Outlet store: 400 State St.* ☎*805/962–5558*), a high-quality outdoorsy catalog company, sells fashionably rugged clothing for men and women.

EN ROUTE

If you choose to drive north via U.S. 101 without detouring to the Solvang/Santa Ynez area, you will drive right past some good beaches. In succession from east to west, **El Capitan, Gaviota, and Refugio state beaches** all have campsites, picnic tables, and fire rings. If you'd like to encounter nature without roughing it, you can try "comfort camping" at **El Capitan Canyon** (⊠ *11560 Calle Real, north side of El Capitan State Beach exit* ☎*805/685–3887 or 866/352–2729*). The safari tents and cedar cabins here have fresh linens and creature comforts. There are also spacious sites for tent and RV camping at the adjacent **Ocean Mesa Campground** (☎*805/879–5751 or 866/410–5783*).

15

SANTA BARBARA COUNTY

Residents refer to the glorious 30-mi stretch of coastline from Carpinteria to Gaviota as the South Coast. The Santa Ynez Mountains divide the county geographically; U.S. 101 passes through a mountain tunnel leading inland. Northern Santa Barbara County used to be known for its sprawling ranches and strawberry and broccoli fields. Today its 100-plus wineries and 22,000 acres of vineyards dominate the landscape from the Santa Ynez Valley in the south to Santa Maria in the north.

The hit film *Sideways* was filmed almost entirely in the North County wine country; when the movie won Golden Globe and Oscar awards in 2005, it sparked national and international interest in visits to the region.

The Santa Barbara Conference & Visitors Bureau (☎*805/966–9222 or 800/676–1266* ⊕*www.santabarbaraca.com*) created a detailed map highlighting film location spots. Maps can be downloaded from visitor bureau Web sites: *www.santaynezvalleyvisit.com* or *www.santa barbaraca.com*.

SANTA YNEZ

31 mi north of Goleta via Hwy. 154.

Founded in 1882, the tiny town of Santa Ynez still has many of its original frontier buildings. You can walk through the three-block downtown area in just a few minutes, shop for antiques, and hang around the old-time saloon. At some of the eponymous valley's best restaurants, you just might bump into one of the many celebrities who own nearby ranches.

Just south of Santa Ynez on the Chumash Indian Reservation lies the sprawling, Las Vegas–style **Chumash Casino Resort** (✉*3400 E. Hwy. 246* ☎*800/248–6274*). The casino has 2,000 slot machines, and the property includes three restaurants, a spa, and an upscale hotel ($$$–$$$$).

WHERE TO STAY & EAT

$$ ✕**Trattoria Grappolo.** Authentic Italian fare, an open kitchen, and fes-
★ tive, family-style seating make this trattoria equally popular with celebrities from Hollywood and ranchers from the Santa Ynez Valley. Italian favorites on the extensive menu range from thin-crust pizza to homemade ravioli, risottos, and seafood linguine to grilled lamb chops in red-wine sauce. The noise level tends to rise in the evening, so this isn't the best spot for a romantic getaway. ✉*3687-C Sagunto St.* ☎*805/688–6899* ▤*AE, MC, V* ⊗*No lunch Mon.*

$$$$ 🔲**Santa Ynez Inn.** This posh two-story Victorian inn in downtown Santa Ynez was built from scratch in 2002. The owners have furnished all the rooms with authentic historical pieces. The inn caters to a discerning crowd with the finest amenities—Frette linens, thermostatically controlled heat and air-conditioning, DVD/CD entertainment systems, and custom-made bathrobes. Most rooms have gas fireplaces, double steam showers, and whirlpool tubs. Rates include a phenomenal evening wine and hors d'oeuvres hour and a full breakfast. **Pros:** Near several restaurants, unusual antiques, spacious rooms. **Cons:** High price for location, not in a historic building. ✉*3627 Sagunto St.* ☎*805/688–5588 or 800/643–5774* ⊕*www.santaynezinn.com* ⇌*20 rooms* ⚷*In-room: Ethernet, Wi-Fi. In-hotel: gym, concierge, laundry service, no-smoking rooms* ▤*AE, D, MC, V* ⦿|*BP.*

SPORTS & THE OUTDOORS

The scenic rides operated by **Windhaven Glider** (✉*Santa Ynez Airport, Hwy. 246* ☎*805/688–2517*) cost between $125 and $245 and last up to 30 minutes.

LOS OLIVOS

4 mi north of Santa Ynez on Hwy. 154.

This pretty village in the Santa Ynez Valley was once on Spanish-built El Camino Real (Royal Highway) and later a stop on major stagecoach and rail routes. It's so sleepy today, though, that the movie *Return to Mayberry* was filmed here. A row of tasting rooms, art galleries, antiques stores, and country markets lines Grand Avenue.

Inside the intimate, 99-square-foot **Carhartt Vineyard Tasting Room** (✉*2990-A Grand Ave.* ☎*805/693–5100* ⊕*www.carharttvineyard. com*), you're likely to meet owners and winemakers Mike and Brooke Carhartt, who pour samples of their small-lot, handcrafted vintages most days.

Historic Heather Cottage, originally an early-1900s doctor's office, houses the **Daniel Gehrs Tasting Room** (✉*2939 Grand Ave.* ☎*800/275–*

8138 ⊕*www.dgwines.com*). Here you can sample Gehrs's various varietals, produced in limited small-lot quantities.

Firestone Vineyard (⊠*5000 Zaca Station Rd.* ☎*805/688–3940* ⊕*www.firestonewine.com*) has been around since 1972. It has daily tours, grassy picnic areas, and hiking trails in the hills overlooking the valley; the views are fantastic.

WHERE TO STAY & EAT

$$$$

FodorśChoice

★

✕**Brothers Restaurant at Mattei's Tavern.** In the stagecoach days, Mattei's Tavern provided wayfarers with hearty meals and warm beds. Chef-owners and brothers Matt and Jeff Nichols renovated the 1886 building, and while retaining the original character, transformed it into one of the best restaurants in the valley. The casual, unpretentious dining rooms with their red-velvet wallpaper and historic photos reflect the rich history of the tavern. The menu changes every few weeks but often includes house favorites such as spicy fried calamari, prime rib, and salmon, and the locally famous jalapeño corn bread. There's also a full bar and an array of vintages from the custom-built cedar wine cellar. ⊠*2350 Railway Ave.93441* ☎*805/688–4820* ⚲*Reservations essential* ▤*AE, MC, V* ☾*No lunch.*

$$

✕**Los Olivos Cafe.** Site of the scene in *Sideways* where the four main characters dine together and share a few bottles of wine, this down-to-earth restaurant not only provided the setting but served the actors real food from their existing menu during filming. Part wine store and part social hub for locals, the café focuses on wine-friendly fish, pasta, and meat dishes made from local bounty, plus salads, pizzas, and burgers. Don't miss the homemade muffuletta and olive tapenade spreads. Other house favorites include an artisanal cheese plate, baked Brie with honey-roasted hazelnuts, and braised pot roast with whipped potatoes. ⊠*2879 Grand Ave.* ☎*805/688–7265* ▤*AE, D, MC, V.*

$$$–$$$$

✕▦**The Ballard Inn.** Set among orchards and vineyards in the tiny town of Ballard, 2 mi south of Los Olivos, this inn makes an elegant wine-country escape. Rooms are furnished with antiques and original art. Seven rooms have wood-burning fireplaces; the inn provides room phones and TVs on request. The inn's tasting room serves boutique wines Friday through Sunday. At the Ballard Inn Restaurant ($$$), which serves dinner Wednesday through Sunday, owner-chef Budi Kazali creates sumptuous French–Asian dishes in one of the area's most romantic dining rooms. **Pros:** Exceptional food, attentive staff; secluded. **Cons:** Some baths could use updating; several miles from Los Olivos and Santa Ynez. ⊠*2436 Baseline Ave., Ballard* ☎*805/688–7770 or 800/638–2466* ⊕*www.ballardinn.com* ◄*15 rooms* ♺*In-room: no phone, no TV, Wi-Fi. In-hotel: restaurant, bicycles, no elevator, public Wi-Fi* ▤*AE, MC, V* ▦*BP.*

$$$$

▦**Fess Parker's Wine Country Inn and Spa.** This luxury inn includes an elegant, tree-shaded French country–style main building and an equally attractive annex across the street with a pool, hot tub, and day spa. The spacious accommodations have fireplaces, seating areas, and wet bars. **Pros:** Convenient wine-touring base; walking distance from restaurants and galleries; well-appointed rooms. **Cons:** Pricey; staff attention is

inconsistent. ✉*2860 Grand Ave.* ☎*805/688–7788 or 800/446–2455*
⊕*www.fessparker.com* ➪*20 rooms, 1 suite* ⚒*In-room: refrigerator,
Ethernet. In-hotel: restaurant, bar, pool, gym, spa, public Wi-Fi, some
pets allowed, no-smoking rooms* ▤*AE, DC, MC, V* ⦿*BP.*

SOLVANG

☾ *5 mi south of Los Olivos on Alamo Pintado Rd.; Hwy. 246, 3 mi east
of U.S. 101.*

You'll know you've reached the town of Solvang when the architecture
suddenly changes to half-timber buildings and windmills. This town
was settled in 1911 by a group of Danish educators (the flatlands and
rolling green hills reminded them of home), and even today, more than
two-thirds of the residents are of Danish descent. Although it's attracted
tourists for decades, in recent years it has become more sophisticated,
with galleries, upscale restaurants, and wine-tasting rooms. Most shops
are locally owned; the city has an ordinance prohibiting chain stores. A
good way to get your bearings is to park your car in one of the many
free public lots and stroll around town. Stop in at one of the visitor centers—at 2nd Street and Copenhagen Drive, or Mission Drive (Highway
246) at 5th Street—for maps and helpful advice on what to see and do.
Don't forget to stock up on Danish pastries from the town's excellent
bakeries before you leave.

Often called the Hidden Gem of
the missions, **Mission Santa Inés**
(✉*1760 Mission Dr.* ☎*805/688–
4815* ⊕*www.missionsantaines.
org* ✇*$4* ⊙*Daily 9–4:30*) has an
impressive collection of paintings,
statuary, vestments, and Chumash
and Spanish artifacts in a serene
bluff-top setting. Take a self-guided
tour through the museum, sanctuary, and tranquil gardens.

Housed in an 1884 adobe, the **Rideau
Vineyard** (✉*1562 Alamo Pintado
Rd.* ☎*805/688–0717* ⊕*www.
rideauvineyard.com*) tasting room
provides simultaneous blasts from
the area's ranching past and from
its hand-harvested, Rhône-varietal
wine-making present.

ON A MISSION

Six important California missions
established by Franciscan friars are
within the Central Coast region.
San Miguel is one of California's
best-preserved missions. La Purisima is the most fully restored;
Mission Santa Barbara is perhaps
the most beautiful in the state; and
Mission San Luis Obispo de Tolosa
has a fine museum with many
Chumash Indian artifacts. Mission
Santa Inés is known for its serene
gardens and restored artworks, and
Mission San Buenaventura has 250-
year-old paintings and statuary.

Just outside Solvang is the **Alma Rosa Winery** (✉*7250 Santa Rosa Rd.*
☎*805/688–9090* ⊕*www.almarosawinery.com*). Owners Richard and
Thekla Sanford helped put Santa Barbara County on the international
wine map with a 1989 pinot noir. Recently the Sanfords started a new
winery, Alma Rosa, with wines made from grapes grown on their 100-
plus-acre certified organic vineyards in the Santa Rita Hills. You can taste

the current releases at one of the most environmentally sensitive tasting rooms and picnic areas in the valley. All their vineyards are certified organic, and the pinot noirs and chardonnays are exceptional.

WHERE TO STAY & EAT

$$$ ✕**The Hitching Post II.** You'll find everything from grilled artichokes to ostrich at this casual eatery just outside of Solvang, but most people come for what is said to be the best Santa Maria–style barbecue in the state. The oak used in the barbecue imparts a wonderful smoky taste. Be sure to try a glass of owner-chef-winemaker Frank Ostini's signature Highliner pinot noir, a star in the 2004 film *Sideways*. ⊠*406 E. Hwy. 246* ☎*805/688–0676* ⊟*AE, MC, V* ⊘*No lunch*.

$$ ✕**Bit O' Denmark.** Perhaps the most authentic Danish eatery in Solvang, this restaurant (the oldest food establishment in Solvang) occupies an old-beam building that was a church until 1929. Two specialties of the house are the *Frikadeller* (meatballs with pickled red cabbage, potatoes, and thick brown gravy) and the *Medisterpølse* (Danish beef and pork sausage with cabbage). ⊠*473 Alisal Rd.* ☎*805/688–5426* ⊟*AE, D, MC, V.*

$$$$ ⊞**Alisal Guest Ranch and Resort.** Since 1946 this 10,000-acre ranch has
★ been popular with celebrities and plain folk alike. There are lots of activities to choose from here: horseback riding, golf, fishing, sailing in the 100-acre spring-fed lake—although you can also just lounge by the pool or book a treatment at the day spa. The ranch-style rooms and suites come with garden views, covered porches, high-beam ceilings, and wood-burning fireplaces, with touches of Spanish tile and fine Western art. A jacket is required at the nightly dinners (which are included in your room rate). **Pros:** Old West atmosphere; tons of activities; ultraprivate. **Cons:** Isolated; cut off from the high-tech world; some units are aging. ⊠*1054 Alisal Rd.* ☎*805/688–6411 or 800/425–4725* ⊕*www.alisal.com* ⊅*36 rooms, 37 suites* ⌂*In-room: no a/c, refrigerator, no TV. In-hotel: no elevator, restaurant, room service, bar, golf courses, tennis courts, pool, gym, spa, bicycles, children's programs (ages 6 and up), public Internet* ⊟*AE, DC, MC, V* ⏃*MAP.*

$$$$ ⊞**Petersen Village Inn.** Like most of Solvang's buildings, this upscale country inn wouldn't seem out of place in a small European village. The canopy beds here are plush, the bathrooms small but sparkling. Weekend rates include a complete French-theme dinner for two in the guests-only Café Provence—prepared by Swiss chef Erminio Dal-Fuoco—and a European buffet breakfast. **Pros:** In the heart of Solvang; easy parking; comfy beds. **Cons:** Right on Highway 246; atmosphere too traditional for some. ⊠*1576 Mission Dr.* ☎*805/688–3121 or 800/321–8985* ⊕*www.peterseninn.com* ⊅*39 rooms, 1 suite* ⌂*In-room: Wi-Fi. In-hotel: restaurant, no-smoking rooms* ⊟*AE, MC, V* ⏃*BP.*

$$ ⊞**Solvang Gardens Lodge.** Lush gardens with fountains and waterfalls, friendly staff, and cheery English-country-theme rooms with antiques make for a peaceful retreat just a few blocks—but worlds away—from Solvang's main tourist area. Rooms range from basic to elegant; each has unique character and furnishings, and many have marble showers and baths. Rates include complimentary access to a gym across the street. **Pros:** Homey; family-friendly; colorful gardens.

15

Cons: Some rooms are tiny; some units need upgrades. ✉️*293 Alisal Rd.* ☎️*805/688–4404 or 888/688–4404* ⊕*www.solvanggardens.com* ➪*16 rooms, 8 suites* ⚐*In-room: no phone, kitchen (some), refrigerator (some), DVD, Wi-Fi. In-hotel: spa, public Internet, no-smoking rooms* ▤*AE, D, MC, V* ⦿*CP.*

$ ▦**Best Western King Fredrik Inn.** Rooms at this comfortable and central motel are fairly spacious. If you want to stay right in Solvang and don't want to spend a fortune, this is a good bet. **Pros:** Great value; near main square; good choice for families. **Cons:** On main highway; miniature lobby; next to major city parking lot. ✉️*1617 Copenhagen Dr.* ☎️*805/688–5515 or 800/549–9955* ⊕*www.bwkingfrederik.com* ➪*46 rooms, 1 suite* ⚐*In-room: refrigerator, Ethernet. In-hotel: pool, no elevator, public Wi-Fi, no-smoking rooms* ▤*AE, D, DC, MC, V* ⦿*CP.*

LOMPOC

20 mi west of Solvang on Hwy. 246.

Known as the flower-seed capital of the world, Lompoc is blanketed with vast fields of brightly colored flowers that bloom from May through August.

For five days around the last weekend of June, the **Lompoc Valley Flower Festival** (☎️*805/735–8511* ⊕*www.flowerfestival.org*) brings a parade, carnival, and crafts show to town.

☾ At **La Purisima Mission State Historic Park** you can see Mission La Purisima Concepción, the most fully restored mission in the state. Founded in 1787, it stands in a stark and still remote location and powerfully evokes the lives of California's Spanish settlers. Docents lead tours every afternoon, and displays illustrate the secular and religious activities that were part of mission life. From March through October the mission holds special events, including crafts demonstrations by costumed docents. ✉️*2295 Purisima Rd., off Hwy. 246* ☎️*805/733–3713* ⊕*www.lapurisimamission.org* ▦*$4 per vehicle* ⊙*Daily 9–5; tour daily at 1.*

SAN LUIS OBISPO COUNTY

PISMO BEACH

U.S. 101/Hwy. 1, about 40 mi north of Lompoc.

About 20 mi of sandy shoreline—nicknamed the Bakersfield Riviera for the throngs of vacationers who come here from the Central Valley—begins at the town of Pismo Beach. The southern end of town runs along sand dunes, some of which are open to cars and off-road vehicles; sheltered by the dunes, a grove of eucalyptus trees attracts thousands of migrating monarch butterflies November through February. A long, broad beach fronts the center of town, where a municipal pier extends into the sea at the foot of shop-lined Pomeroy Street. To the north, hotels and homes perch atop chalky oceanfront cliffs.

Fewer than 10,000 people live in this quintessential surfer haven, but Pismo Beach has a slew of hotels and restaurants with great views of the Pacific Ocean. Still, rooms can sometimes be hard to come by. Each Father's Day weekend the Pismo Beach Classic, one of the West Coast's largest classic-car and street-rod shows, overruns the town. A Dixieland jazz festival in February also draws crowds.

> ### VOLCANOES?
>
> Those funny looking, sawed-off peaks along the drive from Pismo Beach to Morro Bay are the Seven Sisters—a series of ancient volcanic plugs. Morro Rock, the northernmost sibling and a state historic monument, is the most famous and photographed of the clan.

EN ROUTE

The spectacular **Guadalupe-Nipomo Dunes Preserve** stretches 18 mi along the coast south of Pismo Beach. It's the largest and most ecologically diverse dune system in the state, and a habitat for more than 200 species of birds as well as sea otters, black bears, bobcats, coyotes, and deer. The 1,500-foot Mussel Rock is the highest beach dune in the western states. As many as 20 movies have been filmed here, including Cecil B. DeMille's 1923 silent *The Ten Commandments*. The main entrances to the dunes are at Oso Flaco Lake (about 13 mi south of Pismo Beach on U.S. 101/Highway 1, then 3 mi west on Oso Flaco Road) and at the far west end of Highway 166 (Main Street) in Guadalupe. At the **Dunes Center** (⊠ *1055 Guadalupe St., 1 mi north of Hwy. 166* ☎ *805/343–2455* ⊕ *www.dunescenter.org* ☉ *Wed.–Sun. 10–4*), you can get nature information and view an exhibit about *The Ten Commandments* movie set, which weather and archaeologists are slowly unearthing near Guadalupe Beach. Parking at Oso Flaco Lake is $5 per vehicle.

15

WHERE TO STAY & EAT

$$ ✕**Cracked Crab.** This traditional New England–style crab shack imports fresh seafood daily from Australia, Alaska, and the East Coast. Fish is line-caught, much of the produce is organic, and everything is made from scratch. For a real treat, don a bib and chow through a bucket of steamed shellfish with Cajun sausage, potatoes, and corn on the cob, all dumped right onto your table. The menu changes daily. ⊠ *751 Price St.* ☎ *805/773–2722* ⚠ *Reservations not accepted* ▤ *AE, D, MC, V.*

$$ ✕**Giuseppe's Cucina Italiana.** The classic flavors of southern Italy are highlighted at this lively, warm downtown spot. Most recipes originate from Bari, a seaport on the Adriatic; the menu includes breads and pizzas baked in the wood-burning oven, hearty dishes such as osso buco and lamb, and homemade pastas. The wait for a table can be long at peak dinner hours, but sometimes an accordion player gets the crowd singing. Next door, their bakery sells take-out selections. ⊠ *891 Price St.* ☎ *805/773–2870* ⚠ *Reservations not accepted* ▤ *AE, D, MC, V* ☉ *No lunch weekends.*

¢ ✕**Splash Café.** Folks line up all the way down the block for clam chowder served in a sourdough bread bowl at this wildly popular seafood stand. You can also order beach food such as fresh steamed clams,

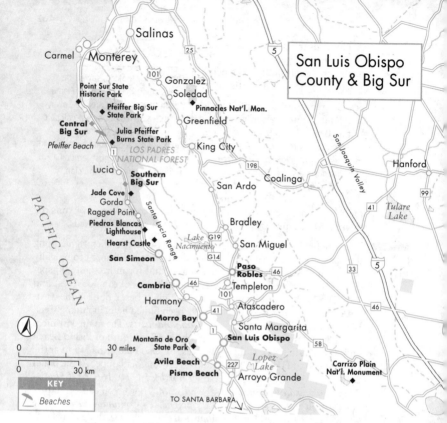

burgers, and fried calamari at the counter (no table service)—and many items on the menu are $7 or less. The grimy, cramped, but cheery hole-in-a-wall, a favorite with locals and savvy visitors, is open daily for lunch and dinner (plus a rock-bottom basic breakfast starting at 8 AM), but closes early on weekday evenings during low season. ⊠*197 Pomeroy St.* ☎*805/773–4653* ⊟*AE, D, MC, V.*

$$$$ ✕🏨 **Dolphin Bay.** Perched on grass-covered bluffs overlooking Shell Beach, this luxury resort looks and feels like an exclusive condominium community. Choose among sprawling one- or two-bedroom residences, each with a gourmet kitchen, laundry room with washer and dryer, and contemporary Mission-style furniture. Many have ocean views. Two-bedroom units include either a spa tub or fireplace; penthouse units have both. Rejuvenate at La Bonne Vie day spa, lounge by the infinity pool, or stroll down a short path to the beach to gaze at the sea—this place was made for upscale escape and relaxation. At Lido ($$$–$$$$), the fancy yet casual restaurant (no flip-flops), Chef Evan Treadwell presents an impressive menu of California wine country cuisine with an international flair; favorites include wild salmon medallions with curry sauce, and pulled-pork empanadas. **Pros:** Lavish apartment units; as upscale as you can get; killer views; walking distance from the beach. **Cons:** Hefty price tag; upper-crust vibe. ⊠*2727 Shell Beach Rd.* ☎*805/773–4300 or 800/516–0112* ⊕*www.thedolphinbay.com* ⌐*61*

residences ⟨In-room: kitchen, DVD, Ethernet, Wi-Fi. In-hotel: restaurant, room service, bar, pool, gym, spa, some pets allowed, no-smoking rooms ⊟AE, D, MC, V.

$$$ ✕⬚**Sea Venture Resort.** The bright, homey rooms at this hotel all have fireplaces and featherbeds; most have balconies with private hot tubs, and some have beautiful ocean views. A breakfast basket is delivered to your room in the morning, and the elegant Sea Venture Restaurant ($$–$$$, no lunch weekdays)—with sweeping ocean vistas from the third floor—features fresh seafood and local wines. **Pros:** On the beach; excellent food; romantic rooms. **Cons:** Touristy area; some rooms and facilities are beginning to age; dark hallways. ✉100 Ocean View Ave. ☎805/773–4994 or 800/662–5545 ⊕www.seaventure.com ⇄50 rooms ⟨In-room: no a/c, refrigerator, Ethernet, Wi-Fi. In-hotel: restaurant, spa, bicycles, no-smoking rooms ⊟AE, D, DC, MC, V ⎪○⎪CP.

$$$$ ⬚**Pismo Lighthouse Suites.** Each of the well-appointed two-room, two-bath suites at this oceanfront resort has a private balcony or patio. Some suites are suitable for couples, others for families, and all have crisp nautical-style furnishings. Ask for a corner oceanfront suite for the best views. On the central sport court you can play a variety of games, including chess on a life-size board. **Pros:** Lots of space for families and groups; nice pool area. **Cons:** Not easy to walk to main attractions; some units are next to busy road. ✉2411 Price St. ☎805/773–2411 or 800/245–2411 ⊕www.pismolighthousesuites.com ⇄70 suites ⟨In-room: refrigerator, Ethernet, Wi-Fi. In-hotel: pool, gym, laundry facilities, no-smoking rooms ⊟AE, D, DC, MC, V ⎪○⎪CP.

$–$$ ⬚**Shell Beach Inn.** Just 2½ blocks from the beach, this basic but cozy motor court is a great bargain for the area. Along with a 2005 room remodel, the property upgraded its name from "motel" to "inn." Choose from king, queen, or two-bedded rooms; all have European country-style furnishings and floral details painted on the walls and ceilings. **Pros:** Walking distance from the beach; clean rooms; friendly and dependable service. **Cons:** Sits on a busy road; small rooms; tiny pool. ✉653 Shell Beach Rd. ☎805/773–4373 or 800/549–4727 ⊕www.shellbeachinn.com ⇄10 rooms ⟨In-room: no a/c, refrigerator, dial-up. In-hotel: pool, some pets allowed ⊟AE, D, DC, MC, V.

AVILA BEACH

⟨ *4 mi north of Pismo Beach on U.S. 101/Hwy. 1.*

Because the village of Avila Beach and the sandy, cove-front shoreline for which it's named face south into the Pacific Ocean, they get more sun and less fog than any other stretch of coast in the area. It can be bright and warm here while just beyond the surrounding hills communities shiver under the marine layer. With its fortuitous climate and protected waters, Avila's public beach draws plenty of sunbathers and families; weekends are very busy. Demolished in 1998 to clean up extensive oil seepage from a Unocal tank farm, downtown Avila Beach has sprung back to life. The seaside promenade has been fully restored and shops and hotels have quickly popped up; with mixed results the

15

town has tried to re-create its former offbeat character. For real local color, head to the far end of the cove and watch the commercial fishing boats offload their catch on the old Port San Luis wharf. A few seafood shacks and fish markets do business on the pier while sea lions congregate below. On Fridays from June through September, a fish and farmers' market livens up the beach area with music, fresh local produce and seafood, and a children's bounce house.

WHERE TO STAY & EAT

$$$ ✕**Olde Port Inn.** Locals swear by this old-fashioned fish house at the end of the Port San Luis Pier. Ask for today's fresh catch, or go for the *cioppino* (spicy tomato-based seafood stew) or fish tacos; simplicity is the key to a decent meal here. You can't beat the views, whether you're looking out over the ocean or through the glass surface of your table into the waters below. ⊠*End of 3rd pier* ☎*805/595–2515* ▤*AE, D, MC, V.*

$$–$$$ ✕▥**Sycamore Mineral Springs Resort.** This wellness resort's hot mineral springs bubble up into private outdoor tubs on an oak-and-sycamore-forest hillside. Whether or not you stay here, it's worth coming for a soak—even though the grounds are well within earshot of a busy road. Each room or suite has its own private balcony with a hot tub; about half have mineral water piped in. New owners have gradually been upgrading furnishings and amenities since taking over in 2003; insist on a renovated room. The spa offers everything from massages and skin care to yoga classes and a variety of integrative healing arts. Creative spa and California cuisine is served in the romantic Gardens of Avila restaurant ($$–$$$). **Pros:** Great place to rejuvenate; nice hiking; incredible spa services. **Cons:** Rooms vary in quality; 2½ mi from the beach. ⊠*1215 Avila Beach Dr., San Luis Obispo* ☎*805/595–7302 or 800/234–5831* ⊕*www.sycamoresprings.com* ⇱*26 rooms, 50 suites* ⌂*In-room: refrigerator (some), Ethernet, Wi-Fi. In-hotel: restaurant, room service, bar, pool, spa, no elevator, no-smoking rooms* ▤*AE, D, DC, MC, V.*

$$$$ ▥**Avila La Fonda.** Modeled after a village in early California's Mexican period, Avila La Fonda surrounds guests with rich jewel tones, fountains, and upscale comfort. The facade of the hotel replicates eight different casitas, including several famous historic homes in Mexico. Inside, stained-glass windows and tiled murals celebrate Mexican art and life in Avila Beach. Guests can choose from two types of rooms: a spa room with a huge tub near the king bed, or a great room with gourmet kitchen, queen Murphy bed, and sofa sleeper. You can also combine adjacent rooms to create your own casita. The lavish Owner's Spa Suite includes a sauna and steam shower—it's available to guests when it's not occupied by the owner or special guests. An added bonus: the beach is just one block away. **Pros:** One-of-a-kind theme and artwork; flexible room combinations; only a block from the beach. **Cons:** Pricey; most rooms don't have an ocean view. ⊠*101 San Miguel St.* ☎*805/595–1700* ⊕*www.avilalafondahotel.com* ⇱*32 rooms, 1 suite* ⌂*In-room: kitchen (some), refrigerator, DVD, dial-up, Wi-Fi. In-hotel: laundry service, public Wi-Fi, no-smoking rooms.* ▤*AE, D, MC, V.*

SAN LUIS OBISPO

8 mi north of Avila Beach on U.S. 101/Hwy. 1.

About halfway between San Francisco and Los Angeles, San Luis Obispo—nicknamed SLO—spreads out below gentle hills and rocky extinct volcanoes. Its main appeal lies in its architecturally diverse and commercially lively downtown, especially several blocks of Higuera Street. The pedestrian-friendly district bustles with shoppers, restaurant goers, and students from California Polytechnic State University, known as Cal Poly. On Thursday from 6 PM to 9 PM a farmers' market fills Higuera Street with local produce, entertainment, and food stalls. SLO is less a vacation destination than a pleasant stopover along Highway 1; it's a nice place to stay while touring the wine country south of town.

★ Special events often take place on sun-dappled Mission Plaza in front of **Mission San Luis Obispo de Tolosa,** established in 1772. Its small museum exhibits artifacts of the Chumash Indians and early Spanish settlers, and docents sometimes lead tours of the church and grounds. ⊠ *751 Palm St.* ☎ *805/543–6850* ⊕ *www.missionsanluisobispo.org* ⊠ *$3 suggested donation* ⊙ *Apr.–late-Oct., daily 9–5; late Oct.–Mar., daily 9–4.*

🔄 The delightful, sparkling new **San Luis Obispo Children's Museum,** reopened in 2008, has 21 indoor and outdoor activities that present a kid-friendly version of the city of San Luis Obispo. Visitors enter through an "imagination-powered" elevator, which transports them to a series of underground caverns beneath the city, while simulated lava and steam sputters from an active volcano. Kids can pick rubber fruit at a farmers' market, clamber up a clockworks tower, race to fight a fire on a fire engine, and learn about solar energy from a 15-foot sunflower. ⊠ *1010 Nipomo St.* ☎ *805/545–5874* ⊕ *www.slocm.org* ⊠ *$8* ⊙ *Tues.–Sat. 9:30–5, Sun. and select Mon. holidays 10:30–5*

🔄 Across the street from the old Spanish mission, **San Luis Obispo County Historical Museum** presents rotating exhibits on various aspects of county history—such as Native American life, California ranchos, and the impact of railroads. A separate children's room has theme activities where kids can earn prizes. ⊠ *696 Monterey St.* ☎ *805/543–0638* ⊕ *www.slochs.org* ⊠ *Free* ⊙ *Wed.–Sun. 10–4.*

San Luis Obispo is the commercial center of **Edna Valley/Arroyo Grande Valley wine country,** whose appellations stretch east–west from San Luis Obispo toward the coast and toward Lake Lopez in the inland mountains. Many of the 20 or so wineries line Highway 227 and connecting roads. The region is best known for chardonnay and pinot noir, although many wineries experiment with other varietals and blends. Wine-touring maps are readily available around town; note that many wineries charge a small tasting fee, and most tasting rooms close at 5.

For sweeping views of the Edna Valley while you sample estate-grown chardonnay, go to the modern tasting bar at **Edna Valley Vineyard** (⊠ *2585 Biddle Ranch Rd.* ☎ *805/544–5855* ⊕ *www.ednavalley.com*).

15

A refurbished 1909 schoolhouse serves as tasting room for **Baileyana Winery** (⊠ *5828 Orcutt Rd.* ☎ *805/269–8200* ⊕ *www. baileyana.com*), which produces concentrated chardonnays, pinot noirs, and Syrahs. Its sister winery, Tangent, creates alternative white wines and shares the tasting room.

> **DEEP ROOTS**
>
> Way back in the 1700s, the Spanish padres who accompanied Father Junípero Serra planted grapevines from Mexico along California's Central Coast, and began using European wine-making techniques to turn the grapes into delectable vintages.

Best-known for its pinot noir– and Syrah-based reds, **Domaine Alfred** (⊠ *7525 Orcutt Rd.* ☎ *805/541–9463* ⊕ *www.domainealfred.com*) grows most of its grapes in the Edna Valley's oldest vineyard, which the winery bought in 1994.

An ecofriendly winery built from straw bales, **Claiborne & Churchill** (⊠ *2649 Carpenter Canyon Rd.* ☎ *805/544–4066* ⊕ *www.claiborne churchill.com*) makes small lots of exceptional Alsatian-style wines such as dry Riesling and gewürztraminer.

While touring Edna Valley wine country, be sure to stop at **Old Edna** (⊠ *Hwy. 227, at Price Canyon Rd.* ☎ *805/544–8062* ⊕ *www.oldedna. com*), a peaceful, 2-acre site that once was the town of Edna. Browse for gifts and antiques, pick up sandwiches at the gourmet deli, and stroll along Old Edna Lane.

A nonprofit entity founded by the San Luis Obispo County Vintners Association, **Taste** (⊠ *1003 Osos St.* ☎ *805/269–8278* ⊕ *www.taste-slo. com* ☉ *Mon.–Sat. 11–9, Sun. 11–5*) pours samples of up to 72 different south county vintages from a nifty dispensing system that keeps oxygen out of the wines. This provides a great downtown wine-tasting alternative for those who don't have time to tour outside of town.

WHERE TO STAY & EAT

$$$
★ ✕ **The Park Restaurant.** This is one of the most sophisticated restaurants in the county. Chef-owner Meghan Loring presents food that she describes as "refined rustic." The always-evolving menu relies on seasonal ingredients sourced from local producers. You might find sweet pea–asparagus soup with mint cream, or organic rib eye with panko-fried shiitakes. The well-crafted wine and beer list includes local and international selections. Service is skillful in the spare, white-table-cloth dining room and on the tree-rimmed patio. ⊠ *1819 Osos St.* ☎ *805/545–0000* ⊟ *AE, MC, V* ☉ *Closed Mon. No lunch.*

$$
★ ✕ **Big Sky Café.** A popular gathering spot three meals a day, this quintessentially Californian, family-friendly (and sometimes noisy) café turns local and organically grown ingredients into global dishes. Spicy Portuguese piri-piri chicken, Thai catfish, New Mexican *pozole* (hominy stew): just pick your continent. Vegetarians have lots to choose from. ⊠ *1121 Broad St.* ☎ *805/545–5401* ⊿ *Reservations not accepted* ⊟ *AE, MC, V.*

$$
✕ **Buona Tavola.** Homemade pasta with river shrimp in a creamy tomato sauce and porcini-mushroom risotto are among the northern Italian

dishes served at this casual spot. Daily fresh fish and salad specials and an impressive wine list attract a steady stream of regulars. In good weather you can dine on the flower-filled patio. The Paso Robles branch is equally enjoyable. ⊠*1037 Monterey St.* ☎*805/545–8000* ⊠*943 Spring St., Paso Robles* ☎*805/237–0600* ▤*AE, D, MC, V* ◷*No lunch weekends.*

$ ✕**Novo Restaurant and Bakery.** In the colorful dining room or on the large creek-side deck, this animated downtown eatery will take you on a culinary world tour. The salads, small plates, and entrées come from nearly every continent. The wine and beer list also covers the globe (you can sample various international wines paired with tapas Sunday evenings)—and includes local favorites. Many of the decadent desserts are baked at the restaurant's sister property in Cambria, the French Corner Bakery. ⊠*726 Higuera St.* ☎*805/543–3986* ▤*MC, V.*

¢ ✕**Mo's Smokehouse BBQ.** Barbecue joints abound on the Central Coast, but this one excels. A variety of southern-style sauces seasons tender hickory-smoked ribs and shredded meat sandwiches; sides such as baked beans, coleslaw, homemade potato chips, and garlic bread extend the pleasure. ⊠*1005 Monterey St.* ☎*805/544–6193* ▤*AE, MC, V.*

$$$–$$$$ ⌂**Apple Farm.** Decorated to the hilt with floral bedspreads and watercolors by local artists, this Victorian country-style hotel is one of the most popular places to stay in San Luis Obispo. Each room has a gas fireplace and fresh flowers; some have canopy beds and cozy window seats. There's a working gristmill in the courtyard; within the inn are a restaurant serving American food (the hearty breakfasts are best), a gourmet food and wine shop, a bakery, and a gift shop. **Pros:** Flowers everywhere; convenient to Cal Poly and Hwy. 101; creek-side setting. **Cons:** Hordes of tourists stop here during the day; too floral for some people's tastes. ⊠*2015 Monterey St.* ☎*800/374–3705* ⊕*www.applefarm. com* ⇆*66 rooms, 3 suites* ⌂*In-room: dial-up. In-hotel: restaurant, pool, spa, public Wi-Fi, no-smoking rooms* ▤*AE, D, MC, V.*

$$–$$$ ⌂**Garden Street Inn.** From this fully restored 1887 Italianate Queen Anne, the only lodging in downtown SLO, you can walk to many restaurants and attractions. The individually decorated rooms, each with private bath, are filled with antiques; some have stained-glass windows, fireplaces, and decks. Each evening, wine and hors d'oeuvres are served in the intimate dining room; there's also a lavish homemade breakfast when you rise. **Pros:** Classic B&B; walking distance from everywhere downtown; nice wine-and-cheese reception. **Cons:** City noise filters through some rooms; not a great place for families. ⊠*1212 Garden St.* ☎*805/545–9802 or 800/488–2045* ⊕*www.gardenstreetinn.com* ⇆*9 rooms, 4 suites* ⌂*In-room: no TV (some), dial-up, Wi-Fi. In-hotel: no elevator, no-smoking rooms* ▤*AE, D, MC, V* ⦿*BP.*

$$–$$$ ⌂**Petit Soleil.** A cobblestone courtyard, country-French custom furnishings, and Gallic music piped through the halls evoke a Provençal mood at this cheery inn on upper Monterey Street's motel row. With extensive experience in luxury lodging, the owners are serious about the details: the individually themed rooms, sprinkled with lavender water, have CD players and L'Occitane bath products. Rates include wine and appe-

15

tizers at cocktail hour and a full homemade breakfast in the sun-filled patio or dining room. **Pros:** French details throughout; scrumptious breakfasts; cozy rooms. **Cons:** Sits on a busy avenue; cramped parking. ⊠*1473 Monterey St.* ☎*805/549–0321 or 800/676–1588* ⊕*www. petitsoleilslo.com* ➪*15 rooms, 1 suite* ⌂*In-room: no a/c, Wi-Fi. In-hotel: no elevator, no-smoking rooms* ⊟*AE, MC, V* ⦿|*BP.*

NIGHTLIFE & THE ARTS

NIGHTLIFE   The club scene in this college town is centered on Higuera Street off Monterey Street. The **Frog and Peach** (⊠*728 Higuera St.* ☎*805/595–3764*) is a decent spot to nurse an English beer and listen to live music. **Linnaea's Cafe** (⊠*1110 Garden St.* ☎*805/541–5888*), a mellow java joint, sometimes holds poetry readings, as well as blues, jazz, and folk music performances. Chicago-style **Mother's Tavern** (⊠*725 Higuera St.* ☎*805/541–8733*) draws crowds with good pub food and live entertainment in a turn-of-the-20th-century setting (complete with antique U.S. flags and a wall-mounted moose head).

THE ARTS   The **Performing Arts Center** (⊠*1 Grand Ave.* ☎*805/756–7222, 805/756–2787 for tickets outside CA, 888/233–2787 for tickets in CA* ⊕*www. pacslo.org*) at Cal Poly hosts live theater, dance, and music performances by artists from around the world. The **San Luis Obispo Mozart Festival** (☎*805/781–3008* ⊕*www.mozartfestival.com*) takes place in late July and early August. Not all the music is Mozart; you'll also hear Haydn and other composers. **San Luis Obispo Art Center** (⊠*1010 Broad St., at Mission Plaza* ☎*805/543–8562* ⊕*www.sloartcenter.org* ⊙*Closed Tues. early Sept.–late June*) displays and sells a mix of traditional work and cutting-edge arts and crafts by Central Coast, national, and international artists.

SPORTS & THE OUTDOORS

A hilly greenbelt with vast amounts of open space and extensive hiking trails surrounds the city of San Luis Obispo. For information on trailheads, call the city **Parks and Recreation Department** (☎*805/781–7300* ⊕*www.slocity.org/parksandrecreation*) or visit its Web site to download a trail map.

EN
ROUTE   Instead of continuing north on Highway 1 from San Luis Obispo to Morro Bay, consider taking Los Osos Valley Road (off Madonna Road, south of downtown) past farms and ranches to dramatic **Montaña de Oro State Park** (⊠*7 mi south of Los Osos on Pecho Rd.* ☎*805/528–0513 or 805/772–7434* ⊕*www.parks.ca.gov*). The park has miles of nature trails along rocky shoreline, wild beaches, and hills overlooking some of California's most spectacular scenery. Check out the tide pools, watch the waves roll into the bluffs, and picnic in the eucalyptus groves.

MORRO BAY

14 mi north of San Luis Obispo on Hwy. 1.

Commercial fishermen slog around Morro Bay in galoshes, and beat-up fishing boats bob in the bay's protected waters.

At the mouth of Morro Bay, which is both a state and national estuary, stands 576-foot-high **Morro Rock** (⊠*Northern end of Embarcadero*) one of nine such small volcanic peaks, or morros, in the area. A short walk leads to a breakwater, with the harbor on one side and the crashing waves of the Pacific on the other. You may not climb the rock, where endangered falcons and other birds nest. Sea lions and otters often play in the water at the foot of the peak.

The center of the action on land is the **Embarcadero** (⊠*On waterfront from Beach St. to Tidelands Park*), where vacationers pour in and out of souvenir shops and seafood restaurants. From here, you can get out on the bay in a kayak or tour boat.

☾ South of downtown Morro Bay, interactive exhibits at the spiffy **Morro**
★ **Bay State Park Museum of Natural History** teach kids and adults about the natural environment and how to preserve it—both in the Morro Bay estuary and on the rest of the planet. ⊠*State Park Rd.* ☎*805/772–2694* ⊕*www.ccnha.org* ⊠*$2* ⊙*Daily 10–5.*

WHERE TO STAY & EAT

$$$ ✕**Windows on the Water.** From giant picture windows at this second-floor spot, watch the sun set over the water. Fresh fish and other dishes based on local ingredients emerge from the wood-fired oven in the open kitchen; a variety of oysters on the half shell beckon from the raw bar. About 20 of the wines on the extensive, mostly California list are poured by the glass. Service is uneven and can be amateurish for the setting. ⊠*699 Embarcadero* ☎*805/772–0677* ⊟*AE, D, DC, MC, V* ⊙*No lunch.*

$$ ✕**Dorn's Original Breakers Cafe.** This seafood restaurant overlooking the harbor has satisfied Morro Bay appetites since 1948. In addition to excellent, straight-ahead fish dishes such as petrale sole or calamari steaks sautéed in butter and wine, Dorn's serves breakfast. ⊠*801 Market Ave.* ☎*805/772–4415* ⊟*D, MC, V.*

¢ ✕**Taco Temple.** The devout stand in line at this family-run diner that
★ serves some of the freshest food around. Seafood anchors a menu of dishes—salmon burritos, superb fish tacos with mango salsa—hailing from somewhere between California and Mexico. Desserts get rave reviews, too. Make an effort to find this gem tucked away in the corner of a supermarket parking lot north of downtown—it's on the frontage road parallel to Highway 1, just north of the Highway 41 junction. A renovation and expansion are planned; call ahead to be sure they're open. ⊠*2680 Main St., at Elena* ☎*805/772–4965* ⌦*Reservations not accepted* ⊟*No credit cards* ⊙*Closed Tues.*

$$$ ▥**Ascot Suites.** A hop and a skip from the Embarcadero, this hotel wins loyal guests with its high-end conveniences. There are large jetted tubs in most bathrooms, well-stocked wet bars, and gas fireplaces. A complimentary breakfast basket arrives at your door each morning. **Pros:** Romantic rooms; close to the waterfront; upscale amenities. **Cons:** Drab neighborhood; not especially child-friendly. ⊠*260 Morro Bay Blvd.* ☎*805/772–4437 or 800/887–6454* ⊕*www.ascotinn.com* ⇌*32 units* ⌂*In-room: refrigerator, VCR, Wi-Fi (some). In-hotel: pool, concierge, public Wi-Fi, no-smoking rooms* ⊟*AE, D, DC, MC, V* ⦿*CP.*

15

$$–$$$ ▧ **The Inn at Morro Bay.** Surrounded by eucalyptus trees on the edge of Morro Bay, the inn abuts a heron rookery and Morro Bay State Park. It's a beautiful setting, even though the birds can cause a din (and make a mess of parked cars). Many of the contemporary-style rooms have fireplaces, private decks with spa tubs, and bay views. The most affordable rooms (petite queens) can seem small and dark, but you'll probably be spending much of your time elsewhere: getting a massage at the on-site wellness center, playing a round (fee) at the golf course across the road, or peddling through the state park on a complimentary bicycle. **Pros:** Great for wildlife enthusiasts, stellar bay views from restaurant and some rooms. **Cons:** Some rooms are cramped and dark, some sections need updating, birds can wake you early. ⊠*60 State Park Rd.* ☎*805/772–5651 or 800/321–9566* ⊕*www.innatmorro bay.com* ⇨*97 rooms, 1 cottage* ⚒*In-room: refrigerator, Ethernet. In-hotel: 2 restaurants, room service, bar, pool, spa, bicycles, laundry service, no-smoking rooms* ☰*AE, D, DC, MC, V.*

SPORTS & THE OUTDOORS

Kayak Horizons (⊠*551 Embarcadero* ☎*805/772–6444* ⊕*www.kayak horizons.com*) rents kayaks and gives lessons and guided tours. **Sub-Sea Tours** (⊠*699 Embarcadero* ☎*805/772–9463* ⊕*www.subseatours. com*) operates glass-bottom boat and catamaran cruises and has kayak and canoe rentals and summer whale-watching cruises. **Virg's Sport Fishing** (⊠*1215 Embarcadero* ☎*805/772–1222* ⊕*www.virgs.com*) conducts deep-sea fishing and whale-watching trips.

PASO ROBLES

30 mi north of San Luis Obispo on U.S. 101; 25 mi northwest of Morro Bay via Hwy. 41 and U.S. 101.

In the 1860s tourists began flocking to this dusty ranching outpost to "take the cure" in a luxurious bathhouse fed by underground mineral hot springs. An Old West town, complete with opera house, emerged; grand Victorian homes went up, followed in the 20th century by Craftsman bungalows. A 2003 earthquake demolished or weakened several beloved downtown buildings, but historically faithful reconstruction has proceeded rapidly.

Today the wine industry booms and mile upon mile of vineyards envelop Paso Robles; golfers play the four local courses and spandex-clad bicyclists race along the winding back roads. A mix of down-home and upmarket restaurants, bars, antiques stores, and little shops fills the streets around oak-shaded City Park, where special events of all kinds—custom car shows, an olive festival, Friday night summer concerts—take place on many weekends. Still, Paso (as the locals call it) more or less remains cowboy country: each year in late July and early August, the city throws the two-week California Mid-State Fair, complete with livestock auctions, carnival rides, and corn dogs.

Take a look back at California's rural heritage at the **Paso Robles Pioneer Museum.** Displays of historical ranching paraphernalia, horse-drawn vehicles, hot springs artifacts, and photos evoke the town's old days; a one-room schoolhouse is part of the complex. ✉*2010 Riverside Ave.* ☎*805/239–4556* ⊕*www. pasoroblespioneermuseum.org* ✉*Free* ◷*Thurs.–Sun. 1–4.*

The lakeside **River Oaks Hot Springs & Spa,** on 240 hilly acres near the intersection of U.S. 101 and Highway 46E, is a great place to relax before and after wine tasting or festival going. Soak in a private indoor or outdoor hot tub fed by natural mineral springs or indulge in a massage or facial. ✉*800 Clubhouse Dr.* ☎*805/238–4600* ⊕*www.pasohot springs.com* ✉*Hot tubs $13 to $20 per person per hr* ◷*Sun.–Thurs. 9– 9, Fri. and Sat. 9–10.*

In **Paso Robles wine country,** nearly 170 wineries and more than 26,000

LAID-BACK WINE COUNTRY

Hundreds of vineyards and wineries dot the hillsides from Paso Robles to San Luis Obispo, through the scenic Edna Valley and south to northern Santa Barbara County. The wineries offer much of the variety of northern California's Napa and Sonoma valleys—without the glitz and crowds. Since the early 1980s the region has developed an international reputation for high-quality wines, most notably pinot noir, chardonnay, and zinfandel. Wineries here tend to be small, but most have tasting rooms (some have tours), and you'll often meet the winemakers themselves.

vineyard acres pepper the wooded hills west of U.S. 101 and blanket the flatter, more open land on the east side. The region's brutally hot summer days and cool nights yield stellar grapes that make noteworthy wines, particularly robust reds such as cabernet sauvignon, merlot, zinfandel, and Rhône varietals such as Syrah. An abundance of exquisite whites also comes out of Paso, including chardonnay and Rhône varietals such as Viognier. Small-town friendliness prevails at most wineries, especially smaller ones, which tend to treat visitors like neighbors. Pick up a regional wine-touring map at lodgings, wineries, and attractions around town. Most tasting rooms close at 5 PM; many charge a small fee.

Most of the local wineries pour at the **Paso Robles Wine Festival,** held mid-May in City Park. The outdoor tasting—the largest such California event—includes live bands and diverse food vendors. Winery open houses and winemaker dinners round out the weekend. ✉*Spring Street, between 10th and 12th Sts., City Park* ☎*805/239–8463* ⊕*www. pasowine.com* ✉*$55, designated driver $15.*

Small but swank **Justin Vineyards & Winery** (✉*11680 Chimney Rock Rd.* ☎*805/238–6932 or 800/726–0049* ⊕*www.justinwine.com*) makes Bordeaux-style blends at the western end of Paso Robles wine country. This reader favorite offers winery, vineyard, and barrel-tasting tours ($15 to $50). In the tasting room there's a deli bar; a tiny high-end restaurant is also part of the complex.

Tucked in the far-west hills of Paso Robles, **Tablas Creek Vineyard** (✉*9339 Adelaida Rd.* ☎*805/237–1231* ⊕*www.tablascreek.com*) makes some of the area's finest wine by blending organically grown,

15

hand-harvested Rhône varietals such as Syrah, Grenache, Roussanne, and Viognier. Tours include a chance to graft your own grapevine.

★ While touring the idyllic west side of Paso Robles, take a break from wine by stopping at **Willow Creek Olive Ranch** (⊠ *8530 Vineyard Dr.* ☎*805/ 227–0186* ⊕*www.pasolivo.com*). Find out how they make their Tuscan-style Pasolivo olive oils on a high-tech Italian press, and taste the widely acclaimed results.

In southeastern Paso Robles wine country, **Wild Horse Winery & Vineyards** (⊠ *1437 Wild Horse Winery Ct., Templeton* ☎*805/434–2541* ⊕*www. wildhorsewinery.com*) was a pioneer Central Coast producer. You can try delicious, well-priced pinot noir, chardonnay, and merlot in their simple tasting room.

As they say around Paso Robles, it takes a lot of beer to make good wine, and to meet that need the locals turn to **Firestone Walker Fine Ales** (⊠ *1400 Ramada Dr.* ☎*805/238–2556* ⊕*www.firestonewalker.com*). In the brewery's taproom, sample medal-winning craft beers such as Double Barrel Ale. They close at 7 PM.

Even if you don't drink wine, stop at **Eberle Winery** (⊠ *Hwy. 46E, 3½ mi east of U.S. 101* ☎*805/238–9607* ⊕*www.eberlewinery.com*) for a fascinating tour of the huge wine caves beneath the east-side Paso Robles vineyard. Gary Eberle, one of Paso wine's founding fathers, is obsessed with cabernet sauvignon.

For an aerial view of vineyards, ranches, and mountains, make an advance reservation with **Let's Go Ballooning!** Flights carrying up to four passengers launch at sunrise and last about an hour. ⊠*Paso Robles Airport, 4912 Wing Way* ☎*805/458–1530* ⊕*www.sloballoon.com* ☞*$189 per person* ⊙*Daily.*

WHERE TO STAY & EAT

$$$ ✕ **Bistro Laurent.** Owner-chef Laurent Grangien has created a handsome,
★ welcoming French bistro in an 1890s brick building across from City Park. He focuses on traditional dishes such as osso buco, cassoulet, rack of lamb, goat-cheese tart, and onion soup, but always offers a few updated dishes as daily specials. Wines come from around the world. Le Petit Marcel, a tiny nook next door to the main restaurant, is open just for lunch Monday through Saturday. ⊠*1202 Pine St.* ☎*805/226– 8191* ⊟*MC, V* ⊙*Closed Sun. No lunch.*

$$$ ✕ **McPhee's Grill.** The grain silos across the street and the floral oilcloths on the tables belie the sophisticated cuisine at this casual chophouse. In an 1860s building in the tiny cow town of Templeton (just south of Paso Robles), the restaurant serves creative, contemporary versions of traditional Western fare—such as oak-grilled filet mignon and cedar-planked salmon. House-label wines, made especially for McPhee's, are quite good. ⊠*416 Main St., Templeton* ☎*805/434–3204* ⊟*AE, D, MC, V.*

$$$ ✕ **Villa Creek.** With a firm nod to the Southwest, chef Tom Fundero conjures distinctly modern magic with locally and sustainably grown ingredients. The seasonal menu has included butternut-squash enchi-

ladas and braised rabbit with mole negro, but you might also find duck breast with sweet-potato latkes. Central Coast wines dominate the list, with a smattering of Spanish and French selections. All brick and bare wood, the dining room can get loud when winemakers start passing their bottles from table to table, but it's always festive. For lighter appetites or wallets, the bar serves smaller plates—not to mention a killer margarita. ⊠*1144 Pine St.* ☎*805/238–3000* ⊟*AE, D, MC, V* ⊘*No lunch.*

$ ✗**Panolivo.** Scrumptious French bistro fare draws a loyal crowd of locals to this cheery downtown café, just a block north of the town square. For breakfast, try a fresh pastry or quiche, or build your own omelet. Lunch choices include traditional French dishes like snails baked in garlic-butter sauce or cassoulet as well as sandwiches, salads, and fresh pastas—including the house-made beef cannelloni. ⊠*1344 Park St.* ☎*805/239–3366* ⊟*AE, D, MC, V* ⊘*No dinner Sun.–Thurs.*

$$$$ ⊞**Hotel Cheval.** Equestrian themes surface throughout this intimate, sophisticated, European-style inn just a half-block from the main square and a short walk to some of Paso's best restaurants. Each of the 16 spacious rooms is named after a famous racehorse (its history and picture hang on the wall) and includes custom European contemporary furnishings, king beds with exquisite linens and comforters, and original works of art. Most rooms have fireplaces and window seats; some have vaulted cedar ceilings. At the on-site Pony Club, you can sip local and international wines and champagne at the horseshoe-shaped zinc bar. **Pros:** Walking distance from downtown restaurants; European-style facilities; personal service. **Cons:** Next to construction site; views aren't great; no pool or hot tub. ⊠*1021 Pine St.* ☎*805/226–9995* ⊕*www.hotelcheval.com* ➳*16 rooms* ⌂*In-room: DVD (some), Ethernet, Wi-Fi. In-hotel: bar, no elevator, public Wi-Fi, no-smoking rooms* ⊟*AE, D, MC, V* ⏀*CP.*

$$ ⊞**Paso Robles Inn.** On the site of a luxurious old spa hotel by the same name, the inn is built around a lush, shady garden with a hot mineral pool. The water is still the reason to stay here, and each deluxe room (new and old) has a spring-fed hot tub in its bathroom or on its balcony. Have breakfast in the circular 1940s coffee shop, and on weekends dance with the ranchers in the Cattlemen's Lounge. **Pros:** Private spring-fed hot tubs; historic property; across from park and town square. **Cons:** Fronts a busy street; rooms vary in size and quality. ⊠*1103 Spring St.* ☎*805/238–2660 or 800/676–1713* ⊕*www.pasoroblesinn. com* ➳*92 rooms, 6 suites* ⌂*In-room: refrigerator, Ethernet. In-hotel: restaurant, bar, pool, public Wi-Fi, no-smoking rooms* ⊟*AE, D, DC, MC, V.*

¢–$ ⊞**Adelaide Inn.** Family-owned and -managed, this clean, friendly oasis
Fodor's Choice with meticulous landscaping offers spacious rooms and everything you
★ need: coffeemaker, iron, hair dryer, and peace and quiet. In the lobby, complimentary muffins and newspapers are set out in the morning; cookies come out in the afternoon. The motel has been around for decades, but nearly half the rooms were built in 2005. It's a tremendous value, so it books out weeks or even months in advance. A short walk from the fairgrounds, the Adelaide is tucked behind a conglomeration

15

of gas stations and fast-food outlets just west of the U.S. 101 and Highway 46E interchange. **Pros:** Great bargain; attractive pool area; ideal for families. **Cons:** Not a romantic retreat; near a busy intersection and freeway. ✉1215 Ysabel Ave. ☎805/238–2770 or 800/549–7276 ⊕www.adelaideinn.com ✍109 rooms ☖In-room: refrigerator, Ethernet, Wi-Fi. In-hotel: pool, no elevator, laundry facilities, laundry service, no-smoking rooms ▤AE, D, DC, MC, V ⦿CP.

CAMBRIA

28 mi west of Paso Robles on Hwy. 46; 20 mi north of Morro Bay on Hwy. 1.

Cambria, set on piney hills above the sea, was settled by Welsh miners in the 1890s. In the 1970s, the gorgeous, isolated setting attracted artists and other independent types; the town now caters to tourists, but it still bears the unmistakable imprint of its bohemian past. Both of Cambria's downtowns, the original East Village and the newer West Village, are packed with art and craft galleries, antiques shops, cafés, restaurants, and B&Bs. Late-Victorian homes stand along side streets, and the hills are filled with redwood-and-glass residences.

Lined with low-key motels, **Moonstone Beach Drive** runs along a bluff above the ocean. The boardwalk that winds along the beach side of the drive makes a great walk.

Leffingwell's Landing (✉*North end of Moonstone Beach Dr.* ☎*805/927–2070*), a state picnic ground, is a good place for examining tidal pools and watching otters as they frolic in the surf.

Arthur Beal (aka Captain Nit Wit, Der Tinkerpaw) spent 51 years building **Nit Wit Ridge,** a home with terraced rock gardens. For building materials, he used all kinds of collected junk: beer cans, rocks, abalone shells, car parts, TV antennas—you name it. The site, above Cambria's West Village, is a State Historic Landmark. You can drive by and peek in; better yet, call ahead for a guided tour of the house and grounds. ✉*881 Hillcrest Dr.* ☎*805/927–2690* ☖*$10* ⊙*Daily by appointment.*

WHERE TO STAY & EAT

$$$ ✕**The Black Cat.** Jazz wafts through the several small rooms of this intimate East Village bistro where leopard-print cushions line the banquettes. Start with an order of the fried olives stuffed with Gorgonzola, accompanied by a glass from the eclectic list of local and imported wines. On the daily-changing, always exciting menu, you might find braised short ribs with goat-cheese polenta or duck breast with dried-cherry couscous. ✉*1602 Main St.* ☎*805/927–1600* ☖*Reservations essential* ▤*AE, D, DC, MC, V* ⊙*Closed Tues. and Wed. No lunch.*

$$$ ✕**The Sea Chest.** By far the best seafood place in town—readers give it a big thumbs-up—this Moonstone Beach restaurant fills soon after it opens at 5:30. Those in the know grab seats at the oyster bar, where they can take in spectacular sunsets while watching the chefs broil fresh halibut and steam garlicky clams. If you can't get there early, play some

cribbage or checkers while you wait for a table. ⊠ *6216 Moonstone Beach Dr.* ☎ *805/927–4514* ⚏ *Reservations not accepted* ⊟ *No credit cards* ⊘ *Closed Tues. mid-Sept.–Apr. No lunch.*

$$ ✕ **Robin's.** A truly multiethnic and vegetarian-friendly dining experience awaits you at this East Village cottage filled with country antiques. At dinner, choose from lobster enchiladas, Brazilian-style pork tenderloin, Thai red tofu curry, and more. Lunchtime's extensive salad and sandwich menu embraces burgers and tempeh alike. Unless it's raining, ask for a table on the secluded (and heated) garden patio. ⊠ *4095 Burton Dr.* ☎ *805/927–5007* ⊟ *MC, V.*

¢ ✕ **French Corner Bakery.** Place your order at the counter and then sit outside to watch the passing East Village scene (if the fog has rolled in, take a seat in the tiny deli). The rich aroma of coffee and fresh breakfast pastries makes mouths water in the morning; for lunch, try a quiche with flaky crust or a sandwich on house-baked bread. ⊠ *2214 Main St.* ☎ *805/927–8227* ⚏ *Reservations not accepted* ⊘ *No dinner.*

$$–$$$ ▦ **Cambria Pines Lodge.** With lots of recreational facilities and a range of accommodations—from basic state park–style cabins to motel-style standard rooms to large fireplace suites—this 25-acre retreat up the hill from the East Village is a good choice for families. Walls can be thin in buildings dating as far back as the 1940s; a separate cluster of luxury suites and rooms opened in 2006. The lodge is always busy: its extensive gardens are popular with wedding parties; groups and conferences are big business; and bands play light rock, folk, and jazz in the lounge. **Pros:** Short walk from downtown; verdant gardens; spacious grounds. **Cons:** Front desk service and housekeeping not always top-quality; some units could use an update. ⊠ *2905 Burton Dr.* ☎ *805/927–4200* ⊕ *www.cambriapineslodge.com* ⬳ *72 rooms, 19 cabins, 62 suites* ⛭ *In-room: refrigerator (some), VCR (some), Ethernet. In-hotel: no elevator, restaurant, room service, bar, pool, spa, concierge, public Wi-Fi, some pets allowed, no-smoking rooms* ⊟ *AE, D, DC, MC, V.*

$$–$$$ ▦ **Moonstone Landing.** Friendly staff, lots of amenities, and reasonable ★ rates make this up-to-date motel a top pick with readers who like to stay right on Moonstone Beach. All rooms have Mission-style furnishings, DVD players, fireplaces, and Internet access. From their balconies or patios, a few of the deluxe rooms, which have marble whirlpool tubs and showers, offer some of the best views in Cambria. **Pros:** Sleek furnishings; across from the beach; cheery lounge. **Cons:** Narrow property; some rooms overlook a parking lot. ⊠ *6240 Moonstone Beach Dr.* ☎ *805/927–0012 or 800/830–4540* ⊕ *www.moonstonelanding. com* ⬳ *29 rooms* ⛭ *In-room: refrigerator, DVD, Wi-Fi. In-hotel: no-smoking rooms* ⊟ *AE, D, MC, V* ⦿ *CP.*

¢–$ ▦ **Bluebird Inn.** This sweet motel in Cambria's East Village sits amid beautiful gardens along Santa Rosa Creek. Rooms include simply furnished doubles and nicer creek-side suites with patios, fireplaces, and refrigerators. The Bluebird isn't the fanciest place, but if you don't require beachside accommodations, it's a bargain. **Pros:** Excellent value; well-kept gardens; friendly staff. **Cons:** Few frills; basic rooms; on Cambria's main drag. ⊠ *1880 Main St.* ☎ *805/927–4634 or 800/552–5434* ⊕ *www.bluebirdmotel.com* ⬳ *37 rooms* ⛭ *In-room:*

refrigerator (some), VCR (some), Wi-Fi. In-hotel: no-smoking rooms ⊟*D, MC, V.*

SAN SIMEON

Hwy. 1, 9 mi north of Cambria and 65 mi south of Big Sur.

Whalers founded San Simeon in the 1850s but had virtually abandoned the town by the time Senator George Hearst reestablished it 20 years later. Hearst bought up most of the surrounding ranch land, built a 1,000-foot wharf, and turned San Simeon into a bustling port. His son, William Randolph Hearst, further developed the area during the construction of Hearst Castle. Today the town, 4 mi south of the entrance to Hearst San Simeon State Historical Monument, is basically a strip of gift shops and mediocre motels along Highway 1.

★ **Hearst San Simeon State Historical Monument** sits in solitary splendor atop La Cuesta Encantada (the Enchanted Hill). Its buildings and gardens spread over 127 acres that were the heart of newspaper magnate William Randolph Hearst's 250,000-acre ranch. Hearst devoted nearly 30 years and about $10 million to building this elaborate estate. He commissioned renowned architect Julia Morgan—who also designed buildings at the University of California at Berkeley—but he was very much involved with the final product, a hodgepodge of Italian, Spanish, Moorish, and French styles. The 115-room main building and three huge "cottages" are connected by terraces and staircases and surrounded by pools, gardens, and statuary. In its heyday the castle was a playground for Hearst and his guests, many of whom were Hollywood celebrities. Construction began in 1919 and was never officially completed. Work was halted in 1947 when Hearst had to leave San Simeon because of failing health. The Hearst family presented the property to the State of California in 1958.

Access to the castle is through the large visitor center at the foot of the hill, which contains a collection of Hearst memorabilia and a giant-screen theater that shows a 40-minute film giving a sanitized version of Hearst's life and of the castle's construction. Buses from the visitor center zigzag up the hillside to the neoclassical extravaganza, where guides conduct four different daytime tours of various parts of the main house and grounds. Tour No. 1 (which includes the movie) provides a good overview of the highlights; the others focus on particular parts of the estate. Daytime tours take about two hours. In spring and fall, docents in period costume portray Hearst's guests and staff for the slightly longer evening tour, which begins at sunset. All tours include a ½-mi walk and between 150 and 400 stairs. Reservations for the tours, which can be made up to eight weeks in advance, are necessary. ⊠*San Simeon State Park, 750 Hearst Castle Rd.* ☎*805/927–2020 or 800/444–4445* ⊕*www.hearstcastle.com* ▢*Daytime tours $24, evening tours $30* ⊙*Tours daily 8:20–3:20, later in summer; additional tours take place most Fri. and Sat. evenings Mar.–May and Sept.–Dec.* ⊟*AE, D, MC, V.*

☾ A large and growing colony (at last count 15,000 members) of elephant seals gathers every year at **Piedras Blancas Elephant Seal Rookery,** on the beaches near Piedras Blancas Lighthouse. The huge males with their pendulous, trunklike noses typically start appearing on shore in late November, and the females begin to arrive in December to give birth—most babies are born in the last two weeks of January. The newborn pups spend about four weeks nursing before their mothers head out to sea, leaving them on their own; the "weaners" leave the rookery when they are about 3½ months old. The seals return once or twice in the spring and summer months to molt or rest, but not en masse as in winter. You can watch them from a boardwalk along the bluffs just a few feet above the beach; do not attempt to approach them, as they are wild animals. Docents are often on hand to give background information and statistics. The rookery is just south of Piedras Blancas Lighthouse (4½ mi north of Hearst San Simeon State Historical Monument); the nonprofit Friends of the Elephant Seal runs a small visitor center and gift shop at their San Simeon office. ⊠*Friends of the Elephant Seal, 250 San Simeon Ave., Suite 3* ☎*805/924–1628* ⊕*www. elephantseal.org.*

WHERE TO STAY

$$ ⓣ**Best Western Cavalier Oceanfront Resort.** Reasonable rates, an ocean-front location, evening bonfires, and well-equipped rooms—some with wood-burning fireplaces and private patios—make this motel by far the best choice in San Simeon. **Pros:** On the bluffs; fantastic views; close to Hearst Castle; bluff bonfires. **Cons:** Room amenities and sizes vary; pools are small and sometimes crowded. ⊠*9415 Hearst Dr.* ☎*805/927–4688 or 800/826–8168* ⊕*www.cavalierresort.com* ⬌*90 rooms* ♿*In-room: refrigerator, DVD, Ethernet (some), Wi-Fi (some). In-hotel: 2 restaurants, pools, gym, no elevator, laundry facilities, some pets allowed, no-smoking rooms* ▤*AE, D, DC, MC, V.*

BIG SUR COASTLINE

SOUTHERN BIG SUR

Hwy. 1 from San Simeon to Julia Pfeiffer Burns State Park.

This especially rugged stretch of oceanfront is a rocky world of mountains, cliffs, and beaches.

Fodor'sChoice One of California's most spectacular drives, **Highway 1** snakes up the
★ coast north of San Simeon. Numerous pullouts along the way offer tremendous views and photo ops. On some of the beaches, huge elephant seals lounge nonchalantly, seemingly oblivious to the attention of rubberneckers—but keep your distance. In rainy seasons, the southern Big Sur portion of Highway 1 is regularly shut down by mud slides. Contact **CalTrans** (☎*800/427–7623* ⊕*www.dot.ca.gov*) for road conditions.

In Los Padres National Forest just north of the town of Gorda is **Jade Cove** (⊠*Hwy. 1, 34 mi north of San Simeon*), a well-known jade-hunting spot. Rock hunting is allowed on the beach, but you may not remove anything from the walls of the cliffs.

Julia Pfeiffer Burns State Park provides some fine hiking, from an easy ½-mi stroll with marvelous coastal views to a strenuous 6-mi trek through the redwoods. The big attraction here, an 80-foot waterfall that drops into the ocean, gets crowded in summer; still, it's an astounding place to sit and contemplate nature. Migrating whales, as well as harbor seals and sea lions, can sometimes be spotted not far from shore. ⊠*Hwy. 1, 53 mi north of San Simeon, 15 mi north of Lucia* ☎*831/667–2315* ⊕*www.parks.ca.gov* ⊠*$10* ☉*Daily sunrise–sunset.*

WHERE TO STAY & EAT

$$–$$$ ✕⊡ **Ragged Point Inn.** At this cliff-top resort—the only inn and restaurant for miles around—glass walls in most rooms open to awesome, unobstructed ocean views. Though not especially luxurious, some rooms have spa tubs, kitchenettes, and fireplaces. The restaurant ($$–$$$) is a good place to fill up on standard American fare—sandwiches, salads, pastas, and main courses—before or after the long, winding Highway 1 drive. Even if you're just passing by, stop to stretch your legs on the 14 acres of lush gardens above the sea; you can pick up souvenirs, a burger, or an espresso to go. **Pros:** On the cliffs, great food, idyllic views. **Cons:** Busy road stop during the day, often booked for weekend weddings. ⊠*19019 Hwy. 1, 20 mi north of San Simeon, Ragged Point* ☎*805/927–4502, 805/927–5708 restaurant* ⊕*www.raggedpointinn. com* ⊅*30 rooms* ⚹*In-room: no phone, kitchen (some). In-hotel: restaurant, no elevator, laundry facilities, public Wi-Fi, no-smoking rooms* ▭*AE, D, DC, MC, V.*

$$–$$$ ⊡ **Treebones Resort.** Perched on a hilltop, surrounded by national forest and stunning, unobstructed ocean views, this yurt resort opened in 2004. The yurts here—circular structures of heavy-duty fabric, on individual platforms with decks—are designed for upscale camping. Each has one or two queen beds with patchwork quilts, wicker furniture, and pine floors. Electricity and hot and cold running water come to you, but you have to walk to squeaky-clean bathhouse and restroom facilities. The sunny main lodge, where breakfast and dinner (not included) are served, has a big fireplace, games, and a well-stocked sundries and gift shop. Younger children have difficulty on the steep paths between buildings. There is a two-night minimum for stays on weekends and between April and October. **Pros:** 360-degree views; spacious pool area; comfortable beds. **Cons:** Steep paths; no private bathrooms; more than a mile from the nearest store. ⊠*71895 Hwy. 1, Willow Creek Rd., 32 mi north of San Simeon, 1 mi north of Gorda* ☎*877/424–4787* ⊕*www.treebonesresort.com* ⊅*16 yurts* ⚹*In-hotel: restaurant, pool, spa, no elevator, laundry facilities, public Internet, some pets allowed* ▭*AE, MC, V* ⊚*CP.*

CENTRAL BIG SUR

Hwy. 1, from Partington Cove to Bixby Bridge.

The countercultural spirit of Big Sur—which instead of a conventional town is a loose string of coast-hugging properties along Highway 1—is alive and well today. Its few residents include the very wealthy, the enthusiastically outdoorsy, and the thoroughly evolved: since the 1960s the Esalen Institute, a center for alternative education and East–West philosophical study, has attracted seekers of higher consciousness and devotees of the property's hot springs. Today, posh and rustic resorts hidden among the redwoods cater to visitors drawn from near and far by the extraordinary scenery and serene isolation.

Through a hole in one of the gigantic boulders at secluded **Pfeiffer Beach,** you can watch the waves break first on the sea side and then on the beach side. Keep a sharp eye out for the unsigned road to the beach: it is the only ungated paved road branching west off Highway 1 between the post office and Pfeiffer Big Sur State Park. The 2-mi, one-lane road descends sharply. ⊠ *Off Hwy. 1, 1 mi south of Pfeiffer Big Sur State Park* 🖫 *$10 per vehicle per day.*

Among the many hiking trails at **Pfeiffer Big Sur State Park** ($10 per vehicle for day use) a short route through a redwood-filled valley leads to a waterfall. You can double back or continue on the more difficult trail along the valley wall for views over miles of treetops to the sea. Stop in at the Big Sur Station visitor center, off Highway 1, less than ½ mi south of the park entrance, for information about the entire area; it's open 8–4:30. ⊠ *47225 Hwy. 1* 🕾 *831/667–2315* ⊕ *www.parks.ca.gov* 🖫 *$10 per vehicle* ☉ *Daily dawn–dusk.*

★ **Point Sur State Historic Park** is the site of an 1889 lighthouse that still stands watch from atop a large volcanic rock. Four lighthouse keepers lived here with their families until 1974, when the light station became automated. Their homes and working spaces are open to the public only on 2½- to 3-hour ranger-led tours. Considerable walking, including up two stairways, is involved. Strollers are not allowed. ⊠ *Hwy. 1, 7 mi north of Pfeiffer Big Sur State Park* 🕾 *831/625–4419* ⊕ *www. parks.ca.gov* 🖫 *$10* ☉ *Tours generally Nov.–Mar., Sat. at 10 and 2, Sun. at 10; Apr.–Oct., Wed. and Sat. at 10 and 2, Sun. at 10, July–Aug. add'l tour Thurs. at 10; call to confirm.*

The graceful arc of **Bixby Creek Bridge** (⊠ *Hwy. 1, 6 mi north of Point Sur State Historic Park, 13 mi south of Carmel*) is a photographer's dream. Built in 1932, it spans a deep canyon, more than 100 feet wide at the bottom. From the parking area on the north side you can admire the view or walk across the 550-foot span.

WHERE TO STAY & EAT

$$$$ ✕**Sierra Mar.** Ocean-view dining doesn't get much better than this. Perched at cliff's edge 1,200 feet above the Pacific at the ultra-chic Post Ranch Inn, Sierra Mar serves cutting-edge American food made from mostly organic, seasonal ingredients, including a stellar four-course prix-fixe menu. The restaurant's wine list is one of the most extensive

in the nation. ⊠ *Hwy. 1, 1½ mi south of Pfeiffer Big Sur State Park* ☎*831/667–2200* ⌂ *Reservations essential* ▭*AE, MC, V.*

$$$ ✕**Deetjen's Big Sur Inn.** The candlelighted, creaky-floor restaurant in the main house at the historic inn of the same name is a Big Sur institution. It serves roast duck, steak, and rack of lamb for dinner and wonderfully light and flavorful pancakes for breakfast. The chef procures much of the fish, meats and produce from purveyors who practice sustainable farming and fishing practices. ⊠ *Hwy. 1, 3½ mi south of Pfeiffer Big Sur State Park* ☎*831/667–2377* ▭*MC, V* ⊙*No lunch.*

$$$ ✕**Nepenthe.** It may be that no other restaurant between San Francisco and Los Angeles has a better coastal view; no wonder Orson Welles and Rita Hayworth once owned the place. The food and drink are overpriced but good; there are burgers, sandwiches, and salads for lunch, and fresh fish and hormone-free steaks for dinner. For the real show, settle on the terraced deck in the late afternoon, order a glass from the extensive wine list, and watch the sun slip into the Pacific Ocean. The less expensive, outdoor Café Kevah serves breakfast and lunch. ⊠*Hwy. 1, 2½ mi south of Big Sur Station* ☎*831/667–2345* ▭*AE, MC, V.*

$$ ✕**Big Sur Roadhouse.** In their colorful, casual bistro, Marcus and Heather Foster serve up innovative, well-executed California Latin–fusion fare. Crispy striped bass atop a pillow of carrot-coconut puree, tangy-smoky barbecue chicken breast beneath a julienne of jicama and cilantro: the zesty, balanced flavors wake up your mouth. Emphasizing new-world vintages, the wine list is gently priced. The chocolate-caramel layer cake may bring tears to your eyes. ⊠*Hwy. 1, 1 mi north of Pfeiffer Big Sur State Park* ☎*831/667–2264* ⊙*Closed Tues. No lunch.*

$$$$ ✕▣**Post Ranch Inn.** This luxurious retreat, designed exclusively for adult
Fodor's Choice   getaways, has remarkably environmentally conscious architecture. The
★   redwood guesthouses, all of which have views of the sea or the mountains, blend almost invisibly into a wooded cliff 1,200 feet above the ocean. Each unit has its own fireplace, stereo, private deck, and massage table. On-site activities include everything from yoga to stargazing. **Pros:** World-class resort; spectacular views; gorgeous property with hiking trails. **Cons:** Expensive; austere design; not a good choice if you're scared of heights. ⊠*Hwy. 1, 1½ mi south of Pfeiffer Big Sur State Park* ⌂*Hwy. 1, Box 219, 93920* ☎*831/667–2200 or 800/527–2200* ⊕*www.postranchinn.com* ⇥*40 units* ⌂*In-room: refrigerator, no TV. In-hotel: restaurant, bar, pools, gym, spa, no elevator, public Internet, no-smoking rooms* ▭*AE, MC, V* ⊙*BP.*

$$$$ ✕▣**Ventana Inn & Spa.** Hundreds of celebrities, from Oprah Winfrey to
Fodor's Choice   Sir Anthony Hopkins, have escaped to Ventana, a romantic resort on
★   243 tranquil acres 1,200 feet above the Pacific. The activities here are purposely limited. You can sunbathe (there is a clothing-optional deck and pool), walk or ride horses in the nearby hills, or pamper yourself with mind-and-body treatments at the Allegria Spa or in your own private quarters. All rooms have walls of natural wood and cool tile floors; some have private hot tubs on their patios. The inn's Cielo restaurant ($$$–$$$$) showcases fine California cuisine and wine. **Pros:** Nature trails everywhere; great food; secluded. **Cons:** Simple break-

fast; some rooms need updating. ⊠*Hwy. 1, almost 1 mi south of Pfeiffer Big Sur State Park* ☎*831/667–2331 or 800/628–6500* ⊕*www. ventanainn.com* ⬦*25 rooms, 31 suites, 3 houses* ⏚*In-room: DVD, Ethernet, Wi-Fi. In-hotel: restaurant, bar, pools, gym, spa, no elevator, no-smoking rooms* ⊟*AE, D, DC, MC, V* ⬦*2-night minimum stay on weekends and holidays; children allowed only in houses* ⫿◎⫿*BP.*

$–$$$ ✗⫿⫿ **Deetjen's Big Sur Inn.** This historic 1930s Norwegian-style property is endearingly rustic and charming, especially if you're willing to go with a camplike flow. The room doors lock only from the inside, and your neighbors can often be heard through the walls—if you plan to bring children, you must reserve an entire building. Still, Deetjen's is a special place. Its village of cabins is nestled in the redwoods, and many of the very individual rooms have their own fireplaces. **Pros:** Surrounded by Big Sur history; tons of character; wooded grounds. **Cons:** Rustic; thin walls; some rooms don't have private baths. ⊠*Hwy. 1, 3½ mi south of Pfeiffer Big Sur State Park* ☎*831/667–2377* ⊕*www. deetjens.com* ⬦*20 rooms, 15 with bath* ⏚*In-room: no phone, no TV. In-hotel: restaurant, no elevator, no-smoking rooms* ⊟*MC, V.*

CENTRAL COAST ESSENTIALS

To research prices, get advice from other travelers, and book travel arrangements, visit www.fodors.com.

TRANSPORTATION

BY AIR

Alaska Air, Allegiant Air, American, Delta, Horizon Air, United Express, and U.S. Airways fly to Santa Barbara Municipal Airport, 12 mi from downtown. American/American Eagle, Delta Connection, Skywest, United Express, and U.S. Airways provide service to San Luis Obispo County Regional Airport, 3 mi from downtown San Luis Obispo. *See Air Travel in California Essentials for airline phone numbers.*

Contacts San Luis Obispo County Regional Airport (⊠*903–5 Airport Dr., San Luis Obispo* ☎*805/781–5205* ⊕*www.sloairport.com*). **Santa Barbara Airport** (⊠*500 Fowler Rd., Santa Barbara* ☎*805/683–4011* ⊕*www.flysba.com*).

AIRPORT TRANSFERS Santa Barbara Airbus shuttles travelers between Santa Barbara and Los Angeles for $48 one way and $90 round-trip (slight discount with 24-hour notice, larger discount for groups of six or more). The Santa Barbara Metropolitan Transit District Bus 11 ($1.25) runs every 30 minutes from the airport to the downtown transit center. A taxi between the airport and the hotel district runs $18 to $25.

Contacts Santa Barbara Airbus (☎*805/964–7759, 800/733–6354, 800/423–1618 in CA* ⊕*www.sbairbus.com*). **Santa Barbara Metropolitan Transit District** (☎*805/683–3702 or 805/963–3364* ⊕*www.sbmtd.gov*).

BY BUS

Greyhound provides service from San Francisco and Los Angeles to San Luis Obispo, Ventura, and Santa Barbara. From Monterey and Carmel, Monterey-Salinas Transit operates buses to Big Sur between May and mid-October. From San Luis Obispo, Central Coast Transit runs buses around Santa Maria and out to the coast. Santa Barbara Metropolitan Transit District provides local service. The Downtown/State Street and Waterfront shuttles cover their respective sections of Santa Barbara during the day. South Coast Area Transit buses serve the entire Ventura County region.

Information Central Coast Transit (☎ *805/781-4472* ⊕ *www.slorta.org*). **Gold Coast Transit** (☎ *805/487-4222 or 805/643-3158 for Ojai, Ventura, and Oxnard* ⊕ *www.scat.org*). **Greyhound** (☎ *800/231-2222* ⊕ *www.greyhound.com*). **Monterey-Salinas Transit** (☎ *888/678-2871* ⊕ *www.mst.org*). **San Luis Obispo Transit** (☎ *805/781-4472* ⊕ *www.slorta.org*). **Santa Barbara Metropolitan Transit District** (☎ *805/963-3366* ⊕ *www.sbmtd.gov*).

BY CAR

Highway 1 and U.S. 101 run north–south and more or less parallel along the Central Coast, with Highway 1 hugging the coast and U.S. 101 running inland. The most dramatic section of the Central Coast is the 70 mi between Big Sur and San Simeon. Don't expect to make good time along here: the road is narrow and twisting with a single lane in each direction, making it difficult to pass the many lumbering RVs. In fog or rain the drive can be downright nerve-racking; in wet seasons mud slides can close portions of the road. Once you start south from Carmel, there is no route east from Highway 1 until Highway 46 heads inland from Cambria to connect with U.S. 101. At Morro Bay, Highway 1 turns inland for 13 mi and connects with U.S. 101 at San Luis Obispo. From here south to Pismo Beach the two highways run concurrently. South of Pismo Beach to Las Cruces the roads separate, then run together all the way to Oxnard. Along any stretch where they are separate, U.S. 101 is the quicker route.

U.S. 101 and Highway 1 will get you to the Central Coast from Los Angeles and San Francisco. If you are coming from the east, you can take Highway 46 west from I–5 in the Central Valley (near Bakersfield) to U.S. 101 at Paso Robles, where it continues to the coast, intersecting Highway 1 a few miles south of Cambria. Highway 33 heads south from I–5 at Bakersfield to Ojai. About 60 mi north of Ojai, Highway 166 leaves Highway 33, traveling due west through the Sierra Madre to Santa Maria at U.S. 101 and continuing west to Highway 1 at Guadalupe. South of Carpinteria, Highway 150 winds from Highway 1/U.S. 101 through sparsely populated hills to Ojai. From Highway 1/U.S. 101 at Ventura, Highway 33 leads to Ojai and Los Padres National Forest. South of Ventura, Highway 126 runs east from Highway 1/U.S. 101 to I–5.

Contacts Caltrans (☎ *800/427-7623* ⊕ *www.dot.ca.gov/hq/roadinfo*).

BY TRAIN

The Amtrak *Coast Starlight,* which runs between Los Angeles and Seattle via Oakland, stops in Paso Robles, San Luis Obispo, Santa Barbara, and Oxnard. Amtrak runs several *Pacific Surfliner* trains daily between San Luis Obispo, Santa Barbara, Los Angeles, and San Diego. Metrolink Regional Rail Service trains connect Ventura and Oxnard with Los Angeles and points between.

Contacts **Amtrak** (☎ 800/872–7245, 805/963–1015 in Santa Barbara, 805/541–0505 in San Luis Obispo ⊕ www.amtrakcalifornia.com). **Metrolink** (☎ 800/371–5465 within service area, 213/347–2800 ⊕ www.metrolinktrains.com).

CONTACTS & RESOURCES

EMERGENCIES

In case of emergency dial 911.

Contacts **Big Sur Health Center** (✉ Hwy. 1, ¼ mi south of River Inn, Big Sur ☎ 831/667–2580) is open weekdays 10–5. **Cottage Hospital** (✉ Pueblo and Bath Sts., Santa Barbara ☎ 805/682–7111, 805/569–7210 emergencies). **Sierra Vista Regional Medical Center** (✉ 1010 Murray Ave., San Luis Obispo ☎ 805/546–7600).

TOUR OPTIONS

Cloud Climbers Jeep and Wine Tours offers four types of daily tours: wine-tasting, mountain, sunset, and a discovery tour for families. These trips to the Santa Barbara/Santa Ynez mountains and wine country are conducted in open-air, six-passenger jeeps. Fares range from $89 to $120 per adult. The company also arranges biking, horseback riding, and trap-shooting tours by appointment. Wine Adventures operates customized Santa Barbara County tours and narrated North County wine-country tours in 25-passenger minicoaches. Fares for the wine tours are $95 per person. The Grapeline Wine Country Shuttle leads daily wine and vineyard picnic tours with flexible itineraries in San Luis Obispo County and Santa Barbara County wine country; they stop at many area hotels and can provide private custom tours with advance reservations. Fares range from $42 to $85, depending on pickup location and tour choice.

Spencer's Limousine & Tours offers customized tours of the city of Santa Barbara and wine country via sedan, limousine, van, or minibus. A four-hour basic tour with at least four participants costs about $60 per person. Sultan's Limousine Service has a fleet of super stretches; each can take up to eight passengers on Paso Robles and Edna Valley–Arroyo Grande wine tours and tours of the San Luis Obispo County coast. Hiring a limo for a four-hour wine country tour typically costs $380 to $430 with tip.

Contacts **Cloud Climbers Jeep and Wine Tours** (☎ 805/965–6654 ⊕ www.ccjeeps.com). **The Grapeline Wine Country Shuttle** (☎ 805/239–4747 Paso Robles, 805/238–2765 San Luis Obispo, 888/894–6379 Santa Barbara/Solvang ⊕ www.gogrape.com). **Spencer's Limousine & Tours** (☎ 805/884–9700 ⊕ www.spencerslimo.com). **Sultan's Limousine Service** (☎ 805/466–3167 North SLO

County, 805/544–8320 South SLO County, 805/771–0161 coastal SLO County cities ⊕ www.sultanslimo.com). **Wine Adventures** (✉ 3463 State St., #228, Santa Barbara ☎ 805/965–9463 ⊕ www.welovewines.com).

VISITOR INFORMATION

Contacts **Big Sur Chamber of Commerce** (☎ 831/667–2100 ⊕ www.bigsur california.org). **Cambria Chamber of Commerce** (☎ 805/927–3624 ⊕ www. cambriachamber.org). **Central Coast Tourism Council** (🖰 1601 Anacapa St., Santa Barbara 93101 ⊕ www.centralcoast-tourism.com). **Ojai Valley Chamber of Commerce** (☎ 805/646–8126 ⊕ www.ojaichamber.org). **Paso Robles Wine Country Alliance** (✉ 744 Oak St. ☎ 805/239–8463 ⊕ www.pasowine. com). **Paso Robles Visitors and Conference Bureau** (✉ 1225 Park St., 93446 ☎ 805/238–0506 ⊕ www.pasorobleschamber.com). **San Luis Obispo Chamber of Commerce** (✉ 1039 Chorro St., 93401 ☎ 805/781–2777 ⊕ www.visitslo.com). **San Luis Obispo County Visitors and Conference Bureau** (✉ 811 El Capitan Way #200, 93401 ☎ 805/541–8000 or 800/634–1414 ⊕ www.sanluisobispocounty. com). **San Luis Obispo Vintners Association** (☎ 805/541–5868 ⊕ www.slowine. com). **Santa Barbara Conference and Visitors Bureau** (✉ 1601 Anacapa St., 93101 ☎ 805/966–9222 ⊕ www.santabarbaraca.com). **Santa Barbara County Vintners' Association** (☎ 805/688–0881 ⊕ www.sbcountywines.com). **Santa Ynez Valley Visitors Association** (☎ 800/742–2843 or 805/686–0053 ⊕ www. santaynevalleyvisit.com). **Solvang Conference & Visitors Bureau** (✉ 1511 Mission Dr., 93463 ☎ 805/688–6144 or 800/468–6765 ⊕ www.solvangusa.com). **Ventura Visitors and Convention Bureau** (✉ 101 S. California St., 93001 ☎ 805/648–2075 or 800/483–6214 ⊕ www.ventura-usa.com).

The Monterey Bay Area

FROM CARMEL TO SANTA CRUZ

Monterey Bay Aquarium

WORD OF MOUTH

"The Monterey Bay Aquarium is a great experience for young kids and adults. Venues for the sea creatures are very well done. It is quite a fun and an educational experience. I suggest going early in the day to avoid the lines. Either way, it's well worth the wait."

—Tom

WELCOME TO THE MONTEREY BAY AREA

TOP REASONS TO GO

★ **Marine life:** Monterey Bay is home to the world's third-largest marine sanctuary, home to whales, otters, and other underwater creatures.

★ **Getaway central:** For more than a century, urbanites have come to the Monterey Bay area to unwind, relax, and have fun. It's a great place to browse unique shops and galleries, ride a giant roller coaster, or play a round of golf on a world-class course.

★ **Nature preserves:** More than the sea is protected here—the region boasts nearly 30 state parks, beaches, and preserves, fantastic places for walking, jogging, hiking, and biking.

★ **Wine and dine:** The area's rich agricultural bounty translates to abundant fresh produce, great wines, and fabulous dining. It's no wonder more than 300 culinary events take place here every year.

★ **Small-town vibes:** Even the cities here are friendly, walkable places where you'll feel like a local.

1 Carmel. Exclusive Carmel-by-the-Sea and Carmel Valley Village burst with historic charm, fine dining, and unusual boutiques that cater to celebrity residents and well-heeled visitors.

2 Monterey. A former Spanish military outpost, Monterey's well-preserved historic district is a hands-on history lesson. Cannery Row, the former center of Monterey's once-thriving sardine industry, has been reborn as a tourist attraction with shops, restaurants, hotels, and the Monterey Bay Aquarium.

3 Mid-Monterey Bay. Much of California's lettuce, berries, artichokes, and Brussels sprouts come from Salinas and Watsonville. Salinas is also home of the National Steinbeck Center, and Moss Landing and Watsonville encompass pristine wildlife wetlands.

4 Aptos/Capitola/ Soquel. These former lumber towns became popular seaside resorts more than a century ago. Today they're filled with antiques shops, restaurants, and wine-tasting rooms. You'll also find some of the bay's best beaches along the shore here.

GETTING ORIENTED

North of Big Sur the coastline softens into lower bluffs, windswept dunes, pristine estuaries, and long, sandy beaches, bordering one of the world's most amazing marine environments—the Monterey Bay. On the Monterey Peninsula, at the southern end of the bay, are Carmel-by-the-Sea, Pacific Grove, and Monterey; Santa Cruz sits at the northern tip of the crescent. In between, Highway 1 cruises along the coastline, passing windswept beaches piled high with sand dunes. Along the route are wetlands, artichoke and strawberry fields, and workaday towns such as Castroville and Watsonville.

16

Biking Highway 1

THE MONTEREY BAY AREA PLANNER

Timing Your Trip

Summer is peak season; mild weather brings in big crowds. In this coastal region, a cool breeze generally blows and fog often rolls in from offshore; you will frequently need a sweater or windbreaker. Off-season, from November through April, fewer people visit and the mood is mellower. Rainfall is heaviest in January and February, but autumn through spring days are crystal-clear more often than in summer.

Helpful Contacts

Bed and Breakfast Innkeepers of Santa Cruz County (☎831/688–0444 ⊕ www.santacruz bnb.com), an association of innkeepers, can help you find a B&B. **Monterey County Conventions and Visitors Bureau Visitor Services** (☎877/666–8373 ⊕ www.montereyinfo.org) operates a lodging referral line and publishes an informational brochure with discount coupons that are good at restaurants, attractions, and shops. **Monterey Peninsula Reservations** (☎888/655–3424 ⊕ www. monterey-reservations.com) will assist you in booking lodgings.

About the Hotels

Monterey-area accommodations range from no-frills motels to luxurious hotels. Pacific Grove, filled with ornate Victorian houses, has quietly turned itself into the region's B&B capital; Carmel also has charming inns. Lavish resorts with everything from featherbeds to heated floors cluster in Pebble Beach and Carmel Valley.

High season runs April through October. Rates in winter, especially at the larger hotels, may drop by 50 percent or more, and B&Bs often offer midweek specials in the off-season. However, special events throughout the year can fill lodgings far in advance. Whatever the month, even the simplest of the area's lodgings are expensive, and most properties require a two-night stay on weekends. ⚠ **Many of the fancier accommodations are not suitable for children, so if you're traveling with kids, be sure to ask before you book.**

About the Restaurants

Some of the finest dining to be found in California is around Monterey Bay. The waters are full of fish, wild game roams the foothills, and the inland valleys are some of the most fertile in the country—local chefs draw on this bounty for their fresh, truly California cuisine. Except at beachside stands and inexpensive eateries, where anything goes, casual but neat dress is the norm.

WHAT IT COSTS				
¢	$	$$	$$$	$$$$
Restaurants				
under $10	$10–$15	$16–$22	$23–$30	over $30
Hotels				
under $90	$90–$120	$121–$175	$176–$250	over $250

Restaurant prices are for a main course at dinner, excluding sales tax of 7.5%–8.25% (depending on location). Hotel prices are for two people in a standard double room in high season, excluding service charges and 10%–10.5% tax.

Updated
by Cheryl
Crabtree

IN THE GOOD LIFE OF Monterey Bay's coast-side towns, in the pleasures of its luxurious resorts, and in the vitality of its resplendent marine habitat, this piece of California shows off its natural appeal. The abundance is nothing new: an abiding current of plenty runs through the many histories of the region. Military buffs see it in centuries' worth of battles for control of the rich territory. John Steinbeck saw it in the success of a community built on the elbow grease of farm laborers in the Salinas Valley and fishermen along Cannery Row. Biologists see it in the ocean's potential as a more sustainable source of food.

Downtown Carmel-by-the-Sea and Monterey are walks through history. The bay itself is protected by the Monterey Bay National Marine Sanctuary, the nation's largest undersea canyon—bigger and deeper than the Grand Canyon. And of course, the backdrop of natural beauty is still everywhere to be seen.

CARMEL & PACIFIC GROVE

If you want to see small towns and spectacular vistas, be sure to visit the stretch of coast between Big Sur and Monterey. Each of the communities here is distinct, and you'll see everything from thatch-roof cottages to palatial estates, rolling hills to craggy cliffs.

16

CARMEL-BY-THE-SEA

26 mi north of Big Sur on Hwy. 1.

Although the community has grown quickly through the years and its population quadruples with tourists on weekends and in summer, Carmel-by-the-Sea, commonly referred to as Carmel, retains its identity as a quaint village. Self-consciously charming, the town is populated by many celebrities, major and minor, and has more than its share of quirky ordinances. For instance, women wearing high heels do not have the right to pursue legal action if they trip and fall on the cobblestone streets; drivers who hit a tree and leave the scene are charged with hit-and-run; and live music is banned in local watering holes. Buildings still have no street numbers (street names are written on discreet white posts) and consequently no mail delivery (if you really want to see the locals, go to the post office). Artists started this community, and their legacy is evident in the numerous galleries. Wandering the side streets off Ocean Avenue, where you can poke into hidden courtyards and stop at cafés for tea and crumpets, is a pleasure.

For a look past the shops and into the town's colorful history, the **Carmel Heritage Society** (⊠ *Lincoln St., at 6th Ave.* ☎ *831/624–4447* ⊕ *www.carmelheritage.org*) leads 1½-hour walking tours the first Saturday of the month (and additional Saturdays certain months) at 9:30 AM; $10 suggested donation.

Downtown Carmel's chief lure is shopping, especially along its main street, **Ocean Avenue,** between Junipero Avenue and Camino Real; the

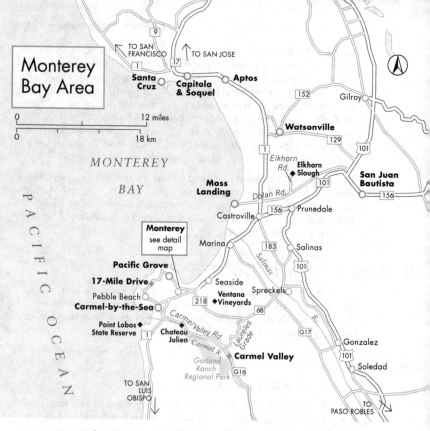

architecture here is a mishmash of ersatz Tudor, Mediterranean, and other styles.

Carmel Plaza (✉ *Ocean and Junipero Aves.* ☎ *831/624–1385* ⊕ *www. carmelplaza.com*), in the east end of the village proper, holds more than 50 shops and restaurants.

★ Long before it became a shopping and browsing destination, Carmel was an important religious center during the establishment of Spanish California. That heritage is preserved in the Mission San Carlos Borroméo del Rio Carmelo, more commonly known as the **Carmel Mission.** Founded in 1771, it served as headquarters for the mission system in California under Father Junípero Serra. Adjoining the stone church is a tranquil garden planted with California poppies. Museum rooms at the mission include an early kitchen, Serra's spartan sleeping quarters, and the first college library in California. ✉ *3080 Rio Rd., at Lasuen Dr.* ☎ *831/624–3600* ⊕ *www.carmelmission.org* ✉ *$5* ☉ *Mon.–Sat. 9:30–5, Sun. 10:30–5.*

Scattered throughout the pines in Carmel-by-the-Sea are houses and cottages originally built for the writers, artists, and photographers who discovered the area decades ago. Among the most impressive dwellings is **Tor House,** a stone cottage built in 1919 by poet Robinson Jeffers on a craggy knoll overlooking the sea. Portraits, books, and unusual art objects fill the low-ceiling rooms. The highlight of the small estate is Hawk Tower, a detached edifice set with stones from the Carmel coastline—as well as one from the Great Wall of China. The docents who lead tours (six people maximum) are well informed about the poet's work and life. Reservations for tours are recommended. ✉*26304 Ocean View Ave.* ☎*831/624-1813* ⊕*www.torhouse.org* ✉*$7* ⊙*Tours on the hour Fri. and Sat. 10–3* ☞*No children under 12.*

WORD OF MOUTH

"The beauty of Point Lobos State Reserve was so stunning, I could not believe it. Here you have a mix of tall cliffs, crashing waves, gorgeous wild flowers, abundant wild life (seals, sea otters, deer), and sheltered emerald-green coves with white sandy beaches."

—Birder

Carmel-by-the-Sea's greatest attraction is its rugged coastline, with pine and cypress forests and countless inlets. **Carmel Beach** (✉*End of Ocean Ave.*), an easy walk from downtown shops, has sparkling white sands and magnificent sunsets.

Carmel River State Beach stretches for 106 acres along Carmel Bay. The sugar-white beach is adjacent to a bird sanctuary, where you might spot pelicans, kingfishers, hawks, and sandpipers. ✉*Off Scenic Rd. south of Carmel Beach* ☎*831/624-4909 or 831/649-2836* ⊕*www.parks. ca.gov* ✉*Free* ⊙*Daily 8 AM–½ hr after sunset.*

★ **Point Lobos State Reserve,** a 350-acre headland harboring a wealth of marine life, lies a few miles south of Carmel. The best way to explore the reserve is to walk along one of its many trails. The Cypress Grove Trail leads through a forest of Monterey cypress (one of only two natural groves remaining), which clings to the rocks above an emerald-green cove. Sea Lion Point Trail is a good place to view sea lions. From those and other trails you may also spot otters, harbor seals, and (in winter and spring) migrating whales. An additional 750 acres of the reserve is an undersea marine park open to qualified scuba divers. ■TIP➜ **Arrive early (or in late afternoon) to avoid crowds; the parking lots fill up.** No pets are allowed. ✉*Hwy. 1* ☎*831/624-4909, 831/624-8413 for scuba-diving reservations* ⊕*www.pointlobos.org* ✉*$10 per vehicle* ⊙*Daily 8 AM–½ hr after sunset.*

WHERE TO STAY & EAT

$$$$ ✕**Aubergine.** To eat and sleep at the luxe L'Auberge Carmel is a weekend in itself, but even those staying elsewhere should consider splurging on the inn's intimate, 12-table restaurant. Aubergine epitomizes farm-fresh gourmet dining. Chef Christophe Grosjean grows more than 20 different herbs in his own garden, which he harvests and brings to the restaurant. His menu offers diners various options; you can create your own three-, four-, or five-course menu, for example, wild watercress and oysters, eggplant and lamb, and lemongrass ice cream with peaches. You can also ask the chef to design a surprise gastronomic "journey." There's a 4,500-bottle wine cellar. ✉ *Monte Verde, at 7th*

16

Ave , ☎*831/626–7880* ⚮*Reservations essential* ▤*AE, MC, V* ⊘*No lunch.*

$$$$ ✕**Casanova.** Built in a former home, this cozy restaurant inspires Euro-
★   pean-style celebration and romance—chairs are painted in all colors,
accordions hang from the walls, and tiny party lights dance along the
low ceilings. All entrées include antipasti and your choice of appetiz-
ers, which all but mandate you to sit back and enjoy a long meal. The
food consists of delectable seasonal dishes from southern France and
northern Italy. Private dining and a special menu are offered at Van
Gogh's Table, a special table imported from France's Auberge Ravoux,
the artist's final residence. ✉*5th Ave., between San Carlos and Mission
Sts.* ☎*831/625–0501* ⚮*Reservations essential* ▤*AE, MC, V.*

$$$ ✕**Anton and Michel.** Carefully prepared European cuisine is the draw at
this airy restaurant. The rack of lamb is carved at the table, the duck
prosciutto is cured in-house, and the desserts are set aflame before
your eyes. In summer, you (and your dog!) can have lunch served in
the courtyard; inside, the dining room looks onto a lighted fountain.
✉*Mission St. and 7th Ave.* ☎*831/624–2406* ⚮*Reservations essential*
▤*AE, D, DC, MC, V.*

$$$ ✕**Bouchée.** Prepared by Chef Christopher Dettmer—whose pedigree
★   includes work at San Francisco's Campton Place Hotel and other first-
rate Bay Area establishments—the food here presents an innovative bis-
tro-style take on local ingredients. Monterey red abalone is prepared with
black truffles, potatoes, and Noilly Prat beurre blanc; smoked California
squab breast is served with apricots, heirloom carrots, and kumquats.
With its copper bar, the dining room feels more urban than most of Carmel; perhaps this is why Bouchée is the "cool" place in town to dine. The
stellar wine list sources the selection at adjoining Bouchée Wine Merchant. ✉*Mission St., between Ocean and 7th Aves.* ☎*831/626–7880*
⚮*Reservations essential* ▤*AE, MC, V* ⊘*No lunch.*

$$$ ✕**L'Escargot.** Chef-owner Kericos Loutas personally sees to each plate
of food served at this romantic and mercifully unpretentious French
restaurant (which also has a full bar). Take his recommendation and
order the duck confit in puff pastry or the bone-in steak in truffle but-
ter; or, if you can't decide, choose the three-course prix-fixe dinner.
Service is warm and attentive. ✉*Mission St., between 4th and 5th
Aves.* ☎*831/620–1942* ⚮*Reservations essential* ▤*AE, DC, MC, V*
⊘*No lunch.*

$$$ ✕**Lugano Swiss Bistro.** Fondue is the centerpiece here. The house spe-
cialty is a version made with Gruyère, Emmentaler, and Appenzeller.
Rotisserie-broiled meats are also popular and include rosemary chicken,
plum-basted duck, and fennel pork loin. Ask for a table in the back
room, which contains a hand-painted street scene of Lugano, or on the
sunny patio. ✉*Barnyard Shopping Center, Hwy. 1 and Carmel Valley
Rd.* ☎*831/626–3779* ▤*AE, DC, MC, V.*

$$ ✕**Bahama Billy's.** The energy is electric at this always-bustling Carib-
bean bar and restaurant. An excellent and diverse menu combined with
a lively crowd makes it a prime spot for fun and good eating in Car-
mel. Particularly good is the ahi tuna, which is rolled in Jamaican jerk
seasoning, seared, and served with aioli. There's often live music in

the bar. ⊠*Barnyard Shopping Center, Hwy. 1 and Carmel Valley Rd.* ☎*831/626–0430* ⚑*Reservations essential* ▤*AE, D, MC, V.*

\$\$ ✕**Flying Fish Grill.** Simple in appearance yet bold with its flavors, this Japanese–California seafood restaurant has quickly established itself as one of Carmel's most inventive eateries. Among the best entrées is the almond-crusted sea bass served with Chinese cabbage and rock shrimp stir-fry. The warm, wood-lined dining room is broken up into very private booths. For the entrance, go down the steps near the gates to Carmel Plaza. ⊠*Mission St., between Ocean and 7th Aves.* ☎*831/625–1962* ▤*AE, MC, V* ⊘*No lunch.*

\$ ✕**The Cottage Restaurant.** If you're looking for the best breakfast in Carmel, this is the place: the menu offers six different preparations of eggs Benedict, and all kinds of sweet and savory crepes. Sandwiches and homemade soups are served at lunch, but you'll have the best meals here in the morning. ⊠*Lincoln St., between Ocean and 7th Aves.* ☎*831/625–6260* ▤*MC, V* ⊘*No dinner.*

\$ ✕**Jack London's.** If anyone's awake after dinner in Carmel, he's at Jack London's. This publike local hangout is the only Carmel restaurant to serve food until midnight. The menu includes everything from nachos to steaks. ⊠*Su Vecino Court on Dolores St., between 5th and 6th Aves.* ☎*831/624–2336* ▤*AE, D, DC, MC, V.*

\$ ✕**Katy's Place.** Locals flock to Katy's cozy, country-style eatery to fill up on hearty eggs Benedict dishes. (There are 16 types to choose from, each made with three fresh eggs). The huge breakfast menu also includes omelets, pancakes, and eight types of Belgian waffles. An assortment of salads, sandwiches, and burgers is available at lunch—try the grilled calamari burger with melted Monterey Jack cheese. ⊠*Mission St., between 5th and 6th Aves.* ☎*831/624–0199* ▤*No credit cards* ⊘*No dinner.*

\$ ✕**Tuck Box.** This bright little restaurant is in a cottage right out of a fairy tale, complete with a stone fireplace that's lighted on rainy days. Handmade scones are the house specialty and are good for breakfast or afternoon tea. ⊠*Dolores St., between Ocean and 7th Aves.* ☎*831/624–6365* ▤*No credit cards* ⊘*No dinner.*

\$\$\$\$ ✕▥ **Park Hyatt Carmel Highlands Inn.** High on a hill overlooking the Pacific, this place has superb views. Accommodations include king rooms with fireplaces, suites with personal Jacuzzis, and full town houses with all the perks. The excellent menus at the inn's Pacific's Edge restaurant (\$\$\$\$; jackets recommended) blend French and California cuisine; the sommelier helps choose the perfect wines. **Pros:** Killer views; romantic getaway; great food. **Cons:** Thin walls; must drive to Carmel; some rooms need updating. ⊠*120 Highlands Dr.* ☎*831/620–1234, 800/682–4811, 831/622–5445 for restaurant* ⊕*http://highlandsinn.hyatt.com* ⥱*48 rooms, 105 suites* ⚑*In-room: no a/c, safe, kitchen (some), refrigerator, DVD, Ethernet, Wi-Fi. In-hotel: 2 restaurants, room service, bars, pool, gym, bicycles, concierge, laundry service, no-smoking rooms* ▤*AE, D, DC, MC, V.*

\$\$\$\$ ▥ **L'Auberge Carmel.** Stepping through the doors of this elegant inn is like being transported to a little European village. The rooms are luxurious yet understated, with Italian sheets and huge, classic soaking tubs; sitting in the sun-soaked brick courtyard makes you feel like a movie

Fodor's Choice
★

16

star. **Pros:** In town but off the main drag; four blocks from the beach; full-service luxury. **Cons:** Touristy area; not a good choice for families. ✉*Monte Verde, at 7th Ave.* ☎*831/624–8578* ⊕*www.laubergecarmel. com* ⟿*20 rooms* ♿*In-room: safe, refrigerator, Wi-Fi. In-hotel: restaurant, room service, bar, no elevator, concierge, no-smoking rooms* ▤*AE, MC, V* ⦿*CP.*

$$$$ 🖼**Tickle Pink Inn.** Atop a towering cliff, this inn has views of the Big Sur coastline, which you can contemplate from your private balcony. After falling asleep to the sound of surf crashing below, you'll wake to a Continental breakfast and the morning paper in bed. If you prefer the company of fellow travelers, breakfast is also served buffet-style in the lounge, as are complimentary wine and cheese in the afternoon. Many rooms have wood-burning fireplaces, and there are six luxurious spa suites. **Pros:** Close to great hiking; intimate; dramatic views. **Cons:** Close to a big hotel; lots of traffic during the day. ✉*155 Highland Dr.* ☎*831/624–1244 or 800/635–4774* ⊕*www.ticklepink.com* ⟿*24 rooms, 11 suites* ♿*In-room: no a/c, refrigerator, DVD, Wi-Fi. In-hotel: room service, concierge, public Wi-Fi, no-smoking rooms* ▤*AE, DC, MC, V* ⦿*CP.*

$$$$ 🖼**Tradewinds Inn.** Its sleek decor inspired by the South Seas, this con-
★ verted motel encircles a courtyard with waterfalls, a meditation garden, and a fire pit. Each room has a tabletop fountain and orchids, to complement antique and custom furniture from Bali and China. Some private balconies afford a view of the bay or the mountains. The chic boutique hotel, owned by the same family since it opened in 1959, is on a quiet downtown side street. **Pros:** Serene; within walking distance of restaurants; friendly service. **Cons:** No pool; long walk to the beach. ✉*Mission St., at 3rd Ave.* ☎*831/624–2776 or 800/624–6665* ⊕*www. carmeltradewinds.com* ⟿*26 rooms, 2 suites* ♿*In-room: no a/c, safe, refrigerator, dial-up, Wi-Fi. In-hotel: no elevator, concierge, some pets allowed, no-smoking rooms* ▤*AE, MC, V* ⦿*CP.*

$$$ 🖼**Cypress Inn.** The decorating style here is luxurious but refreshingly simple. Rather than chintz and antiques, there are wrought-iron bed frames, wooden armoires, and rattan armchairs. Some rooms have fireplaces, some hot tubs, and one (Room 215) even has its own sunny veranda that looks out on the ocean. The in-town location makes walking to area attractions easy, and pet owners will be pleased to hear that in the spirit of the dog-loving owner, movie star Doris Day, animal companions are always welcome. **Pros:** Luxury without snobbery; popular lounge; traditional British-style afternoon tea. **Cons:** Not for the pet-phobic. ✉*Lincoln St. and 7th Ave., Box Y* ☎*831/624–3871 or 800/443–7443* ⊕*www.cypress-inn.com* ⟿*39 rooms, 5 suites* ♿*In-room: no a/c (some), dial-up. In-hotel: bar, gym, concierge, laundry service, public Wi-Fi, some pets allowed, no-smoking rooms* ▤*AE, D, DC, MC, V* ⦿*CP.*

$$$ 🖼**Pine Inn.** A favorite with generations of Carmel-by-the-Sea visitors, the Pine Inn has Victorian-style furnishings, complete with grandfather clock, padded fabric wall panels, antique tapestries, and marble tabletops. Only four blocks from the beach, the property includes a brick courtyard of specialty shops and a modern Italian restaurant.

Pros: Elegant; close to shopping and dining. **Cons:** On the town's busiest street; public areas a bit dark. ⊠*Ocean Ave. and Monte Verde St.* ☎*831/624–3851 or 800/228–3851* ⊕*www.pine-inn.com* ⌨*43 rooms, 6 suites* ⚷*In-room: no a/c, refrigerator (some), Wi-Fi. In-hotel: restaurant, bar, no elevator, laundry service, public Wi-Fi, no-smoking rooms* ▤*AE, D, DC, MC, V.*

$$–$$$ ⬛**Cobblestone Inn.** Stones from the Carmel River cover the exterior
★ walls of this English-style country inn; inside, the work of local painters is on display. Guest rooms have stone fireplaces, patterned wallpaper and fabrics, and fluffy duvets on the beds. Antiques in the cozy sitting room, and afternoon wine and hors d'oeuvres, contribute to the homey feel. **Pros:** Cozy; convenient access to Highway 1; great breakfast. **Cons:** Tour buses park nearby; not ideal for families. ⊠*Junipero Ave., between 7th and 8th Aves.* ☎*831/625–5222 or 800/833–8836* ⊕*www.cobblestoneinncarmel.com* ⌨*22 rooms, 2 suites* ⚷*In-room: no a/c, refrigerator, DVD, dial-up, Wi-Fi. In-hotel: no elevator, bicycles, no-smoking rooms* ▤*AE, DC, MC, V* ⑩*BP.*

$$ ⬛**Mission Ranch.** The property at Mission Ranch is gorgeous and includes a sprawling sheep pasture, bird-filled wetlands, and a sweeping view of the ocean. The ranch is nicely decorated but low-key, with a 19th-century farmhouse as the central building. Other accommodations include rooms in a converted barn, and several cottages, many with fireplaces. Though the ranch belongs to movie star Clint Eastwood, relaxation, not celebrity, is the focus here. **Pros:** Farm setting; pastoral views; great for tennis buffs. **Cons:** Busy parking lot; must drive to the heart of town. ⊠*26270 Dolores St.* ☎*831/624–6436 or 800/538–8221* ⊕*www.missionranchcarmel.com* ⌨*31 rooms* ⚷*In-room: no a/c, refrigerator (some), dial-up. In-hotel: restaurant, bar, tennis courts, gym, no elevator, no-smoking rooms* ▤*AE, MC, V* ⑩*CP.*

$–$$ ⬛**Sea View Inn.** In a residential area a few hundred feet from the beach, this restored 1905 home has a double parlor with two fireplaces, Oriental rugs, canopy beds, and a spacious front porch. Rooms are individually done in cheery colors and country patterns; taller guests might feel cramped in those tucked up under the eaves. Afternoon tea and evening wine and cheese are offered daily. Because of the fragile furnishings and quiet atmosphere, families with kids will likely be more comfortable elsewhere. **Pros:** Quiet; private; close to the beach. **Cons:** Small building; uphill trek to the heart of town. ⊠*Camino Real, between 11th and 12th Aves.* ☎*831/624–8778* ⊕*www.seaviewinncarmel.com* ⌨*8 rooms, 6 with private bath* ⚷*In-room: no a/c, no phone, no TV, Wi-Fi. In-hotel: no elevator, no-smoking rooms* ▤*AE, D, MC, V* ⑩*CP.*

THE ARTS

Carmel Bach Festival (☎*831/624–2046* ⊕*www.bachfestival*.org) has presented the works of Johann Sebastian Bach and his contemporaries in concerts and recitals since 1935. The festival runs for three weeks, starting mid-July. **Monterey County Symphony** (☎*831/624–8511* ⊕*www. montereysymphony*.org) performs classical concerts from October through May at the Sunset Center.

16

The **Pacific Repertory Theater** (☎ *831/622–0100 or 866/622–0709* ⊕ *www. pacrep.org*) puts on the Carmel Shakespeare Festival from August through October and performs contemporary dramas and comedies at several area venues from February through July. **Sunset Center** (⊠ *San Carlos St., at 9th Ave.* ☎ *831/620–2048* ⊕ *www.sunsetcenter.org*), which presents concerts, lectures, and headline acts, is the Monterey Bay Area's top venue for the performing arts.

SHOPPING

ART GALLERIES   **Carmel Art Association** (⊠ *Dolores St., between 5th and 6th Aves.* ☎ *831/624–6176* ⊕ *www.carmelart.org*) exhibits the paintings, sculptures, and prints of local artists. **Galerie Plein Aire** (⊠ *Dolores St., between 5th and 6th Aves.* ☎ *831/625–5686* ⊕ *www.galeriepleinaire. com*) showcases oil paintings by a group of seven local artists. **Masterpiece Gallery** (⊠ *Dolores St. and 6th Ave.* ☎ *831/624–2163* ⊕ *www. masterpiecegallerycarmel.com*) shows early-California-impressionist art. Run by the family of the late Edward Weston, **Weston Gallery** (⊠ *6th Ave., between Dolores and Lincoln Sts.* ☎ *831/624–4453* ⊕ *www.westongallery.com*) is hands down the best photography gallery around, with contemporary color photography complemented by classic black-and-whites.

SPECIALTY   **Bittner** (⊠ *Ocean Ave., between Mission and San Carlos Sts.* ☎ *831/626–* SHOPS   *8828 or 888/248–8637*) has a fine selection of collectible and vintage pens from around the world. **Intima** (⊠ *Mission St., between Ocean and 7th Aves.* ☎ *831/625–0599*) is the place to find European lingerie that ranges from lacy to racy. **Jan de Luz** (⊠ *Dolores St., between Ocean and 7th Aves.* ☎ *831/622–7621*) monograms and embroiders fine linens (including bathrobes) while you wait. **Madrigal** (⊠ *Carmel Plaza and Mission St.* ☎ *831/624–3477*) carries sportswear, sweaters, and accessories for women.

♥   **Mischievous Rabbit** (⊠ *Lincoln Ave., between 7th and Ocean Aves.* ☎ *831/624–6854*) sells toys, nursery accessories, books, music boxes, china, and children's clothing, and specializes in Beatrix Potter items.

CARMEL VALLEY

10 mi east of Carmel, Hwy. 1 to Carmel Valley Rd.

Carmel Valley Road, which heads inland from Highway 1 south of Carmel-by-the-Sea, is the main thoroughfare through this valley, a secluded enclave of horse ranchers and other well-heeled residents who prefer the area's sunny climate to the fog and wind on the coast. Once thick with dairy farms, the valley has recently proved itself as a venerable wine appellation. Tiny Carmel Valley Village, about 13 mi southeast of Carmel-by-the-Sea via Carmel Valley Road, has several crafts shops and art galleries, as well as tasting rooms for numerous local wineries.

At **Bernardus Tasting Room**, you can sample many of the wines—including older vintages and reserves—from the nearby Bernardus Winery and Vineyard. ✉ *5 W. Carmel Valley Rd.* ☎ *800/223–2533* ⊕ *www. bernardus.com* ⊙ *Daily 11–5.*

Pick up fresh veggies, ready-to-eat meals, gourmet groceries, flowers, and gifts at 32-acre **Earthbound Farm** (✉ *7250 Carmel Valley Rd.* ☎ *831/625–6219* ⊕ *www.ebfarm. com* ▨ *Free* ⊙ *Mon.–Sat. 8–6:30, Sun. 9–6*), the world's largest grower of organic produce. You can also take a romp in the kid's garden, cut your own herbs, and stroll through the chamomile aromatherapy labyrinth. On Saturdays from April through December the farm offers special events, from bug walks to garlic-braiding workshops.

WINE TOURING WITH THE MST

Why risk driving while wine tasting when you can hop aboard the Carmel Valley Grapevine Express? This Monterey-Salinas Transit bus travels between downtown Monterey and Carmel Valley Village, with stops near wineries, restaurants, and shopping centers. Buses depart daily every hour from 11 to 6. At $4.50 for a ride-all-day pass, it's an incredible bargain. For more information, call 888/678–2871 or visit www.mst.org.

Garland Ranch Regional Park (✉ *Carmel Valley Rd., 9 mi east of Carmel-by-the-Sea* ☎ *831/659–4488*) has hiking trails across nearly 4,500 acres of property that includes meadows, forested hillsides, and creeks.

The extensive **Château Julien** winery, recognized internationally for its chardonnays and merlots, gives weekday tours at 10:30 and 2:30 and weekends at 12:30 and 2:30, all by appointment. The tasting room is open daily. ✉ *8940 Carmel Valley Rd.* ☎ *831/624–2600* ⊕ *www.chateau julien.com* ⊙ *Weekdays 8–5, weekends 11–5.*

WHERE TO STAY & EAT

$$$ ✕ **Will's Fargo.** On the main street of Carmel Valley Village since the 1920s, this restaurant calls itself a "dressed-up saloon." Steer horns and gilt-frame paintings adorn the walls of the Victorian-style dining room; you can also eat on the patios. The menu is mainly seafood and steaks, including a 24-ounce porterhouse. ✉ *16 E. Carmel Valley Rd.* ☎ *831/659–2774* ▭ *AE, DC, MC, V* ⊙ *No lunch.*

$ ✕ **Café Rustica.** Italian-inspired country cooking is the focus at this lively roadhouse. Specialties include roasted meats, pastas, and thin-crust pizzas from the wood-fired oven. Because of the tile floors, it can get quite noisy inside; opt for a table outside if you want a quieter meal. ✉ *10 Delfino Pl.* ☎ *831/659–4444* ⚠ *Reservations essential* ▭ *MC, V* ⊙ *Closed Mon.*

¢ ✕ **Wagon Wheel Coffee Shop.** This local hangout decorated with wagon wheels, cowboy hats, and lassos serves up terrific hearty breakfasts, including date-walnut-cinnamon French toast and a plate of trout and eggs. The lunch menu includes a dozen different burgers and other sandwiches. ✉ *Valley Hill Center, Carmel Valley Rd., next to Quail Lodge* ☎ *831/624–8878* ▭ *No credit cards* ⊙ *No dinner.*

$$$$ ✕▦ **Bernardus Lodge.** Even before you check in at this luxury spa resort, Fodor'sChoice the valet hands you a glass of chardonnay. Spacious guest rooms have ★ vaulted ceilings, featherbeds, fireplaces, patios, and bathtubs for two.

16

The restaurant, Marinus ($$$$; jacket recommended), is perhaps the best in the Monterey Bay area, with a menu that changes daily to highlight local meats and produce. Reserve the chef's table in the main kitchen and you can talk to the chef as he prepares your meal. **Pros:** Exceptional personal service; outstanding food and wine. **Cons:** Some guests can seem snooty; pricey. ⊠ *415 Carmel Valley Rd.* ☎ *831/659–3131 or 888/648–9463* ⊕ *www.bernardus.com* ↩ *54 rooms, 3 suites* ☒ *In-room: safe, refrigerator, DVD, Wi-Fi. In-hotel: 2 restaurants, room service, bar, tennis courts, pool, gym, spa, no elevator, concierge, laundry service, public Internet, no-smoking rooms* ▭ *AE, DC, MC, V.*

$$$$ ✕🏨 **Quail Lodge.** What began as the Carmel Valley Country Club—a
★   hangout for Frank Sinatra, among others—is now a semiprivate golf club and resort in the valley's west side. Winding around swimming pools and putting greens, the buildings' exteriors recall the old days, but indoors the luxury is totally updated with a cool, modern feel: plasma TVs swing out from the walls, the toiletries include giant tea bags to infuse your bath with herbs, and each room has a window seat overlooking a private patio. The Covey at Quail Lodge ($$$–$$$$; jacket recommended) serves contemporary California cuisine in a romantic lakeside dining room. **Pros:** On the golf course; on-site Land Rover Driving School; pastoral views. **Cons:** Some rooms need updating; 5 mi from the beach and Carmel Valley Village. ⊠ *8205 Valley Greens Dr.* ☎ *831/624–2888 or 888/828–8787* ⊕ *www.quaillodge.com* ↩ *83 rooms, 14 suites* ☒ *In-room: safe, refrigerator, DVD, Ethernet, Wi-Fi. In-hotel: 2 restaurants, room service, bars, golf course, tennis courts, pools, gym, spa, bicycles, no elevator, concierge, laundry service, public Internet, some pets allowed, no-smoking rooms* ▭ *AE, DC, MC, V.*

$$$$ 🏨 **Stonepine Estate Resort.** Set on 330 pastoral acres, this former estate of
Fodor'sChoice   the Crocker banking family has been converted to a luxurious inn. The
★   oak-paneled main château holds eight elegantly furnished rooms and suites, and a dining room for guests (although with advance reservations, it's also possible for nonguests to dine here). The property's "cottages" are equally opulent, each with its own luxurious identity (the Hermes House has four fireplaces and a 27-foot-high living-room ceiling). Fresh flowers, afternoon tea, and evening champagne are offered daily. This is a quiet property, best suited to couples traveling without children. **Pros:** Supremely exclusive. **Cons:** Difficult to get a reservation; far from the coast. ⊠ *150 E. Carmel Valley Rd.* ☎ *831/659–2245* ⊕ *www.stonepinecalifornia.com* ↩ *3 rooms, 9 suites, 3 cottages* ☒ *In-room: no a/c, safe (some), VCR, dial-up, Wi-Fi. In-hotel: restaurant, room service, golf course, tennis courts, pools, gym, bicycles, concierge, laundry service, public Internet, no-smoking rooms* ▭ *AE, MC, V* ⦿ *BP.*

THE ARTS

Hidden Valley Performing Arts Institute (⊠ *Carmel Valley Road, at Ford Rd.* ☎ *831/659–3115* ⊕ *www.hiddenvalleymusic.org*) gives classes for promising young musicians and holds a year-round series of classical and jazz concerts by students, masters, and the Monterey Peninsula Choral Society.

SPORTS & THE OUTDOORS

The **Golf Club at Quail Lodge** (⊠*8000 Valley Greens Dr.* ☎*831/624–2770*) incorporates several lakes into its course. Depending on the season and day of the week, green fees range from $140 to $175 for guests and $175 to $200 for nonguests, including cart rental. **Rancho Cañada Golf Club** (⊠*4860 Carmel Valley Rd., 1 mi east of Hwy. 1* ☎*831/624–0111 or 800/536–9459*) is a public course with 36 holes, some of them overlooking the Carmel River. Fees range from $35 to $80, plus $36 for cart rental, depending on course and tee time.

17-MILE DRIVE

Fodor'sChoice
★

Off North San Antonio Rd. in Carmel-by-the-Sea or off Sunset Dr. in Pacific Grove.

Primordial nature resides in quiet harmony with palatial late-20th-century estates along 17-Mile Drive, which winds through an 8,400-acre microcosm of the Monterey coastal landscape. Dotting the drive are rare Monterey cypress, trees so gnarled and twisted that Robert Louis Stevenson described them as "ghosts fleeing before the wind." Some sightseers balk at the $9-per-car fee collected at the gates—this is the only private toll road west of the Mississippi—but most find the drive well worth the price. An alternative is to grab a bike: ■TIP➔ cyclists tour for free, as do those with confirmed lunch or dinner reservations at one of the hotels.

You can take in views of the impeccable greens at **Pebble Beach Golf Links** (⊠*17-Mile Dr., near Lodge at Pebble Beach* ☎*800/654–9300* ⊕*www. pebblebeach.com*) over a drink or lunch at the Lodge at Pebble Beach. The ocean plays a major role in the 18th hole of the famed links. Each winter the course is the main site of the AT&T Pebble Beach Pro-Am (formerly the Bing Crosby Pro-Am), where show business celebrities and golf pros team up for one of the nation's most glamorous tournaments.

Many of the stately homes along 17-Mile Drive reflect the classic Monterey or Spanish Mission style typical of the region. A standout is the **Crocker Marble Palace,** about a mile south of the Lone Cypress (⇨*below*). It's a private waterfront estate inspired by a Byzantine castle, easily identifiable by its dozens of marble arches.

The most-photographed tree along 17-Mile Drive is the weather-sculpted **Lone Cypress,** which grows out of a precipitous outcropping above the waves about 1½ mi up the road from Pebble Beach Golf Links. You can stop for a view of the Lone Cypress at a parking area, but you can't walk out to the tree.

Sea creatures and birds—as well as some very friendly ground squirrels—make use of **Seal Rock,** the largest of a group of islands about 2 mi north of Lone Cypress.

16

Bird Rock, the largest of several islands at the southern end of the Monterey Country Club's golf course, teems with harbor seals, sea lions, cormorants, and pelicans.

WHERE TO STAY & EAT

$$$$ ✕⌂ **Inn at Spanish Bay.** This resort sprawls across a breathtaking stretch of shoreline, and has lush, 600-square-foot rooms. Peppoli's restaurant ($$–$$$), which serves Tuscan cuisine, overlooks the coast and the golf links; Roy's Restaurant ($$$–$$$$) serves more casual and innovative Euro-Asian fare. When you stay here, you're also allowed privileges at the Lodge at Pebble Beach, which is under the same management. **Pros:** Attentive service; tons of amenities; spectacular views. **Cons:** Huge hotel; far from other Pebble Beach resorts' facilities. ⊠*2700 17-Mile Dr., Pebble Beach* ☎*831/647–7500 or 800/654–9300* ⊕*www.pebblebeach.com* ⇌*252 rooms, 17 suites* ☖*In-room: no a/c, refrigerator, VCR, Ethernet, dial-up, Wi-Fi. In-hotel: 3 restaurants, room service, bar, golf course, tennis courts, pool, gym, beachfront, bicycles, concierge, laundry service, public Internet, no-smoking rooms* ▤*AE, D, DC, MC, V.*

$$$$ ✕⌂ **Lodge at Pebble Beach.** All rooms have fireplaces and many have
★ wonderful ocean views at this circa 1919 resort. The golf course, tennis club, and equestrian center are posh. Overlooking the 18th green, the intimate Club XIX restaurant ($$$$; jackets recommended) serves expertly prepared French cuisine. When staying here, you also have privileges at the Inn at Spanish Bay. **Pros:** World-class golf; borders the ocean and fairways; fabulous facilities. **Cons:** Some rooms are on the small side; very pricey. ⊠*1700 17-Mile Dr., Pebble Beach* ☎*831/647–7500 or 800/654–9300* ⊕*www.pebblebeach.com* ⇌*142 rooms, 19 suites* ☖*In-room: no a/c, refrigerator, DVD (some), VCR (some), Ethernet, dial-up, Wi-Fi. In-hotel: 3 restaurants, bars, golf course, tennis courts, pool, gym, spa, beachfront, bicycles, concierge, laundry service, public Internet, some pets allowed, no-smoking rooms* ▤*AE, D, DC, MC, V.*

$$$$ ⌂ **Casa Palmero.** This exclusive spa resort evokes a stately Mediterra-
★ nean villa. Rooms are decorated with sumptuous fabrics and fine art; each has a wood-burning fireplace and heated floor, and some have private outdoor patios with in-ground Jacuzzis. Complimentary cocktail service is offered each evening in the main hall and library. The spa is state-of-the-art, and you have use of all facilities at the Lodge at Pebble Beach and the Inn at Spanish Bay. **Pros:** Ultimate in pampering; more private than sister resorts; right on the golf course. **Cons:** Pricey; may be *too* posh for some. ⊠*1518 Cypress Dr., Pebble Beach* ☎*831/622–6650 or 800/654–9300* ⊕*www.pebblebeach.com* ⇌*21 rooms, 3 suites* ☖*In-room: no a/c, refrigerator, VCR, dial-up, Wi-Fi. In-hotel: room service, bar, golf course, pool, spa, bicycles, concierge, laundry service, no-smoking rooms* ▤*AE, D, DC, MC, V.*

SPORTS & THE OUTDOORS

GOLF The **Links at Spanish Bay** (⊠*17-Mile Dr., north end* ☎*831/624–3811, 831/624–6611, or 800/654–9300*), which hugs a choice stretch of shoreline, is designed in the rugged manner of a traditional Scottish course, with sand dunes and coastal marshes interspersed among the greens. The green fee is $260, plus $35 per person for cart rental (cart is included for resort guests); nonguests can reserve tee times up to two months in advance.

Pebble Beach Golf Links (⊠*17-Mile Dr., near Lodge at Pebble Beach* ☎*831/624–3811, 831/624–6611, or 800/654–9300*) attracts golfers from around the world, despite a green fee of $495, plus $35 per person for an optional cart (complimentary cart for guests of the Pebble Beach and Spanish Bay resorts). Nonguests can reserve a tee time only one day in advance on a space-available basis (up to a year for groups); resort guests can reserve up to 18 months in advance.

Peter Hay (⊠*17-Mile Dr.* ☎*831/625–8518 or 831/624–6611*), a 9-hole, par-3 course, charges $25 per person, no reservations necessary. **Poppy Hills** (⊠*3200 Lopez Rd., at 17-Mile Dr.* ☎*831/625–2035*), a splendid 18-hole course designed in 1986 by Robert Trent Jones Jr., has a green fee of $200; an optional cart costs $34. Individuals may reserve up to one month in advance, groups up to a year.

Spyglass Hill (⊠*Stevenson Dr. and Spyglass Hill Rd.* ☎*831/624–3811, 831/624–6611, or 800/654–9300*) is among the most challenging Pebble Beach courses. With the first five holes bordering on the Pacific and the other 18 reaching deep into the Del Monte Forest, the views offer some consolation. The green fee is $330, and an optional cart costs $35 (the cart is complimentary for resort guests). Reservations are essential and may be made up to one month in advance (18 months for guests).

HORSEBACK RIDING
The **Pebble Beach Equestrian Center** (⊠*Portola Rd. and Alva La.* ☎*831/624–2756*) offers guided trail rides along the beach and through 26 mi of bridle trails in the Del Monte Forest. Rates are $55–$110 per rider.

PACIFIC GROVE

3 mi north of Carmel-by-the-Sea on Hwy. 68.

This picturesque town, which began as a summer retreat for church groups more than a century ago, recalls its prim and proper Victorian heritage in its host of tiny board-and-batten cottages and stately mansions. However, long before the church groups flocked here the area received thousands of annual pilgrims—in the form of bright orange-and-black monarch butterflies. They still come, migrating south from Canada and the Pacific Northwest to take residence in pine and eucalyptus groves from October through March. In Butterfly Town USA, as Pacific Grove is known, the sight of a mass of butterflies hanging from the branches like a long, fluttering veil is unforgettable.

A prime way to enjoy Pacific Grove is to walk or bicycle the 3 mi of city-owned shoreline along Ocean View Boulevard, a cliff-top area landscaped with native plants and dotted with benches meant for sitting and gazing at the sea. You can spot many types of birds here, including colonies of web-foot cormorants crowding the massive rocks rising out of the surf.

Among the Victorians of note is the **Pryor House** (⊠*429 Ocean View Blvd.*), a massive, shingled, private residence with a leaded- and beveled-glass doorway.

Green Gables (⊠*5th St. and Ocean View Blvd.* ☎*831/375–2095* ⊕*www.greengablesinnpg.com*), a romantic Swiss Gothic–style mansion with peaked gables and stained-glass windows, is a B&B.

☾ The view of the coast is gorgeous from **Lovers Point Park** (☎*831/648–5730*), on Ocean View Boulevard midway along the waterfront. The park's sheltered beach has a children's pool and picnic area, and the main lawn has a sandy volleyball court and snack bar.

> ## BUTTERFLY SPOTTING
>
> ☾ The **Monarch Grove Sanctuary** (⊠*1073 Lighthouse Ave., at Ridge Rd.* ⊕*www.pgmuseum.org*) is a fairly reliable spot for viewing the butterflies between October and February. Contact **Friends of the Monarchs** (☎*831/375–0982* ⊕*www.pgmuseum.org*) for the latest information. If you're in Pacific Grove when the monarch butterflies aren't, you can view the well-crafted butterfly tree exhibit at the **Pacific Grove Museum of Natural History.** ⊠*165 Forest Ave.* ☎*831/648–5716* ⊕*www.pgmuseum.org* ☜*$2 suggested donation* ☉*Tues.–Sun. 10–5.*

☾ At the 1855-vintage **Point Pinos Lighthouse,** the oldest continuously operating lighthouse on the West Coast, you can learn about the lighting and foghorn operations and wander through a small museum containing U.S. Coast Guard memorabilia. ⊠*Lighthouse Ave., off Asilomar Blvd.* ☎*831/648–5716* ⊕*www.pgmuseum.org* ☜*$2* ☉*Thurs.–Mon. 1–4.*

Asilomar State Beach (☎*831/646–6440* ⊕*www.parks.ca.gov*), a beautiful coastal area, is on Sunset Drive between Point Pinos and the Del Monte Forest in Pacific Grove. The 100 acres of dunes, tidal pools, and pocket-size beaches form one of the region's richest areas for marine life—including surfers, who migrate here most winter mornings.

WHERE TO STAY & EAT

$$–$$$ ✕**Red House Café.** When it's nice out, sun pours through the big windows of this cozy restaurant and across tables on the porch; when fog rolls in, the fireplace is lighted. The American menu is simple but selective, including grilled lamb fillets atop mashed potatoes for dinner and a huge Dungeness crab cake over salad for lunch. Breakfast on weekends is a local favorite. ⊠*662 Lighthouse Ave.* ☎*831/643–1060* ▭*AE, D, DC, MC, V* ☉*Closed Mon.*

$–$$$ ✕**Fandango.** The menu here is mostly Mediterranean and southern French, with such dishes as calves' liver and onions and paella served in a skillet. The decor follows suit: stone walls and country furniture give the restaurant the earthy feel of a European farmhouse. This is where locals come when they want to have a big dinner with friends, drink wine, have fun, and generally feel at home. ⊠*223 17th St.* ☎*831/372–3456* ▭*AE, D, DC, MC, V.*

$$ ✕**Fishwife.** Fresh fish with a Latin accent makes this a favorite of locals for lunch or a casual dinner. Standards are the sea garden salads topped with your choice of fish and the fried seafood plates with fresh veg-

gies. Large appetites appreciate the fisherman's bowls, which feature fresh fish served with rice, black beans, spicy cabbage, salsa, vegetables, and crispy tortilla strips. ⊠*1996½ Sunset Dr., at Asilomar Blvd.* ☎*831/375–7107* ▤*AE, D, MC, V.*

\$\$ ✕**Joe Rombi's.** Pastas, fish, and veal are the specialties at this modern trattoria, which is the best in town for Italian food. The look is spare and clean, with colorful antique wine posters decorating the white walls. Next door, Joe Rombi's La Piccola Casa serves lunch and early dinner Wednesday through Sunday. ⊠*208 17th St.* ☎*831/373–2416* ▤*AE, MC, V* ☉*Closed Mon. and Tues. No lunch.*

\$\$ ✕**Passionfish.** South American artwork and artifacts decorate the room,
★   and Latin and Asian flavors infuse the dishes at Passionfish. Chef Ted Wolters—lauded for his commitment to using eco-friendly, sustainable ingredients—shops at local farmers' markets several times a week to find the best produce, fish, and meat available, then pairs it with creative sauces. The ever-changing menu might include crispy squid with spicy orange-cilantro vinaigrette. ⊠*701 Lighthouse Ave.* ☎*831/655–3311* ▤*AE, D, MC, V* ☉*No lunch.*

\$\$ ✕**Taste Café and Bistro.** A favorite of locals, Taste serves hearty European-inspired food in a casual, airy room with high ceilings and an open kitchen. Meats, such as grilled marinated rabbit, roasted half chicken, and filet mignon, are the focus. ⊠*1199 Forest Ave.* ☎*831/655–0324* ▤*AE, MC, V.*

\$–\$\$ ✕**Fifi's Café.** Candlelight and music fill this small bistro known for its generous wine pours and French cuisine. The menu ranges from escargot to petrale sole piccata (sautéed and served with a sauce made from lemon juice, parsley, and pan drippings) to steak frites; lunch and the early-bird dinner (until 6 PM) are an exceptional value. ⊠*1188 Forest Ave.* ☎*831/372–5325* ⌲*Reservations essential* ▤*AE, D, DC, MC, V.*

\$ ✕**Peppers Mexicali Cafe.** A local favorite, this cheerful white-walled storefront serves traditional dishes from Mexico and Latin America, with an emphasis on fresh seafood. Excellent red and green salsas are made throughout the day, and there's a large selection of beers. ⊠*170 Forest Ave.* ☎*831/373–6892* ▤*AE, D, DC, MC, V* ☉*Closed Tues. No lunch Sun.*

\$\$\$–\$\$\$\$ ▦**Martine Inn.** The glassed-in parlor and many guest rooms at this 1899 Mediterranean-style villa have stunning ocean views. The inn is furnished with exquisite antiques, and the owner's collection of classic race cars is on display in the patio area. In the rooms, thoughtful details such as robes, rocking chairs, and nightly turndown combine in luxuriant comfort. Lavish breakfasts—and winemaker dinners of up to 12 courses—are served on lace-clad tables set with china, crystal, and silver. Because of the fragility of the antiques, the inn is not suitable for children, except in the two-bedroom family suite. **Pros:** Romantic; fancy breakfast; ocean views. **Cons:** Not child-friendly; sits on a busy thoroughfare. ⊠*255 Ocean View Blvd.* ☎*831/373–3388 or 800/852–5588* ⊕*www.martineinn.com* ⇆*24 rooms* ⌂*In-room: no a/c, refrigerator, no TV, Ethernet, Wi-Fi. In-hotel: no elevator, public Internet, no-smoking rooms* ▤*AE, D, MC, V* ⍐*BP.*

$$$ ⊞**Green Gables Inn.** Stained-glass windows and ornate interior details
★   compete with spectacular ocean views at this Queen Anne–style man-
sion, built by a businessman for his mistress in 1888. Rooms in a car-
riage house perched on a hill out back are larger, have more modern
amenities, and afford more privacy, but rooms in the main house have
more charm. Afternoon wine and cheese are served in the parlor. **Pros:**
Exceptional views; impeccable attention to historic detail. **Cons:** Some
rooms are small; thin walls. ⊠*301 Ocean View Blvd.,* ☎*831/375–
2095 or 800/722–1774* ⊕*www.greengablesinnpg.com* ⌁*7 rooms, 4
with bath; 4 suites* ⌂*In-room: no a/c, DVD (some), dial-up (some),
Wi-Fi. In-hotel: no elevator, bicycles, no-smoking rooms* ⊟*AE, D,
DC, MC, V* ⊚*BP.*

$$–$$$ ⊞**The Inn at 213 Seventeen Mile Drive.** Set in a residential area just past
town, this carefully restored 1920s Craftsman-style home and cottage
are surrounded by gardens and redwood, cypress, and eucalyptus trees.
Spacious, well-appointed rooms have simple, homey furnishings. The
innkeepers offer complimentary wine and hors d'oeuvres in the evening
and tea and snacks throughout the day. **Pros:** Off the beaten path; his-
toric charm; verdant gardens. **Cons:** Far from restaurants and shops;
few extra amenities. ⊠*213 17-Mile Dr.* ☎*831/642–9514 or 800/526–
5666* ⊕*www.innat17.com* ⌁*14 rooms* ⌂*In-room: no a/c, Wi-Fi. In-
hotel: no elevator, no-smoking rooms* ⊟*AE, MC, V* ⊚*BP.*

$$–$$$ ⊞**Lighthouse Lodge and Suites.** Near the tip of the peninsula, this com-
plex straddles Lighthouse Avenue—the lodge is on one side, the all-
suites facility on the other. Suites have fireplaces and whirlpool tubs.
Standard rooms are simple, but they're decently sized and much less
expensive. ■TIP➔ **With daily afternoon barbecues at the lodge, this is a
woodsy alternative to downtown Pacific Grove's B&B scene.** (The suites
do not have a daily barbecue but instead feature a wine-and-cheese
spread.) **Pros:** Near lighthouse and 17-Mile Drive; friendly reception;
upgraded beds and linens in 2006. **Cons:** Next to a cemetery; lodge
rooms are basic. ⊠*1150 and 1249 Lighthouse Ave.* ☎*831/655–2111
or 800/858–1249* ⊕*www.lhls.com* ⌁*64 rooms, 31 suites* ⌂*In-room:
no a/c, refrigerator, Wi-Fi. In-hotel: room service, pool, no elevator,
some pets allowed, no-smoking rooms* ⊟*AE, D, DC, MC, V* ⊚*BP.*

SPORTS & THE OUTDOORS

GOLF   Green fees at the 18-hole **Pacific Grove Municipal Golf Links** (⊠*77 Asilo-
mar Blvd.* ☎*831/648–5777* ⊕*www.ci.pg.ca.us/golf*) run between $35
and $40 (you can play 9 holes for $20–$23), with an after-2 PM twilight
rate of $20. Optional carts cost $34 ($20 for 9 holes). The course has
spectacular ocean views on its back 9. Tee times may be reserved up to
seven days in advance.

TENNIS   The municipal **Morris Dill Tennis Courts** (⊠*515 Junipero St.* ☎*831/648–
5729*) are available for public play for a small hourly fee. The pro shop
here rents rackets and offers lessons.

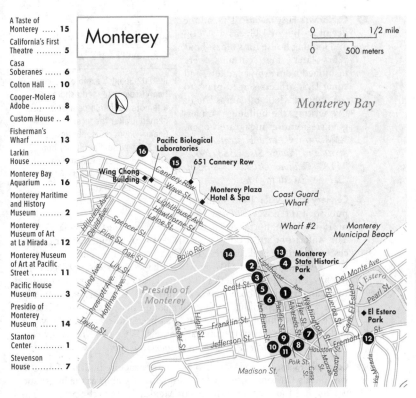

MONTEREY

Early in the 20th century Carmel Martin, the first mayor of the city of Monterey, saw a bright future for his town: "Monterey Bay is the one place where people can live without being disturbed by manufacturing and big factories. I am certain that the day is coming when this will be the most desirable place in the whole state of California." It seems that Mayor Martin was not far off the mark.

HISTORIC MONTEREY

2 mi southeast of Pacific Grove via Lighthouse Ave.; 2 mi north of Carmel-by-the-Sea via Hwy. 1.

WHAT TO SEE

15 **A Taste of Monterey.** Without driving the back roads, you can taste the wines of up to 70 area vintners while taking in fantastic bay views. Purchase a few bottles and pick up a map and guide to the county's wineries and vineyards. ⊠*700 Cannery Row, Suite KK* ☎*831/646–5446 or 888/646–5446* ⊕*www.tastemonterey.com* 🍷 *Wine tastings $10–$15* ☉*Daily 11–6.*

⑤ California's First Theatre. This adobe began its life in 1846 as a saloon and lodging house for sailors. Four years later stage curtains were fashioned from army blankets, and some U.S. officers staged plays to the light of whale oil lamps. As of this writing, the building is undergoing restoration and is rarely open. ✉ *Monterey State Historic Park, Scott and Pacific Sts.* ☎ *831/649-7118* ⊕ *www.parks.ca.gov/mshp* ✆ *Free* ⊙ *Call for hrs.*

> **MONTEREY: FORMER CAPITAL OF CALIFORNIA**
>
> In 1602 Spanish explorer Sebastian Vizcaíno stepped ashore on a remote California peninsula. He named it after the viceroy of New Spain—Count de Monte Rey. Soon the Spanish built a military outpost, and the site was the capital of California until the state came under American rule.

Cannery Row. When John Steinbeck published the novel *Cannery Row* in 1945, he immortalized a place of rough-edged working people. The waterfront street once was crowded with sardine canneries processing, at their peak, nearly 200,000 tons of the smelly silver fish a year. During the mid-1940s, however, the sardines disappeared from the bay, causing the canneries to close. Through the years the old tin-roof canneries have been converted into restaurants, art galleries, and malls with shops selling T-shirts, fudge, and plastic sea otters. Recent tourist development along the row has been more tasteful, however, and includes several stylish inns and hotels. ✉ *Cannery Row, between Prescott and David Aves.* ⊕ *www.canneryrow.com.*

⑥ Casa Soberanes. A classic low-ceiling adobe structure built in 1842, this was once a Custom House guard's residence. Exhibits at the house survey life in Monterey from the era of Mexican rule to the present. The building is open only during the free 45-minute tours, but feel free to stop at the peaceful rear garden, which has a lovely rose-covered arbor and sitting benches. ✉ *Monterey State Historic Park, 336 Pacific St.* ☎ *831/649-7118* ⊕ *www.parks.ca.gov/mshp* ✆ *Free* ⊙ *Tours Mon.–Wed., and Fri. at 11:30; Sat. and Sun. at noon.*

⑩ Colton Hall. A convention of delegates met in 1849 to draft the first state constitution at California's equivalent of Independence Hall. The stone building, which has served as a school, a courthouse, and the county seat, is a city-run museum furnished as it was during the constitutional convention. The extensive grounds outside the hall surround the Old Monterey Jail. ✉ *500 block of Pacific St., between Madison and Jefferson Sts.* ☎ *831/646-5648* ⊕ *www.monterey.org/museum* ✆ *Free* ⊙ *Daily 10–4.*

⑧ Cooper-Molera Adobe. The restored 2-acre complex includes a house dating from the 1820s, a visitor center, a bookstore, and a large garden enclosed by a high adobe wall. The mostly Victorian-era antiques and memorabilia that fill the house provide a glimpse into the life of a prosperous early sea merchant's family. The building is open only during organized 45-minute tours, which leave from the Cooper Museum Store. ✉ *Monterey State Historic Park, Polk and Munras Sts.*

☎831/649–7118 ⊕ *www.parks. ca.gov/mshp* ▱*Free* ◐*Tours Fri.– Wed. at 3; additional tours Sun. at noon.*

④ **Custom House.** This adobe structure built by the Mexican government in 1827—now California's old- est standing public building—was the first stop for sea traders whose goods were subject to duties. At the beginning of the Mexican-American War, in 1846, Commodore John Sloat raised the American flag over the building and claimed California for the United States. The house's lower floor displays cargo from a 19th-century trading ship. ⊠ *Mon- terey State Historic Park, 1 Custom House Plaza, across from Fisher- man's Wharf* ☎831/649–7118 ⊕*www.parks.ca.gov/mshp* ▱*Free* ◐*Sat.–Thurs., 10–4, Fri. 10:30–4.*

> ## JOHN STEINBECK'S CANNERY ROW
>
> "Cannery Row in Monterey in California is a poem, a stink, a grating noise, a quality of light, a tone, a habit, a nostalgia, a dream. Cannery Row is the gath- ered and scattered, tin and iron and rust and splintered wood, chipped pavement and weedy lots and junk heaps, sardine canneries of corrugated iron, honky tonks, restaurants and whore houses, and little crowded groceries, and laboratories and flophouses."
>
> —John Steinbeck, *Cannery Row*

16

⑬ **Fisherman's Wharf.** The mournful barking of sea lions provides a steady sound track all along Monterey's waterfront, but the best way to actu- ally view the whiskered marine mammals is to walk along one of the two piers across from Custom House Plaza. Fisherman's Wharf is lined with souvenir shops, seafood restaurants, and whale-watching tour boats. It's undeniably touristy, but still a lively and entertaining place. Up the harbor to the right is Wharf No. 2, a working municipal pier where you can see fishing boats unloading their catches to one side, and fishermen casting their lines into the water on the other. The pier has a couple of low-key restaurants, from whose seats lucky customers may spot otters and harbor seals. ⊠ *At end of Calle Principal* ☎*831/649– 6544* ⊕*www.montereywharf.com.*

⑨ **Larkin House.** A veranda encircles the second floor of this architecturally significant two-story adobe built in 1835, whose design bears witness to the Mexican and New England influences on the Monterey style. The rooms are furnished with period antiques, many of them brought from New Hampshire by the building's namesake, Thomas O. Lar- kin, an early California statesman. The building is open only during organized 45-minute tours. ⊠ *Monterey State Historic Park, 464 Calle Principal, between Jefferson and Pacific Sts.* ☎*831/649–7118* ⊕*www. parks.ca.gov/mshp* ▱*Free* ◐*Tours Tues., Wed., Sat., Sun. at 2.*

⑯ **Monterey Bay Aquarium.** The minute you hand over your ticket at this extraordinary aquarium you're surrounded by sea creatures; right at the entrance, you can see dozens of them swimming in a three-story- tall, sunlit kelp forest tank. The beauty of the exhibits here is that they are all designed to give a sense of what it's like to be in the water with the animals—sardines swim around your head in a circular tank, and

Fodor'sChoice
★

jellyfish drift in and out of view in dramatically lighted spaces that suggest the ocean depths. A petting pool gives you a hands-on experience with bat rays, and the million-gallon Outer Bay tank shows the vast variety of creatures (from sharks to placid-looking turtles) that live in the eastern Pacific. A Splash Zone with 45 interactive bilingual exhibits opened in 2008: here, kids (and kids-at-heart) can commune with sea dragons, pot-bellied seahorses, and other fascinating creatures. The only drawback to the experience is that it must be shared with the throngs of people that crowd the place daily; most think it's worth it. To avoid the crowds, arrive as soon as the aquarium opens or visit in mid-afternoon, after the field trip groups depart and youngsters head home for their naps. ⊠*886 Cannery Row* ☎*831/648–4888, 800/756–3737 in CA for advance tickets* ⊕*www.montereybayaquarium.org* ⊠*$25* ⊙*Late May–June and early Sept., daily 9:30–6; July–Aug. weekdays 9:30–6, weekends 9:30–8; early Sept.–late May, daily 10–6.*

② **Monterey Maritime and History Museum.** Maintained by the Monterey History and Art Association, this collection of maritime artifacts belonged to Allen Knight, who was Carmel-by-the-Sea's mayor from 1950 to 1952. Highlights are a collection of outstanding scrimshaw, including fully jointed pocketknives and a toy guillotine, and a lively movie from 1943 chronicling a day in the life of the cannery that used to stand where the aquarium is. The jewel in the museum's crown is the enormous, multifaceted Fresnel lens from the lighthouse at Point Sur Light Station. ⊠*Stanton Center, 5 Custom House Plaza* ☎*831/372–2608* ⊕*www.montereyhistory.org* ⊠*Free* ⊙*Tues.–Sun. 10–5.*

⑫ **Monterey Museum of Art at La Mirada.** Asian and European antiques fill this 19th-century adobe house. A newer 10,000-square-foot gallery space, designed by Charles Moore, houses Asian and California regional art. Outdoors are magnificent rose and rhododendron gardens. A single fee covers admission to the La Mirada and Pacific Street facilities of the Monterey Museum of Art. ⊠*720 Via Mirada, at Fremont St.* ☎*831/372–3689* ⊕*www.montereyart.org* ⊠*$5* ⊙*Wed.–Sat. 11–5, Sun. 1–4.*

⑪ **Monterey Museum of Art at Pacific Street.** Photographs by Ansel Adams and Edward Weston, as well as works by other artists who have spent time on the peninsula, are on display here. There's also a colorful collection of international folk art; the pieces range from Kentucky hearth brooms to Tibetan prayer wheels. A single fee covers admission to the Pacific Street and La Mirada facilities of the Monterey Museum of Art. ⊠*559 Pacific St., across from Colton Hall* ☎*831/372–5477* ⊕*www. montereyart.org* ⊠*$5* ⊙*Wed.–Sat. 11–5, Sun. 1–4.*

Monterey State Historic Park. You can glimpse Monterey's early history in the well-preserved adobe buildings scattered along several city blocks. Far from being a hermetic period museum, the park facilities are an integral part of the day-to-day business life of the town—within some of the buildings are a store, a theater, and government offices. At some of the historic houses, the gardens (open daily 10 to 5) are worthy sights themselves. Departing from the Pacific House Museum, guided

45-minute walking tours of Old Monterey take place Monday, Tuesday, Wednesday, and Friday at 10:30 AM. ⊠ *20 Custom House Plaza* ☎ *831/649–7118* ⊕ *www.parks.ca.gov/mshp* ⊡ *Free* ⊘ *Call for hrs.*

❸ **Pacific House Museum.** Once a hotel and saloon, this visitor center and museum now commemorates early-California life with gold-rush relics and photographs of old Monterey. The upper floor displays Native American artifacts, including gorgeous baskets and pottery. ⊠ *Monterey State Historic Park, 10 Custom House Plaza* ☎ *831/649–7118* ⊕ *www. parks.ca.gov/mshp* ⊡ *Free* ⊘ *Fri.–Wed. 10–4, Thurs. 10:30–4.*

❿④ **Presidio of Monterey Museum.** This spot has been significant for centuries as a town, a fort, and the site of several battles, including the skirmish in which the pirate Hipoleto Bruchard conquered the Spanish garrison that stood here. Its first incarnation was as a Native American village for the Rumsien tribe; then it became known as the landing site for explorer Sebastien Vizcaíno in 1602, and father of the California missions, Father Serra, in 1770. The indoor museum tells the stories; the outdoor sites are marked with plaques. ⊠ *Corporal Ewing Rd., Presidio of Monterey* ☎ *831/646–3456* ⊕ *www.monterey.org/museum/pom* ⊡ *Free* ⊘ *Mon. 10–1, Thurs.–Sat. 10–4, Sun. 1–4.*

❶ **Stanton Center.** This is the place to go to load up on maps and area information. Especially worthwhile are the brochures on self-guided walking tours of historic Monterey and Cannery Row; admission to most sites along the walks is free, and most are open daily. The Maritime Museum of Monterey is in the Stanton Center; you can also view a free 20-minute film about Old Monterey. ⊠ *5 Custom House Plaza* ☎ *831/372–2608* ⊕ *www.montereyhistory.org* ⊡ *Free* ⊘ *Tues.–Sun. 10–5.*

❼ **Stevenson House.** This house was named in honor of author Robert Louis Stevenson, who boarded here briefly in a tiny upstairs room. Items from his family's estate furnish Stevenson's room; period-decorated chambers elsewhere in the house include a gallery of the author's memorabilia and a children's nursery stocked with Victorian toys and games. The building is open only during free 45-minute tours and on Saturday from 11:30 to 2. ⊠ *Monterey State Historic Park, 530 Houston St.* ☎ *831/649–7118* ⊕ *www.parks.ca.gov/mshp* ⊡ *Free* ⊘ *Sat. 11:30–2; tours Mon. and Fri. at 2, weekends at 10:30.*

WHERE TO STAY & EAT

$$$$ ✕ **Fresh Cream.** For years this dining room with a view of glittering Heritage Harbor has provided one of the most refined dining experiences in Monterey. The wine list is carefully chosen, the service is attentive yet restrained, and everything carries an air of luxury. The menu centers around imaginative variations on classic French cuisine, such as lobster and prawns with white-corn bisque. Though there's no requirement for dress, men will feel more comfortable in a jacket. ⊠ *99 Pacific St., Suite 100C* ☎ *831/375–9798* ⚜ *Reservations essential* ⊟ *AE, D, DC, MC, V* ⊘ *No lunch.*

$$$ ✕ **Stokes Restaurant & Bar.** This 1833 adobe building glows with well-being, its many fireplaces, booths, and banquettes bringing coziness to the numerous intimate dining rooms. Regional ingredients handled

16

with Mediterranean techniques combine in dishes such as Monterey Bay sardines escabèche (a spicy marinade) and pork shoulder with celery-root gratin. Small plates are a specialty, and wines come from all over the world. ⊠ *500 Hartnell St.* ☎ *831/373–1110* ▤ *AE, D, DC, MC, V* ⊘ *No lunch.*

$$ ✕ **Monterey's Fish House.** Casual yet stylish, and removed from the hubbub of the wharf, this always-packed seafood restaurant attracts locals and frequent visitors to the city. If the dining room is full, you can wait at the bar and savor deliciously plump oysters on the half shell. The bartenders and waitstaff will gladly advise you on the perfect wine to go with your poached, blackened, or oak-grilled seafood. ⊠ *2114 Del Monte Ave.* ☎ *831/373–4647* ▤ *AE, D, DC, MC, V* ⊘ *No lunch weekends.*

$$ ✕ **Montrio Bistro.** This quirky, converted firehouse, with its rawhide walls
Fodor'sChoice and iron indoor trellises, has a wonderfully sophisticated menu. Chef
★ Tony Baker uses organic produce and meats to create imaginative dishes that reflect local agriculture, such as baby artichoke risotto and whole stuffed quail with savory French toast and apple-blackberry reduction. Likewise, the wine list draws primarily on California, and many come from the Monterey area. ⊠ *414 Calle Principal* ☎ *831/648–8880* ⌕ *Reservations essential* ▤ *AE, D, DC, MC, V* ⊘ *No lunch.*

$$ ✕ **Tarpy's Roadhouse.** Fun, dressed-up American favorites—a little something for everyone—are served in this renovated early-1900s stone farmhouse several miles outside town. The kitchen cranks out everything from Cajun-spiced prawns to meat loaf with marsala-mushroom gravy to grilled ribs and steaks. Eat indoors by a fireplace or outdoors in the courtyard. ⊠ *2999 Monterey–Salinas Hwy., Hwy. 68* ☎ *831/647–1444* ▤ *AE, D, DC, MC, V.*

¢ ✕ **Café Lumiere.** Attached to the lobby of Monterey's art-house cinema, this café shows work by local artists. Eat a light breakfast or lunch, drink coffee, or choose a pot of tea from the extensive selection. The menu includes baked goods, cakes, sandwiches, granola, and other breakfast items. Most patrons bring their laptops for the free Wi-Fi, and most tables are shared. Close to downtown bars, it's open until 10 PM. ⊠ *365 Calle Principal* ☎ *831/920–2451* ▤ *No credit cards.*

¢ ✕ **Old Monterey Café.** Breakfast here gets constant local raves. Its fame rests on familiar favorites in many incarnations: a dozen kinds of omelets, and pancakes from blueberry to cinnamon-raisin-pecan. The lunch and dinner menus have good soups, salads, and sandwiches, and this is a great place to relax with an afternoon cappuccino. ⊠ *489 Alvarado St.* ☎ *831/646–1021* ⌕ *Reservations not accepted* ▤ *AE, D, MC, V.*

¢ ✕ **Thai Bistro.** This cheery mom-and-pop restaurant serves excellent, authentic Thai cuisine from family recipes. Though technically just over the city line in Pacific Grove, it's within walking distance of Cannery Row and the Monterey Bay Aquarium. ⊠ *159 Central Ave., Pacific Grove* ☎ *831/372–8700* ▤ *AE, D, MC, V.*

$$$$ ⌂ **Old Monterey Inn.** This three-story manor house was the home of
Fodor'sChoice Monterey's first mayor, and today it remains a private enclave within
★ walking distance of downtown. Lush gardens are shaded by huge old

trees and bordered by a creek. Rooms are individually decorated with tasteful antiques; many have fireplaces, and all have featherbeds. Those with private entrances have split doors; you can open the top half to let in cool air and the sound of birds. In the spa room, indulge in a massage or wrap in front of the fireplace. The extensive breakfast is delivered to the rooms, and wine, cheese, and cookies are served each afternoon in the parlor. **Pros:** Gorgeous gardens; refined luxury; serene. **Cons:** Must drive to attractions and sights; fills quickly. ✉*500 Martin St.* ☎*831/375–8284 or 800/350–2344* ⊕*www.oldmontereyinn.com* ⬅*6 rooms, 3 suites, 1 cottage* ♿*In-room: no a/c, DVD (some), VCR (some), Ethernet, Wi-Fi. In-hotel: no elevator, concierge, no-smoking rooms* ▭*MC, V* ⦿*BP.*

THE FIRST ARTICHOKE QUEEN

Castroville, a tiny town off Highway 1 between Monterey and Watsonville, produces about 95% of U.S. artichokes. Back in 1948, the town chose its first queen to preside during its Artichoke Festival—a beautiful young woman named Norma Jean Mortenson, who later changed her name to Marilyn Monroe.

$$$–$$$$ ★ 🏨**Monterey Plaza Hotel and Spa.** This full-service hotel commands a waterfront location on Cannery Row, where you can see frolicking sea otters from the wide outdoor patio and many room balconies. The architecture blends early California and Mediterranean styles, and also echoes elements of the old cannery design. Meticulously maintained, the property offers both simple and luxurious accommodations. On the top floor, the spa offers a full array of treatments, perfect after a workout in the penthouse fitness center. **Pros:** On the ocean; lots of amenities; attentive service. **Cons:** Touristy area; heavy traffic. ✉*400 Cannery Row* ☎*831/646–1700 or 800/334–3999* ⊕*www.montereyplazahotel.com* ⬅*280 rooms, 10 suites* ♿*In-room: no a/c, DVD, Ethernet. In-hotel: 2 restaurants, room service, gym, spa, concierge, laundry service, public Internet, no-smoking rooms* ▭*AE, D, DC, MC, V.*

16

$$$–$$$$ 🏨**Spindrift Inn.** This boutique hotel on Cannery Row, under the same management as the Hotel Pacific and the Monterey Bay Inn, has beach access and a rooftop garden that overlooks the water. Designed with traditional American style, spacious rooms have sitting areas, hardwood floors, fireplaces, and down comforters, among other pleasures. This property caters to adults and is therefore inappropriate for children. **Pros:** Close to aquarium; steps from the beach; friendly staff. **Cons:** Throngs of visitors outside; can be noisy. ✉*652 Cannery Row* ☎*831/646–8900 or 800/841–1879* ⊕*www.spindriftinn.com* ⬅*45 rooms* ♿*In-room: no a/c, refrigerator, VCR, Wi-Fi. In-hotel: concierge, no-smoking rooms* ▭*AE, D, DC, MC, V* ⦿*CP.*

$$–$$$ 🏨**Best Western Beach Resort Monterey.** The rooms here may be nondescript, but this hotel has a great waterfront location about 2 mi north of town that affords views of the bay and the city skyline. Amenities are surprisingly ample. The grounds are pleasantly landscaped, and there's a large pool with a sunbathing area. **Pros:** On the beach; great value; family-friendly. **Cons:** Several miles from major attractions; big-box mall neighborhood. ✉*2600 Sand Dunes Dr.* ☎*831/394–3321 or*

800/242–8627 ⊕*www.montereybeachresort.com* ↝*196 rooms* ⅋*In-room: safe, refrigerator, Wi-Fi. In-hotel: restaurant, room service, bar, pool, beachfront, laundry service, public Internet, public Wi-Fi, some pets allowed, no-smoking rooms* ⊟*AE, D, DC, MC, V.*

$–$$ ⚏**Monterey Bay Lodge.** Location (on the edge of Monterey's El Estero
★ Park) and superior amenities give this cheerful facility an edge over other motels in town. Lots of greenery, indoors and out, views over El Estero Lake, and a secluded courtyard with a heated pool are other pluses. **Pros:** Within walking distance of beach and playground; quiet at night; good family choice. **Cons:** Near busy boulevard. ⊠*55 Camino Aguajito* ☎*831/372–8057 or 800/558–1900* ⊕*www.montereybay lodge.com* ↝*43 rooms, 2 suites* ⅋*In-room: safe, refrigerator, VCR (some), Ethernet, Wi-Fi. In-hotel: no elevator, restaurant, pool, some pets allowed, no-smoking rooms* ⊟*AE, D, DC, MC, V.*

$–$$ ⚏**Quality Inn Monterey.** This attractive motel has a friendly, country-inn feeling. Rooms are light and airy, some have fireplaces—and the price is right. **Pros:** Indoor pool; bargain rates; cheerful innkeepers. **Cons:** Street is busy during the day; some rooms are dark. ⊠*1058 Munras Ave.* ☎*831/372–3381* ⊕*www.qualityinnmonterey.com* ↝*55 rooms* ⅋*In-room: refrigerator, VCR, Ethernet, Wi-Fi. In-hotel: pool, no elevator, no-smoking rooms* ⊟*AE, D, DC, MC, V* ⎮◯⎮*CP.*

NIGHTLIFE & THE ARTS

NIGHTLIFE **Planet Ultralounge and Restaurant** (⊠2110 N. Fremont St. ☎831/373–1449 ⊕*www.theplanetmonterey.com*) presents comedy shows on weekends and dancing to a DJ or live music most nights. An Italian restaurant with a big bar area, **Cibo** (⊠301 Alvarado St. ☎831/649–8151 ⊕*www.cibo.com*) brings live jazz, Latin, soul, and more to downtown Tuesday through Sunday. Loungey **Monterey Live** (⊠414 Alvarado St. ☎831/375–5483 ⊕*www.montereylive.org*), in the heart of downtown, presents jazz, rock, and comedy acts, including some big names, nightly.

THE ARTS **Dixieland Monterey** (☎831/675–0298 or 888/349–6879 ⊕*www.dixie*
★ *land-monterey.com*), held on the first full weekend of March, presents traditional jazz bands at waterfront venues on the harbor. The **Monterey Bay Blues Festival** (☎831/394–2652 ⊕*www.montereyblues.com*) draws blues fans to the Monterey Fairgrounds the last weekend in June. The **Monterey Jazz Festival** (☎831/373–3366 ⊕*www.monterey jazzfestival.org*), the world's oldest, attracts jazz and blues greats from around the world to the Monterey Fairgrounds on the third full weekend of September.

Monterey Bay Theatrefest (☎831/622–0100) presents free outdoor performances at Custom House Plaza on weekend afternoons and evenings from late June to mid-July. The **Bruce Ariss Wharf Theater** (⊠*One Fisherman's Wharf* ☎831/649–2332) focuses on American musicals past and present.

SPORTS & THE OUTDOORS

Throughout most of the year, the Monterey Bay area is a haven for those who love tennis, golf, surfing, fishing, biking, hiking, scuba diving, and kayaking. In the rainy winter months, when the waves grow larger, adventurous surfers flock to the water. The **Monterey Bay National Marine Sanctuary** (☎ *831/647–4201* ⊕ *http://montereybay.noaa.gov*), home to mammals, seabirds, fishes, invertebrates, and plants, encompasses a 276-mi shoreline and 5,322 square mi of ocean. Ringed by beaches and campgrounds, it's a place for kayaking, whale-watching, scuba diving, and other water sports.

> ### WHALE-WATCHING
>
> Thousands of gray whales pass close by the Monterey Coast on their annual migration between the Bering Sea and Baja California. The gigantic creatures are sometimes visible through binoculars from shore, but a whale-watching cruise is the best way to get a close look at these magnificent mammals. The migration south takes place from December through March; January is prime viewing time. The whales migrate north from March through June. In addition, some 2,000 blue whales and 600 humpbacks pass the coast and are easily spotted in late summer and early fall.

BICYCLING For bicycle and surrey rentals, visit **Bay Bikes** (✉ *585 Cannery Row* ☎ *831/655–2453*, ⊕ *www.baybikes.com*). **Adventures by the Sea, Inc.** (✉ *299 Cannery Row* ☎ *831/372–1807 or 831/648–7236* ⊕ *www.adventuresbythesea.com*) rents tandem and standard bicycles.

FISHING **Randy's Fishing Trips** (✉ *66 Fisherman's Wharf* ☎ *831/372–7440* ⊕ *www.randysfishingtrips.com*) has been operating under the same skippers since 1958.

GOLF The green fee at the 18-hole **Del Monte Golf Course** (✉ *1300 Sylvan Rd.* ☎ *831/373–2700*) is $110, plus $25 per person for an optional cart. The $25 twilight special (plus cart rental) begins two hours before sunset.

KAYAKING **Monterey Bay Kayaks** (✉ *693 Del Monte Ave.* ☎ *831/373–5357, 800/ 649–5357* ⊕ *www.montereybaykayaks.com*) rents equipment and conducts classes and natural-history tours.

SCUBA DIVING Monterey Bay waters never warm to the temperatures of their Southern California counterparts (the warmest they get is low 60s), but that's one reason why the marine life here is among the world's most diverse. The staff at **Aquarius Dive Shop** (✉ *2040 Del Monte Ave.* ☎ *831/375– 1933, 831/657–1020 diving conditions* ⊕ *www.aquariusdivers.com*) gives diving lessons and tours, and rents equipment. Their scuba-conditions information line is updated daily.

WALKING From Custom House Plaza, you can walk along the coast in either direction on the 29-mi-long **Monterey Bay Coastal Trail** (☎ *831/372–3196* ⊕ *www.mtycounty.com/pgs-parks/bike-path.html*) for spectacular views of the sea. It runs all the way from north of Monterey to Pacific Grove, with sections continuing around Pebble Beach.

16

<table>
<tr><td>

WHALE-
WATCHING

★

</td><td>

Monterey Bay Whale Watch (⌧*84 Fisherman's Wharf* ☎*831/375–4658* ⊕*www.montereybaywhalewatch.com*), which operates out of the Monterey Bay Whale Watch Center at Fisherman's Wharf, gives three- to five-hour tours led by marine biologists. **Monterey Whale Watching** (⌧*96 Fisherman's Wharf #1* ☎*831/372–2203 or 800/979–3370,* ⊕*www.montereywhalewatching.com*) provides three tours a day on a 150-passenger high-speed cruiser and a large 75-foot boat.

</td></tr>
</table>

SHOPPING

Bargain hunters can sometimes find little treasures at the **Cannery Row Antique Mall** (⌧*471 Wave St.* ☎*831/655–0264*), which houses 150 local vendors under one roof. Historical society–operated, **The Pickett Fence** (⌧*Monterey State Historic Park, 1 Custom House Plaza, across from Fisherman's Wharf* ☎*831/649–3364*) sells high-end garden accessories and furnishings.

AROUND THE BAY

As Highway 1 follows the curve of the bay between Monterey and Santa Cruz, it passes through a rich agricultural zone. Opening right onto the bay, where the Salinas and Pajaro rivers drain into the Pacific, a broad valley brings together fertile soil, an ideal climate, and a good water supply to create optimum growing conditions for crops such as strawberries, artichokes, brussels sprouts, and broccoli. Several beautiful beaches line this part of the coast.

MOSS LANDING

17 mi north of Monterey on Hwy. 1.

Moss Landing is not much more than a couple blocks of cafés and antiques shops plus a busy fishing port, but therein lies its charm. It's a fine place to stop for lunch and get a dose of nature.

★ In the **Elkhorn Slough National Estuarine Research Reserve** (⌧*1700 Elkhorn Rd., Watsonville* ☎*831/728–2822* ⊕*www.elkhornslough.org* ⌧*$2.50* ☉ *Wed.–Sun. 9–5*), 1,400 acres of tidal flats and salt marshes form a complex environment that supports some 300 species of birds. A walk or a kayak trip along the meandering waterways and wetlands can reveal hawks, white-tailed kites, owls, herons, and egrets. Sea otters, sharks, rays, and many other animals also live or visit here. On weekends guided walks from the visitor center to the heron rookery begin at 10 and 1. Although the reserve lies across the town line in Watsonville, you reach its entrance through Moss Landing.

Aboard a 27-foot pontoon boat operated by **Elkhorn Slough Safari** (⌧*Moss Landing Harbor* ☎*831/633–5555* ⊕*www.elkhornslough. com*), a naturalist leads an up-close look at wetlands denizens. Advance reservations are required for the two-hour tours ($32).

Sanctuary Cruises (⌧*"A" Dock* ☎*831/643–0128* ⊕*www.sanctuary cruises.com*) offers three- and four-hour whale-watching trips ($40

SALINAS & JOHN STEINBECK'S LEGACY

Salinas (17 mi east of Monterey), a hard-working city surrounded by vegetable fields, honors the memory and literary legacy of John Steinbeck, its most well-known native, at the modern **National Steinbeck Center** (⊠ *1 Main St., 17 mi east of Monterey via Hwy. 68, Salinas* 🕾 *831/796–3833* ⊕ *www.steinbeck. org* 🎫 *$11* ⊙ *Daily 10–5*). Exhibits document the life of the Pulitzer- and Nobel-prize winner and the history of the local communities that inspired Steinbeck novels such as *The Grapes of Wrath*. Highlights include reproductions of the green pickup-camper from *Travels with*

Charley and of the bunkroom from *Of Mice and Men*; you can watch actors read from Steinbeck's books on video screens throughout the museum. The museum is the centerpiece of the revival of Old Town Salinas, where handsome turn-of-the-20th-century stone buildings have been renovated and filled with shops and restaurants. Two blocks from the National Steinbeck Center is the author's Victorian birthplace, **Steinbeck House** (⊠ *132 Central Ave.* 🕾 *831/424–2735*). It operates as a lunch spot Monday through Saturday and displays some Steinbeck memorabilia.

16

three hours, $46 four hours) on Monterey Bay, some on catamarans and others on boats powered by biodiesel.

Tom's Sportfishing (⊠ *Moss Landing Harbor* 🕾 *831/633–2564* ⊕ *www. tomssportfishing.com*) takes anglers out onto Monterey Bay ($65 to $70). Depending on the season, king salmon, albacore, or halibut may be the quarry.

WHERE TO EAT

$ ✕ **Phil's Fish Market & Eatery.** Exquisitely fresh, simply prepared seafood (try the cioppino) is on the menu at this warehouselike restaurant on the harbor; all kinds of glistening fish are on offer at the market in the front. ■ TIP➔ **Phil's Snack Shack, a tiny sandwich-and-smoothie joint, serves quicker meals at the north end of town.** ⊠ *7600 Sandholdt Rd.* 🕾 *831/633–2152* 🚬 *AE, D, DC, MC, V.*

WATSONVILLE

7 mi north of Moss Landing on Hwy. 1.

If ever a city was built on strawberries, Watsonville is it. Produce has long driven the economy here, and this is where the county fair takes place each September.

↺   One feature of the Santa Cruz County Fairgrounds is the **Agricultural History Project,** which preserves the history of farming in the Pajaro Valley. In the Codiga Center and Museum you can examine antique tractors and milking machines, peruse an exhibit on the era when Watsonville was the "frozen food capitol of the West," and watch experts restore farm implements and vehicles. ⊠ *2601 E. Lake Ave.* 🕾 *831/724–5898* ⊕ *www.aghistoryproject.org* 🎫 *$2 suggested donation* ⊙ *Thurs.–Sun. noon–4.*

SAN JUAN BAUTISTA

About as close to early-19th-century California as you can get, San Juan Bautista (15 mi east of Watsonville on Hwy. 156) has been protected from development since 1933, when much of it became a state park. Small antiques shops and restaurants occupy the Old West and art-deco buildings that line 3rd Street.

The wide green plaza of San Juan Bautista State Historic Park is ringed by 18th- and 19th-century buildings, many of them open to the public.

The cemetery of the long, low, colonnaded mission church contains the unmarked graves of more than 4,300 Native American converts. Nearby is an adobe home furnished with Spanish-colonial antiques, a hotel frozen in the 1860s, a blacksmith shop, a stable, a pioneer cabin, and a jailhouse.

The first Saturday of each month, costumed volunteers engage in quilting bees, tortilla making, and other frontier activities.

Every Memorial Day weekend, aerial performers execute elaborate aerobatics at the **Watsonville Fly-in & Air Show.** More than 300 classic, experimental, and military aircraft are on display; concerts and other events fill three days. ⊠ *Watsonville Municipal Airport, 100 Aviation Way* ☎*831/763–5600* ⊕*www.watsonvilleflyin.org* ⊠*$15.*

APTOS

7 mi north of Watsonville on Hwy. 1.

Backed by a redwood forest and facing the sea, downtown Aptos—known as Aptos Village—is a place of wooden walkways and false-fronted shops. Antiques dealers cluster along Trout Gulch Road, off Soquel Drive east of Highway 1.

Sandstone bluffs tower above **Seacliff State Beach** (⊠*201 State Park Dr.* ☎*831/685–6442* ⊕*www.parks.ca.gov* ⊠*$6 per vehicle*), a favorite of locals. You can fish off the pier, which leads out to a sunken World War I tanker ship built of concrete.

WHERE TO STAY & EAT

$$$ ✕ **Bittersweet Bistro.** A large old tavern with cathedral ceilings houses
★ this popular bistro, where chef-owner Thomas Vinolus draws culinary inspiration from the Mediterranean. The menu changes seasonally, but regular highlights include the pan-seared sand dabs (a species of flounder), seafood puttanesca (pasta with a spicy sauce of garlic, tomatoes, anchovies, and olives), and grilled lamb tenderloin. The decadent chocolate desserts are not to be missed. You can order many of the entrées in small or regular portions. Lunch is available to go from the express counter. ⊠*787 Rio Del Mar Blvd.* ☎*831/662–9799* ⊟*AE, MC, V.*

$$$$ ▦ **Seascape Resort.** On a bluff overlooking Monterey Bay, Seascape is
☾ a full-fledged resort that makes it easy to unwind. The spacious suites sleep from two to six people; each has a kitchenette and fireplace, and many have ocean-view patios with barbecue grills. Treat yourself to

an in-room manicure, facial, or massage, or a bonfire with s'mores on the beach. **Pros:** Time-share-style apartments; access to miles of beach-front; superb views. **Cons:** Far from city life; most bathrooms are small. ⊠*1 Seascape Resort Dr.* ☎*831/688–6800 or 800/929–7727* ⊕*www. seascaperesort.com* ⬩*285 suites* ⬩*In-room: no a/c, kitchen (some), DVD, Ethernet, Wi-Fi. In-hotel: restaurant, room service, pools, gym, spa, beachfront, no elevator, children's programs (ages 5–10), laundry service, public Internet, no-smoking rooms* ⊟*AE, D, DC, MC, V.*

$$$ 🏨 **Best Western Seacliff Inn.** A favorite lair of families and business travelers, this 6-acre Best Western near Seacliff State Beach is more resort than motel. Six two-story lodge buildings encircle a large pool and lush gardens with a koi pond and waterfall—ask for a room in a building away from the busy restaurant and bar, which can get noisy at night. The decent-size rooms, totally redecorated in 2006, sport a fresh—if somewhat generic—contemporary look. **Pros:** Walking distance from the beach; family-friendly; includes full breakfast. **Cons:** Close to the freeway; occasional nighttime bar noise. ⊠*7500 Old Dominion Ct.* ☎*831/688–7300 or 800/367–2003* ⊕*www.seacliffinn.com* ⬩*139 rooms, 10 suites* ⬩*In-room: refrigerator, Ethernet. In-hotel: restaurant, room service, bar, pool, gym, laundry facilities, laundry service, public Wi-Fi, no-smoking rooms* ⊟*AE, D, MC, V* ⦿*BP.*

$$–$$$ 🏨 **Flora Vista.** Multicolored fields of flowers, strawberries, and fresh veggies unfold in every direction at this luxury neo-Georgian inn set on two serene acres in a rural community just south of Aptos; Sand Dollar Beach is just an eight-minute walk away. Innkeepers Deanna and Ed Boos transformed the 1867 home, a replica of Abe Lincoln's Spring-field farmhouse, adding modern conveniences like Wi-Fi and spa tubs while retaining the house's original redwood floors and country charm. Guests wake to a full breakfast—which might include the neighbor's strawberries—and enjoy a wine and cheese spread in the late afternoon. Each room has its own sparkling bathroom and gas fireplace; three have a spa tub with shower. Stroll through the eclectic gardens (something's always in bloom) or play tennis on the two tournament-quality HarTru tennis courts. The inn is on the Pacific Coast Bike Route and welcomes cyclists for stopovers. **Pros:** Super-private; near the beach; flowers everywhere. **Cons:** No restaurants or nightlife within walking distance; not a good place for kids. ⊠*1258 San Andreas Rd. La Selva Beach* ☎*831/724–8663 or 877/753–5672* ⊕*www.floravistainn.com* ⬩*5 rooms* ⬩*In-room: no a/c, Wi-Fi. In-hotel: tennis courts, no-smoking rooms* ⊟*AE, MC, V* ⦿*BP.*

CAPITOLA & SOQUEL

4 mi northwest of Aptos on Hwy. 1.

On the National Register of Historic places as California's first seaside resort town, the village of Capitola has been in a holiday mood since the late 1800s. Its walkable downtown is jam-packed with casual eat-eries, surf shops, and ice-cream parlors. Inland, across Highway 1, antiques shops line Soquel Drive in the town of Soquel. Wineries dot the Santa Cruz Mountains beyond.

New Brighton State Beach (⊠*1500 State Park Dr.* ☎*831/464–6330,* ⊕*www.parks.ca.gov* ⊠*$6 per vehicle*), once the site of a Chinese fishing village, is now a popular surfing and camping spot. Its Pacific Migrations Visitor Center, opened in 2006, traces the history of the Chinese and other peoples who settled around Monterey Bay, as well as the migratory patterns of the area's wildlife, such as monarch butterflies and gray whales. ■TIP➔ **New Brighton Beach connects with Seacliff Beach, and at low tide you can walk or run along this scenic stretch of sand for nearly 16 mi south (you might have to wade through a few creeks). The 1½-mile stroll from New Brighton to Seacliff's cement ship is a local favorite.**

> **CALIFORNIA'S OLDEST RESORT TOWN**
>
> As far as anyone knows for certain, Capitola is the oldest seaside resort town on the Pacific Coast. In 1856 a pioneer acquired Soquel Landing, the picturesque lagoon and beach where Soquel Creek empties into the bay, and built a wharf. Another man opened a campground along the shore, and his daughter named it Capitola after a heroine in a novel series. After the train came to town in the 1870s, thousands of vacationers began arriving to bask in the sun on the glorious beach.

WHERE TO STAY & EAT

$$$ ✕**Shadowbrook.** To get to this romantic spot overlooking Soquel Creek, you can take a cable car or walk the stairs down a steep, fern-lined bank beside a running waterfall. Dining room options include the rooftop Redwood Room, the wood-paneled Wine Cellar, and the airy, glass-enclosed Garden Room. Prime rib and grilled seafood are the stars of the simple menu. A cheaper menu of light entrées is available in the lounge. Champagne brunch is served on Sunday. ⊠*1750 Wharf Rd.* ☎*831/475–1511 or 800/975–1511* ▤*AE, D, DC, MC, V* ⊗*No lunch.*

$$$ ✕**Theo's.** Theo's is on a quiet side street in a residential neighbor-
★ hood. It serves mainly five- and seven-course prix-fixe dinners; seasonal standouts include duck with garden vegetables and currants, as well as rack of lamb with ratatouille. Much of the produce comes from the ¾-acre organic garden behind the restaurant (where you can stroll between courses); the rest comes from area farmers and ranchers. Service is gracious and attentive, and the wine list has won awards from *Wine Spectator* 15 years in a row. ⊠*3101 N. Main St., Soquel* ☎*831/462–3657* ⊛*Reservations essential* ▤*AE, MC, V* ⊗*Closed Sun. and Mon. No lunch.*

$$ ✕**Michael's on Main.** Classic comfort food with a creative gourmet twist, reasonable prices, and attentive service draw a lively crowd of locals to this upscale-but-casual creek-side eatery. Chef Michael Clark's commitment to locally sustainable fisheries and farmers has earned him community accolades and infuses dishes with the inimitable taste that comes from using fresh local ingredients. The menu changes seasonally, but you can always count on finding such home-style dishes as Yankee-style pot roast and mashed potatoes as well as unusual entrées like pistachio-crusted salmon with mint vinaigrette. For a quiet conversation

spot, ask for a table on the romantic patio overlooking the creek. The busy bar area hosts Wednesday karaoke nights and live music Thursday through Saturday. ⊠*2591 Main St.* ☎*831/479–9777* ▭*AE, D, MC, V* ⊘*Closed Mon.*

¢ ✕**Carpo's.** Locals line up in droves at Carpo's counter, hankering for mouthwatering, casual family meals. The menu leans heavily toward seafood, but also includes burgers, salads, and steaks. Favorites include the fishermen's baskets of fresh battered snapper, calamari and prawns, seafood kabobs, and homemade olallieberry pie. Nearly everything here costs less than $10. Go early to beat the crowds, or be prepared to wait for a table. ⊠*2400 Porter St.* ☎*831/476–6260* ▭*D, MC, V.*

¢ ✕**Gayle's Bakery & Rosticceria.** Whether you're in the mood for an orange-olallieberry muffin, a chicken-satay (marinated and served with spicy peanut sauce) salad, or tri-tip on garlic toast, this bakery-cum-deli's varied menu is likely to satisfy. Munch your chocolate macaroon on the shady patio or dig into the daily blue-plate dinner amid the whirl inside. ⊠*504 Bay Ave.* ☎*831/462–1200* ▭*AE, MC, V.*

$$$–$$$$ ⌂**Capitola Venetian Motel.** Brightly painted Venetian Court, a funky 1923 cluster of garden apartments, is a landmark on Capitola's waterfront. The complex's pseudo-Mediterranean style extends next door to this old (but well-maintained and up-to-date) motel on the beach. Popular with families, it offers studios to three-bedroom units with kitchen. Ocean-view rooms have balconies, and some rooms have fireplaces. **Pros:** Steps from the beach; within walking distance of everything in Capitola Village; quintessential California seaside digs. **Cons:** Near nightlife hub; busy street, few frills. ⊠*1500 Wharf Rd.* ☎*831/476–6471 or 800/332–2780* ⊕*www.capitolavenetian.com* ➹*19 apartments* ⚷*In-room: kitchen, Ethernet. In-hotel: no elevator, beachfront* ▭*D, MC, V.*

$$$–$$$$ ⌂**Inn at Depot Hill.** This inventively designed B&B in a former rail depot sees itself as a link to the era of luxury train travel. Each double room or suite, complete with fireplace and featherbeds, is inspired by a different destination—Italy's Portofino, France's Côte d'Azur, Japan's Kyoto. One suite is decorated like a Pullman car for a railroad baron. Some accommodations have private patios with hot tubs. This is a great place for an adults-only weekend. **Pros:** Short walk to beach and village; historic charm; excellent service. **Cons:** Fills quickly; hot tub conversation on the patio may irk second-floor guests. ⊠*250 Monterey Ave., 95010* ☎*831/462–3376 or 800/572–2632* ⊕*www.innatdepothill.com* ➹*8 rooms, 4 suites* ⚷*In-room: no a/c, VCR, Wi-Fi. In-hotel: no elevator, public Wi-Fi, no-smoking rooms* ▭*AE, D, MC, V.*

SANTA CRUZ

The big city on this stretch of the California coast, Santa Cruz (pop. 57,500) is less manicured than Carmel or Monterey. Long known for its surfing and its amusement-filled beach boardwalk, the town is a mix of grand Victorian-era homes and rinky-dink motels. The opening of the University of California campus in the 1960s swung the town sharply to the left, and the counterculture more or less lives on here.

At the same time, the revitalized downtown and an insane real-estate market reflect the city's proximity to Silicon Valley and to a growing wine country in the surrounding mountains.

THE WATERFRONT, DOWNTOWN & THE UNIVERSITY

5 mi west of Capitola on Hwy. 1; 48 mi north of Monterey on Hwy. 1.

The sleepy small-town personality of Santa Cruz changed forever in 1965, when a new University of California campus opened on a redwood-studded hillside above town. Tie-dye, yoga, and social progressivism arrived with the students and faculty, many of whom settled here permanently. In 1989 another radical event—the 7.1 Loma Prieta earthquake—wreaked havoc on downtown, which reinvented itself during reconstruction. Today, a lively mix of families, vacationers, students, surfers, and time-warp victims makes Santa Cruz hum.

WHAT TO SEE

ℭ Santa Cruz has been a seaside resort since the mid-19th century. Along one end of the broad, south-facing beach, the **Santa Cruz Beach Boardwalk** has entertained holidaymakers for almost as long—it celebrated its 100th anniversary in 2007. Its Looff carousel and classic wooden Giant Dipper roller coaster, both dating from the early 1900s, are surrounded by high-tech thrill rides and easygoing kiddie rides with ocean views. Video and arcade games, a mini-golf course, and a laser-tag arena pack one gigantic building. You have to pay to play, but you can wander the entire boardwalk for free while sampling delicacies such as corn dogs and chowder fries. ⊠*Along Beach St.* ☎*831/423–5590 or 831/426–7433* ⊕*www.beachboardwalk.com* ✍*$30 day pass for unlimited rides* ⊘*Late May–early Sept., daily; early Sept.–late May, weekends, weather permitting; call for hrs.*

ℭ Jutting half a mile into the ocean near one end of the Santa Cruz Beach Boardwalk, the **Santa Cruz Municipal Wharf** (⊠*Beach St., at Pacific Ave.* ☎*831/420–6025* ⊕*www.santacruzwharf.com*) is topped with seafood restaurants; souvenir shops; and outfitters offering bay cruises, fishing trips, and boat rentals. A salty sound track drifts up from under the wharf, where barking sea lions lounge in heaps on crossbeams.

West Cliff Drive winds along the top of an oceanfront bluff from the municipal wharf to Natural Bridges State Beach. It's a spectacular drive, but it's much more fun to walk, blade, or bike the paved path that parallels the road. Groups of surfers bob and swoosh in Monterey Bay at several points near the foot of the bluff, especially at a break known as Steamer Lane. Named for a surfer who died here in 1965, nearby Mark Abbott Memorial Lighthouse stands at Point Santa Cruz, the cliff's major promontory. From here you can watch pinnipeds hang out, sunbathe, and frolic on Seal Rock.

★ The **Santa Cruz Surfing Museum,** inside the Mark Abbott Memorial Lighthouse, traces local surfing history back to the early 20th century. Historical photographs show old-time surfers, and a display of boards includes rarities such as a heavy redwood plank predating the fiberglass era and the remains of a modern board chomped by a great white shark. Surfer-docents are on site to talk about the old days. ⊠*701 W. Cliff Dr.* ☎*831/420–6289* ⊕*www.santacruzsurfingmuseum.org* ✉*$1 suggested donation* ⊘*Thurs.–Mon. noon–4.*

At the end of West Cliff Drive lies **Natural Bridges State Beach,** a stretch of soft sand edged with tide pools and sea-sculpted rock bridges. ■TIP→ From October to early March a colony of monarch butterflies roosts in a eucalyptus grove. ⊠*2531 W. Cliff Dr.* ☎*831/423–4609* ⊕*www.parks.ca.gov* ✉*Beach free, parking $6* ⊘*Daily 8 AM–sunset. Visitor center Oct.–Feb., daily 10–4; Mar.–Sept., weekends 10–4.*

Seymour Marine Discovery Center, part of Long Marine Laboratory at UCSC's Institute of Marine Sciences, looks more like a research facility than like a slick aquarium. Interactive exhibits demonstrate how scientists study the ocean, and the aquarium displays creatures of particular interest to marine biologists. The 87-foot blue whale skeleton is the world's largest. ⊠*100 Shaffer Rd., off Delaware St. west of Natural Bridges State Beach* ☎*831/459–3800* ⊕*http://seymourcenter.ucsc.edu* ✉*$6* ⊘*Tues.–Sat. 10–5, Sun. noon–5.*

In the Cultural Preserve of **Wilder Ranch State Park** you can visit the homes, barns, workshops, and bunkhouse of a 19th-century dairy farm. Nature has reclaimed most of the ranch land, and native plants and wildlife have returned to the 7,000 acres of forest, grassland, canyons, estuaries, and beaches. Hike, bike, or ride horseback on miles of ocean-view trails. ⊠*Hwy. 1, 1 mi north of Santa Cruz* ☎*831/426–0505 Interpretive Center, 831/423–9703 trail information* ⊕*www.parks.ca.gov* ✉*Parking $6* ⊘*Daily 8 AM–sunset.*

When you've had your fill of the city's beaches and waters, take a stroll in downtown Santa Cruz, especially on **Pacific Avenue** between Laurel and Water streets. Vintage boutiques and mountain sports stores, sushi bars and Mexican restaurants, day spas and nightclubs keep the main drag and the surrounding streets hopping midmorning until late evening.

Pop into **Vinocruz** (⊠*725 Front St., #101* ⊘*Mon.–Thurs. 11–7, Fri. and Sat. 11–8, Sun. noon–6*) for one-stop tasting of Santa Cruz Mountain wines. They pour vintages from more than 65 local wineries, including small operations that don't have their own tasting rooms. The slick, contemporary space in Abbott Square off Cooper Street in historic downtown was once part of an old jail.

On the northern fringes of downtown, **Santa Cruz Mission State Historic Park** preserves the site of California's 12th Spanish mission, built in

16

the 1790s and destroyed by an earthquake in 1857. A museum in a restored 1791 adobe and a half-scale replica of the mission church are part of the complex. ⊠*144 School St.* ☎*831/425–5849* ⊕*www.parks. ca.gov* ☜*Free* ☉*Thurs.–Sun. 10–4.*

Hokey tourist trap or genuine scientific enigma? Since 1940, curious throngs baffled by the **Mystery Spot** have made it one of the most visited attractions in Santa Cruz. The laws of gravity and physics don't appear to apply in this tiny patch of redwood forest, where balls roll uphill and people stand on a slant. ⊠*465 Mystery Spot Rd.* ☎*831/423–8897* ⊕*www.mysteryspot.com* ☜*Mystery Spot $5, parking $5* ☉*Late May–early Sept., daily 9–7, early Sept.–late May, daily 9–5.*

The modern 2,000-acre campus of the **University of California at Santa Cruz** nestles in the forested hills above town. Its sylvan setting, sweeping ocean vistas, and redwood architecture make the university worth a visit. Campus tours, offered several times daily (reserve in advance), offer a glimpse of college life and campus highlights. They run about an hour and 45 minutes and combine moderate walking with shuttle transport. Half a mile beyond the main campus entrance, the **UCSC Arboretum** (⊠*1156 High St.* ☎*831/427–2998* ⊕*www2.ucsc.edu/arboretum* ☜*$5* ☉*Daily 9–5, guided tours Sat. at 11*) is a stellar collection of gardens arranged by geography. A walking path leads through areas dedicated to the plants of California, Australia, New Zealand, and South Africa. ⊠*Main entrance at Bay and High Sts.* ☎*831/459–0111* ⊕*www.ucsc.edu.*

OFF THE BEATEN PATH

★

Santa Cruz Mountains. Highway 9 heads northeast from Santa Cruz into hills densely timbered with massive coastal redwoods. The road winds through the lush San Lorenzo Valley, past hamlets consisting of a few cafés, antiques shops, and old-style tourist cabins. Here, residents of the hunting-and-fishing persuasion coexist with hardcore flower-power survivors and wannabes. Along Highway 9 and its side roads are about a dozen **wineries,** most notably Bonny Doon Vineyard, Organic Wineworks, and David Bruce Winery. ■TIP➜ The Santa Cruz Mountains Winegrowers Association (www.scmwa.com) distributes a wine-touring map at many lodgings and attractions around Santa Cruz.

WHERE TO STAY & EAT

$$ ✕**Gabriella Café.** The work of local artists hangs on the walls of this petite, romantic café in a tile-roof cottage. Featuring organic produce from area farms, the seasonal Italian menu has offered steamed mussels, braised lamb shank, and grilled portobello mushrooms. ⊠*910 Cedar St.* ☎*831/457–1677* ▤*AE, D, MC, V.*

$$ ✕**Soif.** Wine reigns at this sleek bistro and wine shop that takes its name from the French word for thirst. The lengthy list includes selections from near and far, dozens of which you can order by the taste or glass. Infused with the tastes of the Mediterranean, small plates and mains are served at the copper-top bar, the big communal table, and private tables. A jazz combo or solo pianist play some evenings. ⊠*105 Walnut Ave.* ☎*831/423–2020* ▤*AE, MC, V* ☉*No lunch Sun.–Tues.*

$ ✕**O'mei.** This is Chinese food like you've never had it. Imagine red-oil
★ dumplings stuffed with pork and vegetables, oolong-smoked chicken
wok-cooked with cremini mushrooms and rosemary, impossibly fluffy
fried potatoes topped with house-cured bacon and black-date sauce.
Service in the tasteful west side dining room is excellent; you can also
order take-out. ✉*2316 Mission St.* ☎*831/425–8458* ▤*AE, D, DC,
MC, V* ⊘*No lunch. Closed Monday.*

¢ ✕**Seabright Brewery.** Great burgers, big salads, and stellar house-made
microbrews make this a favorite hangout in the youthful Seabright
neighborhood east of downtown. Sit outside on the large patio or
inside at a comfortable, spacious booth; both are popular with families. ✉*519 Seabright Ave.* ☎*831/426–2739* ▤*AE, MC, V.*

¢ ✕**Zachary's.** This noisy café filled with students and families defines
the funky essence of Santa Cruz. It also dishes up great breakfasts:
stay simple with sourdough pancakes, or go for Mike's Mess—eggs
scrambled with bacon, mushrooms, and home fries, then topped with
sour cream, melted cheese, and fresh tomatoes. ⚠ **If you arrive after 9 AM,
expect a long wait for a table; lunch is a shade calmer, but closing time is 2
PM.** ✉*819 Pacific Ave.* ☎*831/427–0646* ⚇*Reservations not accepted*
▤*MC, V* ⊘*Closed Mon. No dinner.*

$$$$ ▦**Pleasure Point Inn.** Tucked in a residential neighborhood at the east
end of town, this modern Mediterranean-style B&B sits right across the
street from the ocean and a popular surfing beach (where surfing lessons
are available). The rooms are handsomely furnished and include such
deluxe amenities as fireplaces and private patios. You have use of the
large rooftop sundeck and hot tub, which overlook the Pacific. Because
this is a popular romantic getaway spot, it's best not to bring kids. **Pros:**
Fantastic views; ideal for checking the swells; quirky neighborhood.
Cons: Few rooms; several miles from major attractions. ✉*2–3665 E.
Cliff Dr.,* ☎*831/475–4657* ⊕*www.pleasurepointinn.com* ⇥*4 rooms*
⚐*In-room: no a/c, safe, refrigerator, DVD, Wi-Fi. In-hotel: no elevator, beachfront, no-smoking rooms* ▤*MC, V* ⚑*CP.*

$$$–$$$$ ▦**Babbling Brook Inn.** Though it's smack in the middle of Santa Cruz,
this B&B has lush gardens, a running stream, and tall trees that make
you feel like you're in a secluded wood. All rooms have fireplaces
(though a few are electric) and featherbeds; most have private patios.
Complimentary wine, cheese, and fresh-baked cookies are available in
the afternoon. **Pros:** Close to UCSC; walking distance from downtown
shops; woodsy feel. **Cons:** Near a high school; some rooms are close to
a busy street. ✉*1025 Laurel St.* ☎*831/427–2437 or 800/866–1131*
⊕*www.babblingbrookinn.com* ⇥*11 rooms, 2 suites* ⚐*In-room: no
a/c, VCR. In-hotel: no elevator, no-smoking rooms* ▤*AE, D, DC, MC,
V* ⚑*BP.*

$$$–$$$$ ▦**Chaminade.** A full-on renovation in 2005 sharpened this hilltop
resort's look and enhanced its amenities. Secluded on 300 acres of
redwood and eucalyptus forest, the mission-style complex commands
expansive views of Monterey Bay. Guest rooms are furnished in a mod-
ern Spanish style, with dark wood, deep colors, and patterned fab-
rics; some have private patios or decks. The spa employs all-natural
products in its complete menu of body and beauty treatments. **Pros:**

16

Far from city life; spectacular property; ideal spot for romance and rejuvenation. **Cons:** Must drive to attractions and sights; near major hospital. ⊠*1 Chaminade La.* ☎*800/283–6569* ⊕*www.chaminade. com* ⇆*112 rooms, 44 suites* ⌂*In-room: safe, refrigerator (some), Ethernet, Wi-Fi. In-hotel: 3 restaurants, bar, tennis courts, pool, gym, spa, concierge, laundry service, public Wi-Fi, airport shuttle, no-smoking rooms* ⊟*AE, D, DC, MC, V.*

$$$–$$$$ **West Cliff Inn.** Perched on the bluffs across from Cowell's Beach, this posh nautical-theme inn commands sweeping views of the boardwalk and Monterey Bay. Built in 1877, the Italianate three-story Victorian emerged from a top-to-bottom renovation in 2007 in classic California-beach style with color schemes that hint of ocean, sky, and reflecting light. All rooms have a comfy king bed, fireplace, and fancy marble tile bathroom, many with spa tubs and some with sitting areas; rooms facing the bay have the best views. For the ultimate in privacy, ask for the room that has a private patio and hot tub. In the morning, enjoy a lavish breakfast in the elegant dining room and watch the surfers and seals catching the waves below. **Pros:** Killer views; walking distance from the beach; close to downtown. **Cons:** Boardwalk noise; street traffic. ⊠*174 West Cliff Dr.* ☎*800/979–0910* ⊕*www.westcliffinn.com* ⇆*7 rooms, 2 suites* ⌂*In-room: DVD, Wi-Fi. In-hotel: no-smoking rooms* ⊟*AE, D, MC, V* ⧀*BP.*

$$$ **Sea & Sand Inn.** The main appeal of this aging motel perched on a waterfront bluff is its location: every room has an ocean view, and the boardwalk is just down the street. Blond-wood furniture and floral fabrics create a vaguely country look; some rooms have private hot tubs or fireplaces. A few studios and suites include kitchenettes. **Pros:** Beach is steps away; friendly staff; tidy landscaping. **Cons:** Tight parking lot; fronts a busy road; can be noisy. ⊠*201 W. Cliff Dr.* ☎*831/427–3400* ⊕*www.santacruzmotels.com* ⇆*15 rooms* ⌂*In-room: kitchen (some), VCR (some), Wi-Fi. In-hotel: no elevator, no-smoking rooms* ⊟*AE, MC, V* ⧀*CP.*

NIGHTLIFE & THE ARTS

NIGHTLIFE   Dance with the crowds at **The Catalyst** (⊠*1011 Pacific Ave.* ☎*831/423–*
★   *1338* ⊕*www.catalystclub.com*), a huge, grimy downtown club that has regularly featured big names, from Neil Young to Nirvana to Ice T. Renowned in the international jazz community, and drawing performers such as Herbie Hancock, Pat Metheny, and Charlie Hunter, the nonprofit **Kuumbwa Jazz Center** (⊠*320–2 Cedar St.* ☎*831/427–2227* ⊕*www.kuumbwajazz.org*) bops with live music most nights; "Jazz and Dinner" Thursday includes a meal with the show. Blues, salsa, reggae, funk: you name it, **Moe's Alley** (⊠*1535 Commercial Way* ☎*831/479–1854* ⊕*www.moesalley.com*) has it all, six nights a week.

THE ARTS   Each August, the **Cabrillo Festival of Contemporary Music** (☎*831/426–6966, 831/420–5260 box office* ⊕*www.cabrillomusic.org*) brings some of the world's finest artists to the Santa Cruz Civic Auditorium to play groundbreaking symphonic music, including major world premieres. Using period and reproduction instruments, the **Santa Cruz Baroque Festival** (☎*831/457–9693* ⊕*www.scbaroque.org*) presents a wide range of classical music at various venues throughout the year. As the name suggests, the focus is on 17th- and 18th-century composers such as Bach and Handel.

Shakespeare Santa Cruz (⊠ *SSC/UCSC Theater Arts Center, 1156 High St.* ☎ *831/459–2159, 831/459–2121 tickets* ⊕ *www.shakespearesanta cruz.org*) stages a six-week Shakespeare festival in July and August that may also include the occasional modern dramatic performance. Most performances are outdoors under the redwoods. A holiday program is also performed in December.

SPORTS & THE OUTDOORS

BICYCLING   Park the car and rent a beach cruiser at **Bicycle Shop Santa Cruz** (⊠ *1325 Mission St.* ☎ *831/454–0909,* ⊕ *www.thebicycleshopsantacruz.com*). Mountain bikers should head to **Another Bike Shop** (⊠ *2361 Mission St.* ☎ *831/427–2232* ⊕ *www.anotherbikeshop.com*) for tips on the best trails around and a look at cutting-edge gear made and tested locally.

BOATS & CHARTERS   **Chardonnay Sailing Charters** (☎ *831/423–1213* ⊕ *www.chardonnay.com*) cruises Monterey Bay year-round on a variety of trips, such as whale-watching, astronomy, and winemaker sails. The 70-foot *Chardonnay II* leaves from the yacht harbor in Santa Cruz. Food and drink are served on many of their cruises. Reservations are essential. **Original Stagnaro Fishing Trips** (⊠ *June–Aug., Santa Cruz Municipal Wharf; Sept.–May, Santa Cruz West Harbor* ☎ *831/427–2334*) operates salmon, albacore, and rock-cod fishing expeditions; the fees ($49 to $75) include bait. The company also runs whale-watching cruises ($39) year-round.

GOLF   Tee off at woodsy **DeLaveaga Golf Course** (⊠ *401 Upper Park Rd.* ☎ *831/423–7212* ⊕ *www.delaveagagolf.com*), an 18-hole, par-72 public course in a hilly park setting overlooking the town and bay. Green fees are $51 to $68, and an electric cart (optional) costs $18 per rider.

Designed by famed golf architect Dr. Alister MacKenzie in 1929, semi-private **Pasatiempo Golf Club** (⊠ *20 Clubhouse Rd.* ☎ *831/459–9155* ⊕ *www.pasatiempo.com*), set amid undulating hills just above the city, often ranks among the nation's top championship courses in annual polls. Golfers rave about the spectacular views and challenging terrain. The green fee is $200; an electric cart is $30 per player.

KAYAKING   Explore hidden coves and kelp forests with **Venture Quest Kayaking** (⊠ *#2 Santa Cruz Wharf* ☎ *831/427–2267 or 831/425–8445* ⊕ *www. kayaksantacruz.com*). The company's guided nature tours depart from Santa Cruz Wharf or Harbor, depending on the season. A two-hour kayak nature tour and introductory lesson costs $50. A three-hour kayak rental is $30 and includes wet suit and gear. Venture Quest also arranges tours at other Monterey Bay destinations, including Capitola and Elkhorn Slough.

SURFING   Surfers gather for spectacular waves and sunsets at **Pleasure Point** (⊠ *E. Cliff and Pleasure Point Drs.*). **Steamer Lane,** near the lighthouse on West Cliff Drive, has a decent break. The area plays host to several competitions in summer.

16

Find out what all the fun is about at **Club-Ed Surf School and Camps**
(✉*Cowell Beach, at Coast Santa Cruz Hotel* ☎*831/464–0177 or
800/287–7873* ⊕*www.club-ed.com*). Your first private or group lesson ($85 and up) includes all equipment. The most welcoming place
in town to buy or rent surf gear is **Paradise Surf Shop** (✉*3961 Portola
Dr.* ☎*831/462–3880* ⊕*www.paradisesurf.com*). The shop is owned
by local amateur longboarder Sally Smith and run by women who aim
to help everyone feel comfortable on the water. **Cowell's Beach Surf Shop**
(✉*30 Front St.* ☎*831/427–2355* ⊕*www.cowellssurfshop.com*) sells
bikinis, rents surfboards and wet suits, and offers lessons.

MONTEREY BAY AREA ESSENTIALS

*To research prices, get advice from other travelers, and book travel
arrangements, visit www.fodors.com.*

TRANSPORTATION

BY AIR

Monterey Peninsula Airport is 3 mi east of downtown Monterey (take
Olmstead Road off Highway 68). It's served by American Eagle, United,
United Express, and US Airways. *See Air Travel in California Essentials
for airline phone numbers.* Taxi service to downtown runs about $12
to $14; to Carmel the fare is $20 to $29. To and from San Jose Inter-
national Airport and San Francisco International Airport, Monterey
Airbus starts at $35 and the Surf City Shuttle runs $68 to $108.

Contacts **Carmel Taxi** (☎*831/624–3885*). **Monterey Airbus** (☎*831/373–7777*
⊕www.montereyairbus.com). **Monterey Airport Taxi** (☎*831/626–3385*). **Monterey Peninsula Airport** (✉*200 Fred Kane Dr., Monterey* ☎*831/648–7000*
⊕www.montereyairport.com). **Surf City Shuttle** (☎*831/419–2642*). **Yellow
Checker Cabs** (☎*831/646–1234*).

BY BUS

Greyhound serves Santa Cruz and Monterey from San Francisco three
or four times daily. The trips take about 3 and 4½ hours, respectively.
Monterey-Salinas Transit provides frequent service between the peninsula's towns and many major sightseeing spots and shopping areas.
The base fare is $2, with an additional $2 for each zone you travel into.
A day pass costs $4.50 to $9, depending on how many zones you'll be
traveling through. Monterey-Salinas Transit also runs the MST Trolley,
which links major attractions on the Monterey waterfront. The free
shuttle operates late May through early September, weekdays from 10
to 7 and weekends and holidays from 10 to 8.

Contacts **Greyhound** (☎*800/231–2222* ⊕www.greyhound.com). **Monterey-
Salinas Transit** (☎*831/899–2555 or 888/678–2871* ⊕www.mst.org).

BY CAR

Highway 1 runs south–north along the coast, linking the towns of
Carmel-by-the-Sea, Monterey, and Santa Cruz; some sections have only
two lanes. The freeway, U.S. 101, lies to the east, roughly parallel to

Highway 1. The two roads are connected by Highway 68 from Pacific Grove to Prunedale; Highway 152 from Watsonville to Gilroy; and Highway 17 from Santa Cruz to San Jose. Highway 17 crosses the redwood-filled Santa Cruz Mountains; ⚠ **traffic near Santa Cruz can crawl to a standstill during commuter hours.**

The drive south from San Francisco to Monterey can be made comfortably in three hours or less. The most scenic way is to follow Highway 1 down the coast past flower, pumpkin, and artichoke fields and small seaside communities. Unless you drive on sunny weekends when locals are heading for the beach, the two-lane coast highway may take no longer than the freeway. A sometimes-faster route is I–280 south from San Francisco to Highway 17, north of San Jose. A third option is to follow U.S. 101 south through San Jose to Prunedale and then take Highway 156 west to Highway 1 south into Monterey.

From Los Angeles the drive to Monterey can be made in five to six hours by heading north on U.S. 101 to Salinas and then west on Highway 68. The spectacular but slow alternative is to take U.S. 101 to San Luis Obispo and then follow the hairpin turns of Highway 1 up the coast. Allow about three extra hours if you take this route.

16

BY TRAIN

Amtrak's *Coast Starlight* runs between Los Angeles, Oakland, and Seattle. From the train station in Salinas, connecting Amtrak Thruway buses serve Monterey and Carmel-by-the-Sea; from San Jose, connecting buses serve Santa Cruz.

Contacts **Amtrak** (☎ 800/872–7245 ⊕ www.amtrakcalifornia.com). **Salinas Amtrak Station** (✉ 11 Station Pl., Salinas ☎ 831/422–7458).

CONTACTS & RESOURCES

EMERGENCIES

In the event of an emergency, dial 911. The Monterey Bay Dental Society provides dentist referrals throughout the area. The Monterey County Medical Society and the Santa Cruz County Medical Society can refer you to a doctor in Monterey and Santa Cruz counties, respectively. There are 24-hour Walgreens pharmacies in Seaside, about 4 mi northeast of Monterey via Highway 1, and in Freedom, on the eastern edge of Watsonville.

Contacts **Community Hospital of Monterey Peninsula** (✉ 23625 Holman Hwy., Monterey ☎ 831/624–5311 ⊕ www.chomp.org). **Dominican Hospital** (✉ 1555 Soquel Dr., Santa Cruz ☎ 831/462–7700 ⊕ www.dominicanhospital.org). **Monterey Bay Dental Society** (☎ 831/658–0168 ⊕ http://mbdsdentists.com). **Monterey County Medical Society** (☎ 831/455–1008 ⊕ www.montereymedicine.org). **Santa Cruz County Medical Society** (☎ 831/479–7226 ⊕ www.cruzmed.org). **Watsonville Community Hospital** (✉ 75 Nielson St., Watsonville ☎ 831/724–4741 ⊕ www.watsonvillehospital.com).

Pharmacies **Walgreens** (✉ 1055 Fremont Blvd., Seaside ☎ 831/393–9231). **Walgreens** (✉ 1810 Freedom Blvd., Freedom ☎ 831/768–0183).

TOUR OPTIONS

California Parlor Car Tours operates motor-coach tours from San Francisco that include one or two days in Monterey and Carmel. Ag Venture Tours runs wine-tasting, sightseeing, and agricultural tours in the Monterey, Salinas, Carmel Valley, and Santa Cruz areas.

Contacts **Ag Venture Tours** (☎ *831/761–8463* ⊕ *www.agventuretours.com*). **California Parlor Car Tours** (☎ *415/474–7500 or 800/227–4250* ⊕ *www. calpartours.com*).

VISITOR INFORMATION

Contacts **Aptos Chamber of Commerce** (✉ *7605-A Old Dominion Ct., Aptos* ☎ *831/688–1467* ⊕ *www.aptoschamber.com*). **Capitola-Soquel Chamber of Commerce** (✉ *716-G Capitola Ave., Capitola* ☎ *831/475–6522* ⊕ *www.capitola chamber.com*). **Carmel Chamber of Commerce** (✉ *San Carlos, between 5th and 6th, Carmel* ☎ *831/624–2522 or 800/550–4333* ⊕ *www.carmelcalifornia. org*). **Monterey County Convention & Visitors Bureau** (☎ *877/666–8373* ⊕ *www.montereyinfo.org*). **Monterey County Vintners and Growers Association** (☎ *831/375–9400* ⊕ *www.montereywines.org*). **Moss Landing Chamber of Commerce** (✉ *Box 41, Moss Landing, 95039* ☎ *831/633–4501* ⊕ *www.moss landingchamber.com*). **Pajaro Valley Chamber of Commerce** (✉ *449 Union St., Watsonville, 95076* ☎ *831/724–3900* ⊕ *www.pajarovalleychamber.com*). **Salinas Valley Chamber of Commerce** (✉ *119 E. Alisal St., Salinas 93901* ☎ *831/424–7611* ⊕ *www.salinaschamber.com*). **San Lorenzo Valley Chamber of Commerce** (✉ *Box 661, Ben Lomond, 95005* ☎ *831/345–2084* ⊕ *www.slvchamber. org*). **Santa Cruz County Conference and Visitors Council** (✉ *1211 Ocean St., Santa Cruz, 95060* ☎ *831/425–1234 or 800/833–3494* ⊕ *www.santacruz.org*). **Santa Cruz Chamber of Commerce** (✉ *1519 Pacific Ave., Santa Cruz, 95060* ☎ *831/457–3713* ⊕ *www.santacruzchamber.org*). **Santa Cruz Mountain Winegrowers Association** (✉ *7605-A Old Dominion Ct., Apto,s 95003* ☎ *831/685–8463* ⊕ *www.scmwa.com*).

Southern California Essentials

PLANNING TOOLS, EXPERT INSIGHT, GREAT CONTACTS

There are planners and there are those who, excuse the pun, fly by the seat of their pants. We happily place ourselves among the planners. Our writers and editors try to anticipate all the issues you may face before and during any journey, and then they do their research. This section is the product of their efforts. Use it to get excited about your trip to Southern California, to inform your travel planning, or to guide you on the road should the seat of your pants start to feel threadbare.

GETTING STARTED

We're really proud of our Web site: Fodors.com is a great place to begin any journey. Scan Travel Wire for suggested itineraries, travel deals, restaurant and hotel openings, and other up-to-the-minute info. Check out Booking to research prices and book plane tickets, hotel rooms, rental cars, and vacation packages. Head to Talk for on-the-ground pointers from travelers who frequent our message boards. You can also link to loads of other travel-related resources.

▌ RESOURCES

ONLINE TRAVEL TOOLS

All About California ⊕*www.ceres.ca.gov/ceres/calweb/Natl_Parks.html*: links to pages for California's national parks, preserves, historic sites, and other natural areas operated by the federal government. ⊕*www.parks.ca.gov*: California Parks Department site, with the lowdown on state-run parks and other recreational areas. ⊕*www.californiasnow.com*: the California Ski Industry Association gives you a real-time look at snow conditions and reservation information for member resorts. ⊕*www.visitcalifornia.com*: the official state travel site takes you to each region of California, with digital visitor guides, driving tours, maps, welcome center locations, information on local tours, links to bed-and-breakfasts, and a complete booking center. ⊕*www.dot.ca.gov*: the Caltrans site is an excellent source for information about road closures due to construction or accidents. It links to real-time freeway speed maps, live traffic cams, and current weather/travel conditions in urban areas. ⊕*www.surfrider.org*: the Surfrider Foundation monitors conditions at state beaches for health problems such as pollution, runoff, and water quality. This is a good resource if you plan to visit local beaches following a storm. ⊕*www.gorp.com*: the Great Outdoor Recreation Page, a must-visit site for outdoor- and adventure travel enthusiasts. ⊕*www.calagtour.org*: agricultural tourism information and links to small farms, roadside fruit and vegetable stands, stock farms, and wineries that welcome visitors. ⊕*www.usgs.gov*: detailed information about earthquake location and intensity. ⊕*www.wineinstitute.org*: events listings and detailed information about the California wine industry, with links to the regional wine association home pages.

Safety Transportation Security Administration (⊕www.tsa.gov).

Time Zones Timeanddate.com (⊕www.timeanddate.com/worldclock) can help you figure out the correct time anywhere.

Weather Accuweather.com (⊕www.accuweather.com) is an independent weather-forecasting service. **Weather.com** (⊕www.weather.com) is the Web site for the Weather Channel.

VISITOR INFORMATION

The California Travel and Tourism Commission's Web site has travel tips, events calendars, and other resources, and links you—via the Explore California menu—to the Web sites of city and regional tourism offices and attractions. *For the numbers of regional and city visitor bureaus and chambers of commerce see the "Essentials" section at the end of each chapter.*

Contacts California Travel and Tourism Commission (✉980 9th St., Suite 480, Sacramento ☎916/444–4429 information, 800/862–2543 brochures ⊕www.visitcalifornia.com).

▮ ONLINE

You really have to shop around. A travel wholesaler such as Hotels.com or Hotel-Club.net can be a source of good rates, as can discounters such as Hotwire or Priceline, particularly if you can bid for your hotel room or airfare. Indeed, such sites sometimes have deals that are unavailable elsewhere. They do, however, tend to work only with hotel chains (which makes them just plain useless for getting hotel reservations outside of major cities) or big airlines (so that often leaves out upstarts like JetBlue and some foreign carriers like Air India).

Also, with discounters and wholesalers you must generally prepay, and everything is nonrefundable. And before you fork over the dough, be sure to check the terms and conditions, so you know what a given company will do for you if there's a problem and what you'll have to deal with on your own.

▮TIP➔ To be absolutely sure everything was processed correctly, confirm reservations made through online travel agents, discounters, and wholesalers directly with your hotel before leaving home.

Booking engines like Expedia, Travelocity, and Orbitz are actually travel agents, albeit high-volume, online ones. And airline travel packagers like American Airlines Vacations and Virgin Vacations—well, they're travel agents, too. But they may still not work with all the world's hotels.

An aggregator site will search many sites and pull the best prices for airfares, hotels, and rental cars from them. Most aggregators compare the major travel-booking sites such as Expedia, Travelocity, and Orbitz; some also look at airline Web sites, though rarely the sites of smaller budget airlines. Some aggregators also compare other travel products, including complex packages—a good thing, as you can sometimes get the best overall deal by booking an air-and-hotel package.

▮ WITH A TRAVEL AGENT

If you use an agent—brick-and-mortar or virtual—you'll pay a fee for the service. And know that the service you get from some online agents isn't comprehensive. For example Expedia and Travelocity don't search for prices on budget airlines like JetBlue, Southwest, or small foreign carriers. That said, some agents (online or not) *do* have access to fares that are difficult to find otherwise, and the savings can more than make up for any surcharge.

A knowledgeable brick-and-mortar travel agent can be a godsend if you're booking a cruise, a package trip that's not available to you directly, an air pass, or a complicated itinerary including several overseas flights. What's more, travel agents that specialize in a destination may have exclusive access to certain deals and insider information on things such as charter flights. Agents who specialize in types of travelers (senior citizens, gays and lesbians, naturists) or types of trips (cruises, luxury travel, safaris) can also be invaluable.

▮TIP➔ Remember that Expedia, Travelocity, and Orbitz are travel agents, not just booking engines. To resolve any problems with a reservation made through these companies, contact them first.

Agent Resources **American Society of Travel Agents** (☎703/739–2782 ⊕www.travelsense.org).

▮ ACCOMMODATIONS

The lodgings we list are the cream of the crop in each price category. We always list the facilities that are available, but we don't specify whether they cost extra; when pricing accommodations, always ask what's included and what costs extra. Properties marked ✕▦ are lodging establishments whose restaurants warrant a special trip. ⇨For price information, see the planner in each chapter.

Online Booking Resources

Aggregators

Kayak	www.kayak.com	also looks at cruises and vacation packages.
Mobissimo	www.mobissimo.com	also looks at car rental rates and activities.
Qixo	www.qixo.com	also compares cruises, vacation packages, and even travel insurance.
Sidestep	www.sidestep.com	also compares vacation packages and lists travel deals.
Travelgrove	www.travelgrove.com	also compares cruises and packages.

Booking Engines

Cheap Tickets	www.cheaptickets.com	a discounter.
Expedia	www.expedia.com	a large online agency that charges a booking fee for airline tickets.
Hotwire	www.hotwire.com	a discounter.
lastminute.com	www.lastminute.com	specializes in last-minute travel; the main site is for the U.K., but it has a link to a U.S. site.
Luxury Link	www.luxurylink.com	has auctions (surprisingly good deals) as well as offers on the high-end side of travel.
Onetravel.com	www.onetravel.com	a discounter for hotels, car rentals, airfares, and packages.
Orbitz	www.orbitz.com	charges a booking fee for airline tickets, but gives a clear breakdown of fees and taxes before you book.
Priceline.com	www.priceline.com	a discounter that also allows bidding.
Travel.com	www.travel.com	allows you to compare its rates with those of other booking engines.
Travelocity	www.travelocity.com	charges a booking fee for airline tickets, but promises good problem resolution.

Online Accommodations

Hotelbook.com	www.hotelbook.com	focuses on independent hotels worldwide.
Hotel Club	www.hotelclub.net	good for major cities worldwide.
Hotels.com	www.hotels.com	a big Expedia-owned wholesaler that offers rooms in hotels all over the world.
Quikbook	www.quikbook.com	offers "pay when you stay" reservations that let you settle your bill at checkout, not when you book.

Other Resources

Bidding For Travel	www.biddingfortravel.com	a good place to figure out what you can get and for how much before you start bidding on, say, Priceline.

Car Rental Resources

Automobile Associations		
American Automobile Association	315/797–5000	www.aaa.com; most contact with the organization is through state and regional members
National Automobile Club	650/294–7000	www.thenac.com; membership open to CA residents only
Major Agencies		
Alamo	800/462–5266	www.alamo.com
Avis	800/331–1084	www.avis.com
Budget	800/472–3325	www.budget.com
Hertz	800/654–3131	www.hertz.com
National Car Rental	800/227–7368	www.nationalcar.com

Most hotels require you to give your credit-card details before they will confirm your reservation. If you don't feel comfortable e-mailing this information, ask if you can fax it (some places even prefer faxes). However you book, get confirmation in writing and have a copy of it handy when you check in.

■TIP➡ Assume that hotels operate on the European Plan (EP, no meals) unless we specify that they use the Breakfast Plan (BP, with full breakfast), Continental Plan (CP, Continental breakfast), Full American Plan (FAP, all meals), Modified American Plan (MAP, breakfast and dinner) or are all-inclusive (AI, all meals and most activities).

BED & BREAKFASTS

California has more than 1,000 bed-and-breakfasts. You'll find everything from simple homestays to lavish luxury lodgings, many in historic hotels and homes. The California Association of Bed and Breakfast Inns has about 300 member properties that you can locate and book through their Web site.

Reservation Services **Bed & Breakfast. com** (☎512/322–2710 or 800/462–2632 ⊕www.bedandbreakfast.com) also sends out an online newsletter. **Bed & Breakfast Inns Online** (☎615/868–1946 or 800/215–7365 ⊕www.bbonline.com). **BnB Finder.com** (☎212/432–7693 or 888/547–8226 ⊕www.bnbfinder.com). **California Association of Bed and Breakfast Inns** (☎800/373–9251 ⊕www.cabbi.com).

■ RENTAL CARS

When you reserve a car, ask about cancellation penalties, taxes, drop-off charges (if you're planning to pick up the car in one city and leave it in another), and surcharges (for being under or over a certain age, for additional drivers, or for driving across state or country borders or beyond a specific distance from your point of rental). All these things can add substantially to your costs. Request car seats and extras such as GPS when you book.

Rates are sometimes—but not always—better if you book in advance or reserve through a rental agency's Web site. There are other reasons to book ahead, though: for popular destinations, during busy times of the year, or to ensure that you get certain types of cars (vans, SUVs, exotic sports cars).

■TIP➡ Make sure that a confirmed reservation guarantees you a car. Agencies sometimes overbook, particularly for busy weekends and holiday periods.

A car is essential in most parts of Southern California. In sprawling cities such as Los Angeles and San Diego, you'll have to take the freeways to get just about anywhere.

Rates statewide for the least expensive vehicle begin at around $69 a day and $115 a week. This does not include additional fees or tax on car rentals, which is 8.25% in Los Angeles and 7.75% in San Diego. You can sometimes get lower rates in San Diego; compare prices by city before you book, and ask about "drop charges" if you plan to return the car in a city other than the one where you rented the vehicle. If you pick up at an airport, there may also be a facility charge of as much as $12 per rental; ask when you book. When you're returning your rental, be aware that gas stations can be few and far between near airports.

In California, you must have a valid driver's license and be 21 to rent a car; rates may be higher if you're under 25. Some agencies will not rent to those under 25; check when you book. Non-U.S. residents must have a license with text that is in the Roman alphabet that is valid for the entire rental period. Though it need not be entirely written in English, it must have English letters that clearly identify it as a driver's license. An international license is recommended but not required.

Specialty Car Agencies In Los Angeles **Specialty Rentals** (☎800/400–8412 ⊕www.specialtyrentals.com); in Los Angeles (several locations) **Beverly Hills Rent a Car** (☎800/479–5996 ⊕www.bhrentacar.com) or in Los Angeles (several locations) **Midway Car Rental** (☎800/824–5260 ⊕www.midway carrental.com).

CAR-RENTAL INSURANCE

Everyone who rents a car wonders whether the insurance that the rental companies offer is worth the expense. No one—including us—has a simple answer. It all depends on how much regular insurance you have, how comfortable you are with risk, and whether or not money is an issue.

If you own a car and carry comprehensive car insurance for both collision and liability, your personal auto insurance will probably cover a rental, but read your policy's fine print to be sure. If you don't have auto insurance, then you should probably buy the collision- or loss-damage waiver (CDW or LDW) from the rental company. This eliminates your liability for damage to the car.

Some credit cards offer CDW coverage, but it's usually supplemental to your own insurance and rarely covers SUVs, minivans, luxury models, and the like. If your coverage is secondary, you may still be liable for loss-of-use costs from the car-rental company (again, read the fine print). But no credit-card insurance is valid unless you use that card for *all* transactions, from reserving to paying the final bill.

■**TIP→** Diners Club offers primary CDW coverage on all rentals reserved and paid for with the card. This means that Diners Club's company—not your own car insurance—pays in case of an accident. It *doesn't* mean that your car-insurance company won't raise your rates once it discovers you had an accident.

You may also be offered supplemental liability coverage; the car-rental company is required to carry a minimal level of liability coverage insuring all renters, but it's rarely enough to cover claims in a really serious accident if you're at fault. Your own auto-insurance policy will protect you if you own a car; if you don't, you have to decide whether you are willing to take the risk.

U.S. rental companies sell CDWs and LDWs for about $15 to $25 a day; supplemental liability is usually more than $10 a day. The car-rental company may offer you all sorts of other policies, but they're rarely worth the cost. Personal accident insurance, which is basic hospitalization coverage, is an especially egregious rip-off if you already have health insurance.

■ TIP→ You can decline the insurance from the rental company and purchase it through a third-party provider such as Travel Guard (www.travelguard.com)—$9 per day for $35,000 of coverage. That's sometimes just under half the price of the CDW offered by some car-rental companies.

Some states, including California, have capped the price of the CDW and LDW, but the cap has a floating value, depending on the cost of the vehicle; for those valued at more than $35,000, there's no maximum. Verify the cost of the CDW/LDW at the time you book. Make sure you have enough coverage to pay for the car. If you do not have auto insurance or an umbrella policy that covers damage to third parties, purchasing liability insurance and a CDW or LDW is highly recommended.

Each car-rental company sets its own cap on the insurance it offers. Some agencies may not provide full coverage for their most expensive vehicles. Thus you may rent a car valued at $50,000, but only be able to purchase a CDW or LDW for coverage up to $35,000. The cap varies agency to agency, so as you shop around, ask each agency about its insurance limits, and when you book, make sure you have enough coverage to pay for the *specific* car that you're renting.

Rental agencies in California aren't required to include liability insurance in the price of the rental. If you cause an accident, you may expose your assets to litigation. When in doubt about your own policy's coverage, take the liability coverage that the agency offers. If you plan to take the car out of California, ask if the policy is valid in other states or countries. Most car-rental companies won't insure a loss or damage that occurs outside of their coverage area—particularly in Mexico. If you do plan to drive in Mexico, you'll also need special Mexican insurance coverage; it's available from auto clubs and at kiosks at the border.

▌VACATION PACKAGES

Packages *are not* guided excursions. Packages combine airfare, accommodations, and perhaps a rental car or other extras (theater tickets, guided excursions, boat trips, reserved entry to popular museums, transit passes), but they let you do your own thing. During busy periods packages may be your only option, as flights and rooms may be sold out otherwise.

Packages will definitely save you time. They can also save you money, particularly in peak seasons, but—and this is a really big "but"—you should price each part of the package separately to be sure. And be aware that prices advertised on Web sites and in newspapers rarely include service charges or taxes, which can up your costs by hundreds of dollars.

■ TIP→ Some packages and cruises are sold only through travel agents. Don't always assume that you can get the best deal by booking everything yourself.

Each year consumers are stranded or lose their money when packagers—even large ones with excellent reputations—go out of business. How can you protect yourself?

First, always pay with a credit card; if you have a problem, your credit-card company may help you resolve it. Second, buy trip insurance that covers default. Third, choose a company that belongs to the United States Tour Operators Association, whose members must set aside funds to cover defaults. Finally, choose a company that also participates in the Tour Operator Program of the American Society of Travel Agents (ASTA), which will act as mediator in any disputes.

You can also check on the tour operator's reputation among travelers by posting an inquiry on one of the Fodors.com forums.

Organizations **American Society of Travel Agents** (ASTA ☎703/739–2782 or 800/965–2782 ⊕www.astanet.com). **United States Tour Operators Association** (USTOA ☎212/599–6599 ⊕www.ustoa.com).

■TIP→ Local tourism boards can provide information about lesser-known and small-niche operators that sell packages to only a few destinations.

GUIDED TOURS

Guided tours are a good option when you don't want to do it all yourself. You travel along with a group (sometimes large, sometimes small), stay in prebooked hotels, eat with your fellow travelers (the cost of meals sometimes included in the price of your tour, sometimes not), and follow a schedule.

But not all guided tours are an if-it's-Tuesday-this-must-be-Belgium experience. A knowledgeable guide can take you places that you might never discover on your own, and you may be pushed to see more than you would have otherwise. Tours aren't for everyone, but they can be just the thing for trips to places where making travel arrangements is difficult or time-consuming (particularly when you don't speak the language).

Whenever you book a guided tour, find out what's included and what isn't. A "land-only" tour includes all your travel (by bus, in most cases) in the destination, but not necessarily your flights to and from or even within it. Also, in most cases prices in tour brochures don't include fees and taxes. And remember that you'll be expected to tip your guide (in cash) at the end of the tour.

SPECIAL-INTEREST TOURS

BIKING

Bicycling is a popular way to see the California countryside, and commercial tours are available throughout the state. Most three- to five-day trips are all-inclusive— you'll stay in delightful country inns, dine at good regional restaurants, and follow experienced guides. When booking, ask about level of difficulty, as nearly every trip will involve some hill work. Tours fill up early, so book well in advance.

■TIP→ Most airlines accommodate bikes as luggage, provided they're dismantled and boxed.

Contacts **Bicycle Adventures** (⊠Box 11219, Olympia, WA ☎800/443–6060 ⊕www.bicycleadventures.com).

CRUISES

A number of major cruise lines offer trips that begin or end in California. Most voyages sail north along the Pacific Coast to Alaska or south to Mexico. California cruise ports include Los Angeles, San Diego, and San Francisco.

Cruise Lines **Carnival Cruise Line** (☎305/599–2600 or 800/227–6482 ⊕www.carnival.com). **Celebrity Cruises** (☎305/539–6000 or 800/437–3111 ⊕www.celebrity.com). **Crystal Cruises** (☎310/785–9300 or 800/446–6620 ⊕www.crystalcruises.com). **Holland America Line** (☎206/281–3535 or 877/932–4259 ⊕www.hollandamerica.com). **Norwegian Cruise Line** (☎305/436–4000 or 800/327–7030 ⊕www.ncl.com). **Princess Cruises** (☎661/753–0000 or 800/774–6237 ⊕www.princess.com). **Regent Seven Seas Cruises** (☎954/776–6123 or 800/477–7500 ⊕www.rssc.com). **Royal Caribbean International** (☎305/539–6000 or 800/327–6700 ⊕www.royalcaribbean.com). **Silversea Cruises** (☎954/522–4477 or 800/722–9955 ⊕www.silversea.com).

TRANSPORTATION

Wherever you plan to go in California, getting there will likely involve driving (even if you fly). With the exception of San Diego, major airports are usually located far from main attractions. (For example, four airports serve the Los Angeles area—but three of them are outside the city limits.) Southern California's major airport hub is LAX in Los Angeles, but satellite airports can be found around most major cities. When booking flights, it pays to check these locations, as you may find cheaper flights, more convenient times, and a better location in relation to your hotel. Most small cities have their own commercial airports, with connecting flights to larger cities— but service may be extremely limited, and it may be cheaper to rent a car and drive from L.A.

There are two basic north–south routes in California: I–5, an interstate highway, runs inland most of the way from the Oregon border to the Mexican border; and Highway 101 hugs the coast from Oregon to Mexico. (In portions of Southern California, the two roads are the same.) From north to south, the state's east–west interstates are I–80, I–15, I–10, and I–8. Much of California is mountainous, and you may encounter very winding roads, frequently cliffside, and steep mountain grades. In winter, roads crossing the Sierra east to west may close at any time due to weather, and chains may be required on these roads when they are open. Also in winter, I–5 north of Los Angeles closes during snowstorms. The flying and driving times in the following charts are best-case-scenario estimates, but know that the infamous California traffic jam can occur at any time.

■ TIP➜ Ask the local tourist board about hotel and local transportation packages that include tickets to major museum exhibits or other special events.

FROM LOS ANGELES TO:	BY AIR	BY CAR
Big Sur		6 hours
Death Valley		5 hours
Monterey	1 hour 30 minutes	5 hours 30 minutes
Sacramento	1 hour 20 minutes	6 hours
San Diego	50 minutes	2 hours
San Francisco	1 hour 30 minutes	6 hours
Santa Barbara	45 minutes	1 hour 30 minutes

■ BY AIR

Flying time to California is roughly six hours from New York and four hours from Chicago. Travel from London to Los Angeles is 12 hours and from Sydney approximately 14. Flying between San Francisco and Los Angeles takes about 90 minutes.

■ TIP➜ If you travel frequently, look into the TSA's Registered Traveler program. The program, which is still being tested in several U.S. airports, is designed to cut down on gridlock at security checkpoints by allowing prescreened travelers to pass quickly through kiosks that scan an iris and/or a fingerprint. How sci-fi is that?

Airlines & Airports Airline and Airport Links.com (⊕ www.airlineandairportlinks.com) has links to many of the world's airlines and airports.

Airline Security Issues Transportation Security Administration (⊕ www.tsa.gov) has answers for almost every question that might come up.

AIRPORTS

Southern California's gateways are Los Angeles International Airport (LAX) and San Diego International Airport (SAN). Other Los Angeles airports include Long Beach (LGB), Bob Hope Airport (BUR), LA/Ontario (ONT), and John Wayne Airport (SNA).

Airport Information **Bob Hope Airport** (☎818/840-8840 ⊕www.burbankairport. com). **John Wayne Airport** (☎949/252-5200 ⊕www.ocair.com). **LA/Ontario International Airport** (☎909/937-2700 ⊕www.flyontario. com). **Los Angeles International Airport** (☎310/646-5252 ⊕www.lawa.org/lax). **Long Beach Airport** (☎562/570-2619 ⊕www.longbeach.gov/airport). **San Diego International Airport** (☎619/231-2100 ⊕www.san.org).

FLIGHTS

United, with a hub in San Francisco and Los Angeles, has the greatest number of flights into and within California. But most national and many international airlines fly here. Southwest Airlines connects smaller cities within California, often from satellite airports near major cities.

Airline Contacts **Air Canada** (☎888/247-2262 ⊕www.aircanada.com). **Alaska Airlines** (☎800/252-7522 or 206/433-3100 ⊕www.alaskaair.com). **American Airlines** (☎800/433-7300 ⊕www.aa.com). **ATA** (☎800/435-9282 or 317/282-8308 ⊕www.ata.com). **British Airways** (☎800/247-9297 ⊕www.britishairways.com). **Cathay Pacific** (☎800/233-2742 ⊕www.cathaypacific.com). **Continental Airlines** (☎800/523-3273 for U.S. and Mexico reservations, 800/231-0856 for international reservations ⊕www.continental.com). **Delta Airlines** (☎800/221-1212 for U.S. reservations, 800/241-4141 for international reservations ⊕www.delta.com). **Japan Air Lines** (☎800/525-3663 ⊕www.japanair.com). **JetBlue** (☎800/538-2583 ⊕www.jetblue.com). **Midwest Airlines** (☎800/452-2022 ⊕www.midwestairlines.com). **Northwest Airlines** (☎800/225-2525 ⊕www.nwa.com). **Qantas** (☎800/227-4500 ⊕www.qantas.

com). **Southwest Airlines** (☎800/435-9792 ⊕www.southwest.com). **Spirit Airlines** (☎800/772-7117 or 586/791-7300 ⊕www.spiritair.com). **United Airlines** (☎800/864-8331 for U.S. reservations, 800/538-2929 for international reservations ⊕www.united.com). **US Airways** (☎800/428-4322 for U.S. and Canada reservations, 800/622-1015 for international reservations ⊕www.usairways.com).

▌ BY BUS

Greyhound is the major bus carrier in California. Megabus offers express service between San Francisco and Los Angeles. Regional bus service is available in metropolitan areas.

Bus Information **Greyhound** (☎800/231-2222 ⊕www.greyhound.com). **Megabus** (☎877/462-6342 ⊕www.megabus.com).

▌ BY CAR

Three major highways—I–5, U.S. 101, and Highway 1—run north–south through California. The main east–west routes are I–15, I–10, and I–8 in Southern California and I–80 in northern California.

FROM LOS ANGELES TO:	RTE.	DISTANCE
Big Sur	Hwy. 101 to Hwy. 1	297 mi
Death Valley	I-10 to I-15 to Hwy. 127 to Hwy 190	288 mi
Las Vegas	I-10 to I-15	290 mi
Monterey	Hwy. 101 to Salinas Hwy. 68	334 mi
Sacramento	I-5	386 mi
San Diego	I-5 or I-15	120 mi
San Francisco	I-5 to Hwy. 156 to Hwy. 101	403 mi
Santa Barbara	Hwy. 101	95 mi

GASOLINE

Gasoline prices in California vary widely, depending on location, oil company, and whether you buy it at a full-serve or self-serve pump. It's less expensive to buy fuel in the southern part of the state than in the north. If you're planning to travel near Nevada, you can save a bit by purchasing gas over the border. Gas stations are plentiful throughout the state. Most stay open late (24 hours along major highways and in big cities), except in rural areas, where Sunday hours are limited and where you may drive long stretches without a chance to refuel.

ROAD CONDITIONS

Rainy weather can make driving along the coast or in the mountains treacherous. Some of the smaller routes over mountain ranges and in the deserts are prone to flash flooding. When the rains are severe, coastal Highway 1 can quickly become a slippery nightmare, buffeted by strong winds and obstructed by falling debris from the cliffs above. When the weather is particularly bad, Highway 1 may be closed due to mud and rock slides.

Many smaller roads over the Sierra Nevada are closed in winter, and if it's snowing, tire chains may be required on routes that are open, most notably those to Yosemite and Lake Tahoe. From October through April, if it's raining along the coast, it's usually snowing at higher elevations. Consider renting a four-wheel-drive vehicle, or purchase chains before you get to the mountains. (Chains or cables generally cost $30 to $70, depending on tire size; cables are easier to apply than chains, but chains are more durable.) If you delay and purchase them in the vicinity of the chain-control area, the cost may double. Be aware that most rental-car companies prohibit chain installation on their vehicles. If you choose to risk it and do not tighten them properly, they may snap—your insurance likely will not cover any resulting damage. Uniformed chain installers on I–80 and U.S. 50 will apply them at the checkpoint for $30 or take them off for less than that. (Chain installers are independent business people, not highway employees, and set their own fees.) On smaller roads, you're on your own. Always carry extra clothing, blankets, water, and food when driving to the mountains in the winter, and keep your gas tank full to prevent the fuel line from freezing.

Road Conditions **Statewide Hotline** (☎800/GAS–ROAD or 916/445–1534 ⊕www. dot.ca.gov/hq/roadinfo).

Weather Conditions **National Weather Service** (☎707/443–6484 northernmost California, 831/656–1725 San Francisco Bay area and central California, 775/673–8100 Reno, Lake Tahoe, and northern Sierra, 805/988–6610 Los Angeles area, 858/675–8700 San Diego area ⊕www.weather.gov).

ROADSIDE EMERGENCIES

Dial 911 to report accidents on the road and to reach the police, the California Highway Patrol (CHP), or the fire department. On some rural highways and on most interstates, look for emergency phones on the side of the road. In Los Angeles, the Metro Freeway Service Patrol provides assistance to stranded motorists under nonemergency conditions. Call 399 on your cell phone to reach them 24 hours a day.

RULES OF THE ROAD

Children under age six or weighing less than 60 pounds must be secured in a federally approved child passenger restraint system and ride in the back seat. Seat belts are required at all times, and children must wear them regardless of where they're seated (studies show that children are safest in the rear seats). Unless otherwise indicated, right turns are allowed at red lights after you've come to a full stop. Left turns between two one-way streets are allowed at red lights after you've come to a full stop. Drivers with a blood-alcohol level higher than 0.08 who are stopped by police are subject to arrest, and police officers can detain those with a level of 0.05 if they appear impaired. California's drunk-driving laws are extremely tough—violators may have their licenses immediately suspended, pay hefty fines, and spend the night in jail. The speed limit on many interstate highways is 70 mph; unlimited-access roads are usually 55 mph. In cities, freeway speed limits are between 55 mph and 65 mph. Many city routes have commuter lanes during rush hour.

Effective July 2008, those 18 and older must use a hands-free device for their mobile phones while driving, while teenagers under 18 are not allowed to use mobile phones or wireless devices while driving. Smoking in a vehicle where a minor is present is an infraction. For more information refer to the Department of Motor Vehicles driver's handbook at ⊕*www.dmv.ca.gov/dmv.htm*.

▌ BY TRAIN

One of the most beautiful train trips in the country is along the Pacific Coast from Los Angeles to Oakland via Amtrak's *Coast Starlight,* which hugs the waterfront before it turns inland at San Luis Obispo for the rest of its journey to Seattle. (Be aware that this train is frequently late arriving at and departing from Central Coast stations.) The *Pacific Surfliner* connects San Diego and San Luis Obispo via Los Angeles and Santa Barbara with multiple departures daily; and the *Sunset Limited* runs from Los Angeles to New Orleans via Arizona, New Mexico, and Texas.

Information **Amtrak** (☎800/872–7245 ⊕www.amtrak.com).

ON THE GROUND

■ COMMUNICATIONS

INTERNET

Internet access is widely available in California's urban areas, but it's usually more difficult to get online in the state's rural areas. Most hotels offer some kind of connection—dial-up, broadband, or Wi-Fi (which is becoming much more common). Most hotels charge a daily fee (about $10) for Internet access. Cybercafés are also located throughout California.

Contacts Cybercafes (⊕www.cybercafes. com) lists over 4,000 Internet cafés worldwide.

■ HOURS OF OPERATION

Banks in California are typically open weekdays from 9 to 6 and Saturday morning; most are closed on Sunday and most holidays. Smaller shops usually operate from 10 to 6, with larger stores remaining open until 8 or later. Hours vary for museums and historical sites, and many are closed one or more days a week, or for extended periods during off-season months. It's a good idea to check before you visit a tourist site.

■ MONEY

Los Angeles and San Diego tend to be expensive cities to visit, and rates at coastal and desert resorts are almost as high. A day's admission to a major theme park can run upward of $60 a head, hotel rates average $150 to $250 a night (though you can find cheaper places), and dinners at even moderately priced restaurants often cost $20 to $40 per person. Costs in the Gold Country, the Far North, and the Death Valley/Mojave Desert region are considerably less—many fine Gold Country bed-and-breakfasts charge around $100 a night, and some motels in the Far North and the Mojave charge $70 to $90.

ITEM	AVERAGE COST
Cup of Coffee	$2–$3
Glass of Wine	$8
Glass of Beer	$4
Sandwich	$8–$10
One-Mile Taxi Ride in the City	$5
Museum Admission	$8–$12

Prices throughout this guide are given for adults. Reduced fees are almost always available for children, students, and senior citizens.

CREDIT CARDS

Throughout this guide, the following abbreviations are used: **AE**, American Express; **D**, Discover; **DC**, Diners Club; **MC**, MasterCard; and **V**, Visa.

It's a good idea to inform your credit-card company before you travel, especially if you're going abroad and don't travel internationally very often. Otherwise, the credit-card company might put a hold on your card owing to unusual activity—not a good thing halfway through your trip. Record all your credit-card numbers—as well as the phone numbers to call if your cards are lost or stolen—in a safe place, so you're prepared should something go wrong. Both MasterCard and Visa have general numbers you can call (collect if you're abroad) if your card is lost, but you're better off calling the number of your issuing bank, since MasterCard and Visa normally just transfer you to your bank; your bank's number is usually printed on your card.

Reporting Lost Cards American Express (☎800/992–3404 in the U.S. or 336/393–1111 collect from abroad ⊕www.american express.com). **Discover** (☎800/347–2683 in the U.S. or 801/902–3100 collect from abroad ⊕www.discovercard.com). **Diners Club** (☎800/234–6377 in the U.S. or 303/799–1504 collect from abroad ⊕www.dinersclub.com). **MasterCard** (☎800/622–7747 in the U.S. or 636/722–7111 collect from abroad ⊕www.mastercard.com). **Visa** (☎800/847–2911 in the U.S. or 410/581–9994 collect from abroad ⊕www.visa.com).

TRAVELER'S CHECKS & CARDS

Both Citibank (under the Visa brand) and American Express issue traveler's checks in the United States.

Traveler's Check Contacts **American Express** (☎888/412–6945 in the U.S. or 801/945–9450 collect outside of the U.S. to add value or speak to customer service ⊕www.americanexpress.com).

▌SAFETY

California is a safe place to visit, as long as you take the usual precautions. In large cities ask the concierge or desk clerk to point out areas on your map that you should avoid. Lock valuables in a hotel safe when you're not using them. (Some hotels have in-room safes large enough to hold a laptop computer.) Keep an eye on your handbag when you're out in public. Security is high (but mostly invisible) at theme parks and resorts.

▌TIP➔ Distribute your cash, credit cards, IDs, and other valuables between a deep front pocket, an inside jacket or vest pocket, and a hidden money pouch. Don't reach for the money pouch once you're in public.

▌TAXES

Sales tax in California varies from about 7.25% to 8.5% and applies to all purchases except for food purchased in a grocery store; food consumed in a restaurant is taxed but take-out food purchases are not. Hotel taxes vary widely by region, from 10% to 15%.

▌TIPPING

Most service workers in California are fairly well paid compared to those in the rest of the country, and extravagant tipping is not the rule here. Exceptions include wealthy enclaves such as Beverly Hills, and La Jolla as well as the most expensive resort areas.

TIPPING GUIDELINES FOR CALIFORNIA	
Bartender	$1–$5 per round of drinks, depending on the number of drinks
Bellhop	$1–$5 per bag, depending on the level of the hotel
Hotel Concierge	$5 or more, if he/ she performs a service for you
Hotel Door-man	$1–$2 if he/she helps you get a cab
Valet Parking Attendant	$1–$2 when you get your car
Hotel Maid	$1–$2 per person, per day
Waiter	15%–20% (20% is standard in upscale restaurants); nothing additional if a service charge is added to the bill
Skycap at Airport	$1–$3 per bag
Hotel Room-Service Waiter	$1–$2 per delivery, even if a service charge has been added
Taxi Driver	15%–20%, but round up the fare to the next dollar amount
Tour Guide	10% of the cost of the tour

INDEX

NOTES

ABOUT OUR WRITERS

Native Californian Cheryl Crabtree, who updated the Central Coast and Monterey Bay chapters this year, has worked as a freelance writer since 1987. She has contributed to *Fodor's California* since the 2003 edition and has also written for *Fodor's Complete Guide to the National Parks of the West*. Cheryl is editor of *Montecito Magazine*. She currently lives in Santa Barbara with her husband, two sons, and Jack Russell terrier.

Reed Parsell, who updated the Central Valley, Gold Country, and Southern Sierra chapters, is a longtime travel writer whose stories have appeared in dozens of newspapers in the United States and abroad. He's also a going-green columnist for *Sacramento* magazine, has taught copy editing at Sacramento State, and is a copy editor for *The Sacramento Bee*. Reed spent much of the summer of 2008 researching and writing the new Fodor's InFocus guide to Yosemite, Sequoia, and Kings Canyon National Parks.

Bobbi Zane, who updated the Experience Southern California and Palm Springs/Southern Desert chapters, has been living in and visiting the region since her childhood. Her articles on Palm Springs have appeared in the *Orange County Register* and *Westways* magazine. She recently contributed to *Fodor's Complete Guide to the National Parks of the West*, *Fodor's San Diego*, and *Escape to Nature Without Roughing It*. A lifelong Californian, Bobbi has visited every corner of the state on behalf of Fodor's.